The Chemical Behavior of
ZIRCONIUM

by

WARREN B. BLUMENTHAL

Chief of Chemical Research
Titanium Alloy Manufacturing Division
National Lead Company
Niagara Falls, N. Y.

D. VAN NOSTRAND COMPANY, INC.
PRINCETON, NEW JERSEY

TORONTO   LONDON

NEW YORK

D. VAN NOSTRAND COMPANY, INC.
120 Alexander St., Princeton, New Jersey (*Principal office*)
257 Fourth Avenue, New York 10, New York

D. VAN NOSTRAND COMPANY, LTD.
358, Kensington High Street, London, W.14, England

D. VAN NOSTRAND COMPANY (Canada), LTD.
25 Hollinger Road, Toronto 16, Canada

Published simultaneously in Canada by
D. VAN NOSTRAND COMPANY (Canada), LTD.

Library of Congress Catalogue Card No. 58-14168

PRINTED IN THE UNITED STATES OF AMERICA

Preface

I have written this book with the intent of providing students and research workers with a broad and detailed account of the chemistry of zirconium as an element and as a component of compounds, interstitial solutions, and alloys. I have endeavored to give comprehensive treatment of the behavior of the element in these various conditions by means of descriptions of the preparation and properties of the zirconium-containing substances, their uses, and measured and deduced details of their structure and the nature of their chemical bonding.

A broad survey of the chemical behavior of zirconium and its compounds suggests that there are reliable basic rules that govern their properties and that useful tentative formulations of these rules are now possible. These rules permit satisfactory explanations of observed chemical behaviors, allow accurate predictions of previously uninvestigated behaviors, and aid in the integration and clarification of the large mass of miscellaneous data on zirconium chemistry that have been reported in the literature. They also help in deciding which reports are more likely to be correct in the numerous cases of conflicting results and conclusions of different investigators. I have made extensive use of the rules without intending to imply that their present formulation is final. Indeed, the existence of a tentative formulation of rules constitutes a challenge for their criticism and refinements in their formulation.

No similar work on the chemistry of zirconium has been available. Only one book has previously appeared on zirconium chemistry, written by F. P. Venable and published in 1922. At that time the scientific literature contained only about 1000 articles on zirconium and its compounds, while at the time of publishing this book the number is about 7000. During the interim since the appearance of Venable's book, there has been an enormous growth of theoretical chemistry, particularly in the areas of chemical bonding and concepts of the solid state. I have striven not only to give broad coverage of both the earlier and later literature on zirconium chemistry but also to recast the earlier literature into the language and perspectives of recent years.

Throughout the text of this book, the conventional cgs units are used. All temperatures are given in degrees centigrade without using the abbreviation C, e.g., 1000°, unless other units are specifically designated. The word *solution* is to be understood as referring to aqueous solution, unless it is stated to be otherwise.

iii

I am indebted to many persons for encouragement and helpful suggestions in writing this book. Messrs. Karl B. Thews and Daniel D. Wheeler recognized the need for an up-to-date book on the chemistry of zirconium long before I began to write one and persistently urged that I undertake this task. Dr. Stephen F. Urban also encouraged the work and was always generous in advising me out of his extensive knowledge, particularly in the fields of metallurgy and ceramics. Messrs. Howard J. Smith and Ray F. Seifert, and Drs. A. Clearfield and S. Y. Tyree read parts or all of the manuscript and made many useful comments and corrections. I owe especial thanks to my employer, the Titanium Alloy Manufacturing Division of the National Lead Company, for generously allowing me the large freedom of time that was essential to the collection and sorting of material and the writing of the manuscript.

WARREN B. BLUMENTHAL

Table of Contents

v

1

The Element, Zirconium

HISTORY

Zirconium in chemically combined form is widely distributed in nature as a component of the lithosphere. Hence, prehistoric man must have handled it and noticed its existence in some vague way long before he was able to recognize the element or its compounds as distinct substances. At the early dawn of recorded history, he was already familiar with varieties of zircon, a gem stone occurring as attractive colorless or colored crystals and consisting of chemically combined zirconia and silica. One of the twelve stones in the breastplate of the ancient high priests of Israel is thought to have been the hyacinth or jacinth (1), a variety of zircon. Some have thought, too, that the lyncurium mentioned by Theophrastus about 300 B.C. was a zircon, but this is very doubtful (2, 3). Possibly the *hyacinthus* and other minerals listed by Pliny (4) were the same as hyacinth and other forms of zircon recognized in later times. St. John the Divine mentioned a hyacinth as one of the twelve precious stones which garnished the walls of the new Jerusalem (5). It appears highly likely that zircons were known and used in the times of these writers, but it is unlikely that we can prove today that the terminologies which they used definitely referred to specimens of zircon.

Hyacinth and jargon were well known in the Middle Ages. In the eighteenth century colorless zircons were regarded as inferior or imperfect diamonds and were known as *Matara diamonds* because many were derived from the Matara district of Ceylon. Romé de l'Isle proved them to be a distinct mineral species, to which Werner later applied the name *zircon*, possibly derived from the Arabic *zerk*, a precious stone (3, 6), or Persian *zargūn*, gold-colored.

Not until 1789 was it recognized that zircons contain a distinguishing oxide. In that year M. H. Klaproth published the results of his analyses of

---

1. Exodus 39:12 (Hebrew, *leshem*).
2. Theophrastus, *Peri Dithon*.
3. J. W. Mellor, *A Comprehensive Treatise on Inorganic and Theoretical Chemistry*, Longmans, Green and Co., New York, Vol. VII, 1927.
4. Pliny, *Historia Naturalis*.
5. Revelation 21:20.
6. A. G. Werner, *Letztes Mineralsystem*, Freiburg, 1912.

zircons from Ceylon. He had fused the specimens with sodium hydroxide, extracted the reaction product with hydrochloric acid, and found the solution to contain an element of novel behavior. When precipitated by a base, the precipitate would not dissolve in an excess of sodium hydroxide, like aluminum hydroxide. Klaproth proposed the German name *Zirkonerde* and the Latin *terra circonia* for the new oxide. The English equivalent is *zirconia*. The zircons which he analyzed contained on the average about 68% zirconia (7, 8). Klaproth also established the identity of hyacinth and zirconite with zircon (8, 9).

Thirty-five years elapsed after Klaproth's discovery before the element zirconium was extracted from its compounds. In 1799 Trommsdorff reported the failure of his efforts to reduce zirconia by chemical means (10), and in 1808 Davy reported failure of his electrolytic method (11). But in 1824 J. J. Berzelius heated a mixture of potassium metal and potassium fluozirconate in a small closed iron tube placed inside a platinum crucible. After washing and drying the reaction product, he found that he had obtained a black powder which consisted of impure elementary zirconium (12). Over eighty years later, Weiss and Neumann found Berzelius's procedure to yield metal of the order of 93.7% purity, but 98% purity could be obtained if the reaction product were treated first with absolute alcohol instead of water, and then washed with dilute acid (13).

In reviewing the numerous preparations of zirconium metal during the century and a quarter following Klaproth's identification of zirconium oxide, it is necessary to take cognizance of important changes in views as to what might truly be called elementary zirconium or zirconium metal. As it is now known, pure elementary zirconium exists stably as a hexagonal close-packed crystalline solid below 862° and as a body-centered cubic crystalline solid between 862° and the melting point (about 1830°). These phases have characteristic physical and chemical properties. It is to be noted that the element has always been prepared at a red heat or higher, and at these temperatures it is extremely reactive chemically, picking up carbon, oxygen, and nitrogen with great avidity from its environs. After absorbing relatively small amounts of these elements, its hardness and ductility are severely changed, and with moderately higher contamination the crystal structure alters to a face-centered cubic type with major differences in physical and chemical properties. In this condition the crystal structure and physical and

7. M. H. Klaproth, *Beobacht. Entdeck. Naturkunde* **3,** 2 (1789).
8. Klaproth, *Ann. chim. phys.* **8** (1789).
9. Klaproth, *Chem. Ann. Crell* **1,** 7 (1789).
10. J. B. Trommsdorff, *Trommsdorff's Jour.* **6,** 116 (1799).
11. H. Davy, *Phil. Mag.* **32,** 203-7 (1808).
12. J. J. Berzelius, *Ann. chim. phys.* **20,** 43 (1824).
13. L. Weiss and E. Neumann, *Z. anorg. allgem. Chem.* **65,** 248 (1910).

chemical properties become virtually identical with those of zirconium carbide, even though the concentrations of oxygen, carbon, or nitrogen be but a small fraction of the stoichiometric equivalence. Moreover, when compounds of zirconium are reduced by certain metals, notably aluminum, intermetallic compounds of zirconium and the reducing metal may form, and the product cannot be regarded as zirconium metal. If the standard for judging a reduction product is hexagonal zirconium metal, doubtless many of the so-called preparations of the element prior to 1914 can be ruled out, and if we further add certain limitations in the variation of the impurity content and the physical properties of the hexagonal metal, perhaps none of the preparations until the second decade of the twentieth century would qualify.

Since Berzelius did not use a completely sealed tube for conducting his reduction of potassium fluozirconate, his product was at best an altered zirconium. In 1914 Lely and Hamburger reported the preparation of zirconium metal of nearly 100% purity by heating zirconium tetrachloride with sodium in a bomb (13b). Their product was recovered as metallic laminae which could be pressed into rods, drawn into wire, and burnished to a bright, mirrorlike surface. Podszus in 1917 announced a product of 99.3% purity, obtained by heating potassium fluozirconate with sodium in a sealed bomb (14). Marden and Rich obtained metal of 99.76-99.89% purity by volatilizing the aluminum out of a zirconium-aluminum alloy in an arc furnace (15). Finally, van Arkel and de Boer prepared extremely pure, grossly crystalline zirconium metal by the thermal decomposition of zirconium iodide vapor on a tungsten filament (16).

It was not recognized until 1922 that all the zirconium occurring in the lithosphere contains a small proportion of the element of atomic number 72. This element is so extraordinarily like zirconium that no qualitative differences in chemical behavior between the two elements have been observed up to the present. The unrecognized element had been following zirconium in all the processing of its ores and its subsequent handling as though it were a huge isotope of zirconium.

There had been many spurious indications of the presence of one or more unrecognized elements in zirconium, none of which were actually proved to be real. Breithaupt reported an element which he called *ostranium* in the mineral ostranite, a decompositoin product of zircon (17). Svanberg reported *Norerde* or *noria* as a new oxide present in zircon and eudialyte (18), and

13b. D. Lely, Jr., and L. Hamburger, *Z. anorg. allgem. Chem.* **87,** 209-28 (1914).
14. E. Podszus, *Z. anorg. allgem. Chem.* **99,** 123-31 (1917).
15. J. W. Marden and M. N. Rich, *Ind. Eng. Chem.* **12,** 651-6 (1920).
16. A. E. van Arkel and J. H. de Boer, *Z. anorg. allgem. Chem.* **148,** 345-50 (1925).
17. A. Breithaupt, *Pogg. Ann.* **5,** 377 (1825).
18. L. F. Svanberg, *Pogg. Ann.* **65,** 317 (1845).

Sorby reported *jargonia* in zircon from Ceylon (19). Church thought that he had found spectrographic evidence of a new element in zirconium which he called *nigrum* (20). Hofmann and Prandtl concluded that an unrecognized earth, *Euxenerde* or *euxenia*, made up half of the oxide isolated as zirconia from euxenite (21).

In 1911 Urbain announced the spectrographic discovery of element 72 in a fraction of liquor concentrated from an ytterbium solution (22). He named the element *celtium*. Subsequently von Hevesy and Coster noted that the occurrence of element 72 with trivalent ytterbium was not in accord with the expected tetravalency for this element demanded by the quantum theory. Moreover, the indicated rarity of element 72 as a minor constituent of ytterbium concentrates did not agree with the general statistics of abundances of elements of even atomic numbers. They reasoned that element 72 was more likely to occur with zirconium than with the rare earths and undertook a careful X-ray study of zircon. They soon found two very distinct α_1 and α_2 lines situated exactly at the positions interpolated by means of Moseley's law. Not long afterward they also identified the β_1, β_2, β_3, and γ_1 lines and found that the relative intensities were those anticipated by the theory. They announced the discovery of element 72 in January, 1923, and called it *hafnium* from Hafnia, an ancient name of Copenhagen, the city in which von Hevesy and Coster did their work on the discovery (23). A literary controversy between Urbain and von Hevesy on the relative merits of their respective discoveries was finally resolved decisively in favor of the latter.

Hafnium compounds have been concentrated by von Hevesy and others through tedious recrystallizations, particularly of the alkali fluozirconates-fluohafnates. Up to 1930 only about 70 g of pure hafnium oxide had been prepared in Europe (24). In recent years satisfactory, though still costly, large-scale separations of compounds of zirconium and hafnium have been made by liquid-liquid extraction methods. But the zirconium metal and compounds of industry still usually contain the same concentration of hafnium as existed in the ores from which they were derived. When derived from zircon sand, the hafnium content is commonly 2% by weight of the combined metals. For all purposes other than use in atomic reactors and exacting academic researches, the hafnium content is ignored because of the extreme similarity of the two elements. It should be assumed by the reader of this book that all observations on the element and its compounds were

19. H. C. Sorby, *Proc. Roy. Soc. London* **17**, 511 (1869).
20. A. H. Church, *Chem. News* **19**, 21 (1869).
21. K. A. Hofmann and W. Prandtl, *Ber.* **34**, 1064 (1901).
22. G. Urbain, *Compt. rend.* **152**, 141 (1911).
23. G. von Hevesy, *Chem. Rev.* **2**, 1-41 (1925).
24. P. M. Tyler, *U.S. Bur. Mines Information Circ.* **6457**, 11 pp. (1931).

made on materials containing 0.5 to 2.0 parts of hafnium per 100 of the combined metals, unless it is specifically stated to the contrary.

Only after the discovery of hafnium was it possible to obtain a true value for the atomic weight of zirconium; and all determinations prior to 1923 were in error by amounts equivalent to misleading effects of hafnium on the determination, in addition to other possible experimental errors. Historically significant determinations of the atomic weight of zirconium are summarized in Table 1.1. The value reported by Hönigschmid, Zintl, and Gonzalez in

TABLE 1.1. ATOMIC WEIGHT DETERMINATIONS OF ZIRCONIUM

Year	Analyst	Ratio Used	Atomic Weight Found
1825	J. J. Berzelius	$Zr(SO_4)_2:ZrO_2$	89.46
1844	R. Hermann	$ZrCl_4:ZrO_2$	88.64
1844	R. Hermann	$ZrOCl_2 \cdot 8H_2O:ZrO_2$	89.98
1860	J. C. G. Marignac	$K_2ZrF_6:H_2SO_4$	90.03
1860	J. C. G. Marignac	$K_2ZrF_6:ZrO_2$	91.54
1881	M. Weibull	$Zr(SO_4)_2:ZrO_2$	89.54
1881	M. Weibull	$Zr(SeO_4)_2:ZrO_2$	90.79
1889	G. H. Bailley	$Zr(SO_4)_2:ZrO_2$	90.45
1898	F. P. Venable	$ZrOCl_2 \cdot 8H_2O:ZrO_2$	90.81
1917	F. P. Venable and J. M. Bell	$ZrCl_4:Ag$	91.76
1924	O. Hönigschmid, E. Zintl, and F. Gonzalez	$ZrBr_4:AgBr$	91.22

1924 (25) has been proved to be accurate and is still the accepted value.

OCCURRENCE

Compounds of zirconium are widely and fairly abundantly distributed in the lithosphere. Clarke and Washington have estimated that zirconium constitutes about 0.017% of the lithosphere (26, 27), about the same as carbon. Other estimates have ranged from 0.0019-0.1% (28, p. 17; 29). The element does not occur in the free state as a consequence of its vigorous chemical

25. O. Hönigschmid, E. Zintl, and F. Gonzalez, Z. anorg. allgem. Chem. 139, 293 (1924).

26. F. W. Clarke, U.S. Geol. Survey Bull. 695, 30 (1920).

27. F. W. Clarke and H. S. Washington, Proc. Nat. Acad. Sci. 8, 108 (1922).

28. W. Vernadsky, La Geochimie, Alcan, Paris, 1924.

29. G. von Hevesy, J. Chem. Soc. 1931, 1

activity at the temperatures of its environments during the solidification of the earth's crust. The chief occurrences are in the minerals zircon, $ZrO_2 \cdot SiO_2$, baddeleyite, ZrO_2, and a variety of complex minerals, particularly silicates, which will be discussed hereunder. Studies by von Hevesy and Wuerstlin of 1175 rock specimens, stony meteorites, and moldavites showed granite to contain about 1 g of zirconium per 3000 g, volcanic rocks about 1 g per 4000 g, effusive rocks 1 g per 4500 g, and stony meteorites 1 g per 12,000 g (30). Some mineral waters contain a few tenths of a part per million of dissolved zirconium in the form of carbonate complexes, and the element is also found in minute proportions in living organisms and in coal. Its existence in stars has been widely noted spectrographically. Hafnium has been found with zirconium in all its terrestial occurrences, and the studies of von Hevesy and Wuerstlin led them to believe that hafnium occurs in the solar system in about the same proportion to zirconium as it occurs in the rocks of the earth, that is, about 2:100. Hafnium has always been found to be present in its minerals in smaller proportions than zirconium, except in the rare mineral thortveitite, a scandium silicate (31).

ZIRCON is the most common zirconium mineral. It has been found to occur in all types of rocks, but chiefly in granitic and syenitic rocks. It is frequently found in microscopic inclusions in minerals such as cordierite and the micas. In certain pegmatites, notably those of Henderson County, North Carolina, zircon crystals have been found several inches in length, and crystals weighing as much as several pounds have been found in Madagascar.

In the use of zirconia as a ceramic opacifier, it has been observed that the oxide dissolves in the molten glass and zircon precipitates from the melt as it cools. Doubtless a similar process occurred in nature during the cooling of molten siliceous magmas. Moreover, in the natural process quantities of zirconia were retained in solution during the separation of zircon, and ultimately appeared in solid solution in the cooled rock or as a component of complex minerals. Radioactivity studies have indicated that zirconium tended to concentrate in the late cooling parts of rock masses (32). It tended to separate as zircon from the more acid molten environments and as complex silicates from alkaline environments (33). Other factors in the composition of the magmas, such as the alumina content, also appear to have played roles (34).

During the disintegration of rocks by weather and hydrolytic action, the extremely unreactive zircon crystals were often preserved while the parent rock crumbled, dissolved, and ultimately became clay and soil. In some

30. G. von Hevesy and K. Wuerstlin, *Z. anorg. allgem. Chem.* **216**, 305-11 (1934).
31. M. Fleischer, *U.S. Geol. Survey Bull.* **1021-A**, 13 pp. (1955).
32. W. H. Gross, *Proc. Geol. Assoc. Can.* **3**, 123-99 (1950).
33. V. I. Gerasimovskii, *Compt. rend. acad. sci. U.S.S.R.* **30**, 820-1 (1941).
34. E. E. Kostyleva, *Bull. acad. sci. U.S.S.R.* **1940**, No. 2, 1118-24

regions the disintegration products of zirconiferous rocks were carried by streams and rivers into the sea, where grains of zircon and other heavy, chemically resistant minerals were dropped to form shoals along the sea-coasts. Later some of these shoals became beaches. Beaches containing considerable proportions of zircon are now known in Travancore, India; Miriupol (now Zhdanov), Ukraine; Malaya; Australia, near Byron Bay; Florida, near Jacksonville; and elsewhere. Table 1.2 cites references to reports on zircons found in various parts of the world.

TABLE 1.2. SOURCES OF ZIRCON SPECIMENS DESCRIBED IN THE LITERATURE

Locality	Literature
AFRICA	
Madagascar	*Bull. soc. franc. minéral. et crist.* **41**, 186-96 (1918)
	Rev. matériaux construct. et trav. publ. **1932**, 61-2B
	Compt. rend. **205**, 1333-6 (1937)
Nigeria	*Geol. Survey Nigeria Bull.* **19**, 79-80 (1948)
Nubia	*Bull. inst. Égypt* **27**, 229-64 (1945)
Nyasaland	*S. African Mining Eng. J.* **61**, I, 433-9 (1950)
Senegal Coast	*Bull. soc. Ing. Colon.* **106**, 256-70 (1932)
	Congr. intern. mines. mét. et géol. appl., 7e Congr. Paris, Oct. 1935; *Geol.* **1**, 187-96
South Africa	*J. Chem. Met. Mining Soc. S. Africa* **24**, 90-5 (1923)
	Ann. Univ. Stellenbosch **22A**, 105-34, 135-42, 143-58, 159-68, 171-82 (1944); **26A**, 307-22 (1950)
	Mineral. Mag. **28**, 486-91 (1949)
Uganda	*Bull. Imp. Inst.* **46**, 342-7 (1948)
NORTH AMERICA	
Alaska	*U.S. Geol. Survey Circ.* **184**, 1-14 (1952)
Canada	
Ontario	*Univ. Toronto Studies, Geol. Ser.* **16**, 21-4 (1923); **30**, 21-4 (1931); **32**, 19-21 (1932)
	Am. Mineralogist **13**, 384-9 (1928)
	Geol. Mag. **73**, 193-213 (1936)
	Geochim. et Cosmochim. Acta **5**, 49-73 (1954)
Greenland	*Mineral. Mag.* **27**, 198-203 (1946)
	Medd. Grønland **115**, No. 3, 108 pp. (1944)
United States	
Alabama	*Bull. Am. Ceram. Soc.* **18**, 429-31 (1939)
Arkansas	*Am. Mineralogist* **33**, 374-7 (1948)
	Rev. Metal. **51**, 173-8 (1954)
Colorado	*Bull. Geol. Soc. Am.* **53**, 765-814 (1942)
Florida	*Eng. Mining J.* **104**, 153-5 (1917)
	Am. Mineralogist **30**, 65-75 (1945)
	Am. Inst. Mining Met. Engrs., Tech. Publ. **2456**, 4 pp. (1948)

TABLE 1.2. Continued

Locality	Literature
Idaho	*Am. Mineralogist* **10**, 187-94 (1925)
	Idaho Bur. Mines Geol. Pam. **87**, 1-23 (1949)
	Idaho Bur. Mines Geol., Mineral Resources Reports **5**, 1-12 (1948)
Maryland	*Am. Mineralogist* **30**, 65-75 (1945)
Massachusetts	*Am. J. Sci.* **28**, 449
Minnesota	*Bull. Geol. Soc. Am.* **60**, 999-1016 (1946)
New England	*Bull. Geol. Soc. Am.* **54**, 1049-66 (1943)
	Geochim. et Cosmochim. Acta **5**, 49-73 (1954)
New Jersey	*Am. J. Sci.* **238**, 260-71 (1940)
New York	*Am. J. Sci.* **238**, 260-71 (1940)
Oklahoma	*Am. Mineralogist* **38**, 118-25 (1953)
Oregon	*Oregon Dep. Geol. Mineral Ind., Bull.* **30**, 1-6 (1946)
Pennsylvania	*Proc. Penn. Acad. Sci.* **15**, 73-5 (1941)
Texas	*Am. Mineralogist* **22**, 122-32 (1937)
Virginia	*Bull. Am. Inst. Mining Engrs.* **1916**, 1237-43
	Am. Mineralogist **20**, 741-68 (1935)
	U.S. Bur. Mines. Rep. Invest. **5001**, 41 pp. (1953)
Wisconsin	*Eng. Mining J.-Press* **119**, 405-6 (1925)
SOUTH AMERICA	*Stahl u. Eisen* **62**, 369-73 (1942)
Argentina	*Univ. nacl. Tucumán Inst. geol. y mineria, Publ.* **458**, 304 pp. (1948)
Brazil	*Neues Jahrb. Mineral. Geol., Monatsh.* **A64**, 423-76 (1931)
	Mineração e met. (Rio de Janeiro) **4**, 1820 (1939)
	Rev. quím. ind. (Rio de Janeiro) **13**, No. 15, 19-20 (1944)
Poços de Caldas	*Avulsa do S.T.P.M. Rio de Janeiro* **8**, 1-33 (1936)
	Mineração e met. (Rio de Janeiro) **1**, 1-4 (1936)
	Univ. São Paulo, Fac. filosof. ciênc. e letras, Bol. **49**, Mineralogia No. 7, 7-26 (1945)
	Brazil, Ministério agr., Dep. nacl. prod. mineral. Div. fomento prod. mineral, Bol. **55**, 1-63 (1943)
	Trans. Am. Inst. Mining Met. Engrs., Tech. Pub. **187**, No. 2856-H (1950)
	Ministério agr., Dept. nacl. prod. mineral. Lab. prod. mineral (Brazil) Bol. **7**, 57-66 (1943)
	Am. Mineralogist **33**, 142-51 (1948)
Peru	*Bol. soc. quím. Peru* **14**, 1-7 (1948)
ASIA	
Borneo	*Trav. Mus. acad. sci. Petrograd* **6**, 49-95 (1912)
Ceylon	*Mineral. Mag.* **27**, 198-203 (1946)
Formosa	*J. Chem. Soc. Japan* **55**, 644-8 (1934)

TABLE 1.2. Continued

Locality	Literature
	Mem. Faculty Sci. Taihoku Imp. Univ. Ser. III, **1,** No. 1, 1-22 (1943)
India	*Records Geol. Survey India* **64,** 312-3 (1930)
	Quart. J. Geol. Mining Met. Soc. India **18,** 37-41, 85-95 (1946)
	J. Sci. Ind. Research (India) **5B,** No. 2, 36 (1946)
	Trans. Mining Geol. Inst. India **42,** 105-89 (1948)
	Half-Yearly J. Mysore Univ. **12B,** 35-55 (1952)
Travancore	*Science and Culture* **12,** 22-9 (1946)
	Trans. Indian Ceram. Soc. **5,** 36-40 (1946)
Vizagapatam Coast	*Current Sci.* (India) **19,** 48-9 (1950)
Indochina	*Deut. Goldschmiede-Ztg.* **38,** 303-4, 474-5 (1935)
Japan	*Jap. J. Chem.* **2,** 73-9 (1925)
	J. Chem. Soc. Japan **57,** 1195-9 (1936); **59,** 1127-31 (1938)
	Sci. Papers, Inst. Phys. Chem. Research (Tokyo) **34,** 619-22 (1938)
	J. Faculty Sci. Hokkaido Imp. Univ., Ser. IV, **3,** 221-362 (1936)
	J. Japan. Assoc. Mineralogists, Petrologists, Econ. Geologists **32,** 209-30 (1944)
Korea	*J. Chem. Soc. Japan* **57,** 1195-9, 1205-7 (1936); **64,** 1-6 (1943)
Manchuria	*J. Geol. Soc. Japan* **56,** 79-83 (1950)
Siam	*Am. Mineralogist* **21,** 721-6 (1936)
Sumatra	*Ing. Ned.-Indië* **8,** No. 4, IV, 33-8 (1941)
	J. Sediment. Petrol. **18,** 241-9 (1948)
Tatary	*Doklady Akad. Nauk. S.S.S.R.* **45,** 355-7 (1944)
Turkey	*Maden Tetkit Arama Enotitüsü Necmuasi (Ankara)* **6,** 37-44 (1941)
	Bull. Geol. Soc. Turkey **4,** 37-54 (1953)
AUSTRALIA	*Australian Mineral Resources Survey, Summary Reports* **1,** 16 pp. (1945); **2,** 21 pp. (1945)
East Coast	*Australian J. Sci.* **8,** 99-103 (1946)
	Am. Inst. Mining Met. Engrs., Tech. Pub. **2455,** 11 pp. (1948)
New South Wales	*Chem. Eng. Mining Rev.* **31,** 216-20, 250-6 (1939)
Queensland	*Proc. Roy. Soc. Queensland* **61,** No. 7, 59-104 (1949)
New Zealand	*New Zealand J. Sci. Tech.* **25B,** 89-90 (1943)
	Bull. Geol. Soc. Am. **61,** 635-710 (1950)
EUROPE	*Metall. u. Erz.* **41,** 169-74, 193-200 (1944)
Austria	*Z. angew. Mineral.* **1,** 134-43 (1938)
Belgium	*Bull. sect. sci. acad. roumaine* **23,** 300-2 (1941)

TABLE 1.2. Continued

Locality	Literature
Czechoslovakia	*Bull. internat. acad. sci. Prague* **12**, 1-5
	Vestnik Stát. geol. ústavu Ceskoslov. rep. **22**, 315-27 (1947)
	Khimiĭ Uspekhi Khim. (*U.S.S.R.*) **4**, 531-62 (1934)
	Sbornik ústřed. ústavu geol. **19**, 337-450 (1952)
England	*Mineral. Mag.* **20**, 27-31 (1923)
	J. Soc. Glass Technol. **29**, 266-7 (1945)
France	*Bull. soc. géol. min. de Bretagne* **9**, 10-14 (1928)
	Compt. rend. **215**, 1491-3 (1942)
	Bull. soc. franç. minéral. et crist. **41**, 173-7, 597-604 (1946)
	Génie civil **127**, 391-2 (1950)
Germany	*Centr. Mineral. Geol.* **1919**, 1-14
	Centr. Mineral. Geol. **1938A**, 115-20
	Z. deut. geol. Ges. **92**, 477-99 (1940)
	Geologica **9**, 1-114 (1951)
	Neues Jahrb. Mineral. Geol. Monatsh. **1952**, 241-52
Greece	*Ann. géol. peninsule balkan.* **20**, 137-44 (1952)
	Berg. u.-hüttenmänn. Monatsh. Montan. Hochschule Leoben **97**, 205-10 (1952)
Hungary	*Ann. Hist. Nat. Musei Nat. Hung.* **19**, 78-102 (1922)
	Centr. Mineral. Geol. **1930A**, 112-7
Ireland	*Am. Mineralogist* **22**, 686-700 (1937)
Italy	*Boll. soc. nat. Napoli* **41**, 180-4
	Atti. soc. ital. sci. nat. e museo civico storia nat. Milano **85**, 136-46 (1946)
	Rend. soc. mineral. ital. **3**, 124-38 (1946)
	Atti. soc. nat. e mat. modena **79**, 85-88 (1948)
	Atti. soc. toscana sci. nat. Pisa, Mem. Se. **57A**, 145-73, 174-81 (1950)
Lapland	*Bull. comm. géol. Finlande* **135**, 5-86 (1945)
Portugal	*Compt. rend.* **164**, 102-3 (1917)
Scotland	*Trans. Edinburgh Geol. Soc.* **11**, 200-13 (1923)
	Trans. Roy. Soc. Edinburgh **61**, Pt. II, 533-75 (1944-48)
Sicily	*Notiz. mineral. siciliana e calabrese* **1**, 5-41 (1947)
Soviet Union	
Caucasus	*Compt. rend. acad. sci. U.R.S.S.* **35**, 284-7 (1942)
Chibin Tundra	*Bull. acad. sci. Russ.* **16**, 341-58 (1922)
Ilmen Mountains	*Bull. acad. sci. Petrograd* **1915**, 1907-12
	Mém. soc. russe minéral. **67**, 229-35 (1938)
Kola Peninsula	*Redkie Metal.* **2**, 27-38 (1935)

TABLE 1.2. Continued

Locality	Literature
Soviet Russia	*Keram. Rundschau* **37,** 659-63 (1929)
	Z. Krist, Festband P. v. Groth **58,** 386-403 (1923)
	Mém. soc. russe minéral. **62,** 218-56 (1933)
	Soviet Geol. **8,** No. 9, 132-8 (1938)
	Pedology (*U.S.S.R.*) **1945,** 348-54
	Doklady Akad. Nauk. S.S.S.R. **72,** 945-8 (1950)
Transbaikalia	*Compt. rend. acad. sci. U.R.S.S.* **32,** 361-4 (1941)
Ukraine	*Mineral. petrog. Mitt.* **155,** 274-83 (1943)
West Azov Coast	*J. Geol. Ukrain. Acad. Sci.* **6,** No. 4, 131-63 (1940)
Spain	*Met. y elec.* (*Madrid*) **16,** No. 58, 31-4 (1944)
	Anales edafol. y fisiol. vegetal (*Madrid*) **9,** 15-28 (1950)
Sweden	*Arkiv. Kemi, Mineral. Geol.* **A23,** No. 9, 160 pp. (1946)
	Arkiv. Mineral. Geol. **1,** 227-32 (1951)

BADDELEYITE, ZrO_2, was found in 1892 by N. Hussak at Jacupiranga, Brazil (35), and he named the Brazilian mineral *brazilite*. Subsequently the name *caldasite* has also been used. Slightly later the same mineral was discovered in Ceylon by Fletcher (36), who gave it the name *baddeleyite*. The latter name came to be the generally accepted one. Still another name, *zirkite*, has also been used to designate zirconia ore. The chief known occurrence of baddeleyite is in the Poços de Caldas region of the states of São Paulo and Minas Gerais in Brazil, but it has been found in many other locales, for example near Bozeman, Montana; Alno, Sweden; Kuda Padi Oya, India; and Vesuvius, Italy. In the Poços de Caldas region, boulders of baddeleyite weigh up to about 30 tons, and alluvial pebbles known as *favas* (> Portuguese *fava*, a bean) are found up to about 3 inches in diameter in streams and along the slopes. The favas commonly consist of over 90% zirconia. Wedekind observed Brazilian baddeleyite to contain up to about 94% of ZrO_2, and the concentration could be rendered even higher by treating the ore with acids. He reported the analysis of a zirconia-rich specimen to show ZrO_2 94.12%, $ZrO_2 \cdot SiO_2$ 1.97%, SiO_2 0.43%, TiO_2 0.98%, and Fe_2O_3 3.22% by weight (37). The hafnium content of Brazilian baddeleyite is about 0.5% of the combined zirconium and hafnium content.

The known COMPLEX MINERALS containing significant amounts of zirconium are listed in Table 1.3. None of them are currently used as sources of zirconium.

35. E. Hussak, *Neues Jahrb. Min.* **2,** 141 (1892).
36. L. Fletcher, *Mineral. Mag.* **10,** 148 (1892).
37. E. Wedekind, *Z. angew. Chem.* **21,** 2270 (1908).

TABLE 1.3. COMPLEX MINERALS CONTAINING ZIRCONIUM

Name	*Composition or Observed ZrO_2 Content*
Aahrenite	3-4% ZrO_2
Anderbergite	A complex vanadium-zirconium silicate
Annerodite	1-2% ZrO_2
Arfvedsonite or Riebeckite	To 7% ZrO_2
Astrophyllite	$(K,Na)(Fe,Mn,Al)_4(Zr,Ti,Si)_{14}(OH,F)_2$
Auerlite	Up to 3% ZrO_2
Beckelite	2.5% ZrO_2
Catapleiite	$Na_2ZrSi_6O_{15} \cdot 3H_2O$ with up to 40% ZrO_2
Cerite	Up to 8% ZrO_2
Chalcolamprite	A zirconium niobate-silicate, 5.7% ZrO_2
Columbite	To 11% ZrO_2
Dalyite	$K_2ZrSi_6O_{15}$
Elpidite	$Na_2ZrSi_6O_{15} \cdot 3H_2O$ with 20% ZrO_2
Endeolite	3.8% ZrO_2
Erdmannite and Michaelsonite	A basic silicate of cerium earth metals with up to 5.5% ZrO_2
Eucolite and Eudialyte	$Na_{13}(Ca,Fe)_6Cl(Si,Zr)_{20}O_{52}$, up to 17% ZrO_2
Euxenite	Up to 2% ZrO_2
Fergusonite	Up to 2% ZrO_2
Guarinite and Hiortdahlite	$Na_2Ca_4F_2(Si,Zr)_5O_{14}$, up to 22% ZrO_2
Hainite	$M(Si,Zr)O_3 \cdot Zr(SiO_3)_2 \cdot MTa_2O_6$, up to 32% ZrO_2
Johnstrupite	2.8% ZrO_2
Lavenite	$Na(Mn,Ca,Fe)ZrOF(SiO_3)_2$
Leucosphenite	3.5% ZrO_2
Loranskite and Wiikite	Up to 20% ZrO_2
Lorenzenite (Ramsayite)	11.9% ZrO_2
Monazite	Up to 8% ZrO_2
Mosandrite	7.4% ZrO_2
Nohlite and Samarskite	Up to 4% ZrO_2
Oegirite	2.7% ZrO_2
Polymignite	$5MTiO_3 \cdot 5MZrO_3 \cdot M(Nb,Ta)O_6$ with 29% ZrO_2
Pyrochlore	Up to 5% ZrO_2
Sipylite	2-3% ZrO_2
Thorianite	Up to 3% ZrO_2
Thortveitite and Benfanamite	$(Se,Y)_2Si_2O_7$ with 2.5% $(Zr,Hf)O_2$
Tritonite	Up to 3.6% ZrO_2
Uhligite	$Ca(Ti,Zr)O_5 \cdot Al_2TiO_5$, up to 33% ZrO_2
Uraninite	Up to 8% ZrO_2
Wadeite	$K_2CaZrSi_4O_{12}$
Wöhlerite	$13(Ca,Na_2)O \cdot 9SiO_2 \cdot 3ZrO_2 \cdot Nb_2O_5$
Xenotime	$Y_2O_3 \cdot P_2O_5$ with up to 8% ZrO_2
Zirkelite	$(Ca,Fe)O \cdot 2(Zr,Ti,Th)O_2$ with up to 53% ZrO_2

Zirconium has been found dissolved in spring water at Aguas de Prata, Brazil (38), Saratoga, New York (39), Taiwan (40), and Kamchatka (41). It has been widely noted as a minor constituent of soils and clays, usually present in only trace amounts (42, 43, 44). It is present in traces, too, in living organisms (45, 46, 47), but specimens of coal from various sources have been observed to contain zirconium in amounts ranging from below the level of detection to several hundredths of a per cent of the total ash (48, 49, 50). It is believed that the minerals of zirconium are too insoluble to influence plant growth (51).

THE EXTRACTION OF THE ELEMENT
FROM ITS COMPOUNDS

It is very difficult to extract zirconium from its ores or from compounds derived from the ores in a state of purity sufficiently high for it to exhibit the characteristic properties of the element. Relatively pure zirconium has been found to exist as a hexagonal α-phase below 862° and as a β-body-centered cubic phase above 862°. If a sufficient amount of carbon or nitrogen is dissolved in the solid metal, it assumes a face-centered cubic symmetry, but if hydrogen or boron are dissolved, other types of lattices may also form. Oxygen can be dissolved in considerable proportions in both the α- and β-phases, but it does not induce the formation of other crystalline phases of the element. It does, however, markedly affect the physical and chemical properties of the metal, decreasing its chemical activity and its

38. A. Salles Teixeira, *Rev. brasil. chim. (São Paulo)* **4**, 365-6 (1937).

39. L. W. Strock and S. Drexler, *J. Opt. Soc. Am.* **31**, 167-73 (1941).

40. Kuan Pan, *Bull. Agr. Chem. Dept. Natl. Taiwan Univ.* **1**, 22-6 (1952).

41. T. I. Ustinova, *Trudy Lab. Gidrogeol. Problem. im. F. P. Savarenskogo Akad. Nauk S.S.S.R.* **2**, 144-57 (1947).

42. A. Fioletova, *Trans. Mendeleev Cong. Theoret. Appl. Chem. VI 1932*, **2**, v, 499-503 (1935).

43. L. H. Rogers, O. E. Gali, L. W. Gaddum, and R. M. Barnette, *Fla. Univ. Agr. Exp. Sta., Tech. Bull.* **341**, 31 pp. (1939).

44. L. H. Ahrens, *S. African J. Sci.* **41**, 152-60 (1945).

45. J. M. Lopez de Azcona, A. Santos Ruiz, and M. Dean Guelbenzu, *Anales real soc. españ. fís. y quím. (Madrid)* **45B**, 919-34 (1949).

46. A. P. Vinogradov, *Pedology (U.S.S.R.)* **1945**, 348-54 (1949).

47. S. A. Borovik and T. F. Borovik-Romanova, *Trudy Biogeokhim. Labor. Akad. Nauk S.S.S.R.* **9**, 149-54 (1949).

48. M. Lopez de Azcona and A. Camunas Puig, *Anales fís. y quím. (Madrid)* **43**, 48-50 (1947).

49. Yasumitsu Uzumasa, *Chem. Researches (Japan)* **5**, Inorg. and Anal. Chem. 1-17 (1949).

50. A. J. W. Headlee and R. G. Hunter, *Ind. Eng. Chem.* **45**, 548-51 (1953).

51. N. Gammon, Jr., T. R. Henderson, R. A. Cardigan, R. G. Leighty, and F. B. Smith, *Florida Univ. Agr. Exp. Sta. Bull.* **524**, 5-124 (1953).

ductility and increasing its hardness and melting point. The effects of oxygen may be regarded as quantitative rather than qualitative: it changes the value of physical constants without inducing decisive changes in the crystal lattice or other identifying characteristics. It does tend to stabilize the α-phase against conversion to the β-phase.

It appears appropriate to recognize as elementary zirconium that reduction product of zirconium compounds which exhibits the characteristic α- or β-structures of the element. If dissolved impurities do not alter these morphological manifestations of the element, they must be regarded as impurities only and not as components of a composition of matter other than the element. This concept is the same as that by which mineral halite and calcite are regarded as sodium chloride and calcium carbonate crystals, even though appreciable amounts of foreign substances are distributed through them. But carnallite, $KCl \cdot MgCl_2 \cdot 6H_2O$ (rhombic), is not considered to be bischofite, $MgCl_2 \cdot 6H_2O$ (monoclinic), containing potassium chloride as an impurity, because the identifying characteristics of bischofite have disappeared in the formation of carnallite.

The first zirconium metal prepared by Berzelius in 1824 contained some 6-7% of oxygen. It would not have been suitable for working into shapes for structural use, but it did exhibit characteristic crystalline and chemical properties of zirconium and merited acceptance as a preparation of the element in crude form. Some later attempts at preparation of the metal cannot be regarded as having succeeded because they resulted in compositions of different identity. With carbon, for example, reduction products were obtained consisting of metallic face-centered solid solutions of carbon in zirconium, which we will represent Zr,C, having distinctive characteristics of its own. The atomic ratio $Zr:C = 1$ is a lower limit only, and the same phase can be obtained with considerably higher ratios. The marked differences between this face-centered cubic phase and zirconium are typified by the differences in melting points: zirconium 1830°; Zr,O (1:1) 1900°; Zr,C (1:1) 3800°. Again, in aluminum reduction, a phase Al_3Zr was obtained by the first investigators. But reductions with calcium and magnesium always give elementary zirconium, although it may contain impurities that impair the usefulness of the element for ordinary applications as metal.

It will be the practice in this book to accept as elementary solid zirconium the hexagonal and body-centered cubic phases discussed above. Errors and confusions which can result from the arbitrariness which is in most, if not all, definitions, can best be avoided by keeping in mind the true range of applicability of the definition. For our purposes this will be fixed by the concept of elementary zirconium as a chemical identity. Were the metallurgic aspects of the element to be treated, a different definition might well be sought. Liquid and gaseous zirconium will be regarded as the matter which is obtained when solid zirconium is melted or boiled.

An indication of the energy requirements for reducing zirconium compounds is furnished by Table 1.4. From the data furnished, it is seen that

TABLE 1.4. A COMPARISON OF THE FREE ENERGIES
OF SOME METALLIC COMPOUNDS AT 25°

Free Energies of Formation of Compounds, in kg
cal/mole per Valence Bond in the Molecule

Element	Oxide	Fluoride	Chloride
Aluminum	−62.8	−98.	−50.7
Calcium	−72.2	−138.9	−97.4
Carbon	−23.6		
Iron	−29.6		−36.1
Magnesium	−68.1	−125.4	−70.8
Sodium	−45.0	−129.3	−91.8
Tin	−31.1		−28.3
Zirconium	−61.1	−111.2	−57.5

zirconium dioxide might be reduced to the metal by calcium or magnesium, possibly with aluminum, but not with carbon, iron, sodium, or tin. Zirconium fluorides and chlorides might be reduced to the metal by calcium, magnesium, or sodium, and not by aluminum, iron, or tin. These statements must be altered to the extent that the energy data at other temperatures are significantly different and for cases where reactions occur between zirconium and the reducing agent.

It is apparent from what has already been said that elementary zirconium should be prepared in the absence of an atmosphere from which carbon, oxygen, or nitrogen can be picked up, and to these undesired contaminants we can also add hydrogen. Experience has shown zirconium to be a powerful getter for these gases, and it has found application in eliminating residual traces of gases in vacuum tubes.

Obtaining pure zirconium metal from the dioxide or other oxygen compounds is rendered particularly difficult by the strong tendency to form a solution of oxygen in the metal. Chemists prefer to study the properties of pure substances, and metallurgists have found that zirconium containing over 0.7% oxygen is practically unworkable. The dissolution of oxygen in zirconium entails a decrease in free energy which is reflected in the decreased chemical activity of the composition as compared to the pure metal, higher melting point, greater hardness, and the requirement of powerful reducing conditions for removal of the oxygen. The dissolved oxygen diffuses freely through the metal, but the oxide phase ZrO_2 does not separate, indicating that the solid solution is energetically preferred over the oxide. Up to 29 atom % oxygen can be dissolved in solid zirconium at elevated temperature without the separation of zirconium dioxide, as against a maximum of about 1 atom % of carbon before forming the phase Zr,C. Liquid zirconium and liquid zirconium dioxide appear to be miscible (51b). In obtaining the pure metal from an oxygen-containing composition, severe energetic and mechanical requirements must be met.

In the preparation of zirconium, the containing vessel must be unreactive with both the reagents introduced and the products sought. Fortunately ordinary iron and steel have met these requirements quite well. A much more difficult problem has been posed in the construction of a suitable vessel for melting powders and sponges which are obtained from all the preparations, so that ingots and other useful shapes can be formed. Most ceramics are unsatisfactory because they melt or decompose before the melting temperature of zirconium is reached or because the molten zirconium penetrates the ceramic or reacts with it, causing failure. The relationship to alumina is instructive. According to Table 1.4, the free energy of the zirconium-oxygen bond is nearly equal to that of the aluminum-oxygen bond. But additional free energy is made available in reactions involving these elements by the formation of an intermetallic compound. Actually, either metal can reduce the oxide of the other, as represented by the equations

$$6Al_2O_3 + 13Zr \rightarrow 4Al_3Zr + 9ZrO_2$$
$$3ZrO_2 + 13Al \rightarrow 3Al_3Zr + 2Al_2O_3$$

(1-2)

Zirconia vessels, too, are attacked by molten zirconium with the formation of liquid and solid solutions of oxygen in zirconium. Molten zirconium passes through the pores of ordinary carbon or graphite crucibles, but fortunately zirconium does not dissolve or react directly with elementary carbon. It reacts strongly with carboniferous gases. By use of special dense graphite, it has been possible to contain molten zirconium quite satisfactorily.

The electroreduction of zirconium has been seriously limited by the inability of its atoms to form monatomic ions. It is probable that a direct electrodeposition of the element has never been achieved, but electrochemical processes in which another metal is liberated electrolytically and reacts chemically with a zirconium compound to furnish zirconium have succeeded. The practicality of such processes is rendered small by the difficulties encountered in making the zirconium adhere to the electrode or in segregating

51b. Armour Research Foundation, *Phase Diagrams of the Zirconium-base Binary Alloys. The Zirconium-Oxygen System*, March 31, 1953.

the zirconium in any way so as to permit its economical separation from the electrolytic bath. The Hall process for aluminum is favored by the low melting point of this element (659.7°) which results in the formation of a pool of the liberated metal at the bottom of the cell, from which it can periodically be tapped off. Zirconium forms a powder, and only pains-taking arrangement of conditions in the cell cause the powder to build up dense compacts at the electrode rather than to form loose sinters and to become at least partially dispersed through the electrolyte.

The failure to form discrete ions and the extreme activity toward oxygen make it particularly unlikely that zirconium could be deposited electro-lytically from an aqueous system or from solution in any oxygen-containing solvents. A number of investigators mistakenly concluded that they had deposited zirconium electrochemically from aqueous or organic solutions either by displacement with a more electropositive metal or by passage of an electric current. Warren considered that he had deposited zirconium by displacement with magnesium from an aqueous solution (52), and Gable thought he had obtained a similar effect with zinc in a methanol solution (53). Bradt and Linford reported depositing zirconium by electrolyzing a solution of zirconium sulfate of specified composition (54), but their find-ings could not be substantiated. Misleading effects are easily obtained in electrolyzing solutions containing zirconium compounds. If the zirconium compounds were not fastidiously purified, they are apt to contain small amounts of copper, nickel, or other metallic salts which yield deposits of metallic appearance. In the aqueous electrolysis, the pH rises in the vicinity of the cathode, and almost invisible hydrous zirconia separates and tends to form a layer over the electrode. If the electrode is washed and scraped after the termination of the electrolysis and the scrapings analyzed chemi-cally for zirconium, the findings are positive. The metallic appearance and the chemical evidence for the presence of zirconium are deceptive evidence of the presence of zirconium metal in the deposit.

This review of the difficulties standing in the way of preparing the element serve to explain the failures in the early attempts at chemical re-duction by Trommsdorf (10) and electrolytic reduction by Davy (11), and the long lapse of thirty-five years between Klaproth's discovery of the element in 1789 and Berzelius's preparation in 1824. Approximately another century elapsed before the pure metal was prepared by Lely and Hamburger (13b), Podszus (14), Marden and Rich (55, 56), and van Arkel and de

52. H. N. Warren, *Chem. News* **61**, 183 (1890).

53. H. S. Gable, *J. Am. Chem. Soc.* **52**, 3741 (1930).

54. W. E. Bradt and H. B. Linford, *Trans. Electrochem. Soc.* **70**, 431-40 (1936).

55. J. W. Marden and M. N. Rich, *Ind. Eng. Chem.* **12**, 651 (1920).

56. Marden and Rich, *Investigations of Zirconium with Especial Reference to the Metal and the Oxide,* Washington, D.C., 1921.

Boer (16). In 1914 Wedekind and Lewis reported a study of samples of zirconium prepared by the old methods in which they found 2.6-54% oxygen and 1.24-8.7% zirconium nitride (57).

In Berzelius's original preparation of zirconium, he heated a mixture of potassium fluozirconate, K_2ZrF_6, with potassium metal to a red heat in an iron tube, 6 mm in diameter and 30 mm long, which was closed at one end. He cooled the reaction product, leached it with dilute hydrochloric acid, with ammonium chloride solutions, and finally with alcohol (12). His results were duplicated by numerous later experimenters, notably by Dennis and Spencer (58) and by Weiss and Neumann (13). The latter found that Berzelius's method yielded a product containing 93.7% zirconium. The chief impurity was zirconium dioxide, which formed during the washing of the crude product with the aqueous solutions. By washing the crude metal first with absolute alcohol, they were able to get 98% pure zirconium. In 1917 Podszus reported heating potassium fluozirconate with sodium in a steel bomb and obtaining fine crystalline zirconium of 99.3% purity (14). Berglund used a similar process and obtained the zirconium as a black powder (59).

Potassium fluozirconate was a particularly suitable starting material because it was so readily obtainable in anhydrous condition. However, the element has been prepared similarly by heating sodium fluozirconate, $Na_5Zr_2F_{13}$, with sodium (60).

The removal of alkali fluorides after the preparation of zirconium from its fluozirconates is rendered arduous by their low volatility, low solubility in the case of the sodium salt, and toxic nature. Ultimately the chief interest centered about the reduction of zirconium tetrachloride. Zirconium tetrachloride can be sublimed into the reaction chamber and thus purified at the time of use. Alkali or alkaline earth chloride by-products of its reaction can largely be removed by melting and draining, and the remainder can be removed by volatilizing under reduced pressure.

In 1865 Troost reported the preparation of zirconium metal by passing zirconium tetrachloride vapor over heated sodium, magnesium, or aluminum (61). In 1914 Lely and Hamburger prepared what has been regarded as the first pure zirconium by heating the tetrachloride with sodium in a bomb (13b). They were able to press their product into rods. The techniques of preparing zirconium by reduction of tetrahalogenides in bombs was studied by Barton and by Hunter and Jones (62), whose work did much

---

57. E. Wedekind and S. J. Lewis, *Met. Chem. Eng.* **12**, 260 (1914).

58. L. M. Dennis and A. E. Spencer, *J. Am. Chem. Soc.* **18**, 673 (1896).

59. V. E. Berglund, *Ingeniøren* **1925**, 270-1; *J. Inst. Metals* **34**, 529.

60. J. H. de Boer and J. D. Fast, German patent **609,501**, Feb. 16, 1935.

61. L. Troost, *Compt. rend.* **61**, 109 (1865).

62. M. A. Hunter and A. Jones, *Trans. Electrochem. Soc.* **44**, 23 (1923).

to demonstrate the feasibility of the procedure as an industrial process. It was soon found that calcium or magnesium could be used in place of sodium or potassium (63), and magnesium was particularly satisfactory because of the ease of obtaining and maintaining it in any oxygen-free condition. The reduction of the tetrachloride by magnesium was developed to a high state of perfection by W. J. Kroll and his associates. They performed the reaction under a blanket of argon or other inert gas, to protect the product from atmospheric contamination (64), and removed excess magnesium and magnesium chloride by volatilizing them out of the zirconium sponge (65).

The attractiveness of sodium amalgam as a reducing agent for zirconium tetrachloride has been noted, but no suitable method for its use has been achieved up to this time (66).

Studies of the vapor phase reduction of zirconium halogenides led eventually to their thermal decomposition without the use of a chemical reducing agent. Weintraub reported reducing the halogenide vapors with a mixture of sodium or potassium vapor with hydrogen at about 1325°, obtaining metal of only 0.001% impurity (67). He was also able to form the metal by passing zirconium tetrachloride vapor into an electric arc (68). Maddex found that when gaseous zirconium halogenides were passed into molten magnesium, sodium, calcium, or potassium heated to only 750-900°, reduction to the metal occurred (69), and a French patent disclosed that when zirconium chloride or bromide vapors impinged on any adequately heated, inert refractory surface in a reducing environment, the metal was deposited (70). In 1921 the British Thompson-Houston Company obtained a patent on a process for depositing zirconium metal on a tungsten wire by heating the wire in a mixture of zirconium chloride and hydrogen gases (71). In such processes the hydrogen was actually dispensable.

A practical process for obtaining zirconium metal by pyrolysis of a halogenide was worked out by van Arkel and de Boer. They recognized that the deposition of a metal from its compound in the gaseous phase requires that at the temperature of the operation the metal be solid and its vapor pressure be less than the partial pressure of the metal in the gas phase. They reasoned that since zirconium iodide vapor dissociates to a greater extent

63. J. H. de Boer and J. D. Fast, *Z. anorg. allgem. Chem.* **187**, 177-89 (1930).
64. A. W. Schlechten and W. J. Kroll, U.S. Patent Application **688,870**; *Official Gazette* **628**, 1531 (1949).
65. Schlechten, Kroll, and L. A. Yerkes, U.S. Patent **2,482,127**, Sept. 20, 1949.
66. R. B. MacMullin, *Chem. Eng. Progr.* **46**, 440-55 (1950).
67. E. Weintraub, U.S. Patent **1,306,568**, June 10, 1919.
68. Weintraub, British Patent **25,033**, Oct. 27, 1910.
69. P. J. Maddex, U.S. Patent, **2,556,763**, June 12, 1951.
70. French Patent **749,383**, June 22, 1933.
71. British Patent **182,699**, July 19, 1921.

than the chloride or bromide at a given temperature, it should prove most satisfactory for the pyrolytic preparation of the metal. They heated a tungsten filament to 2000° in a chamber maintained at 650° containing vapor formed by heating the tetraiodide. After a few hours they obtained layers of 2 to 4 cm of zirconium of extremely high purity. The metal exhibited a hexagonal lattice and was identical with zirconium prepared by other methods. It was extraordinarily flexible (72, 73, 74). It was eventually ascertained that the filament temperature need be no higher than 1200-1300°, and that a chamber temperature of about 340° was most satisfactory (75). When the filament temperature exceeds 1800°, rapid crystal growth of zirconium occurs, but a tungsten-zirconium eutectic forms, resulting in the melting of the filament. Below 1800° a relatively fine crystal structure is obtained (72, 76, 77, 78). On a tungsten wire consisting of a single crystal, long zirconium crystals form, but on a polycrystalline tungsten wire, fine crystals develop (63).

In the later practice of the van Arkel-de Boer process, the chamber was made of Pyrex or Hastalloy. Crude zirconium metal, prepared by some other process, was sealed into the evacuated chamber along with about 82.5 g iodine per liter of chamber volume. When the chamber was heated, the iodine attacked the crude metal, forming zirconium iodide vapor. This vapor impinged on a heated tungsten, or better, a zirconium filament in the upper part of the chamber, and decomposed, depositing zirconium on the filament and liberating iodine. The iodine attacked more of the crude metal until the cyclic process had transferred all the zirconium from the crude raw material to the pure deposit on the filament. Zirconium so prepared is outstandingly free of carbon, nitrogen, oxygen, and hydrogen, since it is in the nature of the process that these elements are not transferred from the raw materials to the product. Impurities such as aluminum, iron, silicon, or tin, if present in the crude metal, however, will be carried into the product (63).

In the reductions of the halogenides, all possible care is taken to keep oxygen and oxygen-containing substances out of the reacting system. In the reduction of zirconium dioxide, the presence of oxygen as part of the reacting system necessitates an extreme refinement of operating conditions. Not only the reduction of zirconium dioxide as such is required, but the

72. A. E. van Arkel and J. H. de Boer, *Z. anorg. allgem. Chem.* **153**, 1-8 (1926).

73. J. H. de Boer, *Ind. Eng. Chem.* **19**, 1256-9 (1927).

74. J. H. de Boer and A. E. van Arkel, U.S. Patent **1,709,781**, April 16, 1929.

75. W. M. Raynor, in *Zirconium and Zirconium Alloys,* American Society for Metals, Cleveland, 1953, p. 79.

76. British Patent **260,062**, August 7, 1925.

77. German Patent **476,099**, Oct. 27, 1925.

78. A. E. van Arkel and J. H. de Boer, U.S. Patent **1,671,213**, May 29, 1928.

prevention of the dissolution of oxygen in the zirconium metal, which might be represented

$$Zr + ZrO_2 \rightarrow Zr,O \qquad (3)$$

or, if the solution Zr,O forms, to deoxygenate it. This result has been achieved, and the following will serve to trace the development of the achievement.

The Thermit process of Goldschmidt and Vautin has long been successfully applied to the preparation of metals from oxides, but when applied to the reduction of zirconium dioxide, zirconium-aluminum alloys were obtained rather than zirconium metal. The products were also contaminated with aluminum and zirconium oxides which could not be separated from the metal (80). In spite of the persistence of these inadequacies of the method, a patent on the aluminothermic reduction was obtained by Kuhne in 1909 (81). A year later Weiss and Neumann reported a general method of freeing refractory metals such as titanium and zirconium from impurities. They fabricated rods of the impure metal and used them as electrodes of an electric arc. When the arc was struck, the metal of the upper electrode was melted and dropped onto the surface of the lower electrode. During the process impurities were volatilized by the heat of the arc and stalactites of pure metal built up on the lower electrode surface (13). Marden and Rich applied this method to the removal of aluminum from zirconium-aluminum alloy, conducting the purification in an atmosphere of nitrogen at only 10 to 11 mm pressure. They recovered zirconium at 99.76-99.89% purity (55, 56).

In 1907 Burger reported obtaining zirconium of 98.77% purity by heating zirconia with an excess of calcium. In the first stage of the reaction, zirconium metal formed and by-product calcium oxide reacted with unreduced zirconia to form calcium zirconate. But on elevating the temperature to 1050°, more calcium reacted with the calcium zirconate, yielding zirconium metal (83). M. Petinot described the reduction of calcium zirconate with carbon, but it is unlikely that he obtained metal of reasonable purity (84). Kroll found calcium hydride to be somewhat better than calcium metal for reducing zirconium dioxide (in the presence of alkaline earth chlorides). The metal which he obtained was workable but contained enough residual oxygen to render it brittle (85). Zabel has described the preparation of pure zirconium by heating zirconium dioxide with calcium hydride in an atmosphere of hydrogen, followed by leaching the reaction

80. S. A. Tucker and H. R. Moody, *J. Am. Chem. Soc.* **81,** 14 (1902).
81. K. A. Kuhne, U.S. Patent **910,394,** 1909.
83. A. Burger, *Reduktionen durch Calcium,* Basel, 1907, p. 30.
84. N. Petinot, U.S. Patent **1,335,982,** April 6, 1920.
85. W. J. Kroll, *Z. anorg. allgem. Chem.* **234,** 42-50 (1937).

product with dilute acid. If excess calcium hydride is present, the product is contaminated with zirconium hydride (86). Lindsay and Alexander used lithium hydride in a similar process (87). Alexander also found that if zirconium dioxide were heated with an alkaline earth metal to 500° under a hydrogen atmosphere, the alkaline earth hydride formed, giving off enough heat to bring the mixture to a temperature of 800-900° at which the hydride reacted with the zirconia to form zirconium metal (88). Reduction of zirconium dioxide with calcium alone was brought to a very high state of perfection by Lilliendahl and Rentschler (89).

Zirconium metal which contained up to 0.5% oxygen has been purified so as to contain only about 0.02% oxygen by heating it with molten calcium or in contact with calcium vapor at 1000-1300° for five hours or longer. When liquid calcium was used, it was found that it must be nitrogen-free or else the zirconium would be contaminated with nitrogen. The calcium could be purified of nitrogen by heating it with scrap zirconium prior to its use for removal of oxygen to form high grade zirconium (90, 90b).

Wedekind and Kuzel obtained zirconium of 99.09% purity and with 97.5% yield by heating a mixture of zirconia and magnesium in an iron tube to 1000° under reduced pressure. They extracted the pulverized reaction product with water and dilute acids (91, 92, 93). De Boer and Fast used a mixture of magnesium and sodium for the reaction (63).

In 1923 Ruff and Brintzinger compared the reducing properties of sodium, calcium, and magnesium on zirconia at 900-950° and found that sodium could not be used (94), as would be expected from the free-energy relationships involved (Table 1.4). However, if sodium is mixed with an alkaline earth chloride and zirconia, satisfactory reductions can be obtained (95, 96, 97). This is doubtless the result of the liberation of alkali earth metal by the interaction of the sodium and the salt.

It was noted by Bailey in 1886 that zirconium dioxide is not reduced by

86. H. W. Zabel, *Chem. Inds.* **60**, 37-9 (1947).
87. T. Lindsay and P. P. Alexander, U.S. Patent **2,545,821**, March 20, 1951.
88. P. P. Alexander, U.S. Patent **2,584,411**, Feb. 2, 1952.
89. W. C. Lilliendahl and H. C. Rentschler, *Trans. Am. Electrochem. Soc.* **91**, 285-94 (1947).
90. W. C. Lilliendahl, E. D. Gregory, and D. M. Wroughton, *J. Am. Electrochem. Soc.* **99**, 187-90 (1952).
90b. Lilliendahl and Gregory, U.S. Patent **2,707,679**, May 3, 1955.
91. H. Kuzel, British Patent **23,215**, Oct. 11, 1909.
92. H. Kuzel, U.S. Patent **1,088,909**, Mar. 3, 1914.
93. H. Kuzel and E. Wedekind, *Ann.* **395**, 149 (1913).
94. O. Ruff and H. Brintzinger, *Z. anorg. allgem. Chem.* **129**, 267 (1923).
95. J. W. Marden and C. C. van Voorhis, U.S. Patent **1,573,083**, Feb. 16, 1929.
96. A. S. Cachemaille, British Patent **238,347**, July 7, 1924.
97. Cachemaille, British Patent **238,663**, July 7, 1924.

hydrogen. However, zirconium alloys with tungsten (98), iron, or nickel (99) have been prepared by heating zirconium dioxide with hydrogen in the presence of the alloying metal. The tungsten alloy was formed at 2500°. The free energy of formation of the alloy when added to the free energy of reduction by hydrogen is apparently sufficient to reduce the zirconium. The critical role of hydrogen is by no means proved, however. Even in the absence of hydrogen, tungsten will react with zirconium at a very high temperature to form tungsten-zirconium alloy, although the reverse reaction occurs at lower temperature (100).

The reaction of carbon with zirconium dioxide gives largely the face-centered cubic crystalline solution of carbon in zirconium which is represented Zr,C. Up to one atom of carbon may be dissolved per atom of zirconium, and at or near this maximum carbon content the product has been known as *zirconium carbide*. At lower carbon contents, the product of identical crystal structure is known as *zirconium cyanonitride*. The name was given in deference to its nitrogen content, which may be 0.5-2.5%, derived from the atmosphere during the preparation of the product in an open arc furnace. Attempts have been made to prepare elementary zirconium by heating the carbide with zirconium dioxide (101). Only impure products have been obtained in this fashion. Heating zirconia or zircon with calcium carbide gives primarily zirconium carbide (102, 103). In one preparation, zirconia heated with calcium carbide in a calcium oxide crucible gave a product consisting 20% of zirconium and 71% of zirconium carbide. A refined portion containing 70% zirconium was obtained by physical separation (104).

Reductions of zirconium in the electric furnace with boron or silicon have yielded alloy products only.

The improbability of a direct electrodeposition of zirconium has already been discussed above, as well as the feasibility and actual achievement of a stepwise process in which a metal such as sodium, potassium, calcium, or magnesium is liberated electrolytically in the presence of a zirconium compound with which it then reacts to yield zirconium metal. A process of the latter type was first achieved by Troost, who electrolyzed molten sodium and potassium fluozirconates (61). Subsequently, Wedekind (104b) and Marden and Rich (56) obtained amorphous zirconium powder by this

98. H. von Wartenburg, J. Broy, and R. Reinicke, *Z. Elektrochem.* 9, 633 (1903).
99. W. Rohn, French Patent 730,718, Jan. 29, 1932.
100. H. von Wartenburg and H. Moehl, *Z. physik. Chem.* 128, 439-44 (1927).
101. W. Rohn, German Patent 600,369, Sept. 29, 1934.
102. L. Renaux, *Contribution à l'étude de la zircone,* Paris, 1900.
103. H. Moissan, *Le four electrique,* Paris, 1897.
104. W. Dawihl, *Tonind. Ztg.* 58, 449 (1934).
104b. E. Wedekind, *Z. anorg. allgem. Chem.* 33, 81 (1902).

method. Driggs and Lilliendahl obtained zirconium by electrolyzing molten salt baths containing sodium and potassium chlorides and potassium fluozirconate (105, 106). Plotnikov and Kirichenko electrolyzed a melt containing aluminum and potassium chlorides, sodium fluoride, and zirconia, held at 300-550° in a porcelain cell. They used a copper cathode and an aluminum or graphite anode. At relatively low current densities (>5 amp/sq dm) and temperatures (300-400°), only zirconium was found deposited on the cathode, while at higher current densities and temperatures both aluminum and zirconium were found. Their data indicated a decomposition potential of 1 volt for zirconium tetrachloride and 1.95 volts for the dioxide (107). They also obtained zirconium under similar conditions by the electrolysis of molten mixtures of potassium fluozirconate, sodium chloride, and potassium chloride (108). Steinberg, Sibert, and Wainer have studied intensively the practical operation of electrolytic cells of this type and have found the apparent decomposition potential for zirconium tetrachloride in molten potassium chloride-sodium chloride mixtures to range from 1.41 volts at 843° to 2.33 volts at 621°. Higher potentials were required in fluoride-containing systems (108b). They succeeded in preparing zirconium of 99.8-99.9% purity with carbon content 0.05%, oxygen 0.05%, and nitrogen 0.003% (108c).

As against the performance of the electrochemical process, Potvin and Farnham simply added molten sodium to a mixture of potassium fluozirconate, sodium chloride, and potassium chloride at 800° and obtained zirconium metal (109).

When fused salts containing zirconium are electrolyzed, using molten electrodes of zinc or cadmium, alloys of zirconium with these metals are obtained (110).

Bradt and Linford electrolyzed aqueous solutions containing sodium and zirconium sulfates. In an electrolysis which they regarded as particularly favorable for the deposition of zirconium, their electrolyte contained 18 g of ZrO_2 per 100 ml, the pH was 1.20, the temperature 32°, and the current density used was 0.012 amp-sq cm. They mistook a cathode deposit for zirconium metal (54). Subsequently a technique for the electroreduction of ketones between electrodes allegedly plated with zirconium by the method

105. F. H. Driggs, U.S. Patent 1,835,025, Dec. 8, 1931.

106. F. H. Driggs and W. C. Lilliendahl, Canadian Patent 323,060, June 7, 1932.

107. V. A. Plotnikov and E. I. Kirichenko, *Mem. Inst. Chem. Acad. Sci. Ukrain. S.S.R.* 6, 13-15 (1939).

108. V. A. Plotnikov and E. B. Gutman, *J. Appl. Chem. U.S.S.R.* 19, 826-32 (1946).

108b. M. A. Steinberg, M. E. Sibert, and E. Wainer, in *Zirconium and Zirconium Alloys,* American Society for Metals, Cleveland, 1953, pp. 37-72.

108c. Steinberg, Sibert, and Wainer, *J. Electrochem. Soc.* 101, 63-78 (1954).

109. R. Potvin and G. S. Farnham, *Trans. Can. Inst. Mining, Met.* 49, 516-23 (1946).

110. British patent 660,908, Nov. 14, 1951.

of Bradt and Linford was patented (111). Their findings, however, could not be established by other investigators (108, 112, 113), nor were there any subsequent developments by Bradt and Linford themselves of this process. It therefore appears that they did not, in fact, obtain deposits of zirconium metal. Other reported processes for the electrolytic deposition of zirconium from aqueous or organic solutions appear similarly to have been misinterpreted by those who reported them (114, 115, 116).

THE CHEMICAL BEHAVIOR OF ELEMENTARY ZIRCONIUM

Nearly all studies of zirconium and its compounds have been made on specimens containing 0.4-2.0% of hafnium. Since there are no indications that the presence of hafnium makes for qualitative differences in the behavior of zirconium, and even the quantitative differences are usually trifling, the presence of hafnium will be ignored in the following discussion. The effects of other impurities will be dealt with as required, according to the availability of information. The physical properties of elementary zirconium will not be elaborated upon in the work, but a summary of the more pertinent physical properties is given in Table 1.5. For detailed treatment of the physical properties of zirconium, the reader may consult reference (117) and the numerous sources cited in that work.

TABLE 1.5. PHYSICAL PROPERTIES OF ZIRCONIUM (118)

M.p. (β), °C	1830 ± 40
B.p. °C	2900
α-β transformation, °C	862
density, hot rolled, g/cc	6.586
density, cold rolled, g/cc	6.505
Crystal structure	
α	hexagonal close-packed
β	body-centered cubic
Cell dimensions, A	
α	a = 3.228, c = 5.120, c/a = 1.59
β	a = 3.61

111. O. C. Slotterbeck, U.S. Patent **2,408,101**, Sept. 24, 1946.

112. Tatsuyuki Kita, Tadashi Tokumitsu, and Tominosuke Katsurai, *Bull. Inst. Phys. Chem. Research Chem. Ed.* (*Tokyo*), **23**, 239-40 (1944).

113. M. L. Holt, *J. Electrochem. Soc.* **98**, 33C-35C (1951).

114. Katsunaga Koizumi, Japanese patents **172,312**, Feb. 12, 1946; **172,621**, May 9, 1946; and **172,982**, June 26, 1946.

115. Keiki Kamibayashi, Japanese patents **172,299**, Feb. 8, 1946, and **176,653**, Sept. 11, 1948.

116. R. S. Miner, Jr., and L. E. Klakmap, Jr., U.S. Patent **2,510,128**, June 6, 1950.

117. G. L. Miller, *Zirconium*, Academic Press, Inc., New York, 1954.

TABLE 1.5. *Continued*

Specific heat (at room temperature) cal/g/°C . . . .   0.67 ± 0.001
Thermal expansion, linear coefficient, per °K
   α, 298-1143°K, along a axis . . . . 5.5×10^{-6}
                 along c axis . . . . 10.8×10^{-6}
   β, 1143-1600°K . . . . 9.7×10^{-6}
Thermal conductivity, at 125°C (cal/sec)(sq cm)(°C/cm)   0.035 ± 5%
Magnetic susceptibility, room temperature, cgs units . . 1.3×10^{-6}
Thermionic work function, ev 4.1
Electrical resistivity (crystal bar) ohm-cm . . . . 45×10^{-6}
Hardness (crystal bar), Rockwell B   25-30
Tensile strength, 0.25 in. rolled bar, machined to 0.16 in.,
   lb/sq in   128,900
Vapor pressure, 1949-2054°K . . . .   log P (atm) = $-(31{,}066/T)$
                                         + 7.3351 − 2,415
                                       $\times 10^{-4}T$ (119)

Elementary zirconium has been known and studied in massive form, as granules or powder, and as a colloid. In all these forms the same hexagonal crystal symmetry has been found to prevail at the ordinary temperature (120). All show substantially the same chemical properties except for the effects of variations in particle size. Variations in chemical behavior which are of quantitative origin may assume qualitative importance by indirection. Thus, in contact with certain reagents, such as fluorine or molten caustic alkali, there is an incipient reaction of zirconium. When the zirconium is massive, the formation of an adherent film of reaction product passivates the surface and the reaction ceases. To the superficial observer little or no reaction has occurred. But if the diameter of the zirconium particle is less than twice the usual film thickness, quantitative reaction will be observed to occur. Moreover, since the reaction proceeds at a velocity which is proportional to the specific surface, when the zirconium particles are smaller there will be a more rapid evolution of heat and a higher peak temperature will be obtained. At the higher peak temperature there may be a qualitatively different behavior than at lower temperatures. The size of zirconium particles therefore has an empirical effect on their chemical properties, although actually the small particles are behaving no differently than the larger masses would behave if the same physical conditions could be made to be in effect.

118. *Encyclopedia of Chemical Technology,* Interscience Publishers, Inc., vol. 15, New York, 1956.

119. G. B. Skinner, J. W. Edwards, and H. I. Johnston, *J. Am. Chem. Soc.* **73,** 174-6 (1951).

120. A. W. Hull, *Phys. Rev.* **18,** 88 (1921).

In Berzelius's first preparation of zirconium in 1824, he noticed that if he washed the crude preparation with water alone, the entire product was carried in finely suspended state through the pores of a filter, while if a solution of ammonium chloride in dilute hydrochloric acid was used, the colloid was coagulated into large flakes. The colloid could also be flocculated by heat. In the light of later data on zirconium, the behavior was to be expected. Zirconium is a highly refractory metal. The crystal nuclei which form have no melt from which to recrystallize and no appreciable vapor phase to support their growth. Thus, regardless of the reaction by which zirconium is produced, there is little opportunity to form particles larger than colloidal size. This ceased to be the case only in the very much later high-temperature formation of zirconium developed by van Arkel and de Boer (*supra*). In 1890 Winkler obtained results similar to those of Berzelius, recovering colloidal zirconium upon reducing zirconium tetrachloride or zirconia with magnesium (121). A decade later Wedekind obtained colloidal solutions of zirconium after reducing potassium fluozirconate with magnesium and washing the reduction product with dilute acid. The colloid appeared dark blue by transmitted light, and he observed the particles to be positively charged and to have an average mass of less than 10^{-11} mg. The colloid was coagulated by hydrogen peroxide, by salts of alkaline reaction, and by heating. On drying the aqueous colloid, the last traces of water were held very tenaciously and were released only after heating *in vacuo* to at least 200°. The dried powder was very pyrophoric (122, 123).

Under the reported conditions of preparing zirconium colloids, significant amounts of hydrogen, oxygen, nitrogen, and carbon may have been dissolved in the metallic product and not have been detected by the experimenters. The presence of some or all of these elements may have influenced the observations.

It has been shown by Kuzel that many metallic elements, including zirconium, can be dispersed colloidally by mechanical means (124, 125), and he has described techniques of fabricating articles from the colloids by expressing the water and heating the shaped objects in nonoxidizing atmospheres (126). Brown observed tantalic acid to peptize zirconium particles (127). Natanson coagulated zirconium hydrosols by stirring them with xylene in the presence of phenylhydrazine. He was able to repeptize the

121. C. Winkler, *Ber.* **23**, 2642 (1890); **24**, 808 (1908).
122. E. Wedekind, *Rev. Internat. Congr. Appl. Chem.* **5**, IV, 439 (1903).
123. Wedekind, *Z. Chem. u. Ind. Kolloide* **2**, 289-93 (1908).
124. H. Kuzel, German patent **186,980**, April 28, 1906.
125. Kuzel, German patent **197,379**, Dec. 13, 1905.
126. Kuzel, German patent **200,466**, May 1, 1906.
127. J. L. Brown, U.S. Patent **1,934,294**, Nov. 7, 1933.

coagulate in xylene, using rubber as the peptizing agent (128, 129). Zirconium has been deposited electrophoretically from a suspension in alcohol and ether containing small amounts of hydrogen chloride and nitrocellulose (130).

Dry colloidal zirconium and finely pulverized zirconium are black and resemble carbon in appearance. They burn in air, nitrogen, or carbon dioxide (131). Dust clouds of zirconium powder in air, containing 45 to 300 mg/1, are explosive. It has been observed that a thin coating of copper on zirconium powder reduces the ignition sensitivity, but when ignition is accomplished, the explosion is nearly as powerful as without the copper (132). Zirconium powder is usually shipped in water to avoid fire and explosion hazards.

Massive zirconium is a silver-gray metal similar to steel in appearance. It is known in the allotropic forms listed in Table 1.5, and it has been found that no other polymorphic changes occur when zirconium is submitted simultaneously to pressures up to 50,000 kg/sq cm and shearing stresses up to the point of plastic flow (133). At ordinary temperatures massive zirconium appears not to be active chemically, but this is due to an invisible, adherent coating of oxide which forms on the metal when it is exposed to air; the metal itself is actually quite active. When the metal is in contact with water or other liquids, zirconium cations do not dissolve into the liquid and the mass does not assume the characteristic negative charge of the more active metals of the electromotive series (122, 134). Zirconium does not undergo galvanic corrosion or exhibit any behavior reflecting an ionic (Nernst) solution pressure.

Latimer has calculated the potential of the change, $Zr(O) \to Zr$ (IV), to be 1.43 volts, based on the free-energy change (135). He properly represented the over-all reaction

$$Zr + 2H_2O \rightleftharpoons ZrO_2 + 4H^+ + 4e^- \tag{4}$$

To express the mechanism of the reaction, it is perhaps more reasonable to write the equation in terms of a reacting hydroxyl ion

$$Zr + 4OH^- \to ZrO_2 + 2H_2O + 4e^- \tag{5}$$

128. E. M. Natanson, *Kolloid Zhur.* **11**, 336-45 (1949).

129. Natanson, *Doklady Akad. Nauk. S.S.S.R.* **64**, 831-3 (1949).

130. French patent **938,907**, Oct. 28, 1948.

131. I. Hartmann and H. P. Greenwald, *Mining and Met.* **26**, 331-5 (1945).

132. I. Hartmann, J. Nagy, and M. Jacobson, *U.S. Bureau of Mines, Rep. Invest.* **4835**, 16 pp. (1951).

133. P. W. Bridgman, *Phys. Rev.* **48**, 825-47 (1935).

134. D. Schlain, C. B. Kenahan, and Doris V. Steele, *J. Electrochem. Soc.* **102**, 102-9 (1955).

135. W. M. Latimer, *The Oxidation States of the Elements and Their Potentials in Aqueous Solutions*, Prentice-Hall, Inc., New York, 1938.

Hatwell measured the electrical potential of a freshly abraded zirconium metal surface in a 3% sodium chloride solution under an argon atmosphere. The potential was −0.990 volts. When the abraded surface was exposed to air for 15 minutes and again measured against the same electrolyte, its potential was −0.450 volts (136).

Anodized films can be formed by making zirconium metal the anode in electrolyte solutions containing oxy anions, such as sulfate or chromate, but the films do not form if only anions such as chloride are present (137). The oxide film on anodically polarized zirconium has been demonstrated to be monoclinic zirconium dioxide, i.e., baddeleyite (138). Misch and Ruther anodized zirconium in nitric acid solutions of less than 14% strength, using a current density of 1 ma/sq cm. Oxide layers of low resistance formed. At higher concentrations of acid, oxide layers formed which progressively changed from white to black, the latter being particularly hard and coherent. All the films consisted of monoclinic zirconia as the only phase. The color was probably due to anion defects, the white oxide having very few or none (139).

Zirconium has been etched and polished for metallographic study by being made the anode in a cell containing perchloric acid mixed with acetic acid and ethanol or butoxymethanol (140, 141).

The effects of various liquids on zirconium are summarized in Table 1.6. It is seen that zirconium strongly resists attack by most organic and inorganic reagents such as methyl alcohol, salt solutions, and both strong and weak acids. The resistance to the last three is attributable to the nongalvanic quality of zirconium and the protection of the surface film. However, zirconium is corroded by chloride solutions containing oxidizing agents. This might be regarded as susceptibility to even infinitesimal concentrations of chlorine, i.e.,

$$Zr + 4[Cl] \rightarrow ZrCl_4 \qquad (6)$$

but alternatively, it may be regarded as an ionic attack analogous to that of equation 5:

$$Zr + 4Cl^- \rightarrow ZrCl_4 + 4e^-$$

and $\qquad 4Fe^{+3} + 4e^- \rightarrow 4Fe^{+2}$ $\qquad\qquad (7-9)$

and $\qquad ZrCl_4 + H_2O \rightarrow ZrO^{++} + 2H^+ + 4Cl^-$

The oxidizing ions, Fe^{+3}, Cu^{+2}, NO_3^-, etc., make it possible for the re-

136. H. Hatwell, *Compt. rend.* **236**, 1881-3 (1953).
137. A. Charlesby, *Acta Met.* **1**, 340-7 (1953).
138. W. G. Burgers, A. Claasen, and I. Zernike, *Z. Phys.* **74**, 593-603 (1932).
139. R. D. Misch and W. E. Ruther, *J. Electrochem. Soc.* **100**, 531-7 (1953).
140. H. P. Roth, *Metal Progress* **58**, 709-11 (1950).
141. P. A. Jacquet, *Metallurgia* **42**, 268-70 (1950).

action represented by equation **7** to proceed to the right. As against this, the attack by hydrofluoric acid and hot concentrated sulfuric, phosphoric, and trichloracetic acids is due to the formation of soluble complex acids of zirconium, e.g.,

$$Zr + 3H_2SO_4 + H_2O \rightarrow H_4ZrO(SO_4)_3 + 2H_2$$

$$Zr + 6HF \rightarrow H_2ZrF_6 + 2H_2 \text{ (142)}$$

(10-11)

Zirconium does not form stable complex anions with aqueous hydrochloric acid and hence it is not attacked by this acid.

TABLE 1.6. CORROSION OF COMMERCIAL INDUCTION-MELTED ZIRCONIUM BY VARIOUS AGENTS (AQUEOUS SOLUTIONS UNLESS OTHERWISE INDICATED.) (142b)

Agent	Attack
Acetic acid, all strengths, hot and cold	0
Alcohol, methyl, 99%, boiling	0
Aluminum chloride, 20-30%, hot and cold	0
Aluminum potassium sulfate (alum), 10% and 50%, boiling	0
Aqua regia, 19-26°	4 (strong)
Bromine water, saturated, boiling	0
Calcium hypochlorite	0
Chlorine saturated with water vapor, room temp	4 (strong)
Chromic acid, 10-30%, hot and cold	0
Cupric chloride, 2.5-10%, 35°	2
same, 60-100°	4
Ferric chloride, 1-10%, 35-60°	1
>5%, 100°, also >15%, 35°	3-4
Formic acid, 90%, 20-50°, boiling	0
Hydrochloric acid, 1-20%, 35-100°, aerated	0-1
60°, 3 atm pressure; 110°	2-4
Hydrofluoric acid, 3%, hot or cold	4
Hydrogen peroxide, 10-50%	0
Lactic acid, 10-85%, 35°, boiling	0
Magnesium chloride, 5-42%, 35-100°	0
Manganese chloride, 20%, 35-100°	0
Mercuric chloride, 1%-saturated, 35-100°	0
Monochloracetic acid, 100%, boiling	0
Nitric acid, 10-69.5%, 35°-100° (except >40% at 35°)	0
Nitric acid, red fuming, room temp	0
Nitric acid, white fuming with $\frac{1}{3}$ red, boiling	0
Nitric acid, plus 1-10% sulfuric acid, 100°	0
Oxalic acid, 1-25%, 25-100°	0

142. M. E. Straumanis and J. I. Ballass, *Z. anorg. allgem. Chem.* **278**, 33-41 (1955).
142b. Zirconium Metals Corp. of America, *Properties and Prices of Zirconium Metal,* unpublished revised manuscript.

TABLE 1.6. *Continued*

Agent	Attack
Phosphoric acid, 10-85%, 25-60°...............................	0
75-100%, 100° to boiling..	3-4
Sodium hydroxide, 10-40%, 25° and 100°.........................	0
fused at 319° and 370°..	0
Sodium hypochlorite, 0.5%, 35-100°..............................	0
Stannic chloride, 24%, 35-100°..................................	0
Sulfuric acid, 1-50%, room temp................................	0
hot and concd..	4 (strong)
Sulfurous acid, 6%, 100°..	0
Trichloracetic acid, 10% and 50%, boiling.......................	0
glacial, boiling...	4
Zinc chloride, 5% and 20%, 100°................................	0

Key: $0 = \leq 0.5$ mils penetration per year; $1 = 0.5$-5 mils penetration per year; $2 = 5$-20 mils penetration per year; $3 = 20$-50 mils penetration per year; $4 = >50$ mils penetration per year.

The oxide film on zirconium impedes its reaction with HYDROGEN, but the oxide-coated metal reacts slowly with hydrogen at 250°. If the metal is heated to 500° in a high vacuum, the film dissolves into the metal, and the metal is then able to react rapidly with hydrogen at 150°. The reaction leads to the formation of interstitial solutions of ultimate composition corresponding to the formula ZrH_2. Oxygen, nitrogen, or carbon dissolved in the zirconium decrease the hydrogen-absorbing capacity (143). The dissolved hydrogen exists in dynamic equilibrium with gaseous hydrogen of the environment, and only contaminated zirconium exhibits a hysteresis phenomenon during the absorption and desorption of hydrogen. Hydrogen is soluble in both α- and β-zirconium, the solubility being greater in the latter. In both the solubility increases with rising temperature (144). No film of hydride forms analogous to the oxide films. The hydrogen appears to diffuse into the lattice as atoms, and the reaction obeys the square root of pressure law (145). The presence of hydrogen in zirconium renders it brittle, but unlike other embrittling elements, it can be removed from the metal by heating *in vacuo*.

Dravnieks followed the progress of reactions between metallic zirconium and gases at 986° by measuring the change in the electrical conductivity of the metal. He found the gases to react with zirconium in the following order of decreasing activity: oxygen, air, steam, nitrogen (containing 0.5%

143. C. F. P. Berington, S. L. Martin, and D. H. Matthews, *Proc. Intern. Congr. Pure and Appl. Chem.* (London) **11**, 3-6 (1947).

144. E. A. Gulbransen and K. F. Andrew, *Rev. métal.* **51**, 101-7 (1954).

145. Gulbransen and Andrews, *J. Metal.* **1**, 515-26 (1949).

oxygen), carbon dioxide, carbon monoxide, and ethylene. He noted an increase in the rate of attack by carbon dioxide when the gas was ionized, but ionization decreased the rate of attack by carbon monoxide, steam, and nitrogen. In other cases ionization had no effect (146).

It has already been noted that zirconium powder is highly combustible in air. Kinetic studies of the reaction rate of ductile zirconium with OXYGEN show the oxidation rate to be appreciable at 200°. The energy of activation of the reaction has been calculated to be 18,200 cal/mole and the entropy of activation −25.6 cal/mole (145).

When zirconium is heated in air, both oxygen and nitrogen enter into the formation of a scale. In time a two-layer scale may form, an outer white or buff scale of zirconium dioxide and an inner black scale containing both zirconium dioxide and the face-centered cubic solid solution of nitrogen in zirconium represented Zr,N. The white formation has been observed to predominate below about 1050° and the black above that temperature. It requires about 100 hours of exposure of the metal to air at 400° for the white scale to appear, and less than 5 minutes at 1300° (147). Zirconium scales are very adherent, tough, and resistant to chemical attack. One zirconium dioxide scale was observed to be 125μ thick and to have a dielectric constant of 12.3 (148). Pickling baths for removal of zirconium scale have been formulated with hydrofluoric and nitric acids, and the addition of lead nitrate and metallic lead has been recommended (149). A polishing solution for hafnium and zirconium for use at 15-30°, consisting of 300-600 cc of concentrated nitric acid, 175-300 cc of 30% fluosilicic acid, and 50-100 g of ammonium acid fluoride, is said to be particularly suitable for metal containing carbide inclusions (149b).

Specimens of the solid zirconium metal have been made to absorb up to at least 29 atom % of oxygen without forming a new phase. The lattice constants increase, but a becomes constant at 10 atom % while c continues to increase regularly. The specific gravity increases in such fashion as to indicate that oxygen is absorbed in the interstices of the zirconium lattice, and zirconium atoms are not replaced. At 1000° the oxygen atoms have great mobility in the lattice and under an electric potential they migrate as ions toward the positive pole. Measurable increase of oxygen concentration occurs at the anode end, and measurable decrease at the cathode end. The transfer can be reversed at will (150). The anionic condition of the oxygen

146. A. Dravnieks, *J. Phys. and Colloid Chem.* **55**, 540-9 (1951).

147. C. A. Phalnikar and W. M. Baldwin, *Proc. Am. Soc. Testing Materials* **51**, 1038-5 (1951).

148. A. Guntherschulze and H. Betz, *Z. Elektrochem.* **37**, 726-34 (1931).

149. E. A. Dilling and G. L. Frederic, U.S. Patent **2,653,134**, Sept. 22, 1953.

149b. J. G. Beach, U.S. Patent **2,711,364**, June 21, 1955.

150. J. H. de Boer and J. D. Fast, *Rec. trav. chim.* **59**, 161-7 (1940).

can be regarded as the result to two electronic exchanges within the metal phase: (1) in typical metal fashion, the zirconium transfers one or more orbital electrons to free, extraorbital positions, and (2) the oxygen accepts one or two of the electrons into its 2p orbital vacancies.

Isotherms and isobars on the solubility of hydrogen, oxygen, nitrogen, and carbon in zirconium indicate all to take up interstitial positions in the octahedral holes where they assume negative charges. They are strongly bound, but are nonetheless mobile. They expand the metal lattice but increase the density, and the electrical conductivity decreases (143). In zirconium as well as in a number of other elements, the dissolution of oxygen, nitrogen, or hydrogen in the lattice causes a slight lowering of the photoelectric work function (151).

Zirconium is able to acquire oxygen not only from the gas, but from oxygen-containing compounds as well. The massive metal is unaffected by liquid water, but, as already noted, the finely divided metal becomes contaminated with oxygen when leached with aqueous solutions. The massive metal reacts with steam at red heat and with carbon monoxide or dioxide at 600-800°. In the latter cases zirconium carbide as well as dioxide are formed (152). Zirconium readily takes up oxygen from fused salts such as the chlorate or nitrate, and it has been employed as a reducing metal in Thermit processes (153). Molten zirconium penetrates beryllia, alumina, zirconia, and thoria vessels, and reacts chemically with all except thoria (154). Solid zirconium, however, does not react with zirconia at 1400° (155).

Zirconium metal dissolves in 50 times its weight of molten sodium bisulfate. With fused sodium carbonate, zirconium has been observed to lose 5% of its weight in 2 hours, and with fused sodium peroxide, 4%. In fused caustic soda, it formed a black scale and then appeared to be entirely stable. It has been suggested that zirconium be used for making crucibles for caustic fusions (156). Zirconium reacts with fused borax to form boron, zirconium borides, and zirconium dioxide (157).

Zirconium can absorb at least 20 atom % of NITROGEN without forming a new phase (158). Nitrogen diffuses into zirconium at a much slower rate than oxygen between 425° and 1300°. A marked increase in the rate of penetration occurs at about 900°, for oxygen as well as for nitrogen, doubt-

151. H. C. Rentschler and D. E. Henry, *Trans. Electrochem. Soc.* **87,** 289-297 (1945).

152. W. G. Guldner and L. A. Wooten, *J. Electrochem Soc.* **93,** 223-34 (1948).

153. O. Maresch and F. Viehbock, Australian patent **180,993,** Feb. 10, 1955.

154. F. H. Norton, W. D. Kingery, G. Economos, and M. Humenik, Jr., *U.S. Atomic Energy Comm. Natl. Sci. Foundation, NYO-3144,* 83 pp. 1953.

155. G. Economos, *Ind. Eng. Chem.* **45,** 458-9 (1953).

156. R. S. Young and K. G. A. Strachan, *Chem. and Ind.* **1953,** 154-5.

157. J. L. Andrieux, *Colloq. intern. centre natl. récherche sci. (Paris)* **39,** Electrolyse C7-C10 (1952).

158. J. D. Fast, *Metallwirtschaft* **17,** 641-4 (1938).

less due to the allotropic change (159). The rate is very sensitive to the presence of even traces of oxygen or hydrogen in the reacting gas (145). When hot, nitrogen-containing zirconium is corroded with steam and ammonia can be identified in the steam (160). Conversely zirconium can be nitrided by reaction with ammonia.

The reaction of zirconium with halogens at low temperatures is obscured by the formation of impervious films of halogenation products. The dominating effects of the films is the more significant because of the insolubility of zirconium halogenides in many solvents. To illustrate, titanium powder and some titanium alloys can be dissolved by a solution of iodine in carbon disulfide, since titanium tetraiodide is soluble in this solvent (161), but zirconium is unattacked by such a solution, due to the insolubility of zirconium iodides in carbon bisulfide. Zirconium reacts with fluorine at 190°, but complete solution is prevented by a fluoride coating on the metal (162). At higher temperatures the reaction goes to completion. Zirconium does not react appreciably with molten iodine chloride (163), and it is attacked only superficially by iodine bromide (164). Liquid bromine attacks zirconium slowly (165). As the temperature of the reaction of halogens with zirconium is raised, the effective rate of attack increases and rapid evolution of gaseous tetrahalogenides occurs. With the exception of iodine, the reactions with the halogens are sufficiently exothermic to sustain themselves without external heat being supplied. Similar reactions occur with the hydrogen halogenides, hydrogen and zirconium tetrahalogenide vapor being evolved.

Zirconium is not a strongly catalytic element. The relatively few reactions which zirconium metal has been shown to catalyze are usually better catalyzed by other elements. In particular, zirconium has found virtually no use or promise of use as a single catalyst. In combination with copper it has been observed to catalyze the decomposition of diethyl acetal to diethyl acetate (166) and the esterification of alcohols (167). The latter catalysis occurred also with zirconium alone. In combination with kieselguhr, zirconium catalyzed the formation of n-propane from n-butanol at 120-300°,

159. A. Gulbransen and K. F. Andrew, *J. Electrochem. Soc.* **96**, 364-76 (1949).

160. L. E. Colteryahn, W. Joseph, W. E. Ray, and H. J. Read, *U.S. Atomic Energy Comm.* **NYO-838**, 3-16 (1952).

161. W. B. Blumenthal and H. Smith, *Ind. Eng. Chem.* **42**, 249-51 (1950).

162. H. M. Haendler, S. F. Bartram, R. S. Becker, W. J. Bernard, and S. W. Bukata, *J. Am. Chem. Soc.* **76**, 2177-8 (1954).

163. V. Gutman, *Z. anorg. allgem. Chem.* **264**, 169-73 (1951).

164. Gutman, *Monatsh.* **82**, 280-6 (1951).

165. L. M. Dennis and A. E. Spencer, *J. Am. Chem. Soc.* **18**, 673 (1896).

166. Yu. N. Berg and M. N. Vishnyakov, *J. Gen. Chem. U.S.S.R.* **17**, 1618-25 (1947).

167. S. L. Lel'chuk, D. N. Vaskerich, A. P. Belen'kaya, and F. A. Dashkovskaya, *Izvest. Akad. Nauk. U.S.S.R., Otdel Khim. Nauk* **1946**, 191-200, 411-17.

but was inferior to nickel for this purpose (168). Zirconium, mixed with alumina and silica, catalyzed the conversion of high molecular weight paraffins to unsaturated hydrocarbons (169). It failed to catalyze the formation of dimethyl tin from methyl chloride and tin (170). It had little effect on the yield of platinum-catalyzed oxidation of ammonia, but its presence in this process was associated with an attack on the platinum gauze (171).

GENERAL THEORY OF ZIRCONIUM CHEMISTRY

For the most part the literature has treated zirconium chemistry as a conglomeration of empirically determined facts. While assuming the basic laws of chemistry and physics to apply also to zirconium, it has done relatively little toward making the behavior of zirconium intelligible within this framework of the laws of chemistry and physics. Some proposals for efforts in this direction were published by the author in 1954 (172). In the later sections of this book, the behavior of individual compounds and classes of compounds will be described in connection with the development of a broad pattern into which their behavior appears to fit. In this section of the book, some of the more general fundamentals of this behavior will be sketched.

The electronic configurations of zirconium and hafnium are:

$$\text{Zr} \quad 1s^2 2s^2 2p^6 3s^2 3p^6 3d^{10} 4s^2 4p^6 4d^2 5s^2$$

$$\text{Hf} \quad 1s^2 2s^2 2p^6 3s^2 3p^6 3d^{10} 4s^2 4p^6 4d^{10} 4f^{14} 5s^2 5p^6 5d^2 6s^2$$

and their remarkable chemical similarity is associated with the perfectly similar arrangements of the electrons of the outermost quantum levels and near identity of their atomic radii, zirconium 1.452 A and hafnium 1.442 A. These factors alone, however, do not give sufficient explanation for the similarity, for other pairs of elements, such as silver and gold, also have similar electronic configurations and even closer values for atomic radii. While the exceptional similarity of zirconium and hafnium cannot be explained at this time, its existence suggests that the field affect of the underlying quantum levels of electrons on the valence electrons is more nearly identical in the case of zirconium and hafnium than in that of any other pair of similar elements. It is pertinent also that zirconium and hafnium occur in their compounds almost exclusively with oxidation number 4 and covalently bonded to the maximum extent that is sterically possible. These conditions limit the possibilities for hybridizations of the valence types

168. V. N. Ipatieff, G. S. Monroe, L. E. Fischer, and E. E. Meisinger, *Ind. Eng. Chem.* **41**, 1802-5 (1949).

169. Japanese patent **161,378,** Jan. 28, 1944.

170. A. C. Smith, Jr., and E. G. Rochow, *J. Am. Chem. Soc.* **75**, 403-5 (1953).

171. K. Ruthardt and A Schott, *Festschrift 100 Jährigen Jubiläums W. C. Heraeus G. m. b. H.* **1951,** 15-63.

172. W. B. Blumenthal, *Ind. Eng. Chem.* **46,** 528-539 (1954).

which might tend to multiply the differences between the compounds of the two elements. Differences in electronic arrangements in pairs of elements placed near to zirconium and hafnium in the periodic table, e.g., Nb $4d^25s^1$, Ta $5d^36s^2$ and Mo $4d^55s^1$, W $5d^46s^2$, do not occur in the cases of zirconium and hafnium.

The atomic number of zirconium requires that it be placed in Group IV and period 5 of the periodic table, whence its characteristic valence should be 4 and its maximum coordination number 8. At coordination number 8, the 16 valence electrons will have the arrangements $4d^{10}5p^6$, $4d^{10}5s^25p^4$, or $4d^85s^25p^6$. Table 1.7 lists examples of compounds of zirconium for which there are evidences of coordination numbers 4, 5, 6, 7, and 8, respectively.

TABLE 1.7. EXAMPLES OF THE COORDINATION NUMBERS OF ZIRCONIUM

Coordination Number	Examples
4	$ZrCl_4$ vapor, zirconium alkoxides derived from high molecular weight branched-chain alcohols
5	$KZrF_5$ vapor
6	K_2ZrF_6 vapor
7	K_3ZrF_7 liquid
8	$Zr(CH_3COCH_2COCH_2)_4$

Under terrestrial conditions nearly all zirconium compounds contain the element at oxidation number 4, but di- and trichlorides, bromides, and iodides are known. Their low volatility indicates that they form giant molecules through polymerization, and that the coordination number of zirconium in these compounds is higher than the oxidation number. These compounds are very active chemically, being powerful reducing agents. They disproportionate when heated to form the element and (directly or indirectly) the tetrahalogenides. All their chemical reactions with other substances, such as water, result in the oxidation of the zirconium to the tetravalent state.

Zirconium appears never to form a monatomic ion in its compounds or even to form a valence bond of the classical electrovalent type. Stated otherwise, it appears never to be bonded to other atoms by an electrostatic charge at a characteristic distance such as is typical of other elements which form electrovalencies. Sidgwick thought of the zirconium atom as "not large enough for ionization with a quadruple charge" (172b). According to Mathieu, the elements of atomic numbers 39 to 46 and 72 to 78 cannot exist in their compounds as ions. Much of the electrochemical behavior of these

---

172b. N. V. Sidgwick, *The Electron Theory of Valency,* Oxford University Press, London, 1932, p. 273.

elements might be ascribed to this rule, and in the case of zirconium the entire behavior of the element points to its nonionic character in its compounds. The first four elements of period 5 exhibit the following ionization potentials:

TABLE 1.8. IONIZATION POTENTIAL OF SOME FIFTH PERIOD ELEMENTS

Element	Atomic radius, Ångstrom units	Ionization potentials in volts for various degrees of ionization			
		1	2	3	4
Rubidium	2.16	4.176			
Strontium	1.914	5.672	10.98		
Yttrium	1.616	6.6	12.3	20.4	
Zirconium	1.454	6.95	13.97	24.0	33.8

Zirconium may serve as the central atom in complex ions. In such cases it is covalently bound to its ligands and the group as a whole has an electric charge. Since the zirconium atoms do not give up electrons, they never exhibit a net positive charge. But they do accept electrons and may exhibit net negative charges. This state of affairs is reflected in some of the chemical behavior of zirconium. Hydroxides of zirconium are unknown, as indeed are any compounds in which a multiplicity of hydroxyl groups are bound to a single zirconium atom. The negative charge of the hydroxyl group tends to pass to the zirconium atom, causing it to repel other hydroxyl groups or to relieve the repulsion by the passage of a proton from one of the hydroxyl groups to the oxygen atom of the neighboring hydroxyl group, resulting in the formation of an oxo group and an aquo group.

Zirconium cannot be regarded as a truly amphoteric element, in so far as it does not tend both to give up electrons and to receive them. Although zirconium occurs both in cations and in anions, it is incorrect to associate the positive charge of zirconium-containing cations with the zirconium atom. It is rather to be associated with the oxygen atom. Zirconium is therefore only pseudoamphoteric.

In aqueous solutions, some simple behaviors govern the choice between forming complex cations or complex anions, and they may be summarized in this wise:

1. The zirconium atom tends to realize the highest coordination number that is sterically possible by the addition of ions or molecules from the environment.

2. Zirconium exhibits an order of preference for ions or molecules from

which it will accept electron pairs. The following order of preference (the top member of the list having the greatest affinity for zirconium) is suggested by experience:

Glycoxide, $-\overset{\overset{O}{\cdot}}{C}-\overset{\overset{O}{\cdot}}{C}-^{-2}$

Hydroxide, OH^-

Carbonate and alphaoxycarboxylate, CO_3^{-2} and $-\overset{\overset{O}{\cdot}}{C}-\overset{\overset{O}{\cdot}}{C}=O^{-2}$

Fluoride, F^-

Hydrosulfate, carboxylate, and nitrate, HSO_4^-, $-\overset{\overset{O}{\cdot}}{C}=O$, and NO_3^-
Water, HOH
Alcohols, ROH
The halide ions Cl^-, Br^-, I^-

Thus, in aqueous solutions that are normal or stronger than normal in hydroxyl ions, a soluble compound of zirconium and glycol is quite stable, but compounds with the other ions or molecules are not stable. The carbonate and alphaoxycarboxylate complexes are decomposed by high hydroxyl ion concentrations but are stable at pH values above those at which the fluorine complexes are stable. The hydrosulfate, carboxylate, and nitrate complexes are stable at hydroxyl-ion concentrations of a lower order than the fluorine complexes, but they are stable in water in the absence of considerable hydroxyl-ion concentrations. The alcohol complexes are generally decomposed by water, but the anhydrous halogen compounds are decomposed by alcohols. In aqueous solutions of halogen compounds of zirconium, complete hydrolysis occurs, and the halogen atoms are completely dissociated from the zirconium atoms:

$$ZrCl_4 + 2H_2O \rightarrow 4Cl^- + ZrOOH^+ + 3H^+ \qquad (12)$$

Other ions and molecules may eventually be introduced into the series and values for the displacements may be made quantitative by establishing equilibrium constants under standardized conditions. The oxalate ion is similar to the sulfate ion in forming oxalatozirconic acids, and oxalic acid is a better solvent for some zirconium compounds than sulfuric.

Zirconium does not form chains of atoms like the typical elements of Group IV, carbon and silicon, nor will it form conventional valence bonds with carbon. The so-called zirconium carbide is really an interstitial solution of carbon in a matrix of zirconium metal. The composition is metallic in appearance; it alloys like a metal, and does not have the characteristic properties of a true carbide, such as ready dissolution in water or acids with the formation of hydrocarbons. No covalently bonded organozirconium compounds are known, although zirconium alkoxides and amines are well known. In recent years an interesting new group of compounds has been derived from cyclopentadiene, and among them are biscyclopentadienyl zirconium dichloride, $(C_5H_5)_2ZrCl_2$. X-ray studies of this and similar compounds reveal that the two monoelectronegative cyclopentadienyl groups sandwich in the dipositive chlorozirconyl cation, and there is no actual bond between zirconium and any of the carbon atoms.

Molecular and ion species which exist in gas or solution phases are not necessarily carried into the solid phases which separate from them. Many examples of this are known in general chemistry, but it is particularly common in zirconium chemistry. The monomolecular zirconium tetrachloride vapor condenses directly to a solid which behaves as a chlorozirconyl chlorozirconate of the type $ZrCl_2ZrCl_6$. The characteristic cation in zirconyl chloride solutions of moderate concentrations is $ZrOOH^+$, but in crystalline zirconyl chloride the cation is $Zr_4(OH)_8{}^{-8}$. If potassium chloride solution is added to a solution of sodium pentasulfatotetrazirconate, $Na_2(ZrO)_4(SO_4)_5$, a precipitate forms and then redissolves. Apparently the species which precipitated from solution became altered in the crystal so that a new soluble species formed. Examples of the converse of this process are also known. If crystals of oxalic acid are added to an aqueous slurry of carbonated hydrous zirconia, $HOOZrOCO_2ZrOOH$, a clear solution forms, but after a short time a solid crystallizes out. Here the species which was dissolved must have undergone intramolecular rearrangement in the solution to form a new, insoluble species. The covalent nature of the zirconium compounds is reflected in the slow reactions and rearrangements which they undergo.

BIOLOGICAL AND PHYSIOLOGICAL EFFECTS OF ZIRCONIUM AND ITS COMPOUNDS

There has been no evidence to date that zirconium has played a role in the organic life on this planet, and some students have come to the conclusion that zirconium minerals are too insoluble to influence plant growth (51). It is well established, however, that zirconium has found its way into living organisms. A study of soil along the fortieth meridian in Russia showed it to contain about 0.03% of zirconium, and organisms living on the soil contained less than 10^{-4}% of zirconium (46). An examination of wheat, oats, barley, rye, and corn in Spain showed detectable amounts of zirconium in 1.6% of the samples, but in amounts only slightly exceeding the lower limits of sensitivity of the analytical instruments (173, 174). Zirconium could not be detected in the plants *Centaurea paniculata, Alyssum bentolinis, Euphorbia nicœensis,* and *Helicrysum italicum* (175). Another study of a variety of plants showed an average zirconium content of 0.005% (176). Analyses of coals have shown variations in zirconium content ranging from none to several hundredths of a per cent of the total ash (48, 49, 50). Traces of zirconium have been noted in the analyses of insects (47).

The absorption of zirconium by plants has been studied under controlled conditions. Carrots grown in soil containing radioactive zirconium contained high activity in the roots and low activity in the shoots. The appearance of zirconium in the roots was the more remarkable in the light of the observation that although zirconium was not absorbed to a great extent by clay or soil, when once absorbed, it was held very tenaciously and resisted leaching with various solutions. No zirconium activity could be found in aqueous extracts (178). Other studies have corroborated the observations with carrots to the effect that the greatest fixation of zirconium is in the roots and translocation is very limited (179). Zirconium stimulated the production of roots in stems of *Alternanthera spathulata* (180). Zirconyl chloride solutions inhibited the geocurvature of roots for the first eight hours, and after that curvature occurred as usual (181).

Unpublished studies reported to the author have shown zirconium to have exerted no bacteriostatic effects under the conditions of the studies. It has been noted elsewhere that zirconium nitrate in peptone baths reduced the indole formation of *Escherichia coli,* increased pyrocyanine formation of *Pseudomonas aeruginosa,* and lowered the virulence of chicken cholera and of *Bacillus anthracis* (182).

Frear and Seiferle found all zirconium compounds to exhibit insecticidal properties (183), and Yasue noted zirconium dioxide to be insecticidal against *Tribolium ferrugineum* (flour beetles), its action being greater than that of titanium or silicon dioxides (184).

173. J. M. Lopez de Azcona, A. Santos Ruiz, and M. Deán Guelbenzu, *Anales real soc. españ. fís. y quím.* **453,** 919-34 (1949).
174. M. Deán Guelbenzu, *Anales real acad. farm.* **17,** 237-66 (1951).
175. C. Minguzzi and O. Vergnano, *Nuovo giorn. botan. ital.* **60,** 287-319 (1953).
176. J. U. Laiseca, *Inst. forestal invest. y experiencas (Madrid)* **21,** No. 21, 1-91 (1950).
178. J. Vlamis and G. A. Pearson, *Science* **111,** 112-3 (1950).
179. L. Jacobson and R. Overstreet, *Soil Sci.* **65,** 129-34 (1948).
180. M. Arena, *Rend. accad. sci. fis. nat. Napoli* **33** (3), 37-9 (1927).
181. V. Bambacioni-Mezzetti, *Atti accad. Lincei* **20,** 125-8 (1934).
182. P. G. Paternoster, *Rev. Facultad Cienc. Quim* **2,** 51-75 (1924).
183. D. E. H. Frear and E. J. Seiferle, *J. Econ. Entom.* **40,** 336-41 (1947).
184. Yasunobu Yasue, *Science (Japan)* **20,** 184 (1950).

Zirconium compounds have been observed to inhibit egg-cultivated tumors without affecting the embryos (185).

In the higher animals the insoluble compounds of zirconium appear to have no effects when administered orally, intratracheally, intravenously, or topically. The water-soluble compounds are harmless when administered orally or topically if they do not contain toxic constituents along with the zirconium, but it is to be noted that some zirconium compounds are strongly acidic and others are strongly basic and in their administration the same cautions must be observed as in the administration of any acids or alkalies. Only small amounts of zirconium compounds can be tolerated when injected intravenously or intraperitoneally, but these small tolerances are large compared to bodily tolerances for most other heavy metal compounds. Zirconium metal produced only mild reactions when implanted in the cerebral hemispheres of dogs for 8 to 97 days. Under similar conditions silver caused inflammation (186). The metal is regarded of considerable potential value for sutures.

Large and repeated administrations of carbonated hydrous zirconia, $2ZrO_2 \cdot CO_2 \cdot nH_2O$, in the diets of cats and mice were without observable effects on the health and comfort of the animals (187). While this compound is insoluble in water, it is soluble in hydrochloric acid and hence must have been converted at least in part to soluble chloride salts in the stomach. The author has known several persons to consume without ill effects quantities of carbonated hydrous zirconia in amounts equivalent to up to an ounce of chemically combined zirconia. Soluble salts have been administered orally to various animals without ill effects, including a citrate to dogs (188) and a lactate to mice (189). In the latter case both gram-positive and gram-negative gut flora were markedly reduced, and the therapeutic implications for bacterial disturbances of the intestinal tract have been noted.

Rats have been exposed to very high concentrations of zircon dust for 6 to 8 hours per day, 5 days a week over a period of 184 days without serious ill effects. The lungs showed dense, radiological shadows produced by aggregates of phagocytes containing zircon, but apart from the phagocytes and possibly slight small cell accumulation, there was no evidence of

185. A. Taylor and Nell Carmichael, *Univ. Texas Biochem. Inst. Studies 5,* Pub. No. **5314;** *Cancer Studies* **2,** 36-79 (1953).

186. F. H. Lewey and C. R. Reiners, *J. Neurosurgery* **5,** 349-53 (1948).

187. J. W. E. Harrison, B. Trabin, and E. W. Martin, *J. Pharmacol. Exp. Therap.* **102,** 179-84 (1951).

188. C. Richet, Gardner, and Goodbody, *Compt. rend.* **181,** 1105-6 (1925).

189. W. B. Blumenthal and C. S. Leonard, "An Investigation of the Physiological and Therapeutic Properties of Zirconium Compounds," *Report to the XIIth International Congress of Pure and Applied Chemistry,* Sept. 13, 1951.

reaction to the presence of zircon in the lungs (190). Aqueous slurries of zirconia and of zircon have been administered intratracheally to mice, rats, cavies, and a rabbit with no more effect than that caused by iron oxide or industrial dusts which have been regarded as harmless (191, 192).

Slurries of hydrous zirconia injected into the tail veins of rats were without ill effects on the animals (187). Colloidal suspensions of zirconium compounds in the blood appear to be cleared by two processes, one slow and one rapid and both following exponential rate laws. The time for removal of rapidly disappearing particles is of the order of $\frac{1}{2}$ to 1 minute, and this period has been associated with uptake by the liver and spleen cells of the relatively large particles. Half of the more slowly disappearing particles disappeared in 30 to 80 minutes, and this has been related to the removal of the smaller-sized particles by liver, spleen, and marrow. Both sizes of particles remained in the clearing organs, fixing the radioactive tracer atoms in those organs. In general, particle size rather than the identity of the metallic element in the colloid was found to determine the localization (193). After injection of sodium zirconium mandelate and hafnium catecholdisulfonate into the tail veins of anesthetized rats, little Hf^{181} tracer was found in the bile, but the liver activity was high (193b).

McClinton and Schubert found the intravenous toxicity of sodium zirconium citrate to rats to be approximately $LD_{50} = 171$ mg Zr/kg body weight. Rats that survived 36 hours after large, repeated doses of the salt invariably recovered and showed no signs of injury 6 months later. There were no hematologic or histologic effects. Sodium zirconium gluconate was slightly less toxic than the citrate (194). The value $LD_{50} = 2.7$ g/kg has been reported for sodium zirconium citrate administered intraperitoneally to mice (194b). When administered to dogs, nearly all the sodium zirconium citrate was excreted through the bowels in 5 to 6 hours (194b). The principal organ of retention of zirconium is the bone, and elimination is gradual, requiring over 100 days (194c). Sodium zirconium tartrate administered intravenously caused motor paralysis and death to frogs, mice, and rats. Small doses increased respiration (195). Similar results were obtained when sodium zir-

190. H. E. Harding and T. A. Lloyd Davies, *Brit. J. Ind. Med.* **9**, 70-3 (1952).

191. Harding, *Brit. J. Ind. Med.* **5**, 75-6 (1948).

192. The Trudeau Foundation, *Assay of the Biological Activity of Zirconium Oxide and of Superpax,* 1950 (unpublished).

193. E. L. Dobson, J. W. Gofman, H. B. Jones, L. S. Kelly, and L. A. Walker, *J. Lab. Clin. Med.* **34**, 305-12 (1949).

193b. J. W. Archdeacon, J. B. Nash, and G. C. Wilson, *Texas Rep. Biol. Med.* **10**, 281-5 (1952).

194. L. T. McClinton and J. Schubert, *J. Pharmacol. Exp. Therapy* **94**, 1-6 (1948).

194b. S. W. Hunter, J. Miree, and H. Bloch, *Surgery* **26**, 682-4 (1949).

194c. J. G. Hamilton, *New England J. Med.* **240**, 863-70 (1949).

195. E. Taro Marvi, *Folia. pharmacol. japon.* **8**, 20-35 (1928).

conium lactate was administered intravenously to a cat (189). Intraperitoneal administration of solutions of aqueous salts produced effects similar to the intravenous injections, but in mice the toxicity was about four times as high by intraperitoneal injection (194b). Leonard found the LD_{50} for intraperitoneal injections of sodium zirconium lactate in mice to be about 51 mg Zr/kg of body weight, but the toxicity varied with the concentration of the solution used. Large doses caused the animals to become jerky in their motions, after which they made convulsive rushes and sometimes went into respiratory paralysis (189).

Walbum found injection of less than lethal doses of zirconium salts to have favorable effects on staphylococcic infection, and attributed this to stimulation of the defense mechanism (195b).

Effects of zirconium salts on specific organs and bodily processes have been reported. Solutions of normal zirconyl nitrate at concentrations 1.83 to 9.1×10^{-4} M have been observed not to inhibit amolytic action, but to inhibit invertase and saccharase reactions slightly. They markedly inhibited blood phosphatase activity (196). Zirconyl and hafnyl chloride solutions caused cessation of the pendular movements of the rabbit uterus; they caused an increase in the tone of the guinea-pig uterus, followed by relaxation. They appeared to have paralyzing effects which could be washed away with fresh Ringer-Locke solution. These salt solutions also produced stimulation of the small intestines of cats, followed by depression. On the perfused rabbit heart, they caused a slight increase in auricular and ventricular contractions and decreased frequency of contraction and of coronary flow. They caused constrictions of the blood vessels of frogs. When injected into the femoral vein, they caused no effect on the blood pressure of a decerebrated, vagosympathectomized cat (197). The minimum dose for causing reversible change in heart muscle was 1:60,000 (198).

Topical applications of water-soluble and water-insoluble compounds have produced no ill effects but have shown certain therapeutic values. Large quantities of carbonated hydrous zirconia rubbed into the shaved skins of guinea pigs had no ill effects (187). Applications of sodium zirconium lactate lotion to the shaved skins of rabbits and guinea pigs showed no acute or chronic toxicity effects or sensitization (199). Ointments containing carbonated hydrous zirconia have proved highly effective in treating poison-ivy dermatitis (200) and solutions containing sodium zirconium lactate are said to be effective body deodorants (199, 201).

195b. L. E. Walbum, *Wiener Arch. inn. Med.* **21**, 169-89 (1931).
196. B. S. Gould, *Proc. Soc. Exp. Biol. Med.* **34**, 381-5 (1936).
197. J. van Niekerk, *Arch. exp. Path. Pharmakol.* **184**, 686-93 (1937.)
198. E. Mezey and K. Mezey, *Magyar Biol. Kutato intezet Munkai* **10**, 371-5 (1938).
199. W. B. Blumenthal, *J. Soc. Cosmetic Chem.* **4**, 69-75 (1953).
200. G. A. Cronk and D. E. Naumann, *J. Lab. Clin. Med.* **37**, 909-13 (1951).
201. H. L. van Mater, U.S. Patent **2,498,514**, Feb. 21, 1950.

Some of the properties of zirconium compounds have indicated them to be of value in radiography. Solutions of zirconium compounds are more opaque to X-rays than those of barium or iodine compounds of equal molarity, and they approach the opacities of lead compounds. Intravenous injections of sodium zirconium citrate administered in the hope of opacifying brain tumors in rabbits failed to accomplish this; but zirconium was found to remain in the kidneys for about an hour, making it possible to obtain an X-ray picture of the renal parenchyma. The salt was finally excreted by the kidneys (194b). Comparative studies of the value of zirconia and of barium sulfate meals administered orally prior to radiography showed, by count of radioactive tracers and by spectrographic analysis, that barium entered into the tissues and zirconium did not (202).

Zirconium compounds cause displacement of certain other elements from the bone, tissues, organs, and blood of experimental animals, and have been proposed for the treatment of certain metal poisonings, particularly radio-active-metal poisoning. The findings are largely the results of the persistent and painstaking efforts of Dr. Jack Schubert. In 1947 he reported that intra-venous injection of sodium zirconium citrate in nontoxic doses to rats and a dog, 2 to 4 hours after intravenous injections of a plutonium compound, caused increased rate of the urinary excretion of the plutonium (203). His subsequent studies have thrown considerable light both on the nature of the action and on the importance of the schedule of treatment. A zirconium solution administered 30 minutes after the injection of plutonium and yttrium compounds increased the urinary extraction of the former by a factor of 50 and the latter by 2.5. Even after considerable delay, adminis-tration of the zirconium salt caused significant increases in the rates of elimination of both elements. The plutonium and yttrium were found to have been eliminated from the skeleton, but no changes appeared in the fecal excretion or in the liver, spleen, or kidney. Control tests showed that the citrate ion itself had no affect on fecal or urinary excretion. Schubert regarded the effects as resulting from competitive displacement of the plutonium and yttrium by zirconium, all three of these elements tending to concentrate in the osteoid matrix. Sodium zirconium citrate had no effect on metals such as strontium which became fixed in the mineral structure of the bone (204). The excretion of plutonium and yttrium was proportional to the dosage. Following zirconium injection, the plutonium blood level was reduced to half in 5 minutes and to a tenth in 90 minutes. It appeared that plutonium was displaced by zirconium from colloidal aggregates found in the blood (205).

202. L. A. Crandall, Jr., *Gastroenterology* **13**, 513-26 (1949).
203. J. Schubert, *Science* **105**, 389-90 (1947).
204. Schubert, *J. Lab. Clin. Med.* **34**, 313-25 (1949).
205. Schubert and Marcia R. White, *J. Biol. Chem.* **184**, 191-6 (1950).

Further studies showed that zirconium solutions injected intravenously into rats 2 to 5 hours after plutonium injections caused immediate and continued urinary excretion of the plutonium, with reduction of liver and bone plutonium content, but not of the muscle content. Fecal excretion again was unaffected. The zirconium was excreted rapidly in the urine without causing chronic toxic effects (206). When injected into rats prior to the administration of plutonium and yttrium compounds, the zirconium caused a decrease in the amounts of the latter elements subsequently deposited in the skeleton, but increased the amount of plutonium in the kidneys. When injected 24 hours after plutonium and yttrium, zirconium prevented further depositions of these elements in bones, but had no favorable effect on the organ distribution. Organic salts of manganese, iron, titanium, aluminum, and thorium also reduced bone deposition of plutonium and showed various effects on the amounts deposited in other organs (207). Injection of zirconium solutions during the month following the administration of plutonium to rats effected a sixfold reduction of the skeletal deposition of the plutonium and increased the retention of plutonium in the soft tissues. Therapy beginning a month after the injection of plutonium had little or no effect on the distribution of this element (208).

A zirconium citrate solution was found to be twice as effective as a calcium disodium ethylenediaminetetracetate solution in preventing skeletal deposit of plutonium in rats, but only half as effective in preventing deposit in the soft tissues. A mixture of the two agents was most effective in reducing total body deposit of plutonium (209). The effectiveness of these two compounds was independent of the concentration of the dose of plutonium (210). A zirconium malate solution proved to be more toxic than the citrate solution and to have no advantages (209).

Zirconium salts had no effect on the urinary excretion of coproporphyrin III, but caused porphorin excretion in animals which had been treated with lead compounds several months previously (211). Zirconium treatment did not cause removal of previously administered lead from the blood or tissues nor affect the rate of its excretion except for an increase in the amount excreted the first day and a decrease in the kidney concentration. Sodium citrate, used as a control, was without effect (212).

---

206. J. Schubert, *Natl. Nuclear Energy Ser. Div. IV*, **20,** Ind. Med. on the Plutonium Project, 472-5 (1951).

207. Marcia R. White and J. Schubert, *J. Pharmacol. Exp. Therapy* **104,** 317-24 (1952).

208. Patricia L. Hackett, *Proc. Soc. Exp. Biol. Med.* **83,** 710-12 (1953).

209. J. Katz, M. H. Weeks, and W. D. Oakley, *Radiation Research* **2,** 166-70 (1955).

210. M. H. Weeks, W. D. Oakley, and R. C. Thompson, *Radiation* **2,** 237-9 (1955).

211. S. Schwartz and R. M. Zagaria, *Natl. Nuclear Energy Ser., Div. IV,* **23,** 290-36 (1952).

212. J. Schubert and Marcia R. White, *J. Lab. Clin. Med.* **39,** 260-6 (1952).

2

Interstitial Solutions and Intermetallic Compounds

TYPES OF PHASES AND COMPOUNDS FORMED BY ZIRCONIUM WITH ELEMENTS ASSIGNED TO VARIOUS REGIONS OF THE ATOMIC CHART

A broad inspection of the chemical behavior of the zirconium atom and the properties of zirconium compounds and quasi-compounds indicates that elements normally assigned to certain regions of the atomic chart exhibit characteristic regional behaviors in their reactions with zirconium. In describing these behaviors, we shall apply the term *phase* to homogeneous reaction products which may or may not meet all the requirements for the term *compound*, and shall apply the term *compound* to homogeneous reaction products which (1) have stoichiometric compositions or ranges of composition which embrace stoichiometric compositions, (2) have compositions which exhibit or probably would exhibit maximum melting points on melting-point diagrams, and (3) have properties, such as solubilities, bearing marked similarity to other substances already known to be true compounds.

Regions of the atomic chart in which the assigned elements show similarities of behavior in their reactions and reaction products with zirconium are delineated in Figure 2.1. Elements whose atoms have small radii—hydrogen, boron, carbon, nitrogen, and oxygen—tend to dissolve in zirconium metal without forming compounds and simply occupy the interstices of the zirconium crystal lattice. Their dispositions in space are determined by the geometry of the metallic matrix, and not by chemical bonds, bond distances, and bond angles, as in the true compounds. All except hydrogen occupy octahedral holes, while hydrogen can occupy both octahedral and tetrahedral holes. Fluorine atoms are small enough to occupy octahedral holes, but this element is not included in the present grouping because its uniquely high electron affinity causes it to form extremely stable valence bonds, and an interstitial solution of fluorine cannot exist. Oxygen is on the borderline of showing the same property. Oxygen can occupy about 60% of the octahedral holes in a zirconium lattice

46

TABLE 2.1. PERIODIC ARRANGEMENT OF THE ELEMENTS, SHOWING ATOMIC AND IONIC RADII

Scheme of Representation:
atomic radius
symbol
ionic radius
valence (at which the given ionic radius was determined)

Period	I A	II A	III A	IV A	V A	VI A	VII A	VIII	VIII	VIII	I B	II B	III B	IV B	V B	VI B	VII B	O
1																	0.3 H 1.3 −1	1.79 He
2	1.225 Li 0.78 1	0.889 Be 0.34 2											0.80 B	0.771 C	0.74 N 1.7 −3	0.74 O 1.32 −2	0.72 F 1.33 −1	1.60 Ne
3	1.572 Na 0.98 1	1.364 Mg 0.78 2	1.248 Al 0.83 3											1.173 Si	1.10 P 2.1 −3	1.04 S 1.74 −2	0.994 Cl 1.81 −1	1.91 A
4	2.025 K 1.33 1	1.736 Ca 1.06 2	1.439 Sc 0.78 3	1.324 Ti 0.64 4	1.224 V	1.172 Cr 0.65 3	1.168 Mn	1.165 Fe 0.83 2	1.157 Co 0.82 2	1.149 Ni 0.78 2	1.173 Cu 1.0 1	1.249 Zn 0.83 2	1.245 Ga 0.62 3	1.223 Ge	1.21 As 2.2 −3	1.17 Se 1.91 −2	1.142 Br 1.96 −1	1.97 Kr
5	2.16 Rb 1.49 1	1.914 Sr 1.27 2	1.616 Y 0.93 3	1.454 Zr 0.87 4	1.342 Nb	1.291 Mo 0.68 4	Tc	1.241 Ru 0.65 4	1.247 Rh 0.69 3	1.278 Pd	1.339 Ag 1.13 1	1.413 Cd 1.03 2	1.497 In 0.92 3	1.412 Sn 0.74 4	1.41 Sb 2.4 −3	1.37 Te 2.11 −2	1.334 I 2.220 −1	2.18 Xe
6	2.35 Cs 1.65 1	1.981 Ba 1.43 2	1.690 La* 1.22 3	1.442 Hf	1.343 Ta	1.299 W 0.68 4	1.278 Re	1.255 Os 0.67 4	1.260 Ir 0.66 4	1.290 Pt	1.336 Au	1.440 Hg 1.12 2	1.549 Tl 1.05 3	1.538 Pb 0.84 4	1.52 Bi	1.53 Po	At	Rn
7	Fr	Ra 1.52 2	Ac**															

* La is succeeded by the lanthanide series of inner transitional elements, the atoms of which differ from La chiefly in the number of 4f electrons which they contain; these electrons having principal quantum number 2 units lower than that of the electrons in the outermost or valence orbitals. The final member of this series is Lu, at. radius 1.557, ionic radius 0.99 for valence 3.

** Ac is succeeded by the actinide series of inner transitional elements, whose relationship to Ac is similar to that of the lanthanide series to La.

without the solution rearranging to form the compound zirconium dioxide. A combination of oxygen, carbon and nitrogen atoms can fill a larger proportion of the octahedral holes while the solution structure remains stable. When all the octahedral holes are filled by small atoms, the composition has a stoichiometric proportion, but this is due to a geometric situation and not to a balancing of valences between the metal and the nonmetal. It is because valence is not the determining factor in composition that we have phases corresponding to the formulas ZrB, ZrC, ZrN, and Zr(C,N,O)*. The properties of these phases do not correspond to the properties which would be expected of compounds, as will be shown hereunder.

The atoms of the rare gases are all too large to fit into the interstitial spaces of zirconium lattices, and their chemical inertness precludes the possibility of valence-bonded compounds. Hence there are no phases or compounds consisting of zirconium and rare gases.

Halogens form very stable covalences with zirconium, resulting in true compound formation. Since the maximum coordination number of zirconium (8) is larger than its oxidation number (4), the possibility exists for polymerization of monomer molecules and also for formation of complex ions by disproportionation of the combined halogen atoms or ions between the zirconium atoms. Manifestations of these possibilities are discussed in Chapter 4.

The elements silicon, phosphorus, sulfur, selenium, and possibly arsenic, antimony, and tellurium permit of a less clear-cut treatment than do the small atoms and the halogens. The atoms of these elements are too large to fit into interstitial holes of metallic zirconium, and chemically they are not active enough to decompose the refractory structure of metallic zirconium to form discrete molecules of zirconium silicide, phosphide, etc. The reactions of these elements with zirconium appear to take the form of adding themselves to the previously existing metal structure, rather than of decomposing it to form entirely new structures. Atoms of these elements become inserted between planes of zirconium atoms and between zirconium atoms grouped about one another on the planes, giving rise to new phases (which may be regarded as compounds only if special definition of the term is understood) in which more or less of the original zirconium metal structure survives. Such reaction products may be thought of as semimetallic and to be held together by metallic as well as covalent bonding.

The remaining elements are entirely metallic in character and their

---

* The representation Zr (C,N,O) is sometimes given for the composition which has the name *zirconium cyanonitride*. The subscript after the parenthesis is generally less than 1, and the given representation with the implied subscript 1 is an idealized formula which is approached, but rarely, if ever, quite achieved. Zirconium cyanonitride will be discussed in detail later in this chapter.

reaction products with zirconium are to be regarded as compounds in which bonding of the atoms is primarily of a metallic type. The reactions of zirconium with groups of atoms, or radicals, are largely of a character determined by the specific atom of the group with which the zirconium atom interacts. As discussed in Chapter 1, hafnium is to be regarded as though it were simply a heavy isotope of zirconium, for chemical considerations.

In this chapter we are concerned with the interstitial solutions and the intermetallic (or simply "metallic") and semimetallic phases and compounds formed by zirconium. We shall confine our attention mostly to those aspects of their behavior which are conceived as chemical rather than physicochemical or metallurgical, and in so doing shall endeavor to chart the behavior of the zirconium atoms as major participants in the formation of compositions of matter and in determining the amenability of these compositions of matter to further changes. For the physicochemical and metallurgical behavior of these compositions, the reader is referred to the extensive literature on these subjects, and in particular to the recent, more comprehensive works of Miller (1) and of Lustman and Kerze (2).

THE INTERSTITIAL SOLUTIONS

ZIRCONIUM CARBIDE AND CYANONITRIDE

Zirconium metal normally crystallizes as the hexagonal α-phase below 862° and the body-centered cubic β-phase above this temperature, both of these being close-packed lattices. But if the metal is formed in the presence of substantial amounts of carbon, it forms a face-centered lattice of the sodium chloride type, with carbon occupying the octahedral holes between the zirconium atoms. Diagrams for the system C-Zr have been roughed out by several investigators, and are reproduced here as Figures 2.1 and 2.2. When 1 atom of carbon is taken up per atom of zirconium, the lattice is saturated with carbon, and the product has the empirical formula ZrC. It would be misleading, however, to regard this as a stoichiometric proportion, since it is not determined by valence requirements, but by the number of octahedral holes in the metal lattice. This substance has been given the name *zirconium carbide*, and this name will be retained for the following discussion while recognizing that the expression *carbide* does not carry the connotation of carbon in a chemically combined state, as in such compounds as sodium, calcium, or aluminum carbides.

1. G. L. Miller, *Zirconium*, Academic Press, Inc., New York, 1954.
2. B. Lustman and F. Kerze, Jr., *The Metallurgy of Zirconium*, McGraw-Hill Book Company, Inc., New York, 1955.
3. *Reactor Handbook*, 1st ed., vol. 3, Materials Technical Information Service, A.E.C., Oak Ridge, Tenn., 1953.
4. H. J. Goldsmith, *J. Iron and Steel Inst.* (London) **160**, 345-62 (1948).

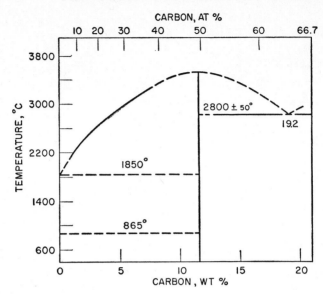

FIG. 2.1. The system C-Zr. From (3); compare (2), p. 449.

When less than 1 carbon atom is taken into solution per atom of zirconium, i.e., per octahedral hole, the crystal lattice remains substantially the same, and the unoccupied holes are tantamount to so many Schottky defects. The undersaturated solution is a powerful getter, when hot, for atmospheric gases, and if it is not well protected from the atmosphere during its preparation it will contain oxygen and nitrogen as well as carbon. While its avidity for oxygen is probably greater than its avidity for nitrogen, the oxygen in the atmosphere is partially removed as carbon monoxide and the opportunity for nitrogen absorption is thereby improved. The product of composition $Zr(C,N,O)_x$, where x is a variable less than unity, has been called *zirconium cyanonitride*. The name was taken from the parallelism of this substance to *titanium cyanonitride*, which had previously been noted to deposit in copper-red, or bronzy cubic, or octahedral crystals in blast furnaces in which titanium-bearing iron ores were smelted (5). It is actually a misnomer, as there has been no evidence for a cyanide radical in these substances.

Berzelius reported formation of zirconium carbide as early as 1817 by reducing zirconium compounds with potassium containing carbon (6). He noted that his product had a metallic appearance, and that it dissolved in hydrofluoric acid, leaving a residue of carbon. Berzelius reported on a

5. F. Wöhler, *Liebig's Ann.* **73**, 34 (1850).

6. J. J. Berzelius, *Schweigger's J.* **21**, 40 (1817); *Ann. chim. phys.* **29**, 337 (1825); *Pogg. Ann.* **4**, 117 (1825).

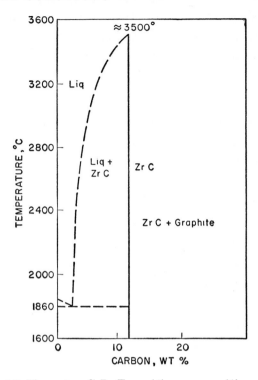

FIG. 2.2. The system C-Zr. From (4); compare (1), p. 241.

number of properties of this product, but since it certainly contained other materials in addition to zirconium carbide, his observations had limited significance.

It is actually quite difficult to prepare the pure phase of composition ZrC. In the reaction of zirconium dioxide with carbon, the ideal reaction is given by the equation

$$ZrO_2 + 3C \rightarrow ZrC + 2CO \qquad (1)$$

Unless an excess of carbon is available for the reaction, however, the solid solution, ZrC, is apt to be undersaturated with respect to carbon. If an excess of carbon is used, some of it will persist through the reaction and be contained in the product as free carbon, which is very difficult to separate completely from the zirconium carbide. Some of the carbon is actually dissolved by the molten zirconium carbide, the melting point of which can be lowered by as much as 1000° by the dissolved excess carbon (7, 8). Some

7. H. Moissan and M. Lengfeld, *Compt. rend.* **122**, 651 (1896).
8. C. Agte and K. Moers, *Z. anorg. allgem. Chem.* **198**, 233 (1931).

investigators have been misled by the presence of the uncombined carbon into thinking that they had obtained a dicarbide, ZrC_2.

Troost made some of the early preparations of zirconium carbide by heating zirconia with sugar charcoal in an electric furnace. He obtained a product which assayed 72.6% zirconium and he presumed this to show that he had formed the dicarbide. His product was attacked by hydrofluoric acid, concentrated or dilute, but not by other acids (9). Similar results were obtained by Moissan and Lengfeld (7; cf. 10 and 11), but in addition, they obtained a product of composition approaching that required for the formula ZrC. Agte avoided the effects of excess carbon to a considerable extent by using less than the amount of carbon required according to reaction 1, but conducted the reaction in a graphite tube from which the reaction product was able to pick up enough additional carbon to approach the theoretical composition. For the final heating he passed the electric current through the product itself to aid in volatilizing off impurities (8). Laughlin found that much of the uncombined carbon could be separated from zirconium carbide by pulverizing it and agitating the powder in 0.5-1.5% soap solutions and allowing the mixture to settle. After the heavy metallic layer had settled, he decanted off the remaining suspension of carbon (12). Oxygen and nitrogen contamination have been avoided by conducting the reaction under vacuum (13) or an inert gas (8).

Most of the experimental preparations of zirconium carbide which have been reported were made by heating zirconia with carbon in resistor furnaces, but the bulk of industrial manufacture has been accomplished by heating zircon with carbon in arc furnaces. The techniques have varied in minor ways as conditions were changed in efforts to obtain optimum purity and maximum yields. Moissan agglomerated mixtures of zirconia and sugar charcoal with oil and compressed them into briquets before heating them (7). Wedekind heated zircon, carbon, and lime together (14, 15), and Renaux used zircon and calcium carbide (16). A summary of the types of reactions that have been used in preparing zirconium carbide is given in Table 2.2. Hafnium carbide containing 0.0002% zirconium has been prepared by heating hafnium oxide with lampblack in the temperature range

9. L. Troost, *Compt. rend.* **116**, 1227 (1893).

10. J. J. Gangler, C. F. Robards, and J. E. McNutt, Nat. Advisory Comm. Aeronautics, Techn. Note No. 1911, 33 pp. (1949).

11. J. J. Gangler, *J. Am. Ceram. Soc.* **33**, 367-75 (1950).

12. C. C. Laughlin, U.S. Patent **2,310,964**, Feb. 16, 1943.

13. G. A. Meerson and G. V. Samsonov, *J. Applied Chem. U.S.S.R.* **25**, 823-6 (1952).

14. E. Wedekind, *Z. anorg. allgem. Chem.* **33**, 81 (1903).

15. Wedekind, *Chem. Ztg.* **31**, 654-55 (1907).

16. L. Renaux, *Contribution à l'étude de la zircone*, Vincennes, 1900.

1500-2800°. The product prepared at **2800°** contained **98%** of the theoretical amount of carbon (17; cf. 18).

The most common temperature range for conducting the reaction of zirconium dioxide with carbon to form zirconium carbide has been 1800-2100° (8, 13, 19, 20, 21, 22).* When the preparation was performed in a hairpin resistor furnace at 1800-2000°, a yield of approximately 100% was obtained with an energy consumption of 5.7 kw hr per lb of zirconium (21). Some efforts have been made to establish thermodynamic data for the equilibrium involved in the preparation. Prescott compressed pellets of zirconia and carbon and studied the equilibria which he obtained at 1880°, 1914°, 1948°, 1982°, and 2015°K. He believed that he came within 10% of equilibrium for the reaction

$$ZrO_2 \text{ (monoclinic)} + 3C \text{ (graphite)} \rightleftharpoons ZrC \text{ (cubic)} + 2CO \text{ (gas)} \quad (2)$$

At 1 atm pressure of carbon monoxide, he found the free energy ΔF to be $151,800 - 76.68\ T$ and the heat of reaction ΔH to be 151,800 cal/mole over the temperature range studied (23). In a later study of a similar type in the range 1800-2500°K, the carbon monoxide pressures were measured and the solid products were analyzed by X-ray diffraction methods as well as chemically. The products were found to contain less than the theoretical carbon content in all cases, and compositions such as $ZrC_{0.71}O_{0.08}$ were obtained (24). Samsonov and Rozinova found that when compositions consisting of carbon and zirconium contained 0.64-3.12% carbon, two solid phases were present: α-zirconium metal containing dissolved carbon and the face-centered cubic zirconium carbide phase. With 3.50-11.62% carbon (theoretical for carbon in ZrC is 11.63%) only the face-centered cubic phase

---

* There is no validity for an assumption by Coley (25) that zirconium carbide does not form below the melting point of zirconium oxide.

17. P. G. Cotter and J. A. Cohn, *J. Am. Ceram. Soc.* **37**, 415-20 (1954).
18. C. E. Curtis, L. M. Doney, and J. R. Johnson, *J. Am. Ceram. Soc.* **37**, 458-65 (1954).
19. German patent **286,054**, July 10, 1914.
20. O. Ruff, E. Friederich, and L. Sittig, *Z. anorg. allgem. Chem.* **144**, 169-89 (1925).
21. W. J. Kroll, W. W. Stephens, and J. P. Walsted, *J. Metals, Trans.* **188**, No. 11, 139-45 (1950).
22. R. A. Schoenlaub, U.S. Patent **2,756,126**, July 24, 1956.
23. C. H. Prescott, Jr., *J. Am. Chem. Soc.* **48**, 2534-50 (1956).
24. V. S. Kutsev, B. F. Ormont, and V. A. Epel'baum, *Doklady Akad. Nauk. S.S.S.R.* **104**, 567-70 (1955).

TABLE 2.2. A SUMMARY OF THE TYPES OF REACTIONS THAT HAVE BEEN
USED IN THE PREPARATION OF ZIRCONIUM CARBIDE

Type of Reaction	Literature
Zirconium heated with carbon	13, 26
Zirconium heated with carbon-containing gas	27
Zirconium hydride heated with carbon	28
Zirconium tetrachloride vapor mixed with a carbon-containing gas and allowed to impinge on a hot filament	29, 30, 31, 32
Zirconia heated with carbon	7, 14, 15, 17, 19, 33
Zirconia heated with carbon and another reducing substance, such as hydrogen	20
Zirconia heated with carbon and lime	22
Zirconia heated with calcium carbide	16
Zircon heated with carbon	35, 36, 37, 38

was present. This gives 21-50 atom % carbon for the range of existence of
the homogeneous face-centered cubic solid solution of carbon in zirconium
(39).

Crystals of pure zirconium carbide have been prepared by allowing a
mixture of gaseous zirconium tetrachloride, hydrogen, and an oxide of
carbon to impinge on a hot tungsten filament (30), or alternatively, a
mixture of gaseous zirconium tetrachloride and toluene (31). The filament
temperature was 2000-2700°K. The gases had to be scrupulously freed of
nitrogen in order to obtain the pure carbide. (However, nitrogen does not
displace carbon from zirconium carbide; once an atom such as carbon,
oxygen, or nitrogen has filled an octahedral hole in the face-centered cubic
lattice, it is immobilized and not subject to displacement). Interestingly,
when a mixture of zirconium tetrachloride and titanium tetrachloride and
a carbonaceous gas was allowed to impinge on a hot tungsten filament,
only zirconium carbide was deposited over a wide range of temperatures

25. H. E. Coley, *Chem. Trade J.* **65**, 742 (1919).
26. P. D. Williams, U.S. Patent **2,447,973**, Aug. 24, 1948.
27. W. G. Guldner and L. A. Wooten, *J. Electrochem. Soc.* **93**, 223-34 (1948).
28. N. O. F. Carlborg and G. Gisnor, Swedish patent **128,002**, Apr. 18, 1950.
29. A. E. van Arkel, *Physica* **4**, 286-301 (1924).
30. A. E. van Arkel and J. H. de Boer, *Z. anorg. allgem. Chem.* **148**, 345 (1925).
31. K. Moers, *Z. anorg. allgem. Chem.* **198**, 243-61 (1931).
32. W. G. Burgers and J. C. M. Basart, *Z. anorg. allgem. Chem.* **216**, 209-22 (1934).
33. Shizuo Fujiwara, *J. Chem. Soc. Japan,* Pure Chem. Sect. **71**, 580-4 (1950).
35. W. J. Kroll, A. W. Schlechten, W. R. Carmody, L. A. Yerkes, H. P. Holmes, and
H. L. Gilbert, *Trans. Electrochem. Soc.* **92**, 99-113 (1947).
36. M. L. Hartmann, U.S. Patent **1,576,275**, March 9, 1926.
37. B. Malétra, French patent **714,283**, July 8, 1930.
38. G. Volkert, *Metal. u. Eng.* **40**, 246-52 (1943).
39. G. V. Samsonov and N. S. Rozinova, *Izvest. Sektora Fiz-Khim. Anal., Inst. Obsh-cheǐ i Seorg. Chim., Akad. Sauk. S.S.S.R.* **27**, 126-32 (1956).

(31). Notwithstanding, titanium has been reported to be more effective than zirconium as a small addition to molybdenum metal for the purpose of mitigating embrittlement of the latter by oxygen, nitrogen, and carbon (40). Hafnium carbide crystals can also be formed on a hot filament (41).

Zirconium carbide separates as a well-defined phase when steels containing zirconium and carbon are quenched (42). In welds where nitrogen and carbon are present, solid solutions are obtained which contain both carbon and nitrogen (43).

Zirconium carbide, ZrC, formula weight 103.23, is a gray metallic substance. Its metallic character is manifest in a metallic luster and metallic conductance of the electric current (14, 30). Values for the parameters of the face-centered cubic crystals are given in Table 2.3 along with other physical data. No crystalline transformations have been reported for zirconium or hafnium carbides. Studies of the lattice have been interpreted as showing that the lattice points consist of neutral atoms rather than ions (44)*. The substance acts in many ways like a solution or occlusion of carbon in zirconium metal (45). The distance between nearest zirconium atoms is 3.43 A, as compared to 3.1788 A for nearest neighbors in α-zirconium. The Zr-C distance is 2.32 A, as compared to a calculated covalent bond distance of 2.225 A.** If we think of the carbon atom as trapped in a space slightly larger than itself, we must still reckon with the possibility of unstable, transitory electron bonding of some type contributing to the stability of the structure. Although stable, conventional carbon-zirconium bonds are unknown in organic chemistry, evidence for the momentary formation of unstable bonds is quite considerable (Chapter 4, in connection with the catalytic effects of zirconium dioxide on the reactions of hydrocarbons). However, since the zirconium atoms are only 0.25 A farther apart than in the hexagonal metal, it is not surprising that the metallic character

---

* A C^{-4} quanticule has been assumed to be present by Fajans (44b), but there has been no support for this assumption.

** It has been noted in one study of octahedral solid solutions that the Zr-O bond length is 2.29, Zr-B 2.33, and Zr-N 2.32 A. These compare closely with the bond distances predicted by Pauling and suggest a slightly strained covalent bond. Partial molar volumes were in some cases much larger than would be expected from the degree of misfit alone, suggesting transfer of electrons from the lattice to the solute-metal bonds (48b). Some investigators have assumed resonance between homopolar and heteropolar bonds (48c) or between heteropolar and electronic bonding (48d).

40. J. Harwood, *Metal Progress* **70**, No. 6, 97-101 (1956).

41. British patent **312,273**, May 23, 1928; German patent **499,069**, May 24, 1928.

42. R. Vogl and K. Hoehberg, *Arch. Eisenhüttenw.* **7**, 473-8 (1934).

43. W. Hummitzsch, *Stahl u. Eisen.* **74**, 1723-30 (1954).

44. K. Becker and F. Ebert, *Z. Physik* **31**, 268-73 (1925).

44b. K. Fajans, *Ceramic Age* **54**, 288-93 (1949).

45. C. F. P. Berington, *Proc. Int. Congr. Pure & Applied Chem.* (*London*) **11**, 3-16 (1947).

prevails, and the properties of the substance are predominantly reflections of the metallic matrix and not of the more incidental and transitory carbon-zirconium bonds. It is instructive to compare zirconium carbide with aluminum carbide. The covalently bonded aluminum carbide forms pale-yellow crystals which sublime *in vacuo* at 1800° and melt at 2200° (46). In this

TABLE 2.3. PHYSICAL CONSTANTS OF ZIRCONIUM CARBIDE*

Property	Value	Literature
Boiling point, °C**	5100[760mm]	47
	5650	48a, pp. 64-8
Crystal parameter, a	4.694 A	49; cf. 17, 18, 20, 29, 44, 50
Density, calcd. from crystal parameter	6.51	20
	6.90	20
	(12.70)	18
Electrical resistivity, ohm-cm		
at 20°	0.634×10^{-4}	34, 51
at liquid air temperature	0.378	51
at fusion temperature	$6\text{-}7 \times 10^{-14}$	20
Hardness, Mohs	7-9	7, 20, 34, 52
Knoop, 100 gm load	(2830)	17
Melting point, °C	3527	55; cf. 20, 53, 54
	(3887 ± 125)	53
Thermodynamic constants, kg cal/mole		
Entropy of formation, $\Delta S^{\circ}_{298.16}$	−1.7	2, p. 61
Free energy of formation, $\Delta F^{\circ}_{298.16}$	−44.5	2, p. 61
Heat of formation, ΔH at 20°	45	56; cf. 15, 57, 58

* Values in parentheses are for hafnium carbide.

** Richardson (48a) estimated the boiling point of zirconium carbide and of other highly refractory substances by driving a spectrographic plate vertically at a constant rate during controlled discharge of the arc. The time during the exposure that a component was in the arc was determined by locating the beginning and the ending of the spectral lines from this component on the plate. Elements were found to have an arrangement on the plates such that the time interval of appearance of each was a function of the boiling temperature. By plotting the time of appearance in the arc against the boiling points of elements for which the values were known, a curve was obtained which permitted estimation of previously unknown boiling points of the charge. Richardson's method was a development of a procedure based on the same principles previously reported by Mott (47).

46. E. Tiede and E. Birnbräuer, *Z. anorg. allgem. Chem.* **87,** 167 (1914).
47. W. R. Mott, *Trans. Am. Electrochem. Soc.* **34,** 255 (1918).

compound the metallic nature and the extreme refractoriness characteristic of zirconium carbide are absent. Zirconium carbide is considerably higher melting than zirconium metal (zirconium carbide 3527°, and metal 1855°) as well as harder (Mohs hardness for zirconium carbide about 7-9, metal estimated at about 3), indicating that the bonding effect of the carbon is quite large.

The nature of the bonding effect of carbon in the zirconium carbide interstitial solution has not been adequately clarified, but a few facts are known which point strongly toward the validity of certain suppositions on this bonding. First, it is striking that the interstitial solutions of the type of which zirconium carbide is a representative are typically formed by the transitional metals. Such metals are characterized by incomplete (n-1) quantum levels, where n is the principal quantum number of the valence electron orbitals. Atoms of such elements are well known to form inner orbital complexes, and it appears not unreasonable that they should form inner orbital bonds with carbon. This would tend to leave the valence electrons free to move into the interstitial spaces of the metal lattice, that is, to higher energy levels than those represented by the valence orbitals. This would favor the retention of metallic characteristics such as luster, conductivity, and thermionic emission, in accord with the empirical facts.

Zirconium carbide is weakly paramagnetic, and the susceptibility is independent of temperature and the valence electrons (59). It is a good thermionic emitter (55, 60). It does not become superconductive at the lowest temperatures at which observations have been made, i.e., 1.2-1.3°K (48c). Although earlier investigators reported superconductivity, this was probably

48a. D. Richardson, *Proc. of the 5th Summer Conference at M.I.T. on Spectroscopy and Its Applications,* John Wiley & Sons, New York, 1938.

48b. K. A. Moon, *J. Phys. Chem.* **59,** 71-6 (1955).

48c. W. T. Ziegler and R. A. Young, *Phys. Rev.* **90,** 115-19 (1953).

48d. G. V. Samsonov, *Izvest. Sektora Fiz.-Khim. Anal., Inst. Obshchei̇ i Neorg. Khim., Akad. Nauk S.S.S.R.* **27,** 97-125 (1956).

49. P. Duwez and F. Odell, *J. Electrochem. Soc.* **97,** 299 (1950).

50. A. E. Kuval'skiĭ and Y. S. Umanskiĭ, *J. Phys. Chem. (U.S.S.R.)* **20,** 769-72 (1940).

51. K. Moers, *Z. anorg. allgem. Chem.* **198,** 262-75 (1931).

52. H. Moissan, *Bull. Soc. Chim.* (3) **15,** 1275 (1896).

53. C. Agte and H Alterthum, *Z. tech. Physik* **11,** 182-91 (1930).

54. H. W. Greenwood, *Engineer* **187,** 349-51 (1949).

55. D. L. Goldwater and R. E. Haddad, *J. Applied Phys.* **22,** 70-3 (1951).

56. W. A. Roth and G. Becker, *Z. physik. Chem.* **145A,** 461-9 (1929).

57. *Ibid.* **159,** 21 (1932).

58. F. D. Rossini, D. D. Wagman, W. H. Evans, S. Levine, and I. Jaffe, *Nat. Bur. Standards Circ.* **600** (1952).

59. W. Klemm and W. Schüth, *Z. anorg. allgem. Chem.* **201,** 24-31 (1931).

60. R. E. Haddad, D. L. Goldwater, and F. H. Morgan, *J. Applied Phys.* **20,** 884 (1949).

an error due to a distribution of superconducting impurities in the observed specimens (48c, 61).*

The crystal lattice of zirconium carbide is similar to that of the mono-hydride, boride, and nitride (62), and to the monocarbides of titanium, vanadium, niobium, and tantalum. The binary systems TiC-ZrC, NbC-ZrC, and TaC-ZrC form continuous series of solid solutions, but the system VC-ZrC shows only small solubilities of the one component in the other. At 2100° no more than 5% vanadium carbide dissolves in zirconium carbide, and less than 1% zirconium carbide in vanadium carbide. A similar situation exists for the corresponding nitrides (50, 53, 63, 64, 65). This has been explained on the basis of the size rule which governs the formation of solid solutions. In the binary systems of two miscible carbides or nitrides, the metal atoms may not differ by more than 15% in atomic diameter (65). The composition 4TaC + 1ZrC exhibits a maximum melting point for the system, 4205°, and 4TaC + 1HfC melts at 4215°, the highest melting substance known. There is no evidence for compound formation in the mono-carbide systems (53). The carbides ZrC and W_2C do not mix in any proportions (53).

The possibility, realized in many preparations, for large numbers of unfilled octahedral holes to exist in the carbide preparation has led some to view these solutions as bertholide or nonstoichiometric compounds (67). When the lattice spacing is plotted as a function of the mole fraction of carbon contained, nearly a straight line is obtained (50).

Zirconium carbide is unattacked by water** or by moist or dry air at the ordinary temperature or at 100°. If heated to a red heat in air, it burns and leaves a residue of zirconium dioxide (52, 68). It has been observed to react with fluorine at the ordinary temperature, with chlorine at about 250°, with bromine at about 300°, and with iodine at 400°. At dull red heat it is slightly attacked by sulfur vapor, and it burns with a brilliant flame in oxygen (7, 52).† Zirconium carbide has been observed

---

* Studies have been made of the increase of temperature of transition to superconductivity in the series MSi, MB, MC, MN, where M is titanium, zirconium, vanadium, tungsten, or molybdenum. B. Lustman and F. Kerze, Jr., *The Metallurgy of Zirconium*, McGraw-Hill, N.Y., 1955.

** For the wetting properties of zirconium carbide, see (70).

† The temperature of reaction of zirconium carbide with gases depends to a considerable extent on its purity, its degree of saturation with carbon, and the condition of the surface. For such reasons, values other than the above, viz. 400-500°, have been reported for the reaction temperature with chlorine (31).

61. G. F. H. Hardy and J. K. Hulm, *Phys. Rev.* **93**, 1004-61 (1954).
62. G. Hägg, *Z. physik. Chem.* **B6**, 221-32 1930).
63. H. Nowatry and R. Kieffer, *Metallforschung* **2**, 257-65 (1947).
64. J. T. Norton and A. L. Mowry, *J. Metals, Trans.* **1**, 133-6 (1949).
65. P. Duwez and F. Odell, *J. Electrochem. Soc.* **96**, 364-76 (1949).
67. J. S. Anderson, *Chem. and Ind.* **56**, 766-9 (1937).
68. W. Watt, G. H. Crockett, and A. R. Hall, *Métaux* **28**, 22-37 (1953).

not to be affected by nitrogen or ammonia at temperatures ranging from red heat (7) to 1800° (69), and reports to the contrary (15) are probably incorrect. Zirconium nitride has been reported to form when the carbide is heated with hydrazine to 600-700° (33). Nitrogen can occupy empty octahedral holes in the zirconium carbide lattice, and it must be introduced at the time of formation of the crystal since it is exceedingly difficult to dislodge carbon atoms and replace them by other small atoms. Water, aqueous solutions of salts, aqua ammonia, and hydrochloric acid do not attack zirconium carbide, even when heated to the boiling points, but both concentrated and dilute hydrofluoric acid (71, 72), concentrated sulfuric and nitric acids (52), and aqua regia (7, 73) attack it. But not all investigators have found the same effects with these aqueous acids, and differences in observations are probably due primarily to the differences of degrees of saturation of the lattice with carbon and the impurity content, particularly at the surface. Some specimens have been reported to show reactivity with hydrochloric acid, and others have been reported resistant to hydrofluoric acid (73). Zirconium carbide is attacked when used as an anode in the electrolysis of sulfuric acid (15). It is unattacked by fused potassium cyanide, but it is attacked by molten potassium hydroxide, and it is oxidized vigorously when heated with potassium nitrate, perchlorate, or permanganate (52). The reaction with perchlorate is explosive (7). The carbide has been noted to be resistant to molten lead-bismuth alloy (74).

The attack of nitric and sulfuric acids on zirconium carbide is at least partially an oxidation attack, and there is no reason to believe that metal ions replace hydrogen ions from the acid. Table 2.5 shows that no hydrogen is included in the gases which are evolved during the attack of hot concentrated sulfuric acid on zirconium carbide which is saturated with carbon. On the other hand, the attack by hydrofluoric acid is a true reaction of an acid with a metal, although not a simple hydrogen ion replacement reaction, and the reaction can be represented

$$ZrC + 6HF \rightarrow ZrF_6^{-2} + 2H_2 + 2H^+ + C \tag{3}$$

A component of the mechanism of this reaction may be supposed to be

$$ZrC + 6F^- \rightarrow ZrF_6^{-2} + 4e + C$$
$$4e + 4H^+ \rightarrow 4H \rightarrow 2H_2 \tag{4a-b}$$

The carbon atoms are liberated atom by atom from the cells of the zir-

69. R. Lorenz and J. Woolcock, *Z. anorg. allgem. Chem.* **176**, 289-304 (1928).

70. H. H. Hausner, H. S. Kalisch, and R. P. Angier, *J. Metals, Trans.* **3**, 625-73 (1951).

71. Titanium Alloy Mfg. Div. of the National Lead Co., unpublished researches.

72. Raizo Ishii, *Sci. Papers Inst. Phys. Chem. Research* (Tokyo) **41**, 1-21 (1943).

73. Isaburo Wada and Raizo Ishii, *Bull. Inst. Phys. Chem. Research* (Tokyo) **21**, 877-83 (1942).

74. J. J. Gangler, *J. Am. Ceram. Soc.* **37**, 312-16 (1954).

conium carbide lattice, and in the presence of nascent hydrogen react to some extent to form hydrocarbons.

The reactions of zirconium carbide with niobium have been observed at 2038°, 2149°, and 2088°, and have been found to proceed in accordance with the equation

$$ZrC + Nb \rightarrow NbC + Zr \tag{5}$$

Metallographic examination of the product showed that the zirconium metal was formed at the grain corners of the carbide structure. The size and distribution of the metal phase are dependent on the time and temperature, and these in turn influence the strength of the product. A fine dispersion gives greater strength than a coarse one (75).

Zirconium carbide reacts with zirconium dioxide at 2200° with liberation of carbon monoxide:

$$ZrO_2 + 2ZrC \rightarrow 3Zr + 2CO \tag{6}$$

The product is a substance of metallic appearance, but the reaction is not quantitative and up to about 5% carbon is apt to remain (76). Lower residual carbon is obtained from reactions with calcium or magnesium oxides (loc. cit.):

$$ZrC + CaO \rightarrow Zr + Ca + CO$$
$$ZrC + MgO \rightarrow Zr + Mg + CO \tag{7-8}$$

The calcium or magnesium as well as the carbon monoxide vaporize off at the temperatures at which the reactions are conducted. Obtaining pure metal by oxidation of zirconium carbide has not yet proved possible because of practical difficulties encountered in forcing all the oxygen to go over to carbon monoxide. A contrary tendency is reflected in the observation that zirconium carbide decreases the oxidation resistance of titanium carbide-cobalt alloys (77).

The chief use of zirconium carbide has been in the preparation of zirconium tetrachloride, an important material in the production of zirconium metal, zirconium alloys, and a variety of zirconium chemicals. A summary of actual and proposed uses of zirconium carbide is given in Table 2.4.

Zirconium cyanonitride is substantially nothing more than zirconium carbide with less than the saturation amount of carbon in the octahedral holes of the lattice. It usually contains oxygen and nitrogen because it has proved quite difficult to prepare the product under conditions where it does not pick up these elements by its gettering effect. Zirconium cyanoni-

75. W. G. Lidman and H. J. Hamjian, *J. Am. Ceram. Soc.* **35**, 236-40 (1952).

76. H. R. Hoge and Z. M. Shapiro, *Naval Reactor Program, Contract AT-11-1-GEN-14*, **Report WAPD-TD-51**, March 20, 1952, and **Report TID-5084**, vol. 2, pp. 79-94 (1952).

77. J. Hinnüber and O. Rüdiger, *Arch. Eisenhüttenw.* **24**, 267-74 (1953).

tride has been found more suitable for certain industrial applications than the carbide, particularly since it is less hard and more easily reduced to sizes suitable for further processing. It has been manufactured since 1918.* The atmospheric gases which are dissolved by the product have little practical significance for most of the intended applications. What is substantially the same product has also been called *zirconium carbonitride* (78, 79).

Zirconium cyanonitride is prepared similarly to the carbide but less carbon is used. Care must be taken not to reduce the proportion of carbon charged into the preparation excessively lest the product retain a large amount of oxygen and be excessively hard and unreactive (37). In an early, patented manufacturing procedure, baddeleyite or zircon were mixed with about 20% of their weight of coke and heated in an electric furnace in contact with a nitrogen-containing gas. Products obtained were reported to contain 82-84% zirconium, 3-5% carbon, and 8-10% nitrogen. The nitrogen figures are doubtless too high and were probably estimated by dif-

TABLE 2.4. INDUSTRIAL AND EXPERIMENTAL USES
REPORTED FOR ZIRCONIUM CARBIDE

Uses	Literature
Catalyst for vapor phase hydration of olefins	80
Component of hard alloys for tools and dies	81, 82, 83, 84, 85, 86
Getter	26
Refractory	11, 87
crucibles	88, 89, 90
coatings, for electrodes	26, 91, 92
for metals	93
for structural carbon or graphite	94, 95
filaments and wire	41, 96
powder	83
Thermionic emitter	60
Wick for molten aluminum	98

* In recent years an extensive study of manufacturing conditions for the production of zirconium cyanonitride has been made by Mr. Howard J. Smith (71), in collaboration with the author. The important contributions of Mr. Smith to that study and to ideas which have evolved from the study are gratefully acknowledged.

78. C. J. Kinzie and D. Hake, U.S. Patents **2,110,733**, March 8, 1938; **2,168,603**, Aug. 8, 1939; British patent **710,020**, June 2, 1954.
79. Kinzie and Hake, U.S. Patent **2,143,013**, Jan. 10, 1939.
80. R. F. Deering, U.S. Patent **2,583,359**, Jan. 22, 1952.
81. K. Schröter and W. Jenssen, U.S. Patent **1,551,333**, Aug. 25, 1925.
82. British patent **361,363**, May 16, 1930.
83. R. Kieffer, Austrian patent **170,248**, Jan. 25, 1952.
84. R. Kieffer and F. Kölbl, Austrian patent **166,036**, May 25, 1950.
85. E. H. M. Hägglund, and N. G. Rehnqvist, U.S. Patent **2,580,171**, Dec. 25, 1951.
86. A. Cibula, *Foundry Trade J.* 98, 713-26 (1955).

ference. The products were golden-yellow to bronze in color, and their specific gravities were 5.95-6.35 (99; cf. 78, 79). In a variation on this procedure, the charge was fed into an arc furnace and air was forced through the electrodes during the heating, to provide the nitrogen (100).

Crystals identified as zirconium cyanonitride have been found in cast iron, and photomicrographs of these crystals have been exhibited (101).

Much of the impurity in commercial zircon is lost during the manufacture of zirconium cyanonitride by volatilization (71, 78, 99), and the cyanonitride can be converted into a fairly pure grade of zirconium dioxide by simply allowing the hot pig to burn in air. The zirconium dioxide so obtained consists of particles about 5-30 microns in diameter (78). Alternatively, the zirconium cyanonitride can be chlorinated to give a good commercial grade of zirconium tetrachloride.

While zirconium cyanonitride characteristically has a golden metallic color, it may be copper-red in shade and, indeed, any number of other shades such as blue, purple, or red, due to surface oxidation (71). Similar colors have been obtained with titanium cyanonitride (102).

The nitrogen content of zirconium cyanonitride prepared in industry in recent years in the arc furnace has been observed to vary from 0.44 to 3.95% by weight, depending on operating conditions (71). This corresponds to 0.03-0.3 atoms of nitrogen per atom of zirconium. A correlation has been noted between higher nitrogen content and greater susceptibility to chemical attack, e.g., by hydrochloric acid. But since the nitrogen content commonly increases as the carbon content decreases, and the excess of metal over small atoms increases, the change in chemical activity is not necessarily related directly to the nitrogen content. The oxygen content is commonly 4.0-5.5% by weight, or about 0.23-0.31 atoms of oxygen per atom of zirconium, and the sum of carbon, nitrogen, and oxygen atoms is usually 7-32% less than the number of zirconium atoms (71).

87. R. Kieffer and F. Benešovsky, Austrian patent 187,692, Nov. 10, 1956.
88. O. Ruff, *Forsch. Gebi. des Ing.* No. 147, 31 pp. (1914).
89. German patent 622,275, Nov. 23, 1935.
90. A. H. Ballard, U.S. Patent 2,538,959, Jan. 23, 1951.
91. P. D. Williams, U.S. Patent 2,497,111, Feb. 14, 1950.
92. Swiss patent 278,754, Feb. 1, 1952.
93. H. D. Miller and P. D. Williams, U.S. Patent 2,497,090, Feb. 14, 1950.
94. C. H. Prescott, Jr., U.S. Patent 2,587,534, Feb. 26, 1952.
95. L. D. Stoughton and T. V. Sheehar, *Mech. Eng.* 78, 699-702 (1956).
96. K. Moers, U.S. Patent 1,987,576, Jan. 8, 1935.
98. P. Godley, U.S. Patent 2,665,225, Jan. 5, 1954.
99. L. E. Barton, U.S. Patent 1,342,084, June 1, 1920; 1,351,091, Aug. 31, 1920.
100. C. J. Kinzie, R. P. Easton, and V. V. Effimoff, U.S. Patent 2,270,527, Jan. 20, 1942; British patent 544,823, April 29, 1942.
101. W. D. Forgeng, *Iron Age* 162, No. 16, 130-3 (1948)
102. C. J. Kinzie, personal communication.

There are no data available on the composition of gases evolved when zirconium carbide or cyanonitride are dissolved in hydrofluoric acid. Dissolution in this solvent would be most satisfactory for production of hydrocarbon gases because there would be no oxidizing affects on the carbon. Gases from the dissolution of zirconium carbide and cyanonitride in hot concentrated sulfuric acid (at about 300°) have been collected and analyzed.

TABLE 2.5. ANALYTICAL DATA ON ZIRCONIUM CARBIDE AND ZIRCONIUM CYANONITRIDE AND ON THE GASES EVOLVED WHEN THEY ARE DISSOLVED IN HOT, CONCENTRATED SULFURIC ACID

Component	Percentage of the Component Found on Analysis*			
	Zirconium carbide	Zirconium cyanonitride		
		Specimen 1	Specimen 2	Specimen 3
STARTING MATERIAL				
Zr	83.77	89.10	86.43	85.99
	(0.9183)	(0.9769)	(0.9475)	(0.9427)
C	15.20**	5.45	4.24	3.10
	(1.261)	(0.4542)	(0.3533)	(0.2583)
N	0.15	0.44	2.51	3.95
	(0.010)	(0.030)	(0.179)	(0.282)
O	0.32	4.08	5.56	4.49
	(0.020)	(0.255)	(0.348)	(0.281)
EVOLVED GASES				
Acidic gas†	89.9	2.5	35.3	30.9
Olefins	1.4	0.0	0.0	0.0
Paraffins††	4.1	43.0	42.2	20.0
CH_4	85	94	98	100
C_2H_6	15	6	2	0
Carbon monoxide	4.2	2.0	2.3	0.8
Hydrogen	0.0	52.1	19.1	37.0
Oxygen	0.4	0.4	0.5	0.7
Nitrogen	0.0	0.0	0.6	10.6

* Percentages are given by weight for solids and by volume for gases; figures in parentheses are the numbers of gram-atoms of the component per 100 grams of the specimen.
** The zirconium carbide specimen contained excess (free) carbon.
† Presumably CO_2 and SO_2.
†† The total percentages of paraffin gases are given, followed by a breakdown to methane and ethane, calculated from the carbon to hydrogen ratios found in these gases.

About 200 ml of gas was recovered from the dissolution of 1 gm of the solutes, and the analytical data are summarized in Table 2.5. It is seen that the greater the proportion of interstitial holes filled by carbon, nitrogen, and oxygen, the greater the proportion of acidic gases and the lower the proportion of hydrogen evolved, indicating the attack by the acid to be increasingly an oxidation attack. The oxidation reaction is associated with low hydrocarbon formation, the carbon tending to form carbon monoxide and dioxide rather than hydrocarbons. The oxygen and nitrogen in the evolved gases were probably present in the specimens as adsorbed atmospheric gases. Any nitrogen in the interstitial holes was converted to ammonia and held as ammonium ion in the sulfuric acid medium.

A few ternary or pseudoternary carbides containing zirconium have been reported. A series regarded as ϵ-carbides was prepared by compressing together suitable metals with animal charcoal under a pressure of 20 tons per sq cm and sintering the pellets so obtained in a vacuum graphite furnace at 1500-1800°. Two types of products were obtained of idealized formulas A_3B_3C and A_2B_4C, in which A is a transition metal of period 4 of the atomic chart and B a metal of periods 5 or 6. A and B have diagonal positions in the chart. Among the products obtained by this method were V_3Zr_3C, Cr_3Nb_3C, Mn_3Mo_3C, Mn_3W_3C, Fe_2Mo_4C, Co_2Mo_4C, Ni_3Mo_3C, and Ni_2Mo_4C (103). Zr_3WC_4 was prepared by sintering under vacuum an intimate mixture of zirconium and tungsten oxides and carbon at 2000-2300°. It was described as having a glistening appearance and was wetted well by alloys of the iron group. The compositions Ti_2ZrWC_4, $TiZr_2WC_4$, and $Ti_3Zr_3W_2C_8$ were prepared similarly. These substances were reported to be of value in preparing sintered hard alloys, suitable for high-speed cutting tools (104, 105).

Isothermal sections of the pseudoternary systems TiC-VC-ZrC, TaC-VC-ZrC, and NbV-VC-ZrC have been examined. Isoparametric lines were determined, showing the curvature of the single-phase field and the direction of the tie lines in the two-phase field. No relationships were found between atom size and the extent of the two-phase field (106). Examination of sintered TiC-WC-ZrC specimens by X-ray diffraction and metallographic methods showed only two phases to occur: hexagonal WC and face-centered cubic solid solution containing the three components. Increasing the amount of ZrC at the expense of TiC decreased the solubility of WC in this phase (107).

103. V. A. Kargin and V. V. Kiselava, *Acta Physiochem. U.R.S.S.* **12**, 377-96 (1940).
104. French patents **898,423** and **898,425**, April 23, 1945.
105. M. Oswald, U.S. Patent **2,507,218**, May 9, 1950.
106. J. T. Norton and A. L. Mowry, *J. Metals, Trans.* **3**, 923-5 (1951).
107. F. Tombrel, *Plansee. Proc.* **1955**, 205-15.

OXYGEN IN THE INTERSTITIAL SOLUTIONS

It is quite striking that oxygen forms an interstitial solution with titanium metal of composition TiO and face-centered cubic lattice like that of the carbide, but does not form a corresponding composition with zirconium. With titanium, when oxygen is dissolved in the metal, the hexagonal alpha metal inverts to the face-centered cubic lattice when the oxygen content exceeds the value represented by the formula $TiO_{0.42}$. The phase so formed exists in equilibrium with the alpha metal at the lower oxygen contents and passes over to the compound Ti_2O_3 at higher oxygen contents in that range of the system Ti-O over which it is stable. The upper limit of composition at which the phase TiO exists corresponds to the formula $TiO_{1.46}$. As distinguished from this, hexagonal α-zirconium can dissolve about 30 atomic % of oxygen, giving a composition corresponding to the formula $ZrO_{0.3}$ without forming a new phase. Thereafter the compound ZrO_2 is formed without the intermediate formation of a face-centered cubic interstitial solution or a suboxide of zirconium. These behaviors may be regarded as indicating that, as a result of the high stability of only one valence state of zirconium in its compounds, corresponding to oxidation number +4, the phase of composition ZrO_2 becomes the stable one at relatively low oxygen contents in the system Zr-O, rather than the face-centered cubic interstitial solution. The ability of the interstitial solutions of zirconium and small atoms to contain oxygen has been illustrated above in the case of zirconium cyanonitride in which 30% or more of the octahedral holes appear to be occupied by oxygen in some specimens.

ZIRCONIUM NITRIDES

A number of nitrides of zirconium have been reported in the literature, but of these only one, ideally of composition ZrN, has been well characterized. In the following pages the simple name *zirconium nitride* will be used in reference to the substance of this composition, and mathematically descriptive names will be used for other compositions, for example, trizirconium tetranitride for the composition Zr_3N_4. Although the compositions other than ZrN have not been demonstrated to be interstitial solutions, it is more convenient to consider the small amount of information available on them in connection with our consideration of ZrN than to treat them separately elsewhere.

When zirconium ClBrI tetrahalogenides are exposed to ammonia, they form addition products of empirical formulas $ZrX_4 \cdot nNH_3$, where X represents a halogen atom and n an integer of maximum value 12. If these addition products be heated in the absence of air or other oxygen-containing gases, they are said to decompose in a series of steps, with formation of trizirconium tetranitride as the end product (108, 109, 110, 111):

$$ZrCl_4 \cdot nNH_3 \rightarrow ZrCl_4 \cdot 4NH_3 + (n-4)NH_3$$
$$ZrCl_4 \cdot 4NH_3 \rightarrow Zr(NH_2)_4 + 4HCl$$
$$Zr(NH_2)_4 \rightarrow Zr(NH)_2 + 2NH_3 \tag{9-12}$$
$$Zr(NH)_2 \rightarrow Zr_3N_4$$

While the formation of Zr_3N_4 has been reported by the several authors cited, its composition and character have not been adequately established. It has been described as a grayish-white solid, insoluble in water and apparently unattacked by it. It is attacked by potassium hydroxide with liberation of ammonia (110). Still other compositions have been reported as final end products of the decomposition of ammino zirconium halides, i.e., Zr_2N_3 (114) and Zr_3N_8 (112, 113), but according to the later studies of Chauvenet, the only nitride obtained has the composition Zr_3N_4, and the other compositions reported actually contained undecomposed zirconium amide and zirconium imide (109, 110).

If trizirconium tetranitride is a true compound, its composition suggests that it has a structure corresponding to the graphical representation $N\equiv Zr\text{—}N\equiv Zr\equiv N\text{—}Zr\equiv N$, in which a triple bond exists between zirconium and the terminal nitrogen atoms.

Preparation of a nitride of zirconium by means other than the thermal decomposition of the ammino compounds generally yields the face-centered cubic interstitial solution of limiting composition ZrN, referred to simply as *zirconium nitride*.

In 1913 Wedekind reported that zirconium metal does not combine with nitrogen below 700°. At 1050° he obtained a reaction product of density $d_{15} = 6.75$. (The density of zirconium metal, containing the usual 2% of hafnium, d_{20} is 6.69.) It had the appearance of a metallic powder, conducted the electric current, and was less reactive toward oxygen and chlorine than zirconium metal. It showed no tendency to dissociate at 1100°, although it reacted reversibly with hydrogen at 1050°, with formation of ammonia. It was resistant to attack by acids other than hydrofluoric acid, but it was attacked by molten potassium hydroxide. Ammonium salts were found in the reaction products of the attack by hydrofluoric acid (114). Later studies

108. F. P. Venable and R. O. Deitz, *J. Elisha Mitchell Sci. Soc.* **38**, Nos. 1 and 2, 74-5 (1922).

109. P. Bruère and E. Chauvenet, *Compt. rend.* **167**, 201-3 (1918).

110. E. Chauvenet, *Ann. chim. phys.* (9) **13**, 59 (1920).

111. J. W. Mallet, *Am. J. Sci.* **28**, 346 (1859).

112. F. Wöhler, *Ann. Chem. Pogg.* **48**, 94 (1839).

113. J. M. Matthews, *J. Am. Chem. Soc.* **20**, 843-46 (1898).

114. E. Wedekind, *Ann.* **395**, 149-94 (1913).

have shown that under the conditions of Wedekind's experiments, an interstitial solution of nitrogen in zirconium is obtained which is isomorphous to zirconium carbide. Agte and Moers heated zirconium metal to 1100-1200° under a current of nitrogen, both in the presence and absence of hydrogen, and helped the reaction to completion by passing an electric current through the product to provide additional heat *in situ*. Their product had a citron-yellow color (8; cf. 33 and 115).

Clausing heated a zirconium filament to 1700° in an atmosphere of nitrogen at 43 mm pressure and obtained an increase in weight of the filament which agreed with that expected for the composition ZrN. His product had a specific gravity of 7.18 (116). Other investigators prepared very pure zirconium nitride by the thermal decomposition of zirconium tetrachloride on an incandescent filament of an unreactive metal in the presence of hydrogen and nitrogen. Homogeneous layers of crystal deposits were obtained, depending on the conditions of operation (29, 30, 31). Hafnium nitride was prepared similarly (31).

Zirconium nitride has been prepared by forming zirconium metal in the presence of nitrogen or ammonia, so that the metal immediately absorbed nitrogen to form the interstitial solution. The zirconium metal for this purpose has been prepared by reducing the oxide with magnesium (117) or gas black (118). Products prepared in this manner have been of low purity (8, 69, 118). For example, a product prepared by reducing zirconia with gas black at 1300° in the presence of nitrogen was assayed to be only 91.6% pure and was described as a yellowish-brown substance of density 6.93, hardness 8-9, melting point 2900°, insoluble in concentrated hydrochloric acid or dilute sulfuric, and rapidly soluble in concentrated sulfuric acid (118). Attempts to purify low-grade zirconium nitride have been reported. Acid-soluble impurities have been leached out with acids (119, 120), carbon has been burned out at 700°, followed by treatment with acids to decompose impurities such as silicides, phosphides, and sulfides without decomposing the nitride (120).

Zirconium nitride has also been prepared by the action of nitrogen on zirconium hydride (28).

Zirconium nitride, ZrN, formula weight 105.23, is a metallic solid solution having a face-centered cubic crystal lattice. The lattice is stable even when the solid solution contains considerably less than the saturation proportion of nitrogen. The variable composition of the phase has led to its

115. A. D. Mah and N. L. Gellert, *J. Am. Chem. Soc.* **78**, 3261-3 (1956).
116. P. Clausing, *Z. anorg. allgem. Chem.* **208**, 401-19 (1932).
117. P. P. Alexander, U.S. Patent **2,461,019**, Feb. 8, 1949.
118. E. Friederich and L. Sittig, *Z. anorg. allgem. Chem.* **143**, 293-320 (1925).
119. German patent **237,436**, July 10, 1909.
120. C. Bosch and A. Mattasch, U.S. Patent **1,102,715**, July 7, 1914.

being regarded as a "bertholide compound" (67). Values for physical constants of zirconium nitride are given in Table 2.6.

X-ray diffraction studies have indicated that the lattice points are occupied by neutral atoms and not by ions (44). The composition becomes superconducting on being cooled to 8.9° (61; cf. 122, 123, 124).* The superconductivity of zirconium nitride has been proved by magnetic as well as resistance manifestations (125). It is weakly paramagnetic and the susceptibility is independent of the valence electrons (59). No boiling point exists for the composition. It has been observed to decompose in the temperature range 1963-2193° with formation of zirconium and nitrogen, with $\Delta H_0° = 79.53$ kg cal/mole (126; cf. 127).

As in the case of the corresponding carbides, ZrN, NbN, TaN, and TiN form continuous series of solid solutions, but VN and ZrN are almost insoluble in one another. This appears to be due to the atom size rule (65), which has already been discussed in connection with the carbides.

Finely divided zirconium nitride can be made to form stable aqueous suspensions, which are said to be stabilized by adsorption of hydrogen ions, which renders the particles mutually repulsive. It does not form stable suspensions in liquids which do not contain available hydrogen ions (128).

Calculations based on the Wiedemann-Franz-Lorenz ratio indicate that thermal conduction of zirconium nitride is due to both electronic and lattice conduction, whereas in silicon carbide it is substantially only crystal lattice conduction. Both electric and thermal conduction are approximately inversely proportional to the absolute temperature (129). According to Samsonov, the conduction behavior reflects the incompletion of the (n-1)d level of electron orbitals (130).

Little attention has been given to the chemical properties of zirconium nitride. It is known to be dissolved by aqua regia (73) and hydrofluoric acid (72). Much of its chemical behavior may be safely inferred from the behavior of zirconium carbide.

There are no well-established uses of zirconium nitride, but a few uses

---

121. O. B. Bush, R. B. Vandergrift, and T. E. Hanley, *J. Applied Phys.* **20**, 295-6 (1949).

122. W. Meissner and H. Franz, *Z. Physik* **65**, 30-54 (1930).

123. W. Meissner, H. Franz, and H. Westerhoff, *Z. Physik* **75**, 521-30 (1932).

124. B. T. Matthias, *Phys. Rev.* **92**, 974-6 (1953).

*In general, the temperature of transition to superconductivity is higher for the transition metals than for their respective nitrides (122).

125. B. T. Matthias and J. K. Hulm, *Phys. Rev.* **87**, 799-806 (1952).

126. M. Hoch, D. P. Dingledy, and H. L. Johnson, *J. Am. Chem. Soc.* **77**, 304-6 (1955).

127. M. Picon, *Compt. rend.* **196**, 2003-6 (1933).

128. T. Vasilos and W. D. Kingery, *J. Phys. Chem.* **58**, 486-8 (1954).

129. Vasilos and Kingery, *J. Am. Ceram. Soc.* **37**, 409-14 (1954).

130. G. V. Samsonov, *Zhur. Tekh. Fiz.* **26**, 716-22 (1956).

TABLE 2.6. PHYSICAL CONSTANTS OF ZIRCONIUM NITRIDE

Property	Value	Literature
Density	7.18	116
Hardness, diamond pyramid, 30 kg load, kg/sq mm	1983 ± 18	29
Lattice parameter, a	4.59 A	29
	4.63 A	44
Melting point	2923°	135
Resistivity, ohm cm, room temperature	0.136 × 10⁻⁴	51
liquid air temperature	397 × 10⁻⁴	51
Thermodynamic values		
Entropy, kg cal/mole, standard state	9.23	58
free energy of formation at 25°	−81.4 ± 0.5	137; cf. 115, 137
Heat of combustion at 25°, for		
$ZrN(c) + O_2(g) \rightarrow ZrO_2(c) + \frac{1}{2}N_2$	174.25	115
Heat of formation at 25°	−87.3 ± 0.4	115; cf. 126, 138
Molal heat at 0°, cal/degree	9.655	139
Specific heat from 0° to 500°*	0.9946-9.242 × 10⁻⁵t-9.75t²	140

* For studies on heat content, see references 133, 139.

have been described, namely, as a conducting element in thoria cathodes (121), as the substance of a wick for picking up molten aluminum to provide a source of aluminum vapor in a metallizing process (98), as a protective coating on steel or graphite (95), and as the substance of crucibles for holding molten uranium (131).

Complex solid solutions having compositions corresponding to TaZrNO and CbZrNO have been described as hard metals (132).

ZIRCONIUM BORIDES

The boron atom is slightly larger than the carbon, nitrogen, and oxygen atoms, and is different from the latter atoms in certain other respects which are important in determining the type of solid phases that are formed in

131. A. G. Buyers, F. J. Keneshea, Jr., and R. A. Barney, *U.S. Atomic Energy Comm. NAA-SR-926*, 26 pp. (1954).

132. G. Hägg, *Iva* **24**, 345-6 (1953).

133. J. P. Coughlin and E. G. King, *J. Am. Chem. Soc.* **72**, 2262 (1950).

135. E. Friederich, *Z. Physik* **31**, 813-27 (1925).

137. G. L. Humphrey, *J. Am. Chem. Soc.* **75**, 2806-7 (1953).

138. B. Neumann, C. Kröger, and H. Kunz, *Z. anorg. allgem. Chem.* **218**, 379-401 (1934).

139. S. S. Todd, *J. Am. Chem. Soc.* **72**, 2914-5 (1950).

140. Shun-Ichi Satî, *Sci. Papers Inst. Phys. Chem. Research* (Tokyo) **34**, 399-405 (1938).

combination with zirconium. While carbon, nitrogen, and oxygen have as many or more electrons in the valence shells than zirconium, boron has fewer electrons in the valence shell. To a certain extent, therefore, the sites occupied by boron atoms in crystal lattices containing boron and zirconium are regions of electron deficiencies, i.e., they contain less than the 4 electrons that would be required to fill the valence orbitals of the boron atoms to the same numerical extent as the similarly placed zirconium atoms. As against this, the atoms of the other three elements must lose electrons to attain this same arrangement of electrons. Further, boron has a peculiar tendency toward forming 1-electron bonds, which also bears on the nature of its bonding to zirconium atoms. It is not surprising, therefore, that boron forms several compounds or phases with zirconium, in addition to a face-centered cubic interstitial solution, ZrB, which is analogous to zirconium carbide and zirconium nitride. That this reflects some generalized properties of boron is supported by the fact that the system of borides of titanium is similar to that of zirconium, and the titanium and zirconium borides form continuous series of solid solutions (141). Other examples of such similarities will appear below. In accordance with our usage in discussing zirconium nitrides, we shall here refer to the composition ZrB simply as *zirconium boride,* while using the mathematically more meaningful names *zirconium diboride* and *zirconium dodecaboride* for the substances of compositions ZrB_2 and ZrB_{12}, respectively. Although these latter substances appear to be true chemical compounds rather than interstitial solutions, they will be treated in this section along with zirconium boride, because of the convenience of grouping all the borides together. The phase diagram for the system Zr-B has been roughed out (142), as is shown in Figure 2.3. The earlier investigators of zirconium borides were unaware of either the true compositions of the products which they prepared or of their structural nature, and they used the term *zirconium boride* quite loosely to describe any reaction product composed of zirconium and boron. The later studies permit considerable correction of the earlier impressions. The reported methods for preparing borides of zirconium include reactions of boron with zirconium dioxide (143), zirconium with boron trioxide (144), zirconium hydride with boron (145), depositions on hot tungsten filaments exposed to mixtures of volatile zirconium compounds, boron compounds, and hydro-

141. G. A. Meerson, G. V. Samsonov, and R. B. Kotel'nikov, *Izvest. Sektora Fiz.-Khim. Anal. Inst. Obshchei i Neorg. Khim. Akad. Nauk. U.S.S.R.* **25,** 89-93 (1954).

142. F. W. Glaser and B. Post, *J. Metals, Trans.* **5,** 1117-8 (1953).

143. E. Zintl, W. Morawietz, and E. Gastinger, *Z. anorg. allgem. Chem.* **245,** 8 (1940).

144. J. L. Andrieux, *Colloq. intern. centr natl. récherche sci.* (Paris) **39,** Electrolyses C7-C10 (1952).

145. H. S. Cooper, U.S. Patent **2,678,870,** May 18, 1954.

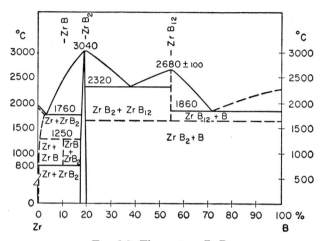

FIG. 2.3. The system Zr-B.

gen (31), and electrolyses of melts containing boron and zirconium compounds (146, 147, 148).

Trizirconium Tetraboride, Zr_3B_4

The existence of trizirconium tetraboride, Zr_3B_4, was presumed by earlier investigators of zirconium borides on the basis of the normal valences of the two elements. Although compounds of this composition have been reported, they have never been adequately identified and probably do not exist. The products were prepared by heating the elements, boron* and zirconium together, or by striking an arc between rods made of these elements (147, 149, 150). For example, equivalent weights of zirconium and boron were compressed into rods and heated by passing an electric current through them. A reaction product was obtained which, in its compact form, was not attacked by hydrochloric acid, and when powdered was dissolved by hydrochloric acid but was not attacked by nitric acid or aqueous alkalies. It was attacked with difficulty by fused sodium carbonate; when hot it was attacked by chlorine (151). Again, in another preparation, 15 g of zir-

---

* The supposed crystalline boron which was described in many of the older textbooks is now known not to be boron, but one or more compounds, especially the black AlB_{12} and the transparent $Al_3C_2B_{44}$ (152; 153, p. 337).

146. J. L. Andrieux, Thesis, 1909, Massonet Cie.

147. Andrieux, *Ann. chim.* **12**, 423 (1929).

148. Andrieux, *J. four élec.* **57**, 54 (1948); *Rev. métal* **45**, 49-59 (1948).

149. S. A. Tucker and H. R. Moody, *J. Chem. Soc.* **81**, 14 (1902).

150. L. Brewer, D. L. Sawyer, D. H. Templeton, and C. H. Dauben, *J. Am. Ceram. Soc.* **34**, 173-9 (1951).

151. E. Wedekind, *Ber.* **46**, 1198-1207 (1913).

conium and 2.2 g of boron were mixed and heated electrically in a carbon crucible. A brittle button was recovered which was more or less black on the visible surface and steel-gray on the fracture. Microscopic examination revealed an agglomerate of brilliant, tabular, transparent or translucent crystals, many of which were colorless. It was attacked slowly by concentrated acids and by aqua regia, and feebly by liquid bromine (149). Molten calcium, magnesium, or lithium borate containing zirconia and zirconium tetrafluoride was electrolyzed and a reaction product isolated by dissolving away the electrolyte with hydrochloric acid. Silvery-white products were recovered which were reported to be attacked only slightly by dilute acids, but which were dissolved by a mixture of dilute nitric and sulfuric acids. Mixtures of concentrated nitric and sulfuric acids attacked them vigorously, as did also molten caustic alkalies, carbonates, and sulfates. They reacted violently with lead dioxide or sodium peroxide (146, 147, 148). The products were supposed to be trizirconium tetraboride, but they varied considerably in physical properties. For example, reported densities were 3.7 (149), 4.98-5.00 (151), 5.97 (147), and reported hardnesses 7 (147, 149) and 8 (151).

Zirconium Diboride, ZrB_2

Niobium, tantalum, titanium, vanadium, and zirconium form diborides of the generic formula MB_2, all occurring as isomorphous hexagonal crystalline phases in which the unit cell contains one MB_2 unit. The atoms are arranged in alternate layers of metal and boron atoms parallel to the basal plane of the lattice. These substances all have characteristic metallic properties (154). The length of the a axis is determined primarily by the B-B contacts in the cases of the smaller metal atoms, and it is determined by the metal atoms in the case of the larger metal atoms. The high melting points of these borides have been ascribed to the affect of the boron-metal bond (155). It is conceivable, however, that the high melting points may be largely due to the migration of valence electrons from the metal atoms to the boron atoms to bring the latter toward an electronic arrangement which is the same as that of the zirconium atoms in the valence orbitals. The oxidized zirconium atoms then tend to make up their deficit of electrons by sharing electron pairs with one another. In so doing they become strongly bound together by covalent bonds. The ratios of melting points of diborides to melting points of the elements for titanium, zirconium, hafnium, va-

152. F. Halla and R. Weil, *Z. Krist.* **101**, 435 (1939).

153. N. V. Sidgwick, *The Chemical Elements and Their Compounds,* Oxford University Press, New York, 1950.

154. J. T. Norton, H. Blumenthal, and S. J. Sindeband, *J. Metals, Trans.* **1**, No. 10, 749-51 (1949).

155. B. Post, F. W. Glaser, and D. W. Moskowitz, *Acta Met.* **2**, 20-5 (1954).

nadium, niobium, tantalum, chromium, molybdenum, and tungsten are respectively 1.62, 1.57, 1.40, 1.33, 1.20, 1.06, 1.02, 0.083, and 0.067. The mutual solubility of these diborides depends mainly on the sizes of the metal atoms. In solid solutions of pairs of the diborides in which one has a more highly ordered structure in the pure state that the other, the more ordered structure is favored (155). Considerable solubilities have also been reported for molybdenum monoboride and tungsten monoboride in zirconium diboride (156).

Zirconium diboride has been prepared by a number of procedures. When zirconium metal was heated to 2000° with boron carbide and boric oxide under an atmosphere of hydrogen, zirconium diboride formed, according to the equation

$$7 \ Zr + 3 \ B_4C + B_2O_3 \rightarrow 7 \ ZrB_2 + 3 \ CO \tag{13}$$

It was found that the reaction should be conducted using a mixture which contained sufficient boric oxide to convert all the carbon to the monoxide, yet avoiding an excess which would consume boron carbide. Zirconium dioxide could be used in the place of boric oxide, but this resulted in products which contained about 1% of carbon (157, 158). Zirconium diboride assaying within 0.2% of ideal has been prepared by heating together a mixture of zirconia, boron carbide, and lampblack in a vacuum furnace. The mean particle size was 2.2 microns (159, 160). Solid solutions of titanium and zirconium diborides have been prepared by heating a mixture of titania, zirconia, carbon, and boric oxide to 1800-2050° (160). On the other hand, solid solutions of molybdenum and zirconium diborides could not be prepared in this fashion. Hafnium diboride can be prepared similarly to zirconium diboride (161).

When a gram-atom of zirconium and a gram-atom of boron are heated together at 900°, zirconium diboride forms and some boron dissolves in the excess of zirconium metal, expanding the lattice. At 1000° the metal disappears and a new phase forms (162). Zirconium diboride has been produced by an electrochemical process (163) quite similar to that which was once reported to yield Zr_3B_4 (147). The product analyzed 80.3% Zr (0.8705 gram-atoms per 100 grams), 18.9% B (1.747 gram-atoms per 100 grams), and 0.45% F.

156. R. S. Steinitz, *Powder Met. Bull.* **6**, 54-6 (1951).
157. R. Kieffer, F. Benesovsky, and E. R. Honak, *Z anorg. allgem. Chem.* **268**, 191-200 (1952).
158. C. T. Barock and T. E. Evans, *J. Metals* **7**, *AIME Trans.* **203**, 908-11 (1955).
159. G. A. Meerson and G. V. Samsonov, *Zhur. Priklad. Khim.* **27**, 1115-20 (1954).
160. H. Blumenthal, *Powder Met. Bull.* **7**, 79-81 (1956).
161. H. R. Montgomery, U.S. Patent **2,613,154**, Oct. 7, 1952.
162. B. J. Post and F. W. Glaser, *J. Chem. Phys.* **20**, 1050-1 (1952).
163. F. W. Glaser, *Powder Met. Bull.* **6**, 51-4 (1951).

Zirconium diboride, ZrB_2, formula weight 112.86, is a metallic substance which is stable over a wide temperature range. It melts at about 3000° and can be sintered at lower temperatures (163). Its electrical resistivity is much less than that of zirconium metal: 9.2 microhm cm vs. 46.6 microhm cm for the metal (51). It does not become superconductive down to 1.8°K (48c, 136), although earlier investigators have erroneously reported it to become superconductive. Some physical constants are listed in Table 2.7. It has been observed that when zirconium diboride is heated in a copper-hearth arc furnace mixed with tantalum or molybdenum disilicide or titanium carbide, no chemical change occurs, but a new phase forms when it is heated in contact with dimolybdenum carbide (164).*

TABLE 2.7. PHYSICAL CONSTANTS OF ZIRCONIUM DIBORIDE

Property	Value	Literature
Crystal parameters, a	3.172	159
b	3.538	
Crystalline symmetry	hexagonal	
structure type	C32	157
Density	5.60	157
	6.24	159
	6.09	163
Electrical conductivity, microhm cm		
at 20°	9	51, 163
at liquid-air temperature	1.8	51
Hardness, micro, 30 kg load, kg/sq cm	2252 ± 22	133
Rockwell A	87-89	254, p. 448
Melting point	~3000°	51, 136, 157, 163

Zirconium Boride (Zirconium Monoboride)

As noted above, when equal numbers of gram-atoms of zirconium and boron are heated together to 900°, zirconium diboride forms, leaving excess metal. On further heating to 1000°, the metal disappears, according to X-ray diffraction evidence, and a face-centered cubic phase appears in its place. It is doubtless of ideal composition ZrB and related structurally and in properties to zirconium carbide and zirconium nitride. The diffraction data available give the value 4.65 ± 0.03 A for a. At 1200° zirconium boride decomposes with the formation of another phase (162).

Little information is available on the properties of zirconium boride. It is said to melt at 2990° (166, p. 858). It becomes superconducting at 3.3°,

---

* For metallographic techniques for examining zirconium diboride, see reference 165.
164. G. A. Geach and F. O. Jones, *Plansee Proc.* 1955, 80-91.
165. R. Wachtell, *Powder Met. Bull.* **6**, 62-6 (1951).
166. W. Hückel, *Structural Chemistry of Inorganic Compounds,* Elsevier Publishing Company, Princeton, N.J. 1951, vol. 2.

although the hafnium analog is not superconducting at 1.2-1.3° (159). It is not as good a thermionic emitter as zirconium carbide (55), which is consistent with the presumption that in zirconium boride electrons which originated in zirconium atoms enter into the valence orbitals of the boron atoms.

Zirconium Dodecaboride

Zirconium dodecaboride, ZrB_{12}, was first reported by Post and Glaser (167). The uranium analog, UB_{12}, had previously been reported (168). Chemical analysis of a preparation of zirconium dodecaboride showed it to contain 44% Zr (0.4825 gram-atoms per 100 grams) and 56% B (5.17 gram-atoms per 100 grams), an empirical atomic ratio of 1:10.7. The theoretical composition is 41% Zr and 59% B. Hence the ordinary product may contain a considerable number of lattice defects. The crystal symmetry is face-centered cubic, with $a_0 = 7.408$ A. It has metallic properties and is black when powdered. The electrical resistivity at 22° is 60 microhm cm, and the temperature coefficient of resistivity is 0.00162 between −79° and 64°. The thermal conductivity at room temperature is 0.122 watts/cm/° (167).

Other Borides

In 1902 Wedekind obtained what he regarded as a borocarbide by reducing a mixture of zirconia and boric acid with carbon in an electric furnace (170). The existence of such a compound or phase has not been corroborated by later work.

Uses of Zirconium Borides

There are no well-established or extensive uses of zirconium borides, but their applications to the manufacture of hard alloys for tools and dies (81), refractories (87, 171, 172), cermets (173, 174), and chemically resistant vessels (172) have been described.

ZIRCONIUM HYDRIDES

A number of phases consisting of zirconium and hydrogen have been shown to exist. Only since the application of modern X-ray diffraction methods for the determination of crystal structure and modern concepts of the solid state have reasonably satisfactory understandings of the nature of

167. B. Post and F. W. Glaser, *J. Metals* 4, *AIME Trans.* 194, 631-2 (1952).
168. F. Bertaut and P. Blum, *Compt. rend.* 229, 666-7 (1949).
170. E. Wedekind, *Ber.* 35, 3929 (1902).
171. K. C. Nicholson, U.S. Patent 2,670,301, Feb. 23, 1954.
172. A. Blum and W. Ivanick, *Powder Met. Bull.* 7, 75-8 (1956).
173. P. Schwartzkopf and F. W. Glaser, *Iron Age* 173, No. 13, 138-9 (1954).
174. J. T. Norton, *Mech. Eng.* 78, 319-22 (1956).

these phases been possible. The term *hydrides* has been used loosely in the literature to designate compounds as well as phases containing zirconium and hydrogen.* We shall continue to make use of the term, with the understanding that it refers to hydrogen-containing substances without inferring the presence of a hydride ion, H^-, or hydrogen in any other specific relationship to other atoms. While hydrogen exhibits the typical behavior of an anion in the alkali and alkaline earth hydrides, hydrogen in palladium has been found to migrate with passage of an electric current as though it were positively charged (175, 176), and, to this extent at least, it behaves as though it were present as a cation (proton). Such cationic manifestations in compositions with metals are doubtless not limited to hydrogen in palladium and might be expected to play a role in the behavior of hydrogen in other transition metals.

Absorption isobars for hydrogen in various metals have been shown to indicate two distinct behaviors. The elements chromium, cobalt, copper, iron, nickel, silicon, and silver show rather weak absorption of hydrogen which increases with rise in temperature in the range 400-1600°, while cerium, lanthanum, neodymium, palladium, praeseodymium, tantalum, thorium, titanium, vanadium, and zirconium show relatively strong absorption which decreases with rising temperature (177).** We might expect to find an extensive range of similarities between compositions containing zirconium and hydrogen and compositions containing other metals of the latter group and hydrogen. For example, the hydrides and deuterides of thorium and zirconium have been shown to be isomorphous and soluble in one another (179).

The system hydrogen-zirconium was first studied by Winkler as early as 1890 (180). He was of the opinion that he had found evidence for the existence of definite gaseous and solid hydrides. A mistaken impression of the formation of volatile zirconium hydrides persisted for years (181), but in

---

* The term *hydride* has been employed to cover such disparate substances as the salt-like hydrides of the alkali and alkaline earth elements, the volatile hydrogen compounds such as ammonia and the hydrocarbons, metallic compositions such as those composed of hydrogen and palladium or other transition metals, and the short-lived, hydrogen-containing substances which are formed by an electric discharge in hydrogen in the presence of certain elements, these latter compounds being detected by their characteristic spectral bands.

175. C. Wagner and G. Heller, *Z. physik. Chem.* **B46**, 242 (1940).
176. A. Cohen and W. Specht, *Z. Phys.* **62**, 1-31 (1930).
177. I. A. D'yakonov and A. Samarin, *Bull. acad. Sci. U.R.S.S.* **1945**, 813-20.
** Other data have been published on the relative solubilities of hydrogen in cerium, copper, iron, nickel, palladium, platinum, thorium, tantalum, titanium, vanadium, and zirconium (178).
178. G. Borelius, *Metallwirschaft* **8**, 105-8 (1929).
179. R. E. Rundle, C. G. Shull, and E. O. Wollan, *Acta Cryst.* **5**, 22 (1952).
180. C. Winkler, *Ber deut. chem. Ges.* **23**, 2642-48 (1890); **24**, 873-98 (1891).
181. R. Schwarz and H. Deisler, *Ber.* **52**, 1896-1903 (1919).

1921 a study was published wherein it was proved that the gases evolved during the decomposition of an alloy of composition $ZrMg_2$ consisted of hydrides of sulfur and phosphorus, and not of zirconium, as had been previously presumed (182). Subsequent studies have given no support of the existence of volatile zirconium hydrides. Paneth has pointed out that volatile hydrides are formed by boron and by all elements not more than 4 places before an inert gas in the atomic chart, and by no other elements (183). But although the later studies of compositions containing hydrogen

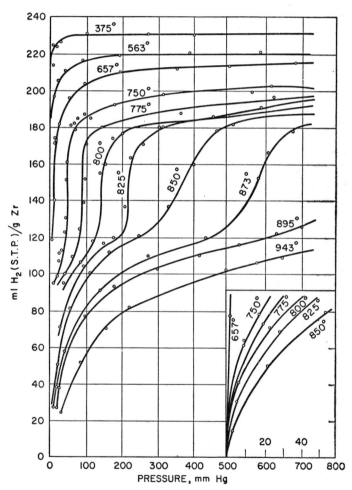

FIG. 2.4. Dissociation pressure of zirconium hydride as a function of temperature and composition. From (208).

182. R. Schwarz and E. Konrad, *Ber.* **54B**, 2122-33 (1921).
183. F. A. Paneth, *Ber.* **53**, 1710 (1920).

and zirconium have indicated no gaseous compounds to exist, at least six solid phases composed of these two elements have been demonstrated to form under suitable circumstances. The following five phases are best established: the α-, hexagonal phase which may contain up to 5-6 atom % of hydrogen at room temperature;* the β-, body-centered cubic phase with about 20 atom % hydrogen; the γ-, close-packed hexagonal with about 33 atom % hydrogen; the δ-, face-centered cubic phase with about 50 atom % hydrogen; and the ϵ-, face-centered tetragonal phase, with about 66.7 atom % hydrogen (184). A simple way of regarding these phases as chemical entities is the following: α is a solution of hydrogen in the ordinary α-, low-temperature, stable form of zirconium metal; β and γ are two varieties of solutions of hydrogen in the β-, high-temperature, stable form of zirconium metal; δ, of typical composition ZrH, is an interstitial solution of hydrogen in zirconium with face-centered cubic symmetry and is analogous to the solutions of carbon, nitrogen, and boron in zirconium; ϵ is a new type of interstitial solution, not previously encountered in zirconium systems, in which the composition approaches if it does not quite attain ZrH_2, and the arrangement of atoms is that of a deformed fluorite structure (179). Thus the larger concentrations of hydrogen in zirconium metal coerce it to assume crystalline symmetries which it does not assume when in the relatively pure condition. There are no compounds of hydrogen in the sense of molecular entities or the polymerization products of hypothetical molecular entities (185). The reversible absorption of hydrogen by zirconium as a function of temperature is shown graphically in Figure 2.4.**

---

* The range of existence of the α-phase extends to about 50 atom % at 700-850°.

184. M. D. Banus, *Encyclopedia of Chemical Technology,* Interscience Publishers, Inc., New York, vol. 15, 298-302 (1956).

185. A. Sieverts and E. Roell, *Z. anorg. allgem. Chem.* **153**, 289-308 (1926).

** The pressure-temperature curves for the system hydrogen-zirconium appear not to depend on the pressure at which the hydride was originally formed. If an excess of hydrogen is avoided, the pressure-temperature curve is reproducible with rising and falling temperature. The system hydrogen-zirconium has been widely studied for the relationship of pressure, temperature, composition of the solid phase, and crystallography (180, 186, 187, 188, 189, 190, 191, 192, 193, 194, 195, 196). The reaction of the two elements at micron pressures has also been reported (27).

186. W. C. Schumb, E. F. Sewell, and A. S. Eisenstein, *J. Am. Chem. Soc.* **69**, 2029-33 (1947).

187. W. Trzebiatowski and B. Stalinski, *Roczniki Chem.* **30**, 691-6 (1956).

188. J. H. de Boer and J. D. Fast. *Rec. trav. chim.* **55**, 350-6 (1936).

189. E. A. Gulbransen and K. F. Andrew, *J. Electrochem. Soc.* **96**, 364-76 (1949).

190. Gulbransen and Andrew, *J. Electrochem. Soc.* **101**, 560-6 (1954).

191. Gulbransen and Andrew, *J. Electrochem. Soc.* **101**, 474-80 (1954).

192. R. K. Edwards, P. Levesque, and D. Cubicciotti, *J. Am. Chem. Soc.* **77**, 1307-11 (1955).

193. H. J. Fitzwilliam, A. R. Kaufmann, and C. F. Squire, *J. Chem. Phys.* **9**, 678-82 (1941).

194. D. A. Vaughan and J. P. Bridge, *J. Metals* **8**, *AIME Trans.* **206**, 528-31 (1956).

All the phases of the system hydrogen-zirconium are of a metallic character. Some investigators of the system have believed their data to support the assumption that the bonding between the metal and the hydrogen is of the nature of the metallic bond, itself (192). Others have assumed the bonding to be ionic, and on this assumption they have calculated a value for the radius of the anion, H^-, equal to 1.29 ± 0.05 A, which is somewhat smaller than the value 1.37 A for hydrogen in lithium hydride (197). In all events the space available for hydrogen atoms is greater than that actually taken up by them (198).

The α-phase of zirconium hydride extends in composition from the pure metal to about the hydrogen content represented by the formula ZrH (192; cf. 187). At room temperature the crystal parameters vary from a = 3.228, c = 5.40 A for the metal to a = 3.247, c = 5.173 A for 5 atom % hydrogen (200). Much higher hydrogen contents are obtainable at 700-850°. The β-phase has a body-centered cubic lattice for which a = 3.61 A at 900° at zero hydrogen content, and the value becomes about 4.66 A for 20 atom % hydrogen (200). This phase has been observed to contain up to slightly more than 1 hydrogen atom per zirconium atom in the temperature range 850-875°. The γ-phase, of hexagonal close-packed structure, has been reported to have the parameters a = 3.335-3.339 and c = 5.453-5.455 A for compositions approximating that of the formula Zr_2H (187, 199). A variant designated γ' has a face-centered tetragonal lattice and exists only in the presence of α- and δ-phases (191). The δ-phase has a face-centered cubic lattice, and at composition approximately equivalent to ZrH it has been observed to have the parameter a = 4.765-4.768 A. Compositions of hydrogen content up to about $ZrH_{1.6}$ have been observed for the δ-phase (191, 192). The ε-phase has a range of homogeneity extending from composition $ZrH_{1.67}$ to almost if not quite ZrH_2 (191). At a composition corresponding to $ZrH_{1.94}$, the parameters were observed to be a = 4.87 and c = 4.58 A (193), while for very nearly ZrH_2 the values a = 4.364 and c = 4.440 A (199) have been reported. Hafnium hydride of composition $HfH_{1.87}$ has been observed by X-ray diffraction methods to have a tetragonal unit cell in which each hafnium atom has 12 nearest hafnium neighbors at 3.289 ± 0.002 A distance, and 4 other hafnium neighbors at 3.461 ± 0.001 A (200). The tetragonal phase persists through variations in composition up to $HfH_{1.98}$ (201).

195. A. P. Young and C. M. Schwartz, U.S. Atomic Energy Comm. **BMI-1100**, 22 pp. (1956).
196. C. E. Ells and A. D. Quillan, J. Inst. Metals **85**, Pt. 3, 89-96 (1956).
197. G. G. Libowitz and T. R. P. Gibbs, Jr., J. Phys. Chem. **60**, 510-11 (1956).
198. W. Biltz, Z. anorg. allgem. Chem. **174**, 42-6 (1928).
199. G. Hägg, Z. physik. Chem. **B11**, 433-54 (1931).
200. L. S. Levitt, J. Phys. Chem. **58**, 573-6 (1954).
201. S. S. Sidhu and J. C. McGuire, J. Appl. Phys. **23**, 1257-61 (1952).

The substitution of deuterium for hydrogen in zirconium hydride results in a decrease in the metal-gas atom distance and a contraction of the structure (202).

The recognition of the six crystal phases in which zirconium hydrides occur emerged only after a long sequence of studies in which an understanding of the true nature of the system was obscured by predisposition to misinterpretation as well as by lack of sufficient data to delineate it. The earlier investigators expected to find compounds consisting of simple molecules of the classical type. They made their studies with impure zirconium, the only kind which was available at first. In 1910 a compound of composition ZrH_2 was reported to form when zirconium metal was heated in an atmosphere of hydrogen (203). A few years later, i.e., in 1914, fairly pure zirconium was available and a more meaningful study was made of the reaction of zirconium with hydrogen under 1 atm pressure. The reaction rate was found to follow a parabolic law, with a rate constant of $2.3 \times 10^5 e^{-17,200/RT}$, giving a value of $17,200 \pm 200$ calories for the activation energy of the reaction (204).*

It has been shown that when a hydrogen molecule enters into a transition metal, it is dissociated into its atoms. This is reflected in the proportionality of the solubility to the square of the hydrogen pressure (185, 192). Neutron diffraction studies on zirconium dihydride have located atomic size particles of hydrogen in slightly flattened metallic tetrahedra (179).

The solubility of hydrogen in both α- and β-zirconium decreases with rising temperature. It is more soluble in the β- than in the α-phase. During the transformation of α-zirconium to β-zirconium, hydrogen is taken up by the metal, and on cooling to below the transition temperature, β-zirconium is transformed to α-zirconium with evolution of hydrogen (188). The dissolved hydrogen lowers the transition temperature, i.e., it increases the stability of the β-phase relative to the α-phase (193, 196, 199). During the absorption of hydrogen by zirconium, there are progressive changes in the magnetic susceptibility (193), photoelectric function (206), free energy, and entropy (207). The element loses its paramagnetism by the time the

---

* In later studies the reaction rate with hydrogen was correlated with the fundamental solution and diffusion processes (189, 191); also, thermodynamic analysis of the system hydrogen zirconium has been made (205).

202. Sidhu, *J. Chem. Phys.* **22**, 1062-3 (1954).

203. L. Weiss and E. Neumann, *Z. anorg. allgem. Chem.* **65**, 248 (1910).

204. J. Belle, B. B. McCleland, and M. W. Mallett, *J. Electrochem. Soc.* **101**, 211-14 (1954).

205. E. A. Gulbransen and K. F. Andrew, *J. Metals* **7**, *AIME Trans.* **203**, 136-44 (1955).

206. H. C. Rentschler and D. E. Henry, *Trans. Electrochem. Soc.* **87**, 289-297 (1945).

207. R. M. Bauer, *Trans. Faraday Soc.* **40**, 374-84 (1944).

hydrogen content has increased to the concentration corresponding to the formula ZrH_2 (193).*

The capacity of zirconium for absorbing hydrogen is considerably diminished by the presence of other atoms in interstitial solution in the metal. The diminution of hydrogen absorption has been observed to increase as the foreign atoms in solution in the metal vary from oxygen to nitrogen to carbon (45). The system hydrogen-oxygen-zirconium has received particular attention (208, 209). The α-, δ-, and ϵ-phases are able to contain considerable amounts of hydrogen and oxygen simultaneously. At 750° the hydrogen saturation boundary of α-zirconium shows that initially 3 hydrogen atoms are replaced by 1 oxygen atom; the hydrogen saturation boundary of the δ-phase shows the replacement of 7 hydrogen atoms by 2 oxygen atoms. There appears to be no interaction between interstitial hydrogen and interstitial oxygen within the metal lattice. While oxygen atoms appear able to occupy only octahedral holes in the α-zirconium lattice (and at most 3 out of every 7 of these), the smaller hydrogen atoms can occupy tetrahedral as well as octahedral holes. The presence of interstitial oxygen atoms appears to set limits not only on the number of holes that can be occupied by other oxygen atoms, but also on the number of holes that can be occupied by hydrogen atoms (209). From the shape of the solubility curves in the system hydrogen-oxygen-zirconium, it appears that more than one solution process is involved when hydrogen is taken up by zirconium which contains oxygen (208).

The methods for making zirconium hydrides have been the following: heating the previously prepared metal with hydrogen (210), forming the metal in the presence of hydrogen, so that it reacts *in situ* to form the hydride (211, 212, 213), and treatment of zirconia with calcium hydride at 600-1000° under a hydrogen atmosphere (214). The latter two methods are used in industrial preparation of zirconium hydride, and the products initially recovered are purified by leaching with hydrochloric acid (212, 213). The products offered in commerce assay about 98% zirconium and hydrogen, about 0.5% nitrogen, 0.6% silica, about 0.5% of miscellaneous metallic impurities, each of which is present in small fractions of a per cent, and the

---

* Data are also available on the systems deuterium-hydrogen (179, 190) and deuterium-hafnium (202).

208. (Mrs.) M. N. A. Hall, S. L. H. Martin, and A. L. G. Rees, *Trans. Faraday Soc.* **41**, 306-16 (1945).
209. R. K. Edwards and P. Levesque, *J. Am. Chem. Soc.* **77**, 1312-16 (1955).
210. F. H. Driggs, U.S. Patent **1,816,830**, Aug. 4, 1931.
211. F. P. Archibald and P. P. Alexander, Canadian patent **435,003**, May 28, 1946.
212. L. W. Davis, U.S. Patent **2,411,524**, Nov. 26, 1946.
213. P. P. Alexander, U.S. Patent **2,427,339**, Sept. 16, 1947.
214. H. W. Zabel, *Chem. Industries* **60**, 37-9 (1947).

balance is presumed to be oxygen. The particle size is typically about 3-5 microns (184). Hafnium hydride is prepared by similar processes, and products have been reported to contain up to 2.16 hydrogen atoms per hafnium atom (215).

Some alloys of zirconium, such as those of compositions ZrV_2, $ZrCr_2$, and Zr_2Ni, have been observed to take up less hydrogen per unit volume of zirconium contained than is taken up by unalloyed zirconium (215).

In addition to the formation of zirconium hydrides by the methods outlined above, zirconium hydrides have been observed to take form under certain special conditions. After exposing zirconium metal to steam at 400° for 180 hours, an incipient formation of a hydride layer between the metal and the oxide surface was noted. Micrographs revealed a needlelike growth of the hydride (216). Widmanstätten patterns for zirconium hydride have been observed on etched surfaces of annealed zirconium crystals. Stereographic projections showed that the formation had occurred on planes of the family $\{10\bar{1}0\}$, and this was verified by comparison with zirconium slip planes of this family (217).

Zirconium foil, clad on tungsten, has been observed to absorb tritium in the atomic ratio 1:1 at 600° (218). Studies have been made on β-rays from tritium absorbed in zirconium (219).

The hydrides of formula ZrH and ZrH_2 have the formula weights 92.23 and 93.24, respectively. Many of the data reported for these hydrides cannot be ascribed specifically to substances of stoichiometric or nearly stoichiometric compositions. While the δ-phase and ϵ-phase discussed above can be idealized to correspond to formula ZrH and ZrH_2, the other phases suggest no such fortuitous stoichiometry. All the phases are metallic substances of well-defined crystalline structure. When heated in air, they burn to zirconium dioxide and water (203), and the reaction may be very violent if the specific surface of the zirconium hydride is high and the surface is not passivified. Zirconium hydride does not react with nitrogen, ammonia, carbon monoxide, or hydrocarbons at room temperature, and it is stable in air under normal atmospheric conditions. Decomposition becomes apparent at temperatures over 100°, and ignition occurs between 300° and 600° (184, 220). It reacts with ammonia, carbon monoxide, nitrogen, and hydrocarbon gases above 600°. The reaction with nitrogen at about 1050° is accompanied by the

215. M. J. Trzeciak, D. F. Dilthey, and M. W. Mallett, *U.S. Atomic Energy Comm.* **BMI-1112,** 32 pp. (1956).
216. C. M. Schwartz and D. A. Vaughan, *U.S. Atomic Energy Comm.* **BMI-1120,** 8 pp. (1956).
217. J. P. Langeron and P. Lehr, *Compt. rend.* **243,** 151-4 (1956).
218. R. S. Rochlin, *Rev. Sci. Instr.* **23,** 100-1 (1951).
219. W. T. Davies and M. A. Grace, *Proc. Phys. Soc.* London **64A,** 846-7 (1951).
220. K. Anderson and W. S. Fleshman, *Ind. Eng. Chem.* **42,** 1381-3 (1950).

formation of ammonia (114). Zirconium hydrides react slowly with oxygen, chlorine, and dry hydrogen chloride at room temperature, but the attack depends to a considerable extent on the condition of the surface of the hydride. These reactive gases attack zirconium hydrides rapidly and quantitatively at higher temperatures. Not only oxygen, but many oxygen-containing compounds react with it at the higher temperatures, and even porcelain has been found to oxidize zirconium hydrides at 1000° (184). Because of the hazard of ignition and explosion, zirconium hydride must be handled with the care that is appropriate to highly combustible substances. There is no evidence of a toxicity hazard in handling zirconium hydrides (184).

Hydrofluoric acid, even as dilute as 1%, dissolves zirconium hydride in the cold; but other mineral acids, concentrated or dilute, are generally without effect on zirconium hydrides at room temperature. The hydrides are attacked and dissolved by hot concentrated sulfuric acid and are decomposed by sulfate fusions.

Of a number of uses described for zirconium hydrides, only a few have been of industrial significance. In 1955 the chief use made of the dihydride was in delayed-action fuses for flare shells, such as those dropped from aircraft by parachute or fired from mortars (184). Zirconium dihydride has been found more satisfactory than zirconium metal for sintering and compacting (70, 221). Vacuum sintering results in metallic products of higher density and larger grain sizes than those obtained from zirconium metal under similar conditions. This superiority in working properties has been ascribed to the high mobility of zirconium atoms, which results from the successive phase changes during the degassing (221). A technique has been described for depositing zirconium dihydride cataphoretically (222). Mixtures of a zirconium hydride with copper or silver can be used as bonding agents for joining nonmetallic bodies such as glasses, porcelains, or diamonds to one another or to metals. The thin layer of bonding agent is decomposed by heating to 400° or higher *in vacuo* or under a hydrogen atmosphere, and the fusible metal mixture which forms accomplishes the bond (223, 224). Zirconium hydride paste has served for applying a surface of getter metal to iron, nickel, or carbon electrodes (225). A hydride has also been used to apply a zirconium metal coating to ceramic ware (226), and in cladding reactor fuel elements with zirconium (227). Baked mixtures of a zirconium hydride and zirconia have been used as coatings on electron discharge de-

221. H. H. Hausner, *Plansee Proc.* **1952**, 146-56 (1953).
222. V. J. DeSantis and F. L. Hunter, U.S. Patent **2,711,980,** June 28, 1955.
223. C. E. Lacy and J. H. Keeler, *Mech. Eng.* **77**, 875-8 (1955).
224. F. C. Kelley, U.S. Patent **2,570,248,** Oct. 9, 1951.
225. W. Espe, *Powder Met. Bull.* **3**, 100-11 (1948).
226. Belgian patent **482,771,** May 28, 1948.
227 H. H. Hausner and M. C. Kells, *Mech. Eng.* **77**, 665-9 (1955).

vices (228). Zirconium hydrides are said to be effective additives to other metals as desulfurizing agents (229).

THE SEMIMETALLIC COMPOUNDS

INTRODUCTION

The atoms of the elements silicon, phosphorus, sulfur, and selenium are significantly larger than the atoms of boron, carbon, nitrogen, and oxygen, and unlike the latter, they cannot fit into the interstices of a zirconium crystal lattice. They are incapable, therefore, of forming such interstitial solutions as are formed characteristically by the atoms of small diameter. On the other hand, they are energetically incapable of forming such compounds as the oxide and halogenides of zirconium.

The zirconium metal lattice is a highly stable one, and an energetic reagent is required to accomplish its breakdown and the rebonding of its constituent atoms in new combinations. It can be inferred from the known interactions of zirconium with silicon, phosphorus, and sulfur that the free energy of formation of the reaction products is insufficient to bring about complete destruction of the elementary zirconium lattice under conditions which have been observed up to the present time. Not being metals, these elements also do not form typical intermetallic compounds. The combinations which are observed to occur are better described by the term *semimetallic* than *metallic*.

An approach to the understanding of the kind of combination with zirconium that is entered into by silicon, phosphorus, and sulfur (and a few of their near neighbors in the periodic table) can be made in the following fashion. These atoms combine with zirconium substantially by forming coordination compounds with zirconium atoms, which may be regarded as bound to one another in the body of the metal. In forming these coordination compounds, they distort and alter the existing interatomic bonding of the zirconium atoms but do not break it down completely. To represent this graphically, we can show a portion of a chain of zirconium atoms. An extension of this chain and its cross-linking in three dimensions would constitute a model of a crystal of zirconium metal. The initial reaction with this chain takes the form

$$
\begin{array}{ccc}
-\mathrm{Zr}-\mathrm{Zr}- + \mathrm{S} \rightarrow -\mathrm{Zr}-\mathrm{Zr}- \rightarrow -\mathrm{Zr}\diagdown\diagup\mathrm{Zr}- \\
\quad\quad\quad\quad\quad\quad\quad | \quad\quad\quad\quad\quad\quad \\
\quad\quad\quad\quad\quad\quad\quad \mathrm{S} \quad\quad\quad\quad\quad\quad \mathrm{S}
\end{array}
\qquad (14)
$$

The bonding electrons might originate entirely or partially from the sulfur atoms, so the usual arrow representation of the coordination bond is not

228. E. G. Widell, U.S. Patent **2,536,673**, Jan. 2, 1951.

229. O. Smalley, British patent **666,095**, Feb. 6, 1952; U.S. Patent **2,604,393**, July 22, 1952.

employed here. The sulfur atoms will tend to link zirconium atoms in certain directions and to push them apart in other directions. Moreover, the bonding of sulfur atoms to zirconium atoms introduces field effects which are reflected in changes in the bond distances between vicinal zirconium atoms, and affects the ease and nature of the bonding of another sulfur atom in a nearby position. The successive additions of sulfur atoms further magnify these effects. The net result of the reaction or reactions is to retain two-dimensional structural features of the original zirconium metal, but in distorted condition, to break down the original metallic arrangement in the third dimension, and to introduce new cross-bonding through sulfur into what now becomes a new solid. Indeed, a whole series of new phases can be formed, depending on how many sulfur atoms are introduced per atom of zirconium. When one sulfur atom has been introduced per atom of zirconium the distance between the zirconium atoms is found to have been increased by 15% (132). The new solid substances are compounds in that the sulfur is chemically bound, i.e., by ordinary covalent bonds, and a definite though not precise stoichiometry is involved.

The arrangements of zirconium atoms and sulfur atoms in the unit cell of

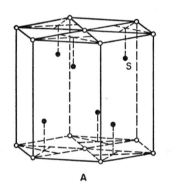

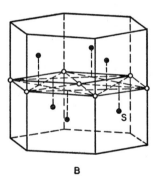

A   B

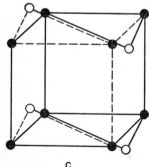

FIG. 2.5. The arrangement of atoms in the unit cells of zirconium disulfide: A, unit cell, showing basal planes of zirconium atoms; B, contiguous half-cells; C, selected parallelepiped of zirconium atoms, showing bonding relationship of sulfur atoms. From (29), (231).

C

231. W. Hückel, *Structural Chemistry of Inorganic Compounds,* Elsevier Publishing Company, Princeton, N.J., 1952, p. 347.

zirconium disulfide have been depicted by van Arkel, and are shown in Figure 2.5. In part C, an additional view is given, showing the arrangement of a parallelepiped of zirconium atoms with respect to one another, and the cross-linkage through sulfur atoms.

Compounds of this type are capable of existing in the solid state only. Vague observations on melting or subliming some of the zirconium sulfides have been reported, but insufficient information is available to permit a description of the processes involved in such phase changes. The zirconium sulfides are reminiscent of sulfur tetrachloride, which is known to exist only as long as its solid state is preserved. The high order of heat stability of the zirconium sulfides is a reflection of the stable chemical bonding. The residual metallic character is manifest in the liberation of hydrogen when some of these compounds are treated with hydrofluoric acid. On the other hand, the loss of metallic character when zirconium metal is converted to compounds of sulfur, phosphorus, or silicon is indicated by partial or complete loss of metallic luster (to varying extents in the different compounds), partial loss of electrical conductivity, and greater resistance to attack by acids. The compounds of this group can be halogenated with formation of the typical halogenides of their components.

The boundary between the elements silicon, phosphorus, and sulfur and between their alloy-forming neighbors in the periodic chart is not sharp, and indeed we need hardly expect a sharp demarcation between elements forming metallic and semimetallic compounds. The interactions of zirconium with germanium, antimony, arsenic, selenium, and tellurium can advantageously be considered along with those of silicon, phosphorus, and sulfur, and will be so treated in the following.

ZIRCONIUM SILICIDES AND GERMANIDES

The heats of formation of silicides of transition elements are generally of the same order of magnitude as those of the corresponding carbides and less than those of the nitrides. For transition elements which form several silicides, the highest heats of formation are associated with the bonding of the first silicon atom. Bond lengths have generally lent themselves to interpretation as indicating strong bonding with metallic character (232).

Silicon has little solubility in either α- or β-zirconium, the value being less than 0.1% in the former at 860° and less than 0.2% in the latter at 1610° (233, 234). The solubility of zirconium in silicon has not been clearly established, but it is considerably less than 5%. At least seven compounds, all

232. H. Nowotny, B. Lux, and H. Kudielka, *Monatsh.* **87,** 447-70 (1956).

233. C. E. Lundin, D. J. McPherson, and M. Hansen, *Trans. Am. Soc. Met.* **45,** 901-14 (1953).

234. F. B. Litton and S. C. Ogburn, *U.S. Air Materiel Command Rept.* **No. AF-TR-5943** (1949).

with high melting points, are formed. The highest melting is Zr_6Si_5, m.p. 2250°. The other compounds are Zr_4Si, Zr_2Si, Zr_3Si_2, Zr_4Si_3, $ZrSi$, and $ZrSi_2$ (233, 235). A diagram of the system Si-Zr has been plotted by Lundin, McPherson, and Hansen, and is reproduced here as Figure 2.6.

Most of these compounds have been prepared by more than one investigator (236, 237), some under conditions in which several members of the

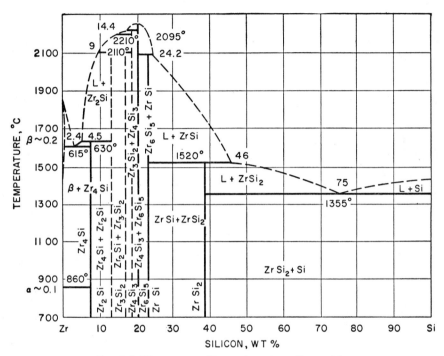

FIG. 2.6. The system silicon-zirconium. From (4).

series may form but not other members. For example, some members will not form in the presence of carbon (232). The hafnium silicides can be prepared by methods similar to those for the zirconium silicides, and their properties are quite similar (238).

Compositions containing silicon and zirconium were prepared by the earlier investigators without precise identification of their products, and it is often difficult to determine in retrospect when a substantially pure com-

235. R. Kieffer, F. Benesovsky, and R. Machenschalk, Z. Metallkunde 45, 493-8 (1954).
236. H. Schachner, H. Nowotny, and R. Machenschalk, Monatsh. 84, 677-8 (1953).
237. G. F. Hardy and J. K. Hulm, Phys. Rev. 89, 884 (1953).
238. B. Post, F. W. Glaser, and D. Moscovitz, J. Chem. Phys. 22, 1264 (1954).

pound was prepared and when a mixture of products. Some of the earlier preparations were accomplished by heating mixtures of potassium fluosilicate and potassium fluozirconate with aluminum (239, 240; cf. 241), sometimes using sulfur in the mixture to increase the temperature attained during reaction. The products were contaminated with aluminum, usually about 2-3%. Another procedure was to heat zircon with coal to a white heat (242). Since the principal product of this method is commonly zirconium carbide, and silicon is lost by volatilization of silicon monoxide, it was difficult to get a satisfactory yield of a zirconium silicide by this method. Another procedure consisted in heating a mixture of zirconia and silica with aluminum (240, 241), and it too gave products contaminated with aluminum. In this latter method, sulfur was added to increase the exothermicity. A typical procedure was to mix together iron-free silica sand, zirconia, sulfur, and aluminum, cover the mixture with magnesium powder, and heat it in a fireclay crucible with a blow torch. The product was regarded as zirconium disilicide, but not proved to be such. Some of the earlier products were extracted with acids and alkalies after the reaction to leach out impurities (242). In still another early preparation, on heating zirconia with an excess of silicon in an electric furnace a sublimate was obtained consisting of characteristic deep-colored crystals of zirconium disilicide (170).

Only the more recent preparations were made and examined with sufficient care to win full credibility for the reports on their identification and properties. More recently the disilicide has been prepared by the following methods:

(1) Zirconium and silicon were heated together under vacuum in an electric furnace (care being taken to avoid the presence of carbon dioxide) at 1000-1200°, and excess silicon was removed with alkalies (243; cf. 237). Hafnium disilicide was prepared similarly (238).

(2) Zirconium hydride and silicon were heated together (28, 241).

Zirconium disilicide, $ZrSi_2$, formula weight 147.40, occurs as orthorhombic crystals in which a = 3.72, b = 14.61, and c = 3.67 A. There are 4 molecules per unit cell, and d_{22} = 4.88 (239, 240, 241, 245). The similar hafnium disilicide has a = 3.67, b = 14.56, and c = 3.64 A, calculated d = 8.03, observed d = 7.2 (238, 241). In both the zirconium and hafnium compounds, discrepancies occurred between calculated and observed densities due to nonstoichiometry in the products. Structure studies have indicated the

239. O. Hönigschmid, *Compt. rend.* 143, 224 (1906).
240. Hönigschmid, *Monatsh.* 27, 1069 (1907).
241. P. G. Cotter, J. A. Kohn, and R. A. Potter, *J. Am. Ceram. Soc.* 39, 11-12 (1950).
242. E. Wedekind, *Z. Chem. Ind. Kolloide* 7, 249-51 (1910).
243. D. A. Robbins and I. Jenkins, *Acta Met.* 3, 598-604 (1955).
245. H. Seyfarth, *Z. Krist.* 67, 295-328 (1928).

crystals to consist of layers of uncharged atoms (246). The compound has a metallic luster, and it has been described as gray or deeply colored. The Mohs hardness is about 6 and the Tukon microhardness with a Knoop identer $K_{100} = 840$. The crystals are brittle, but not hard enough to be attractive for this quality for industrial applications. When heated in air, zirconium disilicide burns with a bright flame. It dissolves in hydrofluoric acid with liberation of hydrogen. It is decomposed by fused potassium hydroxide, and is attacked feebly by bromine. It is not attacked by concentrated or dilute acids other than hydrofluoric, nor by aqueous alkalies (neither 10% nor 50% sodium nor potassium hydroxide), nor by molten potassium bisulfate (240, 241). It is dissolved by molten borax, sodium hydroxide, and potassium hydroxide. It attacks platinum rapidly in the presence of molten borax, although other silicides do not do this, nor do silicon or zirconium (241).* Like other disilicides, it dissolves in nickel. A slight reaction with copper has also been noted (232). It dissolves about 60 mole % of titanium disilicide, but the latter dissolves practically no zirconium disilicide. Zirconium disilicide and vanadium disilicide are completely immiscible (247; cf. 235).**

Zirconium monosilicide, ZrSi, formula weight 119.31, has been prepared by compressing together silicon and zirconium powders and heating the compacts at temperatures up to 1500° (237, 243). Hafnium monosilicide has been prepared similarly. The zirconium compound has a hexagonal lattice with $a_0 = 7.01$, $c_0 = 12.77$ A; for the hafnium compound, $a = 6.86$ and $c = 12.01$ A (238). An orthorhombic structure with 4 molecules per unit cell has also been reported (248).

Little is known of the chemical properties of zirconium monosilicide. It is said to show considerable resistance to heat and to dissolution when heated in contact with chromium, copper, molybdenum, nickel, niobium, silver, tantalum, vanadium, or tungsten (232).

Preparation of other silicides than the above has been made primarily in connection with obtaining data for plotting a diagram of the system Si-Zr, and the most general method of preparation has been to heat the proper proportion of the two powdered elements in compacted mixtures (237, 243). Crystallographic data are available on Zr_5Si_3 (236, 251, 252) and Zr_2Si

---

* For a comparison of zirconium disilicide with other disilicides, see reference 249.
** For details of mutual solubilities of the disilicides of chromium, magnesium, niobium, tantalum, titanium, vanadium, tungsten, and zirconium, see reference 250.

246. I. Náray-Szabo, Z. Krist. 97, 223-8 (1937).
247. H. Nowotny, R. Machenschalk, and R. Kieffer, Monatsh. 85, 241-4 (1954).
248. H. Schachner, H. Nowotny, and H. Kudielka, Monatsh. 85, 1140-53 (1954).
249. R. Kieffer, F. Benesovsky, and E. Gallistl, Z. Metallkunde 43, 284-91 (1952).
250. H. Nowotny, H. Kudielka, and E. Parthé, Plansee Proc. 1955, 166-72.
251. H. Schachner, E. Cerwenka, and H. Nowotny, Monatsh. 85, 245-54 (1954).
252. E. Parthé, H. Nowotny, and H. Schmid, Monatsh. 86, 385-96 (1955).

(236, 248, 253), and also data on the mutual solubilities of Zr_5Si_3 with V_5Si_3 (250) and with Ti_5Si_3 (250, 251).

It has been noted that zirconium silicides do not separate when nickel-silicon-zirconium or copper-silicon-zirconium alloys are heated, even though zirconium disilicide will not react with nickel (232). A commercial silicon-zirconium alloy has been observed not to react with nitrogen or hydrogen up to 1000° and 1100°, respectively (254). Compounds of silicon and zirconium plus boron, carbon, or nitrogen apparently do not form. Sintered bodies containing mixtures of these elements, however, have been prepared (232). A compound ZrBeSi is known. It has a hexagonal lattice in which a = 3.71, and c = 7.19 A, and there are 2 molecules per unit cell (255).

In industry, compositions consisting of silicon and zirconium have been prepared and studied as alloys without regard to their chemical identity. These alloys are made by heating zirconium compounds with silica in an arc furnace (256), in which carbon is furnished by the electrode, or in some other type of furnace in which carbon is added to the other reactants (257). In the arc-furnace preparation, the more silica used the less zirconium carbide in the residue. In other preparations of the alloys, the elements silicon and zirconium have been heated together or else they were formed together in intimate admixture. While aluminothermic processes are useful for forming the elements together, aluminum contamination is difficult to avoid and may be as much as 5% (257). An alloy containing 50% zirconium has been made by reducing zircon with silicon (258). In the trade, the silicon-zirconium alloys are commonly referred to as *silicozirconium*. When formed in the presence of iron compounds, a product known as *ferrozirconium silicide* is obtained (259).

There are no established uses of silicon-zirconium compounds or alloys in chemical industry, but a number of uses have been proposed. Silicozirconium can be prepared inexpensively, and it has been proposed to chlorinate it to obtain silicon tetrachloride and zirconium tetrachloride for industrial use (254). It is said that the alloy is a suitable agent for removing hydroxyl ions from solutions of sodium alcoholates in alcohols (260). A patented

253. P. Pietrokowski, *Acta Cryst.* **7**, 435-8 (1954).

254. W. J. Kroll, W. R. Carmody, and A. W. Schlechten, *U.S. Bureau Mines, Rept. Investigation 4915*, 31 pp. (1952).

255. J. W. Nielsen and N. C. Baenziger, *Acta Cryst.* **7**, 152-3 (1954).

256. F. M. Becket, British patent **427,076**, April 15, 1935; French patent **778,122**, Mar. 9, 1935; U.S. Patent **1,996,037**, Mar. 26, 1935.

257. V. E. Elyutin and R. Grigorash, *Trudy Moskovsakago Inst. Stali im. I. V. Stalin* 1939, No. 12, 59-79.

258. G. Volkert, *Metall. u. Erz.* **40**, 246-52 (1943).

259. Takeshi Kajima, Reiichi Yamasa, and Iwao Asaishi, *J. Electrochem. Soc. Japan* **19**, 262-5 (1951).

260. E. F. Hill, U.S. Patent **2,662,100**, Dec. 8, 1953.

process describes the use of silicozirconium as a flux-forming fuel. This application is based on the principle that when minerals are thermally worked with oxy-fuel flames, inclusion of ferrozirconium, or better, ferrozirconium silicide, in the fuel provides enormous heat and gives more fluid slags due to the combination of the combustion products with the slags. This is said to be particularly beneficial for working concrete, iron ore, and rocks of high silica content (261; cf. 262).

Zirconium digermanide is isomorphous with zirconium disilicide (orthorhombic), and its lattice parameters are $a_0 = 3.80$, $b_0 = 15.01$, and $c_0 = 3.76$ A (263).* On heating, it decomposes peritectically, probably to Zr_2Ge. Another compound, Zr_3Ge, has a hexagonal close-packed lattice with $a_0 = 6.52$ and $c_0 = 5.38$ A (2, p. 455).

PHOSPHIDE, ARSENIDE, AND ANTIMONIDE

The preparation of a phosphide of zirconium was first reported in 1908 by Gewecke, who believed that he had prepared zirconium diphosphide, ZrP_2, by the action of phosphine on zirconium tetrachloride. Gewecke described the compound as a hard, porous, bright-gray mass of density $d_4^{25} = 4.77$. The reaction was obtained by passing the reactants through a porcelain tube (264). In making a similar preparation some years later, Venable and Deitz believed that they obtained first an addition product of the phosphine and zirconium tetrachloride, which decomposed on heating to give the diphosphide (265). Still later, Lilliendahl and Driggs prepared a phosphide by the reaction of slightly more than one gram-atom of zirconium with a gram-atom of red phosphorus at 600-1000° (266). The method was pursued by Strotzer and associates, who reported obtaining zirconium diphosphide as a gray-black powder (267). Some fifteen years later, the proof of the compound nature of zirconium diphosphide was provided by X-ray diffraction (268).

Zirconium diphosphide, ZrP_2, formula weight 153.17, in powder form is stable in air, in water, in some acids, and even in a mixture of bromine and nitric acid at room temperature. It is completely dissolved by warm concentrated sulfuric acid, and even dilute sulfuric acid attacks it slowly with evolution of phosphine (267).

---

* Elsewhere, an incomplete identification of zirconium digermanide indicated a tetragonal lattice with $a_0 = 3.83$ and $c_0 = 14.96$ A (2, p. 455).

261. R. B. Aitchison, U.S. Patent **2,392,353**, Jan. 8, 1946.

262. F. M. Becket, U.S. Patent **1,553,020**, Sept. 8, 1925.

263. C. J. Smithels, *Metals Reference Book*, Butterworth & Co., Ltd., London, 1949.

264. J. Gewecke, *Ann.* **361**, 79-88 (1908).

265. F. P. Venable and R. O. Deitz, *J. Elisha Mitchell Sci. Soc.* **38**, Nos. 1 and 2, 74-5 (1922).

266. W. C. Lilliendahl and F. H. Driggs, Canadian patent **325,502**, Aug. 30, 1932.

267. E. F. Strotzer, W. Biltz, and K. Meisel, *Z. anorg. allgem. Chem.* **239**, 216-24 (1938).

268. N. Schönberg, *Acta Chem. Scand.* **8**, 226-39 (1954).

On heating zirconium diphosphide in vacuum at 750°, phosphorus is evolved vigorously and the monophosphide, ZrP, forms (267). A substance of composition corresponding to $ZrP_{0.9}$ was also prepared by heating powdered zirconium with its equivalence of red phosphorus or by heating powdered zirconium in the presence of phosphine and hydrogen (268). The monophosphide apparently exists in two different crystalline forms, one of which is represented by the composition $ZrP_{0.9}$, prepared as stated above, and it has a sodium-chloride type of crystal lattice. The second type was obtained when zirconium powder was heated with red phosphorus to obtain the composition $ZrP_{0.3-0.5}$. It is isomorphous with titanium monophosphide (267), and its low P content is regarded as indicative of a large number of lattice defects. In zirconium monophosphide, the distance between zirconium atoms is 15% greater than in the pure metal (132), which is also the case in the monosulfide (*infra*).

Zirconium and hafnium phosphides have also been prepared by allowing a mixture of the vapors of the metal tetrachlorides and phosphorus to impinge upon a heated tungsten filament (34).

Zirconium arsenides of ideal formulas $ZrAs_2$ and ZrAs have been reported. The latter has a hexagonal lattice and is isostructural with TiAs. For empirical composition $ZrAs_{0.95}$, the unit cell dimensions were a = 3.80, c = 12.86 A. The diarsenide has a rhombic lattice with a = 6.80, b = 9.02, and c = 3.68 A. The pycnometric density for the composition $ZrAs_{1.86}$ is 6.80, indicating 4 molecules per unit cell (269).

Only a subantimonide, Zr_2Sb, is known (270), showing that a considerable change in relationship occurs when passing from phosphorus and arsenic to antimony, and suggesting that we have crossed the boundary between the elements forming semimetallic compounds and those forming intermetallic compounds.

SULFIDES, SELENIDES, AND TELLURIDES

A number of sulfides of zirconium are known. Their structure has been discussed to some extent above, in the introduction to the semimetallic compounds of zirconium. Sketches of the lattice structure of zirconium disulfide are given in Figure 2.5.

The first preparation of a sulfide of zirconium was reported by Berzelius, who heated the impure metal (available from his earlier experiments) with sulfur in a vacuum and obtained a product which he regarded as zirconium

269. W. Łrzbiatowski, St. Weglowski, and K. Łukaszczewicz, *Roczniki Chem.* **30**, 353-4 (1956).

270. R. F. Russi, Jr., and H. A. Wilhelm, *U.S. Atomic Energy Comm. ISC-204*, Aug. 1951.

disulfide. No definite identification was made of his product (271, 272). Hauser repeated Berzelius's experiments, also using impure metal (273). Only much later were sulfides prepared from pure zirconium metal and a product close in composition to the ideal for the disulfide obtained. It exhibited a distinctive X-ray diffraction pattern (274, 275). A tabulation of methods which have been used to prepare zirconium disulfide is given in Table 2.8. Zirconium sulfides have never been prepared by aqueous precipitation. Since monatomic zirconium cations are unknown, it is not surprising that a precipitated sulfide has never been observed to form in an aqueous medium.

TABLE 2.8. PROCESSES FOR THE PREPARATION OF ZIRCONIUM DISULFIDE

Reaction employed	Literature
Zirconium carbide with sulfur vapor	7
Zirconium tetrachloride with hydrogen sulfide	265, 275, 276
Zirconium tetrachloride with sulfur	30
Zirconium metal with hydrogen sulfide	277
Zirconium dioxide with carbon disulfide	278, 279
Zirconium dioxide with sulfur, under hydrogen	277

The treatment of hot metallic zirconium with hydrogen sulfide or sulfur vapor gives rise to a number of sulfides. At 700° the reaction with sulfur has been observed to give ZrS_3, ZrS_2, Zr_2S_3, $ZrS_{0.75}$, and $ZrS_{0.2-0.33}$ (275, 280). Berzelius noted that no heat or light were evolved during the reaction of zirconium with sulfur (271); recently A. Clearfield and W. B. Blumenthal have observed the formation of zirconium disulfide to be exothermic (71). Zirconium begins to react with hydrogen sulfide at about 1000°. At 1700° trizirconium pentasulfide, Zr_3S_5 is formed. It reacts further with hydrogen sulfide at 900-1300° to form zirconium disulfide. The disulfide can also be obtained directly by the reaction of zirconium metal with hydrogen sulfide

271. J. J. Berzelius, *Oefvers. Akad. Förh. Stockholm* **295** (1824); *Pogg. Ann.* **4,** 117 (1825); *Ann. chim. phys.* (2) **29,** 337 (1825).

272. Berzelius, *Ann. Phys.* **4,** 125 (1825).

273. O. Hauser, *Z. anorg. allgem. Chem.* **53,** 73-77 (1907).

274. W. Biltz, E. F. Strotzer, and K. Meisel, *Z. anorg. allgem. Chem.* **239,** 216 (1938).

275. E. F. Strotzer, W. Biltz, and K. Meisel, *Z. anorg. allgem. Chem.* **242,** 249-71 (1939).

276. S. R. Paykull, *Bull. Soc. Chim.* (2) **20,** 65 (1873).

277. M. Picon, *Compt. rend.* **196,** 2003-6 (1933).

278. E. Fremy, *Ann. chim. phys.* (3) **38,** 326 (1832).

279. A. Clearfield, *Synthesis of Zirconium Sulfides,* 131st National Meeting of the American Chemical Society, April 10, 1957.

280. G. Hägg and N. Schönberg, *Arkiv. Kemi* **7,** 371-80 (1954).

at 900° (280). The reaction of zirconium tetrachloride and sulfur vapor occurs in contact with an incandescent tungsten filament (30).

The preparation of zirconium disulfide from zirconium tetrachloride and hydrogen sulfide is difficult to control, and is not one of the most commendable procedures. The yield from the reaction of zirconium carbide with sulfur is small (7), and it is possible that the reaction was primarily with the excess metal that is present in some specimens of the carbide. Even some of the processes for making zirconium sulfide that appear fundamentally sound have given some odd results. For example, in 1907 Hauser was unable to duplicate the results of Fremy obtained in 1832 (273, 278), in which Fremy obtained steel-gray acicular crystals. The true color of zirconium disulfide is purple or violet (279).

Perhaps the best method of preparing zirconium disulfide in good purity at low cost consists in heating the dioxide with carbon disulfide. Although the method is an old one (44), an important clarification of the process has recently been established by Clearfield and Blumenthal. The ordinary monoclinic zirconium dioxide (baddeleyite) does not yield pure zirconium disulfide when treated with carbon disulfide, but rather a mixture of zirconium disulfide and zirconium sulfoxide. However, tetragonal and cubic zirconium dioxide yield substantially pure zirconium disulfide by this treatment. The cubic oxide is best obtained for this purpose by heating zirconium sulfate under a stream of hydrogen sulfide or carbon disulfide until it has decomposed to the oxide. Then, on continuing a flow of carbon disulfide while maintaining the temperature at about 1100°, pure zirconium disulfide is obtained. Alternatively, monoclinic zirconium dioxide may be heated for about 3 hours at 1100° to convert it to the tetragonal allotrope, then treated with carbon disulfide to obtain pure zirconium disulfide.

Zirconium disulfide, ZrS_2, formula weight 155.35, has been described as a steel-gray (278), brown (275), or violet solid (30, 279). The crystals obtained by the reaction of zirconium tetrachloride with sulfur on a hot tungsten filament are deep violet, not very hard, and rhombohedral-hexagonal with a = 3.68 and c = 5.86 A; a:c = 1.59. There is 1 molecule per unit cell. The Zr-S distance is 2.58 A, and the theoretical covalent bond distance would be 2.49 A (30, 230, 280). The solid is stable in air and in water at the ordinary temperature and also in boiling water. When heated in air, it burns with formation of zirconium dioxide and sulfur dioxide (276). When it is heated in the absence of air, it tends to lose sulfur (277), and zirconium as well as sulfur is reported to volatilize at 1500° (230). Melting has been noted at 1550° (281). Zirconium disulfide is attacked very slowly or not at all by dilute mineral acids* in the cold, except nitric acid which

---

* It has been reported that zirconium disulfide formed in steel is soluble in 1:1 hydrochloric acid, while other sulfides are insoluble (283).

281. R. Vogel and A. Hartung, *Arch. Eisenhüttenw,* **15,** 413-18 (1942).

oxidizes it violently with separation of sulfur (but there is no sulfate formation) (273, 278, 282). Hydrofluoric acid, even when dilute, dissolves the disulfide with liberation of hydrogen sulfide (271). The disulfide is also decomposed by aqua regia (271), slowly by cold 10% sulfuric acid, and rapidly by cold concentrated sulfuric acid (282). Aqueous oxidizing agents, such as potassium permanganate and potassium ferricyanide react slowly with zirconium disulfide, but hydrogen peroxide reacts fairly rapidly, converting the finely divided disulfide in a few minutes to a basic sulfate and other oxidation products (282).

Water at 200° attacks zirconium disulfide with formation of hydrogen sulfide, zirconium dioxide, and zirconium sulfate. Dry hydrogen chloride reacts with the disulfide at 165°. Hot concentrated hydrochloric acid reacts with formation of hydrogen sulfide and zirconium oxychloride. Sulfur dioxide reacts with it at 140°. Ammonia attacks zirconium disulfide at 1000°, forming zirconium nitride. Aqueous ammonia extracts some sulfur from zirconium disulfide. Dry carbon dioxide reacts with it slowly at 500° with formation of zirconium dioxide, carbon monoxide, and sulfur (282).

Carburization of zirconium sulfide has been observed to occur slowly in the presence of graphite at 1600°. Complete desulfurization by carbon was obtained under a hydrogen atmosphere at 2800°, with formation of zirconium carbide. A similar desulfurization under a nitrogen atmosphere gave a solid residue containing zirconium, carbon, and nitrogen (277). Chlorine attacks zirconium disulfide, and zirconium tetrachloride was observed to be evolved at 250°. Bromine attacked the disulfide slowly in the presence of air at room temperature; aqueous bromine reacted more rapidly. The attack of oxygen has been noted to occur at 180°. Sulfur vapor in a stream of hydrogen had no effect up to 800° (282).

Magnesium removes the sulfur from zirconium disulfide at 1000° under a hydrogen atmosphere. Sulfides of tin and lead do not form complex sulfides with zirconium disulfide at this temperature (282).

Zirconium disulfide is a semiconductor, and is considerably different in physical as well as chemical properties from zirconium dioxide (284). In the crystal photoelectric effect on zirconium disulfide, the sign of the charge carrier has been found to be negative (285, 286).*

Zirconium sulfoxide is best prepared by passing hydrogen sulfide or carbon disulfide through or over decomposed disulfatozirconic acid, trihydrate

---

* For energy levels in zirconium disulfide, see reference 286b.
282. M. Picon, *Compt. rend.* **197**, 151-3 (1933); *Bull. soc. chim.* **53**, 1269-77 (1933).
283. A. L. Field, *Trans. Am. Inst. Min. Met. Eng.* **69**, 848 (1923); **70**, 201 (1924).
284. W. L. Fink and L. A. Willey, *Metals Tech.* **6**, 1 (1939).
285. V. P. Zhuze and S. M. Ryvkin, *Doklady Akad. Nauk S.S.S.R.* **62**, 55-8 (1948).
286. S. M. Ryvkin, *Zhur. Tekh. Fiz.* **18**, 1521-42 (1948).
286b. Y. Uyehara, *J. Chem. Soc. Japan* **63**, 1310-3 (1942).

at about 700° (71, 273; cf. 287). The following system of nomenclature has been recommended for compounds of a metal with oxygen and sulfur, where the latter elements are not combined to form radicals or ions such as sulfate or sulfite: (1) if the structure is the same as that of the pure oxide, it should be called a *thio-oxide;* (2) if the structure is that of the pure sulfide, it should be called an *oxysulfide;* and (3) if the structure is different from the oxide and the sulfide, it should be called a *sulfoxide.* The compound of composition ZrOS corresponds in structure to category (3), and accordingly is called *zirconium sulfoxide.* It has a cubic crystal lattice in which a = 5.696 ± 0.02 A. Each zirconium atom is surrounded by 3 sulfur atoms at 2.63 A, 1 sulfur atom at 2.61 A, and 3 oxygen atoms at 2.13 A: altogether by 7 neighbors at the corners of a coordination polyhedron of the symmetry C_{3v-3m} (287, 288).

Zirconium sulfoxide, ZrOS, formula weight 139.29, is obtained as a light-yellow powder of specific gravity 4.87 (calculated value 4.975). It is insoluble in water. If it is removed from the vessel in which it was prepared before it has cooled to room temperature, it is apt to take fire in the air. When cold it is stable in air (273). It can be converted to zirconium disulfide by holding it for considerable lengths of time at a red heat under a stream of hydrogen sulfide (288).

When zirconium disulfide is heated with sulfur at 600-700°, the bright orange-red *zirconium trisulfide,* ZrS_3, slowly forms. For a good yield, two or three days may be required (275). The reaction is exothermic to the extent of 8.5 kg cal/mole. Aside from its density, $d_{25} = 3.71$, few properties have been determined. It is known to resist attack by dilute sulfuric acid and sodium hydroxide solutions.

The reaction of zirconium metal with hydrogen sulfide at 1700° yields *trizirconium pentasulfide,* Zr_3S_5. This compound reacts with hydrogen sulfide at 900-1300° to form the disulfide, as already discussed, and both these compounds lose sulfur at 1400°, under vacuum, with formation of *dizirconium trisulfide,* Zr_2S_3 (277). The latter compound is also one of the products of the reaction of sulfur with zirconium at 700° (275). It is described as a black solid with a bluish sheen. Chlorine gas attacks Zr_3S_5 at 250° and Zr_2S_3 at 210°, and dry hydrogen chloride attacks them at 280° and 210°, respectively, with formation of zirconium tetrachloride (282). At 1000° these two sulfides react with sulfur vapor in hydrogen to form zirconium disulfide. They do not react with cold or boiling water, but they react with water at 200°. Concentrated hydrochloric acid has been observed to decompose trizirconium pentasulfide. In general the reactions of other

287. J. D. McCullough, L. Brewer, and L. A. Bromley, *Acta Cryst.* 1, 287-9 (1948).

288. E. D. Eastman, L. Brewer, L. H. Bromley, P. W. Gilles, and N. L. Lofgren, *J. Am. Chem. Soc.* 73, 3896-8 (1951).

agents, such as sulfuric acid, oxygen, and oxygen-containing gases follow the patterns already described for the disulfide.

In so far as the compounds of silicon, phosphorus, sulfur, and selenium are more or less coordination compounds of these elements with elementary zirconium, it is to be expected that the metallic character of the compounds would be more pronounced the less the proportion of the ligand. This is particularly conspicuous in the sulfides. Compositions of lower sulfur content than that of Zr_2S_3 have a gray-black, "half-metallic" appearance (275) and approach the metal in properties such as visual appearance and electrical conductivity. Phases of compositions ZrS, $ZrS_{0.75}$, and $ZrS_{0.20-33}$ have been prepared by reactions of the constituent elements (132, 275), but their properties have not been extensively studied. Recent unpublished studies indicate Zr_2S_3, ZrS, and $ZrS_{0.75}$ all to be the same phase (71, 288b). ZrS has a tetragonal lattice with a = 3.55 and c = 6.31 A (280). The distance between the zirconium atoms is only 15% greater than in pure zirconium metal (132). The resemblances in compositions and properties between the lower sulfides and the lower phosphides is noteworthy.

There are no established uses for zirconium sulfides and even the recommended uses are few. It has been reported that the addition of 0.40% of zirconium sulfide to a corrosion-resistant steel permitted it to be machined, ground, and polished with approximately the same facility as common screw stock. It did not dissolve in the steel, but was distributed as tiny particles through the metal.* Its effect was likened to the lubricating effect of carbon in cast iron (289). An extreme-pressure lubricant has been described, which consists of zirconium disulfide dispersed in a polar liquid solvent, such as glycerol or glycol (290).

Selenium reacts with zirconium less vigorously than sulfur (291). A small amount of *zirconium diselenide* was reported to form by the reaction of selenium with zirconium dioxide at about 300° (292). Zirconium diselenide has been prepared by the reaction of a gas mixture containing zirconium tetrachloride, hydrogen, and hydrogen selenide when it impinged on an incandescent tungsten filament. The hafnium analog was prepared similarly (30). Zirconium diselenide is a black, crystalline substance of close-packed hexagonal symmetry, with a = 3.69, c = 618 A, and c:a = 1.63. There is 1 molecule to the unit cell, and the cell volume is 46.6 A^3 (30, 230; cf. 293).

---

* For some details of the system Fe-S-Zr, see reference 281.

288b. H. Hahn, *Angew. Chem.* **66**, 351 (1954).

289. F. R. Palmer, *Steel 87,* No. 4, 50-4 (1930).

290. E. M. Kipp, U.S. Patent **2,609,342,** Sept. 2, 1953.

291. E. Wedekind, *Ann. 395,* 49 (1913).

292. O. Ruff and R. Wallstein, *Z. anorg. allgem. Chem.* **128**, 100 (1923).

293. M. Hansen, *Der Aufbau der Zweistofflegierungen,* Julius Springer, Berlin, 1936, and J. W. Edwards, Publisher, Inc., Ann Arbor, Mich., 1943.

It is quite similar to the disulfide, and like the disulfide it is a semiconducting substance, the conductivity of which is affected by light. The sign of the electric carrier is negative (285).

A fragmentary report on the preparation of zirconium tellurides has been offered by Montignie, who stated that he could not obtain a telluride by heating zirconia with tellurium under hydrogen at 500°, but did obtain a product of composition Zr_2Te by heating the subtellurate of composition $5ZrO_2 \cdot TeO_2 \cdot 8H_2O$ in an atmosphere of hydrogen to 500°. It was a black substance which was insoluble in water, acids, and organic solvents. It reacted with hot concentrated sulfuric acid and dissolved. It was also dissolved by fused soda ash, but not by hot 30% potassium hydroxide solution. It burned in air with formation of the oxides of the two metals (294). Possible analogies between the compounds Zr_2Si, Zr_2Ge, Zr_2Sb, Zr_2S, and Zr_2Te deserve attention from future investigators.

THE METALLIC COMPOUNDS

The metallic compounds of zirconium are those homogeneous compositions of zirconium and other metallic elements which form distinct phases and have maximum melting points at their ideal compositions. The chemistry of such compounds is not a well-developed science. The compositions of these compounds, and of metallic compounds generally, are not determined by the group valencies of their elements but rather by other, less simply represented characteristics of their electron orbitals. The Hume-Rothery rule (294B; cf. 295) provides a key to the conditions determining the stoichiometry of many metallic compounds. It postulates that the ratio of the total number of valence electrons to the total number of atoms in the empirical formula of the metallic compound must correspond to certain integers, namely, 3:2 for a β structure, 21:13 for a γ structure, and 7:4 for an ϵ structure. The rule holds for many binary and ternary compounds. It is characteristic, however, for metallic compounds to have a range of compositions embracing an ideal composition which fulfills the requirements of the Hume-Rothery rule. Pauling has pointed out that in the metallic compounds all stable outer orbitals of the transition metals are available for occupancy by unshared electrons and for bond formation (296).

Zirconium is known to form many metallic compounds with the elements shown in the left area of the chart represented in Figure 2.1. Many of these compounds correspond in composition neither to the postulates of the Hume-Rothery rule nor to the ordinary stoichiometry of the conventional valences of the elements of which they are composed. They have

294. E. Montignie. Ann. pharm. franç. 4, 253-5 (1946); Bull. soc. chim. 13, 176 (1946).
294B. W. Hume-Rothery, J. Inst. Metals 35, 295 (1926); Phil. Mag. (7) 3, 301 (1927).
295. A. F. Westgren and G. Phragmén, Z. Metallkunde 18, 279 (1926).
296. L. Pauling, Proc. Royal Soc. A196, 343-62 (1949).

TABLE 2.9. THE METALLIC COMPOUNDS OF ZIRCONIUM

Composition	Melting Point	Notes	Literature
$AgZr_2$			315
			328
$AgZr$	1180°		329
$AlZr_3$			
$AlZr_2$			
Al_2Zr_3			234
Al_3Zr_4	1530°		284
			300
$AlZr$			301
Al_2Zr	1645°	Orthorhombic: $a_0 = 10.40$, $b_0 = 7.21$, $c_0 = 4.97$ A	
Al_3Zr	1580°	Tetragonal: $a = 4.306$, $c = 16.90$ A	
Au_3Zr	1560°		315
Be_2Zr		Hexagonal: $a = 3.82$, $c = 3.24$ A, $Z = 1$	255
Be_6Zr			302
Be_9Zr			303
$Be_{16}Zr$			
Cd_xZr		Value of x undetermined; face-centered cubic crystals: $a_0 = 4.377$ A	304
Cd_yZr		$y > x$; body-centered tetragonal crystals; $a_0 = 3.124$, $c_0 = 4.301$ A	
$CoZr$	1630°		308
Co_2Zr	1580°	Cubic: $a_0 = 6.887$ A	310
Co_4Zr	1560°	Magnetic (313)	311
			312
Cr_2Zr	1700°	Face-centered cubic crystals; also, allotropic modification forming between 900° and 994°, hexagonal: $a_0 = 5.079$, $c = 8.262$ A, also given $a = 5.127$ and $c = 8.372$ A	305 306 307 308 309
$CuZr_2$	1000°	Face-centered tetragonal: $a_0 = 4.536$, $c_0 = 3.716$ A	
$CuZr$	935°		
Cu_3Zr_2			314
Cu_5Zr_3			
Cu_3Zr			
Fe_2Zr	1630°	Face-centered cubic: $a_0 = 7.040$ A; also hexagonal: $a = 4.953$ and $c = 16.42$ A	312 317 318
Ga_3Zr		Tetragonal: $a = 5.605$, $c = 8.712$ A	325
$HgZr_3$		Cubic: $a_0 = 5.558$ A	
$HgZr$		Tetragonal: $a_0 = 3.15$, $c_0 = 4.17$ A	304
Hg_3Zr		Cubic: $a_0 = 4.365$ A	

TABLE 2.9. Continued

Composition	Melting Point	Notes	Literature
InZr$_3$		Face-centered cubic	2, p. 458 316
Ir$_2$Zr		Hexagonal: a$_0$ = 5.179, c$_0$ = 8.509 A	
Mn$_3$Zr$_2$*			
Mn$_5$Zr$_3$*			
Mn$_7$Zr$_4$			319
Mn$_2$Zr		Hexagonal: a = 5.029, c = 8.223 A (312)	
Mo$_3$Zr		Cubic: a = 4.942 A	308
Mo$_2$Zr		Cubic: a$_0$ = 7.59 A	320
NiZr$_2$	1200°		
NiZr	1460°		321
Ni$_3$Zr		Face-centered cubic	318
Os$_2$Zr		Hexagonal	308 322
Ru$_2$Zr		Hexagonal: a$_0$ = 5.131, c$_0$ = 8.48 A	
SbZr$_2$	1900°	Hexagonal: a$_0$ = 8.4, c$_0$ = 5.6 A	270
SnZr$_4$		Tetragonal: a$_0$ = 6.90, c$_0$ = 11.10 A	
Sn$_3$Zr$_5$	1985°	Hexagonal	323 324
SnZr		Orthorhombic: a$_0$ = 7.433, b$_0$ = 5.822, c$_0$ = 5.157 A	
Pt$_3$Zr		Hexagonal: a$_0$ = 5.633, c$_0$ = 9.21 A	308, 322
V$_2$Zr		Hexagonal: a$_0$ = 5.233, c$_0$ = 8.647 A	308
W$_2$Zr		Face-centered cubic: a$_0$ = 7.61 A	327
ZnZr	1050**	Simple cubic: a$_0$ = 3.336 A	304
Zn$_2$Zr		Cubic: a$_0$ = 7.396 A	

* The compound is inferred and not proved.

** Melts incongruently.

300. G. Brauer, *Naturwiss.* **26**, 710 (1938).

301. M. Hansen and D. J. McPherson, *Armour Research Foundation Report COO-89*, April 14, 1952.

302. H. H. Hausner and H. S. Kalisch, *J. Metals* **188**, 59 (1950).

303. J. A. McGurty, S. G. Gordon, G. E. Klein, and K. M. Wizeman, *A.E.C. Report TID-5061* (1951).

304. P. Pietrokowsky, *J. Metals* **6**, 219 (1954).

305. E. T. Hayes, A. H. Roberson, and M. H. Davies, *J. Metals 4, Trans.* **194**, 304-6 (1952).

306. R. F. Domagala, D. J. McPherson, and M. Hansen, *J. Metals* **5**, 279-83 (1953).

307. K. McQuillan, *Aeronautical Research Laboratories, Dept. of Supply, Australia, Report* **SM-165**, Jan. 1951.

308. H. J. Wallbaum, *Naturwiss. 30*, 149 (1942).

309. Rostoker, *J. Metals* **5**, 304 (1953).

been detected and their properties measured in most cases by phase studies and X-ray diffraction. Their chemical properties have generally been ignored. It will suffice, therefore, for the purposes of the present review simply to list the known compounds and some of their more conspicuous physical properties. They are to be found in Table 2.9.

The many uses of zirconium alloys and of zirconium as an alloying element are outside the scope of this book. But it might be noted in passing that zirconium is extensively used in small quantities in structural magnesium and aluminum. Its presence in the melt causes the casting to crystallize with smaller grains, which greatly enhances its strength. The properties of steel and of cast iron are broadly improved by the presence of 0.1-0.3% of zirconium; for example, in steel the impact resistance and ductility are increased and the elastic ratio raised (297). Zirconium has been used as a component of many pyrophoric alloys (298, 299).

Zirconium is insoluble or almost insoluble in alkali and alkaline earth metals and in lead and zinc. The alkali and alkaline earth metals, as well as copper, iron, and molybdenum are insoluble or almost insoluble in α-zirconium.

310. U. Hashimoto, *Nippon Kinzoku Gakki-Shi* **2**, 67 (1938).
311. W. Koster and W. Mulfinger, *Z. Metallkunde* **30**, 348 (1938).
312. H. J. Wallbaum, *Z. Krist.* **103**, 391-402 (1941).
313. W. J. Kroll and A. W. Schlechten, *U.S. Bureau Mines Inform. Circ.* **7341**, Feb. 1946.
314. C. E. Lundin, D. J. McPherson, and M. Hansen, *J. Metals* **5**, 273-8 (1953).
315. E. Raub and M. Engle, *Z. Metallkunde* **39**, 172-7 (1948).
316. J. O. Betterton, Jr., unpublished study.
317. E. T. Hayes, A. H. Roberson, and W. L. O'Brien, *Trans. Am. Soc. Metals* **43**, 888 (1951).
318. H. J. Wallbaum, *Arch. Eisenhüttenw.* **14**, 521-6 (1941).
319. A. H. Roberson, E. T. Hayes, and V. V. Donalson, *Zirconium and Zirconium Alloys,* American Society of Metals, Cleveland, 1953, pp. 283-91.
320. R. F. Domagala, D. J. McPherson, and M. Hansen, *Trans. Am. Inst. Mining. Met. Engrs.* **197**, 73-9 (1953).
321. E. T. Hayes, A. H. Roberson, and O. G. Paasche, *Zirconium and Zirconium Alloys,* American Society of Metals, Cleveland, 1953, p. 275.
322. H. Nowotny, *Z. Metallkunde* **34**, 237 (1942).
323. D. J. McPherson and M. Hansen, *Trans. Am. Soc. Metals* **45**, 915-33 (1953).
324. G. R. Speich and S. A. Kulin, *Zirconium and Zirconium Alloys,* American Society of Metals, Cleveland, 1953, p. 197.
325. H. J. Wallbaum, *Z. Metallkunde* **34**, 118-19 (1942); *Chem. Zentr.* **1942**, II, 1768.
326. H. A. Saller and F. A. Rough, *AEC Report BMI-740* (1952); *TID-5084* (1954).
327. O. N. Carlson and E. Borders, unpublished study.
328. C. Sykes, *J. Inst. Metals* **41**, 179-89 (1929).
329. R. S. Kemper, Thesis, Oregon State College (1952).
297. R. Tull, *Heat Treating and Forging* **18**, 471-3 (1932).
298. P. P. Alexander, U.S. Patent **2,611,316**, Sept. 23, 1952.
299. E. Wainer, U.S. Patent **2,775,514**, Dec. 25, 1956.

3

Zirconium Halogenides

INTRODUCTION

The halogenides of zirconium comprise a large number of compounds of a variety of types. These include the tetrahalogenides, their addition products, and those substitution products in which some of the halogen is retained. Throughout, the fluorides behave differently from the other halogenides and require separate treatment. The chlorides, bromides, and iodides are similar enough to warrant their treatment as a group. The latter will be referred to as the ClBrI halogenides throughout the following pages. In studying the ClBrI halogenides, it is usually convenient to discuss the chlorides as prototypes and the bromides and iodides in comparison with the chlorides.

The addition products formed from the halogenides are of two main types: molecular addition products, such as the ether compound $ZrCl_4 \cdot 2(C_2H_5)_2O$, in which the molecular components retain much of their integrity in the new molecules, and ionic addition products, such as $NaZrCl_5$, in which the formation of new arrangements of atoms largely obscures the identity and integrity of the original components. Progressive substitutions give such series as $Cl_3ZrOC_2H_5$, $Cl_2Zr(OC_2H_5)_2$, and $ClZr(OC_2H_5)_3$, and $ZrOCl_2$ and $ZrOOHCl$.

Among the halogenides are also the only known examples of zirconium compounds in which the oxidation number of the zirconium atom is less than 4. These include the tri- and di-ClBrI halogenides.

THE ClBrI TETRAHALOGENIDES

PREPARATION

Zirconium tetrachloride can be prepared by direct synthesis from its elements, by true or apparent metathesis from the oxide, fluoride, pyrophosphate, or certain other suitable compounds with chlorine compounds, or by the decomposition of certain complex compounds such as the addition compound of zirconium tetrachloride with sulfur dioxide. As shown in Chapter 2, the so-called *zirconium carbide* and *zirconium cyanonitride* are really forms of the metal, and the metal in these forms has been the chief

102

raw material from which zirconium tetrachloride has been prepared in industry.

The conventional synthesis consists in packing a tower with zirconium carbide or cyanonitride, starting a coke fire at the bottom of the water-cooled (steel) tower, and introducing chlorine gas at the bottom of the tower. When the chlorine comes in contact with the hot carbide or cyanonitride, it enflames and the heat of combustion is sufficient to keep the reaction going thereafter without providing heat from an external source. The water-cooled tower withstands attack by the chlorine. The zirconium tetrachloride forms by a reaction which can be represented

$$ZrC + 2Cl_2 \rightarrow ZrCl_4 + C \qquad (1)$$

It rises from the tower, whence it is conducted into an air-cooled condenser where it condenses to a fine powder. This powder is caused to drop into steel drums, into which it is sealed. Table 3.1 shows a typical analysis of an industrial product prepared in this fashion.

Scrap zirconium metal can be used in place of zirconium carbide, and hydrogen chloride can be used in place of chlorine in the described process, but the higher costs of these reagents make their use unattractive.

Instead of chlorinating some form of the metal, the following agents for chlorinations have been demonstrated to be practicable:

1. Zirconium dioxide briquetted with carbon and chlorine
2. Zircon briquetted with carbon and chlorine
3. Zirconium dioxide or zircon and carbon tetrachloride or phosgene
4. Zirconium dioxide and sulfur monochloride or thionyl chloride

Process 1 can be operated as low as about 450°, at which temperature there is no sign of formation of zirconium carbide as an intermediate phase. But chlorine alone does not attack zirconium dioxide appreciably at any observed temperature,* and it follows that carbon can remove oxygen from its combination with zirconium at a much lower temperature in the presence of chlorine than in its absence. The energy released by the bonding of the chlorine to the zirconium supplies the requirements for the removal of oxygen by carbon at a low ambient temperature. Similar remarks apply to process 2. Since processes 3 and 4 are usually conducted at temperatures

---

* The equilibrium constant for the reaction

$$ZrO_2 + 2Cl_2 \rightarrow ZrCl_4 + O_2$$

has been calculated to be 2.41, 7.7, and 20.6×10^{-6}, at the temperatures 1000°, 1100°, and 1200° respectively (1).

1. I. S. Morosov and B. G. Korshunov, *Khim. Redkikh Elementov, Akad. Nauk S.S.S.R.*, Inst. Obshchei i Neorg. Khim. *1955*, No. 2, 102-14.

2. L. P. Twitchell, *U.S. Atomic Energy Comm. Y-574*, 16 pp., March 10, 1950.

3. K. Knox, S. Y. Tyree, Jr., Ram Dularay Srivastava, V. Norman, J. Y. Bassett, Jr., and J. H. Holloway, *J. Am. Chem. Soc.* **79**, 3358-61 (1957).

TABLE 3.1. ANALYSIS OF COMMERCIAL
ZIRCONIUM TETRACHLORIDE

Chemical Assay

Zirconium tetrachloride	98.4%
Hafnium tetrachloride	1.6%
Total chlorine	61.2%

Spectrographic Values for Foreign Elements

Al_2O_3	0.005
B_2O_3	None
BaO	0.003
CaO	0.01
Cr_2O_3	None
CuO	0.0005
Fe_2O_3*	0.03
K_2O	None
Li_2O	None
MgO	0.001
MnO_2	None
Na_2O	0.001
Nb_2O_3	None
NiO	None
P_2O_5*	<0.01
PbO	None
Sb_2O_3	None
SiO_2	0.02
SnO_2	None
TiO_2*	0.015
V_2O_5	None
ZnO	None

* Determined gravimetrically or col-
orimetrically.

at which the carbon or sulfur chlorides are partially or completely decomposed, they become in effect variants on processes 1 and 2, and are
not to be regarded as ordinary metatheses as suggested by the equation

$$ZrO_2 + CCl_4 \rightarrow ZrCl_4 + CO_2** \tag{2}$$

Moreover, zirconium dioxide does not undergo metathesis with any of the
ionic chlorides, such as the alkali and alkaline earth chlorides. It undergoes apparent metathesis with covalent chlorides such as aluminum tri-

** Zirconia has been converted to zirconium tetrachloride with carbon tetrachloride at
ordinary pressure at only 500° (2), and conversion under pressure in small bombs has
been noted as low as 400° (3).

chloride and titanium tetrachloride at red heat, but since these latter chlorides have been recently shown to dissociate slightly, it is possible that even here a combination of reduction and chlorination steps are occurring, rather than true metatheses. These methods have not proved economically feasible for industrial preparations.

Metatheses appear to occur between zirconium tetrafluoride or zirconium pyrophosphate and alkaline earth chlorides:

$$ZrF_4 + 2MgCl_2 \rightarrow ZrCl_4 + 2MgF_2$$

$$K_2ZrF_6 + 2MgCl_2 \rightarrow ZrCl_4 + 2MgF_2 + 2KF \qquad (3\text{-}5)$$

$$ZrP_2O_7 + 2CaCl_2 \rightarrow ZrCl_4 + Ca_2P_2O_7$$

Zirconium pyrophosphate is unique among the oxygen-containing compounds in undergoing metatheses with alkaline earth halides.

Only rarely complex compounds of zirconium decompose with the liberation of zirconium tetrachloride. This occurs with the sulfur dioxide complex of zirconium tetrachloride, alkali chlorozirconates which are rich in zirconium tetrachloride content, and by disproportionation of heated basic zirconyl chlorides, the final stage of which gives rise to the reaction

$$2Zr_2O_3Cl_2 \rightarrow 3ZrO_2 + ZrCl_4 \ (4, 5; \text{cf. } 6) \qquad (6)$$

A similar disproportionation occurs with basic zirconyl bromides.

Zirconium tetrachloride is usually purified for use in making zirconium metal or for certain chemical applications by sublimation. This is particularly effective for the removal of oxygen compounds. Ferric chloride, one of the more undesirable common impurities, boils at 315° and tends to remain with the zirconium tetrachloride (subl. 331°). By conducting the sublimation under a hydrogen atmosphere or in the presence of metallic zinc or other suitable reducing substance, the ferric chloride is reduced to the relatively nonvolatile ferrous chloride. Another method of purification consists in dissolving zirconium tetrachloride in molten alkali chlorozirconates, then raising the temperature to 500-600° to boil out pure zirconium tetrachloride. Products containing only 25 to 200 ppm of metallic impurities have been recovered in this way (7, 8). Still another method makes use of a small quantity of motor oil which is mixed with the zirconium tetrachloride prior to heating and subliming the zirconium tetrachloride in highly purified condition (9).

4. E. Chauvenet, *Compt. rend.* **154**, 1234 (1912).

5. Chauvenet, *Ann. chim. phys.* (8) **28**, 536 (1913).

6. S. Takagi, *J. Chem. Soc. Japan, Pure Chem. Sec.* **76**, 443-4 (1955).

7. I. J. Krchma, U.S. Patent **2,533,021**, Dec. 5, 1950.

8. R. V. Horrigan, *J. Metals 7, AIME Trans.* **203**, 1118-20 (1955). Cf. British patent **771,144**, Aug. 25, 1957.

9. W. Frey, U.S. Patent **2,682,445**, June 29, 1954.

No practical methods have been established for purifying zirconium tetra-chloride by recrystallization from a solution, although it appears possible to do this from liquid sulfur dioxide.

Zirconium tetrabromide has been prepared by the reaction of bromine vapor with heated zirconium carbide or cyanonitride, or with mixtures of zirconium dioxide and carbon. The procedures are substantially the same as those for producing the tetrachloride. It is probable that any of the methods which have been reported as suitable for the preparation of the tetrachloride could be applied satisfactorily to production of the tetra-bromide. It is more difficult, however, to prepare the tetraiodide, excepting from the metal. Iodine or hydrogen iodide will react with zirconium metal at as low a temperature as $340°$, but a temperature of $1000°$ or more is required for a reasonably rapid reaction with zirconium carbide or cyano-nitride. Processes have been described for iodinating zirconium cyanonitride and similar zirconium compositions at about $1000°$ to obtain good yields of zirconium tetraiodide (14b, 14c). According to Karantassis (10), the iodide of a trivalent metalloid will exchange its iodine for chlorine or bromine of the halogenide of greater atomic weight, whence

$$4PI_3 + 3ZrCl_4 \rightarrow 3ZrI_4 + PCl_3 \tag{7}$$

The free energy of the reaction

$$3ZrO_2 + 4AlI_3 \rightarrow 2Al_2O_3 + 3ZrI_4 \tag{8}$$

is -66.9 kg cal/mole at $500°K$, and this has been suggested as the basis of a preparation of zirconium tetraiodide (11). Chaigneau has reported quantita-tive yields by conducting the reaction in sealed tubes at a temperature of at least $191°$ (12).

PROPERTIES

Zirconium tetrachloride, $ZrCl_4$, formula weight 233.05, is a colorless solid at room temperature. Its crystal structure has not been completely de-termined, but Zr-Cl distances varying from 2.27 to 2.396 A have been noted (13; cf. 14). Its magnetic susceptibility is 0.301×10^{-6} cgs electromagnetic

10. T. Karantassis, *Compt. rend.* **182,** 1391-3 (1926).

11. S. Ramamurthy, *J. Sci. Ind. Research* (India) **14B,** 414-15 (1955).

12. M. Chaigneau, *Compt. rend.* **242,** 263-5 (1956). Cf. *Bull. soc. chim.* (France) **1957,** 886-8.

13. M. W. Lister and L. E. Sutton, *Trans. Faraday Soc.* **37,** 393-406 (1941).

14. M. Kimura, K. Kimura, M. Aoki, and S. Shibita, *Bull. Chem. Soc. Japan* **29,** 95-100 (1956).

14b. H. J. Smith, U.S. Patent **2,680,670,** June 8, 1954.

14c. I. E. Campbell, U.S. Patent **2,716,051,** August 23, 1955.

units (15), and its specific gravity is 2.803 at 15°. Its heat of formation from its elements is -231.9 ± 0.5 kg cal/mole (16), and its free energy of formation at 25° is -209 kg cal/mole. The heat of sublimation is 25.3 kg cal/mole and the entropy of sublimation 41.9 kg cal/mole. It is insoluble in covalent solvents which do not contain oxygen or nitrogen atoms, e.g., benzene, carbon tetrachloride, and carbon disulfide. It dissolves in water, alcohol, ether, formaldehyde, acetone, pyridine, phosphorus oxychloride, selenium oxychloride, sulfur dioxide, nitrosyl chloride, and molten alkali and alkaline earth chloride salts. In some solvents, notably water, extensive chemical changes accompany the dissolution.

Zirconium tetrachloride vapor is monomolecular. As the temperature of the vapor is increased, the vapor density decreases at a greater rate than required by the law of Charles (17), which has been interpreted as indicating some dissociation to chlorine and a lower chloride at about 1700° (18). While such dissociation does occur, changes in the molecules themselves, to be discussed below, may also influence the vapor density.

While neither the structure of the vapor molecule nor the arrangements of atoms in the crystal of zirconium tetrachloride have been fully determined by direct means, a consideration of their properties permits some substantial deductions of the structures. The following details are of particular value for this purpose:

1. The melting points and sublimation points of zirconium and of hafnium tetrachlorides are intermediate in value between those of the covalent carbon tetrachloride and titanium tetrachloride, and the ionic thorium tetrachloride, as shown in Table 3.2.

TABLE 3.2. MELTING AND BOILING POINTS OF SOME TETRACHLORIDES

Compound	Melting Point, °C	Boiling Point, °C
CCl_4	-22.6	76.8
$TiCl_4$	-30	136.4
$ZrCl_4$	437^{25} atm	331 (subl.)
$HfCl_4$	432	417 (subl.)
$ThCl_4$	830	720-750 (subl.)

2. Zirconium tetrachloride is insoluble in covalent solvents with which it does not react chemically (*supra*), but soluble in molten alkali and alkaline earth chlorides.

---

15. W. R. de Monsabert and E. A. Boudreaux, *The Magnetic Susceptibilities and Structures of the Anhydrous Zirconium Tetrahalides,* 131st Nat. Meeting of the American Chemical Society, April 8, 1957.

16. H. and U. Siemonsen, *Z. Elektrochem.* **56**, 643-4 (1952).

17. J. A. N. Friend, A. T. W. Colley, and R. S. Hayes, *J. Chem. Soc.* **1930**, 1-26.

18. J. H. de Boer and J. D. Fast, *Z. anorg. allgem. Chem.* **187**, 177-89 (1930).

3. Zirconium tetrachloride forms an addition product with the ionic phosphorus pentachloride ($PCl_4^+PCl_6^-$, melts 148° under pressure, sublimes 160°), but not with covalent phosphorus trichloride (PCl_3, melts −111.8°, boils 76°).

4. Plots of the Raman frequencies as a function of the atomic weights of the metals give smooth curves for the chlorides and bromides of Sc, Si, Ge, Sn, but the frequencies of zirconium tetrachloride and tetrabromide do not fit into the curves.

5. Zirconium and hafnium belong to groups of elements which show no evidence of forming monatomic ions in the sense of parting with their valence electrons and establishing ionic bonds. According to the theory of Cabrera and Bose and the partial experimental substantiation by Mathieu, elements 39-46 (Y-Pd) and 72-78 (Hf-Pt) do not form ions in their compounds (19).

In view of the above and of supporting evidence to be developed below, it appears most likely that in the crystal the zirconium tetrachloride consists of complex cations and anions, formed by exchange of chloride ions between neighboring zirconium atoms. This can be represented

$$2ZrCl_4 \rightleftharpoons (ZrCl_{4-n})^{+n}(ZrCl_{4+n})^{-n} \qquad (9)$$

In view of evidence from other sources of the existence of pentachlorozirconate and hexachlorozirconate anions, equation 9 can tentatively be given the more specific form

$$2ZrCl_4 \rightleftharpoons ZrCl_3ZrCl_5 \rightleftharpoons ZrCl_2ZrCl_6 \qquad (10)$$

The association of molecules through formation of complex ions occurs appreciably only in the crystalline state (virtually nothing is known about liquid zirconium tetrachloride), but it is to be presumed that even in the vapor phase, zirconium in the monomolecular tetrachloride increases its coordination number by forming double bonds with some of its chlorine atoms. It is already recognized that a certain amount of double-bond character is present in the Si-Cl, P-Cl, and S-Cl bonds, and more recently theoretical evidence has been adduced that in the chlorine molecule there is the equivalent of about 20% of double-bond character due to π bonding (20). Double-bond formation by the zirconium tetrachloride monomer

$$\qquad\qquad (11)$$

19. Jean-Paul Mathieu, *Cahiers phys.* **22**, 33-6 (1944).
20. R. S. Mulliken, *J. Am. Chem. Soc.* **77**, 884 (1955).

is to be compared to a similar bonding equilibrium in phosphorus oxy-chloride (21, 22):

$$
\begin{array}{ccc}
\text{Cl} \quad \text{Cl} & & \text{Cl} \quad \text{Cl} \\
\diagdown \diagup & & \diagdown \diagup \\
\text{P} & \rightleftharpoons & \text{P} \\
\diagup \diagdown & & \diagup \diagdown\diagdown \\
\text{Cl} \quad \text{O} & & \text{Cl} \quad \text{O}
\end{array}
\tag{12}
$$

Changes in the amount of double-bond character of the Zr-Cl bonds might affect the b value in the van der Waals equation of state, and play a role in departures from Charles's law, which have been noted above. The tendency of the Zr-Cl to take on double-bond character would tend to favor the disproportionation of chloride atoms in the crystal, the unstable $(\text{Cl-Zr-Cl})^{+2}$ tending to approach the arrangement $(\text{Cl} \rightleftharpoons \text{Zr} \rightleftharpoons \text{Cl})^{+2}$. Some justification for this presumption might be found in values for the Zr-Cl distance in zirconium tetrachloride being slightly less than the calculated values for the single-bond distances (13), while in the alkali chlorozirconates the observed distances correspond closely to the calculated distances (23). Crystalline zirconium tetrachloride thus has a very complex nature, comprising in effect several different cation and anion species containing doubly as well as singly bonded chlorine atoms.

A compound of the structure outlined for zirconium tetrachloride would be expected to have a melting point and boiling point (or sublimation point) higher than those of strictly covalent compounds but lower than those of ionic compounds. It would not be soluble in covalent liquids unless it was first altered chemically by contact with these liquids, but it should form homogeneous phases with ionic chlorides. In the presence of chloride ions from alkali chlorides, for example, the chloride-poor species of zirconium tetrachloride should combine with chloride ions:

$$
\begin{aligned}
\text{ZrCl}_2^{+2} + 4\text{Cl}^- &\rightarrow \text{ZrCl}_6^{-2} \\
\text{ZrCl}_4 + 2\text{Cl}^- &\rightarrow \text{ZrCl}_6^{-2}
\end{aligned}
\tag{13-14}
$$

The over-all effect is to form chlorozirconates, as represented by the simplified equation:

$$
\text{ZrCl}_4 + 2\text{NaCl} \rightarrow \text{Na}_2\text{ZrCl}_6
\tag{15}
$$

The same unsaturation of the covalency of zirconium in the tetrachloride that gives this compound such a structurally complex nature leads to the formation of a large number and variety of coordination compounds when

21. N. V. Sidgwick, *The Chemical Elements and Their Compounds,* Oxford University Press, New York, 1950, p. 751.

22. L. Pauling, *Nature of the Chemical Bond,* Cornell University Press, Ithaca, N.Y., 1940.

23. G. Engel, *Krist.* **90**, 34 (1935).

the tetrachloride is brought into suitable contact with other substances. There seems to be hardly an exception to the rule of forming addition compounds with all oxygen-containing organic compounds, i.e., alcohols, phenols, ethers, esters, aldehydes, ketones, carboxylic acids, and their derivatives. The ability to form addition compounds with nitrogen-containing organic compounds is important but less universal than with the oxygen-containing compounds. Zirconium tetrachloride has been observed not to form complexes with nitrogen dioxide, cyanogen, hydrogen cyanide, cyanogen chloride, and some nitriles. It resists entirely the formation of addition compounds through sulfur or phosphorus atoms, as in hydrogen sulfide, sulfur monochloride, the mercaptans, and phosphorus trichloride (24).* These observations raise the question as to why zirconium tetrachloride will form addition compounds with certain donor atoms and not with others. This might well be related to the double-bonding of chlorine atoms with zirconium in zirconium tetrachloride. Were there no such double bonding, there would be unoccupied positions in zirconium orbitals to receive donations of pairs of electrons from any atoms containing lone pairs. Actually, donor atoms must compete with the previously doubly bonded chlorine for orbital positions on the zirconium atoms, and they will attain to these orbital positions only when conditions are energetically favorable. An energetically favorable situation has never been observed to obtain in the cases of phosphorus, sulfur, or for certain conditions of nitrogen atoms, for coordination to occur with zirconium tetrachloride.

When addition compounds are formed with zirconium tetrachloride, a hydrogen atom on the donor atom tends to form hydrogen chloride with a chlorine atom which is bound to the zirconium, e.g.,

$$Cl_4Zr{\leftarrow}OR \rightarrow Cl_3Zr{-}OR + HCl$$
$$\overset{}{H} \tag{16-17}$$
$$Cl_4Zr({\leftarrow}NH_3)_4 \rightarrow Zr(NH_2)_4 + 4HCl$$

Each addition compound tends to decompose with liberation of hydrogen chloride at a characteristic temperature; for example, the addition product with acetone evolves hydrogen chloride at about 0° or somewhat lower, and tetrammine zirconium tetrachloride loses hydrogen chloride starting at about 225°. These decompositions give rise to zirconium alkoxides, amides, and imides. The alkoxides will be discussed in detail in Chapter 9.

Zirconium tetrachloride absorbs ammonia rapidly at room temperature,

---

* The matter of formation of addition compounds with hydrogen chloride is not entirely clear. The author has observed zirconium tetrachloride to go into solution in toluene at −85° under an atmosphere of hydrogen chloride, suggesting that an addition compound is formed with the hydrogen chloride. An iodozirconic acid, H_2ZrI_6, has been reported but not definitely identified.

24. J. M. Matthews, *J. Am. Chem. Soc.* **20**, 815 (1898).

and the tetrammine and octammine have been prepared in this way. The octammine has also been prepared by adding ammonia to an ether solution of zirconium tetrachloride (24, 25). Ammines have been prepared similarly from zirconium tetrabromide and zirconium tetraiodide.

The ammines having more than 4 ammonia groups per zirconium atom cannot be purely covalent compounds, as this would violate the maximum covalency rule as applied to zirconium. Therefore, the higher ammines such as $ZrCl_4 \cdot 8NH_3$ and $ZrBr_4 \cdot 10NH_3$ must contain complex ions (if they are true compounds and not mixtures of products). Physical studies of the amminozirconium compounds have not been reported, but the chemical evidence which is available indicates that at least 8 ammino groups can combine with zirconium tetrachloride without loss of hydrogen chloride. $ZrCl_4 \cdot 8NH_3$ forms directly from its components or from an ether solution of zirconium tetrachloride (26, 27). It is reported to be stable to hydrolysis (27) and does not lose ammonia when subjected to vacuum (26). According to Chauvenet, the amminozirconium tetrachlorides are decomposed to zirconium tetramide, $Zr(NH_2)_4$, at 225-250°, to the diimide, $Zr(NH_4)_2$, at about 300°, and to a nitride of composition Zr_3N_4 at higher temperatures (28). Fowler and Pollard (26) have reported that on heating the octammino-zirconium tetrachloride under vacuum, a residue of $ZrCl_4 \cdot 2NH_3$ was obtained at 180°, and on further heating ammonium chloride, then zirconium tetrachloride were evolved, and that the residue obtained after attaining a temperature of 350° took fire when it was hydrolyzed. When this residue was heated further in vacuum to 800°, a black substance containing only zirconium and nitrogen was formed.

The existence of octamminozirconium tetrachloride suggests that a disproportionation of hydrogen among the nitrogen atoms must occur to give an ammonium aminozirconate, $(NH_4)_4Zr(NH_2)_4Cl_4$, in which the zirconium atom has a coordination number of 8. Hypothetically, the remaining 4 chlorine atoms can be replaced by amino groups, permitting a maximum of 12 nitrogen atoms with a structure represented by the formula $(NH_4)_4Zr(NH_2)_8$.

Zirconium tetrabromide has been noted to dissolve completely in liquid ammonia at −33°, and when the solution was warmed somewhat crystals separated of the empirical composition $3Zr(NH_2) \cdot 7NH_4Br \cdot 5NH_3$. Precipitation of this substance was inhibited by adding ammonium bromide to the ammonia solution (29). Treating the crystalline product with ammonia

25. A. Stähler and B. Denk, *Ber.* **38,** 2611 (1905).

26. G. W. A. Fowler and F. H. Pollard, *J. Chem. Soc.* **1953,** 4128-32.

27. S. C. Ogburn, Jr., and H. M. Fisher, *Foote Mineral Co., Contract At-(30-1)-543, Rept.,* July 15-Sept. 16, 1949.

28. E. Chauvenet, *Ann. chim.* **13,** 59-86 (1920).

29. E. W. Bowerman and W. C. Fernelius, *J. Am. Chem. Soc.* **61,** 121-24 (1939).

changed it to a substance of composition $3Zr(NH_2) \cdot NH_3$, and treating it with potassium amide resulted in the formation of the imide $Zr(NK)_2 \cdot NH_3$. These observations indicate that the disproportionation of hydrogen among the nitrogen atoms bound to zirconium extends to the formation of imides as well as amides, and the odd ratios of zirconium to nitrogen suggest that chains, of the type $-Zr-\overset{H}{N}-Zr-\overset{H}{N}-Zr-$, may form in analogy to the chains of zirconium atoms linked through oxygen atoms, through sulfato groups, and other atoms or groups to be discussed in later chapters. The compound $Zr(NK)_2 \cdot NH_3$ might be written $K_2Zr(NH_2)_3$, potassium imido-zirconate, and is comparable to potassium metazirconate, K_2ZrO_3.

The organic derivatives of ammonia form addition compounds with zirconium tetrachloride similar to those formed by ammonia itself. The pyridine complexes $ZrCl_4 \cdot 2C_5H_5N$ and $ZrCl_4 \cdot 4C_5H_5N$ have been reported, and measurements of the heat of reaction of pyridine and zirconium tetrachloride have indicated no compound to exist between these two in composition. Tertiary amine addition products with zirconium tetrachloride cannot undergo such alterations to form anions and cations as have been observed with ammonia, and hence we should expect that no more than 4 such amine groups can be bound to the zirconium tetrachloride molecule. This is in accord with existing data. The tetrapyridine complex decomposes to the dipyridine complex at room temperature, and the decomposition is accelerated by heating or by subjecting the complex to vacuum. The dipyridine complex decomposes at 70-80°. Methyl, ethyl, and propylamines form ammines of the type $ZrCl_4 \cdot 4A$ by reaction with zirconium tetrachloride in ether solution. β-naphthylamine and quinoline form $ZrCl_4 \cdot 2A$ complexes (24).

It has been noted above that zirconium tetrachloride does not form addition products by coordination with the phosphorus atoms.* Addition compounds with phosphorus pentachloride and phosphorus oxychloride are well known. For a long time the known formation of a stable, distillable compound with the pentachloride was regarded as an enigma in view of the apparent saturation of the valencies of phosphorus in the pentachloride and the weakness of the donor activity of covalently bound chlorine. It now appears that the compound formation is due to the pairing of anions and cations of the two components (30, 31). Zirconium tetrachloride has been dissolved in phosphorus oxychloride, then titrated with phosphorus pentachloride, and changes in the conductivity of the solution have been observed. Inflections correspond to the compositions $(PCl_4)_2ZrCl_6$, PCl_4ZrCl_5, and

---

* It is possible that an unstable, fleeting addition product is formed with phosphine, which decomposes to form a zirconium phosphide (32), as discussed in Chapter 2.

30. W. B. Blumenthal, *Ind. Eng. Chem.* **46**, 528-39 (1954).

31. V. Gutmann and R. Himml, *Z. anorg. allgem. Chem.* **287**, 199-207 (1956).

$PCl_4ZrCl_6ZrCl_3$ (31). In the last of these, monovalent tetrachlorophosphorus and trichlorozirconium cations share jointly the divalent hexachlorozirconate anion.

The compound $PCl_4ZrCl_6ZrCl_3$ ($= 2ZrCl_4 \cdot PCl_5$) has been prepared by simply heating its components together. It is a colorless, crystalline substance which melts at 164.5° and boils at 416°. It is readily hydrolyzed by moist air (65, 66). It has been fractionally distilled for the separation of the corresponding hafnium and zirconium components, but this has not proved a satisfactory method for an industrial separation.

Phosphorus oxychloride is a good solvent for zirconium tetrachloride, and numerous reactions of zirconium tetrachloride have been conducted in phosphorus oxychloride with little interference by the solvent. If the mixture is distilled, a compound of composition $2ZrCl_4 \cdot POCl_3$ is isolated in the fraction which boils at 363-4°. There is also a well-known series of compounds of generic formula $2POX_3 \cdot MCl_4$ in which X is a halogen and M is hafnium or zirconium. They tend to decompose at room temperature under reduced pressures to $POX_3 \cdot MCl_4$. Some physical constants for the addition products of phosphorus oxychloride and hafnium or zirconium tetrachlorides are given in Table 3.3.

TABLE 3.3. SOME PHYSICAL CONSTANTS OF ADDITION PRODUCTS OF PHOSPHORUS OXYHALOGENIDES WITH ZIRCONIUM AND HAFNIUM TETRACHLORIDES (33)

Formula of Compound	Melting, Subliming, and Decomposition Temperatures
$2POCl_3 \cdot ZrCl_4$	Begins to decomp. 60°
$2POCl_3 \cdot HfCl_4$	Begins to decomp. 60°
$POCl_3 \cdot ZrCl_4$	Sublimes 130°; begins to decomp. 145°
$POCl_3 \cdot HfCl_4$	Sublimes 130°; begins to decomp. 145°
$2POFCl_2 \cdot ZrCl_4$	Melts 74-8°
$2POFCl_2 \cdot HfCl_4$	" 80-3°
$POFCl_2 \cdot ZrCl_4$	" 161-3°
$POFCl_2 \cdot HfCl_4$	" 165-7°
$POF_2Cl \cdot ZrCl_4$	" 106-9°
$POF_2Cl \cdot HfCl_4$	" 110-13°
$POF_3 \cdot ZrCl_4$	" 85°
$POF_3 \cdot HfCl_4$	" 85°

A compound $POCl_3 \cdot 3ZrCl_4$ has been reported, melting at 100° and boiling at 360°. The hafnium analog boils at 365°. Both metal compounds have

---

32. F. P. Venable and R. O. Deitz, *J. Elisha Mitchell Sci. Soc.* 38, 74-5 (1922).

33. E. M. Larsen, J. Howatson, A. M. Gammill, and L. Wittenberg, *J. Am. Chem. Soc.* 74, 3489-92 (1952).

heats of vaporization of 20.5 kg cal/mole. The same investigators also reported $3ZrCl_4 \cdot 2PCl_5$ (34, 35; cf. 36, 37).

Titration and conductivity measurements on phosphorus oxychloride solutions of zirconium tetrachloride with chlorides other than phosphorus pentachloride throw considerable additional light on the ions into which zirconium tetrachloride can be resolved. The following order of basicities have been noted in phosphorus oxychloride solution: $SbCl_5 < FeCl_3 < ZrCl_4 < SbCl_3 < POCl_3 < SnCl_4 < TaCl_5 < NbCl_5 < AlCl_3 < PCl_5 < TiCl_4 < (CH_3)_4NCl < $ pyridine $< (C_2H_5)_4NCl$ (38). The addition of antimony pentachloride to a solution of zirconium tetrachloride should, therefore, give rise to salts containing chlorozirconium cations and chloroantimonate anions. This has been verified by conductimetric and electrolytic studies. On adding antimony pentachloride to a solution of zirconium tetrachloride and phosphorus oxychloride, an orange-yellow color formed in the solution and the conductivity was higher than that of the zirconium tetrachloride or antimony pentachloride solutions alone. An inflection in the conductivity curve corresponded to the composition $ZrCl_4 \cdot SbCl_5$. On evaporating the solution under reduced pressure, the solvated $ZrCl_4 \cdot SbCl_5 \cdot 2POCl_3$ separated. It was a hard, orange-yellow solid which lost $POCl_3$ under vacuum. The final residue was a bright-yellow, hygroscopic solid which was decomposed by water, was insoluble in carbon tetrachloride, chloroform, or diethyl ether, and slightly soluble in xylene, to which it imparted a yellow color. During electrolysis of the solution in phosphorus oxychloride, chlorine and antimony migrated to the anode and zirconium to the cathode (31). The compound formed is to be regarded, therefore, as a solvated $ZrCl_3SbCl_6$.

No evidence could be found for compound formation by addition or ionic reactions of zirconium tetrachloride and aluminum trichloride* in phosphorus oxychloride solution (31). The system $NbCl_5$-$ZrCl_4$ has been examined for compound formation, and no compounds found (39). Zirconium tetrachloride is only slightly soluble in arsenic trichloride and in sulfuryl chloride. When zirconium tetrachloride was suspended in nitrosyl chloride, NOCl, a yellow product was formed which had a composition corresponding to $ZrCl_4 \cdot 1.4NOCl$. It was decomposed by water with evolution of gas, and it gave clear solutions in alcohol, ether, tetrahydrofuran, formamide,

---

*Compounds have been observed to form by the reaction of aluminum chloride or ferric chloride with phosphorus pentachloride (40).

34. D. M. Gruen and J. J. Katz, *J. Am. Chem. Soc.* **71**, 3843-4 (1949).
35. Gruen and Katz, U.S. Patent **2,599,326**, June 3, 1952.
36. S. R. Paykull, *Ber.* **6**, 1467 (1873).
37. E. F. Smith and H. B. Harris, *J. Am. Chem. Soc.* **17**, 654 (1895).
38. V. Gutmann and F. Mairinger, *Z. anorg. allgem. Chem.* **289**, 279-87 (1957).
39. E. S. Morosov and B. Korshunov, *Zhur. Neorg. Khim.* **1**, 145-57 (1956).
40. Ya. A. Fialkov and Ya. B. Bur'yanov, *Zhur. Obshchei Khim.* **25**, 2391-9 (1955).

and phosphorus oxychloride. On evaporation of the solution in the last of these, a residue of $ZrCl_4 \cdot 2POCl_3$ was left. Zirconium tetrachloride was noted to have a slight solubility in liquid nitrosyl chloride, and this was increased by addition of tetramethylammonium chloride. Tetramethylammonium hexachlorozirconate was recovered from this solution (31).

Zirconium tetrachloride dissolves in selenium oxychloride, $SeOCl_2$, giving a solution which conducts the electric current. Removal of the solvent at 80° leaves a bright-yellow solid of composition $ZrCl_4 \cdot 2SeOCl_2$ (31).

Zirconium tetrachloride can be burned in dry air at 950-1100° to form zirconium dioxide (41). When it is passed through hot ceramic tubes, some metathesis occurs with siliceous matter of the tubes with formation of zirconium dioxide and silicon tetrachloride (42). Zirconium tetrachloride undergoes metathesis with hydrogen fluoride to form zirconium tetrafluoride and hydrogen chloride (43). The nature of a reaction product obtained by Ruff from zirconium tetrachloride and sulfur tetrachloride has not been clarified (44).

Relatively few studies have been made of the chemical behaviors of zirconium tetrabromide and zirconium tetraiodide, but in general they behave quite similarly to the tetrachloride except for the relatively easy thermal decomposition of the tetraiodide and its oxidation by dry air at about 200°C (45).

Zirconium tetrabromide, $ZrBr_4$, formula weight 410.88, is a colorless solid at room temperature. Its heat of formation from its elements is 192 kg cal/mole at 25°. It sublimes at 357° under 1 atm pressure and melts under pressure at 450°. The heat and entropy of sublimation are 25.8 and 41.0 kg cal/mole, respectively. The magnetic susceptibility is -0.197×10^{-6} cgs electromagnetic units (15).

Zirconium tetraiodide, ZrI_4, formula weight 598.90, is a yellow to reddish-brown solid (probably due to traces of iodine) at room temperature. Its heat of formation from its elements is 90 kg cal/mole at 25°. It sublimes at 431° under atmospheric pressure, and melts at 499° under elevated pressure. Its heat and entropy of sublimation are 29.0 and 41.2 kg cal/mole, respectively. The magnetic susceptibility is -0.238×10^{-6} cgs electromagnetic units (15). It readily forms the amminozirconium iodides $ZrI_4 \cdot 6NH_3$ and $ZrI_4 \cdot 8NH_3$ when sufficient ammonia is supplied, and the latter compound is reported to decompose into zirconium tetramide when it is washed with liquid ammonia. All its iodine content was washed out as ammonium iodide (25).

41. British patent **655,647**, July 25, 1951.
42. W. Fischer, *Z. anorg. allgem. Chem.* **211**, 349-67 (1933).
43. L. Wolter, *Chem. Ztg.* **32**, 606 (1908).
44. O. Ruff, *Ber.* **34**, 1749 (1901); **37**, 4513 (1904).
45. Titanium Alloy Mfg. Div. of the National Lead Co., unpublished researches.

USES

The major uses of zirconium tetrachloride have been in the preparation of zirconium metal and of zirconium chemicals. The chief chemicals derived directly from zirconium tetrachloride are sodium and potassium chloro-zirconates, zirconyl chloride, hydrous zirconia, carbonated hydrous zirconia, and zirconium tetrafluoride. Secondary derivatives include the oxide and acetate, lactate, sulfate, and soluble carbonate compounds (46).

Zirconium tetrachloride has found some industrial application in catalysis, e.g., Friedel-Crafts catalysis, polymerization catalysis, and isomerization of hydrocarbons, and in proprietary preparations such as printing pastes. Details of these uses are, to a large extent, kept as trade secrets. Literature on these processes is summarized in Table 3.4.

Since zirconium tetrabromide and zirconium tetrachloride are very similar chemically but the former considerably more expensive, the tetrabromide has not been used to any considerable extent. Zirconium tetraiodide has found use only in the preparation of zirconium metal of high purity, and in current procedures it is usually generated and used immediately in the same equipment.

TABLE   3.4. USES OF ZIRCONIUM TETRACHLORIDE
IN CHEMICAL INDUSTRY

Use	Literature
Catalyst	
alkylation	47
chlorination	48
Friedel-Crafts syntheses	49, 50, 51
isomerization of hydrocarbons	52, 53, 54
miscellaneous syntheses	
butadiene	55
isobutane	56
phthalocyanine	57
olefin polymerization	58, 59, 60
oxidation	61
Others	
in printing compositions	62
in regulation of electrical barriers	63
in welding fluxes	64
in separation of hafnium from zirconium	65

46. W. B. Blumenthal, *Chem. Inds.* **65**, 728-30 (1949).
47. W. M. Lanham, British patent **762,147**, Nov. 2, 1956.
48. V. Schvemberger and V. Gordon, *J. Gen. Chem. (U.S.S.R.)* **4**, 529-51 (1934).
49. A. V. Grosse and V. N. Ipatieff, *J Org. Chem.* **1**, 559-66 (1937).

THE ClBrI HALOGENOZIRCONATES

When zirconium tetrachloride is mixed with an alkali or alkaline earth chloride and heated, or when zirconium tetrachloride is introduced into a molten alkali or alkaline earth chloride, chlorozirconates are formed. This is due to the coordination of chloride ions with zirconium atoms, as discussed above and represented in equations 13 and 14. On adding zirconium tetrachloride to molten sodium chloride, the electrical conductivity falls in proportion to the amount of zirconium tetrachloride added, as would be expected when the relatively mobile chloride ions are replaced by the more cumbersome chlorozirconate ions (67). On electrolysis of such a solution, zirconium migrates toward the anode (68; cf. 36, 69). Phase studies have indicated the existence of the compounds $NaZrCl_5$, Na_2ZrCl_6 and $NaZr_2Cl_9$ (8, 39, 70, 71). Na_2ZrCl_6 melts at 695° (70). $NaZr_2Cl_9$ is possibly to be understood as $NaZrCl_6ZrCl_3$, in which there is a zirconium cation as well as a zirconium anion.

Zirconium tetrachloride is soluble in molten sodium chlorozirconates, doubtless reflecting the compatibility of two substances both of which contain chlorozirconate anions. When the solutions are heated strongly, zirconium tetrachloride distills from the melt and may be condensed as a pure, white solid.

The Zr-Cl distances in Rb_2ZrCl_6 and Cs_2ZrCl_6 (cubic) have been de-

50. H. W. Heine, D. L. Cottle, and H. L. van Mater, *J. Am. Chem. Soc.* **68,** 524 (1946).
51. G. S. Kolesnikov and V. V. Korshak, *Izvest. Akad. Nauk S.S.S.R. Odtel. Khim. Nauk* **1953,** 336-43.
52. L. A. Clark, U.S. Patent **2,401,859,** June 11, 1946.
53. H. Pines, U.S. Patent **2,405,516,** Aug. 5, 1946.
54. H. Pines and R. C. Wackher, U.S. Patent **2,418,724,** Aug. 8, 1947.
55. A. R. Workman, U.S. Patent **2,412,762,** Dec. 17, 1946.
56. D. C. Bond and M. Savoy, U.S. Patent **2,425,416,** Aug. 12, 1947.
57. F. H. Moser, U.S. Patent **2,469,663,** May 10, 1949.
58. L. C. Huff, U.S. Patent **2,407,700,** Sept. 17, 1946.
59. J. L. Ernst and R. M. Thomas, U.S. Patent **2,682,531,** June 29, 1954.
60. British patent **778,639,** July 10, 1957.
61. R. A. Greger and F. R. Alsberg, U.S. Patent **2,627,498,** Feb. 3, 1953.
62. J. M. Mecco, U.S. Patent **2,650,152,** Aug. 25, 1953.
63. Dutch patent **58,102,** August 15, 1946.
64. A. P. Edson and I. L. Newell, U.S. Patent **2,674,790,** April 13, 1954.
65. A. E. van Arkel and J. H. de Boer, U.S. Patent **1,582,860,** April 27, 1926.
66. van Arkel and de Boer, *Z. anorg. allgem. Chem.* **141,** 289-96 (1924).
67. N. A. Belozerskiï and B. A. Freidlina, *J. Appl. Chem.* (U.S.S.R.) **14,** 466-8 (1941).
68. R. Ruer, *Z. anorg. allgem. Chem.* **43,** 85, 282 (1904) ; **46,** 456 (1906).
69. M. Weibull, *Acta. Univ. Lund.* (2) **18,** 21 (1882).
70. N. A. Belozerskiï and O. A. Kucherenko, *J. Appl. Chem.* (U.S.S.R.) **13,** 1552-55 (1940).
71. L. T. Howell, R. C. Sommer, and H. H. Kellogg, *J. Metals* **9,** *Trans. 209,* 193-200 (1957).

termined to be 2.44 A and 2.45 A, respectively, in close agreement with the values calculated from the covalent bond lengths of the elements (23).

Tetraethylammonium chlorozirconate has been prepared by adding tetraethylammonium iodide to a solution of zirconium tetrachloride in phosphorus oxychloride. The conductivity of the solution decreased as the organic salt was added and the zirconium compound precipitated. It was filtered, washed, and freed of solvent under vacuum. It contained no phosphorus, and was insoluble in water, mineral acids, and organic solvents, but it dissolved in anhydrous arsenic trichloride (31). The preparation of other complex chlorozirconates in phosphorus oxychloride has already been discussed above in connection with the behavior of zirconium tetrachloride as an ionic solute. The titration of zirconium tetrachloride in solution in selenium oxychloride with potassium chloride gives evidence for the formation of $KZrCl_5$, K_2ZrCl_6, and K_3ZrCl_7 in this medium. A solid of composition $K_2ZrCl_6 \cdot 2SeOCl_2$ was isolated (loc. cit.).

The only important industrial use of the alkali chlorozirconates is in the preparation of aluminum-zirconium and magnesium-zirconium alloys. For this purpose fused lumps of alkali chlorozirconates are used. They may assay up to 88% total $ZrCl_4$ by weight, and they are sold under the trivial name fused salts. In their application the lumps are added directly to the fused aluminum or magnesium metal. Zirconium metal is formed by the chemical reaction and dissolves in the basis metal, usually to the extent of about 0.2%. When the cast metal containing this amount of zirconium cools, the grain development is finer and the strength greater than in the absence of the zirconium.

No studies of the alkali or alkaline earth bromozirconates or iodozirconates have been published. The halogenozirconic acids have never been isolated, but they apparently form when hydrogen halide gas is added to a solution of the zirconium tetrahalogenide in methanol. When organic bases are added to solutions of halozirconic acids prepared in this way, insoluble halogenozirconates are precipitated. Even if a small amount of water is present in the system, the anhydrous salt separates. Pyridinium and quinolinium chlorozirconates, bromozirconates, and chlorohafnates have been prepared in this fashion (72, 73, 74). They are useful intermediates in the preparation of zirconium alkoxides.

The formation of anhydrous halogenozirconates in the presence of small amounts of water, in an alcohol medium, is doubtless due to the conversion

---

72. A. Rosenheim and P. Frank, Ber. 38, 812 (1905).
73. D. C. Bradley, F. M. Abd-el Halim, E. A. Sadek, and W. Wardlaw, J. Chem. Soc. 1952, 2032-2035.
74. D. C. Bradley, R. C. Mehrotra, and W. Wardlaw, J. Chem. Soc. 1953, 1634-36.

of water to hydronium ions, which are only loosely bound by zirconium and are replaceable by halogen.

Stähler and Denk obtained a sublimate from a system containing zirconium tetraiodide which they thought to be ZrI_6 and which Chauvenet and Davidowicz thought to be H_2ZrI_6 (25, 75), but which has not been adequately identified.

THE ClBrI TRI- AND DI-HALOGENIDES

The chloride, bromide, and iodide compounds of trivalent and divalent zirconium are the only compounds of zirconium at valence less than 4 that have been prepared. Efforts to prepare the lower fluorides have not succeeded (76).

Ruff and Wallstein (77) mixed zirconium tetrachloride with finely divided aluminum and heated the mixtures in evacuated bombs under a variety of conditions. In the presence of aluminum chloride they obtained reactions at temperatures of 240° or higher and noted the formation of a red to brown liquid. The cooled product was found to be stable in dry air, but when moisture was admitted there was a vigorous reaction with liberation of hydrogen. An imperfect separation of a substance identified as zirconium trichloride was accomplished by distilling zirconium tetrachloride and aluminum chloride away from the reaction product. In a series of similar preparations they found aluminum to be the best reducing agent, but similar effects were obtained with magnesium, selenium, and zinc.

R. C. Young prepared zirconium tribromide by passing zirconium tetrabromide vapor over a hot aluminum wire coil in a sealed glass system. An excess of zirconium tetrabromide was used to obtain a product free of the dibromide. Zirconium tetrabromide and aluminum tribromide were distilled away from the reaction product and a blue-black powder was recovered. Analysis indicated it to be the tribromide. Reductions to the tribromide were also achieved using magnesium, iron, or aluminum-zirconium alloy as the reducing agents. Magnesium tended to give a greater proportion of the dibromide than did aluminum. No reductions were obtained with mercury, aluminum, or silver in the presence of carbon tetrachloride, benzene, or ethyl bromide (liquids), in which zirconium tetrabromide is insoluble. Hydrogen alone would not reduce zirconium tetrabromide at temperatures up to 1100° (78).

Schumb and Morehouse prepared hafnium tribromide similarly to the

75. E. Chauvenet and J. Davidowicz, *Compt. rend.* **189**, 408-9 (1929).
76. E. M. Larsen and J. J. Leddy, *J. Am. Chem. Soc.* **78**, 5983-6 (1956).
77. O. Ruff and R. Wallstein, *Z. anorg. allgem. Chem.* **128**, 96-116 (1923).
78. R. C. Young, *J. Am. Chem. Soc.* **53**, 2148-53 (1931).

above preparation of the zirconium compound. It, too, is a black-blue solid with physical and chemical properties similar to those of the zirconium analog (79).

De Boer and Fast have noted that zirconium dichloride forms when zirconium tetrachloride is heated with zirconium metal in the presence of aluminum chloride (18).

The preparation of the ClBrI trihalogenides of zirconium from the tetrahalogenides and zirconium metal was investigated in great detail by Larsen and Leddy. They sealed the tetrahalogenide and metal in a glass ampoule which was placed in an outer tube in which a gas pressure could be maintained at a level calculated to be close to that in the ampoule during reaction. The outer tube was heated in a furnace, and in successive runs different

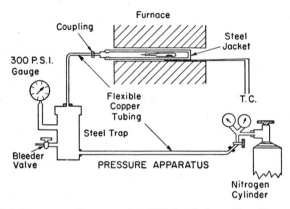

Fig. 3.1. Apparatus for preparing ClBrI trihalogenides. From (76).

temperatures and different heating times were tried for each mixture of tetrahalogenide and zirconium metal. The best yields in each case were obtained at 700°, and a favorable reaction time was about 30 hours. Their results are summarized in Figures 3.2, 3.3, and 3.4. A diagram of their equipment is shown in Figure 3.1.

In a related study by Newnham, advantage was taken of the observation that hafnium tetrachloride is not reduced by zirconium metal to effect a separation of the two elements. After heating a mixture of zirconium tetrachloride (containing hafnium tetrachloride) and zirconium metal at 330° or higher in a suitable bulb, the unreduced hafnium tetrachloride was sublimed out of the mixture, leaving zirconium trichloride of $< 0.1\%$ hafnium content. (In this and other similar reports, $\%$ hafnium is understood to mean the ratio $(100 \times \text{wt. } HfO_2)/(\text{Wt. } ZrO_2 + HfO_2)$. On heating the

---

79. W. C. Schumb and C. K. Morehouse, *J. Am. Chem. Soc.* **69**, 2696 (1947).

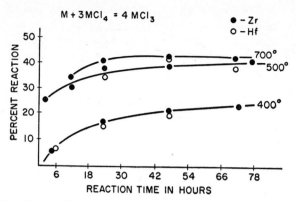

FIG. 3.2. Yields of zirconium and hafnium trichlorides as functions of time and temperature.

residual zirconium trichloride at about 540°, it disproportionates, and hafnium-free zirconium tetrachloride sublimes out of the decomposing solid:

$$2ZrCl_3 \rightarrow ZrCl_4 + ZrCl_2$$

and
$$2ZrCl_2 \rightarrow ZrCl_4 + Zr$$

(18-19)

It was proposed that the final residue of zirconium metal be used as a reducing agent for a succeeding charge of hafnium-containing zirconium tetrachloride (80, 81).

It is reported that sodium or magnesium amalgams can also be used to reduce zirconium tetrachloride (82).

When the lower chlorides or bromides of zirconium are added to water, they give colored solutions which fade out as they are oxidized by the water

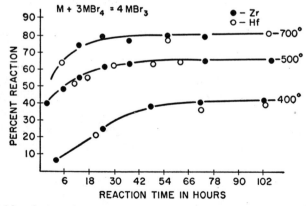

FIG. 3.3. Yields of zirconium and hafnium tribromides as functions of time and temperature.

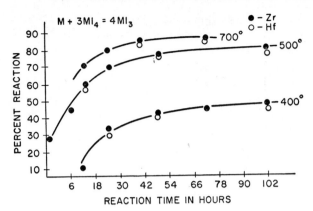

FIG. 3.4. Yields of zirconium and hafnium tetraiodides as functions of time and temperature.

to tetravalent compounds or ions of zirconium. The dichloride takes fire on exposure to dry air, and it reacts so violently with water that it becomes heated to incandescence. The trichloride forms a brownish-yellow aqueous solution and it is oxidized on exposure to air. It has also been noted to dissolve in aluminum chloride (80).

In the van Arkel-de Boer process for preparing pure zirconium metal, iodine vapor is permitted to attack crude zirconium metal so as to form a volatile iodide which eventually impinges on an incendescent filament where it is decomposed to form pure zirconium metal. The liberated iodine is recycled to form more volatile iodide from the crude metal. The activation energy for the formation of zirconium tetraiodide from the elements has been observed to be 21 kg cal/mole below 200° and above 500°, but it has a greater value at temperatures between these limits and attains a maximum of 75 kg cal/mole at 420°. These variations are related to the formation and dissociation of lower iodides. At low temperatures only zirconium tetraiodide forms, but at temperatures starting at about 160° the triodide forms. It is less volatile than the tetraiodide and tends to coat the surfaces of the reacting zirconium metal. At 320° zirconium triiodide vapor begins to disproportionate into zirconium tetraiodide and zirconium diiodide. At 500° the zirconium triiodide solid phase disappears and solid zirconium diiodide appears. As the temperature rises the zirconium diiodide dissociates into tetraiodide and iodine, so that ultimately the vapor contains only zirconium tetraiodide (83).

80. I. E. Newnham, *J. Am. Chem. Soc.* **79**, 5415-17 (1957).
81. I. E. Newnham, U.S. Patent **2,791,485**, May 7, 1957.
82. W. Schmidt, U.S. Patent **2,758,921**, Aug. 14, 1956.
83. H. Döring and K. Molière, *Z. Elektrochem.* **56**, 403-8 (1952).

The relatively low volatilities of the tri- and di-ClBrI halogenides of zirconium as compared to the tetrahalogenides is doubtless due to enhanced intermolecular attraction, which is traceable to the valence electrons of the zirconium atom which are not used in forming the initial halogen bonds. Since zirconium is found at oxidation number less than 4 only in these compounds, these low oxidation states are doubtless stabilized by intermolecular complex formation. It is to be expected that the nature of this complex will eventually be clarified by X-ray diffraction studies.

THE ClBrI OXYHALOGENIDES

INTRODUCTION

The dissolution of zirconium tetrachloride in water leads to the complete decomposition of the original structure, and it has not been possible to reform zirconium tetrachloride from the solution. When approximately 32 moles of water are used to dissolve 1 mole of zirconium tetrachloride under ordinary atmospheric pressure, approximately 1 mole of hydrogen chloride gas is liberated and the rest of the hydrogen chloride formed during the reaction is retained by the solution. The zirconium species which form depend on the concentration of the solution. Evidence for hydrated forms of the ions $ZrOOH^+$, ZrO^{+2}, $ZrOH^{+3}$, Zr^{+4}, and $Zr_4(OH)_8^{+8}$ has been reported. The first of these appears to be the prevailing species in solutions of low total acid concentration, and the latter at higher acid concentrations.

The exact course of the chemical changes which occur when zirconium tetrachloride reacts with water has not been traced experimentally, and because of the rapidity and violence of the reaction, this would be a difficult achievement. It is helpful to begin our consideration of the reaction of zirconium tetrachloride with water and the products of this reaction by constructing from theoretical considerations the probable course of reaction.

When solid zirconium tetrachloride comes into contact with water, liquid, or vapor, an addition reaction doubtless occurs first, in which oxygen atoms of the water molecules donate electrons to zirconium atoms. There is, thus, a fleeting existence of a hydrated tetrachloride $ZrCl_4 \cdot xH_2O$. This decomposes with liberation of hydrogen chloride and instantaneous formation of hydroxychlorides, such as $ZrCl_3OH \cdot (x-1)H_2O$, $ZrCl_{4-n}(OH)_n$, etc. But even as this occurs, more water is becoming associated with the zirconium atom by formation of coordinate bonds, and soon all the chlorine has become disengaged from the zirconium. In liquid water, the course of the reaction is ramified by the action of hydroxyl and hydronium ions, but their effect is ultimately the same as that of the water molecules. As soon as two hydroxyl groups have become attached to the zirconium atom, they react with one another, splitting off water and leaving an oxo oxygen atom bound to the zirconium. Ultimately the zirconium atom becomes associated by covalent bonds with the maximum number of atoms or groups that the geometry of the zirconium atom and its ligands permits. If we assume, from implications of other chemical combinations of the zirconium atom, that zirconium attains to a coordination number of 7 in the aqueous medium, the over-all reaction of zirconium tetrachloride with water can be represented by the equation

$$ZrCl_4 + 9H_2O \rightarrow \begin{bmatrix} H_2O & OH & OH_2 \\ & \searrow \downarrow \swarrow & \\ & Zr & \\ & \nearrow \| \nwarrow & \\ H_2O & O & OH_2 \end{bmatrix}^+ + 3H_3O^+ + 4Cl^- \qquad (20)$$

If the aqueous solution is evaporated to dryness, a solid of empirical composition $ZrOCl_2 \cdot 8H_2O$ (or lower hydrates if evaporation is continued) is precipitated. This crystalline solid, known in the literature as *zirconium oxychloride* or *zirconyl chloride,* is one of the most widely studied and best-known compounds of zirconium. X-ray diffraction studies of the crystal have led to the conclusion that no chlorine atoms are bound to zirconium atoms (84, 85). It is thought, therefore, that there will be no actual bonding of chlorine to zirconium atoms in aqueous solutions of this compound. This view gains support from the measurements of Natta, which have shown that zirconyl chloride solutions and zirconyl bromide solutions show the same Raman spectra (86).

Chauvenet titrated solutions of zirconium tetrachloride in water in which all the hydrogen chloride had been retained. He followed the course of the reactions by calorimetric and conductivity measurements and found an inversion point at a titre corresponding to the addition of 2 moles of sodium hydroxide per mole of zirconium tetrachloride. He took this to indicate the presence of the zirconyl ion, ZrO^{+2} (28). It now appears more likely that the zirconyl ion occurs only during the prevalence of a certain range of acid concentrations. The ZrO group, however, persists through many chemical changes of zirconium compound, and it is convenient to designate compounds of the type $ZrOX_2$ (with water of hydration) as zirconyl compounds.

PREPARATION AND PROPERTIES OF ZIRCONYL ClBrI HALOGENIDES

Zirconyl chloride octahydrate can be crystallized from its aqueous solutions not only by evaporation but also by addition of hydrogen chloride or

84. A. Clearfield and P. A. Vaughan, *Acta Cryst.* **9,** 555-8 (1956).
85. B. T. Meyer, *Naturwiss* **118,** 34 (1930).
86. G. Natta, *Atti Congresso naz. chim. pura applicata* **1930,** 347-64.

soluble organic liquids such as acetone (87, 88). The aqueous solutions may be derived from the dissolution of zirconium tetrachloride in water or from the dissolution of hydrous zirconia, alkali zirconates, or certain other zirconium compounds with hydrochloric acid. High purity is achieved by recrystallizing the zirconyl chloride.

Zirconyl chloride octahydrate, $ZrOCl_2 \cdot 8H_2O$, formula weight 322.26, occurs as colorless tetragonal crystals in which a = 17.08 and c = 7.674 A, and ω = 1.563 and ϵ = 1.552. The zirconium is arranged in a complex cation, 4 zirconium atoms being at the corners of a square and each bound to each of its nearest neighbors through ol groups, one of which is located above the plane of the zirconium atoms and one below. The chlorine atoms are remote from the zirconium atoms and not bonded to them chemically (84). The heat of formation of zirconyl chloride octahydrate from its elements at 25° is 857.2 kg cal/mole. On heating the crystals, they contract along the c axis, and both water and hydrogen chloride are evolved. Hence the compound has no actual melting point or boiling point. It is very soluble in water. If hydrogen chloride is added to the solution, the solubility of the zirconyl chloride is diminished until a minimum solubility is attained in a solution containing 8.5 moles (310 g) of HCl per liter, as shown in Table 3.5. The

TABLE 3.5. SOLUBILITY OF ZIRCONYL CHLORIDE OCTAHYDRATE
AT 20° IN VARIOUS CONCENTRATIONS OF HYDROCHLORIC ACID (89)

HCl Concentration	$ZrOCl_2 \cdot 8H_2O$ Concentration	
Moles/1	Moles/1	g/1
0.2	2.91	939
1.47	2.14	690
4.97	0.329	106
8.72	0.0547	17.6
10.14	0.0988	32.8
10.94	0.205	66.1
11.61	0.334	108

solubility of hafnyl chloride octahydrate in moles/1 is identical with that of zirconyl chloride at HCl concentrations of 8.5 M and lower, but at the higher acid concentrations, the hafnium compound is considerably less soluble than the zirconium compound. The effect of temperature on the

87. H. von Siemens and H. Zander, *Wiss. Veraffentll-Siemens Konzern* **2**, 484 (1922).
88. A. W. Henderson and K. B. Higbie, *J. Am. Chem. Soc.* **76**, 5878-9 (1954).
89. G. von Hevesy, *Det. Kg. Danske Videnska b. Selskab* **VI, 7** (1925).

solubility of zirconyl chloride in 10.16 M hydrochloric acid is shown in Table 3.6.

Zirconyl chloride is soluble in alcohol, but insoluble in ether, hydrocarbons, and chlorinated hydrocarbons.

Although zirconyl chloride always crystallizes from aqueous solutions as the octahydrate, numerous other states of hydration have been observed. A study of evaporation rates in the system $ZrOCl_2$-H_2O gave evidence for the 10, 9.5, 8.5, 8, 7.75, 7.25, 7, 6.5, 6, and 4 hydrates (90, 91). The changes of the magnitude of $\frac{1}{4}$ molecule of water per atom of zirconium agrees well with the picture of an ion species containing 4 zirconium atoms. Other investigators have reported preparations of zirconyl chloride with 6.5, 6, 5.5, 4.5, 3.5, 3, and 2 molecules of water per zirconium atom, but little has been done to demonstrate the molecular nature of these empirical compositions.

TABLE 3.6. SOLUBILITY OF ZIRCONYL CHLORIDE
OCTAHYDRATE IN 10.16 M HYDROCHLORIC ACID (92)

Temperature	Grams $ZrOCl_2 \cdot 8H_2O$ per 100 grams solution
0	2.72
10	3.15
20	4.51
30	6.42
40	9.67
50	14.19
60	20.45
68	23.85

When zirconyl chloride octahydrate is exposed to very humid air, it deliquesces, but at moderate humidities it effloresces and leaves a residue of composition $ZrOCl_2 \cdot 6H_2O$. W. W. Braun mixed zirconyl chloride octahydrate with various amounts of zirconium tetrachloride, and after allowing the mixtures to stand for long periods of time, extracted the unreacted zirconium tetrachloride with ether. He repeatedly obtained residues of composition $ZrOCl_2 \cdot 3\frac{1}{2}H_2O$, from which he concluded that this was the lowest hydrate that could be obtained by dehydration with zirconium tetrachloride at room temperature (45).

When zirconyl chloride octahydrate is heated gently, its decomposition products melt at about 115°, but continued decomposition soon causes the

90. W. S. Castor, Jr., and F. Basolo, *J. Am. Chem. Soc.* **75**, 4804-7 (1953).
91. *Ibid.*, 4807-10 (1953).
92. P. Schmid, *Z. anorg. allgem. Chem.* **167**, 369 (1927).

melt to solidify. On heating the decomposition products to 300° and examining the residue by X-ray diffraction, a pattern is obtained for monoclinic zirconium dioxide and no other substance (93).

Aqueous solutions of zirconyl chloride can be boiled under ordinary atmospheric pressure without formation of solid hydrolysis products, but if the solutions are heated under pressure to 150° or higher, hydrous zirconia is deposited (45, 94, 95).

It has long been known that freshly prepared zirconyl chloride solutions change on standing. Venable thought that they attained equilibrium in 2-3 hours (96). Ruer found that the specific conductivity of freshly prepared 0.25 N zirconyl chloride solution increased from about 1400 mho to 2100 mho during the first hour and then remained unchanged for the next 168 hours at 18° (97). The author has added recrystallized zirconyl chloride to rapidly stirred water and observed the pH of the solution after various lengths of time. The salt dissolved within 1 minute, giving an acidic solution the pH of which continued to fall for considerable lengths of time. The hydrogen ion activities for solutions of various concentrations, temperatures, and ages, as determined by a glass electrode, are listed in Table 3.7. It is seen that the 1-minute-old solutions exhibit hydrogen ion activities which range from about $\frac{1}{10}$ to $\frac{1}{2}$ the strengths attained after 24 hours of aging. The final acid strengths are nearly the same as those of hydrochloric acid

TABLE 3.7. HYDROGEN ION ACTIVITIES IN SOLUTIONS
OF ZIRCONYL CHLORIDE OCTAHYDRATE

Age of the zirconyl chloride solution	Hydrogen Ion Activity					
	1.0 molar		0.1 molar		0.01 molar	
	25°	50°	25°	50°	25°	50°
1 min	0.32	0.45	0.019	0.028	0.0013	0.0023
10 min	0.46	0.63	0.026	0.032	0.0014	0.0028
1 hr	0.50	0.71	0.033	0.031	0.0028	0.0048
24 hr	0.60	0.85	0.063	0.056	0.010	0.010
Values for hydrochloric acid (98)	0.81	0.77	0.080	0.079	0.0090	0.0090

93. G. L. Clark and H. Reynolds, *Ind. Eng. Chem.* **29**, 711-15 (1937).
94. Mme. H. Emmanuel-Zavizziana, *J. chim. phys.* **36**, 111-16 (1939).
95. L. K. Akrad-Simonova, N. A. Fleisher, and M. L. Bulkina, *J. Appl. Chem.* (*U.S.S.R.*) **11**, 941-45 (1938).
96. F. P. Venable, *J. Am. Chem. Soc.* **42**, 2531-4 (1920).
97. R. Ruer, *Z. anorg. allgem. Chem.* **43**, 85, 282 (1904); **46**, 465 (1906).

solutions of the same molarity (45). This indicates that the net empirical effect of the dissolution and hydrolysis of zirconyl chloride is in accordance with the equation

$$ZrOCl_2 + H_2O \rightarrow ZrOOH^+ + H^+ + 2Cl^- \tag{21}$$

Similar equilibrium values for hydrogen activity have been observed for hafnyl chloride solutions by Graham (98), who found the hydrogen ion activity to be equal to 0.83 times the hafnyl chloride concentration.

From the above data and from supplementary data to be cited below, it is possible to establish a tentative picture of the ion species found in zirconyl chloride solutions. When the crystalline solid, $ZrOCl_2 \cdot 8H_2O$, is first dissolved, tetrazirconium ions of formula $Zr_4(OH)_8^{+8}$, with water of hydration, pass into the solution phase. They are surrounded and their charge balanced by a layer of anions, i.e., Cl^- and OH^-. The large zirconium ion reacts with its environment, and at concentrations of the order of 0.01 to 1.0 M with respect to zirconium, it breaks down practically completely to the basic zirconyl ion, $ZrOOH^+ \cdot nH_2O$. Assuming 4 as a probable value of n:

$$Zr_4(OH)_8^{+8} \cdot xH_2O + (16-x)\,H_2O \rightleftharpoons 4ZrOOH^+ \cdot 4H_2O + 4H^+ \tag{22}$$

The reaction is reversible, and the higher the acidity of the solution, the more of the tetramer species will be present. Experimental evidence for this will be cited below.

In aqueous solutions of zirconyl chloride, large numbers of the ions $ZrOOH^+$ associate loosely to form aggregates equivalent to ionic weights of the order of 8000, as determined by Rayleigh light-scattering techniques.* Small changes in the conductivity of the solution over long periods of time probably reflect small changes which develop in these aggregates. It is probable that the aggregates are not true polymers, since (1) in many reactions of zirconyl chloride solutions one may observe the instantaneity of simple ionic reactions, and (2) solutions of the ion $Zr_2O_3^{+2}$ show different chemical behavior from those of the ion $ZrOOH^+$, whereas differences between these ions should disappear if true polymerization occurred.

It appears satisfactory at the present time to regard the prevailing species in zirconyl chloride solutions of moderate concentrations as $ZrOOH^+ \cdot 4H_2O$. Konarev and Solovkin have noted that on addition of potassium iodate to zirconium nitrate solution of pH 2-3, the compound

---

* The author is indebted to Prof. S. Y. Tyree of the University of North Carolina for private communications on his measurements of aggregate sizes and small changes in conductivity.

98. A. W. Graham, III, "Rayleigh Light Scattering of Atomic Polymers in Aqueous Solutions of Hafnium IV Chloride." Doctorate thesis, University of North Carolina, 1954.

$ZrOOHIO_3 \cdot 5H_2O$ is precipitated (99), and as discussed in Chapter 8, on addition of 2 moles of sodium acetate to 1 of zirconyl chloride solution, one obtains not the soluble zirconyl acetate but the insoluble basic zirconyl acetate of empirical formula $ZrOOHC_2H_3O_2 \cdot nH_2O$.

When the acidity of a zirconyl chloride solution is increased either by concentrating it or by adding a noncomplexing acid, such as hydrochloric acid, hydronium ions react with the basic zirconyl ion, $ZrOOH^+$ and convert it to other species. Neglecting water of hydration, the changes may be represented as follows:

$$ZrOOH^+ + H_3O^+ \rightarrow ZrO^{+2} + 2H_2O$$
$$ZrO^{+2} + H_3O^+ \rightarrow ZrOH^{+3} + H_2O \qquad (23\text{-}25)$$
$$ZrOH^{+3} + H_3O^+ \rightarrow Zr^{+4} + 2H_2O$$

It is not to be supposed, however, that a tetrapositive zirconium ion ever exists. The higher positive charges are distributed about the sphere of coordinated aquo groups, and in all events, the more highly charged zirconium cations tend to combine to the tetramer:

$$4ZrO^{+2} + 4H_2O \rightleftharpoons Zr_4(OH)_8^{+8} \qquad (26)$$

W. W. Braun observed electromigration of zirconium toward the cathode in zirconyl chloride solutions (45). Lister and McDonald noted electromigration toward the cathode at 0.5 and 1 N concentrations of hydrochloric acid, but no migration at higher acidities (100). No significant migration of zirconium would be expected at high acidities due to the formation of larger, less mobile zirconium ion species and the availability of the large concentration of hydronium ions to carry the current.

On the basis of the distribution of zirconium thenoyltrifluoroacetonate between an aqueous perchloric acid solution and benzene, evidence has been adduced for the existence of polymers of high molecular weight of the zirconium species in the aqueous solution (101, 102). Viscosity measurements on similar solutions, however, failed to support the conclusion that polymers of high molecular weight were present (103). Subsequent studies of the distribution of zirconium chelates between aqueous and benzene layers (104) and by ultracentrifugation (105, 106) supported the existence of trimeric and tetrameric zirconium cation species in solutions of moderate acidity.

99. M. I. Konarev and A. S. Solovkin, *Zhur. Obshchei Khim.* **24**, 1113-8 (1954).
100. B. A. J. Lister and (Miss) L. A. McDonald, *J. Chem. Soc.* **1952**, 4315-4330.
101. R. E. Connick and W. H. McVey, *J. Am. Chem. Soc.* **71**, 3182-92 (1949).
102. R. E. Connick and W. H. Reas, *J. Am. Chem. Soc.* **73**, 1171-6 (1951).
103. P. A. Vaughan, personal communication.
104. A. J. Zielen, *U.S. Atomic Energy Comm. UCRL-2268* (1953).
105. K. A. Kraus and J. S. Johnson, *J. Am. Chem. Soc.* **75**, 5769 (1953).
106. J. S. Johnson and K. A. Kraus, *J. Am. Chem. Soc.* **78**, 3937-43 (1956).

The latter study indicated the system to be monodisperse—i.e., it contains only one principle species of polymeric aggregate—and suggested that the stability of the polymeric species reflects a closed-ring structure.

Many studies on zirconium ion species have been made in the presence of perchloric acid on the assumption that it would not complex the zirconium ion. In some of these studies, salts, such as lithium perchlorate, were added to maintain a constant ionic strength during the determinations. Actually there appears to be reaction both of the perchlorate anions and the alkali cations with the zirconium species in solution of zirconium ClBrI halogenides. Lister and McDonald (100) have noted pronounced anionic electromigration of zirconium in strong perchloric acid solutions. P. T. Joseph has stated that he was able to dissolve zirconium cupferrate in perchloric acid, whereas he was unable to dissolve it in hydrochloric acid of the same strength (45). Other investigators have reported that on adding ammonium, rubidium, or cesium chlorides to a solution of zirconyl chloride, exothermic reactions occurred, although no heat effect was found under similar conditions on adding lithium, sodium, or potassium chlorides (107). Evaporation of the cesium-containing mixture gave large crystals of composition $8ZrOCl_2 \cdot 5CsCl \cdot 64H_2O$. The crystals lost 53 molecules of water on heating to about 80°, and became anhydrous at 100°. Thermal data indicated that in the mixture with ammonium chloride, 5 ammonium ions were associated with 7 zirconium atoms, and in the rubidium mixture, 1 rubidium ion was associated with 1 zirconium atom. No crystalline compounds containing ammonium or rubidium were isolated, however.

Certain mixtures of zirconyl bromide and alkali bromides exhibit maximum specific heats, as shown in Table 3.8, and the formation of large crystals of composition $2CsBr \cdot 3ZrOBr_2 \cdot 27H_2O$ has been noted. When these crystals were dried in air, they lost water so as to become a 21 hydrate (108).

TABLE 3.8. COMBINATIONS OF ALKALI BROMIDES AND ZIRCONYL
BROMIDE EXHIBITING MAXIMUM SPECIFIC HEATS (108)

Alkali Bromide	Compositions of Maximum Specific Heats
LiBr	None
NaBr	$NaBr + ZrOBr_2$
NH_4Br	$NH_4Br + ZrOBr_2$
KBr	$2KBr + ZrOBr_2$
RbBr	$2RbBr + 3ZrOBr_2$
CsBr	$2CsBr + 3ZrOBr_2$

107. E. Chauvenet and E. Duchemin, *Compt. rend.* **185**, 774 (1927).
108. E. Chauvenet and J. Boulanger, *Compt. rend.* **197**, 410-11 (1933).

Some odd compositions, such as $ZrOCl_2 \cdot 2HgClC_6H_5$ and $Zr_3O_4Cl_4 \cdot 6HgClC_6H_5$ (109) have been reported, but little is known of their nature.

Zirconyl bromide octahydrate, $ZrOBr_2 \cdot 8H_2O$, formula weight 411.18, occurs as colorless tetragonal crystals which are virtually identical in structure with the chloride analog, and very similar in physical and chemical properties. The crystal parameters are a = 17.45 and c = 7.95 A (84). The compound is very soluble in water and in alcohol and insoluble in ether. Its heat of formation from its elements at 25° is 829.5 kg cal/mole (110). The aqueous solution exhibits Raman spectral lines at 453 and 568 cm^{-1}, the same as for aqueous solutions of the corresponding chloride. The solubility of zirconyl bromide in water decreases when hydrogen bromide is added, but unlike the behavior of the chloride system, no inflection point is reached whereafter the solubility increases with further increase of hydrogen bromide content of the solution (111). Data on these solubility effects are summarized in Table 3.9.

TABLE 3.9. SOLUBILITY OF ZIRCONYL BROMIDE OCTAHYDRATE
IN HYDROBROMIC ACID SOLUTIONS OF VARIOUS
HBR CONTENTS (111)

Molarity of HBr	Moles of ZrOBr₂ Dissolved, per Liter
1.046	2.886
3.488	1.546
6.44	0.2176
13.17	0.012

According to Takagi (6) the thermal dissociation of zirconyl bromide proceeds somewhat differently from that of the chloride, but it too decomposes without going through discrete stages when it is heated. The chief dissociation products are zirconium dioxide and hydrogen bromide, but at 350° some zirconium tetrabromide is formed.

Zirconyl iodide octahydrate, $ZrOI_2 \cdot 8H_2O$, formula weight 505.19, occurs as colorless needles which are hygroscopic in air and very soluble in water and in alcohol. Both the crystals and aqueous solutions are oxidized by air with liberation of iodine.

Zirconyl bromide and zirconyl iodide are prepared by methods similar to those used for the preparation of zirconyl chloride, and much of their chemistry appears to be quite similar. The iodides, however, do not lend themselves to the formation of iodozirconates in alcohol solution, as do

109. W. Peters, *Ber.* **41**, 3173-5 (1908).
110. E. Chauvenet, *Compt. rend.* **164**, 816-8 (1917).
111. G. von Hevesy and O. H. Wagner, *Z. anorg. allgem. Chem.* **191**, 194-200 (1930).

the bromides and chlorides of zirconium (112). Because of the relatively low cost and better availability of zirconyl chloride, relatively little attention has been given to the bromide and iodide.

Uses of the zirconyl halogenides have been limited practically entirely to the chloride. It is the starting material for making many other zirconium compounds and has been used in industry for the preparation of water-repellents, lakes and toners (113), and a number of specialty products. Only a few of these have been described in the literature, for example, as a catalyst in the preparation of butadiene (55), for improving bonds in resin compositions (114), as a component of antiperspirants (115), as a component of a vehicle for textile printing (116). For its applications in organic chemistry, see Chapters 8 and 9.

BASIC ZIRCONYL ClBrI HALOGENIDES

Halogenides of zirconium in which there are less than 2 halogen atoms per zirconium atom, and in which the other components of the molecule are oxygen, water, or its components, are designated generically basic zirconyl halogenides. In a more specific fashion, the term *basic zirconyl halogenide* is applied to compounds of the formula $ZrOOHX$, and special descriptive names are given to the other basic halogenides. For example, the compound $Zr_2O_3Cl_2 \cdot nH_2O$ is called *trioxodizirconium chloride.*

It was found by Endemann that on addition of ether to an alcoholic solution of zirconyl chloride, a solid of composition $ZrOOHCl \cdot nH_2O$ separated (117). Values for n ranging from 0.5 to 2.5 have been reported. It has been shown by X-ray to be amorphous (45). Basic zirconyl bromide is prepared similarly. What appears to be the same substance is formed by heating a slurry containing hydrous zirconia and hydrochloric acid in the molecular ratio 1:1. These reagents also react in the cold, but a period of weeks or months is required to dissolve the hydrous zirconia. The reaction is to be regarded as

$$ZrO_2 \cdot xH_2O + HCl \rightarrow ZrOOHCl \cdot nH_2O + (x-n) H_2O \qquad (27)$$

Again the analogous bromide can be prepared similarly. The solids recovered on evaporation of the solutions have glassy appearances. When heated they condense with liberation of water and finally of ZrO_2 according to the following equations (4, 5):

112. T. Karantassis, *Ann. Chim.* **8,** 71 (1927).
113. W. B. Blumenthal, *Ind. Eng. Chem.* **40,** 510-12 (1948).
114. E. F. Kohl and Z. Kazenas, U.S. Patent **2,749,586,** June 12, 1956.
115. E. G. Helton, E. W. Daley, and J. C. Ervin, *Proc. Sci. Sect. Toilet Goods Assoc.* **26,** 27-31 (1956).
116. H. Gintzel, U.S. Patent **2,611,678,** Sept. 23, 1952.
117. H. Endemann, *J. prakt. Chem.* (2) **11,** 219 (1875).

$$2ZrOOHCl \rightarrow Zr_2O_3Cl_2 + H_2O$$

and $\qquad\qquad 2Zr_2O_3Cl_2 \rightarrow ZrCl_4 + 3ZrO_2 \qquad\qquad$ (28-29)

It has been noted by von Hevesy that some water must be present in an alcohol solution of a zirconium chloride for Endemann's basic zirconyl chloride to be formed in it (87).

It appears likely that the simplest molecular arrangement that can actually occur in basic zirconyl chloride is

$$\left[\begin{array}{c} O \\ \| \\ H_2O \rightarrow Zr{-}OH \end{array} \right]^+ Cl^-$$

and that polymers can form this by the elimination of water from hydroxyl groups between the monomers. Condensations of this type would give substances of empirical formulas corresponding to the hemihydrate noted above and would lead to the glassy structures which have been described. Beside the compositions $Zr_2O_3Cl_2$ and $Zr_2O_3Br_2$ obtained by cautiously heating the corresponding zirconyl halogenides (4, 5, 87, 110), compositions $Zr_3O_4Cl_4$ (118, 119), Zr_2OCl_6 (120), $Zr_{10}O_{19}Cl_2$, and Zr_5O_9OHCl (97) have been reported. Little is known of the nature of these substances.

The author has observed that 2 or 3 moles of sodium carbonate can be added to a solution containing 4 moles of zirconyl chloride without obtaining a permanent precipitate. The resulting solutions are stable on standing or boiling. Under these conditions, hydrated $Zr_2O_3Cl_2$ (113, 30, 121) and Zr_2O_3OHCl (30) are formed:

$$2ZrOCl_2 + Na_2CO_3 \rightarrow Zr_2O_3Cl_2 + 2NaCl + CO_2$$
$$4ZrOCl_2 + 3Na_2CO_3 \rightarrow 2Zr_2O_3OHCl + 6NaCl + 3CO_2$$

(30-31)

The same products can be prepared by treating carbonated hydrous zirconia with the appropriate amounts of hydrochloric acid:

$$Zr_2O_3(OH)_2 \cdot CO_2 + HCl \rightarrow Zr_2O_3OHCl + H_2O + CO_2$$
$$Zr_2O_3OHCl + HCl \rightarrow Zr_2O_3Cl_2 + H_2O$$

(32-33)

On evaporating the aqueous solutions to dryness, trioxodizirconium hydroxychloride and trioxodizirconium chloride are recovered as glassy solids containing water of hydration. The corresponding bromides and iodides have been prepared similarly and have similar appearances. X-ray diffraction study has verified their amorphous structure. The solids readily redissolve in water (45).

118. R. Hermann, *J. prakt. Chem,* **31,** 75 (1844).
119. H. Lange, *Z. Naturwiss.* **82,** 1 (1910).
120. L. Troost and P. Hautefeuille, *Compt. rend.* **73,** 563 (1871).
121. W. B. Blumenthal, *J. Chem. Ed.* **26,** 472-5 (1949).

The formation of the trioxodizirconium ion is apparently catalyzed by carbon dioxide, or more specifically, carbonic acid:

$$2ZrOOH^+ \xrightarrow{H_2CO_3} Zr_2O_3{}^{+2} + H_2O \qquad (34)$$

The evidence of this is easily demonstrated. If sodium hydroxide solution is added to zirconyl chloride solution, insoluble hydrous zirconia forms before a mole of alkali has been added per mole of zirconyl chloride. On the other hand, an equivalent amount of alkali can be added to the zirconyl chloride solution in the form of sodium carbonate or sodium bircarbonate without formation of a permanent precipitate. If carbon dioxide is bubbled into a zirconyl chloride solution while sodium hydroxide is being added, the sodium hydroxide does not precipitate hydrous zirconia when added mole for mole. The catalysis presumably entails the formation of an unstable complex:

$$HO{-}Zr^+ + \underset{\underset{H}{HO{-}C{=}O}}{O} + {}^+Zr{-}OH \rightarrow \left[HO{-}Zr \longleftarrow \underset{\underset{H}{HO{-}C{=}O}}{O} \longrightarrow Zr{-}OH \right]^{+2} \quad (35)$$

$$H_2CO_3 + \left[{-}Zr{-}O{-}Zr{-} \right]^{+2} + H_2O$$

The structural differences between ZrOOHCl and $Zr_2O_3Cl_2$, which contain the same ratio of chlorine to zirconium, are reflected in a number of chemical behaviors. The addition of base to the former causes precipitation of hydrous zirconia, while the latter can be converted to water-soluble trioxodizirconium hydroxychloride. The author has prepared stearates from solutions of the two salts and obtained products of the same ratio of stearic acid to zirconium, i.e., $ZrOOHO_2CC_{17}H_{35}$ and $Zr_2O_3(O_2CC_{17}H_{35})_2$, which exhibited different solubility behavior in hydrocarbons, different infrared absorption spectra, and different thermal decomposition patterns (45).

Trioxodizirconium chloride has been used in industry in the preparation of lakes and toners from acid dyes (113), and in water repellents (125).

A chloride of composition $Zr_5O_8Cl_4 \cdot 22H_2O$ has been prepared by dissolution of a zirconium hydroxide of the same cation with hydrochloric acid. The formation of such a hydroxide from complex sulfato compounds of zirconium is discussed in Chapter 6. The chloride compound was purified by recrystallization from hydrochloric acid of specific gravity 1.088 (122, 123, 124). It has not proved possible to form this chloride except through the

122. E. H. Rodd, *J. Chem. Soc.* **111**, 396-407 (1917).
123. R. T. Glazebrook, W. Rosenhain, and E. H. Rodd, British patent **112,973**, Jan. 29, 1917.
124. W. Rosenhain and E. H. Rodd, U.S. Patent **1,307,882**, June 24, 1919.

formation of the Zr_5O_8 radical in a sulfate system. It appears probable that the arrangement of atoms in the Zr_5O_8 radical and ion is that indicated by the formula $(—Zr—O—)_4Zr$, and the zirconium atoms are highly hydrated.

$$\overset{\Vert}{O}$$

On the addition of oxalates or sulfates to solutions of octaoxopentazirconium chloride, precipitates form and then redissolve as excesses of the precipitating solutions are added, indicating the formation of insoluble and soluble oxalato and sulfato complexes, as discussed in Chapters 8 and 6.

FLUORINE COMPOUNDS OF ZIRCONIUM

INTRODUCTION

The chemistry of the fluorine compounds of zirconium is different from that of the ClBrI halogen compounds primarily because of the greater strength of the Zr-F bond and because of the smaller size of the fluorine atom, which permits a greater number of them to be bound to a zirconium atom. A particularly important aspect of the high strength of the Zr-F bond is that it is stable in the presence of water, whereas the other halogens are generally replaced from zirconium by water. The aqueous chemistry of the fluorine compounds of zirconium is therefore much different from that of the other halogen compounds. Because of the small size of the fluorine atom, as many as 8 fluorine atoms may be bound to a single zirconium atom, and compounds are known, with 2, 3, 4, 5, 6, 7, and 8 fluorine atoms bound to a zirconium atom. In compounds containing less than 8 fluorine atoms per zirconium atom, the zirconium atom often attains to a coordination number of 7 or 8 by sharing fluorine atoms with nearby zirconium atoms, or by forming addition compounds with components of the environment.

Although there are no known major occurrences of zirconium in nature in fluorine compounds, rocks containing fluorine compounds of zirconium have been reported to occur at the tops of magma chambers in the Fen district of Norway (126).

THE FLUOZIRCONIC ACIDS

Hydrofluoric acid dissolves zirconium metal, zirconium carbide, dioxide, arsenates, arsenites, phosphates, phosphites, antimonates, mandelates, and other compounds of zirconium which generally resist dissolution by strong mineral acids. It is in a class by itself as a powerful solvent for zirconium compounds, and it is apparent that its extraordinary solvent powers are as-

125. S. F. Urban and W. B. Blumenthal, U.S. Patent **2,641,558**, June 9, 1953.
126. E. Saether, *Intern. Geol. Rept., 184th Session, Gt. Britain 1948*, Pt. II, 123-30 (Pub. 1950).

sociated with the formation of one or more exceedingly stable complex fluozirconic acids.

Prideau and Roper added hydrogen fluoride to a "zirconium fluoride" solution and observed the separation of colorless prismatic needles. The needles lost hydrogen fluoride on exposure to air. These investigators analyzed their product, estimated a correction for the loss of hydrogen fluoride, and concluded that the crystals must originally have been a hexafluozirconic acid, $H_2ZrF_6 \cdot 3H_2O$ (127). Ruff and Lauschke observed a solid of composition $H_3Zr_2F_{11} \cdot 5H_2O$ to separate from a fluoride solution of zirconium which had a strength of 40% with respect to hydrofluoric acid (128). The analyses of Prideau and Roper actually fit this formula better than the one which they proposed. Since salts of polyzirconic acids are known, it is not improbable that a polyacid of this type exists. However, the composition could also be a mixture of acids such as $H_2ZrF_6 \cdot 2H_2O$ and $H_2ZrOHF_5 \cdot 2H_2O$. Recently a phase of composition $H_2ZrF_6 \cdot H_2O$ has been observed to be stable in aqueous systems of high HF contents at low temperatures (133).

Chauvenet dissolved hydrous zirconia in hydrofluoric acid and evaporated the solution. Crystals of oxotetrafluozirconic acid, $H_2ZrOF_4 \cdot 2H_2O$, separated (129). Von Hevesy and Wagner made similar preparations from 5 and 10 N hydrofluoric acid solutions and recovered the same solid phase, which they noted to be stable over a broad range of hydrofluoric acid concentrations. They also prepared the analogous hafnium acid and noted its properties to be similar to those of the zirconium compound, although it was less soluble. In 20 N hydrofluoric acid, the solubility of the oxotetrafluozirconic acid was 2.34 moles per liter whereas that of the oxotetrafluohafnic acid was 1.229 moles per liter (111). No salts of oxotetrafluozirconic or oxotetrafluohafnic acid are known. Under the conditions of salt formation reported up to this time, at least 5 fluorine atoms become associated with each zirconium or hafnium atom. Hydrolysis of oxotetrafluozirconic acid leads to the formation of acids of higher oxygen and lower fluorine contents.

Oxotetrafluozirconic acid, $H_2ZrOF_4 \cdot 2H_2O$, formula weight 221.338, occurs as colorless, prismatic or tabular triclinic crystals of axial ratios a:b:c = 0.7636:1:0.6390, with $\alpha = 104°48'$, $\beta = 110°59'$, and $\gamma = 103°53'$. Identical crystals are obtained on recrystallizing the compound from aqueous solution, but in addition, some $H_2ZrO_2F_2 \cdot H_2O$ forms as a hydrolysis product. It is very soluble in water and in hydrofluoric acid. Solubility data are given in Table 3.10.

---

127. E. B. R. Prideau and E. C. Roper, *J. Chem. Soc.* **129**, 898 (1926).

128. O. Ruff and G. Lauschke, *Z. anorg. allgem. Chem.* **97**, 110 (1916).

129. E. Chauvenet, *Compt. rend.* **164**, 727 (1917).

TABLE 3.10. SOLUBILITY OF $H_2ZrOF_4 \cdot 2H_2O$ IN WATER AND HYDROFLUORIC ACID SOLUTIONS AT 25° (130)

Normality of hydrofluoric acid	Gram-molecules of $H_2ZrOF_4 \cdot 2H_2O$ per liter	Grams of ZrO_2 by assay, per liter	$d_{25}{}^4$
0.0	3.300	406.3	1.488
0.0	3.332	410.7	1.490
1.06	4.078	502.2	1.559
1.06	4.030	496.5	1.608
6.03	4.639	571.8	1.712
6.03	4.639	571.7	1.711
10.05	4.455	548.5	1.685
10.05	4.459	549.6	1.690
15.05	3.608	444.3	1.600
20.07	2.340	288.3	1.430

Oxotetrafluozirconic acid is stable in air, but it loses water on heating. The dehydration begins at about 100° and the composition H_2ZrOF_4 is attained at 140°. On further heating, hydrogen fluoride is liberated and a residue of $ZrOF_2$ remains (129).

Oxotetrafluozirconic acid dihydrate is not structurally similar to the hydrated thorium tetrafluoride (131).

The anhydrous H_2ZrOF_4 has a body-centered tetragonal lattice for which a = 7.715 ± 0.01 A and c = 11.65 ± 0.1 A. There are 8 molecules per unit cell. It decomposes *in vacuo* or on heating in air to 250° (132).

A phase study of the system ZrF_4-HF-H_2O, in which the proportion of HF:H_2O ranged from 0:100 to 100:0 showed the solid phases $H_2ZrO_2F_2 \cdot H_2O$, $H_2ZrOF_4 \cdot 2H_2O$, and $H_2ZrF_6 \cdot H_2O$ to exist. The first occurred when the liquid phase contained concentrations of HF from 2.21-3.395%, and ZrO_2 3.14-6-19%; the second at 5.84-30.00% HF and 7.92-32.37% ZrO_2; and the third at 31.63-84.35% HF and 0.015-31.95% ZrO_2. $H_2ZrF_6 \cdot H_2O$ loses 2HF at 11.2° to become H_2ZrOF_4. The latter loses HF at 262-267° with formation of $HZrOF_3$ and more HF at 304-306° with formation of $ZrOF_2$ (133).

130. G. von Hevesy and O. H. Wagner, Z. anorg. allgem. Chem. 191, 194-200 (1930).

131. R. W. M. D'Eye, and G. W. Booth, J. Inorg. Nuclear Chem. 1, 326-33 (1955).

132. R. W. M. D'Eye, J. P. Burden, and E. A. Harper, J. Inorg. Nuclear Chem. 2, 192-5 (1956).

133. I. V. Tananaev, N. S. Nikolaev, and Yu. A. Buslaev. Zhur. Neorg. Khim. 1, 274-8 (1956).

THE ANHYDROFLUORIDES, ZrF_4 AND $ZrOF_2$

The compounds of composition ZrF_4 and $ZrOF_2$ both react with hydrofluoric acid with formation of complex fluozirconic acids (129), and their relationship to hydrogen fluoride is the same as that of the acid anhydrides to water. They do not exhibit saltlike qualities. They can therefore be regarded as anhydrofluorides.

Zirconium oxide difluoride, $ZrOF_2$, can be prepared by heating the acid $H_2ZrOF_4 \cdot 2H_2O$ or its dehydration products to about 200°. When it is brought to a red heat in air or in superheated steam, it is decomposed with formation of zirconium dioxide. Reportedly zirconium oxide difluoride has value as a cracking catalyst, giving high yields of butene and pentene (134). Otherwise little is known about the compound and its derivatives.

Zirconium tetrafluoride, ZrF_4, has been prepared by numerous methods which are summarized in Table 3.11. Although fluorine reacts with zirconium metal quite readily at low temperatures, the formation of a coating of fluoride brings the reaction to a halt (135). Because of this and of the cost and difficulty entailed in using fluorine, other methods of preparation are preferable. A particularly satisfactory laboratory procedure consists in heating ammonium fluozirconate to 300°. The ammonium fluozirconate can conveniently be precipitated in anhydrous condition from aqueous solutions and the physically held water evaporated off (178).

All compounds of zirconium with oxygen and fluorine are converted to zirconium tetrafluoride when heated to about 500-550° under a flow of hydrogen fluoride gas (136). The process is rendered rather costly by the necessity of supplying a current of anhydrous hydrogen fluoride which becomes contaminated with water vapor by reaction with the oxygen of the zirconium compound. For analytical purposes, zirconium dioxide can, in effect, be volatilized by repeatedly heating it with hydrofluoric acid in the presence of small amounts of sulfuric acid (137).

TABLE 3.11. METHODS FOR PREPARING ZIRCONIUM TETRAFLUORIDE

Description and Equation*	Literature
1. Synthesis from the elements	135
$Zr + 2F_2 \xrightarrow{>190°} ZrF_4$	
2. Displacement of oxygen	135
$ZrO_2 + 2F_2 \xrightarrow{525°} ZrF_4 + O_2$	

134. S. M. Darling, U.S. Patent **2,449,061,** *Sept.* 14, 1948.

135. H. M. Haendler, S. F. Bartram, R. S. Becker, W. J. Bernard, and W. W. Bukata, *J. Am. Chem. Soc.* **76,** 2177-8 (1954).

136. H. A. Wilhelm and K. A. Walsh, U.S. Patent **2,635,037,** April 14, 1953.

137. E. Wedekind, *Ber.* **44,** 1753-7 (1911).

TABLE 3.11. Continued

Description and Equation*	Literature

3. Thermal decomposition of fluozirconates — 43, 138

$$(NH_4)_2ZrF_6 \xrightarrow{<300°} ZrF_4 + 2NH_4F$$

4. Metathesis from the oxide — 137

$$ZrO_2 + 4HF \xrightarrow{550°} ZrF_4 + 2H_2O$$ — 106

5. Metathesis from zircon — 139

$$ZrO_2 \cdot SiO_2 + 8HF \xrightarrow[heat]{white} ZrF_4 + SiF_4 + 4H_2O$$

6. Metathesis from the tetrachloride — 43, 140

$$ZrCl_4 + 4HF \longrightarrow ZrF_4 + 4HCl$$

7. Hydrofluorination of oxyfluozirconic acids — 142b

$$H_2ZrO_2F_2 + 2HF \xrightarrow{550°} ZrF_4 + 2H_2O$$

* Other methods have been reported for the formation of zirconium tetrafluoride but have not yet been proved suitable for actual preparation, e.g., the metathesis of zirconia with chromic fluoride in molten cryolite (141). Metathesis of zirconium tetrachloride with hydrogen fluoride in an organic liquid medium has also been described (142).

Zirconium tetrafluoride, ZrF_4, formula weight 167.29, is a colorless, crystalline solid of specific gravity 4.4333 at 16° (43). Its heat of formation from its elements at 25° is 445 kg cal/mole. It has a monoclinic crystal lattice in which each zirconium atom is coordinated by 8 fluorine atoms in the form of a square Archimedean antiprism, and each fluorine atom is coordinated by 2 zirconium atoms. The structure is a three-dimensional array of antiprism polyhedra which are joined by sharing corners. The crystal parameters are a = 9.57, b = 9.93, c = 7.73 A, and $\beta = 94°28'$ (143, 144). Similar structures are exhibited by cerium, neptunium, plutonium, terbium, thorium, and uranium tetrafluorides (145, 146). Eighteen spectral bands of zirconium tetrafluoride have been observed between 4897 and 5061 A (147). The vapor pressure is given by the equation log $p_{mm} = 13.2206 - 12146.2/T$, over the range 688-826°. The extrapolated boiling point is

138. G. von Hevesy and W. Dullenkopf, *Z. anorg. allgem. Chem.* **221,** 161-6 (1934).
139. H. St. C. Deville, *Ann. chim. phys.* **49,** (3) 84 (1857); **5,** (4) 109 (1865).
140. C. Woolf, U.S. Patent **2,805,121,** Sept. 3, 1957.
141. P. Mergault, *Compt. rend.* **239,** 1215-7 (1954).
142. O. F. Sprague, U.S. Patent **2,789,882,** April 23, 1957.
142b. K. A. Walsh, *U.S. Atomic Energy Comm. AECD-3640,* 57 pp. (1950).
143. R. D. Burbank and F. N. Bensey, Jr., *Union Carbide Nuclear Co. (Oak Ridge) Report,* Oct. 31, 1956; *U.S. Atomic Energy Comm. K-1280,* 19 pp. (1956).
144. G. E. R. Schulze, *Z. Krist.* **89,** 477-80 (1934).
145. W. H. Zachariasen, *Acta Cryst.* **2,** 388-90 (1949).
146. B. B. Cunningham, D. C. Feay, and M. A. Rollier, *J. Am. Chem. Soc.* **76,** 3361-3 (1954).
147. M. Afaf, *Proc. Phys. Soc. London* **63A,** 544-5 (1950).

902° and the heat of sublimation 55.55 kg cal/mole (148, 149). The vapor is monomolecular, and there has been no evidence for dissociation at the highest temperatures observed.

When zirconium tetrafluoride is added to water, it is superficially hydrolyzed and only a minute amount of zirconium goes into solution. It tends to fume in moist air, but if the crystals are annealed before exposure, they appear to become inert. Thus, by completing the conversion of zirconium tetrachloride to the tetrafluoride at 300°, a nonhygroscopic product was obtained which did not fume in moist air (150). At 25° about 1.5 g of zirconium tetrafluoride has been observed to dissolve in 100 g of water, and at 50° 1.388 g. The compound is dissolved by aqueous hydrofluoric acid and by hot, concentrated sulfuric acid. In liquid hydrogen fluoride, 0.009 ± 0.002 g of ZrF_4 dissolves per 100 g of the solvent at 12.4°, and 0.023 ± 0.002 g at $-23.1°$ (149, 151). It dissolves in bromine trifluoride to the extent of 0.0016 moles per mole of the solvent (149). It is virtually insoluble in all organic solvents, but it is soluble in molten alkali fluorides. It appears not to react with gaseous ammonia, but in liquid ammonia it forms a white powder of composition $5ZrF_4 \cdot 2NH_3$ (43). It does not react with liquid hydrogen sulfide nor with pyridine.

When zirconium tetrafluoride is heated with magnesium chloride, it is decomposed with evolution of zirconium tetrachloride vapor (152). When it is heated with boric oxide, it is decomposed with evolution of boron trifluoride vapor (139).

Zirconium tetrafluoride can be used as a starting material in the preparation of zirconium metal by reduction with magnesium, calcium, or other active metals (152b), but since it is relatively difficult to separate the fluoride salts formed in the process from the metal, and because of difficulties encountered in preparing zirconium tetrafluoride free of oxygen, this method has not been used to any significant extent. A number of promising catalytic uses for zirconium tetrafluoride have been described. It is an effective cracking catalyst for heavy hydrocarbons (134, 153). It catalyzes the fluorination of CCl_3CClF_2 to $CClF_2CClF_2$, and is particularly effective in obtaining this product free of assymetrical isomers (154). (For regeneration of zirconium tetrafluoride catalysts, see reference 155.)

148. K. A. Sense, M. J. Snyder, and J. W. Clegg, *U.S. Atomic Energy Comm. AECD-3708*, 18 pp. (1953).

149. I. Sheft, H. H. Hyman, and J. J. Katz, *J. Am. Chem. Soc.* **75**, 5221-3 (1953).

150. H. A. Wilhelm and K. A. Walsh, U.S. Patent **2,602,725**, July 8, 1952.

151. A. W. Jache and G. H. Cady, *J. Phys. Chem.* **56**, 1106-9 (1952).

152. W. B. Blumenthal, U.S. Patent **2,626,203**, Jan. 20, 1953.

152b. C. J. Baroch and G. H. Beyer, *U.S. Atomic Energy Comm. ISC-720*, May 31, 1956.

153. S. M. Darling, U.S. Patent **2,524,771**, Oct. 10, 1950.

154. C. Woolf, U.S. Patent **2,714,618**, Aug. 2, 1955.

155. S. Bandes and C. B. Miller, U.S. Patent **2,709,688**, May 31, 1955.

A zirconium fluoride monosulfonate is said to form on heating zirconium tetrafluoride with an excess of fluosulfonic acid (156).

THE FLUOZIRCONATES

Numerous fluozirconate salts have been prepared in which 5, 6, 7, or 8 fluorine atoms are present per zirconium atom, and also a few in which the ratio of fluorine to zirconium atoms is not a whole number. The simplest preparations are those in which an oxide, hydroxide, or carbonate of a suitable metal is added to a hydrofluoric acid solution of a zirconium compound. Well-formed crystals of metal fluozirconates separate from such mixtures. When neither of the metallic compounds is present in large excess, and when the total fluoride ion in the system is approximately equivalent to the metal content, metal hexafluozirconates usually are formed. Pure species are obtained only with care. Aside from the common contamination of the fluozirconates with fluohafnates, one or more species of fluozirconate may be obtained, and the products may be contaminated with small amounts of hydrolysis products and by occlusions, such as of water. However, many species of fluozirconates are remarkably stable. Such a complex type as $Na_5Zr_2F_{11}$ can be recrystallized from water without change.

Fluozirconates are known only of the univalent and divalent cations. Interestingly, clearly defined fluozirconates of calcium, strontium, and barium have not been reported. Fluozirconates of organic bases such as aniline, brucine, cinchonine, quinine, quinoline, and strychnine have been prepared by adding alcoholic solutions of these organic bases to fluozirconic acid solutions, and evaporating to dryness. Solid organic salts are obtained in this fashion (157, 158, 159). These compounds are all colorless, show some solubility in ethanol, and except the strychnine compound, considerable solubility in water.

Wells and Foote have noted that the alkalies of lower atomic weight (and hence of lower ionic radius) tend to form fluozirconates of higher alkali fluoride contents than the alkalies of higher atomic weight (160). Their data, plus some additions, are summarized in Table 3.12.

It is of particular interest to ascertain, in so far as present knowledge permits, how many atoms of fluorine are actually bound to each zirconium atom in the solid fluozirconates and in their solutions. X-ray diffraction studies of potassium hexafluozirconate, K_2ZrF_6, have shown each zirconium atom to be surrounded by 8 fluorine atoms, 4 of which are shared by adjacent polyhedra. These structural units are connected in chainlike fashion

156. E. Hayek, J. Puschmann, and A. Czaloun, *Monatsh.* **85**, 359-64 (1954).
157. F. Kraze, *Ber. deut. keram, Ges.* **3**, 3 (1922).
158. J. L. K. Snyder, Thesis, University of Pennsylvania (1909).
159. M. M. Windsor, *J. Am. Chem. Soc.* **48**, 310 (1926).
160. H. L. Wells and H. W. Foote, *Am. J. Sci.* **3**, 461 (1897).

in the direction of the c axis of the orthorhombic crystal lattice. The cations are located in the neighborhoods of the junctions of the connecting polyhedra. A similar structure occurs in the isomorphous potassium fluohafnate (161). As in zirconium tetrafluoride, the zirconium atom is coordinated by 8 fluorine atoms in the alkali hexafluozirconates.

Fluozirconates with zirconium atoms at lower coordination number have been observed under other conditions. The vapor pressures over the system $NaF-ZrF_4$ were measured over the range 599-1075°, and it was possible to deduce from the measurements that the vapor contained the molecule $NaZrF_5$. There were indications for the existence of the heptafluozirconate ion, ZrF_7^{-3} in the liquid state (162). Differential thermal analysis of ammonium heptafluozirconate indicated the decomposition to proceed according to the pattern $(NH_4)_3ZrF_7 \rightarrow (NH_4)_2ZrF_6 \rightarrow NH_4ZrF_5 \rightarrow ZrF_4$. The

TABLE 3.12. TYPES OF FLUOZIRCONATES FORMED BY VARIOUS ALKALIES (160)

Alkali Cation	Empirical Mole Ratio of Alkali Fluoride to Zirconium Tetrafluoride						
	4:1	3:1	5:2	2:1	5:3	1:1	2:3
Li^+	Li_4ZrF_8			Li_2ZrF_6			
NH_4^+		$(NH_4)_3ZrF_7$		$(NH_4)_2ZrF_6$		NH_4ZrF_5	
Na^+			$Na_5Zr_2F_{13}$	Na_2ZrF_6			
K^+		K_3ZrF_7		K_2ZrF_6		$KZrF_5$	
Rb^+		Rb_3ZrF_7		Rb_2ZrF_6			
Tl^+		Tl_3ZrF_7			$Tl_5Zr_3F_{17}$	$TlZrF_5$	
Cs^+				Cs_2ZrF_6		$CsZrF_5$	$Cs_2Zr_3F_{14}$

temperatures for the three successive decompositions were 297°, 357°, and 410° at 760 mm, 288°, 355°, and 404° at 515 mm, 235°, 288°, and 380° at 120 mm, and 203°, 244°, and 298° at 20 mm. Approximate values for the heats of decomposition were 21, 21, and 25 kg cal/mole, respectively (163).

From the cited evidence for monomolecules of formula ZrF_4 and $NaZrF_5$ in the vapor phase, there is a presumption that zirconium-fluorine compounds exist in which the zirconium is at coordination number 4 or 5, except in so far as double bonding between the zirconium atom and one or more of its associated fluorine atoms raises this number. In all events, the lower coordination numbers do not persist in the crystal lattice or in aqueous

161. H. Bode and G. Teufer, *Acta Cryst.* **9**, 929-33 (1956).

162. K. A. Sense, C. A. Alexander, R. E. Bowman, and R. B. Filbert, Jr., *J. Phys. Chem.* **61**, 337-44 (1957).

163. H. M. Haendler, C. M. Wheeler, Jr., and D. W. Robinson, *J. Am. Chem. Soc.* **74**, 352-3 (1952).

solutions. A solution of potassium hexafluozirconate containing approximately 1% by weight of the salt has a pH of about 4.0 at room temperature. Since simple hydrolysis of a salt of a strong base cannot yield an acidic reaction, it follows that the acidity must be due to the removal of hydroxyl ions from solution by reaction with the fluozirconate ion:

$$\text{ZrF}_6^{-2} + \text{OH}^- \rightarrow \text{HOZrF}_6^{-3} \tag{36}$$

It remains to be ascertained to what extent loss of fluoride ions from the complex, through dissociation or replacement by hydroxyl, occurs during equilibration of the hexafluozirconate salt with water. If potassium fluoride is added to the solution, the pH rises, indicating the formation of heptafluozirconate:

$$\text{HOZrF}_6^{-3} + \text{F}^- \rightarrow \text{ZrF}_7^{-3} + \text{OH}^- \tag{37}$$

When ammonium hydroxide is added to a solution of potassium hexafluozirconate, a precipitate is obtained which after drying has the composition $\text{H}_3\text{ZrO}_2\text{F}_3 \cdot 3\text{H}_2\text{O}$ (45, cf. 178). All these observations support the hypothesis that in aqueous solutions of fluozirconates, the coordination number of zirconium is at least 7.

While the alkali hexa- and heptafluozirconates generally crystallize as anhydrous solids, the pentafluozirconates are often hydrated, or more specifically, contain hydroxyl groups in the anions:

$$\text{KZrF}_5 \cdot \text{H}_2\text{O} = \text{KHZrOHF}_5 \tag{38}$$

The observations on the behavior of fluozirconates in aqueous solution indicate that the Zr-F bond is more stable than $\text{Zr} \leftarrow \text{OH}_2$, but generally not more stable than the Zr-OH bond. At equal concentrations or activities of hydroxyl and fluoride ion, much of the fluoride will be replaced from the zirconium by hydroxyl. The fluozirconates have been observed to be decomposed by strong caustic alkali, and the decomposition product is said to be hydrous zirconia (164, 165).

A summary of the methods of preparation of fluozirconates is given in Table 3.13.

The chief use of fluozirconates has been in the metallurgy of aluminum and magnesium, for which they supply a small content of zirconium which refines the grain and increases the strength of these structural metals. The alloy is formed by adding alkali or alkaline earth fluozirconates, or mixtures of them, to the molten aluminum or magnesium, whereupon chemical reaction liberates zirconium metal and it dissolves in the metal. The final alloys generally contain about 0.2-0.3% zirconium. It appears to be advantageous

164. H. C. Clafin and D. O. Hubbard, British patent **391,369**, April 27, 1933; German patent **603,476**, Oct. 3, 1934.

165. H. H. Friedel, U.S. Patent **2,610,104**, Sept. 9, 1952.

to use mixtures of fluozirconates for the application to magnesium, so that the fluozirconates will melt at the temperature of the molten metal. Better recovery of zirconium into the basis metal is obtained from the liquid fluozirconates than from the solids (166). The salt mixtures may contain chlorides as well as fluorides (167).

Fluozirconates have been reported to be useful as stabilizers for silicone rubber (168), and as a welding flux for coating ferrous metal or joining pieces of ferrous metal with molten aluminum (169). Potassium fluozirconate increases the durability of beryllium-aluminum-lead fluoride optical glass (170). Ammonium fluozirconate in chromic acid solution has shown value in increasing the resistance of a number of metals (steel, zinc, aluminum alloy) to corrosion (171). Other uses include the stabilization of alginate compositions used as plastics for dental impressions (172), and in analysis for the isolation of fluoride ion (173) or of zirconium, particularly from atomic fission products (174, 175).

166. C. J. P. Ball, A. C. Jessup, E. F. Emley, and J. B. Wilson, U.S. Patent **2,452,894,** Nov. 2, 1948.

167. E. F. Emley, British patent **715,967,** Sept. 22, 1954.

168. R. R. Maneri, U.S. Patent **2,658,882,** Nov. 10, 1953.

169. H. Lundin, U.S. Patents **2,686,354** and **2,686,355,** Aug. 17, 1954.

170. T. Izumitani and R. Terai, *Bull. Osaka Ind. Research Inst.* **3,** 25-8 (1952).

171. J. A. Carroll and N. J. Newhard, Jr., U.S. Patent **2,795,518,** June 11, 1957.

172. A. Fink, U.S. Patent **2,652,312,** Sept. 15, 1953.

173. Yu. A. Chernikov and E. I. Vendel'shtein, *Zavodskaya Lab.* **13,** 815-16 (1947).

174. R. E. Waters and D. N. Hume, *Nat. Nuclear Energy Ser. Div. IV, 9, Radiochem. Studies: The Fission Products,* Book 3, 1507-9 (1951).

175. D. N. Hume, *ibid.,* 1499-503 (1951).

TABLE 3.13. PREPARATION AND PROPERTIES OF FLUOZIRCONATES

Formula	Methods of Preparation	Properties
NH_4ZrF_5	Rapid crystallization from an aqueous HF solution of Zr, containing 75% of the theoretical proportion of NH_4F (176)	Distinctive X-ray pattern (176)
$NH_4HZrOHF_5$	Slow crystallization from a solution similar to the above (176)	Distinctive X-ray pattern; in dry air, $NH_4HZrOHF_5$ loses water to NH_4ZrF_5 (176)
$KHZrOHF_5$	Addition of KF solution to an excess of H_2ZrOF_4 solution, or addition of KCl to a solution containing H_2ZrOF_4, HF, and HCl (177)	Monoclinic prisms; loses water at 100° and the residual composition melts at 470°; aqueous solutions unstable (178)
$TlZrF_5$	Addition of 1 part of TlF to 3-4 parts of H_2ZrOF_4 in aqueous solution, then evaporation until crystallization begins, followed by cooling (160)	Minute, square plates
$TlHZrOHF_5$	Like $TlZrF_5$, but cooling before crystallization of the reacting mixture begins (160)	
$CsHZrOHF_5$	Crystallization from a mixture of solutions containing about the same number of moles each of CsF and H_2ZrOF_4 (160)	Can be recrystallized from water without change
$CdH_2(ZrOHF_5)_2 \cdot 4H_2O$	Recrystallization from a mixture of solutions of CdF_2 and H_2ZrOF_4, containing an excess of the latter (178)	Occurs as lamellated crystals
Li_2ZrF_6	Crystallization from a mixture of 2 solutions, the first containing 0.7-2.0 g LiF and the second 22 g H_2ZrOF_4 (160)	Hexagonal prisms showing prism and pyramid, and rarely the basal plane (160)

TABLE 3.13. Continued

Formula	Methods of Preparation	Properties
$(NH_4)_2ZrF_6$	Evaporation of a mixture of solutions of NH_4F and H_2ZrOF_4 (rhombic bipyramidal crystals separate first, then hexagonal plates) (178)	Rhombic: axial ratios $a{:}b{:}c$ = 0.5739:1:0.6590, isomorphous with K salt (178)
		Hexagonal: perfect cleavage parallel to c axis (179)
		Other properties: stable at 100°, but decomposes at higher temperatures to ZrF_4 and NH_4F; solubility in water in moles per 1 (180):

		temperature	*solubility*
		0°	0.611
		20°	1.050
		45°	1.842
		90°	2.96

decomposes in hot sulfuric acid; not isomorphous with $(NH_4)_2TiF_6$

Formula	Methods of Preparation	Properties
Na_2ZrF_6	Crystallization from a solution containing 1 to 2 parts NaF and 15 parts H_2ZrOF_4 (160); also by heating Zr ores with Na_2SiF_6 (181)	Decomposes on recrystallization from water; crystals may contain up to about 2% mechanically entrapped water
K_2ZrF_6	Crystallization from a solution containing KF and more than its equivalence of H_2ZrOF_4 (178); also, fusing zircon with KHF_2 (182); also heating zirconia or zircon with K_2SiF_6 (181)	No loss of weight at red heat; melts about 840°; solubility in g per 100 g water (182):

temperature	*solubility*
10°	1.22
20°	1.55
30°	1.92
40°	2.37
50°	2.94
60°	3.81
70°	5.06
80°	6.90
90°	11.11
100°	23.53

TABLE 3.13. Continued

Formula	Methods of Preparation	Properties
Rb_2ZrF_6	Crystallization from a solution containing an equal number of moles of RbF and H_2ZrOF_4	Hexagonal plates with negative birefringence; can be recrystallized from water (160)
Cs_2ZrF_6	Crystallization from a solution containing more than 1 mole of CsF per mole H_2ZrOF_4 (160)	Monoclinic plates with curved surfaces; on calcination the salt yields magnesia and zirconia (178)
$MgZrF_6 \cdot 5H_2O$	Addition of magnesia to H_2ZrOF_4 solution; evaporation of a solution containing MgF_2 and H_2ZrOF_4 (178)	Long hexagonal prismatic crystals terminating in rhombohedra; axial ratio a:c = 1:0.5176; perfect cleavage along hexagonal faces; sp. gr. 2.258; on calcination it yields zinc and zirconium oxides (178)
$ZnZrF_6$	Crystallization from a solution containing ZnF_2 and H_2ZrOF_4 (178)	
$MnZrF_6 \cdot 5H_2O$	Addition of manganese carbonate to a solution containing H_2ZrOF_4 and HF (178)	Monoclinic crystals of axial ratio a:b:c = 2.090:1: 1.84, $\beta = 123°10'$; the cleavage sometimes exhibits a tubular habit and twinning; isomorphous with the magnesium salt; decomposed by sulfuric acid; on calcination it yields manganese and zirconium oxides (178)
$NiZrF_6$	Evaporation of a solution containing NiF_2 and H_2ZrOF_4 (178)	Green, thick trigonal prisms of axial ratio a:c = 1:0.5176; cleavage is complete; on calcination it yields nickel and zirconium oxides (178)
$K_2Ni(ZrF_6)_2 \cdot 8H_2O$	Crystallization from a solution containing both K_2ZrF_6 and $NiZrF_6 \cdot 6H_2O$, which have been dissolved together by heating the solution, following which the solution is allowed to cool and stand (178)	Pale-green monoclinic prisms, sparingly soluble in water at room temperature; axial ratios a:b:c = 0.6589:1:1.1789 and $\beta = 95°40'$; the habit of the crystals is variable; no water lost at 100°, and HF evolved at higher temperature (178)

147

Table 3.13. Continued

Formula	Methods of Preparation	Properties
$(NH_4)_3ZrF_7$	Crystallization from a solution containing NH_4F and H_2ZrOF_4, the former in large excess (178)	Holohedral face-centered cubic crystals with 4 molecules in the unit cell and a = 9.365 A, sp. gr. 1.433 (184, 185, 186); isomorphous with K_3ZrF_7 and $(NH_4)_3HfF_7$; stable at 100; solubility in water in moles per 1 (180): <table><tr><td>*temperature*</td><td>*solubility*</td></tr><tr><td>0°</td><td>0.425</td></tr><tr><td>20°</td><td>0.588</td></tr><tr><td>45°</td><td>0.788</td></tr></table>
K_3ZrF_7	Crystallization from a solution containing KF and H_2ZrOF_4, the former in excess	Cubic crystals isomorphous with $(NH_4)_3ZrF_7$, with a = 8.951 A (178, 185); index of refraction 1.433 (184); one form of K_3UF_7 is similar (145)
Rb_3ZrF_7	Crystallization from a solution containing RbF and H_2ZrOF_4, the former in excess (183)	Strongly refracting octahedral crystals; can be used in microdetermination of Zr or Rb
Tl_3ZrF_7	Crystallization from a solution containing 4 to 20 parts of TlF per part of H_2ZrOF_4 (160)	Brilliant octahedral crystals; can be reerystallized from water without change (160)
$Cu_3(ZrF_7)_2 \cdot 16H_2O$	Evaporation of a solution containing CuF_2 and H_2ZrOF_4, the latter in excess (139)	Monoclinic crystals of axial ratios a:b:c = 1.0798:1:1.0337 and $\beta = 91°46'$; can be reerystallized from water without change
Li_4ZrF_8	Crystallization from a solution containing 5 to 7LiF per 22 g H_2ZrOF_4 (160)	Sparingly soluble in water, which decomposes it; difficult to obtain pure; $\frac{2}{3}$ mole water has been noted per mole Li_4ZrF_8 (160)

148

TABLE 3.13. Continued

Formula	Methods of Preparation	Properties
$Cu_2ZrF_8 \cdot 12H_2O$	Crystallization after mixing solutions of CuF_2 and $Cu_3(ZrF_7)_2$ (178)	Monoclinic prisms of axial ratios $a{:}b{:}c = 1.255{:}1{:}1.661$ and $\beta = 121°17'$; isomorphous with corresponding Zn and Ni salts; soluble in cold water and decomposed by hot water, which subsequently deposits $Cu_3(ZrF_7)_2 \cdot 16H_2O$
$ZnZrF_8 \cdot 12H_2O$	Crystallization from a solution containing ZnF_2 and H_2ZrOF_4, the former in excess (178)	Monoclinic prisms, usually twinned with axial ratios $a{:}b{:}c = 1.220{:}1{:}1.644$ and $\beta = 119°31'$; dissolves readily in cold water; decomposes in hot water
$CdZrF_8 \cdot 6H_2O$	Crystallization from a solution containing CdF_2 and H_2ZrOF_4, the former in excess (178)	Monoclinic prisms of axial ratios $a{:}b{:}c = 1.384{:}1{:}0.838$ and $\beta = 119°43'$; isomorphous with Mn salt; can be recrystallized from water without change (178)
$Mn_2ZrF_8 \cdot 6H_2O$	Crystallization from a solution containing MnF_2 and H_2ZrOF_4, the former in excess (178)	Monoclinic prisms of axial ratios $a{:}b{:}c = 1.3710{:}1{:}0.8362$ and $\beta = 118°41'$; perfect cleavage; dissolves in cold water without decomposition; solution can be boiled without developing turbidity, but if boiling water is poured on crystals, they decompose with separation of MnF_2 (178)
$Ni_2ZrF_8 \cdot 12H_2O$	Recrystallization from a solution containing NiF_2, H_2ZrOF_4, and HF, the first of these in excess (178)	Emerald-green monoclinic crystals of axial ratios $a{:}b{:}c = 1.2110{:}1{:}1.6265$ and $\beta = 119°10'$, generally showing twinning; dissolves in cold water without decomposition, but if the solution is boiled, NiF_2 is deposited (178)

TABLE 3.13. Continued

Formula	Methods of Preparation	Properties
$Na_5Zr_2F_{11}$	Crystallization from solutions containing NaF and H_2ZrOF_4 over a wide range of proportions (178)	Monoclinic crystals with axial ratios a:b:c = 2.108:1:1.516 and $\beta = 97°13'$ (178); elsewhere reported to be rhombic (160); stable at red heat; 100 g water dissolves 0.387 g of the salt at 18° and 1.67 g at 100°
$Cs_2Zr_3F_{14} \cdot 2H_2O$	Crystallization from a solution containing CsF and H_2ZrOF_4, the latter in large excess (160)	Small, water-soluble crystals; decomposed by water (160)
$Tl_5Zr_3F_{17} \cdot H_2O$	Crystallization from an aqueous solution of $TlHZrOHF_5$, or from a solution containing 1 to 3.5 parts of TlF per part of H_2ZrOF_4, or from a solution containing 4 parts of TlF per part of H_2ZrOF_4, a different crystalline variety being obtained in the last case from in the preceding	Needlelike crystals when up to 3.5 parts of TlF are used per part H_2ZrOF_4, and twinned hexagonal crystals when higher proportions of TlF are used (160)

176. H. M. Haendler and D. W. Robinson, *J. Am. Chem. Soc.* **75**, 3846 (1953).
177. J. Berzelius, *Oefvers Akad. Forh. Stockholm* 295 (1824); *Pogg. Ann.* **4**, 117 (1825); *Ann. chim. phys.* (2) **26**, 43 (1824).
178. J. C. G. De Marignac, *Ann. chim. phys.* (3) **60**, 257 (1860).
179. B. Gossner, *Z. Kryst.* **38**, 147 (1904).
180. G. von Hevesy, J. A. Christiensen, and V. Berglund, *Z. anorg. allgem. Chem.* **144**, 69 (1925).
181. H. C. Kawecki, U.S. Patents **2,418,073-4**, March 25, 1947.
182. J. Missenden, *Chem. News* **124**, 327 (1922).
183. H. Behrens, *Mikrochemische Analyse*, Leipsig, 1901, p. 113.
184. G. von Hevesy, *Danske Vid. Selsk. Medd.* **7**, 8 (1925).
185. L. Pauling and G. C. Hampson, *J. Am. Chem. Soc.* **60**, 2702-7 (1938).
186. O. Hassel and H. Mark, *Z. Physik* **27**, 89 (1924).

4

Zirconium Oxides and the Zirconates

INTRODUCTION

Phase studies of the system zirconium-oxygen reveal the existence of (1) solid solutions of oxygen in both the hexagonal α-metal and the body-centered cubic β-metal, (2) an oxide, ZrO_2, and (3) a solid solution of the metal in the dioxide (Fig. 4.1). Oxygen is soluble in the α-metal up to 6.75 weight % (29 atomic %) and in the β-metal up to 2 weight % (10.5 atomic %). Zirconium dissolves in the dioxide to the extent of changing the atomic percentage from the theoretical value of 33.33 to a maximum value of 37 at the eutectic temperature, 1900° and 34.5 at 700° (1).

Three crystalline modifications of zirconium dioxide are known: the monoclinic (baddeleyite) which is stable up to 1000°, the tetragonal which is stable between 1000° and 1900°, and the cubic which is stable above 1900°. The existence of zirconium monoxide, ZrO, in the atmosphere of the sun and of many stars has been demonstrated spectrographically. It is unstable under terrestrial conditions and has not been isolated for study, although observations have been made on a fleeting phase which appeared to be the monoxide. Other oxides such as the trioxide, Zr_2O_3, (2, 3) and pentoxide, $Zr_2O_5 \cdot nH_2O$ (4) have been reported, but their existence has never been satisfactorily demonstrated and the preponderance of available information suggests that they do not exist. A composition corresponding to Zr_2O has been reported as a definite oxide, with the parameters of its hexagonally close-packed zirconium atoms determined to be a = 3.27 and c = 5.24 A. However, this appears to be but one composition in the continuous series of solid solutions of oxygen in zirconium reported by Domagala and associates, in which a was 3.241 and c 5.188 at saturation with oxygen (1).

Molten zirconium and molten zirconium dioxide appear to be miscible. The pure oxide melts at about 2900° and boils at about 4300°. No studies of the gas phase have been reported.

1. Armour Research Foundation, *Phase Diagrams of Zirconium-base Binary Alloys. The Zirconium-Oxygen System*, March 31, 1953.
2. G. A. Meerson and G. V. Samsonov, *J. Applied Chem.* (U.S.S.R.) **25**, 823-6 (1952).
3. L. Weiss and E. Neumann, *Z. anorg. allgem. Chem.* **65**, 248 (1910).
4. G. H. Bailey, *J. Chem. Soc.* **49**, 149, 481 (1886).

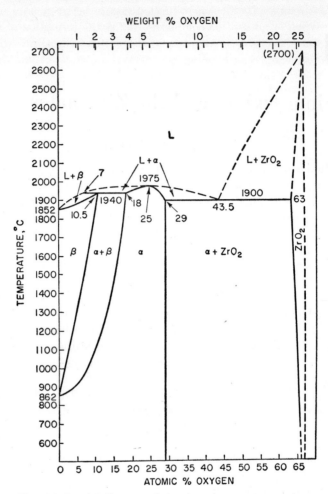

FIG. 4.1. Partial diagram of the zirconium-oxygen system.

Only monoclinic zirconium dioxide occurs in nature, but all three crystalline varieties have been prepared in the laboratory. The cubic phase can be stabilized by incorporation into the solid of various substances such as carbon, lime, or magnesia.

A hydrous peroxide, $ZrO_3 \cdot xH_2O$ is precipitated when a base is added to an aqueous solution of a zirconium salt in which hydrogen peroxide is dissolved. It slowly decays to the dioxide.

Since zirconium has a maximum coordination number of 8, and a coordination number of only 4 is realized in the unit molecule, ZrO_2, the possibility for complex formation exists. This possibility is realized in the formation of crystals of zirconia in which coordination occurs between adjacent atoms, in the formation of adsorption complexes, and in the formation of zirconates and other oxide complexes. All compounds of these categories will be discussed in this chapter, excepting the crystal of composition $ZrO_2 \cdot SiO_2$ known as *zircon*, which is of such exceptional interest as to merit an entire chapter for the discussion of its behavior alone.

ZIRCONIUM MONOXIDE

In 1931 Richardson reported evidence of zirconium monoxide in sun spots in observations using the 75-ft spectrograph at Mt. Wilson, California. The calculated temperature was 4900°K (5). Lowater photographed the zirconium monoxide spectrum from 2600 to 8800 A and measured 250 bands in the interval 3200 to 7600 A. He found that the most prominent bands could be arranged into three systems of vibration levels, all having the same lower electron state, which is probably the ground state of the zirconium monoxide molecule (6). A similar study was reported by Johnson at about the same time (7).

Numerous reports of zirconium monoxide in the atmospheres of stars have been published. Keenan has proposed a system of classifying stars into subgroups on the basis of difference in intensity between titanium monoxide and zirconium monoxide bands in the spectra of stars of class S (8, 9). According to McKellar the distinctive feature of class S stars is the absorption band of zirconium monoxide (10).

Schwarz and Deisler were unable to detect zirconium monoxide in the reduction products of the reaction of magnesium with zirconium dioxide (11). From this and other more extensive studies, it appears that there was no validity to the assumption of Friederich and Sittig that they had produced a lower oxide of zirconium by igniting the dioxide with carbon (12), or the beliefs of Dennis and Spencer (13), Winkler (14), or Wedekind (15) that insoluble residues which they obtained after reduction of zirconia with magnesium were largely the monoxide of zirconium.

In a report by Ewles in which he described the behavior of a number of oxides when excited in the concavity of the cathode of a cathode tube, he

---

5. R. S. Richardson, *Astrophys. J.* **73**, 216-49 (1931).
6. F. Lowater, *Proc. Phys. Soc. London* **44**, 51-66 (1932).
7. L. W. Johnson, *Phil. Mag.* **14**, 286-91 (1932).
8. P. C. Keenan, *Astron. J.* **55**, 172 (1950).
9. Keenan, *Astrophys. J.* **120**, 484-505 (1954).
10. A. McKellar, *J. Roy. Astron. Soc. Canada* **45**, 23-35 (1951).
11. R. Schwarz and H. Deisler, *Ber.* **52**, 1896-1903 (1919).
12. E. Friederich and Lieselotte Sittig, *Z. anorg. allgem. Chem.* **145**, 127-40 (1925).
13. L. M. Dennis and A. E. Spencer, *J. Am. Chem. Soc.* **18**, 673 (1896).
14. C. Winkler, *Ber.* **23**, 2642 (1890).
15. E. Wedekind, *Z. anorg. allgem. Chem.* **45**, 385 (1905).

mentioned sketchily a strong mauve cathodoluminescence which he attributed to zirconium monoxide. It was obtained at a minimum excitation voltage of 1200 and ceased at somewhat above 700°, ostensively due to a phase change (16). Wilber also noted a blackening and what he took to be a reduction during the cathodoluminescence of zirconium dioxide (16b). Jacobs noted that electrons of sufficient kinetic energy cause dissociation of oxide coatings on electrodes, and that the liberated oxygen returns to the cathode, resulting in decreased emission. The critical energy of the electrons starting the dissociation is equal to the heat of formation of the oxide in the coating. From these principles, he derived a value of 135 kg cal/mole for the heat of formation of zirconium monoxide, and a work function of 4.75 e.v. (17).

More recently, Chupka and Berkowitz heated zirconium and zirconia together in a tantalum crucible and found the most volatile species effusing from the mixture on heating to be TaO and ZrO, both being in evidence at about 1700° (17b).

ZIRCONIUM DIOXIDE

PREPARATION

The occurrence of zirconium dioxide in nature has been discussed in Chapter 1. The native oxide is generally associated with zircon, silica, iron, aluminum, and titanium oxides, and various other impurities. The extent to which this or other zirconium minerals must be purified depends on the use for which they are intended.

Acid-soluble impurities, particularly iron oxides, have been removed from naturally occurring zirconium dioxide by crushing and grinding the ore and then extracting it with hydrochloric or sulfuric acid (18). Iron, titanium, and certain other metals present as oxides have been removed by chlorinating the ore with chlorine and sulfur monochloride or similar chlorinating agents (19, 20). An industrial process can hardly tolerate the poor economy of this procedure. Zirkite has been heated in an electric furnace with just enough carbon to cause volatilization of carbon and silicon oxide vapors (21), but this process has not proved successful in producing zirconium dioxide of good quality. Attempts have also been made to produce zirconium dioxide by the

16. J. Ewles, *Phil. Mag.* **45**, 957-68 (1923).

16b. D. T. Wilber, *Phys. Rev.* **33**, 282 (1929).

17. H. Jacobs, *J. Applied Phys.* **17**, 596-603 (1946).

17b. W. A. Chupka, J. Berkowitz, and M. G. Ingraham, *J. Chem. Phys.* **26**, 1207-10 (1957).

18. L. Weiss and R. Lehmann, *Z. anorg. allgem. Chem.* **65**, 178 (1909).

19. O. Ruff and R. Wallstein, *Z. anorg. allgem. Chem.* **128**, 96 (1923).

20. Ruff and Wallstein, German patent **371,604**, Mar. 16, 1923.

21. J. G. Thomson, *Trans. Am. Electrochem. Soc.* **40**, 445 (1921).

thermal decomposition of zircon at 1800° or higher, so that the silica would volatilize (22). Much of the silica, but not all of it, can be economically eliminated in this way.

To obtain zirconium dioxide of reasonable purity, it has generally proved necessary to decompose the ore. Thereafter, one of the following procedures is followed: (1) if the decomposition product is combustible, it is burned to give the dioxide; (2) if the decomposition product is soluble in acid, it is brought into solution, a zirconium compound is precipitated from the solution by addition of a suitable agent, and the compound is calcined to yield the dioxide; or (3) if all of the products of the decomposition reaction are soluble excepting the zirconium dioxide, the soluble substances are leached away from the zirconia.

Zircon can be decomposed by heating it to above 1400° with carbon. This may be done in the electric furnace or the arc furnace, and in practice the latter has proved the more satisfactory. Silicon monoxide is volatilized, and it is reoxidized in air to the dioxide. After the process a dull-gray metallic solid remains in the furnace. If sufficient carbon has been used, its composition will approximate 1 gram-atom of carbon per gram atom of zirconium, and it is actually a solid solution of carbon in zirconium metal, with a face-centered cubic crystalline structure. It may be represented symbolically Zr,C. It is known in industry as *zirconium carbide*. If less than the equivalence of carbon has been used in the furnace process, a more highly lustrous metallic phase will be recovered which is usually a golden yellow and which is also a solid solution. It can be represented $Zr(C,O,N)$ and the combined number of atoms of carbon, oxygen, and nitrogen are less than the number of atoms of zirconium. Products of this type vary considerably in composition, and have been called *zirconium cyanonitride* and *zirconium carbonitride*. When zirconium carbide or cyanonitride are heated in air, they burn to the dioxide and give up to the atmosphere their dissolved elements, carbon and nitrogen. This procedure for preparing the dioxide was developed by E. Ryschkewitsch (23), Kinzie and Hake (24), Kinzie, Easton and Efimoff (25), and Miller (26). A typical analysis of an oxide prepared by burning zirconium carbide is given in Table 4.1.

Instead of burning the zirconium carbide or cyanonitride in air or other oxygen-containing gas, it can be burned in chlorine. Zirconium tetrachloride

22. C. Matignon, *Compt. rend.* **177**, 1290 (1923).

23. C. Lorenz, German patent **543,675**, Jan. 10, 1929.

24. C. J. Kinzie and D. S. Hake, U.S. Patents **2,072,889**, Mar. 9, 1937; **2,168,603**, Aug. 8, 1939, and reissue **21,726**, Feb. 15, 1941; **2,194,426**, Mar. 19, 1940; **2,206,287**, July 2, 1940. British patent **535,011**, Mar. 26, 1941.

25. C. J. Kinzie, R. P. Easton, and V. V. Efimoff, U.S. Patent **2,270,527**, Jan. 20, 1942; British patent **544,823**, Apr. 29, 1942.

26. J. B. Miller, U.S. Patent **2,392,605**, Jan. 8, 1946; British patent **601,876**, May 13, 1948.

TABLE 4.1. SPECTROGRAPHIC ANALYSES SHOWING TYPICAL IMPURITY
CONTENTS OF ZIRCONIUM DIOXIDE PREPARED IN VARIOUS WAYS

Impurity	Percentages Found in Zirconium Dioxide Derived from		
	Zirconium Cyanonitride	Complex Zirconium Sulfate	Complex Zirconium Glycolate
Al_2O_3	0.015	0.03	0.002
B_2O_3	None	None	None
BaO	0.005	0.005	0.002
CaO	0.02	0.03	0.02
Cr_2O_3	None	None	None
CuO	0.002	0.002	0.001
Fe_2O_3	0.06	0.005	0.002
HfO_2	2	2	2
K_2O	None	None	None
Li_2O	None	None	None
MgO	0.03	0.03	0.03
MnO_2	0.0005	None	None
Na_2O	None	None	0.002
Nb_2O_5	None	None	None
NiO	None	None	None
P_2O_5	None	None	None
PbO	None	None	None
Sb_2O_3	None	None	None
SiO_2	4.2	0.15	0.025
SnO_2	None	None	None
SrO	None	None	None
TiO_2	0.6	0.10	0.005
V_2O_5	0.002	None	None
ZnO	None	None	None

forms and sublimes into a receiver, and nitrogen and most of the oxygen and carbon are liberated as gases. Only a small residue consisting of carbon and various oxides remains. The zirconium tetrachloride can be burned to the dioxide in moist or dry air or other oxygen-containing gas. In moist air a temperature of 800° or more is required for the combustion and in dry air, 1000° or more (27, 28). One technique consists in delivering the preheated zirconium tetrachloride vapor and the oxygen via concentric tubes to a

27. W. O. H. Schornstein, British patent 541,343, Nov. 24, 1941.
28. H. Preis, Swiss patent 221,309, Aug. 17, 1942; British patent 567,093, Jan. 29, 1945.

combustion chamber arranged so that complete combustion occurs before any of the reacting gases impinge on the walls of the chamber. Zirconium dioxide particles about 0.4 to 1.0 mu in diameter are formed, the smaller sizes being favored by diluting the zirconium tetrachloride with an indifferent gas such as nitrogen or carbon dioxide (28). Superheated steam has also been used to convert the zirconium tetrachloride vapor to the dioxide (29, 30).

Alternatively, the zirconium tetrachloride can be dissolved in water and zirconium dioxide prepared from the aqueous solution. If the solution is heated under pressure to 150°, it hydrolyzes to hydrous zirconia. The precipitate can be filtered off, washed, and ignited at 1000° to give the anhydrous dioxide. The solution can also be treated with a sulfite (31, 32, 33), a sulfate (34, 35, 36, 37), or an organic acid, such as lactic, glycolic, or mandelic (38, 39) to obtain precipitates which yield zirconium dioxide on calcination. Table 4.1 shows analyses of typical industrial products prepared by calcination of a complex sulfate and a complex glycolate of zirconium. Aside from the various schemes of hydrolyzing zirconium salts by heating (40, 41) and addition of alkalies to aqueous solutions (42, 43, 44, 44b), zirconium tetrachloride has been dissolved in non-aqueous media and the calculated amount of water added for hydrolysis (45). But since the hydrolysis does not directly yield the dioxide, but rather zirconyl salts or esters, this is an expensive and unattractive approach to the preparation of the dioxide.

Instead of heating zircon with carbon in an electric resistance or arc furnace, it can be mixed with an alkali or a salt which yields an alkali on heating, and the mixture sintered at about 1000°. (Sometimes carbon has been used along with the alkali (32), but it is unnecessary.) The procedure results in reaction products consisting of alkali or alkaline earth zirconates,

29. J. Blumenfeld, British patent **307,881,** March 15, 1928.
30. F. Rusberg and P. Schmid, U.S. Patent **1,732,662,** Oct. 22, 1929.
31. A. R. Powell and W. R. Schoeller, *Analyst* **44,** 397-400 (1919).
32. British patent **300,271,** Nov. 11, 1927; French patent **662,507,** Oct. 18, 1928.
33. I. M. Agriomati, I. L. Agriomati, and O. S. Spiridonova, Russian patents **52,593,** Feb. 28, 1928; **53,758,** Aug. 31, 1938.
34. M. N. Rich, U.S. Patent **1,460,766,** July 3, 1923.
35. M. O. Axt and F. W. Berk, Ltd., British patent **550,288,** Jan. 1, 1943.
36. Axt, U.S. Patent **2,384,428,** Sept. 11, 1945.
37. E. Wainer, U.S. Patent **2,387, 046,** Oct. 16, 1945.
38. W. B. Blumenthal, *J. Chem. Educ.* **26,** 472-75 (1949).
39. C. A. Cumins, *Anal. Chem.* **19,** 376 (1947).
40. B. Havas, British patent **9,153,** April 18, 1913.
41. P. Askenasy, U.S. Patent **1,158,769,** Nov. 2, 1915.
42. K. Leuchs, German patent **285,344,** Mar. 7, 1944.
43. H. S. Cooper and L. P. Bensing, U.S. Patent **1,582,126,** Apr. 27, 1926.
44. J. Blumenfeld, British patent **275,672,** Aug. 9, 1926.
44b. L. Weiss, British patent **327,142,** Dec. 27, 1928.
45. British patent **527,855,** Oct. 17, 1940.

complex silicates, such as $Na_2 ZrSiO_5$, and siliceous compounds, such as silica and sodium silicates. Treating these with acids, particularly hydrochloric or sulfuric acid, results in slurries containing dissolved zirconium salts and precipitated silicic acids. The silica can be filtered off and the filtrate treated with a base or with certain salts to form precipitates which yield zirconium dioxide on ignition (46, 47), as in one of the procedures with zirconium tetrachloride which has been discussed above. Baddeleyite can be treated in the same fashion as zircon, in which case the main difference is that smaller quantities of silica need be dealt with in the succeeding operations. Some rarer minerals, such as eudialyte, $Na_{13}(Ca,Fe)_6Cl(Si,Zr)_{20}O_{52}$, are largely acid-soluble, and need not be put through a sintering procedure (33).

Zirconium has been isolated from other elements by precipitation from strongly acid solutions, as the phosphate. The phosphate has been treated with fused sodium carbonate to form sodium zirconate and sodium phosphate, and the latter has been leached out of the mixture with boiling water. The sodium zirconate was amenable to dissolution by acids and precipitation as the hydrous oxide or as a salt yielding the oxide on ignition (48).

Another procedure for preparing the oxide consists in the thermal dissociation of zircon followed by leaching the silica away from the zirconia. Zircon begins to dissociate at about 1550°, but a temperature of 1800° has been found practical for the breakdown of the untreated zircon. However, this operating temperature has been lowered by the addition of a small amount of soda ash, and a 35% sodium hydroxide solution has been used to leach out the silica. The leaching was done at 150° and required 5 hours (49). The procedure is a variation on older methods of treating the zircon with fused sodium hydroxide to form water-soluble sodium silicate (50, 51).

PROPERTIES

The properties of mineral baddeleyite have been determined with great care on specimens obtained from Phalaborwa in the eastern Transvaal. Its density at 25° is 5.379, and its indices of refraction are $\alpha = 2.136$, $\beta = 2.236$, and $\gamma = 2.243$. The chemical analysis is: $(Zr,Hf)O_2 = 95.20$, $SiO_2 = 0.06$, $Fe_2O_3 = 2.10$, $MgO = 0.64$, $CaO = 0.80$, $Mno = 0.23$, $TiO_2 = 1.65$ and ignition loss 0.00% (51b). The Phalaborwa mineral occurs typically as black, prismatic crystals, the blackness being due to the iron and manganese contents.

A detailed treatment of the physical properties of pure zirconium dioxide

46. J. B. Blumenfeld, French patent **671,106**, Mar. 8, 1929.

47. A. Karl, British patent **314,526**, June 30, 1928.

48. V. E. Tishchenko and A. P. Sidorkino, *J. Applied Chem.* (U.S.S.R.) **8**, 1117-25 (1935).

49. British patent **709,882**, June 2, 1954.

50. British patent **562,620**, July 10, 1944.

51. British patent **564,060**, Sept. 12, 1944.

51b. S. A. Hiemstra, *Am. Mineralogist* **40**, 275-82 (1955).

would lie outside the scope of this book which is concerned primarily with chemical behavior. A summary of the more pertinent physical properties is given in Table 4.2, and literature on the history and scientific treatment of other physical properties is cited in Table 4.3.

TABLE 4.2. PHYSICAL CONSTANTS OF ZIRCONIUM DIOXIDE

Property	Value
Boiling point, °C	4300 (52)
Coefficient of thermal expansion	
approx. cm/cm/°C, −130 to −80°	2×10^{-6} (53)
−80 to −50°	8×10^{-6} (53)
up to 1000°	7.2×10^{-6} (54)
Color	white
Crystal parameters, monoclinic	a = 5.174, b = 5.266, c = 5.308 A; $\beta = 80.8°$; 4 molecules per unit cell (55)
tetragonal	a = 5.07, c = 5.16 A (55)
cubic	a = 5.065 ± 0.01 A (56)
Density, gm/cc, monoclinic	5.68 (57)
tetragonal	6.10 (55)
cubic	6.27 (56)
Dielectric constant, approx.	12.5 (57b)
Electric conductivity	(58, 59)
Entropy, cal/mole/°K, at 298.16°K	12.03 ± 0.08 (60)
Entropy of formation, cal., 298.16°K	−46.5 (60)
Formula weight	123.22
Free energy of formation at standard conditions, kg cal/mole	−247.7 (61)
Hardness, Mohs	6.5
Heat of formation from elements, kg cal/mole at 25°	−261.5 ± 0.2 (61)
Heat of fusion, kg cal/mole	20.8
Heat of vaporization, cal/mole	$157{,}300 - 7.80\,T - 4 \times 10^5\,T^{-1}$ (62)
Index of refraction, monoclinic	$\eta = 2.13,\ \omega = 2.19,\ \epsilon = 2.20$
Inversion temperatures, °C	
monoclinic to tetragonal	1000
tetragonal to cubic	1900
Magnetic susceptibility, approx.,	4×10^{-6} (63)
cgs units	-0.112×10^{-6} (64)
Melting point, °C	2900 (65)
Molecular volume, cc, monoclinic	21.7
Solubility	Insol. water, aqueous acids except HF, alkalies, and salts, and all organic solvents; sol. aqueous HF, conc. H_2SO_4, molten borax, molten glasses

TABLE 4.2. Continued

Property	Value
Specific heat, mean, 20 to 600°..............	0.140 (66)
Thermal conductivity,	
cal/sec/cm/cm²/°C, at 100°..............	0.004 (67)
at 1300°.............	0.005 (67)
Young's modulus, dynes/cm², at 0°..........	168×10^{-10} (68)
at 1400°.......	90×10^{-10}
Vapor pressure, atm......................	$\log p = 34{,}383/T - 7.98 \times 10^{-4} T + 11.98$ (62)

TABLE 4.3. SUPPLEMENTARY LITERATURE ON PHYSICAL
PROPERTIES OF ZIRCONIUM DIOXIDE

Subject	Literature
Crushing strength	69
Crystal structure	70-74
Dielectric properties	75-77
Elasticity and torsion	78-80
Excitation by electrons	109
Light emissivity	81-104
Phosphorescence	105
Sintering	99b
Surface electric charges	110
Thermionic emission	106, 107
Triboluminescence	108

52. W. R. Mott, *Trans. Am. Electrochem. Soc.* **34**, 255 (1918).
53. J. Day, *Bull. soc. sci. Bretagne* **24**, 13-19 (1949).
54. J. Pierrey, *Ann. chim.* (12) **4**, 133-95 (1949).
55. O. Ruff and F. Ebert, *Z. anorg. allgem. Chem.* **180**, 19-41 (1929).
56. L. Passerini, *Gazz. chim. ital.* **60**, 672-76 (1930).
57. W. A. Roth and B. Becker, *Z. physik. Chem.* **145A**, 461-9 (1929).
57b. A. Güntherschulze and F. Keller, *Z. Physik* **75**, 78-83 (1932).
58. F. Trombe, M. Foëx, and J. Wyart, *Compt. rend.* **233**, 172-3 (1951).
59. K. Backhaus, *Electrowarme* **8**, 261-6 (1938).
60. K. K. Kelley, *Ind. Eng. Chem.* **36**, 377 (1944).
61. G. L. Humphrey, *J. Am. Chem. Soc.* **76**, 978-80 (1954).
62. Masaru Nakata and H. L. Johnson, *J. Am. Chem. Soc.* **76**, 2651-2 (1954).
63. F. Bourian and O. Hun, *Compt. rend.* **187**, 886-8 (1928).
64. *International Critical Tables*, McGraw-Hill Book Co., Inc., New York, 1929, Vol. VI, p. 356.
65. F. C. Nonamaker, *Chem. Met. Eng.* **31**, 151-5 (1924).
66. J. S. Arthur, *J. Applied Phys.* **21**, 732-3 (1950).
67. M. Adams, *J. Am. Ceram. Soc.* **37**, 74-9 (1954).
68. N. N. Ault and H. F. G. Ueltz, *J. Am. Ceram. Soc.* **36**, 199-203 (1953).
69. V. Bodin, *Trans. Cer. Soc.* **21**, 44 (1922).
70. M. L. Huggins, *Phys. Rev.* **21**, 719-20 (1923).
71. O. Ruff, *Z. Elektrochem.* **30**, 356-64 (1924).

Zirconium dioxide is rarely encountered as a liquid or gas, and its known chemistry is largely that of the monoclinic baddeleyite and the tetragonal modification that is stable above 1000°. The pure cubic modification that is stable above 1900° is rarely encountered, but the cubic modification stabilized by small percentages of lime, magnesia, or certain other oxides dissolved in the lattice is well known and has the fluorite structure. An identifying name, *baddeleyite*, has been applied heretofore only to the monoclinic variety. Hereunder, we shall use the names *ruffite* for the tetragonal variety

72. W. P. Davey, *Phys. Rev.* **27**, 798 (1926).

73. Kathleen Yardley, *Mineral. Mag.* **21**, 169-75 (1926).

74. W. M. Cohn and Sibylle Tolksdorf, *Z. physik. Chem.* **138**, 331-56 (1930).

75. A. Güntherschulze and H. Betz, *Z. Physik* **71**, 106-23 (1931).

76. F. Keller and W. R. Lehrmann, *Z. Physik* **88**, 677-82 (1934).

77. Shigeyuki Nagasawa, *J. Electrochem. Soc. Japan* **18**, 158-60 (1950).

78. E. Ryschkewitsch, *Ber. deut. keram. Ges.* **23**, 243-60 (1942).

79. J. Stavrolakis and F. H. Norton, *J. Am. Ceram. Soc.* **33**, 263-8 (1950).

80. E. Ryschkewitsch, *J. Am. Chem. Soc.* **34**, 322-6 (1951).

81. C. M. T. du Motay, *Chem. News* **19**, 107, 213, 310 (1869).

82. J. T. Taylor and W. H. Harrison, *Mech. Mag.* **21**, 458 (1869).

83. A. Payen, *Genie industriel* (1869) 161.

84. W. Huggins, *Proc. Roy. Soc.* **18**, 546 (1870).

85. A. W. Hofmann, "Bericht über die Entwicklung der chemischen Industrie," *Braunschweig* **1**, 1016 (1875).

86. J. W. Draper, *Am. J. Sci.* (3) **14**, 208 (1877).

87. J. Philipp, *Monit. Scient.* (3) **8**, 481 (1878).

88. A. Bettendorf, *Liebig's Ann.* **256**, 167 (1889).

89. W. Kochs, *Dingler's J.* **278**, 235 (1890).

90. E. Waller, *Eng. Min. J.* **51**, 520 (1891).

91. G. P. Drossbach, *Chem. Ztg.* **15**, 328 (1891).

92. H. Landolt, *Z. anal. Chem.* **35**, 714 (1896).

93. C. E. Mendenhall and L. R. Ingersol, *Phil. Mag.* (6) **15**, 205 (1908).

94. H. E. Ives, E. Kingsbury, and E. Karrer, *J. Franklin Inst.* **186**, 401-38, 585-625 (1918).

95. E. L. Nichols and D. T. Wilbur, *Phys. Rev.* **17**, 707-17 (1921).

96. W. E. Forsythe, *Phys. Rev.* **20**, 101-2 (1922).

97. F. Schröter, *Z. tech. Phys.* **4**, 2 (1923).

98. J. Böhm, *Z. anorg. allgem. Chem.* **149**, 217-22 (1925).

99. L. Wöhler, *Kolloid Z.* **38**, 97-111 (1926).

99b. E. Podszus, *Arch. Physikal. Chem. Glases keram. Massen* **1**, 2.

100. M. L. Phillips, *Phys. Rev.* **32**, 832-9 (1928).

101. D. T. Wilber, *Phys. Rev.* **33**, 282 (1929).

102. H. Hoppe, *Ann. Physik* **15**, 709-28 (1932).

103. I. A. Preobrazhenskiï, *Doklady Akad. Nauk S.S.S.R.* **71**, 671 (1950).

104. A. H. Sully, E. A. Brandes, and R. B. Waterhouse, *Brit. J. Applied Phys.* **3**, 97-101 (1952).

105. K. Holzinger, *Chem. Ztg.* **56**, 1022 (1932).

106. H. J. Spanner, *Ann. physik.* **75**, 609-33 (1924).

107. G. Mesnard, *Le Vide* **8**, 1392-9 (1953).

108. Timozi Inone, Minoru Kunitomi, and Eiiti Sibata, *J. Chem. Soc. Japan* **60**, 149-56 (1939).

109. S. Ziemecki, *Bull. intern. acad. Polonaise* **1928**, 367-75.

110. E. J. W. Verwey, *Rev. trav. chim.* **60**, 625-33 (1941).

and *arkelite* for the cubic variety in recognition of the early studies of O. Ruff and A. E. van Arkel on these crystalline allotropes.

When zirconium dioxide is heated and cooled, it not only undergoes crystallographic changes, but the energy content of the particles is altered by hysteresis effects which are readily observable by their reflection in changes in the coefficient of linear expansion (54). The energy content, and hence to a proportional extent the chemical reactivity, is therefore dependent to a degree on the thermal history of the specimen. In noting some of the inconsistencies in the reported chemical behavior of zirconium dioxide, it is important to take cognizance of thermodynamic differences that may have obtained.

Baddeleyite, ruffite, and arkelite all have face-centered unit cells as the structural units of their crystal lattices (111), and all may be regarded as slightly distorted variants of the same structural type. It is convenient to examine the structure of the cubic zirconia (Fig. 4.2) for correlating the atomic arrangement with the chemical properties of the solid. The zirconium atoms are located at the corners and centers of the faces of the unit cubic cells, and the oxygen atoms are located on the diagonals of the cube at positions between the center of the cube and the corners, the mean distances depending on the kind of bonding relationships prevailing between the oxygen atoms and the nearby zirconium atoms. Referring to the figure, we may regard O^A as an oxygen atom that came into the crystal with the molecule $O^A Zr^A O^{A'}$. The atom $O^{A'}$ is not shown because it lies outside the cell on a projection of the diagonal AG. In the crystal, O^A is approximately as close to zirconium atoms Zr^I, Zr^J, and Zr^M as it is to Zr^A. It is therefore equally likely to form bonds with any of these atoms. A dynamic system therefore obtains, in which the relations can be represented by a series of equations such as the following which show the interactions of fragments of molecules:

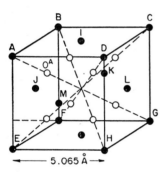

FIG. 4.2. ZrO_2 lattice, $r_+/r_- = 0.66$.

$$Zr^A{=}O^A \rightleftharpoons Zr^A{-}O^A{-} \tag{1-3}$$

$$Zr^A{=}O^A + Zr^M \rightleftharpoons Zr^A{=}O^A \rightarrow Zr^M$$
$$Zr^A{-}O^A + Zr^M \rightleftharpoons Zr^A{-}O^A{-}Zr^M \tag{2-3}$$

That is, the double bonds between a zirconium atom and its oxygen atoms tend to change to and alternate with single bonds. Both the doubly bonded

111. L. W. Coughanour, R. S. Roth, and V. A. DeProsse, *J. Research Nat. Bur. Standards* **52**, No. 1, 37-42 (1954).

oxygen and the singly bonded oxygen are capable of forming an additional bond with a second, nearby zirconium atom. While this process is going on, the zirconium atoms under consideration are also participating in similar exchanges with other oxygen atoms. A resonating system of high stability is thus achieved, and the entire crystal partakes of the nature of a giant molecule. Its stability is reflected in great hardness, high melting point, low vapor pressure, and a low order of chemical reactivity. The properties of zirconium dioxide led early to the realization that some type of bonding of the molecules of zirconium dioxide must occur in the crystal (112).

In crystals of zirconium dioxide, the zirconium atoms have the crystal coordination number 8, i.e., each is surrounded by 8 near oxygen atoms. Since zirconium also has a maximum covalency number of 8, it is electronically possible for the zirconium atom to be bonded simultaneously to all 8 oxygen atoms, but steric factors might limit the bonding to some extent. In all events, the mean covalency number of zirconium is greater than 4. Surface atoms of zirconium will have lower mean covalency numbers than the atoms in the interior of the crystal, and hence they should exhibit some kind of residual chemical activity. But since they are firmly bonded to the vicinal crystal structure, the surface reactivity is usually limited to adsorption or catalytic effects, and only vigorous reagents are capable of bringing about a breakdown of the lattice.

It is unlikely that in the dynamic changes in the zirconium dioxide crystal a zirconium atom is ever altered to the ion Zr^{+4}. No evidence for the existence of such an ion in chemical compounds has ever been adduced, and it would strongly violate the Pauling principle of electroneutrality. It is seen, however, that the effect of the variability of bonding is to form groupings of atoms with positive electrical charges and other groups with negative charges, giving the crystalline compound the nature of a zirconyl zirconate, $ZrOZrO_3$. The net electrical charge associated with a zirconium atom varies. In the

arrangement
$$\begin{array}{c} O \\ \diagdown\!\!\diagup \\ Zr \leftarrow O \\ \diagup\!\!\diagup \\ O \end{array}$$
the electronic charge on the zirconium atom is

$\frac{1}{2} \times 2e = e$ greater than that of the neutral zirconium atom, whereas in the arrangement $O{=}Zr{-}O{-}$ it is e more positive. These values probably represent the extremes of charge on the zirconium atoms in the crystal. In all the arrangements, the actual number of electrons in the valence orbits of the zirconium is greater than the number of valence electrons in the free zirconium atom. It is characteristic of the zirconium atom in all the compounds which it forms to have more than 4 electrons in its valence orbitals.

112. O. Ruff, Z. Elektrochem. 30, 356-64 (1924).

Although the vapor pressure of zirconium dioxide is very small at all temperatures up to the melting point, it is not to be regarded as negligible. At 2000°K, the vapor pressure is about 1.5×10^{-17} (from Table 4.3), whence 22.4 liters of the vapor will contain $1.5 \times 10^{-17} \times 6.023 \times 10^{23} = 9.03 \times 10^6$ molecules. At this temperature much of the chemical activity is to be associated with the vapor. According to Hoch and his co-workers (62), zirconium dioxide vaporizes without appreciable dissociation. (However, the emission of Zr^+, ZrO^+ and ZrO_2^+ has been noted above 1900°K (113), and it has been estimated that zirconia dissociates into metal and oxygen to the extent of 10^{-11} at 2000° and 0.6 at 3000° (114).) The reacting species in the vapor is therefore usually the molecule ZrO_2. It can be conceived as reacting either by the removal of one or both of its oxygen atoms, or by formation of an addition product with the reacting substance, whereafter, depending upon conditions and environment, the fragment or the complex will undergo further chemical change. As examples,

$$ZrO_2 + C \rightarrow Zr + CO_2$$

followed by $\qquad Zr + C \rightarrow Zr,C \qquad\qquad\qquad\qquad\qquad$ (4-6)

and $\qquad\qquad CaO + ZrO_2 \longrightarrow CaO \rightarrow ZrO_2 \longrightarrow CaZrO_3$

But direct reactions of the solid zirconium dioxide doubtless occur also at both ordinary and elevated temperatures. When zirconium dioxide is treated with boiling aqueous hydrofluoric acid, dissolution occurs:

$$ZrO_2 + 6HF \rightleftharpoons H_2ZrF_6 + 2H_2O \qquad\qquad (7)$$

In this case it appears likely that the surface atoms of zirconium, which have residual bonding potential, are complexed by acid fluoride ions and detached from the crystal as complex ions. The new surface thus exposed continues to react in the same way. On the other hand, zirconium dioxide is not usually dissolved by hydrochloric acid, since no chlorozirconates can be formed in aqueous environments. Under some conditions extremely finely divided zirconium dioxide has been observed to dissolve in hydrochloric acid, and this is apparently due to the action of the hydronium ion:

$$ZrO_2 + H_3O^+ \rightarrow H_2O \cdot ZrOOH^+ \qquad\qquad (8)$$

In the reactions of solid zirconium dioxide at higher temperatures, diffusion plays an important role. It is seen from Figure 4.1 that zirconium metal is soluble in solid zirconium dioxide, and it will be shown further that many other substances are soluble in this solid, particularly oxides and elements. When zirconium dioxide is heated with zirconium, the metal diffuses into the lattice of the oxide, and when a suitable concentration is reached, a reaction

113. S. V. Starodubtsev and Yu. I. Timokhina, *Zhur. Tekh. Fiz.* 19, 606-10 (1949).
114. F. Born, *Z. Elektrochemie* 31, 309 (1925).

occurs with formation of a solid solution of oxygen in zirconium. This can be represented by the equation:

$$Zr + ZrO_2 \rightarrow Zr,O \tag{9}$$

in which the amount of oxygen is variable. To avoid indefinite subscripts, the equation is left unbalanced. A similar mechanism doubtless plays a role in the reaction of zirconium with other metals as well as with nonmetals. Thus when calcium oxide is heated with zirconium dioxide, it diffuses into the lattice, and when a suitable temperature and concentration is attained, reaction occurs with formation of calcium metazirconate. Under some conditions, this solid-state reaction and the previously described vapor-state reaction probably proceed simultaneously.

The dissolution of zirconium dioxide in solvents, whether aqueous or other types, always entails loss of the identity of the zirconium dioxide molecule. This loss in identity is of a more catastrophic nature than the alteration that occurs when vapor molecules of zirconium dioxide condense to form a crystal. In the latter case ZrO_2 is still recognizable as a structural unit, and because of the resistance of zirconium to forming ionic bonds or remaining in a positively charged state, a stable zirconate ion does not persist. But when zirconium dioxide is heated with an alkali or added to a fused alkali, the alkali metal readily parts with its oxygen ion and the species ZrO_3^{-2} becomes stable.* It retains its identity when the system is cooled and the crystalline alkali zirconate takes form. When zirconium dioxide is heated with or added to a melt of an oxide of an element which does not form cations, it tends to form addition products with that oxide. In a melt this can be regarded as a solvation. The compounds $SiO_2 \cdot ZrO_2$ and $TiO_2 \cdot ZrO_2$ are formed in this manner.

Unfortunately much of the published data on the behavior of zirconium dioxide in melts is contradictory and poorly established. The dissolution of zirconium dioxide in fused cryolite has been reported to cause a lowering of the melting point of the cryolite to an extent corresponding to 3 dissolved molecules or ions per molecule of zirconium dioxide, and this has been interpreted to indicate the dissociation into a zirconium cation and 2 oxygen

---

* It should not be understoood here or elsewhere in this book that a monomeric ion ZrO_3^{-2}, as a disinct entity is implied. Rather, ZrO_3^{-2} is to be regarded as a hypothetical unit of structure in which 3 oxygen atoms and a net charge of -2 are associated with each zirconium atom, as against 2 oxygen atoms and a net charge of 0 in zirconium dioxide. The zirconates can be thought of as consisting of chains of atoms which can be represented

$$\left[\begin{array}{cccc} O & O & O & O \\ \downarrow & \downarrow & \downarrow & \downarrow \\ Zr\!-\!O\!-\!Zr\!-\!O\!-\!Zr\!-\!O\!-\! & \cdots\cdots & Zr\!-\!O\!-\! \\ \| & \| & \| & \| \\ O & O & O & O \end{array} \right]^{-2n}$$
$$\quad 1 \qquad 2 \qquad 3 \qquad\qquad n$$

anions (115). Another study, in which zirconium dioxide was found to dissolve in molten cryolite at 1000° to the extent of 14 mole % gave values for the depression of the melting point of the solvent which indicated no dissociation or decomposition of the zirconia (116). In any event, there is no evidence to support the dissociation of zirconia to give a tetravalent cation. In such systems it is necessary to take into consideration possible reactions of the type

$$3ZrO_2 + 4Na_3AlF_6 \rightleftharpoons 2Al_2O_3 + 3Na_3ZrF_7 + 3NaF \qquad (10)$$

This would yield 8 new dissolved ions or molecules per 3 molecules of zirconium dioxide.

Ceramists have been interested in evaluating the relative acid strength of zirconium dioxide. On the basis of relative strengths of metal-oxygen bonds, the order of decreasing acid strength TiO_2, Al_2O_3, ThO_2, BeO, ZrO_2 (117) has been proposed. Zirconium dioxide has also been observed to have the slowest reaction rate with silica of any of the following series of oxides, which are given in the order of decreasing reaction rate (118): K_2O, Na_2O, Li_2O, PbO, B_2O_3, BaO, CaO, ZnO, MgO, TiO_2, Al_2O_3, ZrO_2. Zirconium dioxide also generally reacts more slowly with other metallic oxides than do alumina, mullite, or silica (119).

The following is a summary of the reactions of zirconium dioxide with the various elements and their compounds, with details of the crystalline properties of the reaction products. For convenience similar elements have been treated as groups.

ALUMINUM, GALLIUM, INDIUM, AND THALLIUM: Molten aluminum does not react with zirconium dioxide at the melting point (659.7°) of the metal (120), but at higher temperatures it reacts with the formation of aluminum oxide and an intermetallic compound (Chap. 1). No compounds of aluminum oxide and zirconium dioxide are known; the eutectic has been variously reported to melt at 1855° and 1920° (121, 122). Virtually nothing is known of the reactions of zirconium dioxide with gallium, indium, and thallium, **or**

115. E. Darmois and G. Petit, *Compt. rend.* **232**, 1555-6 (1951).

116. Hidehiko Kido, *Sci. Repts. Saitama Univ.* (Japan) **1A**, 165-7 (1954).

117. Kuan-Han Sun, *Glass Ind.* **29**, 73-4, 98 (1948).

118. Abd-El-Moneim and Abou-El-Azm, *J. Soc. Glass Tech.* **37**, 168-81T (1953).

119. *Ibid.*, 269-301T (1953).

120. R. F. Koenig, *Iron Age* **172**, No. 8, 129-33 (1953).

121. R. F. Geller, P. J. Yavorsky, B. L. Steierman, and A. S. Creamer, *J. Research Nat. Bur. Standards* **36**, 277-312 (1946).

122. H. von Wartenberg, H. Linde, and R. Jung, *J. Am. Ceram. Soc.* **176**, 349-62 (1928).

their compounds, except the formation of the compound $In_2Zr_2O_7$ from india and zirconia (123).

ANTIMONY, ARSENIC, AND BISMUTH: No reactions have been reported for any of these elements or their compounds with zirconium dioxide.

BARIUM, CALCIUM, AND STRONTIUM: Calcium reduces zirconium dioxide to zirconium metal at about 800° (124). Details of the behavior of strontium and barium metals have not been reported, yet it is to be expected that they will behave similarly to calcium. Calcium chloride has no action on zirconium dioxide up to at least 1350°. When zirconium dioxide is heated with the oxides of barium, calcium, or strontium, the metazirconates $BaZrO_3$, $CaZrO_3$, and $SrZrO_3$ are formed (125, 126). No compounds other than the metazirconates have been observed. Small proportions of calcium oxide, e.g., 5 weight %, go into solid solution in zirconium dioxide and stabilize the cubic arkelite structure (127, 128). In the system $CaO\text{-}ZrO_2$, the two eutectics occur at 40 and 75 weight % ZrO_2, and melt at 2230° and 2380°, respectively (122). When calcium carbonate is heated with zirconium dioxide, the carbon dioxide pressure becomes higher than that of the pure calcium carbonate, and calcium metazirconate eventually forms (129). The alkaline earth carbonates are convenient starting materials for use in the preparation of the corresponding metazirconates.

BERYLLIUM, CADMIUM, MAGNESIUM, MERCURY, AND ZINC: Of these elements, only magnesium and beryllium combine with oxygen with sufficient release of free energy to cause reduction of zirconium dioxide. Beryllium has been observed not to react with zirconium dioxide at 1600° (130), however, possibly due to failure to wet the dioxide. Magnesium reduces zirconium dioxide to the metal containing some oxygen (131), but it has not proved the equal of calcium in removing practically all of the oxygen. It appears possible that with improved technique, the practical elimination of oxygen will be achieved. Neither the halogenides nor the oxides of the elements of this group react with zirconium dioxide. Literature on the oxide systems is to be found as follows: $BeO\text{-}ZrO_2$ (125, 132); $BeO\text{-}Al_2O_3\text{-}ZrO_2$ (121); $BeO\text{-}CeO_2\text{-}ZrO_2$

123. J. K. Hulm, *Phys. Rev.* **92**, 5045 (1953).
124. W. C. Lilliendahl and H. C. Rentschler, Trans. Am. Electrochem. Soc. **91**, 285-94 (1947).
125. O. Ruff, F. Ebert, and H. von Wartenberg, *J. Am. Ceram. Soc.* **196**, 335-64 (1931).
126. F. Hurd, *Z. Elektrochem.* **55**, 363-6 (1951).
127. A. Gambey and G. Chaudron, *14ᵐᵉ Congr. ind.*, Paris, Oct. 1934, 5 pp.
128. O. Ruff, F. Ebert, and E. Stephen, *J. Am. Ceram. Soc.* **180**, 215-24 (1929).
129. D. Balareff and N. Lukowa, *Analyst* **54**, 704-15 (1929).
130. G. Economos and W. D. Kingery, *J. Am. Ceram. Soc.* **36**, 403-9 (1953).
131. H. Kuzel and E. Wedekind, *Ann.* **395**, 149 (1913).
132. N. R. Thielke, *Bull. Am. Ceram. Soc.* **27**, 277-9 (1948).

(133); $BeO\text{-}MgO\text{-}ZrO_2$ (134); $MgO\text{-}ZrO_2$ (127, 135, 136, 137); $MgO\text{-}Al_2O_3\text{-}ZrO_2$ (138, 139); $MgO\text{-}SiO_2\text{-}ZrO_2$ (140); $ZnO\text{-}ZrO_2$ (141).

BORON: When zirconium dioxide is heated with elementary boron to 1800°, zirconium borides are formed and BO and B_2O_3, chiefly the former, are evolved (57b, 142). Zirconium dioxide does not react with boron oxide (143), but it is attacked by ammonium fluoborate (144).

BISMUTH: See ANTIMONY.

BROMINE, CHLORINE, AND IODINE: Solid zirconium dioxide is inert to these halogens at all temperatures (one investigator has reported incipient reaction of chlorine with zirconium dioxide at 1000° (145), but this appears unlikely to be true). In the presence of carbon, bromine and chlorine react with heated zirconium dioxide to form the zirconium tetrahalogenide. A mixture of zirconium dioxide and carbon must be heated until reduction of the zirconium compound has occurred before the iodine begins to react; hence iodine reacts only with zirconium carbide but not with zirconium dioxide. Ionic halogenides, such as the alkali and alkaline earth bromides, chlorides, and iodides, do not react with zirconium dioxide even at very high temperatures, but the covalent halogenides, such as carbon tetrachloride, titanium tetrachloride, and phosphorus pentachloride (146) react with the heated dioxide with formation of the tetrachloride. Hydrochloric acid, hot or cold, has little if any affect on zirconium dioxide, but a slight solubilization has been noted under some circumstances (143), and the action seems to be only on particles of less than 1 μ (147).

CADMIUM: See BERYLLIUM.

CALCIUM: See BARIUM.

CARBON: Carbon reacts with zirconium dioxide at highly elevated temperatures to form zirconium carbide or cyanonitride and carbon dioxide. The carbide and cyanonitride are best regarded as solid solutions of carbon in the metal in a face-centered cubic lattice. The reaction has been observed to

133. O. Ruff, F. Ebert, and W. Loerpabel, *J. Am. Ceram. Soc.* **207**, 308-12 (1932).

134. F. Trombe, M. Foëx, and C. H. La Blanchetais, *J. recherches centre natl. recherches sci.* (Paris) No. 4/5, 61-89 (1948).

135. F. Ebert and E. Cohen, *J. Am. Ceram. Soc.* **213**, 321-32 (1933).

136. W. Bussen, C. Schusterius, and A. Ungeweiss, *Ber. deut. keram. Ges.* **18**, 433-43 (1937).

137. N. A. Zhirnova. *J. Applied Chem. U.S.S.R.* **12**, 1278-86 (1936).

138. I. Ya. Sal'dan and N. A. Zhirnova, *Bull. acad. sc. U.R.S.S. Classe sci. chim.* **1945**, 669-71.

139. R. F. Mather, *J. Am. Ceram. Soc.* **25**, 93-6 (1942).

140. W. R. Foster, *J. Am. Ceram. Soc.* **34**, 302-5 (1951).

141. H. von Wartenberg and W. Gurr, *J. Am. Ceram. Soc.* **196**, 374-83 (1931).

142. E. Zintl, W. Morawietz, and E. Gastiner, *J. Am. Ceram. Soc.* **245**, 8 (1940).

143. F. P. Venable and T. Clarke, *J. Am. Chem. Soc.* **18**, 434 (1896).

144. D. R. Martin and J. K. Riecke, *J. Am. Chem. Soc.* **73**, 5895-6 (1951).

145. E. Krech, *Doklady Akad. Nauk S.S.S.R.* **78**, 517-18 (1951).

146. E. F. Smith and H. B. Harris, *J. Am. Chem. Soc.* **17**, 654 (1895).

147. E. Podszus, *Z. phys. Chem.* **92**, 227 (1917).

begin at about 1400° (148), but the temperature will depend on the size and condition of the zirconium dioxide particles. The reaction is commonly conducted in either an electric-resistance or an arc furnace. Calcium carbide, too, reacts with zirconium dioxide to form zirconium carbide. When zirconium dioxide is heated with carbides of transition metals, such as tantalum, titanium, vanadium, or zirconium, mixed interstitial solutions tend to form. Carbon tetrachloride and carbon disulfide react with hot zirconium dioxide to form zirconium tetrachloride and zirconium disulfide, respectively.

CERIUM AND THE LANTHANONS: Reactions of the metals with zirconium have not been reported. Ceric oxide forms no compounds with zirconium dioxide. Above 2000° the two oxides are completely soluble in one another, forming cubic crystals of the fluorite structure. They may be recovered at room temperature by cooling them rapidly. Slower cooling leads to mixtures of solid solutions of cubic and tetragonal structures (149; cf. 127 and 150). It has been reported that when ceric oxide and zirconium dioxide are heated together, oxygen is lost (141), but it appears that the tendency to lose oxygen is entirely a property of the ceria, and that this tendency is actually hindered by the zirconia. A compound of zirconia and cerous oxide is formed when barium zirconate is heated with cerous chloride:

$$3BaZrO_3 + 2CeCl_3 \xrightarrow{1000°} Ce_2O_3 \cdot 2ZrO_2 + ZrO_2 + 3BaCl_2 \qquad (11)$$

The compound $Ce_2O_3 \cdot 2ZrO_2$ has a face-centered cubic lattice of parameter 10.669 ± 0.005 A, and the lattice is similar to that of pyrochlore. When the compound is oxidized, it changes over to the same cubic solid solution of cerium and zirconium dioxides which has been described above, and has the lattice parameter 5.272 ± 0.02 A (151). The system La_2O_3-ZrO_2 has been studied by melting-point (152), X-ray (153), and microscope (134) techniques, and no compounds have appeared. Two solid solutions have been noted. A sharp maximum of electric resistance was noted at the composition $2ZrO_2 \cdot La_2O_3$ (154). Studies of other lanthanons are relatively few. Gadolinia and samaria have been noted to form solid solutions with zirconia, with cubic lattices (155).

CESIUM, LITHIUM, POTASSIUM, RUBIDIUM, AND SODIUM: Pure sodium has little or no reducing action on zirconium dioxide, and the other alkali metals have received little attention for this purpose because of their relatively high

148. H. C. Greenwood, *J. Chem. Soc.* **93**, 1493 (1908).

149. P. Duwez and F. Odell, *J. Am. Ceram. Soc.* **33**, 274-83 (1950).

150. L. Passerini, *Gazz. chim. ital.* **60**, 672-6 (1930).

151. J. J. Casey, L. Katz, and W. C. Orr, *J. Am. Ceram Soc.* **77**, 2187-9 (1955).

152. H. von Wartenberg and K. Eckhardt, *J. Am. Ceram. Soc.* **232**, 179-87 (1937).

153. F. Trombe and M. Foëx, *J. recherches centre natl. recherches sci.* (Paris). No. 4/5, 61-89 (1948).

154. F. Trombe and M. Foëx, *Compt. rend.* **233**, 254-6 (1951).

155. P. Duwez, F. H. Brown, Jr., and F. Odell, *J. Electrochem. Soc.* **98**, 356-62 (1951).

cost. Their simple halides are also without effect on zirconium dioxide up to quite high temperatures, i.e., at least 1350°. However, alkali fluosilicates react with zirconium dioxide at about 600° to form alkali fluozirconates. Compounds of the alkalies, such as their carbonates, which serve as sources of alkali oxide when heated, react with zirconium dioxide to form zirconates. These reactions and reaction products are discussed below, pp. 196-198.

COBALT, IRON, AND NICKEL: There are no known reactions of cobalt, iron, or nickel, or their oxides or simple halogenides with zirconium dioxide. For the reaction of a complex fluoferrate, see FLUORINE. Zirconium dioxide is not wetted by nickel at 1450° or 1850° (156, 157). Cobaltous oxide has been observed not to form a compound with zirconium dioxide between 1100° and 1300° (158). Eutectics have been noted in the Fe_2O_3-ZrO_2 system at 1520° and in the NiO-ZrO_2 system at 2050° (141).

COPPER, GOLD, AND SILVER: No reactions have been reported of these elements or any of their compounds with zirconium dioxide.

FLUORINE: Fluorine has been observed not to react with zirconium dioxide at 100°, but quantitative decomposition to the tetrafluoride occurred at 525° (159). Incomplete reaction was noted at 400° and 450°. Hydrogen fluoride gas also converts the dioxide to the tetrafluoride at about 550°, and aqueous hydrofluoric acid near the boil readily dissolves the dioxide with formation of a fluozirconic acid. Many complex fluorides have been observed to react with hot zirconium dioxide to form fluozirconates, e.g., alkali bifluorides, fluoborates, fluoferrates, and fluosilicates (160, 161), a typical reaction being illustrated by the equation

$$K_2SiF_6 + ZrO_2 \leftrightharpoons K_2ZrF_6 + SiO_2 \qquad (12)$$

GALLIUM: See ALUMINUM.

GERMANIUM, LEAD, SILICON, AND TIN: Of these elements, only silicon has been found to react with zirconium dioxide, and in view of the low free energies of formation of the oxides of the others, they would not be expected to react. Wedekind reported that $ZrSi_2$ formed when silicon was heated with zirconium dioxide in an electric furnace (162). Since molten silicon wets zirconium dioxide (156), the reaction is able to proceed with ease. Zirconium silicides have been prepared by heating zirconium dioxide and silicon dioxide together with carbon or aluminum (163, 164). Fluosilicates react

156. M. Humenik, Jr., and W. D. Kingery, *J. Am. Ceram. Soc.* **37**, 18-23 (1954).

157. W. D. Kingery, *J. Am. Ceram. Soc.* **37**, 42-5 (1954).

158. J. A. Hedvall, *Z. anorg. allgem. Chem.* **93**, 313-9 (1915).

159. H. M. Haendler, S. F. Bartram, R. S. Becker, W. J. Bernard, and S. W. Bukata, *J. Am. Chem. Soc.* **76**, 2177-8 (1954).

160. J. Koerner, U.S. Patent **1,467,275**, Sept. 4, 1923.

161. H. C. Kawecki, U.S. Patents **2,418,073/4**, Mar. 25, 1947.

162. E. Wedekind, *Ber.* **35**, 3929 (1902).

163. F. M. Becket, U.S. Patent **1,996,037**, Mar. 26, 1935.

164. V. Elyutin and R. Grigorasch, *Trudy Moskovskago Inst. Stali im. I. V. Stalin* **1939**, No. 12, 59-79.

with zirconium dioxide with formation of fluozirconates (see FLUORINE). When zirconium dioxide is heated with oxides of elements of this group, the compounds $GeO_2 \cdot ZrO_2$ (tetragonal, a = 4.871, c = 10.570 A (165)), $PbZrO_3$ (pseudo-tetragonal at 20°, a = 4.152, c = 4.101 A; changes to cubic at 230° (166)), and $ZrO_2 \cdot SiO_2$ are formed. For details of the compounds of zirconia and silica, see Chapter 5. No compounds of zirconia with tin oxides are known.

GOLD: See COPPER.

HYDROGEN: Hydrogen does not react with zirconium dioxide. There was no perceptible attack at 2000° under 150 atm pressure (167). Calcium hydride reduces the dioxide to zirconium metal (168); hydrogen fluoride and hydrofluoric acid convert the dioxide to fluorine compounds of zirconium (*supra*); and hydrochloric acid attacks zirconium dioxide if the particles are sufficiently small, and are in a suitable energy state. Water forms no compounds with zirconium dioxide (169).

INDIUM: See ALUMINUM.

IODINE: See BROMINE.

IRIDIUM, OSMIUM, PALLADIUM, PLATINUM, RHODIUM, AND RUTHENIUM: No reactions of these elements or any of their compounds with zirconium dioxide have been reported.

IRON: See COBALT.

LANTHANUM AND THE LANTHANONS: See CERIUM.

LEAD: See GERMANIUM.

MAGNESIUM: See CADMIUM.

MANGANESE AND RHENIUM: No reactions of these elements or their compounds with zirconium dioxide are known. A eutectic temperature has been reported to occur at 1620° for mixtures of ZrO_2 and Mn_3O_4 (141).

MERCURY: See CADMIUM.

MOLYBDENUM AND TUNGSTEN: It has been reported that tungsten will react with zirconium dioxide at exceedingly high temperatures to form a tungsten-zirconium alloy (170). Aside from this no reactions of molybdenum or tungsten or their compounds with zirconium dioxide are known.

NICKEL: See COBALT.

NIOBIUM, PHOSPHORUS, TANTALUM, AND VANADIUM: No reactions of these elements or their compounds with zirconium dioxide are known, except the reaction of phosphorus pentachloride to form zirconium tetrachloride (146).

NITROGEN: No reactions of nitrogen or its compounds with zirconium

165. F. Bertaut and A. Durif, *Compt. rend.* **238**, 2173-5 (1954).
166. E. Sawaguchi, H. Maniwa, and S. Hoshino, *Phys. Rev.* **83**, 1078 (1951).
167. E. Newbery and J. N. Pring, *Proc. Roy. Soc.* **92A**, 276 (1916).
168. H. W. Zabel, *Chem. Industries* **60**, 37-9 (1947).
169. H. B. Weiser, *Inorganic Colloid Chemistry*, John Wiley & Sons, Inc., New York, 1935, vol. 2, pp. 264-6.
170. H. von Wartenberg and H. Moehl, *Z. physik. Chem.* **128**, 439-44 (1927).

dioxide are known, other than the reaction of ammonium bifluoride which converts the dioxide to ammonium fluozirconates (*supra*).

OSMIUM: See IRIDIUM.

OXYGEN: Oxygen does not react chemically with zirconium dioxide. For the reactions of oxides of the elements, see elsewhere in this summary.

PALLADIUM: See IRIDIUM.

PLATINUM: See IRIDIUM.

POTASSIUM: See CESIUM.

RHENIUM: See MANGANESE.

RHODIUM: See IRIDIUM.

RUTHENIUM: See IRIDIUM.

SCANDIUM AND YTTRIUM: No reactions of these elements or their compounds with zirconium are known. Yttria, Y_2O_3, forms solid solutions of cubic lattice in the composition ranges 7-55 and 76-100 mole % yttria, at 2000° (126, 155).

SELENIUM, SULFUR, AND TELLURIUM: These elements do not react with zirconium dioxide. Reactions of the anhydrous oxides have not been studied, but hot sulfuric acid attacks zirconium dioxide with the formation of complex sulfatozirconic acids (Chap. 6). Also, zirconium dioxide is converted to water-soluble complex sulfatozirconates by fusing it with alkali metal bisulfates, or by heating a mixture of zirconium dioxide and ammonium sulfate together to 450° (171). The latter reaction goes according to the equation

$$3(NH_4)_2SO_4 + ZrO_2 \rightarrow (NH_4)_3ZrOH(SO_4)_3 + 3NH_3 + H_2O \qquad (13)$$

Carbon disulfide reacts with zirconium dioxide at 1000° with formation of zirconium disulfide (172), and hydrogen sulfide reacts at a red heat with formation of zirconium sulfoxide (173, 174), i.e.,

$$H_2S + ZrO_2 \rightarrow ZrOS + H_2O \qquad (14)$$

In these reactions the condition of the zirconium dioxide appears quite important to the yield. By forming the dioxide in the presence of the sulfide reagent—e.g., by thermal decomposition of zirconium sulfate—a more satisfactory product is obtained than by using calcined zirconium dioxide (175).

SILICON: See GERMANIUM.

SILVER: See COPPER.

STRONTIUM: See BARIUM.

SULFUR: See SELENIUM.

TANTALUM: See NIOBIUM.

TELLURIUM: See SELENIUM.

171. W. B. Blumenthal, U.S. Patent **2,525,474**, Oct. 10, 1950.

172. E. Fiemey, *Ann. chem. Phys.* **38**, 326 (1832).

173. O. Hauser, *Z. anorg. allgem. Chem.* **53**, 74 (1907).

174. L. Brewer, L. A. Bromley, and J. McCullough, *Acta Cryst.* **1**, 287-9 (1948).

175. Titanium Alloy Mfg. Division of the National Lead Co., unpublished researches.

THALLIUM: See ALUMINUM.

THORIUM AND THE ACTINONS: Solid thorium reacts chemically with either baddeleyite or with lime-stabilized arkelite when it is heated with these substances. The liquid metal does not wet nor penetrate zirconium dioxide, however, hence zirconium dioxide crucibles have been used successfully for containing molten thorium (176). No reactions of thorium compounds with zirconium dioxide are known. Thorium dioxide has been observed not to form compounds with zirconium dioxide up to 2400°, but two series of mixed crystals have been observed (177). Thermal expansion data on mixtures of thoria and zirconia led early investigators to the erroneous assumption of compound formation (178). Diagrams of the systems ThO_2-ZrO_2 and MgO-ThO_2-ZrO_2 have been published (133). Uranium dioxide forms no compounds with zirconium dioxide, but a solid solution of cubic lattice forms which can contain up to 52 mole % zirconia, with the lattice parameter varying from 5.46 to 5.32 A with increasing ZrO_2 content. A tetragonal solid solution has been noted for the composition range 53-100 mole % ZrO_2. A eutectic occurs at 52.5 mole % zirconia, melting at 2550° (179). It is reported that zirconium dioxide retards the oxidation of U_3O_8 to UO_3 (180).

TIN: See SILICON.

TITANIUM AND ZIRCONIUM: Molten or highly heated solid titanium and zirconium metals attack zirconium dioxide with formation of solutions of oxygen in the metals. Titanium tetrachloride reacts with hot zirconium dioxide with formation of zirconium tetrachloride (181). When titanium dioxide and zirconium dioxide are heated together, the compound $TiO_2 \cdot ZrO_2$ is formed (111, 182). It has a primitive orthorhombic lattice with a = 4.806, b = 5.032, and c = 5.447 A. The existence of this compound eluded the attention of all investigators of the TiO_2-ZrO_2 system until quite recently. There is a eutectic in the system at 20 mole % ZrO_2 which melts at 1760°. The compound TiO_2-ZrO_2 melts incongruently at about 1820°, and there is some evidence that it exists in two polymorphic forms with a transition temperature between 800° and 1200° (111; cf. 183). Although it has been noted that some oxygen may be lost when titanium dioxide and zirconium dioxide are heated together (141), the tendency to lose oxygen is associated only with the titanium dioxide, and the formation of solid

176. G. R. Pulliam and E. S. Fitzsimmons, *U.S. Atomic Energy Comm. ISC-550*, 16 pp., 1954.

177. O. Ruff, F. Ebert, and H. Woitinek, *J. Am. Ceram. Soc.* 180, 252-6 (1929).

178. G. E. Merritt, *Trans. Am. Electrochem. Soc.* 50, 165-175 (1926).

179. W. A. Lambertson and M. H. Mueller, *J. Am. Ceram. Soc.* 36, 365-68 (1953).

180. I. Sheft and S. M. Fried, U.S. Patent 2,599,946, June 10, 1952.

181. C. Pascause, *Compt. rend.* 231, 1232-3 (1950).

182. F. H. Brown, and P. Duwez, *Progress Report 20-180, Jet Propulsion Laboratory*, California Institute Technology, Aug. 20, 1952.

183. H. G. Sowman and A. I. Andrews, *J. Am. Ceram. Soc.* 34, 298-301 (1951).

solutions or the compound with zirconium dioxide has the effect of preventing loss of oxygen (136). (Titanium dioxide alone begins to decompose at a temperature of about 1640° (183b). For phase diagrams of the system SiO_2-TiO_2-ZrO_2, see reference 183, and for CaO-TiO_2-ZrO_2 and ThO_2-TiO_2-ZrO_2, see reference 183c.

TUNGSTEN: See MOLYBDENUM.

URANIUM: See THORIUM.

VANADIUM: See NIOBIUM.

YTTRIUM: See SCANDIUM.

ZINC: See CADMIUM.

ZIRCONIUM: See TITANIUM.

Zirconium dioxide serves as a catalyst or catalyst promoter in a wide variety of organic reactions. Since the zirconium atom has no unpaired electrons, it should not act as an oxidation-reduction catalyst, and in fact it does not. The catalytic effects which have been observed can be explained on the basis of the electron-accepting capacity of the zirconium atom, and hence are results of the intermediate formation of complex compounds. We have already noted that whereas the crystal coordination number within the zirconium dioxide crystal is 8 and the covalency number is considerably higher than the normal valency of 4, the surface atoms have lower coordination and covalency numbers and possess residual capacity for chemical bonding. The surface atoms are so firmly bound to the underlying stratum, however, that they strongly resist actual removal from the crystal as a result of any chemical reaction at the surface. Thus the residual reactivity finds expression in adsorption and in catalytic effects which are associated with adsorption. Oxygen and nitrogen atoms are particularly suitable donor atoms, provided of course that the geometry of the molecules in which they are combined permits a close enough approach of their outer electrons to the zirconium atoms to form a coordinate bond. Such bonding is readily distinguished from the feeble adsorption resulting from van der Waals forces, both of which have been observed to coexist at 250-500° between basic nitrogen compounds such as quinoline and silica-zirconia catalyst surfaces (184).

It is to be noted that catalytic activity is often favored by the formation of unstable rather than stable bonds. If the intermediate complexes are too stable, they tend to persist rather than to undergo changes leading to

183b. C. D. Hodgman, *Handbook of Chemistry and Physics,* Chemical Rubber Publishing Co., Cleveland, 1955.

183c. W. Rath, *Ber. deut. keram. Ges.* 28, 177-93 (1952).

184. G. A. Mills, E. R. Boedeker, and A. G. Oblad, *J. Am. Chem. Soc.* 72, 1554-60 (1950).

the desired catalyzed reaction product. Compounds containing zirconium-carbon bonds have never been observed to exist, but it can be inferred from some of the catalytic behavior of zirconium dioxide that unstable, short-lived bonds are formed between its zirconium atoms and carbon atoms of olefins. This can be represented graphically:

$$R-\overset{H}{C}=\overset{H}{C}-R + ZrO_2 \rightleftharpoons R-\overset{H}{\underset{\underset{O=Zr=O}{\downarrow}}{C}}-\overset{H}{\overset{+}{C}}-R \tag{15}$$

The formation of the carbonium ion in addition to the unstable zirconium-carbon link activates the olefin for a variety of reactions.

Because the catalytic effects of zirconium dioxide are associated with complex formations which presuppose certain electronic arrangements and molecular geometry, they are characterized by a higher degree of specificity than the oxidation-reduction catalyses of the elements of variable valence. Group IV elements in general have a low order of activity in the catalytic exchange of gaseous oxygen with water vapor (185). Zirconium dioxide has little effect on the interchange of gaseous hydrogen and deuterium (186). It has negligible influence on the oxidation of molten rosin at 200° (187). When zirconium dioxide is used in conjunction with other oxidation catalysts, its effects vary from nil to very considerable. In the latter event, the dioxide is spoken of as a *catalyst promoter*. Zirconium compounds other than the dioxide are known to serve as catalyst promoters, and they will be discussed in Chapter 8. Examples of catalytic indifference are found in the failure of zirconium dioxide to catalyze the oxidation of carbon monoxide in air in the presence of silver permanganate (188) or to promote the catalysis of the reaction of steam with hydrocarbons (189). On the other hand, zirconium abets the hydrogenation of α-picolene, using osmium or nickel as the primary catalyst (190) ; the dehydrogenation of hydrocarbons mixed with steam, using ferric and cupric oxides as primary catalysts (191), the dehydrogenation of paraffins with cobaltous oxide as catalyst (192), and of secondary alcohols, e.g., of $(CH_3)_2CHOH$ to $(CH_3)_2CO$ (193), and

185. Noryosi Morita, *Bull. Chem. Soc. Japan* **15**, 47-55, 71-6 (1940).
186. V. C. F. Holm and R. H. Blue, *Ind. Eng. Chem.* **44**, 107-13 (1952).
187. S. P. Mitra, *Proc. Nat. Acad. Sci. India* **20A**, 140-9 (1951).
188. Morris Katz and Sophie Halpern, *Ind. Eng. Chem.* **42**, 345-52 (1950).
189. H. A. Dirksen, H. R. Linden, and E. S. Pettijohn, *Inst. Gas Technol., Research Bull.* No. 4, 27 pp. (1953).
190. V. S. Sadikov and P. I. Astrakhantzev, *J. Russ. Phys. Chem. Soc.* **62**, 2071-90 (1930).
191. N. F. Linn, U.S. Patent **2,392,750**, Jan. 8, 1946.
192. M. P. Matuszak, U.S. Patent **2,394,625**, Feb. 12, 1946.

the deoxidation of certain aldehydes and ketones to form butadience (194).

Some of the catalytic effects of zirconium dioxide appear to be oxidation-reduction effects without actually being so. Strictly speaking, in an oxidation-reduction catalysis, the catalyst plays a role in the transfer of electrons from the reducing agent to the oxidizing agent. For example, in the catalytic oxidation of hydrogen chloride by gaseous oxygen in the presence of cupric chloride:

$$Cu^{+2} + Cl^- \rightarrow Cu^+ + Cl$$
$$4Cu^+ + O_2 + 4HCl \rightarrow 4Cu^{+2} + 4Cl^- + 2H_2O$$

(16-17)

The copper is alternately bivalent and univalent, and in the former condition it removes electrons from chloride ions whereas in the latter it gives up electrons to oxygen atoms. Such behavior is typical of elements which exist in their compounds at several valencies, and particularly when those elements exhibit valencies of n and n + 1. Zirconium exhibits only a valence of 4 in its compounds, excepting in a few compounds which are irrelevant to its broad catalytic behavior. It does not engage in the type of electron transfer common to the atoms which form paramagnetic ions; rather its catalytic effects are results of its combination with, orientation of, and transfer of atoms. When acetic acid and ethanol are passed over zirconium dioxide prepared by drying hydrous zirconia, or over silica gel impregnated with zirconium dioxide at about 340°, butadiene is formed (195, 196). In terms of an earlier perspective this would have been regarded as an oxidation-reduction reaction, since the structure —C—C=O is "reduced" to

$$\overset{H}{\underset{\cdot}{-C}}=CH,$$ but there is actually no change of carbon valence and there has been only a rearrangement of positions of hydrogen and oxygen atoms. The reaction is believed to proceed in the steps

$$2CH_3COOH + CH_3CH_2OH \rightarrow CH_3CHOHCH_2CHO + CH_3COOH + H_2O$$

(18)

in which ethanol removes oxygen from the acetic acid with the formation of a 4 C chain and a new molecule of acetic acid. The long-chain compound is then dehydrated:

$$CH_3CHOHCH_2CHO \rightarrow CH_3CH:CHCHO + H_2O \qquad (19)$$

193. H. O. Mottern, U.S. Patent 2,633,475, March 31, 1953.
194. W. M. Quattlebaum, W. J. Toussaint, and J. T. Dunn, *J. Am. Chem. Soc.* 69, 593-9 (1947).
195. W. G. Toussaint and J. T. Dunn, U.S. Patent 2,421,361, May 27, 1947.
196. R. Srinivasan and G. D. Hazra, *Science and Culture* 14, 532-3 (1949).

and again deoxygenated by ethanol:

$$2CH_3CH:CHCHO + CH_3CH_2OH \rightarrow 2CH_2:CHCH:CH_2 + CH_3COOH + H_2O \tag{20}$$

In the process the reactants are chemically combined to the zirconium atoms at the surface of the catalyst, and it is the activated complexes that undergo the changes. The total effect reflects the lability of a hydroxyl hydrogen atom when the hydroxyl oxygen atom is bonded to zirconium, and the tendency for the carbonyl oxygen atom to move from a 4 C to a 2 C chain.

Numerous other changes have been noted when oxygen-containing organic compounds are brought into contact with heated zirconia surfaces. Allyl alcohol is decomposed into ethylene, hydrogen, carbon dioxide, and liquid compounds (197); resin acids from tall oil are decarboxylated at 300-310° (198); furan reacts with an acid anhydride or ketenes to form acylated derivatives (199); and thiophene (thiofuran) reacts similarly (200, 201, 202); sulfur reacts with methane at 600° to form carbon bisulfide (203); and olefins of 8 or more carbon atoms react with hydrogen sulfide to form mercaptans (204). Somewhat similar to the formation of butadiene from acetic acid is the catalyzed formation of styrene from acetophenone and primary and secondary alcohols (205). Zirconia catalyzes the reaction of acetylene with water vapor at 400-500° to form acetaldehyde, and if ammonia be present, the process continues with the formation of acetimide and subsequently acetonitrile. Yields up to 99% acetonitrile have been reported for this process (206).

Zirconium dioxide has been found to catalyze many reactions of hydrocarbons, and these generally involve olefin linkages. In the presence of a proton donor, olefins form carbonium ions:

$$\overset{\displaystyle H \quad H}{R—C=C—R'} + H^+ \rightarrow \underset{\displaystyle H \quad +}{\overset{\displaystyle H \quad H}{R—C—C—R'}} \tag{21}$$

197. P. Sabatier and B. Kubota, *Compt. rend.* **173**, 212-6 (1921).

198. Terje Enkvist and Keijo Makela, *Finska Kemistsamfundets Medd.* **57**, No. 1-2, 21-61 (1948).

199. H. D. Hardtough and A. I. Kosak, U.S. Patent **2,460,825**, Feb. 8, 1949.

200. Hardtough and Kosak, U.S. Patent **2,458,512**, Jan. 11, 1949.

201. Hardtough and Kosak, U.S. Patent **2,458,513**, Jan. 11, 1949.

202. J. Kellet and H. E. Rasmussen, U.S. Patent **2,458,514**, Jan. 11, 1949.

203. H. O. Folkins and E. Miller, U.S. Patent **2,668,752**, Feb. 9, 1954.

204. W. A. Schulze, U.S. Patent **2,426,624**, Sept. 2, 1947.

205. British patent **616,844**, Jan. 27, 1949.

206. J. Amiel and G. Nomine, *Compt. rend.* **224**, 483-4 (1947).

The carbonium ions react with aliphatic chains to form new carbonium ions:

$$
\underset{\underset{H \ +}{|\ \ |}}{R-C-C-R'} + \underset{\underset{H\ H}{|\ \ |}}{R''-C-C-R'''} \rightarrow \underset{\underset{H\ H}{|\ \ |}}{R-C-C-R'} + \underset{\underset{H\ +}{|\ \ |}}{R''-C-C-R'''} \tag{22}
$$

They also tend to give rise to rupture of their chain in the β-position:

$$
\underset{\underset{H\ +}{|\ \ |}}{R-C-C-R'} \rightarrow R- \ + \ \underset{\underset{H\ +}{|\ \ |}}{-C-C-R'} \tag{23}
$$

The unsaturated bonds of aromatic compounds can play similar roles to those of the olefins. For further details of these processes, see references 207, 208.

A sequence of reactions of the above types can be started in hydrocarbons by a minute amount of an olefin present as an impurity or deliberately added for the purpose. According to C. L. Thomas (207), mixed zirconia-silica catalysts for hydrocarbon conversions act as though they were the acid $H_4ZrSi_2O_8$, capable of supplying a proton to an olefinic bond. From our present perspective, we can propose the alternative view that the zirconium atoms simply act as electron acceptors, forming carbonium ions by the process indicated by the above equation 15. Among the consequences of the hydrocarbon reactions are isomerization, e.g.,

$$
R-\underset{\underset{Zr}{\underset{|}{H\ +}}}{\overset{H\ H\ H\ H}{C-C-C-CH}} \rightarrow R-\underset{\underset{Zr\ H}{\underset{\downarrow}{H\ +}}}{\overset{H\ CH_3\ \ \ \overset{H}{\diagup}}{C-C-C}} \rightarrow R-\underset{\underset{Zr}{H}}{\overset{H\ CH_3\ \ \ \overset{H}{\diagup}}{C-C=C}}\diagdown H \tag{24}
$$

and cyclization:

$$
\underset{\underset{Zr}{H\ H\ H\ H}}{\overset{H\ H\ H\ H\ H\ H}{HC-C-C-C-C=C}} \rightarrow H_3C \overset{\overset{H_2H_2}{C-C}}{\diagup\diagdown} CH_2 \rightarrow H_2C \overset{\overset{H_2H_2}{C-C}}{\diagup\diagdown} CH_2 \tag{25}
$$

Depending on the relative rates of the several reactions, the main effects may turn out to be synthesis, cracking, alkylation, dealkylation, aromatization, or various combinations of these. For cracking, mixed compositions of alumina, silica, and zirconia have been widely reported to be effective.

207. C. L. Thomas, *Ind. Eng. Chem.* **41**, 2564-73 (1949).
208. B. S. Greenfelder, H. H. Voge, and G. M. Good, *Ind. Eng. Chem.* **41**, 2573-84 (1949).

Typical conditions of reaction are in the temperature range 240-340° under 800 lb/sq in pressure (209, 210). In other processes, olefins have been converted to high antiknock motor fuels (211); paraffin hydrocarbons have been isomerized (212); lignite tar distillate has been converted to gasoline (213); dialkyl paraffins have been broken down to two aromatic compounds (214); xylenes and o-dialkyl-benzenes have been isomerized (215); paraffins have been cyclized and aromatized (216, 217, 218) and maphthenic hydrocarbons aromatized (218); olefins have been polymerized—ethylene (219, 220), propylene and butylene (219, 221)—and combined with phenol at 300-400° to form alkylated phenols (222, 223) or with styrene at 200-260° to form lubricating oils (224). Rosin has been broken down under the influence of an alumina-silica-zirconia catalyst to lower molecular weight compounds, particularly aromatic hydrocarbons (225); and alkyl vinyl ethers have been pyrolyzed at 150-400° to yield monomeric aliphatic compounds (225b).

USES

The uses of zirconium dioxide are indicated by the properties discussed above. The chemical and metallurgical applications as a starting material in the preparation of zirconium metal and zirconium compounds are covered in various places in this book. It remains to take brief note of uses of zirconium dioxide which depend on its physical properties.

The extraordinarily high melting point of zirconium dioxide and its low thermal coefficient of expansion indicated it to be of potential value as a major component of refractories. However, the crystalline inversion at 1000° (and in fewer cases that at 1900°) proved seriously disadvantageous because of the change in density accompanying the phase change. This dif-

209. W. F. Claussen, U.S. Patent **2,400,075,** May 14, 1946.
210. V. Haensel and V. N. Ipatieff, U.S. Patent **2,401,636,** June 4, 1946.
211. C. L. Thomas, U.S. Patent **2,328,754,** Sept. 7, 1943.
212. E. C. Lee and J. E. Ahlberg, U.S. Patents **2,289,918/9,** July 14, 1942.
213. A. Gosselin, *Rev. inst. franç. pétrole* **1,** 145-51 (1946).
214. J. K. Dixon, U.S. Patent **2,422,164,** June 10, 1947.
215. E. D. Reeves, U.S. Patent **2,403,757,** July 9, 1946.
216. H. Fehrer and H. S. Taylor, *J. Am. Chem. Soc.* **63,** 1785-6, 1787-92 (1941).
217. J. K. Dixon, U.S. Patent **2,422,166,** June 10, 1947.
218. J. O. Smith, Jr., U.S. Patents **2,424,636/7,** July 26, 1947.
219. S. C. Fulton and T. Cross, U.S. Patent **2,129,732,** Sept. 13, 1938.
220. A. Zletz, U.S. Patent **2,692,258,** Oct. 19, 1954.
221. C. L. Thomas, *Ind. Eng. Chem.* **37,** 543-5 (1945).
222. W. A. Schulze and C. E. Stoops, U.S. Patent **2,514,419,** Jul. 11, 1950.
223. C. L. Thomas and V. Haensel, U.S. Patent **2,410,111,** Oct. 29, 1946.
224. O. M. Reiff, H. J. Andress, and A. P. Kozacik, U.S. Patent **2,500,203,** March 14, 1950.
225. I. T. Clark and E. E. Harris, *J. Am. Chem. Soc.* **74,** 1030-2 (1952).
225b. D. C. Hull and H. J. Hagemeyer, Jr., U.S. Patent **2,642,460,** June 16, 1953.

ficulty was finally circumvented by firing the zirconia with about 3-5% of certain other oxides which enter into solid solution with it and induce formation of the cubic arkelite structure. Lime is most commonly used for this purpose. The oxide composition prepared in this fashion is known in industry as *stabilized zirconia* and gives good service in refractory bodies up to about 2200°. Up to about 10% zirconia plus titania has been used in refractories of high lime content to stabilize them against hydration (226).

Due to its hardness, zirconium dioxide powder has proved to be of value in glass polishing (227), in general abrasive applications (228), and in attrition-resisting materials (229, 230). It has been added to metals to harden them for use in tools and dies (231, 232, 233).

The high index of refraction of zirconium dioxide has led to its use as a ceramic opacifier for glazes and enamels. In the molten frits, the zirconia frequently combines with silica to form zircon, and this latter compound is the actual opacifying agent. Zirconia has high opacity to X-rays, and its use in X-ray photography has been reported (234). The heated oxide has been reported to be a good source of infrared radiation (235) and of white light (234, 236). It has also been found to intensify the blue luminescence of magnesium oxide (237). Both zirconia and hafnia have been described as suitable sources of blue to green luminescence when irradiated with electrons or with short ultraviolet waves (238). Zirconia is capable of functioning as a phosphor activator, principally in oxygen- and fluorine-dominated host crystals (239). It mitigated the blackening of electrodes of radiation lamps when it was incorporated into the phosphor-containing body (240), and it greatly increased the life of cathodes of fluorescent lamps when incorporated in the cathode coating (241).

The recrystallization of refractory metal electric-lamp filaments, such as tungsten, molybdenum, or tantalum, was retarded by the presence of 0.1-

226. A. J. Hathaway, U.S. Patent **2,678,887**, May 18, 1954.
227. J. B. Miller, U.S. Patent **2,624,661**, Jan. 6, 1953.
228. *Ibid.*, **2,489,307**, Nov. 17, 1949.
229. W. B. Blumenthal, U.S. Patent **2,653,107**, Sept. 22, 1953.
230. S. S. Kistler, U.S. Patent **2,624,097**, Jan. 6, 1953.
231. E. B. Welch, British Patent **345,167**, Sept. 27, 1929.
232. Gregory J. Comstock, U.S. Patent **1,826,456**, Oct. 6, 1931.
233. *Ibid.*, U.S. Patent **1,826,457**, Oct. 6, 1931.
234. H. C. Meyer, *J. Soc. Chem. Ind.* **37**, 698A (1918).
235. M. B. Hall and R. G. Nesten, *J. Optical Soc. Am.* **42**, 257-8 (1952).
236. J. R. Benford, *J. Optical Soc. Am.* **37**, 642-7 (1947).
237. R. H. Bube and K. F. Stripp, *J. Chem. Phys.* **20**, 193-4 (1952).
238. F. A. Kröger and J. T. Overbeck, Dutch patent **73,114**, Aug. 15, 1953.
239. R. Ward, *J. Phys. Chem.* **57**, 773-5 (1953).
240. R. A. Nilender, *Izvest. Akad. Nauk. U.S.S.R.*, *Ser. Fiz.* **15**, 807-14 (1951).
241. E. F. Lowry, *Sylvania Technologist* **3**, No. 1, 2-5 (1950).

3% of hafnia in their composition (242) and it inhibited undesirable off-setting (243).

In certain glasses, zirconia decreases the coefficient of thermal expansion and increases the chemical resistance (244, 245). Up to 5% has been used in eye-protecting ophthalmic glass, in which it absorbs undesired infrared and ultraviolet radiation (246).

Due to its high electrical resistance, zirconia has been used in ceramic insulators (247, 248), and it has been incorporated as a filler in polytetra-fluoroethylene wire-insulating composition (249).

Zirconium dioxide is said to be active in a selective capacity in removing tellurium and mercury, particularly the former, from crude selenium (250).

HYDROUS ZIRCONIA AND THE COMPLEX HYDROXIDES OF ZIRCONIUM

When a base such as ammonium hydroxide is added to an aqueous solution of a zirconyl salt, a gelatinous precipitate forms. Similar precipitates of substantially the same chemical composition may be prepared by adding to the solution a solid base, such as magnesium oxide (251), by raising the pH of the solution electrolytically (252, 253), or by adding solutions of certain salts with alkaline reactions, such as sodium thiosulfate; but in the latter case the product will be modified to some extent by the anions of the salt. Also, the gelatinous material can be formed directly from a solid zirconium salt by treating it with gaseous ammonia or with aqueous ammonium hydroxide (254).

If the precipitate formed on mixing aqueous zirconyl chloride and ammonium hydroxide is filtered and washed, a water pulp is recovered which may contain from 5-40% zirconium dioxide by weight, depending on how the precipitation was conducted. After drying the pulp in air, the residue will contain about 53% zirconium dioxide, corresponding to the composition $ZrO_2 \cdot 6H_2O$. It is, however, not a compound of zirconium dioxide and

242. British patent **220,301**, Aug. 9, 1923.
243. J. A. M. van Liempt, *Nature* **115**, 194 (1925).
244. W. Horak and D. E. Shap, *J. Am. Ceram. Soc.* **18**, 281-4 (1935).
245. M. Fanderlik and Zd. Schaefer, *Sklarske Rozhledy* **20**, 41-5 (1943).
246. W. H. Armistead, U.S. Patent **2,688,561**, Sept. 7, 1954.
247. L. Navias, U.S. Patent **2,515,790**, July 18, 1950.
248. E. J. W. Verwey and R. D. Bugel, *Philips Tech. Rev.* **10**, 231-8 (1949).
249. P. F. Sanders, U.S. Patent **2,567,162**, Sept. 4, 1951.
250. Takeshi Takei, Kozo Aoyama, and Hiroshi Akada, *Repts. Sci. Research Inst.* (Tokyo) **26**, 234-9 (1950).
251. C. N. Kimberlin, Jr., U.S. Patent **2,524,810**, Oct. 10, 1950.
252. R. H. Leutz, German patent **741,670**, Sept. 30, 1943.
253. Marthe Domine-Berges, *Ann. chim.* (12) **5**, 106-51 (1950).
254. P. Schmid, German patent **509,151**, Nov. 11, 1925.

water. Dehydration isobars show that the aqueous vapor pressure over the composition falls continuously as the temperature is slowly raised and dehydration progresses, and there are no discontinuities to indicate the presence of hydrated compounds (255, 256). This is true regardless of the variations in method of preparing the precipitate from a zirconyl salt and an alkali. The absence of actual hydrates of zirconia has also been demonstrated by measurements of the magnetic susceptibility during the dehydration process. The magnetic susceptibility is a linear function of the water content (63). The substance is therefore spoken of as *hydrous zirconia*, and the adjective *hydrous* implies that the water is loosely bound in nonstoichiometric proportions (169). The formula designation is $ZrO_2 \cdot xH_2O$, in which x is a continuously varying quantity. Electron diffraction studies have shown that the particles resulting from the precipitation are of the order of 0.01 microns in diameter (258), and they are too small to give X-ray diffraction patterns (259). Vague diffraction patterns which have been observed by some investigators appear to have been due either to pseudomorphism after the solid zirconyl chloride from which the hydrous zirconia was prepared (169) or to incipient crystal orientation (260). Hydrous zirconia may be regarded as consisting of exceedingly minute crystals of zirconium dioxide, holding onto chemically adsorbed water which is loosely bound by unstable covalencies. The difference between its structural representation and that of a classical hydroxide is shown by I and II of Figure 4.3. For simplicity, 2 molecules of water are shown in

$$
\begin{array}{cc}
\begin{array}{c}
O \\
\parallel \\
H_2O \rightarrow Zr \leftarrow OH_2 \\
\parallel \\
O
\end{array}
&
\begin{array}{c}
OH \\
| \\
HO-Zr-OH \\
| \\
HO
\end{array}
\\
I & II
\end{array}
$$

Fig. 4.3. Structural representations of hydrous zirconia (I) and zirconium hydroxide (II).

the representation of hydrous zirconia. It is of interest that zirconium's neighbor in Group IV of the periodic chart of the elements, titanium, forms a similar precipitated hydrous oxide, but in this case the particles are sufficiently large to exhibit typical patterns to the X-ray, and they

255. J. M. van Bemmeln, *Z. anorg. allgem. Chem.* **45**, 83 (1905).
256. A. Simon and O. Fischer, *Z. anorg. allgem. Chem.* **185**, 130 (1929).
258. Unpublished studies of the Titanium Alloy Mfg. Division of the National Lead Co.
259. H. Freundlich, *Ber.* **61B**, 2219-33 (1928).
260. F. Haber, *Ber.* **55B**, 1717-33 (1922).

are identified as hydrous anatase or hydrous rutile, depending upon the anions present during the precipitation.

When hydrous zirconia is dried at room temperature *in vacuo*, its water content is reduced to that of the composition $ZrO_2 \cdot 1\frac{1}{2}H_2O$ (261); when dried over sulfuric acid (262) or phosphorus pentoxide (258), the composition becomes constant at the composition $ZrO_2 \cdot 2H_2O$. Washing the water pulp thoroughly with petroleum ether has also led to the composition $ZrO_2 \cdot 2H_2O$ (263). A process for preparing dry hydrous zirconia by washing the water pulp with liquids insoluble in water and having no solvent action on the zirconia, followed by evaporating off the liquid, has been patented (264). If a solvent such as alcohol, which is miscible with water and contains an atom capable of donating electrons to a coordinate bond, is used to wash the water pulp, a solid can be recovered containing only 0.1-0.7 moles of water per mole of zirconium dioxide (265). In such a case, there is a chemical replacement of water by alcohol, i.e., an exchange adsorption. The extent of dehydration of zirconia by such a process has shown no relationship to the conditions under which the hydrous zirconia was precipitated (266).

It is seen clearly from the above that such a composition as $ZrO_2 \cdot 2H_2O$ is strictly a fortuitous one, and the amount of water in the composition merely reflects the adsorptive capacity for water at room temperature under the particular environmental conditions described to give this composition. It is of value to examine the differences in bonding that are responsible for the different relationship of zirconium in hydrous zirconia to its water and that of some other metal which forms a true hydrate to its water. Copper sulfate, $CuSO_4 \cdot 5H_2O$ might be used for such a comparison. It is known that in this compound, 4 molecules of water are bound to the copper cation and 1 molecule of water to the sulfate anion. In the copper cation, the arrangement of the aquo groups can be represented

$$\begin{bmatrix} & HOH & \\ H & \downarrow & H \\ O & \rightarrow Cu \leftarrow & O \\ H & \uparrow & H \\ & HOH & \end{bmatrix}^{+2}$$

Bivalent copper forms 4 very stable dsp^2 bonds, whence it would be expected that the tetraquo cupric ion is a stable arrangement. In hydrous

261. S. R. Paykull, *Oefvers. Vet. Akad. For.* **22** (1873).
262. R. Hermann, *J. prakt. Chem.* (1) **31**, 75 (1844).
263. F. P. Venable and A. W. Belden, *J. Am. Chem. Soc.* **20**, 273 (1898).
264. H. A. Bruson and W. D. Niederhauser, U.S. Patent **2,435,553**, Feb. 21, 1948.
265. J. M. van Bemmelen, *Z. anorg. allgem. Chem.* **49**, 125 (1906).
266. R. Ruer, *Z. anorg. allgem. Chem.* **43**, 282 (1905).

zirconia a bonding arrangement exists in the zirconium dioxide crystal skeleton in which maximum stability, i.e., lowest energy content, has been achieved by a preferred orbital hybridization. Even the surface units of the structure are committed to this preferred arrangement. Aquo groups can be bound to the surface zirconium atoms only through zirconium orbitals which remain unoccupied after the bonding within the crystal. Such remaining orbitals are doubtless distorted and decreased in stability by the total adaptation of the zirconium atoms to their lattice fields, and the possibilities of increasing the bond strengths of the residual orbitals by hybridization is minimal.

The preferential formation of structure I rather than structure II in Figure 4.3 has already been discussed in Chapter 1. p. 37. Due to the tendency of zirconium to attain to the sterically highest possible coordination number, were structure II to form, it would tend to alter with the hydroxyl groups becoming ol groups:

$$
\begin{array}{cc}
\text{OH} & \text{OH} \\
| & | \\
\text{HO--Zr--OH} \rightleftharpoons \text{HO} {=} \text{Zr} {=} \text{OH} \\
| & | \\
\text{HO} & \text{HO}
\end{array}
\qquad (26)
$$

resulting in a negative charge on the zirconium atom, an induced negative polarity at the hydroxyl groups, and a positive charge on the ol group. Were this to occur to a hydroxide of another element, such as aluminum, the effect would be relieved by ion formation

$$
\begin{array}{c}
\text{OH} \\
| \\
\text{HO--Al} {=} \text{OH}
\end{array}
\rightleftharpoons (\text{HO--Al} {=} \text{OH})^{+}\text{OH}^{-}
\qquad (27)
$$

The negative charge on the aluminum is thus imparted to a hydroxyl group, converting it to a hydroxyl ion. But it is characteristic of zirconium not to relinquish electron pairs with formation of ionic bonds. Instead, hydrogen ions are repelled from the positively charged ol oxygen atoms rather than hydroxyl ions from the negatively charged zirconium:

$$
\begin{array}{cc}
\text{OH} & \text{HOH} \\
| & \downarrow \\
\text{HO} {=} \text{Zr} {=} \text{OH} \rightarrow \text{O} {=} \text{Zr} {=} \text{O} \\
| & \uparrow \\
\text{HO} & \text{HOH}
\end{array}
\qquad (28)
$$

whence they readily take positions on the negatively polarized hydroxyl groups to form aquo groups.

The formation of hydrous zirconia on the addition of ammonia to an aqueous solution of zirconyl chloride appears to be expressed best by the following equations:

$$ZrOCl_2 \xrightarrow{H_2O} ZrOOH^+ + H^+ + 2Cl^-$$
$$ZrOOH^+ + OH^- \rightarrow ZrO(OH)_2 \rightarrow ZrO_2 \cdot xH_2O + (1-x)\, H_2O$$

(29-30)

Larsen and Gammill demonstrated that on adding slowly 0.1010 M sodium hydroxide to 0.038 M zirconium tetrachloride solution, a dispersed solid first began to form perceptibly when the pH had attained a value of 2.0 and about 2.5 moles of the base had been added per mole of zirconium tetrachloride. In a perchlorate solution, the pH at incipient precipitation was almost the same (the region of the curve showing pH as a function of the amount of alkali added was almost horizontal near the precipitation point), but about 3 moles of sodium hydroxide had been added per mole of zirconium tetrachloride. The solid was initially colloidally dispersed and was perceived only as an opalescence. Coagulation occurred in both the chloride and perchlorate solutions at pH values of about 5.5 to 6.0, nearly 4 moles of sodium hydroxide having been added per mole of zirconium salt. Good duplicability was obtained by this procedure for the precipitation and coagulation points. Hafnium salt solutions were similar in behavior to the corresponding zirconium salt solutions, but the pH of initial precipitation was slightly higher for hafnium (267).

In the experiments of Larsen and Gammill, the concentration of zirconium salt was close to 0.020 M at precipitation, and the hydroxyl ion concentration was 10^{-12}. The ion product, therefore, was

$$[ZrOOH^-] \times [OH^-] = 2 \times 10^{-14}.$$

Since the reaction was not reversible, due to rapid changes in the unstable zirconyl hydroxide which formed instantaneously, this ion product is not a solubility product. The irreversibility of the precipitation reaction is reflected in the failure of any investigators to find evidence of digestion of the solid to larger crystals as it aged in its mother liquor.

Ions and molecules which complex zirconium tend to inhibit or prevent the formation of hydrous zirconia when the pH of a zirconyl salt solution is raised. A slight tendency in this direction appeared to be manifested by the perchlorate ion (*supra*), since more base had to be added to a perchlorate solution than to a chloride solution to precipitate hydrous zirconia. When the stoichiometric amounts of citrate, tartrate, lactate, or certain other complexing ions are present, the precipitation of hydrous zirconia is prevented until the pH attains a strongly alkaline value, about 10-11. Glycol

---

267. E. M. Larsen and A. M. Gammill, *J. Am. Chem. Soc.* **72**, 3615-19 (1950).

and glycerine specifically prevent precipitation of hydrous zirconia in strongly alkaline solution, pH about 14, but not at lower alkalinities.

During the formation of hydrous zirconia, individual molecules must coalesce to form skeletal crystals. In an environment containing the species $ZrOOH^+$, it appears reasonable that a certain number of these ions will take the place of molecules of ZrO_2 as structural units. If we visualize the unidimensional growth of the crystals, we have

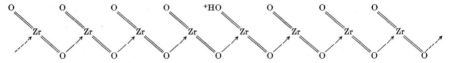

The hydrogen ion can shift its position from one oxygen atom to another, and regardless of its position, it imparts a positive charge to the crystallite. There is some evidence that the crystallite takes the tetragonal ruffite structure, for when the dried precipitate is heated to not higher than 600°, it exhibits the X-ray diffraction pattern of a tetragonal lattice. Above 600° the lattice changes to monoclinic (268). Since ruffite is not stable at ordinary temperatures, the chemical activity of hydrous ruffite would be greater than that of hydrous baddeleyite. Some fragmentary evidence exists for a less reactive variety of hydrous zirconia, formed under special conditions, which may be of the baddeleyite structure. Solutions of zirconyl chloride sealed in glass capillary tubes and heated to 150° undergo hydrolysis to a solid hydrolysate which does not visibly redissolve when the solution is cooled and allowed to stand, although the acid concentration is sufficient to dissolve the ordinary hydrous zirconia. When tetraurea zirconium tetrachloride is dissolved in water, a small amount of solid hydrolysate forms which appears to be hydrous zirconia and is insoluble at a pH (0.7) at which ordinary hydrous zirconia dissolves (258). Commercial aqueous ammonium zirconyl carbonate slowly deposits an insoluble precipitate of hydrous zirconia even though the same solution is capable of dissolving more of the better-known variety of hydrous zirconia. In what follows, discussions of hydrous zirconia will refer only to the more common variety having properties suggestive of the ruffite structure.

On drying, hydrous zirconia shrinks and forms a hard, shiny mass which exhibits a conchoidal fracture (269). It is more or less translucent, depending upon its history. It can be dehydrated completely below 400° without developing sufficient crystallinity to give a pattern when it is subjected to X-ray diffraction techniques (270). It has been observed that when the

268. G. L. Clark and D. H. Reynolds, *Ind. Eng. Chem.* **29**, 711-15 (1937).
269. L. N. Vauquelin, *Ann. Chim. Phys.* (1) **22**, 179 (1797).
270. J. Böhm and H. Niclassen, *Z. anorg. allgem. Chem.* **132**, 1 (1923).

dried hydrous zirconia is subjected to the action of isopropyl benzene vapor at 260°, the apparently homogeneous particles are converted to a heterogeneous mixture of light-gray and black particles. After separation, they can be restored to their original appearance by burning out the carbonaceous coating. There are then no residual differences in available surface, average particle size, or density. But if the fractions are individually treated with isopropyl benzene vapor, the same differentiation by color shows up as before (271).

Depending upon the physical and chemical conditions of formation of hydrous zirconia, the aqueous preparation may be a clear colloidal solution, a jelly, an unfilterable slurry, a difficultly filterable slurry, or an easily filtered slurry. If flocculated hydrous zirconia is washed to a high degree of purity, it is peptized. Peptized hydrous zirconia may be prepared by a number of methods. In one, ammonium hydroxide solution is added to zirconium nitrate solution and the precipitate washed by decantation with water, with cold ammonium nitrate solution, and finally with hot ammonium nitrate solution. Then, on filtering the slurry, an opalescent filtrate is obtained, containing peptized hydrous zirconia. If the solution is evaporated to dryness, it yields a clear gum. When the gum is treated with water, it swells up and finally disperses to form a viscid liquid which becomes turbid on standing (272). Hydrous zirconia is peptized by certain electrolytes, such as uranyl nitrate (273), and by sugars, such as lactose and levulose (274).

Hydrous zirconia sols are obtained by dialysis of zirconyl chloride and other zirconium salt solutions, and jellies are formed when the sols are permitted to set (266, 274, 275). Many anions coagulate the hydrosol, whereas cations are commonly without effect (272). Ferrocyanide, sulfate, oxalate, tartrate, fluoride, chloride, bromide, and iodide have been found to coagulate hydrous zirconia hydrosols in that order of decreasing effectiveness (276). Some metal ions, such as aluminum cations, cause hydrous zirconia to form in fairly stable colloidal condition. If zirconyl chloride solution is added to an aqueous suspension of its chemical equivalence of freshly prepared, washed aluminum hydroxide, the reaction

$$3ZrOCl_2 + 2Al(OH)_3 \rightarrow 3ZrO_2 \cdot xH_2O + 2AlCl_3 + (3 - 3x) H_2O \quad (31)$$

occurs and results in a clear colloidal solution of hydrous zirconia. As the solution stands, it sets to a clear jelly which slowly develops opacity. A clear,

271. G. H. Hüttig and G. Pietzka, *Monatsh.* **78**, 185-92 (1948).
272. A. Müller, *Z. anorg. allgem. Chem.* **52**, 316 (1907).
273. B. Szilard, *J. Chim. Phys.* **5**, 488, 640 (1908).
274. K. C. Sen, *Z. anorg. allgem. Chem.* **174**, 61-74 (1928).
275. R. D. Sharma and N. R. Dhar, *J. Indian Chem. Soc.* **9**, 455-61 (1932).
276. S. Ghosh and N. R. Dhar, *J. Indian Chem. Soc.* **5**, 303-11 (1928).

rigid jelly has also been obtained by adding a piece of aluminum foil to a solution of trioxodizirconium hydroxyiodide and allowing it to stand in a stoppered vessel. The reaction

$$\text{Al} + 3\text{Zr}_2\text{O}_3\text{OHI} + 6x\text{H}_2\text{O} \rightarrow 6\text{ZrO}_2 \cdot x\text{H}_2\text{O} + \text{AlI}_3 + 3\text{H} \qquad (32)$$

results in the formation of hydrous zirconia jelly (258). During the gelation of hydrous zirconia, the particles remain small, and the linear dimensions do not attain to the wavelength of ordinary light (277).

For details of the properties of hydrous zirconia sols, the following literature may be consulted: aging (270, 278, 279); coagulation (280, 281, 283, 284, 285); adsorption (281, 286, 287, 288, 289, 290); cryotropism (279); elasticity (291); Liesegang rings (292, 293); magnetic susceptibility (257); setting time (294, 295); specific heat (296); viscosity (275, 291, 297, 298).

As noted in connection with the precipitation studies of Larsen and Gammill (*supra*), when a base is added to a zirconyl chloride, nitrate, or perchlorate solutions, a colloidal dispersion is first obtained, and a coagulated precipitate is obtained only after the pH has attained a value of about 5.5. If ammonium carbonate is added to zirconyl chloride solution until a precipitate just forms (pH slightly above 2.5 in a solution 0.3 M with respect to zirconium), it is exceedingly gelatinous and practically impossible to filter. On the other hand, if an excess of aqueous ammonia is added to zirconyl chloride solution, or particularly if zirconyl chloride solution is added to an excess of aqueous ammonia, a dense coagulated gelatinous

277. C. R. Kanekar and K. E. Subrahmanian, *J. Univ. Bombay* **19A**, pt. 5, 28-34 (1951).
278. G. F. Hüttig. S. Magierkiewicz, and J. Fichmann, *Z. phys. Chem.* **141A**, 1-34 (1929).
279. S. Prakash, *Indian J. Physics* **8**, 243-58 (1933).
280. E. Schalek and A. Szegvari, *Z. phys. Chem.* **33**, 326 (1923).
281. M. Adolph and W. Pauli, *Zeit. Koll.* **29**, 173 (1921).
282. S. Prakash, *J. Indian Chem. Soc.* **9**, 193-202 (1932).
283. Prakash, *J. Phys. Chem.* **36**, 2483-96 (1932).
284. N. R. Dhar and V. Gore, *J. Indian Chem. Soc.* **6**, 31-43 (1929).
285. M. Prasad, S. Gurnswamy, and N. A. Padwal, *J. Indian Chem. Soc.* **19A**, 89-400 (1944).
286. H. Rheinboldt and E. Wedekind, *Ber.* **47**, 2142 (1914).
287. O. Hahn and M. Biltz, *Z. physik. Chem.* **126**, 323-55 (1927).
288. S. N. Chakravarty and K. C. Sen, *Z. anorg. allgem. Chem.* **186**, 357-64 (1930).
289. J. Shormüller, *Z. Lebensm.-Untersuch. u. Forsch.* **88**, 576-86 (1948).
290. D. A. Hermansen, U.S. Patent **2,487,805**, Nov. 15, 1949.
291. H. Freundlich and E. Schalek, *Z. physik. Chem.* **108**, 153 (1924).
292. M. C. Rastogi, *J. Indian Chem. Soc.* **29**, 206-8 (1952).
293. A. C. Chatterji and M. C. Rastogi, *J. Indian Chem. Soc.* **28**, 283-4 (1951).
294. H. L. Dube and S. Prakash, *Proc. Indian Acad. Sci.* **11A**, 318-30 (1940).
295. C. B. Hurd, W. A. Fallon, and R. W. Hobday, *J. Am. Chem. Soc.* **64**, 110-14 (1942).
296. F. G. Huttig and H. Wehling, *Kolloid Chem. Beihefte* **23**, 354-61 (1926).
297. F. J. Robinson and G. H. Ayres, *J. Am. Chem. Soc.* **55**, 2288-94 (1933).
298. M. Prasad and K. V. Modak, *Proc. Indian Acad. Sci.* **15A**, 445-55 (1942).

precipitate is obtained which can be filtered rapidly and washed free of electrolytes. The latter procedure is used in industry for the preparation of hydrous zirconia.

Hydrous zirconia particles are capable of some interesting and useful alterations. We have seen that they consist of a skeleton of zirconium dioxide with water loosely bound by valence bonds to the crystal surfaces. The surface has been estimated to be 80% hydrated (299). In addition to the chemically bound water, there is an indefinite amount of water held physically in the interstices and as an envelop around the micelle. It will be seen that anions from acids or salts dissolved in the solution may also enter into the micelles.

Water, hydrogen ions (i.e., hydronium ions or protons coordinated with zirconyl oxygen atoms to form ol groups), and hydroxyl ions can be displaced from the micelle by other ions, atoms, or molecules. If alkali salts are added to the aqueous slurry of hydrous zirconia, the pH of the liquid phase is observed to rise (300), indicating that hydroxyl ions have been displaced from the micelle by chloride ions:

$$ZrO_2 \cdot xH_2O + yCl^- \rightleftharpoons ZrO_2 \cdot (x - y)H_2O \cdot yHCl + yOH^- \qquad (33)$$

If the slurry is filtered and the filter cake is washed, chloride ions are found by chemical test to have remained in the solid, and the lower the pH of the slurry, the higher the chloride content of the hydrous zirconia. In the complex, $ZrO_2 \cdot (x-y)H_2O \cdot yHCl$, the hydrogen chloride is not present as such but rather the hydrogen is bound as an ion in the manner already described and the chlorine is either bound coordinately to a zirconium atom or held electrostatically by the positively charged complex. Figure 4.4 shows a series of curves obtained by Thomas and Owens (300) for the pH's of hydrous zirconia sols as functions of the amounts of potassium salts added. It is seen that the feebly coordinating chloride ion has a relatively small effect on the pH; the monocarboxylates, formate, acetate, and propionate, have considerably greater effects; the dicarboxylates have still greater effect; and the hydroxycarboxylates, citrate, tartrate, and glycolate, as a group, have the largest effect in raising the pH. Thus, the displacement of hydroxyl ion is essentially in the order expected from the relative affinities of the ions for the zirconium atom. The curves indicate that the nitrate ion has about the same order of affinity for zirconium as the chloride ion, and sulfate about the same as acetate. When a 0.0086 M solution of hydrochloric acid was passed through a filter cake on a Buchner funnel, the chloride content in the effluent was found first to be reduced to about 0.2 of its original concentration in the wash solution, and then to rise rapidly

299. S. Prakash, *Kolloid Z.* **60**, 184-91 (1932).
300. A. W. Thomas and H. S. Owens, *J. Am. Chem. Soc.* **57**, 1825-8 (1935).

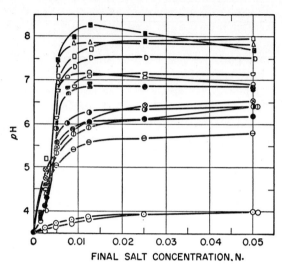

Fig. 4.4. Effect of potassium salts on the *p*H value of Sol D, sol 4 days old: ⓘ, acetate; ⊙, chloride; ◾, citrate; ⊖, formate; ◑, fumarate; ▽, glycolate; △, malate; ◆, maleinate; ⌒, malonate; ○, nitrate; □, oxalate; ⊗, propionate; ◣, succinate; ●, sulfate; D, tartrate.

to the full concentration. The maximum amount of chloride ion retained on the filter cake was 0.016 mg per g of ZrO_2. When the same procedure was followed using 0.0080 M oxalic acid, a comparable volume of effluent was found to contain only 0.005 of the original concentration (258).

The ions which form chelate structures with the zirconium atom, particularly the hydroxycarboxylate ions, displace water as well as hydroxyl ions from the micelles, and this results in a change in the electrostatic charge from positive to negative (301). Table 4.4 lists some anions that have been found to reverse the charge on the micelles of hydrous zirconia, and also some that do not. The reaction which results in the reversal of the charge can be represented

$$ZrO_2 \cdot xH_2O + yA^- \rightleftharpoons (ZrO_2 \cdot (x-y)H_2O \cdot yA)^{-y} + yH_2O \qquad (34)$$

This representation has been simplified by neglecting the probability of an anion A^- displacing some number of aquo groups other than one, and by allowing y to have fractional values in the common case of less than one anion per zirconium atom reacting with a micelle of the hydrous zirconia. Thomas called the negatively charged micelles *zirconeates*, and he gave the order of activity in the displacement of aquo groups: tartrate > citrate > succinate > malate > oxalate > glycolate > lactate. This is also the order

---

301. A. W. Thomas and H. S. Owens, *J. Am. Chem. Soc.* **57**, 2131-5 (1935).

TABLE 4.4. EFFECTS OF VARIOUS ANIONS ON THE ELECTROSTATIC
CHARGE OF HYDROUS ZIRCONIA (301)

Reverse Charge from Positive to Negative	*Do Not Reverse Charge from Positive to Negative*
Citrate	Acetate
Glycolate	β-Hydroxybutyrate
Lactate	Chloride
Malate	Ethoxyacetate
Mucate	Ferricyanide
Pyruvate	Ferrocyanide
Tartrate	Formate
Dihydrogen phosphate	Fumarate
Pyrophosphate	Glycine
	Maleinate
	Monochloracetate
	Monohydrogen phosphate
	Oxalate
	Phosphate
	β-Hydroxyphenylglycine
	Propionate

of effectiveness of the anions in peptizing hydrous zirconia, except that in peptization, succinate would be placed last. In the displacement of aquo groups, hydronium ions would also be forced from the micelles into the liquid phase (301).

It has been demonstrated that the zirconeates will precipitate the colored cations of basic dyes, and processes for preparing intensely colored pigments by this method have been patented (302, 303).

Hydrous zirconia is relatively slightly affected by solutions of alkali hydryoxides, but hydroxyl tends to displace all other adsorbed anions. Were hydroxyl ions to be complexed, the complex would be of the nature of a zirconate, and the pH of the suspending liquid would tend to be lowered by passage of hydroxyl ions into the solid. This does not occur at low and moderate concentrations of strong bases, however. In very concentrated solutions of sodium or potassium hydroxide, there is appreciable dissolution of hydrous zirconia, and this may be presumed to be due to formation of zirconates. But since the zirconates are stable only in the presence of strong alkali, they are not readily isolated from aqueous solutions, and such zirconates have not yet been characterized. Substituted zirconates, such as carbonatozirconates, glycolatozirconates, and mandelatozirconates are well

302. W. B. Blumenthal, *Am. Dyestuff Reptr.* **37**, 285-6 (1948).
303. Blumenthal, U.S. Patent **2,492,959**, Jan. 3, 1950.

known, and many examples of this type of compound have been isolated and described.

The absorption of many substances from aqueous solution have been reported. The adsorption of carbon dioxide from the air (261) is doubtless via carbonic acid formation. Both iodine (286) and bromine (305) are absorbed from aqueous solutions, and hydrous zirconia decolorizes starch iodine solution, acquiring the blue color itself. It has been noted to adsorb arsenious acid without compound formation, and arsenic (306, 307) and phosphoric (308) acids with formation of insoluble compounds. When hydrous zirconia is precipitated with an excess of ammonia in the presence of a cupric salt, the precipitate is colored light blue by cupric ions which cannot be washed out of the precipitate with water or with aqueous ammonia (308b). Hydrous zirconia takes up fatty acids and benzoic acid and its derivatives, and it has been noted that the higher the ionization products of these acids, the greater the apparent capacity of hydrous zirconia for their adsorption, indicating that chemical reaction follows the adsorption (288). The products obtained after adsorption of fatty acids are soluble in solvents such as carbon tetrachloride, and hence the zirconia must have been converted to soaps (258). Rapid but not quantitative adsorption of hydrogen peroxide occurs, and the decomposition of the un-adsorbed peroxide is catalyzed by the hydrous zirconia. The adsorbed peroxide cannot be titrated quantitatively with potassium permanganate unless the hydrous zirconia is dissolved with acid, and it does not react with blood (309). In alkaline solution hydrous zirconia is dissolved by hydrogen peroxide to form perzirconate salts. They can be recovered as crystalline precipitates by adding ethanol. Hydrous hafnia behaves the same as hydrous zirconia in these respects (310). As might be expected, hydrous zirconia readily forms lakes with dyes. Such lakes are useful in the analytical detection of zirconium (311) and in the manufacture of industrial pigments.

The more vigorous chemical reagents dissolve hydrous zirconia with formation of salts, but the rate of attack is often surprisingly slow. It is probable that because of the slowness of attack, some reagents have incorrectly been reported not to react. Stoichiometric equivalents of hydrofluoric, sulfuric, and oxalic acids attack and dissolve hydrous zirconia quite rapidly, but hydrochloric acid reacts quite slowly if only enough is used to form

305. E. Beutel and A. Kutzelnigg, *Monatsh.* **64**, 114-22 (1934).
306. E. Wedekind and H. Wilke, *Kolloid Z.* **34**, 83-97 (1924).
307. K. C. Sen, *Z. anorg. allgem. Chem.* **174**, 75-81 (1928).
308. E. Wedekind and H. Wilke, *Kolloid Z.* **34**, 283-9 (1924).
308b. P. Berthier, *Ann. Chim. Phys.* (2) **50**, 362 (1832).
309. E. Wedekind and H. Wilke, *Kolloid Z.* **35**, 23-4 (1924).
310. G. von Hevesy, *Z. anorg. allgem. Chem.* **147**, 217-32 (1925).
311. A. R. Middleton, *J. Am. Chem. Soc.* **48**, 2125-6 (1926).

ZrOOHCl, about a week being required to approach complete dissolution at room temperature. Dilute aqueous alkalies have no effect on hydrous zirconia, but 2.33 g (ZrO_2 basis) was reported to be dissolved in a liter of 50% potassium hydroxide at 50° and 2.45 g in a liter of 33% sodium hydroxide (312). There was no appreciable solubility in aqueous ammonium hydroxide of specific gravity 0.90, but 100 g of specific gravity 0.96 dissolved 0.01 g of hydrous zirconia (on a ZrO_2 basis) (263). Venable and Belden (*ibid.*) found 100 g of a saturated solution of ammonium carbonate to dissolve 1 g of hydrous zirconia, but the other investigators have found that ammonium carbonate solutions dissolve large quantities of hydrous zirconia on standing for about a week.

Hydrous zirconia and hydrous hafnia have been found to catalyze the condensation of lactams with formation of polymers capable of being spun into fibers and drawn to 4.5 times their original lengths (313). Hydrous zirconia catalyzes the dehydration of diols at temperatures greater than 100°, with formation of olefins (314), and it improves the yield of methanol synthesized from carbon oxides and hydrogen at 250-400° (315). It is the starting material in preparing so-called gel catalysts for cracking hydrocarbons (316, 317, 318). Techniques for preparing various kinds of granules and pellets of dried hydrous zirconia for use as dessicants, adsorbants, and catalysts have been described (277, 319). Like the calcined dioxide, hydrous zirconia appears to have little or no catalytic effect when present in oxidation-reduction processes. It has been reported not to affect the rate of atmospheric oxidation of manganous hydroxide in the presence of varying amounts of alkalies (320).

A variety of uses for hydrous zirconia have been reported, and the lake-forming and catalytic uses have been touched on above. Hydrous zirconia has been used as a binder for asbestos particles (321), in the purification of vitamin B_{12} by adsorption of impurities from its aqueous solution (322), and in the purification of lubricating oils by adsorption of their fatty acid contaminants (323). It has served as a component of ointments for the

312. F. P. Venable and T. Clark, *J. Am. Chem. Soc.* **18,** 434 (1896).
313. T. Koch, U.S. Patent **2,622,076,** Dec. 16, 1952.
314. A. Grun, U.S. Patent **2,086,713,** July 13, 1937.
315. J. C. Woodruff and G. Bloomfield, British patent **279,378,** Sept. 15, 1926.
316. H. A. Shabaker, U.S. Patent **2,616,857,** Nov. 4, 1952.
317. E. A. Hunter, U.S. Patent **2,627,506,** Feb. 3, 1953.
318. J. H. Shapleigh, U.S. Patent **2,628,890,** Feb. 17, 1953.
319. E. A. Bodkin and J. W. Payne, U.S. Patent **2,564,776,** Aug. 21, 1951.
320. N. R. Dhar and N. Kishore, *Proc. Nat. Acad. Sci., India,* **19A,** 89-113 (1950).
321. G. D. Barbaras, U.S. Patent **2,661,288,** Dec. 1, 1953.
322. M. C. Lockart and G. H. Michel, U.S. Patent **2,677,644,** May 4, 1954.
323. G. W. Ayers and W. J. Sandner, U.S. Patent **2,679,471,** May 25, 1954.

treatment of poison ivy dermatitis and body odor (324, 325). The poison ivy plant exudes a substance known as *urushiol*, which is an alkyl catechol. Hydrous zirconia reacts with catechol and with urushiol, forming a chelate structure with the two hydroxyl groups and rendering it biologically inert. Some similar chelation with odoriferous components of perspiration is supposed to be responsible for the suppression of body odor by hydrous zirconia.

When a carbonate is added to a solution of zirconyl chloride, the complex ion $Zr_2O_3^{++}$ is formed in solution, and on further addition of sodium carbonate, a carbonated hydroxide is precipitated. The same substance is percipitated when zirconyl chloride solution is added to a solution or a slurry of a carbonate such as sodium or calcium carbonate. Chauvenet represented this substance as $ZrCO_4 \cdot ZrO_2 \cdot 8H_2O$, and regarded it as a basic orthocarbonate (326; cf. 327). However, over the years since Chauvenet's work there has been no substantiation of the existence of true orthocarbonates or of tetraelectrovalent zirconium cations, and present perspectives indicate that the reaction should be written

$$2ZrOCl_2 + Na_2CO_3 + 8H_2O \rightarrow Zr_2O_3(OH)_2 \cdot CO_2 \cdot 7H_2O + 4NaCl + CO_2$$

and the product should be regarded to be of the structural type   (35)

The product is properly designated carbonated *trioxodizirconium hydroxide heptahydrate*, but it is known in commerce as *carbonated hydrous zirconia*. That 2 atoms of zirconium are present in a single molecule is shown by its ready conversion to a monohalogen derivative (258):

$$Zr_2O_3(OH)_2 \cdot CO_2 + HCl \rightarrow Zr_2O_3OHCl + H_2O + CO_2 \qquad (36)$$

The absence of a carbonate ion in the compound is indicated by its stability in aqueous slurries down to pH 3.5 or slightly lower, whereas all known carbonates are decomposed by acids before a hydrogen ion concentration of this magnitude is attained. This hydroxide does not violate the rule against

324. G. A. Cronk and Dorothy E. Naumann, *J. Clin. Med.* **37**, 909-13 (1951).
325. W. B. Blumenthal, *J. Soc. Cosmetic Chemists* **4**, No. 2, 69-75 (1953).
326. E. Chauvenet, *Bull. soc. chim.* **13**, 454-7 (1913).
327. H. T. S. Britton, *J. Chem. Soc.* **1926**, 125-47.

a multiplicity of hydroxyl groups attached to a zirconium atom, since the two hydroxyl groups are attached to two different zirconium atoms.

Chauvenet found that on heating this dried precipitate, it lost carbon dioxide, and it was impossible to obtain an anhydrous carbonate. But under 30-40 atmospheres of pressure of carbon dioxide, it gained carbon dioxide and formed a product of composition $ZrO_2 \cdot CO_2 \cdot 2H_2O$. No details of the structure of this compound are known, but our present point of view suggests the representation

$$
\begin{array}{ccc}
& O & & O \\
& \| & & \| \\
HO-&Zr&-O-&COH \\
& \uparrow & & \\
& HOH & &
\end{array}
$$

Zirconia does not form carbonate complexes when heated with alkali or alkaline earth carbonates, as do tantalum and niobium oxides (328), and it is indicated empirically that carbon dioxide is bound to zirconium atoms only if a hydroxyl or aquo group is also present. Hydrous zirconia has been observed to adsorb carbon dioxide (261) and Raikow was of the opinion that a carbonate was formed as a result (329).

Since carbonated trioxodizirconium hydroxide is easily prepared and it reacts with strong mineral acids, acetic acid, and ammonium carbonate much more rapidly than hydrous zirconia, it has been used extensively in industry in the preparation of salts and complex acids of zirconium (330), particularly zirconyl acetate and ammonium zirconyl carbonate, for use in the water-repellent treatment of textiles (331).

While the addition of bases to solutions of salts containing complex zirconium cations gives rise to hydroxides of zirconium and their alteration to hydrous zirconia under certain circumstances, the addition of bases to solutions of zirconium salts containing complex anions results in hydroxylation of the anions and a variety of reactions of the hydroxylated anions. When fluozirconic acid is neutralized to give a solution of normal potassium hexafluozirconate, the aqueous solution exhibits a distinctly acid reaction and this can only be accounted for by the supposition that the dissolved zirconium ions are hydroxylated to $ZrOHF_6^{-3}$. If potassium fluoride is added to the solution, the pH rises, due to the replacement of hydroxyl ions from the complex anion with fluoride. Similar effects are found in solutions of "zirconium sulfates" which are really sulfatozirconic acids. As the alkalinity of such solutions are raised, sulfato groups are replaced by hydroxyl

328. M. Bachelot and G. Bouissieres, *Bull. soc. chim.* **11,** 169-71 (1944).
329. P. N. Raikow, *Chem. Ztg.* **31,** 55, 87 (1907).
330. E. Wainer, British patent **569,054,** May 2, 1945.
331. W. B. Blumenthal, *Ind. Eng. Chem.* **42,** 640-2 (1950).

groups, and the hydroxylated species are then able to react as bases with acid species in the same solution. The formation of the complex sulfato species was observed by Larsen and Gammill in the work referred to above (267), but they referred to it as *basic sulfate* formation, as against the *hydroxide* formation from chloride, nitrate, and perchlorate solutions. Hydroxylation is induced also by heating zirconium sulfate solutions. Hagiwara found that on heating sulfate solutions of various transition elements to 90°, precipitation occurred and characteristic pH's were observed, as follows:

Element	La	Ce^{-3}	Pr	Nd	Sm	Y	Cd	Er	Yb	Th	Ce^{-4}	Zr
pH	6.8	—	6.7	6.7	6.4	6.3	6.0	6.0	5.7	4.4	2.4	2.8

Zirconium was precipitated quantitatively at pH 2.8 while thorium required pH 5.5 for quantitative precipitation (332). In all events, hydroxylation of the sulfatozirconate anion results in detachment of sulfato groups and acid-base reactions between the hydroxylated species with formation of chain compounds, for example:

$$HSO_4ZrOOH + HSO_4ZrOSO_4H \rightarrow HSO_4ZrOSO_4ZrOSO_4H + H_2O \quad (37)$$

The terminal HSO_4 groups on such chains can be replaced by hydroxyl groups, giving hydroxides such as $HOZrSO_4ZrSO_4ZrSO_4ZrOH \cdot 14H_2O$, the so-called *Hauser's salt*. Compounds of this type are discussed in greater detail in Chapter 6.

When a solution of the salt $Zr_5O_8(SO_4)_2 \cdot 14H_2O$ is treated with ammonium hydroxide, a hydroxide is precipitated which can be dissolved in hydrochloric acid, and a salt $Zr_5O_8Cl_4 \cdot 22H_2O$ can be crystallized from the solution (332b). Evidently the hydroxide was $Zr_5O_8(OH)_4$, and one hydroxyl group was associated with each of 4 zirconium atoms. Neglecting the hydration, the hydroxide was

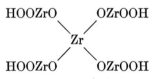

ZIRCONATES

The formation of zirconates from certain oxides when they are heated with zirconia has been touched on above, pp. 167-170. Only the metazirconates are well-characterized compounds. Strictly, a metazirconate is a compound

---

332. Zenji Hagiwara, *Technol. Repts. Tôhoku Univ.* **17**, 70-6, (1953).

332b. R. T. Glazebrook, W. Rosenhain, and E. H. Rodd, British patent **112,973,** Jan. 29, 1917.

containing the ion ZrO_3^{-2}, and it is formed only in the presence of available oxide ions. When zirconia is heated with a strong base to about 1000°, the reactions which occur can be represented

$$M_{\frac{2}{n}}O \rightleftharpoons \frac{2}{n} M^{+n} + O^{-2} \qquad (38\text{-}39)$$

$$ZrO_2 + O^{-2} \rightarrow ZrO_3^{-2}$$

Reaction 39 can be reversed by the action of an electron acceptor, which has the effect of removing an oxide ion from the zirconate ion. Thus, in water

$$ZrO_3^{-2} + 2H^+ \rightarrow ZrO_2 + H_2O \qquad (40)$$

and the zirconates tend to be hydrolyzed to hydrous zirconia and soluble hydroxide compounds. But since the hydrous zirconia is insoluble and coats the reacting surface, the reaction soon comes to a halt. If an acid is present in the water, the hydrous zirconia is dissolved as rapidly as it forms, and the decomposition of the zirconate proceeds to completion. In nonaqueous systems, Lewis acids accomplish the same thing (151) (see reaction 11).

Aqueous solutions of extremely high alkali content, such as 50% potassium hydroxide solution, convert hydrous zirconia to a zirconate:

$$ZrO_2 + 2OH^- \rightarrow ZrO_3^{-2} + H_2O \qquad (41)$$

and a small solubility of hydrous zirconia is observed for this reason in the 50% potassium hydroxide solution (312). The solubility is very limited, however, due to the precipitating effect of the large concentration of alkali cations.

Zirconates are generally formed by heating zirconia with an oxide, hydroxide, carbonate, or some other salt of an alkali or alkaline earth element, which is capable of furnishing the oxide at the elevated temperature. The alkaline earths, calcium, strontium, and barium, are known to form only the metazirconates, $MZrO_3$. Under some circumstances the alkali elements appear to form orthozirconate or acid zirconates, although they too tend to form metazirconates preferentially. When zirconia is heated with an excess of sodium carbonate to a white heat, nearly 2 moles of carbon dioxide are evolved per mole of zirconia (333), indicating a reaction

$$ZrO_2 + 2Na_2CO_3 \rightarrow Na_4ZrO_4 + 2CO_2 \qquad (42)$$

When the product of this reaction was treated with water, hexagonal plates of composition approximately $Na_2O \cdot 8ZrO_2 \cdot 12H_2O$ were obtained, but this composition is entirely empirical and there is no reason to believe that it is expressive of a discrete compound formation. Comparable zirconates of high

---

333. T. Hiortdahl, *Compt. rend.* **61**, 175, 213 (1865).

zirconia content have been obtained from reactions with potash, followed by washing, and they too were of indefinite composition (312).

In addition to the well-known sodium, potassium, and lithium meta-zirconates, a substance of composition $Li_2Zr_2O_5$ has been reported to be recovered on washing the reaction product of zirconia and fused lithium hydroxide with water and acetic acid (334). Here, too, the casual dissolving out of about half the alkali content by the washes may account for the acid zirconate residue.

Magnesium and zinc have never been proved to form true zirconates, but lead metazirconate is well established (166).

The metazirconates are highly refractory, with melting points for calcium 2550°, strontium > 2700°, and barium 2700°. Calcium zirconate has the perovskite structure, differing from perovskite primarily in having a value of 89° for β, and thus being monoclinic rather than cubic.

Some complex minerals containing zirconium dioxide are loosely referred to as zirconates, for example, zirkelite $(Ca,Fe)O \cdot 2(Zr,Ti,Th)O_2$ and uhligite, $Ca(Zr,Ti)_2O_5 \cdot Al_2TiO_5$. Since they are, in effect, solid solutions of several molecular types in one another, their physical and chemical proper-ties will depend on the contributions of all the components, and they are not strictly comparable to the simple zirconates.

PEROXIDES AND PERZIRCONATES

When a base such as ammonium hydroxide is added to a solution of a sulfate or chloride of zirconium containing hydrogen peroxide, a gelatinous precipitate is obtained which has an oxidizing capacity equivalent approxi-mately to 1 oxygen atom per atom of zirconium. When the precipitate is filtered off, washed, and allowed to stand as a water pulp, the oxidizing capacity is continuously diminished. J. A. Peterson (258) found the follow-ing number of peroxide oxygen atoms to remain in the pulp after various lengths of time: 4 days, 0.79; 10 days, 0.42; 22 days, 0.36; 171 days, 0.18 per atom of zirconium.

The earliest studies of such precipitates showed their composition to be $ZrO_3 \cdot 2H_2O$ (335, 336), and the energy content is higher than that of hydrous zirconia:

$$ZrO_2 \cdot xH_2O + HOOH \rightarrow$$
$$ZrO_3 \cdot 2H_2O + (x - 1)H_2O - 21.78 \text{ kg cal } (337; \text{ cf. } 338) \quad (43)$$

The presence of a peroxide structure in the molecule has been proved by the

334. F. P. Venable and C. Baskerville, *J. Am. Chem. Soc.* **17**, 448 (1895).
335. P. T. Cleve, *Bull. soc. Chim.* (2) **43**, 57 (1895).
336. H. Geisow and P. Horkheimer, *Z. anorg. allgem. Chem.* **32**, 372 (1902).
337. L. Pissarjewsky, *Z. anorg. allgem. Chem.* **25**, 378 (1900).
338. W. G. Mixter, *Am. J. Sci.* (4) **27**, 393 (1909).

formation of hydrogen peroxide when the precipitate is dissolved with dilute sulfuric acid. When it is treated with concentrated sulfuric acid, some ozone is formed (337). From the analysis, the peroxide content, and the implications from studies of perzirconate salts, it appears reasonable to regard the com-

$$\underset{\underset{HOH}{\uparrow}}{HO-\overset{\overset{O}{\parallel}}{Zr}-OOH}$$

pound as HO—Zr—OOH, basic zirconyl peroxide.

If the freshly prepared water pulp is dried at room temperature over phosphorus pentoxide (339), or if the water is washed out with liquid ammonia or with acetone followed by petroleum ether (340), a solid of composition HOZrO · OOH · H_2O is recovered. The hafnium analog has been obtained similarly (*loc. cit.*).

The precipitation of basic zirconyl peroxide has been reported to occur in mildly acid and in mildly alkaline media. It has been formed by the addition of hydrogen peroxide to an alkaline tartrate solution of zirconium (341); and it is said that the same substance is obtained by adding sodium hypochloride to a zirconium nitrate solution or by electrolyzing a solution containing sodium chloride and zirconium nitrate (339).

Basic zirconyl peroxide dissolves in potassium hydroxide solution containing hydrogen peroxide. If alcohol is added to the cold (3°) solution, a salt of composition $K_4Zr_2O_{11}$ · $9H_2O$ separates, and the corresponding sodium salt can be prepared in analogous fashion (337). The salt K_4ZrO_8 · $6H_2O$ has also been crystallized from a cold alkaline peroxide solution (340). These salts may be regarded as

$$\underset{KOO}{\overset{KOO}{\diagdown}}Zr-O-Zr\underset{OOK}{\overset{OOK}{\diagup}} \quad \text{and} \quad \underset{KOO}{\overset{KOO}{\diagdown}}Zr\underset{OOK}{\overset{OOK}{\diagup}}$$

HO—Zr—O—Zr—OH

Zirconium peroxide structures form even in strongly acidic solutions. It has been observed that when a strong sulfuric acid solution of zirconium containing hydrogen peroxide was allowed to stand at 0°, a precipitate began to appear after 12 hours and continued to be deposited for 5 or 6 days. After it had been washed with alcohol it was found to have a composition corresponding to $H_2Zr_2O_4(SO_4)_2$ · $3H_2O$. It was very sparingly soluble in water and dilute sulfuric acid, but quite soluble in concentrated sulfuric acid. The suspension in dilute sulfuric acid slowly decomposed with formation of basic zirconyl peroxide (340). When an equivalence of potassium sulfate

339. G. H. Bailey, *J. Am. Chem. Soc.* **49**, 149, 481 (1886); **58**, 705 (1889).
340. R. Schwarz and H. Giese, *Z. anorg. allgem. Chem.* **176**, 209-32 (1928).
341. E. Wedekind, *Z. anorg. allgem. Chem.* **33**, 83 (1903).

was added to a strongly acidic solution of zirconium sulfate containing hydrogen peroxide and the mixture allowed to stand at $0°$, after about 1 hour, a precipitate of composition $K_2ZrO_2(SO_4)_2 \cdot 3H_2O$ separated (*loc.cit.*). The slow formation of these peroxozirconates indicates that they develop as covalently bonded complexes from the components of the system. The bond between zirconium and —O—O— appears to be quite stable, and when the zirconium peroxo compounds decompose, it appears probable that the bond between oxygen atoms is ruptured rather than that between zirconium and oxygen.

When zirconyl chloride solutions are added to mixtures of sodium hydroxide, hydrogen peroxide, and water, the precipitate which first forms dissolves immediately on being stirred into the liquid, apparently with formation of the peroxozirconate, hydrated Na_4ZrO_8. A minimum of 3.6 moles of hydrogen peroxide is required per mole of zirconia held in solution. As the solution stands, an exothermic decomposition occurs, and a series of insoluble decomposition products can be identified, the first containing about 1.2 peroxo oxygen atoms per zirconium atom, the second about 1.0, and the third about 0.6-0.7. The first is observed in the freshly formed slurry, the second in the air-dried product, and the third in products which have been boiled or stand until decomposition ceases. The solids also contain soda (and carbon dioxide which may be held by adsorption only). The sodium ion can be replaced by ion exchange with potassium, magnesium, calcium, or barium chloride. When the slurry is treated with ammonium chloride or ammonium sulfate, the peroxide structure decomposes until only about 0.3 peroxo oxygen atoms are left per zirconium atom (342).

It appears not unreasonable from these observations that the decomposition of the soluble sodium tetraperoxozirconate gives rise to units of the

structure —O—O—Žr—O—O—, the further decomposition of which is accompanied by chain formation, e.g., —O—O—Žr—O—O—Žr—O—O—Žr—O—O. The sodium compound of this anion would have the empirical composition $Na_2O \cdot 3ZrO_2 \cdot 4O_a$, where O_a designates a peroxo (active) oxygen atom. Decomposition of the terminal peroxo structures would leave

Na—O—Žr—O—O—Žr—O—O—Žr—O—Na, empirically $Na_2O \cdot 3ZrO_2 \cdot 2O_a$. Products of both these compositions have been noted, and the latter is the stable end product of decomposition at temperatures up to the boiling point of the aqueous slurry.

---

342. Peggy M. Hurst, "A New Type of Peroxy Compound of Zirconium," Ph.D. Thesis, University of Wisconsin, 1956.

5

Zircon and the Complex Silicates

ZIRCON

IDENTIFICATION AND CRYSTALLOGRAPHY

Until modern times zircon was known only as the naturally occurring gemstone. Its identification was more an art than a science, and it cannot be said with certainty that all that went by the name *zircon* and its synonyms in the ancient and medieval literature was the same substance as is identified by these names today. However, since zircon has an extraordinarily high index of refraction and striking birefringence, it appears likely that many of the historical references to zircon indeed refer to what we call by this name today.

The term *zircon* has been used in both a narrower and broader sense, the former referring to a substance of rather sharply defined chemical composition and crystallographic structure, and the latter to chemically and physically altered varieties. Even the zircon in the more restricted sense occurs in a wide variety of colors, and special names have been associated with the various colors. Colorless zircons are rare in nature, and the colorless zircons seen on the markets are usually heat-treated yellow or brown stones (1, p. 101). Colorless stones do occur in the Matara area in southern Ceylon, and have been called *Matura-diamonds or Matara diamonds* (2, p. 280). The term *white zircons* is now preferred for the colorless stones (3, p. 215). Pale, smoky, and yellow zircons have been called *jargons* or *jargoons;* yellow zircons from Ceylon and orange-yellow to reddish-brown zircons from other sources have been called *hyacinths* or *jacinths;* and the brown variety of zircon has been called *zirconite.* A blue gem variety, the color of which was imparted artificially by a heat treatment, was sold mostly during the 1920s under the name *starlite* (2, pp. 328-9).

Among the characteristics of the gemstone are its ability to cleave readily, its hardness, high refractive index, and striking birefringence (see Table 5.1).

1. M. Weinstein, *Precious and Semi-Precious Stones,* Pitman Publishing Corporation, New York, 1944.
2. G. F. Herbert Smith, *Gemstones,* Pitman Publishing Corporation, New York, 1952.
3. E. H. Kraus and C. B. Slawson, *Gems and Gem Materials,* McGraw-Hill Book Company, New York, 1947.

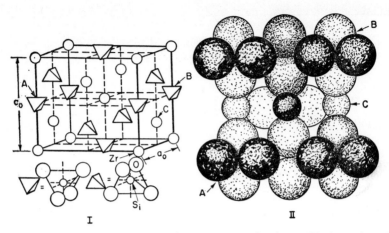

Fɪɢ. 5.1. I. The unit prism of the atomic arrangement in zircon. II. A portion of the zircon structure projected upon the c face through A and B of I. Atoms of Si barely show within the SiO₄ tetrahedra. A zirconium atom C is identified on the two drawings. From (4).

The high birefringence of true zircon results in a strong doubling of the back facets. The juncture of two facets appears to be two lines when the microscope is focused through the gem onto them. Similarly, inclusions in all but the decomposed zircons appear doubled. White zircon may have many inclusions so tiny that they cannot be resolved but which give a total effect referred to as *cottony;* therefore, white zircon, unlike diamond, commonly appears cloudy rather than clear or sharply transparent (20, p. 87). Zircon fracture has a distinctive appearance due to its tendency to pit or crumble at the facet edges. Heat-treated zircons are especially subject to such pitting.

True zircon has a chemical composition corresponding to the formula $ZrO_2 \cdot SiO_2$, and a tetrahedral crystal structure which is shown in Figure 5.1 (4, p. 287), the value of a being 6.60 and of c 5.88 A (c has more recently been given as 5.93 A (5, 6)). The usual silica tetrahedra are found in the structure, but there is no physical basis for regarding them as distinct ions or radicals, but rather the structure may be regarded as consisting of series of chains of the structure illustrated by Figure 5.2. Each successive pair of oxygen atoms is arranged transverse to the previous pair. The structure is bonded in three dimensions by coordination covalencies acting between

4. R. W. G. Wyckoff, *The Structure of Crystals,* Chemical Catalog Co., Inc., New York, 1931.

5. W. Binks, *Mineral. Mag.* 21, 176-87 (1926).

6. W. Hückel, *Structural Chemistry of Inorganic Compounds,* vol. 2, Elsevier Publishing Company, Amsterdam, 1951.

zirconium atoms of one chain and oxygen atoms of a neighboring chain. Thus the entire crystal is held together by valence forces, and breakdown of the structure begins only above about 1550°. The zirconium and silicon atoms are arranged in a tetrahedral lattice of the diamond type, but the lattice symmetry of the crystal is determined by the tetragonal arrangement of the oxygen atoms rather than by that of the zirconium and silicon atoms. The structural unit is the molecule MO_2, in which M is ideally Zr or Si, but may be replaced by other tetravalent elements. The 3 atoms forming 1 molecule are situated on a straight line, with M in the center position (7, 8), and there are 8 MO_2 molecules in the unit prism. This structure was verified by Hassel, who identified the spacial arrangement as D_{4h}^{19}. The zirconium atoms are at 000, $0\frac{1}{4}\frac{1}{2}$, $\frac{1}{2}0\frac{3}{4}$, and $\frac{1}{2}\frac{1}{2}\frac{1}{2}$. Silicon atoms form a similar set, translated through $00\frac{1}{2}$ (9; cf. 5). Huckel has stressed that the silica tetrahedra have no point of contact with one another (6, pp. 742-3), and there is no orthosilicate anion SiO_4^{-4}. Generally, in orthosilicates the cation is situated in space at approximately the same distance from the oxygen atoms as the silicon atoms; therefore it is not proper to speak of elementary cations in such structures, as is done in the case of salts. Although the Si-O distance in zircon (1.62 A) is markedly smaller than the Zr-O distance (2.05 A), this does not imply a disproportionation of oxygen atoms to give Zr^{+4} and SiO_4^{-4} ions, but rather that the zirconium atom with 2 more electron shells than a silicon atom must geometrically require the additional space. The electron distribution along the Si-O axis probably corresponds closely to that along the Zr-O axis (*loc. cit.*, p. 578; cf. 10).

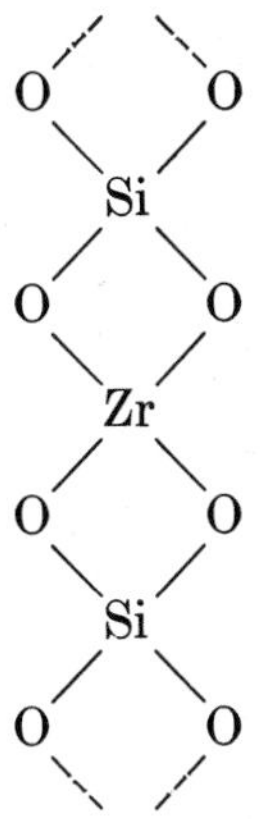

FIG. 5.2. The chain structure formed by zirconia and silica units in zircon.

The most important faces of zircon, having the greatest reticular density, are those having the indices 111, 100, and 110. Almost all the observed variations of crystalline forms are the results of truncation of the edges of these important faces (13).

7. L. Vegard, *Phil. Mag.* **32**, 65-96 (1916).
8. *Ibid.* 505-18 (1916).
9. O. Hassel, *Z. Krist.* **63**, 247-54 (1926).
10. L. Vegard, *Phil. Mag.* (7) **1**, 1151-93 (1926).
11. F. Bertaut and André Durif, *Compt. rend.* **238**, 2173-5 (1954).
12. F. Machatschki, *Zentr. Mineral. Geol.* **1941A**, 38-40.
13. I. I. Shafranovskiĭ, *Mém. soc. russe minerale* **66**, No. 1, 37-44 (1937).

The effect of impurities in zircon, e.g., soda, is often to distort the lattice sufficiently to give an impression of different physical identity as well as chemical composition (14, 15, 16). Natural zircon may also have been altered structurally by heat or exposure to radioactivity so as to lose its crystalline characteristics without changes occurring in its ultimate chemical composition. These effects will be discussed in greater detail below.

Structures similar to that of zircon occur in xenotime (YPO_4), yttrium vanadate, calcium chromate (6, p. 726), germanium thorate and germanium zirconate (11), and monazite (12). Zircon can be distinguished from xenotime by characteristic differences in X-ray absorptions: zircon 0.687 A, xenotime 0.726 A (17). The system CaF_2-BeF_2 has been described as a weakened model of the system ZrO_2-SiO_2, and the compound $CaF_2 \cdot BeF_2$ is similar in some respects to zircon (18).

From our consideration of the above, we can define zircon as a tetragonal crystal of space type D_{4h}^{19} and of chemical composition corresponding to the formula $ZrO_2 \cdot SiO_2$. We shall prefer this representation rather than $ZrSiO_4$, because of the unwarranted implication in this formula that the oxygen atoms are more especially associated with the silicon than with the zirconium. The impurities occurring in natural zircon may be regarded as extraneous matter as long as a lattice of the characteristic space group and composition close to $ZrO_2 \cdot SiO_2$ are exhibited.

COLOR AND LUMINESCENCE

Pure zircon is colorless, and the color of specimens found in nature is to be regarded as an effect superposed by impurities. Purple (19; 20, p. 154), blue (20, p. 164; 21), red or rose (20, p. 207; 22; 23), yellow to orange (20, p. 184), brown (24), and green (20, p. 175; 25, 26) stones are known, the last of these usually being drastically altered in structure. For data on the absorption spectrum of zircon, see reference 27. The colors are often due to

14. E. Brandenberger, *Schweiz. mineral. petrog. Mitt.* **17**, 164-8 (1937).

15. J. J. Schweiz, *Schweiz. mineral. petrog. Mitt.* **17**, 154-63 (1937).

16. M. von Stackelberg and E. R. Rottenbach, *Z. Krist.* **102**, 173-82, 207-8 (1940).

17. R. Coppens, *Compt. rend.* **232**, 1681-2 (1951).

18. W. E. Counts, R. Roy, and E. F. Osborn, *J. Am. Ceram. Soc.* **36**, 12-17 (1953).

19. P. G. H. Boswell, Mineralog. Mag. **21**, 310-7 (1927).

20. R. T. Liddicoot, Jr., *Handbook of Gem Identification*, Gemmological Institute of America, Los Angeles, 1947.

21. H. Michel and K. Przibram, *Anz. Akad. Wiss. Wien.* **62**, 49-52 (1927).

22. K. Chudoba and T. Dreisch, *Zentr. Mineral. Geol.* **1936A**, 65-79.

23. K. Chudoba, *Deut. Goldschmiede-Ztg.* **38**, 474-5 (1935).

24. F. G. Pough and T. H. Rogers, *Am. Mineral.* **32**, 31-43 (1947).

25. W. F. Eppler, *Neues Yahrbuch Min. Geol.* **A61**, 165-226 (1930); *Physik, Ber.* **8**, 734 (1927); *Z. Krist.* **64**, 510-11 (1926).

26. K. Chudoba, *Deut. Goldschmiede-Ztg.* **40**, 410-11 (1937).

27. W. W. Coblenz, *Bull. Bur. Standards* **6**, 301.

impurities such as iron, chromium, and vanadium, but may also be caused by lattice strains and imperfections originating in radioactive bombardment or stresses of physical or chemical nature. Some data on the relationship between the depth of color and the vanadium or chromium content is available (28). Pleochroic haloes in zircon have been found to result from contact with cordierite and biotite (29). The color of zircon is often associated with the area to which it is native. Colorless specimens are found particularly in Ceylon, blue in Siam, rose and green in Moncay, Indochina, and all colors have been found in Madagascar (1, p. 102).

The rose color of zircons from Moncay is thought to be due to the inclusion of iron compounds, and various changes have been induced in the color by exposing them to sunlight, heat, or various radiations. The color changes have been attributed to induced changes in the valence state of the iron. Simple exposure of the mineral to sunlight caused the color to change to gray. On heating the gray crystals to 60-150°, they became colored again, but on raising the temperature to 160-300°, they became brown and then colorless. The last change was irreversible. Exposure to radioactive material of crystals decolorized by sunlight restored the color (22, 23). Specimens of hyacinth have also been observed to change to gray in sunlight. Heating them caused a bluish-white luminescence which began to appear at 200° and disappeared at 300°, the color becoming reddish. This color was unstable to light, and even when the reddened material was stored in the dark it slowly changed to a hyacinth shade. Heating the hyacinth to 900° caused it to become colorless, but heating to 1000° in a reducing atmosphere resulted in a blue shade (30). The color changes on heating Moncay zircons under oxidizing and reducing conditions have been discussed by Eppler (31). Some natural color effects in zircon have been paralleled in synthetic zircon by the introduction of chromium oxide into the composition (32).

Due to the isomorphism of thorium and uranium compounds with zirconium analogs, these elements have tended to separate with zirconium during the solidification of the earth's crust (33), and are frequently found in zircon. The bombardment of the zircon by the radiations of these elements has caused distortion of the lattice and other effects usually made perceptible as color. Sometimes the color can be discharged by annealing the crystal by heat treatment, thus eliminating the lattice distortions and promoting the return of all atoms to their normal positions. Hyacinth which had lost its color completely as a result of heating was restored to its original color by

28. R. Klemm, *Centr. Min. Geol.* **1927A**, 267-78.
29. M. Weber, *Centr. Min. Geol.* **1923**, 388-92.
30. G. D. Wild, *Deut. Goldschmiede-Ztg.* **40**, 411-12 (1937).
31. W. F. Eppler, *Deut. Goldschmiede-Ztg.* **39**, 531-34 (1936).
32. A. Bauer, *Nature* **111**, 252-3 (1927).
33. J. Joly, *J. Chem. Soc.* **125**, 897-907 (1924).

the action of radium emanation (34, 35) or by cathode treatment (35). Purple zircon heated to 300° under oxidizing conditions lost its color, but it was restored by the action of α- and γ-rays (19). Studies of this kind have led to the conclusion that the color of these specimens was of radiochemical origin (34, 36, 37). Pure natural zircon is not radioactive (38). It has been demonstrated that the action of radioactive water on zircon can induce color formation (39). Evidence has been adduced to the effect that black halos in zircon fractures are the results of the action of radioactive disintegrations within the zircon (20, p. 77). X-rays also have color effects on zircon. Blue zircon has been observed to turn brown on irradiation with X-rays while brown zircon was unaffected (24).

Zircon exhibits a characteristic yellow glow under ultraviolet light, which has proved useful in detecting and identifying the mineral (40, 41), and apparatus for ultraviolet luminescence analysis of zircon (42) and its various applications have been described (43, 44, 45). The cause for the luminescence has not been established; specimens of zircon from different locales respond differently. However, Haberlandt found that all specimens of zircon which he subjected to filtered ultraviolet from a mercury lamp showed the same luminescence spectrum and most frequently exhibited the lines of dysprosium and a band which probably belonged to samarium II (46). Specimens from the Jos Plateau, Nigeria, included clear, weakly radioactive zircons which fluoresced, and white, cloudy, more highly radioactive zircons which did not fluoresce (47). Attempts have been made to relate the fluorescence to rare-earth impurities (48).

VARIETIES

When zircon is heated to about 1500-1550°, it dissociates into zirconia and silica. If it is cooled very slowly, it will reassociate to form zircon, but if it

34. R. S. Strutt, *Proc. Royal Soc. London* **89A**, 405-7.
35. E. Newberry and H. Lupton, *Nature* **101**, 198 (1911).
36. R. Brauns, *Centr. Min. Geol.* **1909**, 721-8.
37. R. Grengg, *Centr. Min. Geol.* **1914**, 518-30.
38. C. Doelter, *Mineral petrog. Mitt.* **29**, 258-9.
39. C. Doelter, *Sitz Akad. Wiss. Wien.* I, **124**, 409-23 (1915).
40. V. Kubelka, *Chem. Listy* **23**, 312-8 (1929).
41. F. V. Lutati, *Industria chimica* **5**, 15-9 (1930).
42. V. V. Lozhkin, *Sov. Geol.* **9**, No. 10-11, 142-3 (1939).
43. E. M. Brumberg and Z. M. Sverdlov, *Bull. acad. sci. U.S.S.R.* **4**, 75-82 (1940).
44. R. Webster, *Discovery* **10**, 158-62 (1949).
45. C. Karunakaran and K. Neelakantam, *J. Sci. Ind. Research India* **5B**, No. 2, 36 (1946).
46. H. Haberlandt, *Öster. Akad. Wiss. Math.-Natur. Klasse Sitzber.,* I, **158**, 605-46 (1949).
47. R. Greenwood, *Geol. Survey Nigeria Bull.* **19**, 79-80 (1948).
48. H. Haberlandt, *Sitz. Akad. Wiss. Wien. Math.-Natur. Klasse IIa,* **143**, 11-13 (1934).

is cooled rapidly, a mixture of monoclinic zirconia and glassy silica is usually recovered. It seems likely that the dissociation occurs at lower temperatures in the presence of certain chemical agents, and it may be promoted by bombardment of particles from radioactive substances. A considerable amount of dissociated or partly dissociated zircon is found in nature. The dissociated state is referred to as *metamict*. Much of the green zircon is metamict. Specimens from Moncay which were originally green turned blue and yellow on heating to 1450° (26).

Zircons, according to the broader definition which also includes those in the metamict condition, have been classified by mineralogists and gemmologists according to whether they are entirely undissociated, partially dissociated, or virtually completely dissociated. The first is called *b* or *alpha zircon*, the second *c* or *beta zircon*, and the third *a* or *gamma zircon* (25; 49, p. 254). The alpha is most readily identified by its high specific gravity, about 4.7, and its high birefringence. It is uniaxial, and it is stable to ordinary heating, i.e., to temperatures up to about 1500°. The gamma zircon has a specific gravity of 3.9 to 4.0, or close to that calculated for a mixture of zirconia and vitrous silica. It is uniaxial, has low birefringence, and it also is stable to heating. Beta zircon is partially in the metamict condition and is intermediate between the alpha and gamma in specific gravity and other properties. When heated moderately, the beta zircon goes over to alpha.

Some of the gem zircon from Ceylon has a low specific gravity, is amorphous, and commonly green in color (49, p. 254). A specimen of specific gravity 3.965 showed an X-ray pattern of monoclinic zirconia only (11). For description of specimens of beta zircon, see references 25 and 50. A specimen of hyacinth from Laacher Sea showed a reversible change in index of refraction of 0.0030 at 197°. This is an odd phenomenon which is unrelated to the irreversible recrystallization of metamict zircon (25).

Numerous varieties and altered forms of zircon have been reported in addition to the color varieties already discussed. They include adelphite,* alanite (56), alvite* (57, 58, 60b), anderbergite* (60c, 60d, 60e, 60f),

49. R. M. Shipley, *Dictionary of Gems and Gemmology*, Gemmological Institute of America, 1946.

50. H. C. Meyer, *Foote Prints* **9**, No. 1, 1-9 (1936).

51. F. Zambonini, *Atti Accad. Napoli* **16**, 105 (1890).

52. E. S. Kitchin and W. G. Winterson, *J. Chem. Soc.* **89**, 1568-75.

53. A. C. Cumming, *J. Chem. Soc.* **93**, 350-5.

54. E. S. Dana and W. E. Ford, *A Textbook of Mineralogy*, John Wiley & Sons, Inc., New York, 1921.

55. (Mlle) M. Marquis and P. and G. Urbain, *Compt. rend.* **180**, 1377-80 (1925).

56. Kenjiro Kimura, *Jap. J. Chem.* **2**, 73-9 (1925).

57. W. C. Brogger, T. Vogt, and J. Schetelig, *Vid.-Selsk Skifter, Kristiana, I, Mat.-Nat. Kl.* **1**, 151 (1922).

auerbachite (59, 60g), azorite (60h, 60i), beccarite (60j), calyptolite (60k), cyrtolite (60l), engelhardite (60v, 60w), hagatolite (60m), malacon (60x), naegite (60n), oerstedite* (60p), oliveirite,* orvillite* (60q), ostranite (60r), oyamalite (60m), polykrasilite, ribeiraite, and tachyaphaltite* (60s). The asterisks denote those that have been regarded as altered zircons; the others are substantially unaltered varieties. *Diocroma* and *ligure* have been used synonymously with zircon.

Alvite was first found by Forbes and Dahll at Alve and Naröstö, Norway, as crystals of reddish-brown color (60b). It also occurs at Ytterby, Sweden. It may contain aluminum, beryllium, calcium, copper, magnesium, thorium, and zinc. Alvite from Kragerö has been reported to contain 16% hafnia (60t). The crystals are tetragonal, optically isotropic, and pseudomorphous after zircon. The specific gravity is 3.3-4.3 and the hardness 5-6.

Anderbergite is related to cyrtolite. It is honey-yellow to black in color and is microscopically amorphous, but has a pseudomorphous tetragonal form. Its composition has been observed to approximate $2CaO \cdot R_2O_3 \cdot 6ZrO_2 \cdot 8SiO_2$, and its specific gravity is 3.28-3.33 and hardness 2.5-6. It is thus severely altered chemically and physically from zircon (60c, 60d, 60e, 60f).

Auerbachite was discovered at Mariupol, Ukraine (60g). It contains about 55% zirconia and 43% silica and has a specific gravity of 4.06 and hardness 6.5. *Azorite* has been found in São Miguel in the Azores, and is a pale-green

58. Safder Bedr-Chan, *Z. anorg. allgem. Chem.* **144**, 304-6 (1925).
59. I. P. Chirvinski, *Z. Krist. Festband P. v. Groth* **58**, 386-403 (1923).
60. Kenjiro Kimura, *Japan. J. Chem.* **2**, 81-5 (1925).
60b. D. Forbes and T. Dahll, *Nyt. Mag.* **8**, 228 (1855); **9**, 14 (1855).
60c. C. W. Bloomstrand, *Akad. Handl. Stockholm Bihang* **12**, 10 (1886).
60d. H. Backström, *Z. Kryst.* **15**, 83 (1888).
60e. A. E. Nordenskjold, *Geol. For. Forh. Stockholm* **3**, 229 (1876).
60f. G. K. Almström, *Norsk. Geol. Tids.* **45**, 119 (1923).
60g. R. Hermann, *J. prakt. Chem.* (1) **73**, 210 (1858).
60h. J. D. Dana. *A System of Mineralogy*, New York, 1876, p. 396.
60i. A. Ben-Saude, *Bull. Soc. Min.* **11**, 201 (1888).
60j. G. Grattarola, *Atti. Soc. Toscanna* **4**, 177 (1876).
60k. C. U. Shepard, *Am. J. Sci.* (2) **12**, 210 (1851).
60l. W. J. Knowlton, *Am. J. Sci.* (2) **44**, 224 (1807).
60m. Kenjiro Kimura, *Z. physik. Chem.* **128**, 369-93 (1927).
60n. T. Wada, *The Minerals of Japan*, Tokyo, 1904.
60p. G. Forchhammer, *Pogg. Ann.* **35**, 630 (1835).
60q. T. H. Lee, *Am. J. Sci.* (4) **47**, 126 (1919).
60r. A. Breithaupt, *Pogg. Ann.* **5**, 377 (1825).
60s. N. J. Berlin, *Pogg. Ann.* **88**, 160 (1853).
60t. G. von Hevesy and V. T. Jantzen, *J. Chem. Soc.* **123**, 3218 (1923).
60u. F. W. Clark, *The Constitution of the Natural Silicates*, Washington, 1914, p. 114.
60v. N. von Koskcharoff, *Materialen zur Mineralogie Russlands*, St. Petersberg, 1858, vol. 3, p. 150.
60w. P. von Jeremejeff, *Proc. Russ. Min. Soc.* **15**, 186 (1879).
60x. T. Scheerer, *Pogg. Ann.* **65**, 436 (1845).

variety of zircon (60h, 60i). *Beccarite* was discovered in Point de Galle, Ceylon, and is an olive-green altered zircon (60j). *Calyptolite* was found in minute brown crystals at Haddam, Connecticut (60k).

Cyrtolite was discovered by Knowlton at Rockport, Massachusetts (60l). Its name is derived from the Greek *kyrtos* (bent), and has reference to the curvature of the pyramidal faces. It has been regarded as a brownish-red variety of malacon (see below), and has a considerably higher hafnia content than ordinary zircon. A specimen examined by von Hevesy and Jantzen contained 9% hafnia (60t). Its chemical analysis has been found to approximate $3(Zr,Hf)O_2 \cdot 2SiO_2 \cdot 3H_2O$ (60u). Its specific gravity is about 3.29-4.04 and its hardness 5-5.5. After ignition the hardness becomes 7-7.5.

Engelhardite is a variety of zircon found in Tomsk, Russia (60v, 60w). *Malacon* was discovered by Scheerer and its name derives from the Greek *malakos* (soft), and has allusion to its softness in comparison to zircon (60x). Scheerer's specimen came from Hitterö, now Hidra, Norway. Des Cloizeau subsequently found it occurring in thin plates at Chanteloube, Haute-Vienne (60y), and it has been reported from various other parts of the world. It has been regarded as a hydrated compound pseudomorphous after the original zircon (51, 60z), but various compositions have been reported and have evoked some controversy (52, 53). In addition to hafnium, malacon commonly contains niobium, tantalum, thorium, and uranium (54, p. 522; 55).

Naegite was discovered by Wada as a greenish or brown radioactive mineral containing zirconia, silica, urania, thoria, tantala, columbia, ceria, iron oxide, lime, magnesia, and water. It occurs in Naegi, Mino (now Gifu prefecture), Japan, as tabular or prismatic crystals of tetragonal crystal lattice, specific gravity 4.09 and hardness 7.5 (60n). It has been observed to contain 7% hafnia (60t). *Oerstedite* is the name given to a reddish-brown mineral from Arendal, Norway, by Forchhammer in honor of H. C. Oersted. It has the crystalline form of zircon, and an analysis has given 69% zirconia, 20% silica, 2.0% magnesia, 2.6% lime, and 5.5% water (60p). *Orvillite* is a mineral from the Poços de Caldas region of Minas Gerais, Brazil, described by Lee and named to honor Orville A. Derby. It has a composition corresponding to $8ZrO_2 \cdot 6SiO_2 \cdot 5H_2O$ and appears to be an altered zircon. It is soluble in a mixture of hydrochloric and hydrofluoric acids (60q). *Ostranite* is a weathered variety of zircon from Stoko, Langesund Fiord, Norway (60r). *Tachyaphaltite* was discovered by Weibye as a dark reddish-brown crystalline mineral in gneiss near Kragero, Norway. He gave it the name, derived from Greek *tachys* (quick) and *aphaltos* (flying to pieces) because of the ease of separating it from the gangue by striking it. It is composed

60y. A. des Cloizeau, *Manuel de minéralogie*, Paris, 1862, Vol. 1, p. 157.

60z. C. F. Rammelsberg, *Handbuch der Mineralchemie*, Leipzig, 1860, p. 891.

chiefly of zirconia, silica, thoria, iron oxide, and water; its specific gravity is 3.6 and its hardness 5.5 (60s). *Hagatolite* and *oyamalite* are Japanese zircons containing niobium, tantalum, and rare earths (60).

The descriptions of the varieties and alteration products overlap and merge into the complex silicate minerals to be discussed below. A mineral (composition 27.43% silica, 51.08% zirconia, 4.35% water; brown streak, powder, and fresh fracture; irregular or conchoidal cleavage; density 3.5-3.54; hardness 4.5; index of refraction 1.683) is reported as a specimen of zirconite (61). It is seen from the foregoing that other names might as well have been applied, e.g., malacon.

OCCURRENCE AND GEOCHEMISTRY

Zircon occurs very widely in nature and is found in soils (62), fuller's earth (63), sediments (19), alluvial deposits (1, p. 102), gold slimes (64), sands (65, 66, 67), and rocks, such as granites (68, 69), granitoids, and pegmatites of various kinds (70). Small crystals of zircon are commonly included in diamond and corundum (20, pp. 90, 107). Extensive references to occurrences of zircon in various countries are given in Chapter 1, Table 1.2. Zircon is most commonly found in igneous rocks and in economically important concentrations in beach sands along certain coasts, where grains of zircon have been dropped as alluvial deposits. The zircon sand originated in igneous rocks which were weathered away and from which the zircon particles were carried by rains and streams until they settled out in shallow coastal waters. The survival of the zircon grains is due to their extreme chemical inertness. Gem zircons are usually found in secondary deposits, the most important of which are in the Moncay district of Indochina and Ceylon. They are also found in Burma, Tasmania, New Zealand, and New South Wales, Australia. Zircons of gem quality are rarely encountered in the occurrences in Maine, New York, and North Carolina (3, p. 211).

The zircon found in nature crystallized from magmas which contained dissolved zirconia and silica. As the molten rock cooled, zircon was one of the first crystalline phases to separate. It was particularly prone to separate

---

61. W. Florencio, *Anais acad. brasil cienc.* **24**, 249-59 (1952).

62. J. H. Druif, *Handel 7de Nederl. Ind. Natuurwet. Congr.*, Batavia, Oct. 1935, 666-79 (1936).

63. Maria Foldvari-Vogl, *Magyar Allami Foldt. Intézet. Evi Jelentésé*, Sect. B, Beszamole **10**, 65-76 (1948).

64. V. Zemel, *Sovet. Zolotoprom.* **1935**, No. 7, 23-5.

65. D. M. Liddell, *Eng. Min. J.* **104**, 153-5 (1917).

66. H. A. Hayward, *Microscope* **2**, 169-71 (1938).

67. B. J. N. S. R. Anjaneyulu, *Materials & Methods* **40**, No. 2, 90-2 (1954).

68. G. von Hevesy and K. Wurstlin, *Z. anorg. allgem. Chem.* **216**, 305-11 (1934).

69. Yoshifumi Karakida, *J. Geol. Soc. Japan* **60**, 517-32 (1954).

70. R. Wilcox, *Am. Mineral.* **21**, 459 (1936).

with granites and syenites. It has been noted that zircons occurring in the cretaceous granitic intrusions in Kyushu were of three types of crystal habit, and the relative abundance or *habit ratio* is characteristic of a granitic body. The color as well as the crystalline habit was practically invariant within each granitic body (69). As the host rock weathered away, the zircon grains fell into the soil, clay, or sand, and entered into the history of these products. Artificial weathering tests have shown zircon to be the most resistant of all the minerals studied. On a scale of weather resistance, garnet was assigned the resistance value 1 and zircon 100 (71). Zircon can

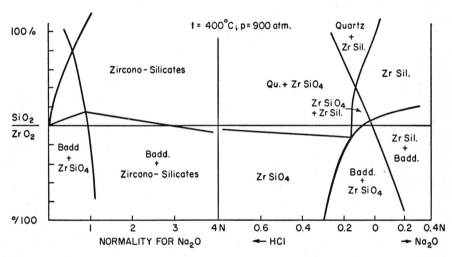

FIG. 5.3. Stability fields of hydrothermal mineralization in the system silica-zirconia-water. From (73).

be corroded under some conditions, notably the conditions of a strong alkalinity associated with laterite development. The corrosion process would be abetted by strains in the zircon caused by intrusions and zoning effects in the rocks (72). Maurice studied the hydrothermal mineralization of silica-containing zirconium compounds occurring in vein deposits, running tests with alkaline solutions at 400° under a vapor pressure of 900 kg/sq cm. Zircon was stable in an acidic environment under these conditions, but it was attacked by alkalinities in excess of 0.001 N (73). Maurice's findings are illustrated in Figure 5.3, which outlines the areas of stability of the various zirconium compounds under the conditions of his experiments. There

71. L. Dryden and Clarissa Dryden, *J. Sediment. Petrol.* **16,** 91-6 (1946).

72. Dorothy Carroll, *J. Sediment. Petrol.* **23,** 106-16 (1953).

73. O. D. Maurice, *Economic Geology and the Bulletin of the Society of Economic Geologists* **44,** 721-31 (1946).

has been, however, no direct proof of the weathering of zircon, although the minute soluble zirconium content of certain spring waters has been attributed to the action of carbonic acid on zircon (74). Metamict zircon is much more likely to be attacked by chemical agents than is true zircon.

Zircon is a common accessory mineral in all types of igneous rocks, although as we have previously noted, it is particularly abundant in granites and syenites. It usually occurs in these rocks as well-formed crystals so tiny that it is difficult to see them well without the aid of a microscope. Larger crystals are sometimes found in limestone and other crystalline rocks. Fine specimens are found in New York, North Carolina, Colorado, and very large ones in Renfrew County, Ontario (75). Crystals several millimeters in length have been found in Henderson County, North Carolina (76), and crystals weighing several kilograms have been reported from Madagascar. Ordinary beach sand usually consists about 99% of silica, but some zircon can usually be separated by panning (66). Relatively high concentrations are found on beaches near Jacksonville, Florida (65), of the Vizagapatam and Travancore coasts of India (67), of Ceylon, and of the eastern coast of Australia, particularly in the vicinity of Byron Bay. Less important or less well-known concentrations occur in many other beaches around the world, such as in Oregon, Mariupol (Ukraine), western France, and various coastal regions of Africa.

The zircon deposits in the beaches of New South Wales are particularly rich. The economically important concentrations are between the outlets of the Clarence and Tweed rivers in northern New South Wales. Zircon is found in amounts ranging 45-75%. The concentration process for the heavy minerals in the sands of this region can be observed as a continuing phenomenon. During good weather the prevailing winds build up the seaward side of the sand dunes with sand consisting mainly of silica, but containing some of the heavy minerals. During the build-up, any stronger winds than usual blow away the silica sand and, if they are not too strong, leave the heavy mineral grains behind. In this way the dunes frequently acquire a banded structure. The foot of the dunes may reach to the high-water mark. When a storm arises, it tends to wash away all the wind-blown sand and to alter the slope of the beach. The beach often appears black for a considerable width above high-tide level because of the almost complete removal of the silica by wave action. The layers of heavy-mineral concentrate may be a mile or more long and up to 80 feet wide, and constitute an enormous

74. L. W. Strock, *Am. J. Science* **239**, 857-98 (1941).
75. E. S. Dana and C. S. Hurlbut, Jr., *Minerals and How to Study Them,* John Wiley & Sons, New York, 1949.
76. P. Pascal, *Traité de chimie minérale,* Masson et Cie, Paris, 1932, Vol. 4.

tonnage of heavy mineral made available by the action of a single storm. The zircon grains of the concentrate are of remarkably high purity. Samples of zircon which have been prepared from the sand contained less than 0.3% iron and titanium oxides, and even then individual grains of the impurity could be detected as rutile and ilmenite. The zircon grains have a cream to grayish-white color in bulk and a specific gravity of 4.66 (77).

The Florida deposits of zircon sand extend for about 6 miles along a beach near Jacksonville. The sand of this area contains about 4.0% of heavy minerals, of which 40% is ilmenite, 4% leucoxene, 7% rutile, 11% zircon, and less than 0.5% monazite. The balance consists of various silicates, including sillimanite, kyanite, staurolite, tourmaline, and garnet. The deposit is approximately ½ mile wide and 20 feet thick, and it is the chief source of supply of zirconium ore for the United States (79b).

Zircon grains and larger crystals are usually of a fairly high purity, yet small amounts of foreign elements are usually found either in the lattice or occluded in the crystal. These inclusions and occlusions affect the color, optical homogeneity, and chemical reactivity of the zircon, and may have bearing on the economic value of the ore deposit. Hafnium is always present in zircon and has been reported to range from 0.5% to 4.0%; Ceylon zircons usually contain about 2.7% hafnia (78); and Florida and Australian zircon contain about 1.3% (79). The accuracy of many of the earlier determinations of hafnia are questionable, but the values given here for Florida and Australian zircon appear to be well established. For literature dealing with the presence of foreign elements in zircon, reference might be made as follows: aluminum (80), barium (80), calcium (25, 80, 81), chromium (28, 32), copper (25, 80), dysprosium (46), helium (82, 83), iron (25), magnesium (80), niobium (81), radium (45, 84), samarium (46), silver (80), sodium (80, 85), strontium (81), tantalum (86), thorium (81), titanium (25, 80), uranium (81), vanadium (28), yttrium (81, 87), and zinc (25).

77. W. R. Poole, *Chem. Eng. Mining Rev.* **31**, 216-20 (1939).

78. B. W. Anderson and C. J. Payne, *Gemmologist* **7**, 297-30 (1937).

79. Titanium Alloy Manufacturing Division of the National Lead Co., unpublished researches.

79b. J. C. Detweiler, *Mining Eng.* **4**, 560-2 (1952).

80. T. G. Kennard and D. E. Howell, *Am. Mineral.* **21**, 721-6 (1936).

81. E. E. Kostyleva, *Compt. rend. sci. U.S.S.R.* **23**, 167-9 (1939).

82. P. Pellas, *Compt. rend.* **235**, 1134-6 (1952).

83. N. B. Keevil, E. S. Larsen, and F. J. Wank, *Am. J. Sci.* **242**, 345-53 (1944).

84. M. Campos and D. G. Figueiredo, *Escola engenharia univ. Minas Gerais, Inst. pesquisas radioativas,* **2**, 35-8 (1953).

85. Nobufusa Saito, *J. Chem. Soc. Japan* **64**, 1-6 (1943).

86. K. Rankama, *Bull. comm. géol. Finlande* **133**, 1-78 (1944).

87. O. Brotzen, *Geol. Fören. i. Stockholm Förh.* **74**, 173-84 (1952).

PHYSICAL AND CHEMICAL PROPERTIES

Zircon, composition $ZrO_2 \cdot SiO_2$ and formula weight 183.28, is the only compound and the only crystalline phase known to form from the elements zirconium, silicon, and oxygen (88, 89, 90, 94). Some of its physical constants are given in Table 5.1.

TABLE 5.1. PHYSICAL CONSTANTS OF ZIRCON

Coefficient of thermal expansion	
parallel to the axis	4.43×10^{-6} (95)
perpendicular to the axis	2.23×10^{-6} (95)
Color (pure)	colorless
Crystal system	tetragonal
parameters	a = 6.60 A, C 5.93 A (96, 97)
formula weights per unit cell	4
Dielectric constant	
parallel to axis	12.6 (98)
perpendicular to axis	12.85 (98)
Hardness (Mohs)	7.5
Melting point	decomp., 1540-1680° (95) (cf. 179)
Refraction	
dispersion	0.048 (3, p. 213)
double	0.0594-0.10 (78)
indices	$\omega = 1.933$, $\epsilon = 1.992$ (78)
Specific gravity	4.7
Thermodynamic constants	
entropy, kg cal/mole at 298.16°K	20.1 ± 0.3 (99)
specific heat, 21-51°C	0.132 (100)
Young's modulus of elasticity	1.98 (101)
modulus of rigidity	0.35 (101)
(values for 99% zircon body)	

88. Nina Zirnowa, Z. anorg. allgem. Chem. **218**, 193-200 (1934).
89. R. F. Geller and P. J. Yavorsky, J. Research Natl. Bur. of Standards **35**, 87-110 (1945).
90. R. F. Geller and S. M. Lang, J. Am. Ceram. Soc. **32**, Supplement No. 1, 157 (1949).
91. C. E. Curtis and H. G. Sowman, J. Am. Ceram. Soc. **36**, 190-3 (1953).
92. Ibid., 193-5 (1953).
93. Ibid., 193-5 (1953).
94. Ibid., 197-8 (1953).
95. J. d'Ans and J. Löffler, Z. anorg. allgem. Chem. **191**, 1-35 (1930).
96. H. George and R. Lambert, Compt. rend. **204**, 688-9 (1937).
97. G. L. Clark and D. H. Reynolds, Ind. Eng. Chem. **29**, 711-15 (1937).
98. D. A. A. S. Narayana Rao, Proc. Indian Acad. Sci. **30A**, 82-6 (1949).
99. K. K. Kelley, J. Am. Chem. Soc. **63**, 2750-2 (1941).
100. H. Kopp, Liebig's Ann. Suppl. **3**, 289 (1865).
101. E. Ryshkewitch, J. Am. Ceram. Soc. **34**, 322-6 (1951).

Metamict zircon exhibits considerably different values for all these constants, and the extent of metamictization is most readily ascertained by specific-gravity measurements. The index of refraction has been found to vary in direct ratio to the specific gravity, between 1.780 and 1.933 for ω and between 1.976 and 1.992 for ϵ (78). Values for the index of refraction of gem zircon are given in reference 102, refractive indices for radiation of 2979 A in 103, and for radiation 2795 to 7699 A in 104. The hardness also varies with the specific gravity (105). The optical anisotropy of zircon is paralleled by anisotropy of thermal conductivity (106; cf. 107), but zircon is nearly isotropic for electrical conductivity (108). Some zircon specimens exhibit recalescence when heated to dull red heat (109, 110, 111). Other details on physical properties of zircon may be found in the following literature: dielectric coefficient (112), energy of immersion and separation of liquids (113, 114), light output and screen potential (115), Raman spectrum (116), reflective power (112), spectrum (117, 118, 119), thermal expansion at high temperatures (120).

The refractory properties of zircon indicate it to be a solid of low energy content, and the representation of its structure as extensively linked and cross-linked by valence bonds implies a high order of chemical as well as physical stability. Empirically, zircon is one of the most stable and chemically inert substances known. It is not attacked by any known agent at the ordinary temperature, nor by any aqueous reagent up to the normal boiling point (121). It is generally unattacked by acidic reagents even at highly elevated temperatures, but it is decomposed when sintered with alkalies, such as sodium or potassium hydroxide or carbonate, or when exposed to

102. C. J. Payne, *Gemmologist* **4**, 263-5 (1935).
103. A. Brun, *Bull. soc. franç. minéral* **54**, 189-90 (1931).
104. Brun, *Bull. soc. franç. minéral* **53**, 35-46 (1930).
105. K. Chudoba, *Deut. Goldschmiede-Ztg.* **41**, No. 1, 10-11 (1938).
106. W. A. Wooster, *Z. Krist.* **95**, 138-49 (1936).
107. W. J. Knapp, *J. Am. Ceram. Soc.* **26**, 48-55 (1943).
108. L. Graetz, *Z. Krist.* **42**, 502 (1907).
109. A. Damour, *Compt. rend.* **58**, 154 (1864).
110. W. Henneberg, *J. prakt. Chem.* **38**, 508 (1847).
111. S. Stevanoic, *Z. Krist.* **37**, 247, 622 (1903).
112. T. Liebisch and R. Rubens, *Sitz. preuss. Akad. Wiss.* **1921**, 211-20.
113. W. D. Harkins and G. E. Boyd, *J. Am. Chem. Soc.* **64**, 1190-4, 1195-1204 (1942).
114. J. J. Chessick, A. C. Zettlemoyer, F. Healey, and G. J. Young, *Can. J. Chem.* **33**, 251-8 (1955).
115. S. T. Martin and L. B. Headrick, *J. Applied Phys.* **10**, 116-27 (1939).
116. Hisamitu Nisi, *Proc. Phys.-Math. Soc. Japan* [3] **14**, 214-18 (1932).
117. G. O. Wild, *Centr. Min. Geol.* **1933A**, 75-7.
118. F. Matossi and O. Bronder, *Z. Physik* **111**, 1-17 (1938).
119. B. W. Anderson and C. J. Payne, *Gemmologist* **9**, 1-5 (1940).
120. R. A. Heindl, *Bur. Standards J. Research* **10**, 715-35 (1933).
121. P. Jost and P. Plöcker, German Patent **285,981**, Feb. 1, 1914.

molten alkalies, borax, cryolite, or glasses (122). It is attacked by aqueous alkalies at 400° under pressure, as noted above. Alkali fluosilicates decompose zircon at about 600° with formation of alkali fluozirconates and silica.

The stability of zircon at high temperatures to most substances other than alkalies makes it a particularly valuable refractory with many applications. Zircon refractories do not react with molten aluminum or with silica (123), but zirconium has been detected spectrographically in a silicon ingot which

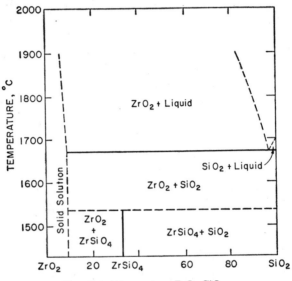

FIG. 5.4. The system ZrO_2-SiO_2.

had been melted in contact with zircon (124); and zircon is decomposed by molten mullite (125). Later in this chapter, we shall examine the kind of chemical attacks on the structure of zircon which result in its decomposition.

Phase diagrams of the system ZrO_2-SiO_2 have been sketched by Geller and his collaborators (90; cf. 89) and by Curtis and Sowman (94). The diagram offered by the latter is shown in Figure 5.4. According to their studies, when zircon is heated to about 1540°, it begins to dissociate into zirconia and silica.* The silica will be liquid or solid at this temperature,

---

* Zircon has been noted to decompose at 1500° in the presence of magnesium and barium fluorides (126), and at lower temperatures in the presence of small percentages of soda (127).

122. M. A. Bezborodov, A. S. Zaporozhtseva, and C. G. Moiseeva, *Tret'ego Soveshchaniya Eksptl. Mineral, Petrog. Inst. Geol. Nauk Akad. Nauk U.S.S.R.* **1940**, 195-203.

123. R. W. Knauft, *Ceram. Ind.* **63**, No. 2, 70-1, 100; No. 3, 59, 99 (1954).

124. J. Hino and H. E. Stauss, *J. Metals, Trans.* **4**, 656 (1952).

125. V. V. Lapin, *Voprosy Petrog. i. Mineral., Akad. Nauk S.S.S.R.* **2**, 367-73 (1953).

126. K. K. Zhirov, *Doklady Akad. Nauk S.S.S.R.* **85**, 889-91 (1952).

127. S. S. Kistler, Canadian Patent **525,999**, June 5, 1956.

depending on whether conditions favor formation of vitreous silica or one of its crystalline varieties. (Of these, cristobalite melts at 1710°, tridymite at 1670°, and quartz at 1470°.) Some appreciable decomposition of the zircon must occur before liquid will be observable. Solid zirconia and silica coexist with zircon until a temperature of about 1675° is attained, when all the zircon is decomposed and molten silica is in equilibrium with solid zirconia. The temperature 1675° is the eutectic temperature for a composition consisting approximately 3% zirconia and 97% silica. There has been no evidence of appreciable solution of silica or zirconia in zircon, but there is some dissolution of silica—not more than 10%—in zirconia (88, 89, 90, 97). Complete fusion of the decomposition products occurs at about 2400° (127).

It has been noted that crystals of zircon sand usually exhibit little or no cleavage. Heat treatment, however, produces cleavage and the phenomenon is influenced both by the nature of the heat treatment and the impurities in the sand. This is thought to be due to the influences of physical and chemical factors on the dissociation of the zircon. The dissociation starts to occur on crystal planes, causing strains conducive to cleavage along these planes (128).

On cooling the decomposition products of zircon, the zircon tends to reform from its components. The recombination can be followed by dilatometric (129) or X-ray (92) observations. Metamict zircon can be distinguished chemically from true zircon by the solubility of the former but not of the latter in hydrofluoric acid (32, 81). The reformation requires the maintenance of the mixture of decomposition products at a temperature sufficiently high for reaction to occur, but even at a suitable temperature recombination can occur only if the components are in suitable physical contact or proximity. For the most favorable physical conditions, the zirconia and silica should be well distributed through one another, and neither should be present as well-developed crystals. Some of the metamict zircon found in nature has been observed to consist of a partially destroyed zircon lattice filled with zirconia and silica. Heating such material moderately causes the reformation of true zircon.

In other natural metamict zircon, total decomposition of the zircon structure has occurred and there has been marked physical separation of the component oxides. The same amount of heating does not cause reassociation of such zircon (97). Lietz observed the appearance of weak X-ray lines of both zirconia and zircon on heating low-density natural zircon to 820°, and he estimated the zirconia particles to be about 170 A in diameter. On heating the specimen to 1250°, sharp X-ray lines of zircon appeared, the

128. A. Hilliard and V. H. Stott, *Trans. Brit. Ceram. Soc.* **48**, 143-52 (1949).
129. R. Chalmin, *Compt. rend.* **236**, 1785-7 (1953).

lattice being slightly enlarged (130).* Natural metamict zircon may contain unoriented minute crystals of either monoclinic or cubic zirconia, of about 10 A diameter, dispersed in silica glass (131, 132), or even smaller particles of zirconia which give only a diffuse X-ray band at the position of the strongest zirconia line, the band being changed to a line if the specimen is heated to about 900° (132). Evidence of structure in metamict zircon has been obtained by electron diffraction where none was detectable by X-ray (133).

When laboratory experiments on the decomposition and reassociation of zircon are conducted in different ways, different physical changes occur in the decomposition products which markedly affect the progress of reassociation. Volatilization of silica from the decomposition products is appreciable at 1900° (134) and is quite rapid at 2000° (135). When zircon was heated briefly to 1800°, the average crystal diameter was found to be 1 micron; after heating to 2000°, it was 2 microns. When the decomposition products were fused completely and allowed to resolidify and cool, zirconia crystals between 25 and 50 microns in diameter formed (127). Foreign solid phases separate if certain impurities are present, e.g., potassium zirconylosilicate (loc. cit.). Zirconia is most commonly found as monoclinic crystals (baddeleyite) in the cooled dissociated zircon (131, 136), but Geller and Yavorsky have reported the tetragonal variety, ruffite, to form and be stabilized under the conditions of their investigation (89), and cubic zirconia, or arkelite, has been found under other conditions (32, 132). The usual allotropic changes of the zirconia on passing through a heating cycle are either disturbed or prevented by dissolution of silica or other substances into the solid (129). The silica is usually recovered as a glassy phase, but cristobalite sometimes develops (92).

Zircon which had been fused was quenched to room temperature and found to be completely dissociated and to contain baddeleyite. It reassociated completely to zircon at 1450° in 3½ hours (136). An impure zircon decomposed at 1750° and was subsequently completely reassociated by holding it at 1500° for a week and then cooling it slowly, but the same material to which 3% barium fluoride or 1.9% aluminum fluoride had been added would not reassociate (131). Curtis and Sowman found thermally

---

*Lietz proposed the name *metazircon* for the metamict substance, but this term has not become conventional (*loc. cit.*).

130. J. Lietz, *Z. Krist* **98**, 201-10 (1937).
131. V. H. Stott and A. Hilliard, *Mineral. Mag.* **27**, 198-203 (1946).
132. M. von Stackelberg and K. Chudoba, *Z. Krist.* **97**, 252-62 (1937).
133. C. L. Crist, E. J. Dwornik, and M. S. Tischler, *Science* **119**, 513 (1954).
134. Camille Matignon, *Compt. rend.* **177**, 1290 (1923).
135. H. von Wartenberg and W. Gurr, *Z. anorg. allgem. Chem.* **196**, 374 (1931).
136. Helen B. Bartlett, *J. Am. Ceram. Soc.* **14**, 837-43 (1931).

dissociated zircon to reassociate within the approximate temperature range 1260-1540°, and the maximum rate was between 1430° and 1540° (92). Coprecipitated silica and zirconia were observed to associate to zircon at 1460° (97, 137), and mixtures of artificial baddeleyite and silica, either as quartz, cristobalite, tridymite, or vitreous silica, were found to associate to zircon at temperatures above 1315°, and particularly in the range 1430-1540° (93, 138, 139). According to Jacobs, zircon tends to crystallize from siliceous glazes in which the acidic components are in stoichiometric excess, while zirconia crystallizes if the basic components are in excess (140; cf. 141). But the formation of zircon is also dependent on the temperature to which the glaze has been heated. Zircon crystallized from certain glazes after firing at 1065-1100°, whereas zirconia, but no zircon, was found in the same compositions after firing at 815-850° (140). Zircon crystals up to 15 microns in length have been noted to form in a zinc-containing glaze that had been heated to 1300° (133).

Zircon of density 4.6 has been synthesized by heating 2 parts of zirconia with 1 part of silica in lithium molybdate at 700-1000° (142). Zircon crystals of measurable length have been obtained by the action of silicon tetrafluoride on zirconia, zirconium tetrafluoride on silica, and silicon tetrafluoride on a mixture of zirconia and silica (143).

Zircon will form from melts containing lime or magnesia, but not from melts containing lithia (4; cf. 127).

Zircon has been synthesized for use as a refractory (144), and it is said that articles of metallic cobalt, molybdenum, niobium, tantalum, or tungsten can be coated with a protective layer of zircon by dipping the article of these metals or their alloys into a molten silicon-zirconium alloy, then oxidizing the surface at 1400° to form zircon (139).

There is no reason to believe that molecular zircon exists in melts, and the characterization of zircon given above identifies it as a crystalline identity rather than a molecular identity. In the formation of zircon from melts, molecules of silica and zirconia alternately take positions in the crystal lattice without the intermediate formation of a zircon molecule. This does not preclude the possibility of the exhibition of pseudocolligative

137. K. von Chrustschoff, *Jahr. Mineral. Geol. Beilage*, **IIA**, 232-61 (1892).

138. C. Frondel and R. L. Collette, *U.S. Atomic Energy Comm. RME-3048*, 27 pp. (1953).

139. E. Nachtigall and R. Kieffer, Austrian Patent **169,916**, Dec. 27, 1951.

140. C. W. F. Jacobs, *J. Am. Ceram. Soc.* 37, 216-20 (1954).

141. Z. A. Nosova and M. E. Yakovleva, *Doklady Akad. Nauk U.S.S.R.* 91, 137-9 (1953).

142. Hautefeuille and Perrey, *Compt. rend.* 107, 1000 (1888).

143. Deville and Caron, *Compt. rend.* 46, 764 (1848).

144. C. Shaw, W. E. Smith, and D. E. B. Greensmith, U.S. Patent 2,593,352, April 15, 1952.

properties of melts into which zircon has been dissolved and decomposed. Zircon and lithium orthosilicate were mixed in a series of proportions, and the melting points of the mixtures were found to decrease linearly with the proportion of zircon, until 30 moles of zircon were used per 100 moles of the lithium compound. At this proportion, a eutectic was obtained which melted at 1021°. It was computed from this that the mixture acted as though it were a solution of a substance of molecular weight very nearly equal to that of $ZrO_2 \cdot SiO_2$ (145). These data indicate that a mole of solute was present per mole of zircon introduced into the system, with no implications as to the structural condition of the solute.

SIGNIFICANCE OF RADIOACTIVITY

It has been noted above that the dissociation and color of natural zircon can often be correlated to the action of particles or rays from radioactive substances, and that zirconium ores are particularly likely to contain uranium or thorium dioxides because of their isomorphism with zirconium dioxide. The concentration of radioactive elements in zirconium minerals is an empirical phenomenon (146), and each radioactive element tends to produce a characteristic halo in the zirconium mineral (33). The residual radioactivity in zircon mined today varies with the locale. A particularly high radioactivity was found in specimens from the gneiss area of Badgastein Hohe Tauern (147). A parallelism was noted between the radioactivity of zircon and its hafnium content (148), but such a relationship is not universal and may have been coincidental in the specimens from which this conclusion was drawn. Radium has been found present in zircon from Nellore, India, to the extent of 1.0 gm per 145 tons, nearly as high a concentration as in Colorado carnotite (45). Some zircons contain surprisingly large amounts of helium of radioactive origin. Zircon from Chelmsford, Massachusetts, has been found to contain 1.2 cc of helium per g (83). Alpha bombardment of zircon causes it to lose helium, and it has been shown that bombarding it with 10^{10} alpha particles per mg causes it to lose nearly all its helium content. From available data, it has been found possible to calculate roughly how much helium a zircon specimen has lost (149).

The intensity of the X-ray diffraction by zircon that has suffered alpha radiations from uranium inclusions decreases progressively with the amount of exposure to the radiations. Diffraction from the (112) plane gives a fairly

145. R. Schwarze and A. Haacke, *Z. anorg. allgem. Chem.* **196**, 374 (1931).

146. N. B. Keevil, A. R. Keevil, W. N. Ingham, and G. P. Crombie, *Am. J. Sci.* **241**, 345-65 (1943).

147. H. Haberlandt and A. Schiener, *Tschermaks mineralog-petrog. Mitt.* **2**, 292-354 (1951).

148. A. Piutti, *Rend. accad. sci. fis. mat. Napoli* **31**, 72-3 (1925).

149. P. M. Hurley, *Trans. Am. Geophys. Union* **33**, 174-83 (1952).

accurate criterion of the damage to the lattice. The age of a homogeneous sample of zircon can be estimated from the measurement of its alpha activity and X-ray diffraction angle (150).

Zircon subjected to prolonged bombardment by the radiations from thorium and uranium was observed to drop 16% in specific gravity during the course of the irradiation, becoming isotropic and so disordered in structure as to yield no X-ray diffraction pattern. The mechanism of the effect has been stated to consist in the displacement of atoms in the zircon by recoil nuclei and by the high temperature generated in the paths of the nuclear particles. The structure first becomes saturated with displacements, then broken down into crystallites of ordered zircon, and finally degraded to a glass (151). According to Pellas, an alpha particle displaces about 500 atoms in zircon, and a flux of not less than $2 \times 10^{17}\alpha$/sq cm is required to convert zircon to the metamict state (152). Hurley and Fairbairn estimated $3 \times 10^{15}\alpha$/sq cm to have the necessary energy for converting zircon half to the metamict state, and 685,000 cal/g is released during the process (153). Both investigators carried the experimental metamictization of zircon to a high degree of completion. Completely undamaged zircon exhibited a value of 35.635° for 2; the radioactively decomposed zircon approached the value 35.1° asymptotically as the metamict condition developed (*loc. cit.*). These and other studies indicate strongly that the degree of metamictization of natural zircons is largely a matter of the amount of irradiation to which they have been exposed, and in particular to the amount of radioactive elements present in the magma at the time of formation of the zircon crystals (154).

CHEMICAL REACTIONS

When a mole of zircon is sintered with a mole of an alkali, such as sodium carbonate or calcium oxide, zirconylosilicates form according to the equations

$$ZrO_2 \cdot SiO_2 + Na_2CO_3 \xrightarrow{900°} Na_2ZrSiO_5 + CO_2$$

and $\qquad ZrO_2 \cdot SiO_2 + CaO \xrightarrow{1100°} CaZrSiO_5$

(1-2)

X-ray diffraction studies of a mixture of zircon and lime at various stages in the heating, starting at 1118°, showed that the complex product had started to form at this temperature, that at 1250° the mixture contained calcium zirconylosilicate and free zirconia, and that from 1300° upward

150. P. M. Hurley and H. W. Fairbairn, *J. Applied Physics* **23**, 1408 (1952).
151. H. D. Holland and D. Gottfried, *Acta. Cryst.* **8**, 291-300 (1955).
152. P. Pellas, *Bull. soc. franç. mineral. et cryst.* **77**, 447-60 (1954).
153. P. M. Hurley and H. W. Fairbairn, *Bull. Geol. Soc. Am.* **64**, 659-74 (1953).
154. J. H. Morgan and M. L. Auer, *Am. J. Sci.* **239**, 305-11 (1941).

there was progressive reduction of the content of calcium zirconylosilicate and increase of zirconia content. At 1415° only traces of zircon remained and a small amount of calcium zirconylosilicate and a large amount of zirconia was present. Although there was no X-ray evidence of calcium silicate after heating to 1300°, chemical examination showed that it must be present (155).* Limestone or dolomite can be used in place of lime. Schoenlaub (156; cf. 156b) took advantage of the decomposition of the calcium zirconylosilicate at the more elevated temperatures to prepare zirconia from zircon by an economical process. He heated a mixture of zircon and lime to above 1430°, and preferably to 1600-1760°, to form a mixture of zirconia and calcium orthosilicate. The over-all reaction was

$$2CaO + ZrO_2 \cdot SiO_2 \xrightarrow{1600°} ZrO_2 + Ca_2SiO_4 \tag{3}$$

Some calcium was taken into solid solution in the zirconia, and the latter was recovered from the process as the *stabilized* variety, or arkelite. After grinding the mixture of products, it was possible to isolate the zirconia by elutriation.

When approximately 1 mole of sodium zirconylosilicate is stirred with 2 moles of a strong solution of tartaric or citric acid, it is dissolved, forming a stable solution of an undetermined complex structure (157). If it is treated with hydrochloric or sulfuric acid, soluble zirconium salts pass into solution, and a precipitate of hydrated silica separates (158).

When 1 mole of zircon is heated with 2 moles of soda ash instead of 1, sodium zirconate and sodium silicate are formed:

$$2\,Na_2CO_3 + ZrO_2 \cdot SiO_2 \xrightarrow{1000°} Na_2ZrO_3 + Na_2SiO_3 \tag{4}$$

The sodium silicate can be leached from the reaction product with water, leaving a residue of acid-soluble sodium zirconate.

The nature of the molecular changes which occur when zircon reacts with alkalies at elevated temperatures may be visualized as shown in Figures 5.5 and 5.6. When 1 mole of alkali reacts with 1 mole of zircon, the oxide ion of the soda adds to the zirconium atom, forming a zirconylosilicate

---

* Alvarez-Estrada obtained the calcium zirconylosilicate after holding the reactants for 64-144 hours at the elevated temperatures. A. J. Hathaway undertook similar preparations in which he held the reactants at the elevated temperatures for 2-3 hours and obtained no detectable complex silicate (79).

155. D. Alvarez-Estrada, *Arkiv. Chemi.* 7, 33-8 (1954).
156. R. A. Schoenlaub, U.S. Patent 2,578,748, Dec. 18, 1941.
156b. British Patent 429,367, May 29, 1935.
157. C. J. Kinzie, U.S. Patents 2,013,856-7, Sept. 10, 1935.
158. M. Kastner, U.S. Patent 2,604,378, July 22, 1952.

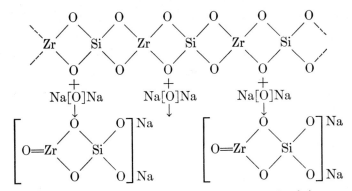

FIG. 5.5. The reaction of a mole of soda with a mole of zircon.

complex. The zircon chain is ruptured between every zirconylosilicate group which forms. With 2 moles of soda, an oxygen ion is added to both the zirconium and the silicon atoms, and the chain breaks down with formation of sodium zirconate and sodium silicate structures. This decomposition of the zircon, then, depends on the availability of an oxygen ion to displace and replace the linkages between successive silica and zirconia groups.

Sodium oxide forms a less stable crystal than calcium oxide, the former subliming at 1275° and the latter melting at 2580°; the liquid boils at 2850°. From this it would be expected that oxide ions would be more readily available from sodium oxide than from calcium oxide, and it is found in practice that the decomposition of zircon with calcium oxide requires a higher temperature than the decomposition with sodium-oxide-containing materials. The decomposition of calcium zirconylosilicate at

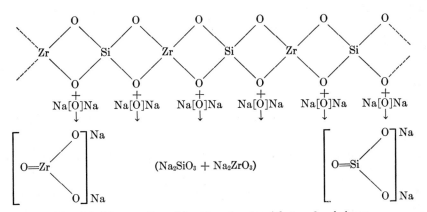

FIG. 5.6. The reaction of 2 moles of soda with 1 mole of zircon.

high temperatures (*supra*) is probably a splitting off of the zirconia in this wise:

$$\text{III} \quad \left[\text{O=Zr} \underset{O}{\overset{O}{<}} \underset{O}{\overset{O}{>}} \text{Si} \right] \text{Ca} \xrightarrow{1600°} \text{O=Zr=O} + \left[\text{O=Si} \underset{O}{\overset{O}{<}} \right] \text{Ca} \quad (4a)$$

It might be expected that fluorides would behave similarly to oxides, decomposing zircon by donating fluoride ions to the zirconium or silicon atoms. In practice this has been found to be true, but in general the refractory fluorides are not suitable for this reaction, and here, too, it can be presumed that the energy of separation of a fluoride ion from its lattice position is the limiting factor. The alkali and alkaline earth fluorides, for example, are not satisfactory for decomposing zircon. (Sodium oxide sublimes at 1270° and the fluoride boils at 1700°; the heavier alkali oxides decompose at low heats, i.e., rubidium and cesium oxides at about 400°, while the fluorides melt at 1250-1500°.) Fluosilicates make fluoride ions available for combination with the zirconium atoms of zircon and react according to the equation

$$ZrO_2 \cdot SiO_2 + K_2SiF_6 \xrightarrow{600°} K_2ZrF_6 + 2SiO_2 \text{ (159, 160, 161b)} \quad (5)$$

The double fluorides of chromium, cobalt, iron, nickel, and zinc with the alkali fluorides may be used in place of fluosilicates (161a), and mixtures of fluorides, such as potassium and magnesium fluorides (162) or potassium and silicon fluorides (163), have also proved satisfactory.

Alkali and alkaline earth halides other than the fluorides do not react with zircon. Were there to be a reaction, it would require the breaking of a bond between zirconium and oxygen to form a bond between zirconium and, say, chlorine. This appears never to happen, except in the displacement of hydronium ions by chloride (see Chap. 3). However, zircon is attacked by carbon tetrachloride with formation of zirconium tetrachloride and silicon tetrachloride:

$$ZrO_2 \cdot SiO_2 + 2CCl_4 \xrightarrow{1100°} ZrCl_4 + SiCl_4 + 2CO_2 \text{ (79)} \quad (6)$$

Alternatively, the zircon can be briquetted with carbon and then submitted to the action of chlorine at about the same temperature (165). No direct

159. P. B. Chakravarti and T. Banerjee, *J. Sci. Ind. Research India* **12B**, 389-90 (1953).
160. J. Koerner, U.S. Patent **1,467,275**, Sept. 4, 1923.
161a. H. C. Kawecki, U.S. Patent **2,418,173**, March 25, 1947.
161b. Kawecki, U.S. Patent **2,418,174**, March 25, 1947.
162. C. Adamoli, U.S. Patent **2,250,581**, July 29, 1941.
163. H. C. Clafin and D. O. Hubbard, British patent **391,369**, April 17, 1933.
165. F. H. McBerty, *Anhydrous Chlorides Manufacture*, Hobart Publishing Co., Washington.

conversion of zircon to zirconium and silicon bromides or iodides has been reported, but it is probable that the bromides can be prepared similarly to the chlorides and that the iodides cannot be prepared in this fashion owing to their instability at high temperatures.

A mixture of zircon and carbon is converted to zirconium carbide or cyanonitride when heated in the arc furnace, the former being a saturated solution of carbon in face-centered, cubic zirconium metal lattice and the latter an undersaturated solution which usually contains some nitrogen which has been gettered from the air. The course of the reaction is very complex and varies with operational conditions (166), but the over-all effects can be represented by the equation

$$2ZrO_2 \cdot SiO_2 + 5C \rightarrow 2Zr, C + \uparrow 2SiO + 3CO_2 \qquad (7)$$

where Zr, C represents the solid solution of carbon in zirconium.

BENEFICIATION AND TREATMENT OF ORES

The beneficiation of zircon-containing ores and the conversion of zircon to other useful zirconium compounds is a highly developed art which has taken extensive advantage of the physical and chemical properties of zircon. Although the zircon sand is the starting material for all present large-scale production of zirconium products, methods for treating zircon-containing rocks have also been described and used to a limited extent. The rock has been ground to sufficiently small particle size to release the zircon particles, and passed over a Wilfley table to separate a zircon-rich fraction (167).

Wet and dry techniques have been used to isolate the grains of zircon sand in a high state of purity by industrial standards—commonly over 99% pure zircon. Zircon particles can be selectively oiled by treatment with an emulsion of an oil such as pine oil or pinene in aqueous soap solution, such as sodium or potassium stearate or palmitate. The oiled particles can then be worked into a froth in which they are separated to a large extent from other mineral particles with which they had been associated (168, 169, 170, 171). Alternatively, the sand can be classified by washing and elutriation (172). The zircon sand, with or without the benefit of previous purification, has been submitted to the action of electrostatic (173, 79b)

166. W. J. Kroll, A. W. Schlechten, W. B. Carmody, L. A. Yerkes, H. P. Holmes, and H. L. Gilbert, *Trans. Electrochem. Soc.* **96**, 99-113 (1947).

167. R. C. Gosbreau, *Eng. Min. J.-Press.* **119**, 405-6 (1925).

168. M. A. Corbett, British Patents **406,018** and **406,043**, Feb. 12, 1934.

169. G. Gutzeit and P. Kovalin, *Arch. sci. phys. nat.* **21**, 260-9 (1939).

170. J. M. Patek, *Am. Inst. Mining Met. Eng., Tech. Rept.* 564, 22 pp. (1934).

171. M. A. Corbett, U.S. Patent **2,082,383**, June 1, 1937.

172. C. J. Kinzie, U.S. Patent **2,036,220**, April 7, 1936.

173. F. A. Fahrenwald, N. F. Parkinson, and G. H. Barnes, U.S. Patent **2,180,804**, Nov. 21, 1939.

and electromagnetic (174) classifiers. Electromagnetic separation takes advantage of differences in the magnetic permeability of different minerals. Ilmenite and garnet are moderately magnetic, monazite weakly magnetic, and zircon, rutile, and cassiterite practically nonmagnetic. Electrostatic separation is based on differences in electrical conductivities of the minerals. If a mixture of minerals is placed on a conducting surface and a highly charged body is brought near it, charges induced on the particles of low conductivity persist while those on the more highly conducting particles run off into the conducting surface. The poorly conducting particles are therefore attracted more strongly to the charged surface (175). Zircon has a lower conductivity than rutile or ilmenite. Sometimes the crude zircon is heated (176) or treated chemically, as with sulfur fumes (177) to improve the efficiency of electric classification. More elaborate chemical methods for substantially complete removal of specific impurities have been described, but they are not in general use because of their high cost. Iron has been removed by leaching with sulfuric acid (178) and by chlorinating with phosgene or with chlorine in the presence of carbon (180, 181, 182) at a temperature too low to affect the zircon. Titanium has been removed by chlorination (181) or by heating the mineral with carbon to 1600°, at which temperature titanium monoxide is formed. The titanium monoxide can be dissolved with acid (183). Silica has been removed with hydrofluoric acid or other fluorides (184). The purity of the zircon is best determined spectrographically (185).

An outline of the steps in the conversion of zircon to other useful products is given in Table 5.2.

Although the zircon crystal has a very stable structure except at highly elevated temperatures, the surface atoms have a certain residual chemical activity due to the lower degree of saturation of bonding capacity of these atoms. Zircon surfaces show a certain type of chemical behavior which is to be associated with this bonding capacity, and it does not involve breakdown of the zircon structure. When zircon is used as a filler for various types of rubber, synthetic rubber, silicone rubber, and other plastics, it increases the

174. D. S. Kutepov, *Tsvetnye Metal* **13**, No. 5, 37-46 (1938).
175. O. A. Jones, *Australian J. Sci.* **8**, 99-103 (1946).
176. E. L. Wiegand, U.S. Patent **2,235,305**, Mar. 18, 1941.
177. F. R. Johnson, U.S. Patent **2,154,682**, April 18, 1939.
178. A. Wakhs, *Chem. Zentr.* **1942**, I, 2052.
179. E. W. Washburn and E. E. Libman, *J. Am. Ceram. Soc.* **3**, 634-40 (1920).
180. K. H. Donaldson, U.S. Patent **2,120,602**, June 14, 1938.
181. C. J. Kinzie, U.S. Patent **2,036,221**, April 7, 1936.
182. H. Funk, C. Muller, and J. Tormyn, *Chem. Tech.* (Berlin) **5**, 530 (1953).
183. C. J. Kinzie and E. Wainer, U.S. Patent **2,127,664**, Aug. 23, 1938.
184. C. H. Peddrick, Jr., and J. H. Weis, U.S. Patent **2,198,972**, April 30, 1940.
185. J. M. Zander and J. H. Terry, *J. Am. Ceram. Soc.* **30**, 366-70 (1947).

TABLE 5.2. AN OUTLINE OF THE STEPS THAT HAVE BEEN USED
TO CONVERT ZIRCON TO OTHER USEFUL PRODUCTS

Step	Literature
A. Opening up the ore by chemical attack	
sintering with sodium hydroxide	186, 187, 188, 189, 190
sintering with sodium hydroxide plus sodium peroxide	191
sintering with sodium carbonate	186, 192, 193, 194
sintering with calcium oxide-containing bases	195, 196, 197
sintering with calcium sulfate	197
sintering with fluorine-containing salts	159, 160, 161, 163
sintering with chlorinating agents	79, 164, 165
B. Opening up the ore by thermal attack	
heating to dissociation	198
heating to volatilize the silica	199
heating with carbon to form Zr (C, N, O)	200, 201
C. Treatment of decomposition products of zircon	
converting sintered products to sulfato compounds of zirconium	188, 196, 202
converting sintered products to chlorides of zirconium	190, 203
Extracting silica from dissociated zircon	
with hydrofluoric acid	198
with strong caustic alkali solution	204
chlorination of Zr (C, N, O)	205, 206
D. Isolation of substantially pure zirconium compounds	
as basic sulfate	191, 207, 208
as basic sulfite	209
as hydrous zirconia	
by adding an alkali	188
by superheating	187
as a fluoride	192, 210
as an oxalate	211
as potassium sulfatozirconate	220b

186. British Patent **350,728,** June 29, 1929.
187. B. Maletra, French Patent **714,285,** July 8, 1930.
188. Yoshikatsu Ogawa, *Repts. Osaka Pref. Ind. Research Inst.* **4,** No. 1, 28-9 (1952).
189. K. S. Rajan, *J. Sci. Ind. Research India* **13B,** 43-5 (1954).
190. H. L. Gilbert, C. Q. Morrison, A. Jones, and A. W. Henderson, *U.S. Bur. Mines, Rept. Invest. 5091,* 31 pp. (1954).
191. Satoru Ishibachi, *J. Ceram. Assoc. Japan* **69,** 138-44 (1951).
192. H. George and R. Lambert, U.S. Patent **2,076,080,** April 7, 1937.
193. C. G. Maier, U.S. Patent **2,501,952,** March 28, 1950.
194. C. J. Kinzie, U.S. Patent **1,618,288,** Feb. 22, 1927.
195. British Patent **282,023,** Dec. 13, 1926.
196. French Patent **60,937,** Aug. 19, 1927.
197. M. O. Axt, British Patent **544,965,** May 5, 1942.
198. H. George and R. Lambert, **44,673,** addition to French Patent **762,066,** April 3, 1934.

thermal stability of these substances (212, 213). Zircon catalyzes the conversion of di-m-xylylmethane and related compounds in combination with water to light oils at about 500° (214), and it serves as an auxiliary catalyst in the dehydration of sulfur-containing hydrocarbons at 900°, where nickel is the main catalyst (215).

USES

The chemical use of zircon is primarily as a raw material from which to derive zirconium dioxide and soluble zirconium salts and complex acids. This use and the use as a filler for rubber and plastics have already been discussed in the preceding section. Both true zircon and metamict zircon have been used as gems. According to Smith, "zircon has not yet attained to a rank in the world of jewelry commensurate with its high qualities. The colorless stones rival even the diamond in splendor and brilliance and display of fire" (2, p. 329; cf. 216). Geologists have used zircon to establish the origins of sedimentary rocks, and petrological provinces can be differentiated on the basis of the zircon which they contain (217). The stability of zircon in the metamorphic processes enables it to serve as a criterion of the igneous or sedimentary origin of the stratum (218). Rock intrusions have been correlated by the type of zircon they contain, e.g., normal,

199. British Patent **345,291**, Dec. 11, 1929.
200. C. J. Kinzie, R. P. Easton, and V. V. Efimoff, U.S. Patent **2,270,527**, Jan. 20, 1942; British Patent **544,823**, April 29, 1942.
201. G. H. Cleaver, *Eng. Min. J.* **155**, No. 7, 98-9 (1954).
202. C. J. Kinzie, U.S. Patent **2,120,602**, June 14, 1938.
203. British Patent **287,424**, Nov. 2, 1927.
204. British Patent **709,882**, June 2, 1954.
205. H. Moissan and F. Lengfeld, *Compt. rend.* **122**, 551 (1896).
206. H. S. Cooper, *Trans. Am. Electrochem. Soc.* **43**, 215 (1923).
207. E. J. Pugh, U.S. Patent **1,316,107**, Sept. 16, 1918; U.S. Patent **1,376,161**, April 26, 1921.
208. E. Wainer, U.S. Patent **2,294,431**, Sept. 1, 1942.
209. J. d'Ans, U.S. Patent **1,819,770**, Aug. 18, 1931.
210. G. I. Voynilovich and Ya. M. Pesin, Russian Patent **46,259**, March 31, 1936.
211. H. Trapp, *Chem. Ztg.* **52**, 365-6 (1928).
212. R. R. Maneri, U.S. Patent **2,658,882**, Nov. 10, 1953.
213. Private communications to the author.
214. M. G. Sturrock and T. Lawe, U.S. Patent **2,422,318**, June 17, 1947.
215. J. H. Shapleigh, U.S. Patents **2,575,324**, Nov. 20, 1951; **2,628,890**, Feb. 17, 1953; **2,639,223**, May 9, 1953.
216. E. P. Youngman, *U.S. Bur. Mines Information Circular 6465*, 20 pp. (1931).
217. J. Zerndt, *Bull. intern. acad. Polonaise*, **1927A**, 363-77.
218. C. B. Coetzee, *Trans. Roy. Soc. S. Africa* **29**, Pt. 2, 91-112 (1942).
219. Margaret S. Woyski, *Bull. Geol. Soc. Am.* **60**, 999-1016 (1949).
220. J. F. Haseman and C. E. Marshal, *Missouri Agr. Exp. Sta., Research Bull. 387*, 75 pp. (1945).
220b. C. J. Kinzie, British Patent **271,873**, May 27, 1926; German Patent **524,986**, May 26, 1927.

hyacinth, or malacon, etc. (219). The origins of soils can also be traced with the help of observations of their zircon contents (220). It has been shown that in computing the age of rocks from measurements of their radio-activity and lead content, a formula $T = cPb/\alpha$ may be used, in which T is the age in millions of years, Pb is the radiogenic lead content in parts per million, α is the number of alpha particles per mg per hour, and c is a specific constant for zircon, sphene, or apatite. Zircon is the most satis-factory mineral for reference in such a determination of age (221, 222).

A large literature exists on the ceramic applications of zircon. A detailed review of the ceramic applications lies outside the scope of this book, and it will be pertinent here merely to list the uses:

1. Casting molds (vehicles such as linseed oil)
2. Chemically resistant ware
3. Electrical resistors and insulators
4. Enamels
5. Glass polishing (223, 224)
6. Glazes
7. Heat transfer pebbles
8. Pigments
9. Porcelains
10. Refractories (brick, caulking compounds, cements, ceramic bodies, coatings, as for foundry molds, and cores).

For details of these applications, reference should be made to the ceramic journals. Some compositions containing zirconia and silica in different pro-portions from those found in zircon have also been used in ceramics, for example, a composition corresponding to $7ZrO_2 \cdot 2SiO_2$ for making bonded engine liners (225).

THE COMPLEX SILICATES

THE DERIVATION OF HETEROPOLYACID ANIONS FROM ZIRCON

It has been shown above that a salt of a heterodiacid is obtained when a mole of zircon is heated to about 1000° with a mole of an alkali such as sodium carbonate (see equation 1 and Fig. 5.5). Consideration of the mechanism of this formation leads to the expectation that a large number of heterodiacids and heteropolyacids might be formed as conditions are varied from those in which the alkali or alkaline-earth compounds of the

221. N. B. Larsen, *Bull. Geol. Soc. Am.* **63**, 1045-52 (1952).
222. H. Yamamoto, *Sci. Rept. Fac. Sci. Kyushu Univ., Geol.* **4**, 81-95 (1953).
223. W. T. Maloney, U.S. Patent **2,427,799**, Sept. *23*, 1947.
224. S. S. Kistler, U.S. Patent **2,696,45**, Dec. 7, 1954.
225. J. D. Morgan, U.S. Patent **1,923,003**, Aug. 15, 1933.

heterodiacids described above were formed. For example, the chain structure present in zircon need not be split only to form units of composition Na_2ZrSiO_5 or Na_2SiO_3 plus Na_2ZrO_3. Under favorable conditions, one might expect the formation of a molecule of composition $Na_4ZrSi_2O_8$:

$$\diagdown ZrO_2SiO_2ZrO_2SiO_2ZrO_2 \diagdown + 4Na_2O \rightarrow 2Na_2ZrO_3 + \qquad (8)$$

$$Na\begin{bmatrix} O & O & O & O \\ \diagdown Si \diagup \diagdown Zr \diagup \diagdown Si \diagup \\ O & O & O & O \end{bmatrix} \begin{matrix} Na \\ \\ Na \end{matrix}$$

The same product might form also in another way:

$$Na\begin{bmatrix} O & O \\ \diagdown Si \diagup \diagdown Zr{=}O \\ O & O \end{bmatrix} + \begin{bmatrix} O \\ O{=}Si \diagup \\ O \end{bmatrix}\begin{matrix} Na \\ \\ Na \end{matrix} \rightarrow \qquad (9)$$

$$Na\begin{bmatrix} O & O & O & O \\ \diagdown Si \diagup \diagdown Zr \diagup \diagdown Si \diagup \\ O & O & O & O \end{bmatrix}\begin{matrix} Na \\ \\ Na \end{matrix}$$

Less alkaline conditions would favor the formation of the asymmetrical structure:

$$Na\begin{bmatrix} O & O \\ \diagdown Si \diagup \diagdown Zr{=}O \\ O & O \end{bmatrix} + SiO_2 \rightarrow Na\begin{bmatrix} O & O & O \\ \diagdown Si \diagup \diagdown Si \diagup \diagdown Zr{=}O \\ O & O & O \end{bmatrix} \quad (10)$$

Titania or other tetravalent metal oxides might take the place of silica in such condensations, giving structures containing the unit $Na_2O_2TiO_2SiO_2ZrO$. Or an oxide of a trivalent or pentavalent metal might form similar structures, with differing alkali requirements depending upon the valence of the metal, e.g.,

$$2Na_2O_2SiO_2ZrO + Nb_2O_3 + Na_2O \rightarrow 2Na_3O_2NbO_2SiO_2ZrO \qquad (11)$$

These processes and combinations of these processes occur in nature, and they have led to the formation of what might be regarded as a continuous and infinite variety of heteropolyacid minerals containing silica and zirconia. Certain more or less definable species have been recognized, however. They are listed in Table 5.3 and will be discussed below. Some of the heteropolyacid compounds probably formed without the actual intermediate crystallization of zircon. Cerium, titanium, thorium, and uranium are particularly prominent among the tetravalent elements coexisting with zirconium in the complex silicates; niobium and tantalum are combined both as trivalent and as pentavalent elements; and various rare earths are found combined in such compounds, probably mostly as trivalent metals. Hydrogen, potassium, calcium, magnesium, iron, and manganese may take the place of sodium. We shall refer to silicate compounds containing ZrO as a structural unit as *zirconylosilicates* and to those containing ZrO_2 as a structural unit as *zirconosilicates*.

Catapleiite was the name given to a mineral from the islands of the Langesund Fiord, Norway. The name was derived from the Greek *kata*, meaning by, with, plus *pleion*, more, and was suggested by the variety of other ores with which it is associated (226). It occurs as calcium and soda varieties, the latter being almost lime-free. There are approximately 3 moles of silicon to 1 of zirconium. The mineral may contain about 9% of water which apparently is not constitutional and can be expelled by heating and at least partially reabsorbed, even at a high temperature, e.g., 270° (227, 228, 229). It varies in color from light-yellow to yellowish-brown, and may be grayish-blue or violet. The crystals are commonly tabular, hexagonal prisms with replaced edges, and are reported to occur in both pseudohexagonal and monoclinic varieties, the former with a:c = 1:1.3593 (230) or 1:1.3605 (228) and the latter with a:b:c = 1.7239:1:1.3618 and $\beta = 90°11\frac{1}{2}'$ (298). Above 140° the crystals are hexagonal. One type has been observed to be uniaxial at 120°, another above 200°, and a third at 10-20° (231). The $(10\bar{1}0)$ cleavage is perfect; the $(10\bar{1}1)$ and $(10\bar{1}2)$ cleavages are imperfect. The specific gravity varies with the analysis. Zircon forms when catapleiite is heated, and pseudomorphs after catapleite have been found (228). Catapleiite is decomposed by hydrochloric acid with formation if gelatinous silica.

Elpidite, a name derived from Greek *elpis*, meaning hope, is the name given to a mineral found near Nagssarsuk, Greenland. It is white or reddish, and contains about 6 silicon atoms per zirconium atom (232, 233). Dehydration studies indicate that the water is not structural, but rather held physically. The crystals are rhombic with a:b:c = 0.510:1:0.9781. The (110)

226. P. C. Weibye and J. Sjögren, *Svenska Akad. Handl.* (1849) 99.
227. M. Weibull, *Geol. For. Forh. Stockholm* **7,** 272 (1884).
228. W. C. Brögger, *ibid.,* **7,** 427 (1884).
229. F. Zambonini, *Atti. Accad. Napoli* (2) **14,** 55 (1908).
230. H. Dauber, *Pogg. Ann.* **92,** 239 (1854).
231. G. Flink, *Zeit. Kryst.* **23,** 359 (1894).
232. G. Lindström, *Geol. För. Förh. Stockholm* **16,** 330 (1894).
233. G. Nordenskjöld, *ibid.* 336 (1894).

cleavage is marked. The specific gravity of the white mineral is about 2.594 and the hardness 7; the optic angle 2V is 75°12′; the indices of refraction are $\alpha = 1.5600$, $\beta = 1.5650$, and $\gamma = 1.5739$. The birefringence is $\gamma - \alpha = 0.0139$ for yellow light (231). Another investigator gives $2V_a = 89°40′$ (234).

Eudialyte and *eucolyte* are chlorine-containing complex minerals of zirconia and silica with high soda contents and varying contents of lime and iron oxide. *Guarinite* and *hiortdahlite* seem to be substantially the same chemical compound. The first of these names was applied to a mineral found in cavities in the sanidine bombs of Monte Somma (235). It has been reported to be rhombic with a:b:c = 0.9892:1:0.3712 (235, 236), or 0.99268:1:0.37008 (237). The optic angle is about 2V = 90″; the specific gravity is 3.487 (235) or 2.9-3.3 (238); birefringence is $\gamma - \beta = 0.0047$, $\beta - \alpha = 0.0048$, and $\gamma - \alpha = 0.0095$ (237). It is pleochroic. *Hiörtdahlite*

TABLE 5.3. NAMES AND COMPOSITIONS OF COMPLEX ZIRCONIA-SILICA MINERALS

Names	*Compositions*
Aarhenite............................	A hydrated cerium-erbium-iron-zirconium silicate
Astrophyllite.........................	$(K,Na)_2(Fe,Mn,Al)_4(Zr,Ti,Si)O_{14}(OH,F)_2$
Catapleiite..........................	$(Na_2Ca)ZrSi_3O_9 \cdot 2H_2O$
Chalcolamprite......................	A zirconium-niobium silicate
Dalyite..............................	$K_2ZrSi_6O_{15}$
Elpidite............................	$Na_2ZrSi_6O_{15} \cdot 3H_2O$
Erdmannite.........................	A cerium earth metal-zirconium silicate
Eudialyte and eucolite	$Na_{13}(Ca,Fe)_6Cl(Si,Zr)_{20}O_{52}$
Guarinite and hiortdahlite............	$Na_2Ca_4F_2(Si,Zr)_5O_{14}$
Hainite.............................	A tantalum-containing salt of a zirconia-silica heteropolyacid
Lavenite............................	$Na(Mn,Ca,Fe)ZrOF(SiO_3)_2$
Mosandrite.........................	A sodium-calcium-cerium-titanium-zirconium-fluoride-silicate
Rosenbuschite.......................	A sodium-calcium-titanium-zirconium-fluoride-silicate
Wadeite............................	$K_2CaZrSi_4O_{12}$
Wöhlerite..........................	A sodium-calcium-niobium-zirconium-fluoride-silicate
Zirfesite............................	$(ZrO_2 \cdot Fe_2O_3) \cdot SiO_2 \cdot nH_2O$

234. O. B. Böggild, *Medd. Gronland* **24**, 102 (1899).
235. G. Guiscardi, *Rend. Accad. Napoli* **2**, 367 (1890).
236. V. von Lang, *Tschermaks Mitt.* **81** (1871).
237. F. Zambonini, *Centr. Min.* **524**, 667 (1902).
238. H. Rosenbusch, *Mikroscopische Physiographie der Mineralien und Gesteine*, Stuttgart, 1905, 384.
239. W. C. Brögger, *Zeit. Kryst.* **16**, 367 (1890).

was found by Brögger (239) on the Arö Islands, Norway. It is reported to be triclinic with axial ratios a:b:c = 0.9985:1:0.35123, $\alpha = 89°22\frac{1}{2}'$, $\beta = 90°36\frac{5}{6}'$, $\gamma = 90°5\frac{5}{6}'$, specific gravity 3.267 (239), and hardness 5-5.6.

A silicate mineral containing sodium, calcium, fluorine, iron, manganese, titanium, and zircon, found in the Langesund Fiord of Norway, has been given the name *lavenite* (240). It has been observed in colorless, pale-yellow, and dark-yellow to brown varieties. The prismatic or tabular crystals are monoclinic with axial ratios a:b:c = 1.0963:1:1.0715 and $\beta = 69°42\frac{1}{2}'$. The (100) cleavage is nearly perfect. The specific gravity is 3.51-3.55 and the hardness 6; the index of refraction is $\beta = 1.750$. The mineral is strongly birefringent with $\gamma - \alpha = 0.03$ (241). The optical character is negative and the crystals are strongly pleochroic. The mineral is incompletely decomposed by acids.

Rosenbuschite is a pale-yellow to brown mineral, and a closely related compound has been reported to form by the reaction of slags with zircon brick (242). A yellow crystalline mineral found on several islands of the Langesund Fiord by Scheerer was named *wöhlerite* in honor of F. Wöhler (243). Its hafnia content has been observed to be 0.7% (60t). Although it was first thought to have a rhombic lattice, it was later shown to be monoclinic with axial ratios a:b:c = 1.0536:1:0.70878 and $\beta = 71°3'$. The color varies through shades of yellow, brown, and gray. The (010) cleavage is distinct, the specific gravity is 3.41-3.33, the hardness 5.5-6, $2H_0 = 121°42'$ and $2V = 78°37'$ (243). The refractive index $\beta = 1.67$-1.74, $\gamma - \alpha = 0.023$ and $\gamma - \beta = 0.14$ (244). The optical character is negative and the crystals are pleochroic. The mineral dissolves in hot concentrated hydrochloric acid with separation of silica and niobium pentoxide.

Eudialyte, rosenbuschite, lavenite, and astrophyllite are very common in the country rocks of Minas Gerais, Brazil (244b). The first two of these are thought to have formed as a result of hydrothermal action on nepheline syenite containing zirconium minerals (244c).

Zirfesite appears to be an alteration product of eudialyte. It has been described as a pale-yellow mineral of low specific gravity (1.620) which is easily powdered and smeared, has a faint argillaceous odor, and tends to stick to the tongue. It has also been observed occurring as flakes and lamellae with a pearly luster. It dissolves readily in hydrochloric acid and

240. *Ibid.* **2**, 275 (1878); **10**, 503 (1897); **16**, 339 (1899).
241. A. Michel-Levy and A. LaCroix, *Les Minéraux des roches,* Paris, 1888, p. 235.
242. P. Koch, *Tonindustrie-Zeitung* **49**, 55-6 (1930).
243. W. C. Brögger, *Zeit. Kryst.* **16**, 355 (1890).
244. G. P. Tschernik, *Compt. rend, acad. sci. Russ.* **1923**, 37-9.
244b. Ruy Ribeiro Franco, *Univ. São Paulo, Fac. filos., cienc. letras* **49**, *mineralogia* No. 7, 7-26 (1945).
244c. Ruy Ribeiro Franco and W. Loewenstein, *Am. Mineral.* **33**, 142-51 (1948).

gelatinizes when heated. Appreciable silica can be extracted from the powdered mineral by aqueous sodium carbonate, and iron and zirconium go into solution when it is treated with tartaric acid. It was found at Mannepachk, Khibina Tundras (244d).

There is some doubt as to the validity of the identity of the minerals *aarhenite*, *chalcolamprite*, and *erdmannite*.

Simpler silica-zirconia complex compounds have been prepared in the

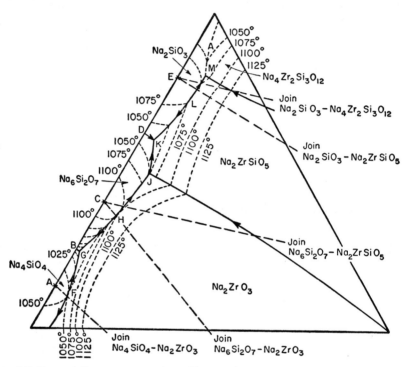

FIG. 5.7. Part of the ternary system silica—sodium oxide—zirconia. From (245).

laboratory or detected in phase studies. A study of the system Na_2O-SiO_2-ZrO_2 has indicated the existence of the compounds Na_2ZrSiO_5, $Na_2ZrSi_2O_7$, and $Na_4Zr_2Si_3O_{12}$, and the conditions for their stability are shown in Figures 5.7 and 5.8, according to d'Ans and Löffler (245). They found the equilibrium to be attained much more readily starting with zircon and a sodium silicate than with zirconia, silica, and a soda alkali.

Sodium zirconylosilicate, Na_2ZrSiO_5, formula weight 245.27, forms as a white powder when 1 mole of sodium carbonate and 1 mole of zircon are

244d. E. E. Kostyleva, *Compt. rend. acad. sci. U.S.S.R.* **48**, 502-4 (1945).
245. J. d'Ans and J. Löffler, *Z. anorg. allgem. Chem.* **191**, 1-35 (1930).

heated together to about 1000°. It is advantageous to use about 1.1 moles of soda ash, and to heat the mixture until all the soda ash has been entirely decomposed (158, 246). Alternatively, sodium zirconate can be prepared by heating a mixture of 1 mole of zirconia and 1 mole of sodium carbonate to 950°; then, on mixing the mole of cooled sodium zirconate with 2 moles of silica and 1 of sodium carbonate and reheating, holding at 1080° for 48 hours, a mixture of sodium zirconylosilicate and sodium silicate is obtained. The sodium zirconylosilicate can be recrystallized with recovery of well-formed crystals by heating a mixture of 20 grams of the

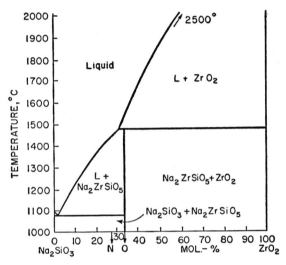

FIG. 5.8. Binary section showing equilibria of sodium metasilicate and zirconia-containing phases. From (245).

zirconylosilicate with 100 grams of sodium metasilicate, and cooling slowly (245). Sodium zirconylosilicate has been reported to form as a by-product in an aqueous medium as a result of the following procedure: 1 mole of zircon was mixed with $\frac{1}{10}$ mole of soldium carbonate and heated to 1800°. The zircon was metamictized by this treatment. It was then leached with 35% aqueous caustic soda solution at 150°. Nearly all the silica was leached out as sodium silicate, but some sodium zirconylosilicate formed (127).

Sodium zirconylosilicate crystals have been observed to be pseudohexagonal and strongly birefringent (247), biaxial and optically negative with $\alpha = 1.741$, $\beta =$ slightly less than 1.790, $\gamma = 1.790$, and density at 240° = 3.605 (245). It is insoluble in water, but dissolves in hydrochloric or sulfuric

246. French patent **698,193,** June 28, 1930.
247. L. Bourgeois, *Bull. Soc. Philomath.* **8,** 50 (1884).

acids with more or less separation of gelatinous silica, depending on conditions during the dissolution. When heated it decomposes to zirconia and sodium metasilicate (245), the decomposition being favored by the presence of sodium carbonate (247).

Potassium zirconylosilicate, K_2ZrSiO_5, has been prepared by heating a mixture of 1 part zircon and 4 parts potassium carbonate to a bright red heat and holding at this temperature for about 15 minutes (248). The conditions for forming the sodium and potassium compounds are not identical, and the difference appears to be due to the amounts of heating required to dissociate the products into zirconia and alkali metasilicate, the sodium compound dissociating more readily. Potassium zirconylosilicate occurs as orthorhombic prisms (249). *Calcium zirconylosilicate* has been recovered as highly birefringent monoclinic crystals by heating a mixture of zircon and calcium oxide to a bright red heat. It is isomorphous with sphene, $CaTiSiO_5$ and with the corresponding tin compound (155, 249). The compound has also been formed by heating together calcium orthosilicate and zircon (250).

Ceramic pigments of composition $BaZrSiO_5$ have been prepared (251, 252, 253), as well as the calcium, lead, magnesium, strontium, and zinc analogs, without regard to whether they were compounds or not. Their effects in glazes have been described by Commons (254).

When mixtures of zirconia, silica, and soda containing very high proportions of silica are heated, *sodium zirconylodisilicate*, $Na_2ZrSi_2O_7$, is formed. For example, a mixture consisting of 57 mole % silica, 15 mole % zirconia, and 28 mole % sodium carbonate was heated initially to 1000° and then held for a long period at 800°. The sodium zirconylodisilicate crystallized from the heated mixture along with sodium disilicate. The latter can be leached from the mixture with water. The two salts appear able to form a true binary eutectic. The needlelike crystals of the sodium zirconylodisilicate exhibit oblique extinction and have the refractive indices $\omega = 1.688$ and $\epsilon = 1.710$ (245).

Sodium dizirconotrisilicate, $Na_4Zr_2Si_3O_{12}$, has been observed to form on prolonged heating of sodium zirconylosilicate with sodium metasilicate:

$$2Na_2ZrSiO_5 + 2Na_2SiO_3 \rightarrow Na_4Zr_2Si_3O_{12} + Na_2SiO_4 \qquad (12)$$

and also when zircon is decomposed by alkali in the presence of excess silica (245, 246). The crystals are rhombohedral, uniaxial, and optically

248. L. Ouvrard, *Compt. rend.* **112**, 1444 (1891).
249. G. Flink, *Z. Krist.* **34**, 672 (1901).
250. R. Schwarze and A. Haacke, *Z. anorg. allgem. Chem.* **115**, 87-99 (1921).
251. C. W. F. Jacobs and W. J. Baldwin, *J. Am. Ceram. Soc.* **37**, 258-66 (1954).
252. C. J. Kinzie, U.S. Patents **2,273,871-2**, Feb. 24, 1942.
253. Kinzie, U.S. Patent **2,127,844**, Aug. 23, 1938.
254. C. H. Commons, *Bull. Am. Ceram. Soc.* **22**, 95-6 (1939).

negative. For sodium D radiation, $\omega = 1.692$ and $\epsilon = 1.715$. The density at 21° is 2.890. It melts congruently at 1540° (245).

Aside from the alkali compounds described above, a number of compositions have been recovered from the treatment of zircon with alkalies which have been described in some detail in the literature without their identification as molecular species. Melliss fused zircon with four times its weight of sodium carbonate, cooled the reaction product, and extracted it with water until no more soluble matter could be removed. He recovered microscopic hexagonal plates of composition $Na_2Zr_8O_{15}SiO_4 \cdot 11H_2O$. He found it to lose water on heating to a low red heat, and to be decomposed by sulfuric acid (255). Gilles was of the opinion that he had recovered a compound of composition $Na_{12}Zr_7O_4(SiO_4)_8$ from a similar fusion (256).

The system Li_4SiO_4-$ZrO_2 \cdot SiO_2$ has been studied by the technique of cooling curves, without finding evidence of complex compounds containing lithium, zirconium, and silicon oxides. Lithium orthosilicate melts at 1249°. A eutectic melting at 1021° consisted of 30% zircon and 70% lithium orthosilicate.

COMPLEX COMPOUNDS OF SILICA AND ZIRCONIA WITH THE LESS BASIC METALS

The strong bases react with zircon by making oxygen ions available for addition to the zirconium and silicon atoms, with the formation of new unit structures. These new structures contain complex anions and their formation is contingent upon the stability of the anions. When zircon reacts with less basic oxides, the molecule of weak base, rather than its oxide ions, is the reacting unit, and the complex product is relatively undissociated. The size and arrangement of the molecule as well as the type of crystalline lattice which it develops should be considerably different from those of the strong alkali derivatives because of these fundamentally different origins. Actually it is observed that the weaker bases do not form complex compounds of silica and zirconia similar to those of the strong bases. Indeed, while compounds of the less basic elements are found to a considerable extent in nature, only magnesium derivatives have been prepared in the laboratory, and magnesium might be regarded as on the borderline between the more strongly basic and less strongly basic metals.

The following summarizes briefly the little that is to be derived from presently available data of the chemical interactions of zirconia plus silica with various metal oxides of feeble basicity.

Alumina. No synthetic compounds have been prepared. A tertiary eutectic

255. D. E. Melliss, *Bull. Soc. Chim.* (2) **14**, 204 (1870).
256. W. Gibbs, *Pogg. Ann.* **71**, 564 (1847).

exists near the composition 70% silica, 15% zircon, and 15% alumina, which melts at cone 27 (roughly 1600°). A second eutectic regarded as a binary between zircon and alumina, containing about 20% alumina, melts at cone 31 (roughly 1680°). Mixtures high in zircon content are very viscous, zircon being like silica in the viscosity effects on the mixture. With increase of alumina content, both the melting point and the viscosity are markedly lowered (257).

A mixture containing alumina, silica, zirconia, and zinc oxide is known as *zirconium spinel*. X-ray examination has shown it to contain zircon and zinc aluminate (251). It is used in ceramic glazes (251, 254).

Beryllia. No synthetic compounds have been prepared. A phosphor has been prepared containing beryllia, zirconia, and silica, and was reported to be characterized by a low *flash ratio* (fluorescence/phosphorescence) (259).

Magnesia. There is only poorly developed evidence for the formation of compounds of magnesia, zirconia, and silica. Roussin and Chesters (260) heated mixtures of magnesite and zircon and observed at least two new substances which formed in maximum amounts in mixtures containing ratios 20:80 and 50:50 of these ingredients, by weight. One was microscopically similar to zircon, but exhibited a different X-ray pattern. Under somewhat similar conditions, Rees and Chesters obtained a solid of mean density between that of magnesia and zircon, and also a phase which they thought to be a magnesium zirconium silicate (261). Microscopic and X-ray studies of refractory bricks made from magnesite and zircon indicated the presence of the compounds *magnesium zirconylosilicate*, $MgZrSiO_5$, and *magnesiozirconosilicate*, of composition $4MgO \cdot ZrO_2 \cdot SiO_2$ (260, 261). As against this, no evidence for a magnesium zirconium silicate was found in a study of the system $MgO-SiO_2-ZrO_2$ at 1450° (262).

No compounds of the four components were found in a study of the system $B_2O_3-MgO-SiO_2-ZrO_2$. An increase of temperature from 820° to 1200° caused only a trifling increase of solubility of zirconia in the melt, and the addition of alumina sharply decreased the solubility of zirconia (263).

Niobia. Although a number of niobia-containing zirconium silicates have been observed in nature, no compounds of these constituents have been prepared synthetically. Niobium occurs with some zircon and is found in chalcolamprite and wöhlerite. An unnamed mineral was reported to occur in the Lovoser Tundra, consisting of niobia, tantala, silica, and zirconia. It

257. R. F. Rea, *J. Am. Ceram, Soc.* **22**, 95-6 (1939).
259. H. W. Leverenz, U.S. Patent **2,402,760**, June 25, 1946.
260. A. L. Roussin and J. H. Chesters, *Trans. Ceram. Soc.* (England) **30**, 217-24 (1931).
261. W. J. Rees and J. H. Chesters, *Trans. Ceram. Soc.* (England) **29**, 309-16 (1930).
262. W. R. Foster, *J. Am. Ceram. Soc.* **34**, 302-5 (1951).
263. B. W. King, Jr., and A. I. Andrews, *J. Am. Ceram. Soc.* **24**, 367-72 (1941).

was brown and had brown striae; the fracture was irregular and the luster resinous; its hardness was about 5 and it was infusible (264).

Titania. A number of the zirconium silicate minerals contain titania, but no compounds of zirconia, silica, and titania were found in a study of the system SiO_2-TiO_2-ZrO_2. A eutectic near the silica apex of the triangular diagram has a melting point of 1500° (265).

264. V. I. Gerasimovskiĭ, *Redkie Metal* **6**, No. 4, 42-3 (1937).
265. H. G. Sowman and A. I. Andrews, *J. Am. Ceram. Soc.* **34**, 298-301 (1951).

6

The Sulfatozirconic Acids, Sulfates and Sulfonates

INTRODUCTION

In our study of the ClBrI halogenides of zirconium, we noted that the greater affinity of zirconium for oxygen than for these halogens resulted in the severing of zirconium-halogen bonds in the presence of water and, less universally, in the presence of other oxygen-containing substances. This gives rise to the formation of zirconium cations and covalent molecules:

$$\mathrm{ZrCl_4 + 2H_2O \rightarrow ZrOOH^+ + 3H^+ + 4Cl^-}$$

$$\mathrm{ZrCl_4 + 4C_2H_5OH \xrightarrow{base} Zr(OC_2H_5)_4 + 4HCl}$$

(1-2)

The pairing of ions such as $\mathrm{ZrOOH^+}$ with $\mathrm{Cl^-}$, $\mathrm{Br^-}$, or $\mathrm{I^-}$ gives rise to the basic zirconyl salts of generic formula ZrOOHX. However, zirconium has a greater affinity for fluorine than for oxygen, and the zirconium-fluorine bond is not ruptured in aqueous or other oxygen-containing environments. Because of this, compounds of zirconium and fluorine tend to yield complex anions such as $\mathrm{ZrF_7^{-3}}$, $\mathrm{ZrF_6^{-2}}$, and $\mathrm{ZrOF_4^{-2}}$ rather than cations.

Perhaps the most fundamental observation in the approach to the study of sulfate compounds of zirconium is that the relationship of the sulfate ion to zirconium resembles that of fluoride rather than chloride, bromide, or iodide. Its affinity for the zirconium atom is greater than that of water, and it remains bound to zirconium in aqueous solutions and in the presence of oxygen-containing organic compounds. In water

$$\mathrm{Zr(SO_4)_2 + 4H_2O \rightarrow 2H^+ + ZrO(SO_4)_2 \cdot 3H_2O^{-2}}$$

(3)

At the ordinary temperature, there is negligible tendency for water to displace sulfate from the complex, but hydroxyl ions do compete with sulfate ions for zirconium bonding orbitals. Only in strongly acidic solution is the effect of hydroxyl ions in decomposing sulfato complexes negligible. In the presence of very low concentrations of hydroxyl ion, additional sulfato groups can become attached to the zirconium atom:

$$\mathrm{ZrO(SO_4)_2 \cdot 3H_2O^{-2} + SO_4^{-2} \rightarrow ZrO(SO_4)_3 \cdot 2H_2O^{-4} + H_2O}$$

(4)

240

As in the case of the zirconyl halogenides, the zirconyl or oxo oxygen atom appears to react reversibly with hydrogen ions to form hydroxo:

$$ZrO(SO_4)_2^{-2} + H^+ \rightleftharpoons ZrOH(SO_4)_2^- \tag{5}$$

But in the presence of hydroxyl ions, part or all of the sulfato groups are displaced, and in the ultimate case,

$$ZrO(SO_4)_2^{-2} + 2OH^- \rightarrow ZrO_2 \cdot xH_2O + 2SO_4^{-2} + (1-x)H_2O \tag{6}$$

It might be stated as an empirical rule that the sulfate ion has no tendency to displace oxo, a negligible tendency to displace hydroxyl, a strong tendency to displace aquo, and an extremely strong tendency to displace hydronium ligands from zirconium. Hence when it is desirable to convert oxygen compounds of zirconium to sulfato compounds, a strongly acid environment is employed. Under such conditions, all bonds between zirconium and oxygen or hydroxyl can be converted to bonds to sulfate:

$$ZrOH(SO_4)_2^- + SO_4^{-2} \rightarrow ZrOH(SO_4)_3^{-3}$$

$$ZrOH(SO_4)_3^{-3} + H^+ \rightarrow H_2O \cdot Zr(SO_4)_3^{-2} \tag{7-9}$$

$$H_2O \cdot Zr(SO_4)_3^{-2} + SO_4^{-2} \rightarrow Zr(SO_4)_4^{-4} + H_2O$$

In all the compounds of the sulfato group with zirconium, it is covalently bound and loses its ionic identity. It is more accurate to speak of sulfatozirconic acids than of zirconium sulfates. In only one peculiar structural arrangement, i.e., the compound $Zr_5O_8(SO_4)_2 \cdot 14H_2O$, is there reason to believe that zirconium cations bind sulfate anions electrostatically. All the other compounds of zirconium with sulfate may be regarded as sulfato derivatives of the hypothetical metazirconic acid, H_2ZrO_3 or H—O—Zr—O—H, with an O above the Zr, in which one, two, three, or four of the bonds with hydroxyl or oxo are replaced by bonds to sulfato.

This gives rise to the series HSO_4ZrOOH, $(HSO_4)_2ZrO$, $(HSO_4)_3ZrOH$, and $(HSO_4)_4Zr$. All these compounds are known (the last only in the form of its salts), and also condensation products containing 2 or more zirconium atoms per molecule. The appropriate names are *monosulfatozirconic acid, disulfatozirconic acid, trisulfatozirconic acid, tetrasulfatozirconic acid, and polysulfatopolyzirconic acids*. In these compounds the hydrogen or hydronium ion are not necessarily associated with a specific oxygen atom, as sometimes conveniently represented by the graphic formula HOSOZrOSOH, with O atoms above and below the two S atoms.

The oxygen bonds of the sulfato group resonate:

$$O-\underset{\underset{O}{\|}}{\overset{\overset{O}{\|}}{S}}-O \rightleftharpoons O-\underset{\underset{O}{\|}}{\overset{\overset{O}{\|}}{S}}=O \rightleftharpoons O-\underset{\underset{O}{\mid}}{\overset{\overset{O}{\|}}{S}}=O \tag{10}$$

and no one of them is uniquely qualified to bind the hydrogen. The hydrogen or hydronium cation is best regarded as attracted to the entire cation, this being represented $(H^+)_2(SO_4ZrOSO_4)$.

Although it is possible to proceed stepwise from hydrous zirconia to tetrasulfatozirconic acid and from tetrasulfatozirconia acid to hydrous zirconia, the processes are not entirely reversible because of the formation of condensation products, for example:

$$2HOZrOSO_4 \rightarrow HSO_4Zr\overset{..}{O}Zr\overset{..}{SO_4}H \tag{11}$$

The size, complexity, and molecular configuration of polysulfatopolyzirconic acids which form depend on the physical and chemical conditions prevailing. In all cases they are the results of (1) the replacement of sulfato by hydroxo, (2) the elimination of water between 2 ions or molecules, and/or (3) the attachment of 1 oxygen atom from 1 ion or molecule to a zirconium atom of another ion or molecule. These unit processes can and do lead to an astonishing variety of heteropolyacids. A review of the known compounds shows that the zirconium atom tends to attain to a coordination number of 5 in the lower molecular weight compounds and 7 in the higher molecular weight compounds, and that the terminal sulfato group tends to be monohydrated.

Because the sulfatozirconic acids are highly complex and often require lengthy names to indicate their structural nature, it is convenient to use a system of numerical symbols to represent them. All the compounds may be reduced to the form $H_nZr_mO_p(SO_4)_q \cdot rH_2O$. The compounds can be represented unambiguously by numbers corresponding to nmqr, the value of p being implicit from the values of the other subscripts. In some compounds oxo becomes hydroxo, but that, too, is indicated by the values of n, m, and q. To illustrate the use of this system, the following examples will suffice:

Molecular formula	Numerical representation
$HZrOOHSO_4$	1110
$HZrOOHSO_4 \cdot H_2O$	1111
$Zr(SO_4)_2$	0120
$H_2ZrO(SO_4)_2 \cdot 3H_2O$	2123
$(HO)_2Zr_4O_4(SO_4)_3 \cdot 14H_2O$	$-243\overline{14}$
$H_2Zr_7O_{10}(SO_3)_5 \cdot 29H_2O$	$275\overline{29}$

The minus sign in the fifth example indicates terminal hydroxyl groups rather than hydrogen ion. In highly hydrated compounds in which the number of aquo groups is a two-digit number, a bar over this number indicates that the two digits belong together. The letter n can be used to indicate that there are several states of hydration. For example, 212n represents a compound disulfatozirconic acid, $H_2ZrO(SO_4)_2 \cdot nH_2O$, where several integral values of n are known to exist.

DISULFATOZIRCONIC ACID (212n)

The best known sulfatozirconic acid is disulfatozirconic acid trihydrate, $H_2ZrO(SO_4)_2 \cdot 3H_2O$, or 2123. It was first reported by Berzelius in 1824 (1). He recovered the crystalline hydrated compound on evaporating a solution obtained by the action of sulfuric acid on zirconium dioxide. The same product was prepared by a number of succeeding investigators who represented its composition as $Zr(SO_4)_2 \cdot 4H_2O$ (2, 3), and until recently it has usually been represented by this formula and called *zirconium sulfate tetrahydrate*. For reasons indicated above and developed in greater detail below, we shall use the name *disulfatozirconic acid trihydrate*.

One of the early preparations consisted in dissolving crude zirconium dioxide powder in an excess of concentrated sulfuric acid over a flame, finally raising the temperature to a level at which nearly all the sulfuric acid evaporated. The mushy residue was cooled, mixed with cold water, and the reaction product dissolved; any unreacted zirconia or silica remained undissolved and was filtered off. The clear solution was evaporated until a white crust appeared on the surface of the liquid. It was thereupon allowed to cool and a large crop of crystals was obtained. The mother liquor was sucked off, the crystals were washed with alcohol and then dried in air (3). It was found that the compound could be recrystallized from dilute sulfuric acid solution but not from water, because of formation of a basic sulfate, i.e., a polysulfatopolyzirconic acid.

Methods similar to the above have been in use to this day with various refinements. If concentrated sulfuric acid is added to any chloride or sulfate solution of zirconium until the solution contains the equivalent of 40-55% SO_3 by weight, an almost quantitative yield of crystalline 2123 is obtained. The crystals are best recovered in a pure state by filtering them off and washing them with small amounts of water or alcohol (4). It is a common practice in industry to precipitate a sparingly soluble polysulfatopoly-

1. J. J. Berzelius, *Oefvers, Akad. Förh. Stockholm* (1824) 295; *Pogg. Ann.* **4**, 117 (1825); *Ann. Chim. Phys.* (2) **29**, 337 (1825).

2. M. Weibull, *Acta Univ. Lund.* (2) **18**, 34 (1881).

2b. Weibull, *Ber.* **20**, 1394 (1887).

3. O. Kulka, *Beitrage zur Kenntnis einiger Zirconium Verdindungen*, Bern, 1902, p. 19.

4. Marie Falinski, *Ann. chim.* **16**, 237-325 (1941).

zirconate from an aqueous solution and to treat this compound with sulfuric acid to form 2123 (5):

$$(HO)_2Zr_5O_6(SO_4)_3 \cdot 15H_2O + 7H_2SO_4 \rightarrow 5H_2ZrO(SO_4)_2 \cdot 3H_2O + 3H_2O \quad (12)$$

It can also be prepared by the reaction of hydrous zirconia with sulfuric acid, a reaction in which 11.67 kg cal is evolved per mole of 2123 formed. Disulfatozirconic acid formed by these processes may be purified by dissolution in water and reprecipitation by the addition of concentrated sulfuric acid (6; cf. 7).

DISULFATOZIRCONIC ACID TRIHYDRATE, formula weight 355.42, forms plate-like crystals belonging to the orthorhombic system. There are 8 formula weights per unit cell, which has the dimensions $a_0 = 26.11$, $b_0 = 11.62$, and $c_0 = 5.56$ A. The cell volume is 1687 A^3, and the axial ratios a:b:c = 2.247:1:0.474.* The indices of refraction for 5893 A radiation are $\alpha = 1.614$, $\beta = 1.655$, and $\gamma = 1.678$. The density calculated from X-ray diffraction data is 2.80 and that determined by physical measurement 2.802 g/cc (11b). The crystals are isomorphous with the corresponding sulfate compounds of hafnium, cerium, thorium, and uranium, and they form solid solutions with these compounds. The ceric and zirconium compounds are completely miscible (8, 9). At 18°, 100 gm of saturated aqueous solution of disulfatozirconic acid trihydrate, 2123, has been observed to contain 52.5 g of the compound (3), and at 39.5°, 59.3 g (10). The solution exhibits Raman frequencies 453 and 568 cm^{-1} (11). The compound is very soluble in methanol, and as the solution stands, it sets to a jelly.

The solubility of disulfatozirconic acid in sulfuric acid solutions decreases with increasing sulfuric acid content, up to about 47% SO$_3$. With further increases of strength of the sulfuric acid the solubility of 2123 increases, as shown by Figure 6.1. The decrease of solubility at higher sulfuric acid concentrations is to be regarded as due to the reversal of all hydrolyses and the common ion effect of the hydrogen of the sulfuric acid. The increase of

---

* These values are consistent with the earlier values reported by Weibull, which are numerically different because of the different orientation selected (2b).

5. E. Wainer, U.S. Patent **2,294,431**, Sept. 1, 1942.
6. H. Trapp, U.S. Patent **1,648,569**, Nov. 8, 1927.
7. W. S. Clabaugh and R. Gilchrist, *J. Am. Chem. Soc.* **74**, 2105-5 (1952).
8. L. Fernandez, *Gazz. chim. ital.* **55**, ii, 290 (1925); *Atti Accad. Lincei* (6) **2**, 182 (1925).
9. G. Beck, *Z. anorg. allgem. Chem.* **174**, 31-41 (1928).
10a. O. Hauser, *Ber.* **37**, 2024 (1904).
10b. Hauser, *Z. anorg. allgem. Chem.* **45**, 185 (1905).
10c. Hauser, *J. prakt. Chem.* (2) **76**, 363 (1907).
10d. Hauser, *Z. anorg. allgem. Chem.* **53**, 74 (1907).
10e. *Ibid.* **54**, 196 (1909).
11. M. Rolla, *Boll. sci. facoltà chim. ind.*, *Bologna*, **1941**, 13-15.
11b. E. Staritzky and D. T. Croner, *Anal. Chem.* **28**, 553-4 (1956).

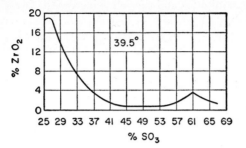

F<small>IG</small>. 6.1. Solubility of zirconium dioxide introduced as disulfatozirconic acid in aqueous sulfuric acid.

solubility at the higher acidities is due to the formation of trisulfatozirconic acid.

Solid 2123 is stable in contact with its saturated aqueous solution at 25° and at 40°, although a slight separation of hydrolysis product from the aqueous solution at 40° has been noted (4). More dilute solutions hydrolyze extensively, and the process continues over great lengths of time. Superficially equilibrium appears to be achieved fairly quickly. Venable and Jackson observed that solutions at 0° and at 20° reached a condition of equilibrium or slow change after 2 to 3 hours (12). The specific conductivity of a 1.75% solution at 18° was 0.03105 mho after 1 hour and 0.03186 mho after 20 hours. When the solution was boiled, its conductivity rose to 0.03418 mho, and at both 24 hours and 72 hours later, it was 0.03432 mho (13). However, these observations did not reveal the complex changes which occur in the solution. The addition of alcohol to a clear solution of 2123 gave a precipitate of complex polysulfatopolyzirconic acids, indicating that these molecular species must already have been present in the solution (1). The presence of various species in sulfate solutions has also been indicated by the irregularities in the elution of zirconium from Amberlite IR-120, using 0.75 to 1.25 N sulfuric acid (15). The following observations according to Falinski (4) are particularly revealing. When she allowed a solution containing 20 g of 2123 in 100 g of water to stand, insoluble hydrolysis products began to be deposited after a few months, and the process was not yet complete after 6 months. More concentrated solutions remained clear and visibly unchanged while standing for great lengths of time, but more dilute solutions hydrolyzed rapidly. A 2% solution began to deposit needlelike crystalline hydrolysate after a few days. Solutions containing between 0.5% and 2.0% took slightly longer to deposit hydrolysate, and an 0.13% solution became

12. F. P. Venable and D. H. Jackson, *J. Am. Chem. Soc.* **42**, 2531 (1920).
13. R. Ruer and M. Levin, *Z. anorg. allgem. Chem.* **46**, 449 (1905).
15. Ying-Mao Chen, *J. Chinese Chem. Soc.* (Taiwan) Ser. II, **1**, 46-56 (1954).

opalescent in a few minutes and the following day it was cloudy and depositing hydrolysate. A 0.07% solution became cloudy instantly on mixing the solid acid with water, and an amorphous precipitate settled out. The higher the dilution, the more colloidal was the hydrolysate. When the mixture contained only 10 ppm of disulfatozirconic acid, a gelatinous suspension was obtained from which a deposit separated only after several months. She also obtained a gelatinous precipitate by throwing the solid acid into a large amount of boiling water. When the concentration was 0.5%, the colloid did not settle, although at this and at lower concentrations all the zirconium was precipitated. Various amounts of sulfate ion remained in the solution phase, depending on the amount of disulfatozirconic acid mixed into the water. Thus, the solid contained less than 2 moles of sulfate per mole of zirconia, and varied in composition with the amount of solute introduced. The hydrolyses were readily reversed by concentrating the solution by evaporation. In mixtures which had deposited solid hydrolysates, the solids were redissolved by the evaporating solutions, with formation of clear solutions.

When 2123 is dehydrated over sulfuric acid, the vapor pressure over the salt decreases in discrete stages, indicating the several hydrates to be true compounds (16). When the compound is heated, it loses 3 molecules of water at about 100° and is completely dehydrated (17, 18, 19) to $H_2ZrO(SO_4)_2$, 2120. At about 380°, 2120 is decomposed to $Zr(SO_4)_2$, 0120 (17). When 2123 was heated in steam to 200-300°, it decomposed and left a residue of composition $Zr_2O_3SO_4$, 0210 (10).

It was first recognized by Ruer that 2123 is not a salt, $Zr(SO_4)_2 \cdot 4H_2O$, but an acid. He was struck by the difference in behavior of solutions of the sulfate compound and that of zirconium chlorides and nitrates. When solutions of the latter were treated with oxalic acid or ammonium oxalate, precipitates were obtained which dissolved on adding excess of the precipitating solution. No precipitate formed from a solution of 2123 under similar conditions. When an electric current was passed through a solution of the latter, zirconium migrated to the anode compartment. He therefore concluded that the compound was a zirconylic acid, $H_2ZrO(SO_4)_2 \cdot 3H_2O$ (20a). The lowering of the freezing point of a solution of 2123 corresponded

16. E. Löwenstein, *Z. anorg. allgem. Chem.* **63,** 69 (1909); *Uber Hydrate, deren Dampfspannung sich kontinuierlich mit der Zusammensetzung ändert,* Göttingen, 1909.
17. S. R. Paykull, *Oefvers. Akad. Förh. Stockholm* (1873) 22; (1878) 53; *Ber.* **12,** 1719 (1879).
18. E. Chauvenet, *Compt. rend.* **164,** 630, 684, 946 (1916).
18b. *Ibid.* **165,** 25 (1917).
18c. *Ann. Chim. Phys.* (9) **13,** 59 (1920).
19. R. Lassere, University Microfilms (Ann Arbor, Mich.), Pub. No. **964,** 95 pp.
20a. R. Ruer, *Z. anorg. allgem. Chem.* **42,** 87 (1904).
20b. *Ibid.* **43:** 282 (1905).

to a molecular weight of about **79**, indicating about **4** dissolved particles per molecule of solute (21):

$$H_2ZrO(SO_4) \cdot 3H_2O \rightleftharpoons 2H^+ + ZrO(SO_4) \cdot 3H_2O^{-2} \qquad (13\text{-}14)$$

$$ZrO(SO_4)_2 \cdot 3H_2O^{-2} \rightleftharpoons ZrOOHSO_4 \cdot nH_2O^- + H^+ + SO_4^{-2} + (3-n)H_2O$$

The behavior of disulfatozirconic acid indicates its structure to be

$$(H^+)_2 \left[HOH\leftarrow O - \underset{\underset{O}{\overset{O}{\|}}}{\overset{\overset{O}{\|}}{S}} - O - \underset{\overset{HOH}{\uparrow}}{Zr} - O - \underset{\underset{O}{\overset{O}{\|}}}{\overset{\overset{O}{\|}}{S}} - O \rightarrow HOH \right]^{-2}$$

The direct establishment of **2123** as a dibasic acid is rendered difficult by the variety of species present in its aqueous solution and the hydrolytic changes which ensue upon the addition of alkalies. Chauvenet titrated the solution of the acid with sodium hydroxide and found an inflection corresponding to neutralization of 2 hydrogen ions per molecule of zirconia (18a), but this is capable of several interpretations. Gable noted that when ammonia is added to a solution of **2123** in methanol, the precipitate which forms is soluble in water when fresh, but after only 5 to 10 minutes it has altered to an insoluble substance, like hydrous zirconia (22). Presumably, an ammonium salt of the acid was first formed, and this decomposed, due to the attack of the hydroxyl ions, with formation of sparingly soluble polysulfatopolyzirconic acids or hydrous zirconia.

It has proved possible to isolate salts of **2123**. This is most readily done by starting with a solution containing an excess of sulfate ions. Such a solution will contain disulfatozirconate ions in equilibrium with trisulfatozirconate ions:

$$ZrOH(SO_4)_3^{-3} \rightleftharpoons ZrO(SO_4)_2^{-2} + HSO_4^- \qquad (15)$$

According to P. T. Joseph (23; cf. 23b, 23c), the addition of a large excess of sodium chloride to such a solution results in the precipitation of the sodium salt, $Na_2ZrO(SO_4)_2 \cdot 3H_2O$. It is particularly interesting that the extent of hydration is the same as in the acid from which this salt was derived, whence it is indicated that the three aquo groups are bound to the sulfatozirconate anion.

The pH values of solutions of **2123** are about equal to those of sulfuric acid solutions of the same molarities (23), and because of this it has been

21. E. Chauvenet and H. Gueylard, *Compt. rend.* **167**, 24, 126, 201 (1918).

22. H. S. Gable, *J. Am. Chem. Soc.* **53**, 1613 (1931).

23. Unpublished researches of the Titanium Alloy Mfg. Division of the National Lead Company.

23b. C. J. Kinzie, U.S. Patent **1,494,426**, May 20, 1924.

23c. C. J. Kinzie, U.S. Patent **1,609,826**, Dec. 7, 1926.

proposed as a substitute for sulfuric acid in certain applications where it is more convenient to transport or handle a solid than liquid sulfuric acid.

As would be expected, 2123 does not react with molecules or with anions which have much less affinity for the zirconium atom than does the sulfate ion. Thus sulfato compounds are readily formed from chloride or nitrate salts of zirconium, but the latter are not obtainable directly from the sulfato compounds. Ions such as acetate and oxalate which have affinities for zirconium of the same order of magnitude as that of sulfate (Chap. 5), give rise to equilibria between sulfatozirconate and oxalatozirconate or acetatozirconate anions. Sparingly soluble monooxalatozirconic acid, $H_2ZrO_2 C_2O_4 \cdot 3H_2O$, which can be precipitated from zirconium chloride solutions, cannot be formed from solutions of 2123 (24, 25). Sulfonated dyestuffs are quantitatively precipitated by solutions of chlorides of zirconium, but they are not precipitated by 2123 (26).

The chief uses of disulfatozirconic acid dihydrate have been in the preparation of other zirconium compounds (27, 28), in the preparation of oxidation-reduction catalysts (29, 30, 31), and in tanning.

Disulfatozirconic acid and its derivatives have been used in the tanning of white leather for many years, but its role is not precisely known. According to Lasserre (32), skins in which carboxyl groups are blocked by methylation show unimpaired combining capacity for zirconium as a sulfate complex, but 25% less combining capacity for chromium. This has been interpreted to indicate a difference between the chemical nature of zirconium tanning and that of chromium, the former involving peptide groups of the protein and the latter carboxyl groups (33). Zirconium salts yielding zirconium cations in solution are not comparable in tanning properties to the sulfatozirconic acids (34), and salts of 2123 and their hydrolysis products are more satisfactory than the straight acid (35).

In analytical chemistry 2123 has been used in the detection of potassium, with which it forms several different sparingly soluble complex salts, depending on conditions in the solution. The precipitation is particularly quantita-

24. A. Rosenheim and P. Frank, *Ber.* **40**, 803 (1907).
25. F. P. Venable and C. Baskerville, *J. Am. Chem. Soc.* **19**, 12 (1897).
26. W. B. Blumenthal, *Ind. Eng. Chem.* **40**, 510-12 (1948).
27. E. Wainer, U.S. Patent **2,316,141**, April 6, 1943.
28. H. L. van Mater, U.S. Patent **2,457,853**, Dec. 14, 1948.
29. A. K. Hawley, U.S. Patent **2,564,331**, Aug. 14, 1951.
30. G. P. Mack and E. Parker, U.S. Patent **2,739,902**, March 27, 1956.
31. Mack and Parker, U.S. Patent **2,739,905**, March 27, 1956.
32. R. Lassere, *Union intern. socs. chimistes inds. cuir, Congr. intern.* **1**, 126-36 (1949).
33. I. C. Sommerville, *J. Soc. Leather Trades Chemists* **38**, 347-58 (1954).
34. A. G. Farbenind, French patent **798,137**, May 9, 1916.
35. I. C. Sommerville and W. J. Rau, *J. Am. Leather Chemists Assoc.*, **44**, 784-95 (1949).

tive in the presence of excess precipitant. In one procedure, a 10% solution of 2123 in dilute sulfuric acid detected 0.48 mg of potassium in 2 cc of reaction mixture. Ammonium ion does not interfere (36).

Attempts to use 2123 in place of tin salts in silk weighting gave negative results (37).

Little attention has been given to the anhydrous acid 2120. The compound $Zr(SO_4)_2$, 0120, is structurally dissimilar to the disulfatozirconic acids, and will be given separate treatment below.

ZIRCONYL PYROSULFATE (0120) AND THE PYROSULFATO ACIDS

It has been noted that when disulfatozirconic acid is heated to about 380°, it loses all of its hydrogen content and attains the composition $Zr(SO_4)_2$. A profound change must occur in the last step of the dehydration, and two dehydration processes might be postulated:

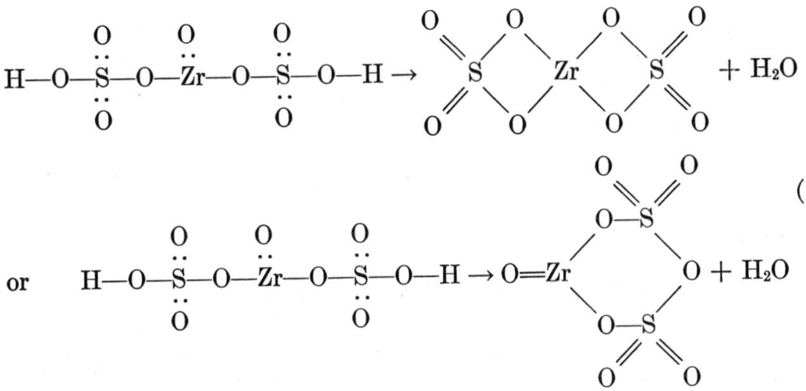

(16-17)

The product of process 16 would be zirconium sulfate, or more properly disulfatozirconium, since zirconium does not form a monatomic cation, and the product of process 17 would be zirconyl pyrosulfate (or pyrosulfato-oxozirconium). No physical data are available for making a selection between the two graphical representations, but it appears preferable to adopt the zirconyl pyrosulfate representation because of the superior stability of a 6-membered ring versus a 4-membered ring and because it is characteristic of the sulfate ion to form monodentate ligands with metals and not bidentate ligands. Moreover, since it is well known that alkali pyrosulfates are obtained on heating the alkali hydrogen sulfates, it is entirely reasonable that zirconyl pyrosulfate should be obtained when zirconyl hydrogen sulfate is heated to about the same temperature.

---

36. R. Reed and J. R. Withrow, *J. Am. Chem. Soc.* **50**, 2785-7 (1928); **51**, 1062-5, 1311-5 (1929).

37. E. Ristenpart, *Farben. Ztg.* **29**, 26 (1918).

When zirconyl pyrosulfate is dissolved in water, the fresh solutions show different hydrolytic properties from those of freshly prepared solutions of disulfatozirconic acid, but eventually the solutions become identical in properties. The slow change is easily associated with the breakdown of the pyrosulfate structure, which can be visualized as occurring in either of the following fashions:

$$(18\text{-}19)$$

followed by

B $OZrOHS_2O_7H + H_2O \rightarrow OZrOHSO_4H + H_2SO_4$

Zirconyl pyrosulfate was first prepared by Berzelius by dissolving zirconia or hydrous zirconia in an excess of concentrated sulfuric acid, evaporating to dryness, and heating the residue for about 15 minutes somewhat below a red heat (1). Later investigators found that the temperature for driving off the excess acid should not exceed 350-400°, lest the residual content of sulfur trioxide become less than that required for $ZrOS_2O_7$ (2, 10, 38, 39, 40). The compound is quite stable in this temperature range (10). Some careful investigators have reported failure to obtain the stoichiometric composition $ZrOS_2O_7$ (41), yet M. Falinski obtained substantially

38. G. H. Bailey, *Chem. News* **60**, 6, 17, 32 (1889); *Proc. Roy. Soc.* **46**, 74 (1889).

39. F. P. Venable, *J. Am. Chem. Soc.* **20**, 119 (1898).

40. Venable, *Zirconium and Its Compounds*, The Chemical Catalog Co., Inc., New York, 1922, p. 77.

41. G. von Hevesy and Erika Kremer, *Z. anorg. allgem. Chem.* **195**, 339 (1931).

pure zirconyl pyrosulfate by evaporating the 2123 compound with sulfuric acid at 350-385°. She treated 100 gm of zirconyl chloride, $ZrOCl_2 \cdot 8H_2O$, with 50 cc of concentrated sulfuric acid, initially forming 2123 and first changing over to 2132 on heating. On further heating, sulfuric acid was evolved and $ZrOS_2O_7$ formed. By holding the temperature at 350-385° until white fumes ceased to come off, she obtained a product which analysis showed to deviate no more than 0.5% from the theoretical composition (4). Thermal decomposition of the pyrosulfate is not rapid at 630° but quite rapid at 750° (32).

ZIRCONYL PYROSULFATE, $ZrOS_2O_7$, formula weight 283.35, is a colorless compound, recoverable as a microcrystalline powder which deliquesces on exposure to air (4). It is very soluble in water, forming clear solutions when added to small amounts of water, and the solid is stable in contact with its saturated solution. Above 40° a small amount of solid hydrolysate has been observed to separate from the solution (4, 10a, 10c). The dissolution in water is accompanied by a large evolution of heat, much of which is doubtless due to the hydration of pyrosulfate to sulfate. According to Chauvenet, of the 32,280 cal evolved when 1 mole of the compound is dissolved, 12,380 cal is due to the hydration reaction (10a, 10b). If solid 0120 is added to such a large quantity of water that there is little rise in temperature, the dissolution is quite slow. The compound is also soluble in methanol (22).

When zirconyl pyrosulfate 0120 is stirred with sulfuric acid of 69%, 79%, or 85% SO_3 content at 40°, no acid sulfate forms. It is a stable phase in contact with these solutions, whereas 2123 in contact with the same solutions is converted to polysulfato acids (4). But in contact with sulfuric acid of less than 45% strength, 0120 is converted to 2123. Also the addition of sulfuric acid to an aqueous solution of 0120 precipitates 2123.

When a solution containing 50 gm of 0120 in 60 cc of water was held at the boil, the temperature gradually fell from 109° to 103°, and after a while the compound $H_2Zr_2O_2(SO_4)_3 \cdot 4H_2O$, 2234, began to separate (10e). Since the temperature began to fall before the deposition of solids occurred, new species must have formed in the solution prior to their appearance in a new phase. When instead of being boiled the solution was held at 39.5° over a long period of time, no solid separated (10a, 10c). At a lower concentration, 0.96 gm per 60 cc (10.2 moles of 0120 per 1000 moles of water), the solution became turbid when held for 5 hours at 90°, and the phase $(HO)_2Zr_4O_4(SO_4)_3 \cdot 14H_2O$, $-243\overline{14}$ was deposited. Dilution of the solution gave a heavy deposit of this compound. At higher temperatures than 39.5°, higher dilutions were necessary to give deposits of $-243\overline{14}$, and above 64° the liquid remained clear indefinitely, even at the boil. If the solution was held for several days at 64° and then cooled to 40°, it no longer deposited $-243\overline{14}$ (10a, 10c). At the high temperature, the compound 2234 formed in solution and it would not precipitate nor alter to a more insoluble compound when the temperature was lowered. Changes of species during heating are also manifest in other behaviors. For example, a fresh cold solution of 0120 underwent complete ion exchange with a resin, but after the same solution was boiled it reacted only partially with the resin, showing that it then contained complexes not capable of ion exchange reactions (64).

M. Falinski found that on treating zirconyl chloride with 79% or stronger sulfuric acid, she obtained a crystalline material which analysis indicated to have the composition $H_2Zr(SO_4)_3$ (4). This is probably a pyrosulfato acid

since a trisulfato compound of the formula $H_2Zr(SO_4)_3$ would contain zirconium at the highly improbable coordination number 3. Salts of composition $MZr(SO_4)_3$ have been obtained by the following procedure: 0.1 g of zirconium nitrate and 0.025-0.4 g of epsom salts were heated in 40 cc of concentrated sulfuric acid (sp. gr. 1.79). A solid formed of composition $MgZr(SO_4)_3$. It was filtered off, washed with sulfuric acid, and dried at 220° until the excess sulfuric acid had evaporated. The zinc, cadmium, cobalt, and manganese analogs were prepared similarly. The cobalt salt was pink, the manganese salt yellow, and the others were colorless. Yields were about 60-70% of the theoretical. The corresponding alkali salts could not be obtained (42). The experimental observations support the representation

The failure of the alkali metals to form corresponding salts is due to their univalency and to their small tendency to form covalencies. The hafnium compound $MgHf(SO_4)_3$ has been prepared, similar to its zirconium analog.

---

42. S. R. Patel, *J. Am. Chem. Soc.* **73**, 2958-9 (1951).

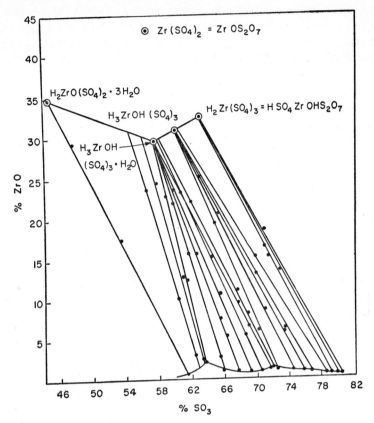

FIG. 6.2. Analytical results in the determination of sulfatozirconic acid phases by the method of residues. From (4).

THE POLYSULFATOZIRCONIC ACIDS

It has been noted above (p. 244) that when 1 mole of hydrous zirconia is treated with 2 moles of sulfuric acid, disulfatozirconic acid is formed and 11.67 kg cal are evolved. It has been observed further that if 3 moles of sulfuric acid are used, only 0.685 kg cal is evolved (43a). A more highly sulfonated acid forms endothermally from the disulfatozirconic acid (43b).

The first experimenters who tried to prepare sulfato compounds of zirconium containing more than 2 sulfato groups per zirconium atom were unsuccessful in their efforts (1, 2, 17, 44), but it was finally demonstrated by

43a. L. Pissarjewsky, J. Russ. Phys. Chem. Soc. 32, 609 (1900).
43b. Pissarjewsky, Z. anorg. allgem. Chem. 25, 378 (1900).
44a. R. Hermann, J. prakt. Chem. (1) 31, 75 (1844).
44b. Ibid. 97, 321, 330 (1886).

O. Hauser that a trisulfatozirconic acid forms very slowly from a strong sulfuric acid solution, and it was due to the slowness of the formation that his predecessors failed to observe it (10). Hauser dissolved 20 g of zirconyl pyrosulfate in 25 cc of water and 10 cc of sulfuric acid (sp. gr. 1.84). After the mixture had stood 14 days at room temperature, a good crop of crystals had formed and he separated them from the mother liquor, washed them with nitric acid, and allowed them to dry on a porous plate over quicklime or sulfuric acid (10e). He reported the product to have the composition $H_2Zr(SO_4)_3 \cdot 3H_2O$, which we prefer to represent $H_3ZrOH(SO_4)_3 \cdot 2H_2O$, 3132. According to the later, more painstaking studies of M. Falinski, Hauser must actually have obtained anhydrous $H_3ZrOH(SO_4)_3$. She also obtained the monohydrate 3131 by treating zirconyl chloride with sulfuric acid of 64-72% SO_3 content. The reaction may be regarded as the addition of a molecule of sulfuric acid to the molecule of 2123, and dehydration of the sulfato groups by the strong sulfuric acid environment:

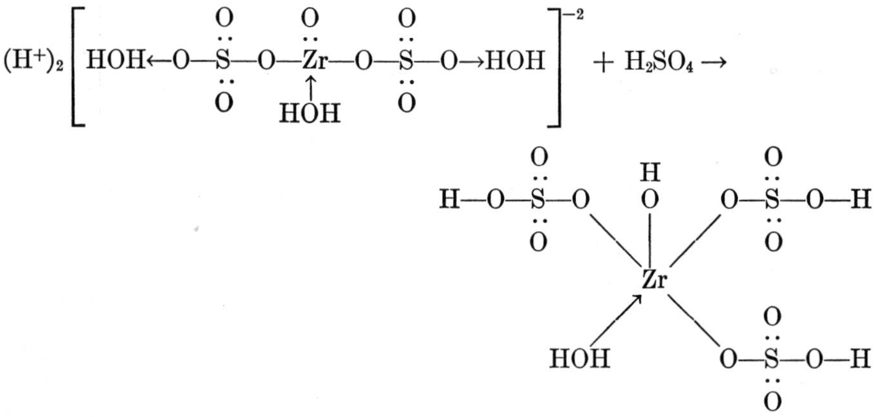

The water bound to the zirconium atom is readily removed by a sulfuric acid environment of sufficiently high strength. The trisulfato acids cannot be regarded as hydrates of $H_2Zr(SO_4)_3$ because of the highly unlikely coordination number of 3 for zirconium in the parent anhydrous acid and the awkward arrangement of hydrogen ions in the hydrated derivatives.

TRISULFATOZIRCONIC ACID MONOHYDRATE, $H_3ZrOH(SO_4)_3 \cdot H_2O$, 3131, formula weight 417.47, forms monoclinic crystals of sp. gr. 2.02 at 19°. It is strongly deliquescent, and on exposure to air it is hydrolyzed to disulfatozirconic acid trihydrate, 2123. It is slowly decomposed by nitric acid, but it is stable in contact with sulfuric acid solutions containing 64-72% SO_3. Sulfuric acid at lower strength hydrolyzes it to disulfatozirconic acid; at higher strength it dehydrates it to the anhydrous acid, 3130. It has been reported that mixtures of borderline composition between the disulfato and trisulfato acids failed to come to equilibrium in a year's time (4). When solutions of the trisulfato acid were electrolyzed, the zirconium was concentrated in the anode compartment (10).

Little is known about the anhydrous acid 3130. For discussion of the further dehydration of this acid, see p. 254.

Salts of trisulfatozirconic acid have been prepared by a variety of methods. A salt of composition $Na_2HZrOH(SO_4)_3 \cdot 3H_2O$ has been crystallized by evaporating a solution containing soda and 3-10 moles of SO_3 per mole of ZrO_2 until the SO_3 concentration attained to the region 33-45% (45, 46). An iron salt $FeHZrOH(SO_4)_3 \cdot 5H_2O$ has been crystallized from solutions containing 50-60% sulfuric acid, and its zinc analog has been prepared similarly (47).

When a mixture of zirconium dioxide and ammonium sulfate is heated to 400-600°, salts of or near the composition $(NH_4)_2HZrOH(SO_4)_3$ are obtained (48):

$$ZrO_2 + 3(NH_4)_2SO_4 \rightarrow (NH_4)_2HZrOH < SO_4)_3 + 4NH_3 + H_2O \quad (20)$$

The sintered products can be dissolved in water and recrystallized to purified products of the same composition. When aqueous solutions of these salts are boiled, they do not yield insoluble hydrolysis products. The third sulfato group in the anion effectively suppresses the hydrolytic attack by water, suggesting that the coordination number of zirconium has attained the sterically possible maximum, i.e., 7.

Discussion of salts of composition $MZr(SO_4)_3$ is given on p. 252.

When a concentrated solution of ammonium sulfate was added to a solution of zirconyl pyrosulfate in water and the mixture evaporated over sulfuric acid, crystals of $(NH_4)_2Zr_2O_2(SO_4)_3 \cdot 4H_2O$ separated first, followed by $(NH_4)_4Zr(SO_4)_4 \cdot 4H_2O$, NH_44144 (49). This appears to be a salt of the structure

45. British Patent **606,681**, Aug. 18, 1948.
46. M. Kastner, U.S. Patent **2,604,378**, July 22, 1952.
47. H. Trapp, *Z. anorg. allgem. Chem.* **209**, 335-6 (1932).
48. W. B. Blumenthal, U.S. Patent **2,525,474**, Oct. 10, 1950.
49. A. Rosenheim and J. Pinsker, *Z. anorg. allgem. Chem.* **106**, 9-14 (1919).

One investigator reported only 3 molecules of water of hydration (18b). A corresponding potassium salt has been reported with 2-7 molecules of water of hydration (24, 49, 50), a sodium salt with 4 (24) or 11 (49) molecules of water, and a thallium salt with 4 molecules of water (51). In general the salts are obtained by dissolving the components in hot water and allowing the solutions to cool. The tetrahydrated sodium salt was obtained by dissolving hydrous zirconia in a hot concentrated solution of sodium bisulfate and allowing the solution to cool and crystallize. The separation of the solid salts obviously depends on having a sufficient concentration of the tetrasulfatozirconate ion after the hydrolytic equilibrium

$$Zr(SO_4)_4^{-4} + OH^- \rightleftharpoons ZrOH(SO_4)_3^{-3} + SO_4^{-2} \tag{21}$$

to exceed the critical ion product $[M][Zr(SO_4)_4]$ which represents saturation for the particular salt. For this reason, the dissolution of a tetrasulfatozirconate salt in hot water, followed by cooling, might not yield crystals of the original solute. Rosenheim and Pinsker dissolved the sodium salt in water and evaporated the solution. They obtained a glassy solid rather than crystals of sodium tetrasulfatozirconate, due to the formation of hydrolyzed species during their operations (49). The potassium salt is very sparingly soluble, and from the low concentrations of its saturated solution only hydrolysis products are recovered. The addition of barium chloride to solutions of the tetrasulfatozirconates results in complete breakdown of the complex anions, and precipitates part or all of the zirconium (49):

$$4BaCl_2 + K_4Zr(SO_4)_4 \cdot 4H_2O \rightarrow$$
$$4BaSO_4 + 4KCl + 4HCl + ZrO_2 \cdot xH_2O + (2 - x)H_2O \tag{22}$$

Due to the hydrolytic breakdown of the tetrasulfato complex, cryoscopic data on the aqueous solutions do not lend themselves to unambiguous interpretation (18c, 21).

Sodium tetrasulfatozirconate has been used as a tanning agent (35), and its preparation for this use has been described (52).

THE POLYSULFATOPOLYZIRCONATES

The sulfatozirconates described above, containing 2 or more sulfate radicals per zirconium atom, have been shown to be in effect derivatives of a hypothetical metazirconic acid which contains a single zirconium atom per molecule. In the older literature they were regarded as normal and acid salts of zirconium. Another class of sulfatozirconates has long been recognized in

50. A. Rosenheim and P. Frank, *Ber.* **38**, 812 (1905).
51. L. Fernandez, *Gazz. chim. ital.* **55**, i, 3 (1925).
52. Toshio Ishino, Jiro Shiokawa, and Ryoyu Shimano, *J. Chem. Soc. Japan, Ind. Chem. Sect.* **56**, 670-1 (1953).

which the molecules contain less than 2 sulfate radicals per zirconium atom and 2 or more zirconium atoms per molecule. Because they contain a higher ratio of ZrO_2 to SO_3 than what was called the normal sulfate, $Zr(SO_4)_2 \cdot 4H_2O$, the older literature has spoken of these compounds as *basic sulfates*. But since the term *basic salt* implies a compound containing a basic cation and one or more basic anions such as O^{-2} or OH^-, it is apparent that the term cannot properly be applied to most of the zirconium compounds of lower sulfate content, for these do not contain basic zirconium cations nor basic anions.

Sulfato groups attached to zirconium are labile and subject to removal by hydrolysis, particularly by the action of hydroxyl ion. The disulfatozirconate ion is attacked according to the following equation:

$$ZrO(SO_4)_2 \cdot 3H_2O^{-2} + H^+ + OH^- \rightleftharpoons HOZrOSO_4 \cdot 3H_2O^- + HSO_4^- \quad (23)$$

The tendency of the reaction to proceed toward the right is greater at higher hydroxyl ion concentrations. Since zirconium has a coordination number of only 5 in disulfatozirconic acid, hydroxyl ion can become attached:

The zirconium atom thus acquires an increased negative charge, which causes it to repel the sulfato group:

The process tends to be reversed by high sulfate ion concentration in the solution phase.

When a solution of disulfatozirconic acid is diluted, the hydrogen ion concentration is diminished and the hydroxyl ion concentration correspondingly increased. As already noted in our discussion of this acid, the higher the dilution the more rapid and the more complete the hydrolysis. The hydrolysis is also promoted by elevation of the temperature, indicating it to be an endothermal process.

It can be inferred from the trihydration of the disulfatozirconate anion that the space around the zirconium atom is sufficiently filled that an additional water molecule cannot penetrate the shield of ligands, i.e., the coordination sphere. Were this not so, the zirconium atom would attain to a higher coordination number by further hydration, as it does in many other compounds. But the hydroxyl ion is small enough to penetrate the shield. By the same token, once a sulfato group has been replaced by the geometrically smaller hydroxo group, a gap is opened for further coordination to occur, and the monosulfatozirconate anion tends to take on other ligands from its environment. Two monosulfatozirconate ions may combine:

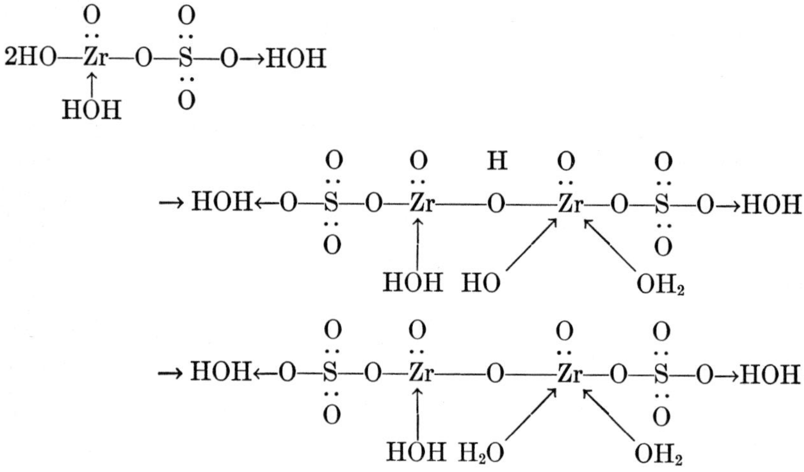

In this process the structural group —Zr—O—Zr— forms, and its 2 zirconium atoms become dihydrated. Alternatively, the 2 monosulfatozirconate anions may combine through sulfato:

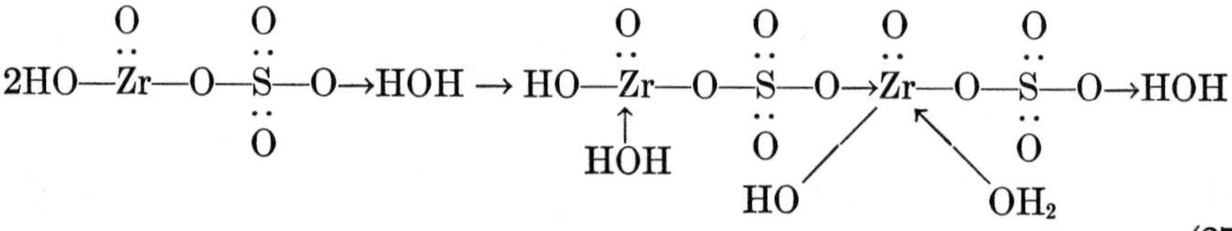

with formation of the structural group $-\overset{\overset{\displaystyle O}{..}}{Zr}-O-\overset{\overset{\displaystyle O}{..}}{\underset{\underset{\displaystyle O}{}}{S}}-O-\overset{\overset{\displaystyle O}{..}}{Zr}-$. Under suit-

able conditions of pH and sulfate concentration, the terminal OH can be replaced by SO_4:

$$H_2SO_4 + HO-\overset{\overset{\displaystyle O}{..}}{\underset{\underset{\displaystyle HOH}{\uparrow}}{Zr}}-\; \rightarrow\; HSO_4-\overset{\overset{\displaystyle O}{..}}{\underset{\underset{\displaystyle HOH}{\uparrow}}{Zr}}-\; + H_2O \qquad (28)$$

In these processes, not only temperature, concentration, and acidity affect the course of chemical changes but also other ions such as chloride which may be present. Their effect is catalytic, and the specific arrangements to which they give rise will be taken up in connection with the study of the specific compounds.

The ion $HOZrOSO_4{}^-$ can be regarded as a monomer from which polymers and their alteration products are derived. It is apparent that the polymers and their alteration products may also be condensed by splitting out of water, and such reactions contribute to the formation of a wide variety of species. Indeed, a competitive growth of various ionic and molecular species can be anticipated from consideration of fundamental reactions of the type reviewed above. It is to be expected that those species can be isolated which have sufficient stability under experimental conditions to make possible their survival in detectable quantities. The broad picture of the competitive processes for development of species explains why it is often exceedingly difficult to establish true equilibrium and to isolate pure species. Aside from the fact of coexistence of a variety of species (with limitations on the number of phases according to the requirements of the phase rule), structural and kinetic factors often prevent the attainment of equilibrium. Let us suppose, for example, that a mixture of reagents is set up under physical conditions that should yield the species **2234** when equilibrium is reached. This species has the structure

$$(H^+)_2\left[HOH\leftarrow O-\overset{\overset{\displaystyle O}{..}}{\underset{\underset{\displaystyle O}{..}}{S}}-O-\overset{\overset{\displaystyle O}{..}}{\underset{\underset{\displaystyle HOH}{\uparrow}}{Zr}}-O-\overset{\overset{\displaystyle O}{..}}{\underset{\underset{\displaystyle O}{..}}{S}}-O-\overset{\overset{\displaystyle O}{..}}{\underset{\underset{\displaystyle HOH}{\uparrow}}{Zr}}-O-\overset{\overset{\displaystyle O}{..}}{\underset{\underset{\displaystyle O}{..}}{S}}-O\rightarrow HOH\right]^{-2}$$

But in preparing the mixture of the components and bringing them to the desired physical condition, we may previously expose them to conditions giving rise to some of the structural unit $-\overset{\overset{\displaystyle O}{..}}{Zr}-O-\overset{\overset{\displaystyle O}{..}}{Zr}-$, which is not found in 2234. Under the conditions making for stability of 2234, no mechanism

$$\overset{\text{O}}{\overset{..}{}}\qquad\overset{\text{O}}{\overset{..}{}}$$

exists for the conversion of —Zr—O—Zr— to the structures required for 2234. Therefore, complete equilibrium will never be attained and the desired product will be contaminated with other species. If a mechanism exists whereby odd structural units can change over to the equilibrium structure, it may still require such a vast amount of time as to be practically unachievable. The slowness of chemical changes which are actually observed in systems of the polysulfatopolyzirconic acids reflects the covalent nature of the bonds between atoms which are participating in the reactions.

In addition to the matter of the type of chain growth, there are also factors of importance which determine the amount of hydration of the atoms in the chain and the lengths to which the chain may attain. It is seen by inspection that in the sulfatozirconates containing 1 or 2 zirconium atoms, the zirconium atoms characteristically attain to coordination number 5 by hydration, whereas in chains containing more than 2 zirconium atoms, these atoms characteristically attain to coordination number 6 or 7. Dehydration usually follows a pattern whereby the coordination number of all the zirconium atoms is reduced by 1 during a single dehydration step. Terminal hydroxyl and hydrosulfate groups are monohydrated, and their dehydration also constitutes a recognizable step in the total dehydration process. Whether the zirconium atoms in a particular compound are hydrated to coordination number 6 or 7 will depend on the energy of attachment of the water forming the seventh ligand and on the aqueous tension over the hydrate under the conditions of its preparation or isolation.

The existence of polysulfatopolyzirconic acids and the monomers from which they are derived was noted by some of the earliest experimenters with the zirconia-sulfuric acid system. Berzelius observed that on addition of potassium sulfate to a solution of disulfatozirconic acid the zirconium was partially precipitated if the solution was strongly acid and completely precipitated if the free acidity was neutralized with potassium hydroxide. He obtained similar crystalline precipitates when he fused zirconia with potassium hydrogen sulfate and treated the reaction product with water (1), and succeeding experimenters obtained analogous results on treating disulfatozirconic acid solution with various alkali sulfates (17, 53, 54). They recognized that they were obtaining more basic compounds than the 2123 with which they started, but were not clear as to the nature of their products. Actually in the more acidic solutions they were obtaining tetrasulfatozirconates, $M_4Zr(SO_4)_4 \cdot nH_2O$ and in the more nearly neutral solutions chains of the general formula $M_2(ZrO)_m(SO_4)_{m+1} \cdot nH_2O$. The potas-

53. C. M. Warren, *Pogg. Ann.* **102**, 449 (1857); *J. prakt. Chem.* (1) **75**, 361 (1858).
54. R. Hermann, *J. prakt. Chem.* (1) **31**, 75 (1844).

sium compounds are generally sparingly soluble in water and almost insoluble in the presence of excess potassium sulfate, due to the common ion effect of the latter salt.

Berzelius found that hydrous zirconia could be dissolved in aqueous solutions of disulfatozirconic acid, 2123, and at 60° he was able to dissolve 1.15 moles of hydrous zirconia per mole of concentrated 2123 solution. On evaporation of the solution, an apparently homogeneous solid was obtained (10). Kulka reported a solid of similar appearance to separate when the excess acidity of the solution was neutralized with ammonia (8). These products were glassy rather than crystalline, and vapor pressure studies indicated them to form no definite hydrates (16). We may explain these results by postulating the initial formation of monosulfatozirconic acid:

$$H_2ZrO(SO_4)_2 \cdot 3H_2O + ZrO_2 \cdot xH_2O \rightarrow 2HZrOOHSO_4 \cdot 2H_2O + (x - 2)H_2O \tag{29}$$

This acid acts as a monomer from which crystalline polymers and their alteration products may be recovered, and also from which such long chains may be built up that they tend to become interlaced and tangled so as to form glasses rather than crystals. Berzelius's solution containing 1.15 moles of hydrous zirconia per mole of 2123 had the composition of a chain containing 15 zirconium atoms and 14 sulfato groups. The numerous possibilities of this system for the formation of glasses, colloids, and crystalline solids have been responsible for numerous interpretations of the available data and rendered definitive interpretation very difficult (10e, 55).

Qualitative evidence of the formation of polysulfatopolyzirconic acids was obtained by Chauvenet, who regarded them as basic zirconium sulfates. He mixed zirconia with sulfuric acid in various proportions, heated the mixtures to 200°, and measured the specific gravities of the products in nitrobenzene at 12.4°. His data indicated the existence of several compounds of higher basicity than that of 2123 (18). He also studied the freezing points of systems containing 2123 and alkali sulfates, and obtained evidence for the formation of relatively basic compounds (21). His most definite results, however, came from the preparation and isolation of these compounds. He isolated a solid of composition $HZrOOHSO_4 \cdot 3H_2O$ by three different methods: (1) by evaporation of a mixture of 1 mole of hydrous zirconia and 1 mole of sulfuric acid, (2) by treating a solution of 2123 with potassium hydroxide, and (3) by adding ammonium sulfate to a solution of 2123 and allowing it to stand for a few days. When the precipitated solid was dried in air at the ordinary temperature, the dihydrated monosulfatozirconic acid was recovered, and at 150° it became anhydrous. During the handling it is probable that some condensation to higher molecular weight acids occurred.

---

55. R. Ruer, Z. anorg. allgem. Chem. **46,** 456 (1905).

The symmetrical condensation of 2 molecules of the monomer would yield $H_2Zr_2O_3(SO^4)_2 \cdot 6H_2O$, 2226:

$$2H_2O \rightarrow HO-\overset{\overset{O}{..}}{\underset{\underset{O}{..}}{S}}-O-Zr-OH \rightarrow$$

(with H_2O and OH_2 coordinated to Zr)

$$H_2O \rightarrow HO-\overset{\overset{O}{..}}{\underset{\underset{O}{..}}{S}}-O-Zr\text{------}O\text{------}Zr-O-\overset{\overset{O}{..}}{\underset{\underset{O}{..}}{S}}-OH \leftarrow OH_2 \quad (30)$$

(with H_2O, OH_2, H_2O, OH_2 coordinated)

Evidence for such a compound was first reported by Ruer and Levin (13) and subsequently by a number of other investigators. Lasserre obtained it by neutralizing to the extent of 63% or more a solution of disulfatozirconic acid containing 2.5% of ZrO_2 by weight (19), and Falinski by electrodialysis of a dilute solution of 2123 (4). The compound 2226 has not been characterized as well as some of the other polysulfatopolyzirconic acids. A number of salts of this acid have been reported to form, namely $K_2Zr_2O_3$ $(SO_4)_2 \cdot 8H_2O$, $Rb_2Zr_2O_3(SO_4)_2 \cdot 15H_2O$, and $Cs_2Zr_2O_3(SO_4)_2 \cdot 11H_2O$ (50, 56).

It is noteworthy that similar behavior has been noted for the element cerium (57). When 50 ml of a solution containing 25 gm of $Ce(SO_4)_2$ and 20 ml of 1 M sulfuric acid was heated in a sealed glass tube at 200°, rod-shaped crystals of $HCeOOHSO_4$ separated. They had orthorhombic symmetry, and the X-ray pattern indicated a zigzag string of n CeO groups lying parallel to the c axis. The strings were so connected that every sulfate oxygen atom was connected to one cerium atom. A contaminant in the product had the composition $H_2Ce_3O_4(SO_4)_3$, which must also be analogous to sulfatozirconic acid chain compounds.

Hauser obtained a composition $2ZrO_2 \cdot SO_3$ by heating the compound 2123 in steam at 200-300° (10) and Chauvenet obtained $2ZrO_2 \cdot SO_3 \cdot 8H_2O$ by hydrolysis of the compound 2434 (18b). Britton found evidence of the existence of a sulfato compound of this ratio in his data on the potentiometric titration of 2123 with alkalies (58). Lasserre isolated a precipitate of composition $(HO)_2Zr_2O_2SO_4 \cdot 2H_2O$, −2212, from a solution of 2123 which was 63% or more neutralized with alkali (19). Falinski found that a solution containing 0.1-0.6% of zirconyl persulfate deposited a mixture of crystals and of finely divided amorphous solid which had the composition

56a. O. Hauser and H. Herzfeld, *Z. anorg. allgem. Chem.* **67**, 369 (1910).
56b. *Ibid.* **106**, 1 (1919).
57. G. Lundgren, *Arkiv. Kemi.* **6**, 59-75 (1953).
58. H. T. S. Britton, *J. Chem. Soc.* **127**, 2120 (1925).

$(HO)_2ZrO_2O_2SO_4 \cdot 6H_2O$ after drying in air (4). D'Ans and Eick obtained the octahydrate by hydrolysis of very dilute 2123. An electron micrograph of their product showed it to be a homogeneous microcrystalline solid (59). From these results it can be said that monosulfatodizirconic acid results from the hydrolysis of the terminal sulfato groups from what would otherwise be the compound 2234:

$$
\text{HO}-\overset{\overset{\displaystyle O}{\cdot\cdot}}{\underset{\underset{\displaystyle H_2O}{\cdot\cdot}}{S}}-O-\overset{\nearrow}{\underset{\searrow}{Zr}}\underset{OH_2}{}-O-\overset{\overset{\displaystyle O}{\cdot\cdot}}{\underset{\underset{\displaystyle H_2O}{O}}{S}}-O-\overset{\nearrow}{\underset{\searrow}{Zr}}\underset{OH_2}{}-O-\overset{\overset{\displaystyle O}{\cdot\cdot}}{\underset{\underset{\displaystyle O}{\cdot\cdot}}{S}}-OH + 9H_2O + 2OH^- \rightarrow
$$

$$
H_2O \rightarrow HO-\overset{\overset{\displaystyle H_2O}{\searrow}}{\underset{\underset{\displaystyle H_2O}{\nearrow}\ \underset{\displaystyle OH_2}{\searrow}}{Zr}}\overset{\parallel}{}-O-\overset{\overset{\displaystyle O}{\cdot\cdot}}{\underset{\underset{\displaystyle O}{\cdot\cdot}}{S}}-O-\overset{\overset{\displaystyle O}{\parallel}}{\underset{\underset{\displaystyle H_2O}{\nearrow}\ \underset{\displaystyle OH_2}{\searrow}}{Zr}}-OH \leftarrow OH_2 + 2HSO_4^-
$$

(31)

This product, −2218, might be expected to become dehydrated readily to −2216, and under more vigorous conditions of hydration to lower hydrates. the dihydrate of Lasserre being the lowest hydrate attainable without change in identity of the fundamental chain structure. Hauser found that prolonged boiling of a solution of 20 g of zirconyl pyrosulfate in 60 g of water gave a crystalline precipitate of composition $2ZrO_2 \cdot 3SO_3 \cdot 5H_2O$, of specific gravity 2.834 at 19°. It dissolved in water but dissolved more readily in dilute acids. The aqueous solution was acidic, but less so than that of the 2120 from which it was prepared (10e). The formation of this product is most easily conceived as resulting from the addition of a mole of disulfatozirconic acid and a mole of the partially hydrolyzed acid:

$$
(H^+)_2 \left[HOH \leftarrow O-\overset{\overset{\displaystyle O}{\cdot\cdot}}{\underset{\underset{\displaystyle O}{\cdot\cdot}}{S}}-O-\overset{\uparrow}{\underset{\underset{\displaystyle HOH}{}}{Zr}}-O-\overset{\overset{\displaystyle O}{\cdot\cdot}}{\underset{\underset{\displaystyle O}{\cdot\cdot}}{S}}-O \rightarrow HOH \right]^{-2}
$$

$$
+ H^+ \left[HO-\overset{\uparrow}{\underset{\underset{\displaystyle HOH}{}}{Zr}}-O-\overset{\overset{\displaystyle O}{\cdot\cdot}}{\underset{\underset{\displaystyle O}{\cdot\cdot}}{S}}-O \rightarrow HOH \right]^{-} \rightarrow
$$

(32)

$$
(H^+)_2 \left[HOH \leftarrow O-\overset{\overset{\displaystyle O}{\cdot\cdot}}{\underset{\underset{\displaystyle O}{\cdot\cdot}}{S}}-O-\overset{\uparrow}{\underset{\underset{\displaystyle HOH}{}}{Zr}}-O-\overset{\overset{\displaystyle O}{\cdot\cdot}}{\underset{\underset{\displaystyle O}{\cdot\cdot}}{S}}-O-\overset{\uparrow}{\underset{\underset{\displaystyle HOH}{}}{Zr}}-O-\overset{\overset{\displaystyle O}{\cdot\cdot}}{\underset{\underset{\displaystyle O}{\cdot\cdot}}{S}}-O \rightarrow HOH \right]^{-2} + 2H_2O
$$

59. J. d'Ans and H. Eick, Z. Elektrochem. 55, 19-28 (1951).

This product is represented by the formula $H_2Zr_2O_2(SO_4)_3 \cdot 4H_2O$ and the numerical symbol 2234. Hauser noted that it was only imperfectly precipitated by ammonia and other alkalies, which reflects the initial formation of a somewhat insoluble salt of this acid. When he heated the acid to 300°, it lost all its water, leaving a residue of composition $2ZrO_2 \cdot 3SO_3$ (10e). Later studies of the dehydration of this compound showed that 2 molecules of water are liberated between 170° and 220° and 2 additional molecules at 225° (59). Thus the water of hydration of the zirconium atoms, the water of hydration of the terminal sulfato groups, and that formed by the hydro-

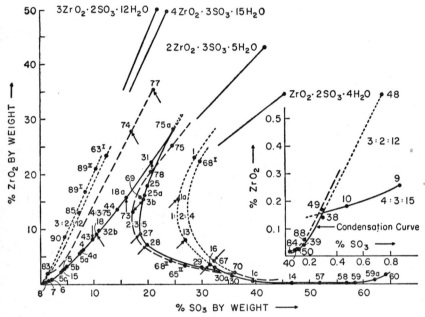

FIG. 6.3a. Isotherms in the system ZrO_2-SO_3-H_2O. ——— 39.7°, – – – – 72°, as determined by d'Ans and Eick (59).

gen ions are lost in stages at three successively higher temperature ranges. On electrolysis of an aqueous solution of 2234, the zirconium goes to the anode. Although Chauvenet contested the existence of this compound, the later work of Falinski (4) and d'Ans and Eick (59) proved its existence and substantiated Hauser's findings. Figure 6.3 shows the isotherms developed by d'Ans and Eick which clearly delineate the existence of a number of the polysulfatopolyzirconic acids, including 2234. In their preparation of the latter compound, they boiled a 50% solution of zirconyl pyrosulfate and found the entire mass to freeze to a white crystalline slush in about half an hour. They tested the solubility of the washed salt, and found it to dissolve slowly in water due to a sparingly soluble crust of hydrolysis product, but it dissolved readily in small amounts of hot water in which a markedly acid reaction was quickly attained, giving viscous, sticky solutions (59).

A number of salts of 2234 have been prepared. The addition of concentrated ammonium sulfate solution to a solution of zirconyl pyrosulfate, 2120, followed by evaporation of the mixture, gave crystals of composition $(NH_4)_2Zr_2O_2(SO_4)_3 \cdot 9H_2O$ (50). The tetrahydrated ammonium salt was

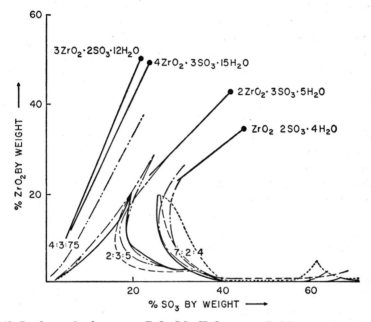

Fig. 6.3b. Isotherms in the system ZrO_2-SO_3-H_2O as compiled from various literature by d'Ans and Eick (59). ······ Hauser, ——— Auergesellschaft 39.5°, −−−−−− Auergesellschaft 87°, −·−·−·−·− d'Ans and Eick 39.7°, ···−··−··· d'Ans and Eick 72°.

obtained by evaporation of a mixture of 10 g of 2120 in 10 ml of water and 14 g of ammonium sulfate in 25 ml of water (49). On cooling a hot solution containing 2123 and thallous sulfate, a solid separated which has been reported to have the composition $Tl_2Zr_2(SO_4)_3 \cdot 8H_2O$ (51), but for which we postulate $(Tl \cdot 2H_2O)_2Zr_2O_2(SO_4)_3 \cdot 4H_2O$, hydrated Tl 2234. Evaporation of cool solutions of thallous sulfate and 2123 gave a solid of composition $Tl_{14}Zr_2(SO_4)_{11}$, the thorium analog of which is also known. Little is known of the structure or properties of these thallium salts, but the solubility of the thallium zirconium compound, expressed in g ZrO_2 per 100 ml of water, has the following values at different temperatures:

Temp.	0°	10°	20°	30°	40°	60°	80°	100°
Soly.	6.2	6.2	6.5	7.2	8.5	15.7	24.5	32.0

The odd number of sulfato groups suggests that one of them must link the 2 zirconium atoms and 5 others must be associated with each zirconium atom,

$$\overset{\overset{\displaystyle O}{\cdot\cdot}}{\underset{\displaystyle O}{}}$$

giving in effect a derivative of 2234: $(Tl^+)_{14}(SO_4)_5 ZrOSOZr(SO_4)_5$.

Berzelius obtained a precipitate of composition $3ZrO_2 \cdot 2SO_3 \cdot nH_2O$, for which a number of discrete values of n were obtained by him and others, by adding alcohol to an aqueous solution of 2123, filtering, washing the precipitate with alcohol and then with water. He obtained a solid of the same composition on diluting a solution of zirconyl chloride containing sulfate ions. The white, flaky precipitate was insoluble in water but soluble in hydrochloric acid. It became anhydrous on heating it to 100°. Similar compositions were reported by some early successors (17, 60). Leuchs formed a compound of composition $3ZrO_2 \cdot 2SO_3 \cdot 12H_2O$ by adding the calculated amount of sulfuric acid to a dilute solution of zirconyl chloride (61), and the existence of a compound of this composition was proved by the phase studies of d'Ans and Eick (59), who showed that the high water content of Leuchs's product is unstable when the compound is not in contact with its mother liquor. They showed that the same compound is obtained when hydrochloric acid is added dropwise to a boiling solution of the compound 2234, best results being obtained when 4 to 6 moles of hydrochloric acid is used per mole of 2234. Ammonium chloride, sodium chloride, calcium chloride, potassium bromide, or sodium iodide can be used in place of hydrochloric acid, but alkali sulfates, nitrates, or acetates did not give the same result (59). The halogen ions appear to catalyze the hydrolytic removal of the terminal sulfato groups. The method of preparation and the behavior of the compound agree with the structural representation

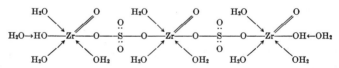

which would be represented by the formula $(HO)_2Zr_3O_3(SO_4)_2 \cdot 11H_2O$ and the numerical symbol $-232\overline{11}$.

The formation of $-232\overline{11}$ in a strongly acid medium is in keeping with the principle of its being a derivative of a zirconic acid rather than a hydroxide of zirconium.

60. H. Endemann, *J. prakt. Chem.* (2) **11**, 219 (1875).
61. K. Leuchs, German Patent **295,246** (1915).

Chauvenet and Gueylard have reported a salt of composition $(NH_4)_4$ $(ZrO)_3(SO_4)_5$ (21), but in view of its odd composition and the absence of other corroborating studies, it appears more likely that this was a mixture rather than a compound.

A solid of composition $K_2Zr_3O_3(SO_4)_4 \cdot 8H_2O$ has been obtained on adding potassium sulfate to a solution of monosulfatozirconic acid or dizirconic acid (18b, 21). It is one of a class of compounds of generic formula $K_2(ZrO)_n(SO_4)_{n+1} \cdot mH_2O$, in which chains of various lengths are built up by alternating zirconyl and sulfato groups, the chain terminating in hydrosulfato groups capable of forming salts. The potassium salts are sparingly soluble. The length of the chain varies with conditions of its formation. The molecule is hydrated by one or more molecules of water per zirconyl group. Blumenthal has noted that if a solution containing 0.1 mole of zirconyl chloride in 250 ml of water at 25° is mixed with 0.125 mole of potassium sulfate dissolved in 250 ml at the same temperature, the mixture remains clear for 15 to 20 seconds, then a precipitate begins to separate from solution. It is a solid of approximately the composition $K_2(ZrO)_4$ $(SO_4)_5 \cdot 4H_2O$. If sodium sulfate is used in place of potassium sulfate, there is no precipitate, but if potassium chloride is added after about 20 seconds, precipitation occurs immediately, showing that the anion $(ZrO)_4$ $(SO_4)_5^{-2}$ has already formed. A dozen or more cations were found not to precipitate this anion, but a precipitate was formed on adding solutions of acid dyes (23). The compound $K_2(ZrO)_4(SO_4)_5 \cdot 4H_2O$ has been reported by Hauser and Herzfeld (56) and by Rosenheim and Pinsker (49); $K_2(ZrO)_8(SO_4)_9 \cdot 22H_2O$ has been reported by Somerville, Turley, and Hurd (62). Kinzie precipitated compounds of this type as means of recovering the zirconium values from solutions of zirconium ores (63).

Hauser noted that when a solution of zirconyl pyrosulfate containing between 7 and 120 molecules of water per molecule of $ZrOS_2O_7$ was allowed to stand for about 10 hours at 39.5°, a compound of composition $4ZrO_2 \cdot 3SO_3 \cdot 15H_2O$ formed. The solid was recovered by filtering, washing, and drying over sulfuric acid of specific gravity 1.256. It has become known as *Hauser's salt*. When 6⅔ molecules of water was present per molecule of zirconyl pyrosulfate, the solution remained clear. The concentration of solution which would deposit this compound varied with temperature, and the rate of deposition was higher at higher temperature. But it would not form at all above 50°, and a dilute solution of 2123 held at 64° would no longer deposit the compound if it was cooled to a temperature at which an unheated solution deposited the compound. Hauser was probably the

62. I. C. Somerville, H. G. Turley, and L. C. Hurd, U.S. Patent **2,264,414**, Dec. 2, 1941.

63. C. J. Kinzie, U.S. Patent **1,618,287**, May 20, 1924.

first to point out that solutions of 2123 which were heated and then diluted gave different hydrolysis products from those which were diluted and then heated (10). It is apparent that at 64°, sulfatozirconic acid species formed which were not convertible to Hauser's salt. The indicated structure for this compound is

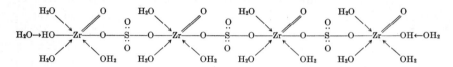

It is represented by the formula $(HO)_2Zr_4O_4(SO_4)_3 \cdot 14H_2O$ and the numerical designation $-243\overline{14}$. It has been recovered as double-refracting monoclinic needles, exhibiting an extinction angle of about 28-29° along the length of the crystals, and its specific gravity is 2.5. Its dehydration is irreversible. It dissolves in water to form a solution of not more than 0.009% strength, and it is stable in the presence of dilute acids (10). It is slightly decomposed by boiling water and completely decomposed by heating it with aqueous solutions of sodium chloride, sodium sulfate, or magnesium sulfate, without dissolution occurring. It is only slightly affected by ammonia and dilute alkali solutions (56b). In addition to the tetradecahydrate, a hexahydrate has been found to be stable at 15-18° and a tetrahydrate at 105-115°. At 300° complete dehydration to $4ZrO_2 \cdot 3SO_3$, specific gravity 4.1 occurs, reported pseudomorphous after the compound of highest hydration. Hauser and Herzfeld tried unsuccessfully to replace the zirconyl oxygen atoms (which they regarded as hydroxo groups) with chlorine (56).

Hauser and Herzfeld reported that a second crystalline variety of $-243\overline{14}$ exists and that they observed it to separate as needles when a 2% solution of 2123 was allowed to stand at room temperature for 6 days. Thereafter the first variety separated from the solution. The second variety showed differences in both chemical and optical properties from the first, its most marked distinction being its perpendicular extinction versus the oblique extinction of the first variety. The second variety was decomposed by boiling water while the first was not (56). Falinski subsequently reported obtaining the crystals of oblique extinction from solutions of 2120 and those of perpendicular extinction from solutions of 2123 (4), but d'Ans and Eick were able to obtain only the crystals with the oblique extinction (59).

The existence of $-243\overline{14}$ was proved by the phase studies of d'Ans and Eick and they were able to observe directly the transformation of 2234 to $-243\overline{14}$ at 39.7°. They prepared a quantity of the compound by allowing a solution of 2123, of strength equivalent to 3% ZrO_2, to undergo hydrolysis at 40°. Both they and Falinski (64) observed that midway during the formation of this compound, the precipitate contained slightly less than the theoretical proportion of SO_3 for $-243\overline{14}$. This would be expected if the chain were building up from smaller units of higher zirconia content. The compounds -2212 and 1222 probably form as intermediates and condense:

$$
\text{HO—Zr—O—S—O—Zr—OH} + \text{H—O—S—O—Zr—O—S—O—Zr—OH} + 9H_2O \rightarrow
$$

$$
H_2O\rightarrow\text{HO——Zr——O——S——O——Zr——O——S——O——Zr——O——S——O——Zr——OH}\leftarrow OH_2 \quad (33)
$$

A slight excess of -2212 in the solid would account for the apparent deficit of SO_3.

A composition $K_4Zr_4(SO_4)_5 \cdot 17H_2O$ has been reported (49), but little is known about this substance and its odd composition suggests it to be a mixture rather than a compound.

A number of compositions containing 5 zirconium atoms per 3 sulfato groups have been reported. Pugh prepared a solution of zirconyl chloride containing excess hydrochloric acid and 3 moles of sulfuric acid per 5 moles of zirconyl chloride. He brought the concentration to the equivalent of 33 g ZrO_2 per 1, and heated it. A precipitate separated which on analysis was found to have a composition corresponding to $5ZrO_2 \cdot 3SO3 \cdot 13H_2O$. It was substantially free of the iron, titanium, and silicon oxides which contaminated the starting materials (65). Wainer made a similar preparation in a less strongly acid solution (5). Blumenthal, using a variation of Wainer's procedure, obtained a precipitate which, after drying in air at room temperature, had the composition $5ZrO_2 \cdot 3SO_3 \cdot 15\text{-}16H_2O$ (23). This composition might be explained on the assumption of a unit composition $10ZrO_2 \cdot 6SO_3 \cdot 31H_2O$, consisting of a complex cation and a complex anion and having the structure represented by the formulation $(HO)_2Zr_5O_8(SO_4ZrOSO_4ZrOSO_4ZrOSO_4ZrOSO_4ZrOSO_4) \cdot 3OH_2O$.

In titrating a solution of 2123 with 0.001 N sodium hydroxide, Chauvenet found an inflection point which indicated the existence of a compound consisting of 6 zirconium atoms per 5 sulfato groups. He added alcohol to a concentrated solution of 2123 and obtained a precipitate of composition $(HO)_2Zr_6O_6(SO_4)_5 \cdot 11H_2O$, which may actually have been the dodecahydrate:

64. Marie Falinski, *Compt. rend.* **206**, 1479-80 (1938).
65. E. J. Pugh, U.S. Patents **1,316,107**, Sept. 16, 1919; **1,376,161**, April 26, 1921.

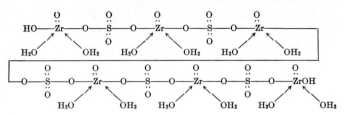

It became anhydrous at 100° (18a).

In her study of the system ZrO_2-SO_3-H_2O by the method of residues, Falinski showed the existence of a phase of composition $7ZrO_2 \cdot 5SO_3 \cdot 3OH_2O$ (4, 64). It was precipitated as needlelike crystals when a 1-10% solution of 2120 was held at 40° or a 1-16% solution was held at 25°. Under very slight pressure the crystals disintegrated into an apparently amorphous powder. Monoclinic crystals of the same substance were reported by Lasserre to separate from a solution of 2123 in which hydrous zirconia had been dissolved. But, when instead of hydrous zirconia, equivalent amounts of sodium hydroxide or sodium carbonate were used, a precipitate of similar composition but of rhombohedral hexagonal symmetry formed, with 32 molecules of water (19). This substance may be a condensation product of a molecule of Hauser's salt and a molecule of Leuchs's compound, in which event it would be

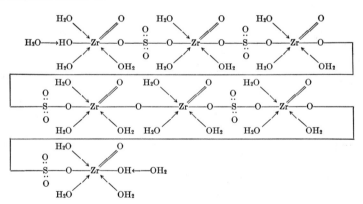

At most, 24 molecules of chemically bonded water can be accounted for, and any additional water which is present may be regarded as held interstitially. The compound can be represented $(HO)_2Zr_7O_8(SO_4)_5 \cdot 23H_2O$, and numerically $-27\overline{523}$.

A compound $-275\overline{13}$ has been reported to separate from a solution of 2123 on the addition of alcohol. It was observed to redissolve in a small amount of water but in large quantities of water it was hydrolyzed to a solid of relatively higher zirconia content. Some alcohol was retained by the washed solid (60). Little is known of this solid or of another substance of 7 zirconium atoms, $-273\overline{16}$, reported by Leuchs (66).

Ruer and Levin boiled a solution of zirconyl chloride containing sulfuric acid and obtained a precipitate corresponding to the composition $8ZrO_2 \cdot 5SO_3 \cdot 36H_2O$ (13). Hauser and Herzfeld obtained a similar composition, but with 19 molecules of water, by dissolving zirconyl pyrosulfate with five times its weight of water and adding alcohol to the solution, then redissolving the precipitate which formed and dialyzing the solution. Over a few days' time $8ZrO_2 \cdot 5SO_3 \cdot 19H_2O$ separated as very characteristic crystals which they described as *sphärecrystalle*. The identical product was obtained by Falinski both by Hauser's method and by diluting liquors from which the compound 2234 had been prepared and separated. She also observed these *sphärecrystalle* as impurities in the solid which was obtained on adding potassium sulfate to a solution of 2123 (4). The indicated structure of this compound is

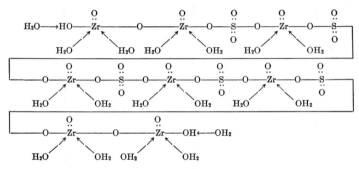

ZIRCONIUM SULFATES

The name *zirconium sulfates* should be reserved for compounds containing zirconium cations and sulfate anions. Such compounds will differ from the sulfatozirconates in that the SO_4^{-2} ion will be held primarily by electrostatic attraction rather than bound covalently as a sulfato group. Only one compound which appears to belong to the category of zirconium sulfates is known, and it has the empirical formula $Zr_5O_8(SO_4)_2 \cdot 14H_2O$.

Compounds containing 5 zirconium atoms have unique theoretical possibilities for the formation of symmetrically branched chain structures:

66. K. Leuchs, German patent **285,344**, March 7, 1914.

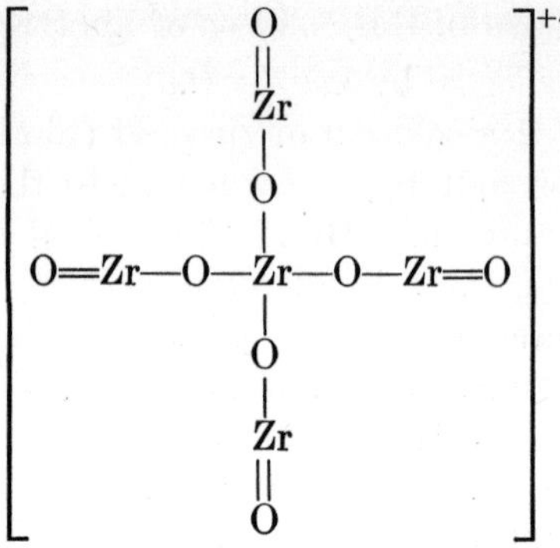

$$\left[\begin{array}{c} O \\ \parallel \\ Zr \\ | \\ O \\ | \\ O=Zr-O-Zr-O-Zr=O \\ | \\ O \\ | \\ Zr \\ \parallel \\ O \end{array} \right]^{+4}$$

and

$$\left[\begin{array}{c} O \\ \parallel \\ Zr \\ | \\ O \\ | \\ O=S=O \\ | \\ \begin{array}{ccc} O & O & O \\ \parallel & | & \parallel \\ O=Zr-O-S-O-Zr-O-S-O-Zr=O \\ \parallel & | & \parallel \\ O & O & O \end{array} \\ | \\ O=S=O \\ | \\ O \\ | \\ Zr \\ \parallel \\ O \end{array} \right]^{+4}$$

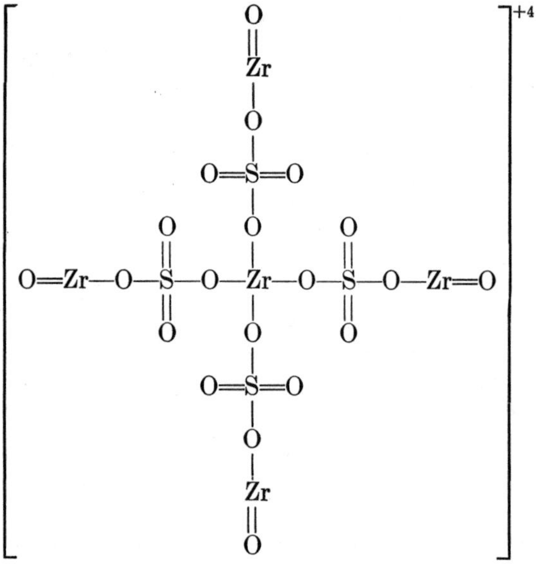

Examples of only the first of these are known. We have noted in our consideration of Leuchs's compound $-232\overline{11}$ that halogen ions in solution with sulfatozirconic acids promote the removal of sulfate groups from zirconium atoms by hydrolysis. Under conditions first noted by Rodd and his collaborators (67, 68), complete desulfating of zirconium has been achieved with formation of a pentazirconyl cation. They accomplished this by preparing a solution of sulfatozirconic acids containing somewhat more than 2 moles of sulfuric acid per mole of zirconium, the zirconium concentration being about 8 moles in 30-40 liters. While stirring, they added to this solution 100 cc of

---

67. E. H. Rodd, *J. Chem. Soc.* **111**, 396-407 (1917).

68a. R. T. Glazebrook, W. Rosenhain and E. H. Rodd, British Pat. **112,973**, Jan. 29, 1918.

68b. W. Rosenhain and E. H. Rodd, U.S. Patents **1,307,881** and **1,307,883**, June 24, 1919.

hydrochloric acid of specific gravity 1.15 followed by enough ammonia to initiate precipitation. They allowed the mixture to stand and precipitation continued. They washed the settled precipitate by decantation and found it to be a crude mixture containing 60-66% ZrO_2 and 15-10% of SO_3 by weight and minor amounts of some contaminating foreign oxides. They dissolved this crude precipitate in a solution of equal volumes of water and hydrochloric acid, specific gravity 1.15, and then concentrated the solution until on cooling abundant crystallization occurred. The solid so obtained was a mixture of zirconyl chloride and pentazirconyl chloride, the latter having the empirical formula $Zr_5O_8Cl_4 \cdot 22H_2O$. By redissolving this mixture and recrystallizing it from hydrochloric acid of specific gravity 1.088, they isolated the pentazirconyl chloride. They dissolved this chloride in thirty times its weight of water and added to the solution either sulfuric acid or a sulfate salt in amounts calculated to be equivalent to the chloride content of the zirconium salt. A precipitate formed of composition $Zr_5O_8(SO_4)_2 \cdot 14H_2O$.

The following interpretation of this process can be offered. When hydrochloric acid was added to the sulfatozirconic acid solution, it promoted the hydrolytic breakdown of the sulfatozirconate structure. Neglecting the hydration of the various species, this can be represented:

$$\text{HO}\overset{\overset{\text{O}}{\|}}{\underset{\underset{\text{O}}{\|}}{\text{S}}}\text{—O—}\overset{\overset{\text{O}}{\cdot\cdot}}{\text{Zr}}\text{—O—}\overset{\overset{\text{O}}{\|}}{\underset{\underset{\text{O}}{\|}}{\text{S}}}\text{—OH} + \text{OH}^- \rightarrow \text{HO—}\overset{\overset{\text{O}}{\cdot\cdot}}{\text{Zr}}\text{—O—}\overset{\overset{\text{O}}{\|}}{\underset{\underset{\text{O}}{\|}}{\text{S}}}\text{—OH} + \text{HSO}_4^-$$

$$\text{and} \quad \text{HO—}\overset{\overset{\text{O}}{\cdot\cdot}}{\text{Zr}}\text{—O—}\overset{\overset{\text{O}}{\|}}{\underset{\underset{\text{O}}{\|}}{\text{S}}}\text{—OH} + \text{OH}^- \rightarrow \text{HO—}\overset{\overset{\text{O}}{\cdot\cdot}}{\text{Zr}}\text{—OH} + \text{HSO}_4^- \quad (34\text{-}35)$$

The hydrolyzed species are unstable and combine:

$$2\text{HO—}\overset{\overset{\text{O}}{\cdot\cdot}}{\text{Zr}}\text{—O—}\overset{\overset{\text{O}}{\|}}{\underset{\underset{\text{O}}{\|}}{\text{S}}}\text{—OH} + 3\text{HO—}\overset{\overset{\text{O}}{\cdot\cdot}}{\text{Zr}}\text{—OH} \rightarrow$$

$$\begin{bmatrix} & & \overset{\text{O}}{\underset{\cdot\cdot}{}} & & \\ & & \text{Zr} & & \\ & & \overset{\cdot}{\text{O}} & & \\ \text{O}=\text{Zr—O—} & & \text{Zr} & \text{—O—Zr}=\text{O} \\ & & \overset{\cdot}{\text{O}} & & \\ & & \text{Zr} & & \\ & & \overset{\cdot\cdot}{\text{O}} & & \end{bmatrix}^{+4} (SO_4)_2 + 5H_2O \quad (36)$$

By trihydration of the 4 peripheral zirconyl groups and monohydration of the sulfate ions, the observed 14 hydrate is attained. In the more highly hydrated chloride compound, some of the water is probably held interstitially. The ready interconversion between the hydroxide, chloride, and sulfate of the pentazirconyl group indicates it to be a cation. Moreover, were the sulfate group to become covalently bound, it would result in an 8-membered ring:

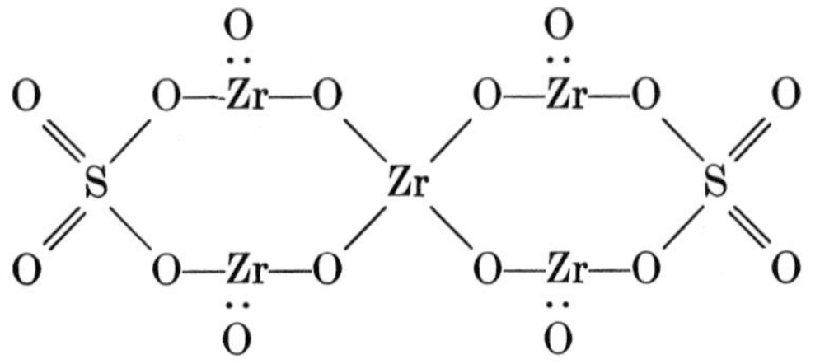

$$
\begin{array}{ccccccc}
 & \overset{\cdot\cdot}{O} & & & \overset{\cdot\cdot}{O} & & \\
O & O\!-\!Zr\!-\!O & & O\!-\!Zr\!-\!O & & O \\
\diagdown\!\!\!\!= & \diagdown\,\diagup & & \diagdown\,\diagup & & =\!\!\!\!\diagup \\
S & Zr & & S \\
=\!\!\!\!\diagup & \diagdown & \diagup & \diagdown & \diagdown\!\!\!\!= \\
O & O\!-\!Zr\!-\!O & & O\!-\!Zr\!-\!O & & O \\
 & \overset{\cdot\cdot}{O} & & & \overset{\cdot\cdot}{O} & &
\end{array}
$$

which is highly improbable.* The pentazirconyl sulfate can be represented

---

* Clearfield and Vaughan have shown that the species $Zr_4(OH)_8^{+8}$ is the stable ion in crystalline zirconyl chloride octahydrate (69). The bonding in this ion is represented in Figure 6.4a. Evidence for existence of this tetramer in aqueous solutions under certain conditions has also been shown (70). It is not unreasonable to expect that a similar ring formation occurs in the pentazirconyl compounds, and that such a structure is re-

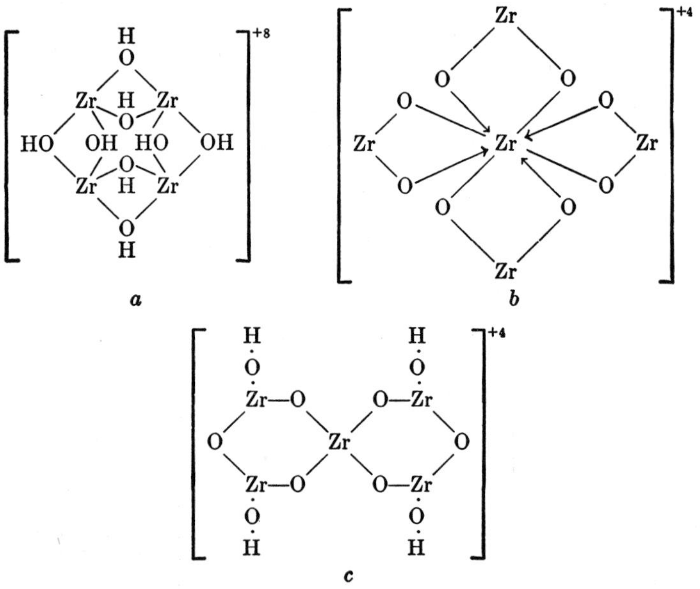

FIG. 6.4. Known and proposed ring structures formed in polyzirconyl cations. *a.* Tetramer structure in crystalline zirconyl chloride. *b* and *c.* Possible structures of the pentazirconyl cation.

numerically as $052\overline{14}$. Its molecular weight is 1028.456. It dissolves in sulfuric acid, doubtless with decomposition and formation of sulfato-zirconates.

According to Rodd (67) when the stoichiometric amount of sulfuric acid is added to a solution of pentazirconyl chloride, an almost quantitative yield of the sulfate $052\overline{14}$ is obtained. If ammonium or magnesium sulfate is used in place of sulfuric acid, the precipitate which first forms redissolves until about half of the equivalence of sulfate ion has been added. Then further addition of sulfate ion results in a permanent precipitate. This suggests the formation of an intermediate compound containing the ion $Zr_5O_8^{+2}$.

In a more recently reported preparation of $052\overline{14}$, a molar solution of zirconyl chloride was heated to 80° and 5 N sulfuric acid was added to obtain in the solution a ratio $Zr:SO_4 = 5:2$. The pH was then adjusted to 1.5 with 10 N sodium hydroxide. As this pH was approached, a precipitate of $052\overline{14}$ separated from the solution very rapidly as a fine, granular solid. After stirring the slurry for 15 minutes, it was once again adjusted to pH 1.5 and then filtered. The filter cake was washed with water adjusted to pH 1.5 with hydrochloric acid, since washing it with water caused it to gel and made the passage of water excessively slow. After drying the filter cake at 80°, a product was recovered the analysis of which showed it to be penta-zirconyl sulfate with 14-16 molecules of water (70b).

ZIRCONIUM SULFONATES

We have seen in our study of the sulfatozirconic acids and of pentazir-conyl sulfate that zirconium can combine with sulfate ions to form complex anions or salts. It might be surmised that the same would be true of the combination of zirconium with the organic sulfonic acids. The anions of these acids might become either covalently or electrovalently bound to zirconium or they might form bonds with both covalent and electrovalent character. Thus possibilities exist for the formation of salts such as $ZrOOHSO_3R$, $ZrO(SO_3R)_2$, and $Zr_5O_8(SO_3R)_2$, and covalent compounds such as

---

sponsible for its stability. A 4-membered or a 6-membered ring can be visualized, as represented in Figure 6.4, *b* and *c*, respectively. Perhaps the likelihood of the 6-membered ring is greater because of the lower degree of strain and the lower coordination number for the central zirconium atom. Although coordination number 8 is known for zirconium in zirconium acetylacetonate and its derivatives and in tetramandelatozirconic acid, it is probably achieved only under very favorable steric conditions.

69. A. Clearfield and P. Vaughan, publication pending in *Acta Cryst.*

70. J. S. Johnson, K. A. Kraus, and R. W. Holmberg, *J. Am. Chem. Soc.* 78, 26 (1956).

70b. G. H. Beyer, E. L. Koerner, and E. H. Olson, *U.S. Atomic Energy Comm. Report ISC-634*, Aug. 18, 1955.

$$R{-}O{-}\overset{O}{\underset{O}{\overset{..}{\underset{..}{S}}}}{-}O{-}Zr{-}O{-}\overset{O}{\underset{O}{\overset{..}{\underset{..}{S}}}}{-}O{-}R$$

The absence of a second functional hydrogen atom or ion in compounds of the class HSO_3R limits the complexity and variety of its zirconium derivatives.

No extensive studies have been made of the sulfonates, particularly as to their chemical behavior and structure. Nearly all the published knowledge of these compounds is on the combinations of zirconium with sulfonated dyes. Some such dyes, for example 2-hydroxy-5-methylazobenzene-4-sulfonic acid, have been used in analysis for the detection of zirconium (71). Many of the sulfonated dyes used in the detection of zirconium contain groups other than the sulfonate group which are capable of forming very stable bonds with zirconium, and hence the role of the sulfonate group in these dyes is obscured. Examples are anthraquinone sulfonic acid (72) and arsenical dyes (73).

Although Crossley and Shafer list zirconium with a group of metals which they believed capable of forming soluble metallized sulfonated dyes (74), it now appears to be generally characteristic of the zirconium compounds of these dyes that they are very sparingly soluble. Wainer and van Mater prepared lake pigments of sulfonated dyes on hydrous zirconia (75), and Blumenthal showed that when solutions of zirconyl chloride or trioxodizirconium chloride are added to solutions of sulfonated dyes, reactions occur in stoichiometric proportions, with formation of very insoluble compounds suitable for use as pigment toners. He added zirconyl chloride solutions to dye solutions held at 50° and trioxodizirconium chloride solutions to dye solutions held at 95°, and obtained precipitates of the compositions shown in Table 6.1 (76, 77). It was observed that using zirconyl chloride at the lower temperature, the compositions recovered correspond to compounds of the ions ZrO^{++} and $ZrOOH^+$, while with trioxodizirconium chloride, $Zr_2O_3Cl_2$, at the higher temperature the compositions corresponded to salts of $(HO)_2Zr_5O_8^{+2}$, except in the case of Ponceau 2R, which gave a compound of $Zr_2O_3^{++}$.

We have seen in the preceding section that disulfatozirconic acid,

71. V. I. Kuznetsov, *J. Applied Chem.* (U.S.S.R.) 13, 1257-61 (1940).
72. J. H. Yoe, *Virginia J. Sci.* 3, No. 1, 8-10 (1942).
73. V. I. Kuznetsov, *Compt. rend. acad. Sci. U.R.S.S.* 31, 898-900 (1941).
74. M. L. Crossley and L. M. Shafer, U.S. Patents 2,086,854, July 13, 1937; 2,136,650, Nov. 15, 1938.
75. E. Wainer and H. van Mater, U.S. Patent 2,452,616, Nov. 2, 1948.
76. W. B. Blumenthal, *Ind. Eng. Chem.* 40, 510-12 (1948).
77. Blumenthal, U.S. Patent 2,626,255, Jan. 20, 1953.

TABLE 6.1. EMPIRICAL FORMULAS OF ZIRCONIUM COMPOUNDS OF SULFONATED DYES

Name of Dye	Precipitant	Empirical Formula of Reaction Product
Acid green	$ZrOCl_2$	$ZrO(ZrOOH)_4[(SO_3)_2C_{37}H_{35}N_2Cl]_3$
Acid green	$Zr_2O_3Cl_2$	$(HO)_2Zr_5O_8(SO_3)_2C_{37}H_{35}N_2Cl$
Erioglaucine	$ZrOCl_2$	$ZrO(ZrOOH)_{10}[(SO_3)_3C_{37}H_{34}N_2Cl]_4$
Erioglaucine	$Zr_2O_3Cl_2$	$[(HO)_2Zr_5O_8]_3[(SO_3)_3C_{37}H_{34}N_2Cl]_2$
Fast light yellow 3G	$ZrOCl_2$	$ZrOOHSO_3C_{16}H_{13}ON_4$
Fast light yellow 3G	$Zr_2O_3Cl_2$	$(HO)_2Zr_5O_8[SO_3C_{16}H_{13}ON_3]_2$
Orange II	$ZrOCl_2$	$ZrOOHSO_3C_{16}H_{11}ON_2$
Orange II	$Zr_2O_3Cl_2$	$(HO)_2Zr_5O_8[SO_3C_{16}H_{11}ON_2]_2$
Ponceau 2R	$ZrOCl_2$	$(ZrOOH)_2(SO_3)_2C_{18}H_{14}N_2$
Ponceau 2R	$Zr_2O_3Cl_2$	$Zr_2O_3(SO_3)_2C_{18}H_{14}N_2$
Quinoline yellow	$ZrOCl_2$	$ZrO(ZrOOH)_2[(SO_3)_2C_{18}H_9O_2]_2$
Tartrazine yellow	$ZrOCl_2$	$ZrO(ZrOOH)_4[CO_2(SO_3)_2C_{15}H_9ON_4]_2$

$H_2ZrO(SO_4)_2 \cdot 3H_2O$ is hydrolyzed to pentazirconyl sulfate, $Zr_5O_8(SO_4)_2 \cdot 14H_2O$ in the presence of chlorides. Apparently a similar hydrolysis and condensation occur in hot solutions containing trioxodizirconium chloride and the sulfonated dye.

The compound of zirconium with the dye Erioglaucine has found considerable use as a printing-ink pigment, and it is prepared as follows: 120 g of the dye is dissolved in hot water and brought to a volume of 4,000 ml, temperature $95° \pm 5°$, and pH 2.8 ± 0.2.

Separately, 330 g zirconyl chloride is dissolved in water, adjusted to 3200 ml at 25°, and to this a solution containing 64 g of soda ash dissolved in 300 ml of water is added slowly until the pH of the mixture is 2.55 ± 0.05. The solution then contains $Zr_2O_3Cl_2$. It is heated to 50° and added slowly to the dye solution while maintaining the pH and temperature of the latter at the values given above. After the addition the slurry is stirred briefly, chilled, filtered, and the precipitate washed well, using wash water which has been adjusted to pH 3.5 with hydrochloric acid.* The precipitate is dried at 55° to obtain a soft, intensely blue pigment of good stability (77).

THIOSULFATES

The thiosulfate ion is decomposed by acids, even at low concentrations. It would not be expected, therefore, that thiosulfates of zirconium could be formed. The anion would be decomposed in acidic environment and replaced by hydroxyl in neutral or alkaline environments.

A number of observers have reported that when sodium thiosulfate is added to a cold zirconyl chloride solution, a precipitate is formed, and

---

* A final rinse with 1% boric acid solution improves the brightness of the pigment in dried oil films.

there has been an impression that the precipitate was a basic thiosulfate mixed with sulfur (2b, 78, 79). However, it appears most likely that the addition of sodium thiosulfate to zirconyl chloride precipitates hydrous zirconia and leads to the decomposition of most if not all of the thiosulfate ion to sulfur and sulfurous acid. The sulfurous acid is then sequestered by the hydrous zirconia and part of the sulfur is entrapped physically by the gelatinous precipitate. If sufficient sodium thiosulfate is added to bring the pH nearly to the neutral point, some thiosulfate ion may survive and be adsorbed by the zirconia. According to Canneri and Fernandes, a composition represented by the formula $Cu_2Zr(S_2O_3)_3 \cdot 3OH_2O$ was obtained by the reaction of zirconium salts with copper sulfate in aqueous solution in the presence of a high concentration of sodium thiosulfate (80).

78. A. Strohmeyer, *Ann.* **113,** 125 (1859).
79. F. P. Venable and C. Baskerville, *J. Am. Chem. Soc.* **17,** 448 (1895).
80. C. Canneri and L. Fernandes, *Gaz. chim. ital.* **55,** 440 (1925).

7

Compounds of Other Inorganic Acids

SOME GENERALIZATIONS

From the exposition of the halogenides (see Chap. 4) and the sulfato-zirconates (see Chap. 6), it has been seen that the zirconium salts may contain either complex cations such as hydrated ZrO^{+2}, $ZrOOH^+$, $Zr_2O_3^{+2}$, and $Zr_5O_8^{+4}$, or complex anions such as hydrated $ZrO(SO_4)^{-2}$, $ZrOH(SO_4)_3^{-3}$, and $Zr(SO_4)_4^{-4}$. In aqueous solutions these species tend to attain the highest coordination number sterically possible by combination with water, and usually coordination numbers of 5, 6, or 7 are attained. Zirconium is not known to form a monatomic ion, and whether it occurs in a complex cation or anion is determined by the bond character of the zirconium compound. There is no predominating tendency for zirconium to form either cations or anions. In the solid state the ClBrI tetrahalogenides appear to consist of both zirconium-containing cations and anions, and the structure can be represented by the formula $(ZrA_n)^{4-n}(ZrA_{8-n})^{n-4}$. There is thus a disproportionation of the halogen atoms which is reflected in the formation of equivalent amounts of cations and anions.

When a zirconium compound is dissolved in water or other ionizing solvent, such as liquid ammonia, certain stereotyped reactions generally occur, which can be illustrated simply by examining the case for a zirconium compound of molecular formula ZrA_4 in water. It will tend to be hydrated to give the structure

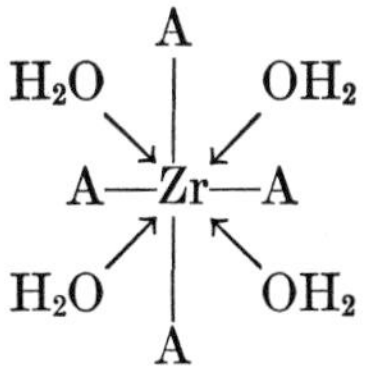

$$
\begin{array}{ccc}
 & A & \\
H_2O & \diagdown \mid \diagup & OH_2 \\
A & \!\!-Zr-\!\! & A \\
H_2O & \diagup \mid \diagdown & OH_2 \\
 & A & \\
\end{array}
$$

If the size and shape of A, however, does not permit the approach of 4 water molecules to a bond length from the zirconium nucleus, fewer than 4 water molecules will become bound, and the pictures for the following changes will be somewhat altered but retain the same general characteristics. Ionizations of the following types will tend to occur:

279

$$ZrA_4 \cdot 4H_2O \xrightarrow{nH_2O} ZrA_{4-n} \cdot (4 + n)(H_2O)^{+n} + nA^-$$

$$ZrA_4 \cdot 4H_2O \longrightarrow nH^+ + (Zr(A - H)_n A_{4-n} \cdot 4H_2O)^{-n}$$

(1-2)

Equation 2 assumes A to be a radical containing an ionizable hydrogen atom, e.g., HSO_4. It is seen from these equations that whether zirconium occurs in a cation or in an anion in aqueous solutions of zirconium compounds is determined by the relative bond strengths of atoms and groups in the molecule under the prevailing environmental conditions. If the Zr—A bond

is strong and the O—H bond relatively weak, as in the case of $Zr-O\overset{O}{\underset{O}{S}}OH$ in

acidic solutions, hydrogen ions and complex zirconium anions will form by dissociation.* If the relative bonding strengths are in the reverse order, A^- anions and complex zirconium cations will form. Stated somewhat differently: if the zirconium compound exchanges an A radical for an aquo group, the zirconium species will become a cation; if it releases a proton for aquation and hydronium ion formation, the zirconium species becomes an anion. While these trends may have superimposed on them other reactions, such as the replacement of A radicals by hydroxo, OH, their importance as determinants of the type of zirconium species remains as part of the complex of reactions.

In the crystalline and glassy states, zirconium compounds retain the same tendency toward attaining to the maximum coordination number as was the case in solution. During crystallization there is competition between two processes by which maximum coordination number may be attained, *solvation* and *giant-molecule formation*. In the former process there is a tendency toward satisfying the maximum coordination number by bonding with molecules of solvent and in the latter a tendency to do the same by formation of bonds with atoms in adjacent positions in the crystal lattice. (However, if the zirconium compound already contains zirconium at its maximum coordination number in the molecule, as in zirconium tetraacetylacetonate, both tendencies will be already completely fulfilled.) The properties of the solid are largely determined by which process prevails for attaining high coordination number. In zirconyl chloride crystals, the prevailing zirconium species is $Zr_4(OH)_8^{+8}$, water molecules are grouped around this polymeric ion, and no cross-linking occurs between unit zirconium species. When the crystal is added to water, it is readily dissolved and the zirconium polymers are simply lifted out of the lattice into the solution, where they are decomposed to $ZrOOH^+$ units. On the other hand, zircon which crystallizes from a melt in nature and has been similarly crystallized in the laboratory has

---

* The cations need not be hydrogen, but can equally well be metallic cations, particularly alkali or alkaline earth metal ions. Strictly, zirconium compounds of this category are salts only when metal cations are present; otherwise they are acids.

extensive internal bonding from zirconium atoms through oxygen to silicon atoms, in three dimensions; it is in effect a giant molecule and strongly resists dissolution and chemical or thermal decomposition. Potassium hexa-fluozirconate appears from its analysis to contain hexacoordinated zirconium atoms. But its aqueous solutions exhibit the apparent anomaly of an alkali salt having an acidic reaction. The 10% solution has a pH of about 4.0. This indicates a higher coordination number than 6 for the zirconium atom in the aqueous solution:

$$ZrF_6^{-2} + H_2O \rightarrow ZrOHF_6^{-3} + H^+ \tag{3}$$

It may be inferred that even in the crystalline solid, zirconium attains a coordination number greater than 6 by bonding with adjacent fluorine atoms, and that this accounts for the refractory character of the crystal. Indeed, the formation of the crystal from an aqueous solution may be described as a chemical reaction represented by the equation

$$4K^+ + 2H^+ + 2ZrOHF_6^{-3} \rightarrow 2K_2ZrF_6 + 2H_2O \tag{4}$$

It may be generalized that strongly internally bonded zirconium compounds will be relatively hard, refractory, and chemically inert and will exhibit low solubilities. Solubilities will be governed to a large extent by the strength of bonds formed by solvation. Zirconyl chloride, with no internal cross-bonding, is readily dissolved not only by water but also by alcohols. Potassium fluozirconate is dissolved by water but not by alcohols. Solids such as zirconia and zircon, which are extensively cross-linked by valence bonds, are insoluble in water and resist dissolution by acids and alkalies. Solvation and dissolution occur only when there is a decrease in free energy in going from the internal cross-linking bond to the solvation bond.

The presence of zirconium cations, such as hydrated ZrO^{+2} or $ZrOOH^+$, is prima-facie evidence of the absence of anions which would replace aquo groups from the zirconium species and reduce their positive charge. Certain anions are capable of reducing the charge to zero and others of reversing the charge:

$$\begin{aligned} ZrOOH^+ + NO_3^- &\rightarrow ZrOOHNO_3 \\ ZrOOH^+ + 2C_2H_3O_2^- &\rightarrow ZrOOH(C_2H_3O_2)^- \end{aligned} \tag{5-6}$$

Some anions, such as chloride, bromide, iodide, molybdate,* tungstate, and ferrocyanide, have been noted empirically to have less affinity for zirconium than water. If simple salts containing these anions are added to an aqueous solution containing zirconium cations, at first no reaction occurs. If the salt has an alkaline hydrolysis, however, the pH of the mixed solution rises

---

* While the simple molybdate ion appears not to displace an aquo group from zirconium, polymolybdate ions have been observed to form complexes with zirconium in aqueous media.

as the salt is added until finally hydrous zirconia is precipitated. An equilibrium is then set up between adsorbed water and adsorbed anion:

$$ZrO_2 \cdot xH_2O + yX^- \rightleftharpoons ZrO_2 \cdot (x - y)H_2O \cdot yX^{-y} + yH_2O \qquad (7)$$

If the proportion of the anion X^- in the solid is high, and particularly if it approaches a real or fancied stoichiometric proportion, the solid is apt to be reported in the literature as a compound, even though no data other than the analytical data were available to support such an assertion.

The charge on the micelles of hydrous zirconia with absorbed X^- ion will not be strictly equivalent to the charge of the adsorbed ions because of another coexisting equilibrium involving protonation of the aquo groups:

$$ZrO_2 \cdot (x - y)H_2O \cdot yX^{-y} + zH_3O^+ \rightleftharpoons$$
$$ZrO_2 \cdot (x - y - z)H_2O \cdot yX \cdot zH_3O^{z-y} + zH_2O \qquad (8)$$

The more strongly acidic the slurry of hydrous zirconia, the farther reaction 8 will be displaced to the right and the more positive or less negative will be the charge on the micelles. Moreover, high positive charge on the micelles favors displacement of reaction 7 to the right and increase of the content of ion X^- in the solid. When alkalies are added to slurries of complexes of the types illustrated in equations 7 and 8, the reactions are displaced toward the left and eventually all the X^- ions and some of the aquo groups are replaced by hydroxyl ions.

COMPOUNDS AND COMPLEXES WITH MONOBASIC ACIDS*

It has been shown in Chapter 3 that in the absence of substances tending to supply donor atoms for coordination reactions (Lewis bases), the halogens form tetrahalogenides of empirical formula ZrX_4 and complex halogenides of empirical formula M_nZrX_{4+n}, where n is 1, 2, or 3. The composition ZrX_4 tends to approach the structure of the M_nZrX_{4-n} complexes by disproportionation of halogen atoms to give $(ZrX_{4-n})(ZrX_{4+n})$. It may be stated broadly that halogenoids tend to act like halogens in this respect, and we may define halogenoids for present consideration as univalent radicals or anions which do not contain halogen atoms or oxygen. Oxygen-containing radicals are excluded because the tendency of oxygen to form undissociatable covalent linkages with zirconium is so great that radicals and ions containing oxygen depart from the behavior typical of halogens. Actually there are only three halogenoid radicals on which any considerable data are

---

* In this section and in the following sections of Chapter 7, the zirconium derivatives of various acids will be studied in groups according to the basicity of the acid. But where an element in a given oxidation state, such as pentavalent phosphorus, forms several oxy acids of differing basicities, all of these acids will be studied together in the group represented by the most common or most characteristic basicity.

available: the amido, thiocyanato, and borohydride radicals. The amido compounds have been discussed in Chapter 3, and the sparse data on thiocyanato compounds show them to be essentially similar in type to the halogen compounds.

Hydrous zirconia has been dissolved in dilute thiocyanic acid and concentrated by evaporation over a sand bath until syrupy. After taking up the syrup in alcohol and then adding ether, a solid of composition $ZrOOHSCN \cdot 2H_2O$ was precipitated, analogous to a chloride obtained in similar fashion (1, 2). Hydrous zirconia was also dissolved in a solution of thiocyanic acid in absolute alcohol and pyridine or quinoline were added. Solids precipitated which appeared to be the hexathiocyanato complexes, $(C_5H_5NH)_2Zr(CNS)_6$ and $(C_9H_7NH)_2Zr(CNS)_6$ (1), also analogous to chlorine compounds. All thiocyanato compounds can be expected to hydrolyze in water to give hydrated zirconium cations, particularly $ZrOOH^+$, and thiocyanate anions.

When aqueous solutions of zirconium and hafnium thiocyanates are equilibrated with hexone, a hexone solution of a zirconium complex impoverished in hafnium is obtained (3). This has been the basis of an important process for obtaining hafnium-free zirconium.

Zirconium and hafnium borohydrides have been prepared by metatheses of the tetrachlorides or pentafluometallates with aluminum borohydride:

$$3ZrCl_4 + 4Al(BH_4)_3 \rightarrow 3Zr(BH_4)_4 + 4AlCl_3$$
$$3NaZrF_5 + 4Al(BH_4)_3 \rightarrow 3Zr(BH_4)_4 + 4AlF_3 + 3NaF$$

$$(9\text{-}10)$$

Unlike thorium tetrafluoride, zirconium and hafnium tetrafluorides will not react directly with aluminum borohydride.

The zirconium and hafnium compounds appear not to be perfectly stoichiometric and analyses corresponding to $Zr_{1.04}B_{4.06}H_{16}$ and $Hf_{1.03}B_{3.98}H_{16}$ have been reported. When the borohydride is prepared from zirconium tetrachloride, some difficulty is experienced in separating it from aluminum chloride, and it has been suspected that there is a tendency toward complex formation between the two compounds (4).

For the preparation of hafnium borohydride, 0.8768 g (2.52 millimoles) of sodium pentafluohafnate was introduced into a reaction chamber, which was evacuated. An excess of aluminum borohydride was distilled into the chamber and condensed on the fluohafnate. The amount of aluminum borohydride used was 211.6 cc at standard temperature and pressure, or 9.45

1. A. Rosenheim and P. Frank, *Ber.* **40**, 803-10 (1907).

2. H. Endemann, *J. prakt. Chem.* (2) **11**, 219 (1875).

3a. W. R. Grimes, C. J. Barton, Sr., L. G. Overholser, J. P. Blakely, and J. D. Redman, *U.S. Atomic Energy Comm. Y-560* (1950).

3b. Overholser, Barton and Grimes, *U.S. Atomic Energy Comm. Y-431* and *Y-477* (1949).

4. H. R. Hoekstra and J. J. Katz, *J. Am. Chem. Soc.* **71**, 2488-92 (1949).

millimoles. The chamber was sealed and the reactants allowed to stand for several days at room temperature. Finally the reaction chamber was placed in a vacuum system, freed of air, and the volatile components pumped off and fractionated through a series of two condensation chambers immersed in an ice-salt mixture and in liquid nitrogen, respectively. The hafnium fluoborate condensed in the former and the aluminum borohydride in the latter chamber. It was found possible to improve the purity of the hafnium borohydride by resublimation. The zirconium compound was prepared similarly (5). The properties which have been given for zirconium and hafnium borohydrides (4) are shown in Table 7.1.

TABLE 7.1. PROPERTIES FOR ZIRCONIUM AND HAFNIUM BOROHYDRIDES

Property	Zirconium borohydride	Hafnium borohydride
Melting point	29°	28.7°
Boiling point (extrap.)	118	123
Heat of subl., kg cal/mole	13	13.6
Heat of fusion, kg cal/mole	3.4	4.3
Values for A*	2844, 2097	2983, 2039
for B*	10.719, 8.247	10.919, 8.032

* For the vapor pressure equation $\log p = -\dfrac{A}{T} + B$; the first values given are for the solid and the second for the liquid.

The borohydrides are the most volatile compounds of zirconium and hafnium known. Their greater volatility than that of the chlorides indicates them to be substantially covalent compounds, resembling titanium tetrachloride (b.p. 136.4°) rather than zirconium tetrachloride (subl. 331°). The disproportionation of chlorine ions of the tetrachloride is not paralleled by a similar disproportionation of borohydride groups in the tetraborohydride because of the absence of an inert pair of electrons on the boron atom. The bonding arrangement shown in the representation below seems reasonable for this compound, and the hydrogen ions are probably situated very close to the zirconium atom, perhaps complexed by the 4p and 4d electrons.

$$(H^+)_4 \begin{bmatrix} H \\ HBH \\ H \quad \downarrow \quad H \\ HB \rightarrow Zr \leftarrow BH \\ H \quad \uparrow \quad H \\ HBH \\ H \end{bmatrix}^{-4}$$

---

5. H. R. Hoekstra and J. J. Katz, U.S. Patent **2,575,760**, Nov. 20, 1951.

Of the oxygen-containing monobasic acids, only those containing 3 or more oxygen atoms have been found to form stable compounds under conditions studied up to the present time. The acids containing 1 or 2 oxygen atoms, such as hypochlorous and nitrous acids, are too weak to form compounds in aqueous environments with the extremely weakly basic zirconia, and moreover these acids are generally unstable in the presence of acid-reacting materials, such as the zirconium salts, which might be used in the preparation of zirconium compounds of low-oxygen acids. It is not improbable, though, that under suitable conditions zirconium compounds of some of the 1-oxygen-atom and 2-oxygen-atom acids could be prepared. Many examples are known of zirconium compounds with 3-oxygen-atom and 4-oxygen-atom acids.

In the earlier studies of zirconium nitrates, the investigators were not clear as to when they were dealing with zirconyl nitrate and when with zirconium tetranitrate, and they were prone to regard a solution containing 4 molecules of nitric acid per zirconium atom as a tetranitrate solution. The clarification of the problem of molecular species in systems containing zirconium and nitrate ions or radicals has progressed somewhat in recent years; but much remains to be learned in order to permit a sound delineation of the structures and species in these systems.

When hydrous zirconia is dissolved in nitric acid solutions containing more than 4 moles of nitric acid per mole of zirconia added, and the solution is evaporated at a temperature not higher than $15°$, crystals of $Zr(NO_3)_4 \cdot 5H_2O$ separate (1, 6, 7). When a 52% solution of nitric acid was used, good yields were obtained after slow evaporation over several weeks of time. If care is not taken to adhere closely to proved conditions for forming these crystals, none of this product is obtained (8). In fuming nitric acid, a hexahydrate is formed (9).

Zirconium nitrate, $Zr(NO_3)_4 \cdot 5H_2O$ or $H_2ZrO(NO_3)_4 \cdot 4H_2O$, formula weight 429.332, is a colorless, hygroscopic, crystalline solid which gives off nitric acid in dry air. Thermal decomposition has been reported to occur in stages at approximately $140°$, $220°$, and $350-400°$, final decomposition to zirconium dioxide occurring at the last temperature (10). The water of hydration can be replaced at room temperature by other molecules. Antipyrine gives $Zr(NO_3)_4 \cdot 6C_{11}H_{12}N_2O$ (11). Because of the instability of zirconium nitrate under most conditions, there are relatively little data on its properties. It has been noted to be diamagnetic and to have a mass sus-

6. S. R. Paykull, *Ber.* **12**, 1719 (1879).
7. H. Pied and M. Falinski, *Compt. rend.* **198**, 1505-6 (1934).
8. E. Chauvenet and L. Nicolle, *Compt. rend.* **166**, 781-3, 821-4 (1918).
9. M. Falinski, *Ann. chim.* **16**, 237-325 (1941).
10. R. Ruff and J. Moczala, *Z. anorg. allgem. Chem.* **133**, 193-219 (1914).
11. A. Kolb, *Z. anorg. allgem. Chem.* **83**, 146 (1913).

ceptibility of -0.211×10^{-6} (12), and to react with hydrogen in the silent discharge to form ammonium nitrate, zirconia, ammonium nitrite, and nitrogen dioxide (13). Observations of Raman frequencies at 720, 1048, and 1400 have indicated the symmetry D_{3n} (14). Many of the studies of aqueous solutions of the salt are not conclusive because the investigators were not informed on the nature of the hydrolysis which changed the structure of the zirconium nitrate. The following literature may be cited: dehydration (16); electrolysis of aqueous solutions (15); effect on aqueous solution of a disaccharide (22); solubility in ether (17) and extraction into ether from 8 M nitric acid (21); Raman spectra of solutions (20); X-ray patterns of the solid (18) and of the aqueous solution (19).

Zirconyl nitrate of composition $Zr(NO_3)_2 \cdot 2H_2O$ is the phase most commonly obtained from aqueous solutions containing zirconium and nitrate ions (8, 23). Even those strong nitric acid solutions, from which zirconium tetranitrate will crystallize at low temperatures, yield zirconyl nitrate above 15° (1). Solutions which yield zirconyl nitrate can be prepared by mixing zirconium chlorides with nitric acid as well as by dissolving hydrous zirconia in nitric acid (24). A hemiheptahydrate, $ZrO(NO_3)_2 \cdot 3\frac{1}{2}H_2O$, can be obtained from aqueous solutions below 10°. It effloresces in room air to form the dihydrate (8, 25). The anhydrous zirconyl nitrate could not be prepared (8).

Zirconyl nitrate, $ZrO(NO_3)_2 \cdot 2H_2O$, formula weight 267.268, is a colorless crystalline compound which is stable in air at ordinary room temperature. When exposed to gaseous ammonia, 1 mole will absorb 2 moles of ammonia (11). Dehydration studies in air showed the composition $2ZrOOHNO_3 \cdot ZrO(NO_3)_2 \cdot nH_2O$ at 110°, $2ZrOOHNO_3 \cdot ZrO_2 \cdot 3H_2O$ at 150°, $2ZrOOH-NO_3 \cdot 6ZrO_2 \cdot 4H_2O$ at 215°, $2ZrOOHNO_3 \cdot 9ZrO_2 \cdot 3H_2O$ at 250°, and ZrO_2 at 300°. In the presence of nitric acid vapor, the composition at 120° was $ZrO(NO_3)_2 \cdot ZrOOHNO_3 \cdot 3H_2O$ (8). Zirconyl nitrate is very soluble in water. When a mole of the salt was mixed with a varying number n of moles

12. S. Meyer, *Wied. Ann.* **69**, 241 (1899); *Monatsh.* **20**, 793 (1899).
13. Susumu Miyamoto, *J. Chem. Soc. Japan* **54**, 1223-32 (1933).
14. M. Rolla, *Atti. accad. Italia, Rend. classe sci. fis. mat. nat.* (7) **1**, 563-74 (1940).
15. A. Müller, *Z. anorg. allgem. Chem.* **52**, 316-24 (1907).
16. E. Löwenstein, *Z. anorg. allgem. Chem.* **63**, 69-139 (1909).
17. R. C. Wells, *J. Wash. Acad. Sci.* **20**, 146-8 (1930).
18. H. T. Mayer, *Naturwiss.* **18**, 34 (1930).
19. J. A. Prins and R. Fonteyne, *Physica* **2**, 1016-28 (1935).
20. M. Rolla, *Boll. sci. facoltà chim. ind., Bologna* **1941**, 13-15.
21. R. and Eleanore Bock, *Z. anorg. allgem. Chem.* **263**, 146-68 (1950).
22. G. A. Abbott, *Proc. N. Dakota Acad. Sci.* **7**, 41-4 (1953).
23. M. Weibull, *Acta Univ. Lund.* **18**, 34 (1881).
24. C. J. Kinzie and D. S. Hake, U.S. Patent **2,285,443**, June 9, 1942; British patent **555,988**, Sept. 15, 1943.
25. J. A. Ayres, *J. Am. Chem. Soc.* **69**, 2879-81 (1947).

of water and the mixtures brought to room temperature and dissolved in water, the following heats of solution were observed:

1. Value of n......0 ......1 ......1.5......2.17.....2.76.....4

2. Heat of solution..2.17... −0.50... −1.92... −2.77... −3.95... −5.90

A curve formed from these data shows a transition point corresponding to the hemiheptahydrate (8).

When an aqueous solution of zirconyl nitrate was passed through Amberlite IR-100 resin cation exchanger and Amberlite JR-4 anion exchanger, only 2% of the zirconium was retained. Only 1% was retained when the sodium salt of the resin was used * (25). This indicates that the zirconium in the solution is almost entirely in a nonionic species, probably $ZrOOHNO_3$. Ignoring hydration,

$$ZrO(NO_3)_2 + H_2O \rightarrow ZrOOHNO_3 + H^+ + NO_3^- \qquad (11)$$

Cryoscopic measurement indicate 3 ions or molecules to be present per molecule of zirconyl nitrate introduced (8). The establishment of equilibrium has been followed by conductivity measurements. For an 0.01 N solution at 29.5°, the conductivity changed from an initial value of 505.19 to 554 in a few hours, and to 600 in a few days, at which time some precipitate of composition $ZrOOHNO_3 \cdot nH_2O$ had separated.** The addition of 0.01 N sodium hydroxide to the solution resulted in conductivity changes at points corresponding to the neutralization of the free hydrogen ion represented in equation 11 and at complete conversion of the $ZrOOHNO_3$ to hydrous zirconia (8; cf. 26). For measurements of the dielectric constant of zirconyl nitrate solution and determination of its molar polarization, see reference 27.

Since zirconyl nitrate is more expensive than zirconyl chloride, the latter has been used in industry whenever there was a choice between the two. Solutions of zirconyl nitrate however, have been used to some extent in industry for undisclosed applications, and there have been several published recommended uses. Solutions of zirconyl nitrate have been noted to gel polyvinyl alcohol and have been recommended for use in preparing photographic plates, films, or paper coated with polyvinyl alcohol emulsion (29). The solutions are also said to improve lamination bonds of polyvinyl

---

* Zirconyl and hafnyl nitrate solutions have been purified by passing them through Amberlite IR-100 resin (28).

** Basic precipitates have been noted to separate from zirconyl nitrate solutions under several conditions, such as on electrolysis and on addition of certain salts (15).

26. Yosiaga Oka, *Bull. Tokyo Univ. Eng.* **8**, 21 (1939).

27. R. T. Lattey and W. G. Davies, *Phil. Mag.* **13**, 444-55 (1932).

28. J. A. Ayres, U.S. Patent **2,567,661**, Sept. 11, 1951.

29. W. G. Lowe, U.S. Patent **2,455,936**, Dec. 14, 1948.

alcohol coated surfaces (30). Another recommended use is for the dissolution of difficultly soluble sulfates, such as those of lead, calcium, strontium, and barium (31).

Basic zirconyl nitrate, $ZrOOHNO_3 \cdot 2H_2O$, has been isolated from a solution of zirconyl nitrate in absolute alcohol by precipitation with ether (2). No data are available giving details of the property of this compound.

No complex nitrates of zirconium are known, aside from the acid $H_2Zr(NO_3)_6 \cdot 4H_2O$ which was identified by M. Falinski as a phase separating from a solution of hydrous zirconia in very strong, fuming nitric acid (9). Nothing has been ascertained of the structure of this compound and no salts are known.

Superficially, chloric acid $HClO_3$ and iodic acid HIO_3 are similar to nitric acid HNO_3, and certain similarities should be found between their zirconium compounds. Actually, the similarities are overlaid by marked differences which are reflections of the larger sizes of the oxyhalogen anions relative to the nitrate anion and the higher coordination numbers attainable by these halogen atoms relative to nitrogen. A zirconyl chlorate, $ZrO(ClO_3)_2 \cdot 6H_2O$, has been reported only once (32). It was made by adding an equivalence of barium chlorate to an aqueous solution of disulfatozirconic acid, filtering off the precipitated barium sulfate, and evaporating the filtrate over caustic potash. The solid obtained was very soluble in water. As against this, potassium chlorate was added to a solution of zirconyl perchlorate, the precipitated potassium perchlorate filtered off, and the filtrate evaporated. The composition of the solid recovered was $ZrO(ClO_3)_2 \cdot ZrOOHClO_3$. The crystals were reported to be unstable, soluble in alcohol, and insoluble in ether (33, 34). Aside from this, little is known about the chlorates.

Hydrous zirconia dissolves in iodic acid. In one of the early studies, zirconium tetraiodate but not zirconyl iodate was recovered from the solution (33), nor was zirconyl iodate subsequently isolated by later investigators. It was found that the addition of iodic acid to zirconyl nitrate solutions gave precipitates of varying compositions, consisting of zirconium hydroxyiodates of low solubility in water or dilute nitric acid (33, 35), but no compounds were isolated having 2 iodate ions per zirconium atom (33, 36, 37, 39). Compounds containing 1, 3, 4, 4½, 6, and 9 iodate ions per zirconium

30. G. F. Nadeau and C. B. Stark, U.S. Patent **2,541,478**, Feb. 13, 1951.

31. A. H. Angerman, U.S. Patent **2,514,115**, July 4, 1950.

32. M. Weibull, *Acta Univ. Lund.* II, 18; V, 53 (1881).

33. F. P. Venable and I. W. Smithey, *J. Am. Chem. Soc.* **41**, 1722-7 (1919).

34. F. P. Venable, *Zirconium and Its Compounds,* Chemical Catalog Co., New York, 1922.

35. M. Weibull, *Ber.* **20**, 1934 (1887).

36. J. T. Davis, *Am. Chem. J.* **11**, 26 (1899).

37. P. H. M. P. Brinton and C. James, *J. Am. Chem. Soc.* **41**, 1080 (1919).

atom have been reported. Konarev and Solovkin (38, 39, 40) added iodic acid or alkali iodates to weak solutions of zirconyl nitrate (0.0076 and 0.0152 M) in the presence of various concentrations of nitric acid, and obtained precipitates of compositions $ZrOOHIO_3 \cdot H_2O$, $ZrOH(IO_3)_3 \cdot 4H_2O$ and $Zr(IO_3)_4$, the latter at an undetermined hydration level, and mixtures of these. The compositions of the precipitates depended on the acidity of the solutions and the iodate ion concentrations. The hydroxyiodate precipitates were initially amorphous. Their separation from such weak solutions indicates a very low solubility. When the precipitates stood for long periods in the presence of iodic acid or alkali iodates, new crystalline compounds formed from them. The change was observed to occur more rapidly in the presence of potassium or rubidium iodates than in the presence of iodic acid, sodium iodate, or lithium iodate. In the iodic acid solutions zirconium tetraiodate formed, but in the presence of alkali iodates complex iodates with 6 or 9 iodate ions per zirconium atom crystallized. Their compositions were described by the generic formulas $Zr(IO_3)_4 \cdot 2MIO_3$, $Zr(IO_3)_4 \cdot MIO_3$- $\cdot HIO_3$, and $Zr(IO_3)_4 \cdot 3MIO_3 \cdot 2HIO_3$. The first two of these are probably salts of hexaiodatozirconic acid. The enneaiodates of the composition represented by the third generic formula are probably of the same basic structure as the hexaiodates, with additional iodic acid and iodate ions added in an undetermined fashion.

A compound of composition $2Zr(IO_3)_4 \cdot KIO_3 \cdot 8H_2O$ has been reported to precipitate quantitatively when potassium iodate is added to a solution of zirconyl nitrate in 5 M nitric acid (41).

Hydrous zirconia is dissolved by perchloric acid solutions, even when quite dilute (e.g., 0.1 N). When an excess of hydrous zirconia was allowed to stand for a period of weeks in the presence of strong perchloric acid (initially 70%), 1 mole of zirconia dissolved per 2 moles of the acid. On evaporating the solution over calcium chloride, crystals of the empirical composition $4ZrO(ClO_4)_2 \cdot HClO_4$ separated. Nothing is known of the structure and little of the properties of this compound, but the tetrameric formula suggests a species similar to that in the tetrameric zirconyl chloride, with a mole of perchloric acid occupying a lattice position similar to that occupied by water in zirconyl chloride. When a heated solution of hydrous zirconia in perchloric acid was allowed to cool, crystals of composition $9ZrO(ClO_4)_2 \cdot ZrO_2 \cdot H_2O$ separated. When recrystallized from water, it yielded the previously noted $4ZrO(ClO_4)_2 \cdot HClO_4$ (33). This compound is

38. M. I. Konarev and A. S. Solovkin, *Zhur. Obshchei Khim.* **24**, 113-18 (1954) and English translation, *J. Gen. Chem. U.S.S.R.* **24**, 1109-12 (1954).

39. M. I. Konarev and A. S. Solovkin, *Zhur. Obshchei Khim.* **24**, 1901-10 (1954) and English translation, *J. Gen. Chem. U.S.S.R.* **24**, 1863-71 (1954).

40. M. I. Konarev and A. S. Solovkin, *Zhur. Obshchei Khim.* **25**, 1279-83 (1954).

41. Yu. A. Chernikov and T. A. Uspenskaya, *Zavodskaya Lab.* **10**, 1653-6 (1918).

soluble in numerous organic solvents, including alcohol, benzene, chloroform, and carbon tetrachloride. The evaporation of the solutions in these solvents did not furnish crystalline solids. The perchlorate compounds tend to explode on heating, even at as low a temperature as 100°.

Wedekind and Wilke were able to obtain unstable crystals containing 2 moles of perchloric acid per mole of zirconia from an aqueous solution, and described them as hygroscopic needles which deliquesced in either water or alcohol vapor. Small quantities could be melted without explosion (42).

Aqueous solutions of zirconyl perchlorate exhibit Raman frequencies at 453 and 568 cm^{-1} (20).

The periodates would be expected to differ from the perchlorates because the chlorine atom can accommodate no more than 4 oxygen atoms around it, whereas the larger iodine atom can accommodate 6 oxygen atoms. Both tetrahedral $IO_4{}^-$ and octahedral $IO_6{}^-$ are known. The addition of trisodium dihydrogen paraperiodate, $Na_3H_2IO_6$, to a solution of zirconyl nitrate containing free nitric acid gave a precipitate of composition $3ZrO_2 \cdot I_2O_7 \cdot 17$-$H_2O$ (43). It appeared quite stable and was unaffected by boiling water. This suggests that it has a structure similar to the polysulfatopolyzirconic acids (see Chap. 6), and that the terminal groups are hydroxyzirconyl:

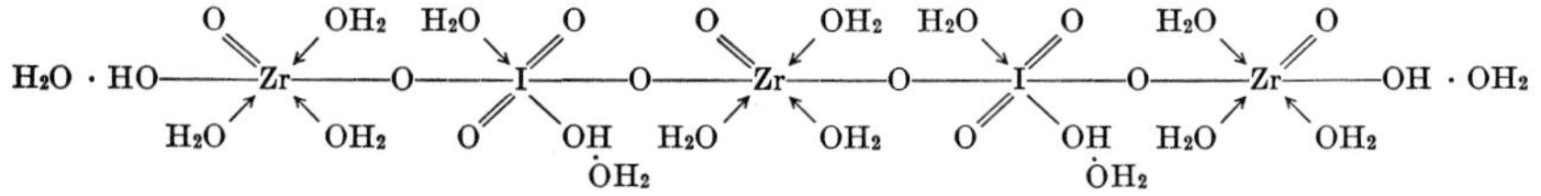

The same compound is reported to form by the action of disodium paraperiodate, $Na_2H_3IO_6$, or potassium metaperiodate, KIO_4, on a zirconyl

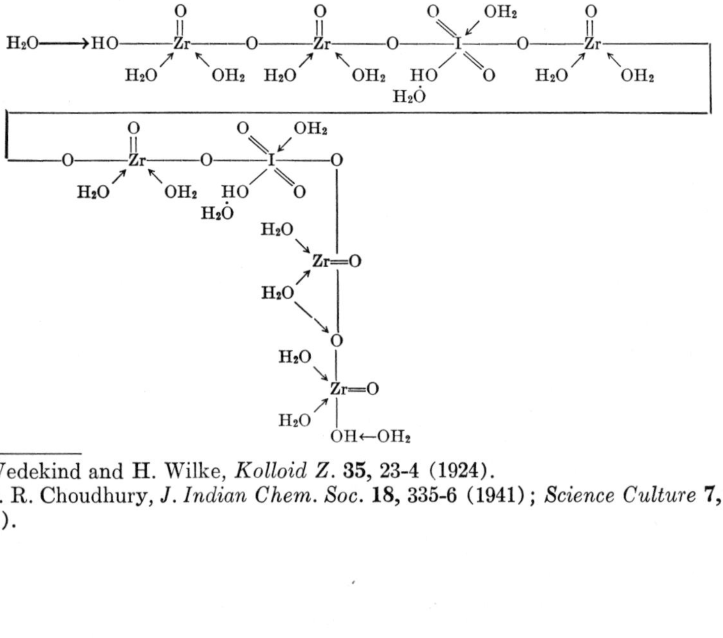

42. E. Wedekind and H. Wilke, *Kolloid Z.* **35**, 23-4 (1924).

43. P. C. R. Choudhury, *J. Indian Chem. Soc.* **18**, 335-6 (1941); *Science Culture* **7**, No. 1, 57 (1941).

nitrate solution, but with 14 or 18 moles of water (44). Iodine and oxygen are liberated when the compound is strongly heated, leaving a residue of zirconium dioxide.

A solid of composition $6ZrO_2 \cdot I_2O_7 \cdot 2OH_2O$ was obtained by the action of paraperiodic acid on freshly precipitated hydrous zirconia. The above structure might be suggested. On dehydration, the 13, 8, 6, 4, and 0 hydrates were observed to form and vapor-pressure studies indicated them to be true compounds (44; cf. 32).

COMPOUNDS AND COMPLEXES WITH DIBASIC ACIDS

As early as 1832 it was reported that "basic sulfites" are precipitated after addition of sulfur dioxide to solutions of zirconium compounds and heating. The solids obtained were of varying and indefinite composition (45). Later it was noted that the precipitates separated from zirconyl chloride solutions more readily than from sulfatozirconic acid solutions (46). The sulfur dioxide could be introduced in the form of ammonium sulfite, but if an excess of this reagent was used the precipitate was redissolved (47). Still later a salt was prepared whose composition, $Zr(SO_3)_2 \cdot 7H_2O$, gave the impression of a normal salt (48). None of these preparations have been studied sufficiently to permit of a satisfactory characterization of the compounds formed. The following outline of the system, however, appears to be in keeping with the available facts. At moderate acidities, e.g., pH 1.6, very sparingly soluble polysulfitopolyzirconic acids are precipitated, containing 2 or more moles of zirconia per mole of sulfur dioxide. In the older literature they were called *basic sulfites*. They tend to change on standing in contact with the mother liquor and may go into solution (46, 48).* In the presence of excess sulfurous acid, soluble sulfitozirconic acids form, and in the presence of excess sulfite salts, soluble complex sulfitozirconates form (49). What has formerly been regarded as the normal sulfite is apparently actually an acid that can be represented $H_2ZrO(SO_3)_2 \cdot 6H_2O$. It was prepared by allowing hydrous zirconia to stand for 2-3 months in contact with sulfurous acid solution. A second solid phase formed which contained 2.2

---

* The sparingly soluble polysulfatopolyzirconic acids are of the form $HOZrO(SO_4ZrO)_n$-SO_4ZrOOH; the soluble polysulfatopolyzirconic acids are of the form $HSO_4(OZrSO_4)_n$-$ZrOSO_4H$. The terminal groups of the chains of the former are hydroxozirconyl; those of the latter are hydrosulfate. A similar scheme is probable for the sulfito compounds, the SO_3 group replacing SO_4.

44. P. K. Bahl, S. Singh, and N. K. Bali, *J. Indian Chem. Soc.* **20**, 141-2 (1943).
45. P. Berthier, *Ann. Chim. Phys.* (2) **50**, 362 (1832); (3) **7**, 77 (1843).
46. C. Baskerville, *J. Am. Chem. Soc.* **16**, 475-6 (1894).
47. R. Hermann, *Jahresber.* **25**, 147 (1886).
48. F. P. Venable and C. Baskerville, *J. Am. Chem. Soc.* **17**, 448 (1895).
49. Titanium Alloy Mfg. Div. of the National Lead Co., unpublished studies.

moles of zirconia per mole of sulfur dioxide. The supernatant liquor was evaporated over sulfuric acid for several months, whereupon warty crystals developed of the composition $Zr(SO_3)_2 \cdot 7H_2O$ (48).

Precipitation of the "basic sulfite" has been used to separate zirconium from aluminum for analytical purposes (46), and an industrial process has been worked out for separation of zirconium from solutions of ores by such a precipitation (50).

Zirconium ClBrI tetrahalogenides dissolve in liquid sulfur dioxide (51, 52). Solvolysis of the tetraiodide yielded anhydrous zirconium sulfite, $Zr(SO_3)_2$, as a light, yellowish-pink solid. It reacted vigorously with water to give sulfur dioxide and hydrous zirconia (52).

Berzelius observed selenious acid to form an amorphous precipitate with zirconyl salts, and stated that the precipitate is soluble in excess of the selenious acid (53). Weibull reported a solid of composition $HZrOOHSeO_3$-
$\cdot H_2O$ to remain after evaporating a solution of its components over sulfuric acid (32). But later studies showed that the addition of selenious acid or sodium selenite to solutions of zirconium chlorides or sulfato compounds gives rise to the quantitative precipitation of a compound of composition $4ZrO_2 \cdot 3SeO_3 \cdot 18H_2O$ (54, 55, 56), which appears to be closely analogous to Hauser's salt, $4ZrO_2 \cdot 3SO_3 \cdot 15H_2O$, and is presumably of the structure

When this compound is treated at 60° with a large excess of selenious acid, it is converted to the water-insoluble selenite $Zr(SeO_3)_2$, which is recovered in the anhydrous condition from concentrated solutions of selenious acid. The monohydrate is obtained as microscopic four-sided prisms with oblique ends when 1 mole of polyselenitopolyzirconic acid is treated with 5 moles of selenious acid at 60°. It is insoluble in water and dissolves only with the greatest of difficulty in boiling hydrochloric acid. Selenitozirconic acids with more than two selenito groups per zirconium atom have not been made. Polyselenitopolyzirconic acid is suitable for isolating zirconium from aqueous solutions for analytical purposes (55, 56).

Diselenatozirconic acid, $H_2ZrO(SeO_4) \cdot 3H_2O$, is formed by the action of

50. British patent **300,271**, Nov. 11, 1927; German patent **509,515**, Nov. 12, 1927.
51. P. A. Bond and W. R. Stephens, *J. Am. Chem. Soc.* **51**, 2910-22 (1929).
52. H. Hecht, R. Greese, and G. Jander, *Z. anorg. allgem. Chem.* **269**, 262-78 (1952).
53. J. J. Berzelius, *Ann. Physik* **4**, 125 (1825); *Ann. Chem. Phys.* (2) **29**, 337 (1825).
54. L. F. Nilson, *Soc. Nova Acta, Upsala* (3) **9**, 7 (1875).
55. O. Kulka, *Beiträge zur Kenntnis einiger Zirkonium Verbindungen*, Berne, 1902.
56. S. G. Simpson and W. C. Schumb, *J. Am. Chem. Soc.* **53**, 921-33 (1931).

selenic acid on hydrous zirconia (32), and is analogous to the sulfate compound. It crystallizes, however, in the hexagonal system whereas the sulfato compound crystallizes as hexagonal plates in the rhombic system. The diselenatozirconic acid can be hydrolyzed to polyselenatopolyzirconic acids, but the latter have not been subjected to detailed study. The trihydrated acid loses its 3 molecules of water at 100°, and on further heating to 120-130° the anhydrous acid is further altered to $Zr(SeO_4)_2$, a hygroscopic solid (32).

Berzelius obtained precipitates on adding sodium tellurite or sodium tellurate to solutions of zirconium salts, but was unable to characterize the products which he obtained (57). Much later Montignie reported briefly on obtaining a precipitate approximating the composition $ZrOTeO_4 \cdot 7H_2O$ on adding a tellurate to a solution of zirconium nitrate containing excess nitric acid, and a composition $3ZrO_2 \cdot TeO_3 \cdot 5H_2O$ from an alkaline solution. The former was a gelatinous solid which was soluble in dilute mineral acids when freshly precipitated, but became insoluble on aging or heating to 100°. When it was heated in a current of hydrogen at 500°, it was converted to a solid of composition $TeZr_2$ (58).

The behavior of chromates, molybdates, and tungstates with zirconium compounds is not well understood from the limited data currently available. There is no evidence that simple compounds such as zirconium or zirconyl chromates, molybdates, or tungstates exist, even though some investigators have obtained precipitates approaching simple stoichiometric compositions such as $Zr(MoO_4)_2 \cdot 2H_2O$ (55, 59).* Some investigators have concluded from their studies that the simple compounds cannot be prepared (60). Table 7.2 summarizes data on reported preparations of the simpler compositions containing zirconium and chromate, molybdate, or tungstate.

To some extent the behavior of zirconium with these ions indicates the formation of adsorption complex on hydrous zirconia. When solutions of zirconyl chloride (0.01 M) were titrated with sodium hydroxide, sodium molybdate, and sodium tungstate, respectively, precipitation was observed to occur at pH 1.86 with the base and at the near value of 1.75 for the salts (62, 63). This suggests that in the case of the salts hydrous

---

* Jellies of compositions approaching that of a simple zirconium molybdate have been prepared and their physical characteristics studied (61).

57. J. J. Berzelius, *Schweigger's J.* **6**, 311 (1822); **34**, 78 (1823); *Pogg. Ann.* **28**, 392 (1833).
58. E. Montignie, *Bull. soc. chim.* **6**, 672-6 (1939); **13**, 176 (1946).
59. S. Tanatar and E. Kurovskii, *J. Russ. Phys. Chem. Soc.* **41**, 813-5 (1909).
60. P. Souchay and A. Tchakirian, *Ann. chim.* (12) **1**, 249-56 (1946).
61. S. Prakash, *J. Indian Chem. Soc.* **8**, 289-92 (1931); *J. Phys. Chem.* **36**, 2483-96 (1932).
62. H. T. S. Britton and W. I. German, *J. Chem. Soc.* **1931**, 709-17.
63. *Ibid.*, 1429-35.

TABLE 7.2. SUMMARY OF REPORTED PREPARATIONS OF ZIRCONIUM CHROMATES, MOLYBDATES, AND TUNGSTATES

Composition	Method of Preparation	Properties	Literature
"Zirconium chromate"	Precipitation from a solution of a zirconium compound with chromic acid or a dichromate	Composition indefinite; flocculant orange-red precipitate, sparingly soluble in dilute acids; CrO_4^{-2} lost on washing with water	58, 67
$3ZrO_2 \cdot CrO_3 \cdot 10H_2O$	Hydrous zirconia dissolved in chromic acid, the solution diluted and boiled	Yellow precipitate; loses much of its water at 110° and all at 200°	58
$3ZrO_2 \cdot CrO_3 \cdot 5H_2O$	Boiling a dilute zirconyl chloride solution containing a slight excess of a dichromate		67
$3ZrO_2 \cdot 2CrO_3 \cdot 4H_2O$	Addition of a large excess of saturated $K_2Cr_2O_7$ solution to a concentrated zirconyl chloride solution		67
$2ZrO_2 \cdot CrO_3 \cdot 3H_2O$	Addition of $K_2Cr_2O_7$ to a dilute zirconyl chloride solution		67
$9ZrO_2 \cdot 5CrO_3 \cdot 12H_2O$	An aqueous precipitate was heated with additional chromic acid at 190°		68
$Zr(MoO_4)_2 \cdot 2H_2O$	Disulfatozirconic acid solution precipitated with ammonium paramolybdate; precipitate washed with hot water and dried	Insoluble in water, slightly soluble in hot concentrated hydrochloric acid	55
$5ZrO_2 \cdot 9WO_3 \cdot 33H_2O$	Zirconyl nitrate solution added to cold ammonium metatungstate solution; gelatinous precipitate washed and dried	Insoluble in water or hydrochloric acid	58
$5ZrO_2 \cdot 7WO_3 \cdot 21H_2O$	Same as preceding but sodium paratungstate used instead of ammonium metatungstate	Insoluble in water or hydrochloric acid	58

zirconia is formed, with immediate adsorption of molybdate or tungstate ions:

$$ZrOCl_2 + Na_2MoO_4 + (x + 1)H_2O \rightarrow$$

$$ZrO_2 \cdot xH_2O + H_2MoO_4 + 2NaCl \quad (12\text{-}13)$$

$$ZrO_2 \cdot xH_2O + yH_2MoO_4 \rightleftharpoons$$

$$ZrO_2 \cdot (x - y)H_2O \cdot yMoO_4^{-2y} + yH_2O + 2yH^+$$

Blumenthal has shown that chromate, molybdate, and tungstate ions impart negative charges to hydrous zirconia in slightly acid media, and the electro-negative micelles precipitate the cations of basic dyes (64). Molybdated and tungstated hydrous zirconia jellies have been prepared by the techniques of dialysis (65).

Adsorption complexes such as those of chromate, molybdate, and tungstate with zirconia are chemically rather than physically bonded (66). The presence of these ions probably tends to rupture the long chains of ZrO_2 units comprising a micelle and to favor the formation of smaller units of certain preferred configuration. The structures of some of the compositions listed in Table 7.2 might be of the following nature:

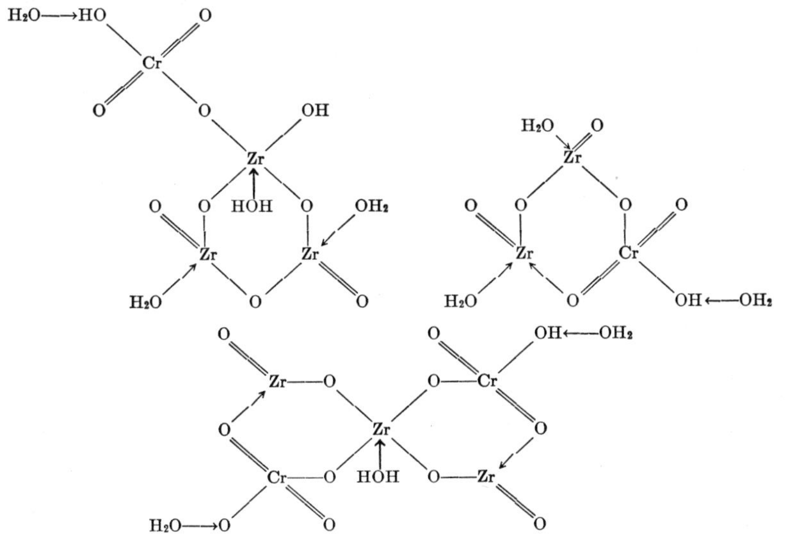

The tungstate compositions shown in Table 7.2 entail the complexities of the tungstate polyanions as well as the fragmentation of the hydrous zirconia chains.

A different pattern of behavior is encountered under conditions which favor the formation of heteropolyacids of zirconium with molybdate and tungstate ions. As early as 1893 Péchard reported the precipitation of solids of compositions $K_2Zr(Mo_2O_7)_6 \cdot 9H_2O$ and $(NH_4)_2Zr(Mo_2O_7)_6 \cdot 5H_2O$

64. W. B. Blumenthal, *Am. Dyestuff Reptr.* **37**, 285-6 (1948).

65. N. R. Dhar and S. Prakash, *J. Indian Chem. Soc.* **7**, 367-78, 417-34 (1930).

66. S. Glasstone, *Textbook of Physical Chemistry*, D. Van Nostrand Company, Inc., Princeton, N.J., 1946, pp. 1201, 1203

(69). Somewhat later a more extensive study of heteropolyacids of this system was undertaken by Hallopeau (70), who followed procedures previously used by Marignac to prepare silicomolybdates. Hallopeau added potash to a potassium fluozirconate solution to precipitate its zirconia content. He regarded the precipitate as hydrous zirconia, but it was probably a fluorine-containing compound. He dissolved the precipitate in a boiling solution of potassium paratungstate, $K_6W_7O_{24} \cdot 6H_2O$ (which was regarded at that time to be $5K_2O \cdot 12WO_3 \cdot 11H_2O$ (71, p. 1041).

The dissolution of the zirconium compound in potassium (likewise ammonium) paratungstate deserves special attention. It is suggestive of the dissolution of hydrous zirconia and carbonated hydrous zirconia in potassium or ammonium carbonate solutions. Soluble complex tungstatozirconate ions are obviously formed. Sodium paratungstate solution does not have a comparable solvent action (70), nor does sodium carbonate solution have solvent action for hydrous zirconia comparable to the potassium and ammonium salts. It is also reported that sodium and ammonium metatungstate solutions do not dissolve hydrous zirconia (55).

On concentrating the filtered solution of the complex, Hallopeau obtained a crystalline precipitate which he recrystallized and obtained the composition $4K_2O \cdot ZrO_2 \cdot 10WO_3 \cdot 15H_2O$. On further concentration of the mother liquor he also obtained small prismatic crystals of the composition $4K_2O \cdot 2ZrO_2 \cdot 10WO_3 \cdot 20H_2O$. It lost $10H_2O$ at $100°$. The first solid acted feebly on polarized light and the latter more strongly. Both substances were only sparingly soluble in cold water, but they were quite soluble at the boil. They appeared similar to silicon analogs, and the composition of the first substance was closely analogous to the previously reported $K_2O \cdot SiO_2 \cdot 10WO_3 \cdot 17H_2O$ (the silicon compound being considerably more water-soluble). The aqueous solutions were immediately decomposed by hydrochloric, nitric, or sulfuric acid with precipitation of yellow tungstic acid. Phosphoric acid slowly reacted to form gelatinous zirconium phosphate.

Following similar procedures, Hallopeau also obtained $3(NH_4)_2O \cdot ZrO_2 \cdot 10WO_3 \cdot 14H_2O$ (70). The recrystallized salt was recovered as octahedral prisms and corresponded to Marignac's ammonium acid silicodecatungstate. It was deliquescent and very soluble in water.

The solids $5ZrO_2 \cdot 9WO_3 \cdot 33H_2O$ and $5ZrO_2 \cdot 7WO_3 \cdot 21H_2O$ have been reported to separate on boiling a mixture of zirconyl nitrate and ammonium

67. L. Haber, *Monatsh.* **18**, 687-99 (1897).
68. H. C. Briggs, *J. Chem. Soc.* **1929**, 242-5.
69. E. Péchard, *Compt. rend.* **117**, 788 (1893).
70. L. A. Hallopeau, *Bull. soc. chim.* (3) **15**, 917-23 (1896).
71. N. V. Sidgwick, *The Chemical Elements and Their Compounds,* Oxford University Press, New York, 1950.

metatungstate solutions. Both were insoluble in water, and only the latter of the two was soluble in hydrochloric acid (55).

Little has been done to elucidate the structure or to verify the compound nature of the complex reaction products of molybdates or tungstates with zirconium compounds. It has been observed, however, that in aqueous solutions containing zirconyl and tungstate ions, reagents which usually precipitate tungstate fail to do so (55), whence it appears quite certain that tungstate forms complexes with zirconium in the solution phase.

Ammonium molybdatozirconate has been converted to molybdatozirconic acid by means of ion exchange, and the complex acid has been noted to be stable up to pH 4.7. At pH 6.2, complete hydrolysis occurs. Polarographic studies indicated the acid to be tetrabasic and to follow the pattern for the dodecamolybdates of generic formula $H_4XO_4(MoO_3)_{12} \cdot nH_2O$. Contrary to the findings of Hallopeau, this study produced no evidence for complexes containing less than this proportion of molybdena (72).

COMPOUNDS AND COMPLEXES WITH TRIBASIC ACIDS

Orthoboric acid, H_3BO_3, with a first dissociation constant of about 6×10^{-10} is too weak an acid to form a salt or a complex acid with zirconium. If an alkali borate is added to a solution of a zirconyl compound, hydrous zirconia is precipitated with chemically adsorbed borate ion. The composition varies with the pH of the suspending solution (73). Sols and gels of borated hydrous zirconia have been prepared by the techniques of dialysis (65).

On adding a solution of zirconyl chloride to a solution of orthophosphoric acid, H_3PO_4, a very insoluble precipitate is obtained in which there are 2 phosphate radicals per zirconium atom. When the washed precipitate is dried at 110°, its composition corresponds to $ZrO_2 \cdot P_2O_5 \cdot 5H_2O$ (74), and it shows the properties of an acid. The chemical behavior is in keeping

with the structure *diphosphatozirconic acid*. It has been conventionally called *zirconium phosphate*. It is probable that when the compound is first

72. A. Liberti, G. Giombini, and Elena Cervone, *Z. anal. Chem.* **147**, 404-9 (1955).
73. H. T. S. Britton, *J. Chem. Soc.* **1926**, 125-7.
74. W. B. Blumenthal, *Ind. Eng. Chem.* **46**, 528-39 (1954).

precipitated, the acid hydrogen atoms are hydrated, i.e., are hydronium ions, and that during drying water is eliminated from these hydrated atoms. An indication of such a change is found in the loss of ion exchange capacity when the solid is dried (75, 76). Anhydrous diphosphatozirconic acid has been reported to precipitate from 6 N hydrochloric acid (77).

Diphosphatozirconic acid has been formed in a number of ways other than by mixing solutions of the component ions. Zirconium metal or alloy was heated with glacial phosphoric acid to 230° to form a clear solution from which diphosphatozirconic acid separated on dilution (78). When hydrous zirconia was treated with phosphoric acid, it appeared first to form an adsorption complex and then to go over to diphosphatozirconic acid. A similar result was obtained with arsenic acid, but the reaction was more sluggish (79). Minerals and other difficultly soluble zirconium-containing substances are often converted to diphosphatozirconic acid by fusing or sintering them with alkalies, dissolving the zirconium compounds so formed with acid, filtering off insoluble matter, and adding phosphoric acid or a phosphate salt (80) to the clear solution. Some minerals, such as baddeleyite or malacon (81), can be dissolved with sulfuric acid without going through the alkali treatment and the solution precipitated with phosphoric acid.

Homogeneous precipitation of diphosphatozirconic acid has been accomplished by adding trimethyl phosphate to a solution of zirconyl chloride in 3.6 N hydrochloric acid and heating the mixture just below the boil for at least 12 hours. The diphosphatozirconic acid precipitate obtained in this way is much denser than that usually obtained by simply mixing solutions of the component ions (82).

Diphosphatozirconic acid also forms on adding the complex compounds $2ZrCl_4 \cdot PCl_5$ or $2ZrCl_4 \cdot POCl_3$ to water (83).

Diphosphatozirconic acid gel has been formed with Liesegang rings separated by clear spaces (84).

Diphosphatozirconic acid, $(H_2PO_4)_2ZrO \cdot nH_2O$, formula weight 355.26 for n = 3, is a white solid which is almost insoluble in water or acids up to approximately 20% sulfuric acid. It and the similar diphosphatohafnic acid

75. K. A. Kraus and H. O. Phillips, *J. Am. Chem. Soc.* **78**, 694 (1956).

76. K. A. Kraus, T. A. Carlson, H. O. Phillips, and J. S. Johnson, *Cation Exchange Properties of Hydrous Oxides, 130th Meeting, Am. Chem. Soc.,* Sept. 1956.

77. G. von Hevesy and K. Kimura, *J. Am. Chem. Soc.* **47**, 2540-44 (1925).

78. M. Wunder and B. Jeanneret, *Compt. Rend.* **152**, 1770 (1911).

79. E. Wedekind and H. Wilke, *Kolloid Z.* **34**, 83-97 (1924).

80. G. H. Bailey, *Proc. Roy. Soc. London* **46**, 74 (1890).

81. J. H. de Boer and P. Koets, *Z. anorg. allgem. Chem.* **165**, 21-30 (1927).

82. H. H. Willard and R. B. Hahn, *Anal. Chem.* **31**, 293-5 (1949).

83. D. M. Gruen and J. J. Katz, U.S. Patent **2,599,326**, June 3, 1952.

84. A. C. Chatterji and M. C. Rastogi, *J. Indian Chem. Soc.* **28**, 283-4 (1951).

are regarded as the most insoluble of the metal phosphates. The solubilities in 6 N hydrochloric acid for the zirconium and hafnium compounds are respectively 0.00012 and 0.00009 g/l, and in 10 N hydrochloric acid 0.00023 and 0.00012 g/l (77). These compounds are ideally suited to the isolation of these elements from other metallic elements for chemical analysis. Their low solubilities may be rendered in effect even lower by precipitating them in the presence of an excess of phosphoric acid. However, concentrated phosphoric acid dissolves diphosphatozirconic acid and many other difficultly soluble zirconium compounds (85, 86). For example, 100 cc of a suspension of a mixture of the hafnium and zirconium diphosphato acids, containing 0.6 g on the metal basis, was entirely dissolved by the solution of 300 cc of phosphoric acid of specific gravity 1.75 (86). On heating zirconia with phosphoric acid to a temperature just short of the dehydration temperature of the acid, 2 parts of the zirconia went into solution per 100 parts of acid (87).

Freshly precipitated diphosphatozirconic acid is soluble in a number of agents which form very stable complexes with the zirconium atom. Solvents of this class include strong sulfuric and oxalic acids (88, 89, 90, 91), hydrofluoric acid (89, 92), concentrated hydrochloric acid (92, 93), alkaline peroxide solutions (90, 91, 94), alkali carbonate solutions, particularly potassium carbonate solution (88, 95), alkaline solutions of polyols or alphahydroxycarboxylic acid, such as glycol, glucose, sucrose, pyrocatechol, pyrogallol (but not hydroquinone, phloroglucinol, or picric acid) or tartaric, malic, or lactic acid (92). There is some evidence that the dissolution of diphosphatozirconic acid with hydrofluoric acid leads to formation of zirconium complexes containing both fluorine and phosphato groups. Not only hydrofluoric acid, but also fluoride salts of sodium, lithium, zinc, copper, nickel, magnesium, barium, pyridinium, and anilinium have been found to form soluble complexes (96). Diphosphatozirconic acid can be reprecipitated from strong acid solutions, such as oxalic, sulfuric, or hydrochloric, by addition of water or certain other diluents, such as alcohol or even nitric acid,

85. British patent 235,217, June 6, 1924.
86. A. E. van Arkel and J. H. de Boer, U.S. Patent 1,636,493, July 19, 1927.
87. P. Hautefeuille and J. Margottet, Compt. rend. 102, 1017 (1886).
88. J. Bardet and C. Toussaint, Compt. rend. 180, 1936-8 (1925).
89. J. H. de Boer, Z. anorg. allgem. Chem. 150, 210-6 (1926).
90. de Boer, U.S. Patent 1,624,162, April 12, 1927.
91. Dutch patent 16,508, July 15, 1927.
92. J. H. de Boer and A. E. van Arkel, Z. anorg. allgem. Chem. 148, 84-6 (1925).
93. J. H. de Boer, Z. anorg. allgem. Chem. 165, 1-15 (1927).
94. E. M. Larsen, W. C. Fernelius, and L. L. Quill, Ind. Eng. Chem., Anal. Ed. 15, 512-15 (1943).
95. A. Karl, Compt. rend. 200, 1668-9 (1935).
96. J. H. de Boer, Z. anorg. allgem. Chem. 144, 190, 196 (1925).

to an oxalic acid solution (89). Barium ion will precipitate phosphate from solutions of diphosphatozirconic acid in alkaline complexing solutions, showing that the phosphate radical has become dissociated from the zirconium by the action of the solvent. When the alkaline solution is neutralized, hydrous zirconia is precipitated (92).

Precipitated diphosphatozirconic acid has been noted to be stable at 120-130° and to lose some water at 700° without changing over to the pyrophosphate (77). The pyrophosphate is obtained by heating the diphosphatozirconic acid to 1000-1380°.

Salts of diphosphatozirconic acid are readily prepared in acid media, but they have generally not been isolated because of difficulties involved in forcing the ionic equilibrium, such as

$$3(H_2PO_4)_2ZrO + 4AlCl_3 \rightleftharpoons Al_4((PO_4)_2ZrO)_3 + 12HCl \qquad (14)$$

completely to the right and maintaining it in this condition while isolating the metal diphosphatozirconate. In forming salts, the diphosphatozirconic acid behaves as a typical ion-exchange substance (75, 76, 97). Alkali, alkaline earth, aluminum, iron, and rare earth derivatives have been prepared (50, 76). In the presence of excess of zirconium ions, it appears that zirconyl salts of diphosphatozirconic acid can be formed, such as

although these have probably never been isolated in substantially pure form (82, 98).

Diphosphatozirconic acid is quite stable in moderately strong acid solution, yet hydrolysis of the general type

$$(H_2PO_4)_2ZrO + nH_2O \rightleftharpoons (H_2PO_4)_{2-n}ZrO(OH)_n + nH_3PO_4 \qquad (15)$$

sets in as the acidity is diminished. This may be regarded

97. F. K. McTaggart and I. E. Newnham, *Proc. Conf. Applications Isotopes, Sci. Research, Univ. Melbourne* **1950**, 167-74 (1951).

98. R. Stumper and P. Mettelock, *Compt. rend.* **224**, 122-4 (1947).

as the replacement of $H_2PO_4^-$ by OH^-. The reaction is displaced far to the right by alkalies, and their action also causes the replacement of hydrogen of the acid groups by alkalies so as to give salts of the phosphatozirconic acids. Thus a multicomponent mixture is obtained on adding alkali to a slurry of precipitated diphosphatozirconic acid in water. It is obvious, therefore, why early investigators noted incomplete precipitation of diphosphatozirconic acid in media containing an insufficiency of an acid (99), and found it necessary to wash the precipitate with ammonium nitrate or phosphoric acid solution to prevent loss of phosphate ion from the filter cake or retention of alkali ion by the precipitate (100). To assure precipitation of stoichiometric diphosphatozirconic acid, strong sulfuric acid (101) or 6 N hydrochloric acid (77) have been used as precipitation media. It has been shown that when the precipitation of zirconyl perchlorate with potassium dihydrogen phosphate is brought about in solutions in the pH range 1 to 3, the precipitate consistently contained the ratio $5ZrO_2:4P_2O_5$, the extreme deviations for the phosphorus pentoxide content being 3.98 and 4.1 per $5ZrO_2$ (102).

Precipitated diphosphatozirconic acid dissolves in hot aqueous alkali carbonate solutions, and when the solutions are cooled, crystals of the generic composition $ZrP_2O_7 \cdot 4M_2CO_3$ separate. Zirconium is not precipitated from the solutions by addition of alkali oxalates, but partial precipitation of the zirconia content is accomplished by adding ammonia or by dilution with water. Caustic soda and caustic potash act on the solutions to precipitate hydrous zirconia (88) or alkali zirconate (95).

According to Stumper and Mettelock, when zirconium is precipitated by a phosphate from a sulfuric acid medium, varying amounts of sulfur trioxide are held in the precipitate, and even after calcining for 2 hours at 1000°, 1 mole of sulfur trioxide remains per 2 moles of zirconium pyrophosphate. They found this composition to be quite stable at 800°, to lose only small proportions of sulfur trioxide at 900°, and gradually to lose all of its sulfur trioxide at 1000°. Dissociation was complete at the latter temperature after 200 hours. Weight-loss curves indicated the thermal dissociation to be a first order reaction, with a kinetic constant $K = 0.0231 \pm 0.003$ at 1000° (103, 104). Diphosphatozirconic acid containing sulfur trioxide has not been reported from other sources.

There are no established uses of diphosphatozirconic acid except as an intermediate compound in certain analytical procedures. Several potential

99. R. D. Reed and J. R. Withrow, *J. Am. Chem. Soc.* **51**, 1311-15 (1929).
100. *Ibid.*, 3238-41 (1929).
101. J. H. de Boer, *Z. anorg. allgem. Chem.* **150**, 211 (1926).
102. P. R. Subbaraman and K. S. Rajan, *J. Sci. Ind. Research India* **13B**, 31-4 (1954).
103. R. Stumper and P. Mettelock, *Compt. rend.* **224**, 654-5 (1947).
104. *Ibid.*, 1224-4 (1947).

uses have been indicated. It has promising properties as an ion-exchange material (76) and as a carrier of radioactive phosphorus for treatment of the skin (105, 106).

Phosphatozirconic acids and their salts, with various ratios of phosphate radical to zirconium, have been obtained on precipitation of zirconium with various orthophosphates in the presence of little or no free acid (102, 107, 108). The specific compositions $5ZrO_2 \cdot 4P_2O_5 \cdot 8H_2O$, $5ZrO_2 \cdot 3P_2O_5 \cdot 9H_2O$, and $3ZrO_2 \cdot 2P_2O_5 \cdot 5H_2O$ have been reported (35, 102). They appear to be chains of $(H_2PO_4)_2ZrO$ units from which pairs of H_2PO_4 radicals have been hydrolyzed off, probably symmetrically, and replaced by OH. Alkali salts of these acids have been prepared both in aqueous media and in melts. Berzelius found zirconia to dissolve in molten sodium ammonium phosphate (109). Knop kept a molten mixture at a white heat for 2 hours, cooled it, washed the product with dilute hydrochloric acid, and separated some colorless crystals having the form of rectangular parallelepipeds and compositions corresponding to $Na_2O \cdot 4ZrO_2 \cdot 3P_2O_5$ (110). The crystals were uniaxial, feebly birefringent, had a density of 3.10 at 13°, and were insoluble in acids and aqua regia (110, 111). More extensive preparations of this type were undertaken later by Troost and Ouvrard. They fused together zirconia, zirconium pyrophosphate, or zirconium tetrachloride and a sodium or potassium orthophosphate, metaphosphate, or pyrophosphate. The reaction products were lixiviated with water or dilute acid. The following products were isolated:

1. $K_2O \cdot ZrO_2 \cdot P_2O_5$, a colorless crystalline substance occurring as hexagonal lamellae, uniaxial negative, density 3.076 at 7°, insoluble in nitric or hydrochloric acids and aqua regia, soluble in hot concentrated sulfuric acid (112).

2. $4Na_2O \cdot ZrO_2 \cdot 2P_2O_5$, a strongly birefringent crystalline solid of density 2.43 at 14°, soluble in acids (113).

3. $6Na_2O \cdot 3ZrO_2.4P_2O_5$, hexagonal lamellae, density 2.88 at 14°, soluble in acids (113).

4. $K_2O \cdot 4ZrO_2 \cdot 3P_2O_5$, uniaxial, strongly birefringent, probably hexagonal crystals of density 3.10 at 12°, and unattacked by acids and aqua regia (112).

105. Dutch patent **60,910**, April 15, 1948.
106. J. F. Schultz, U.S. Patent **2,613,135**, Oct. 7, 1952.
107. R. Hermann, *J. prakt. Chem.* **31**, 75 (1844).
108. S. R. Paykull, *Bull. soc. chim.* (2) **20**, 65 (1873); *Ber.* **6**, 1467 (1873).
109. J. J. Berzelius, *Oefers. Akad. Forh. Stockholm* (1824) 295.
110. A. Knop, *Ann.* **159**, 36 (1871).
111. G. Wunder, *J. prakt. Chem.* **1**, 475 (1870); **2**, 211 (1870).
112. L. Troost and L. Ouvrard, *Compt. rend.* **102**, 1422 (1886).
113. L. Troost and L. Ouvrard, *Compt. rend.* **105**, 30-4 (1887).

Both potassium and phosphorus oxides were observed to split off from the complex salts at high temperatures (112).

At least 2 of the acid hydrogen atoms of diphosphatozirconic acid can be replaced by an ethyl or a methyl group. On hydrolysis of triethyl phosphate in the presence of a zirconium compound, a product of composition $(HC_2H_5PO_4)_2ZrO$ was obtained (114), and hydrolysis of trimethyl phosphate under similar conditions gave the methyl analog (82). Further hydrolysis converts the alkyl compounds to diphosphatozirconic acid.

Zirconium can be extracted into dibutyl phosphate from hydrochloric acid solutions. Observations on this process indicated the extracted species to contain 4 chlorine atoms and 2 tributyl phosphate molecules per atoms of zirconium. The extraction was not very sensitive to the strength of the acid (115). A molecular arrangement

$$
\begin{array}{ccccc}
C_4H_9O & Cl & & Cl & OC_4H_9 \\
| & \diagdown & \diagup & | \\
C_4H_9O{-}P{\rightarrow}O{\rightarrow}Zr{\leftarrow}O{\leftarrow}P{-}OC_4H_0 \\
| & \diagup & \diagdown & | \\
C_4H_9O & Cl & & Cl & OC_4H_9
\end{array}
$$

may be visualized for the extracted species. A method has been demonstrated for the analytical determination of dibutyl hydrogen phosphate by use of a zirconium salt. An unknown solution containing $1 - 6\ \gamma$ of dibutyl hydrogen phosphate was added to 10 ml of a solution of zirconyl nitrate containing 0.7 g Zr per l. Carbon tetrachloride was then added and the mixture was stirred. The phase separation time, t, was compared with that of standards containing known amounts of dibutyl hydrogen phosphate (116).

The addition of phosphorus oxyacids other than orthophosphoric acid to solutions containing zirconium cations appears in all cases to lead to the formation of almost undissociated compounds, some of which are water-soluble and others not. Electrical conductivity measurements have indicated that when a solution of sodium hexametaphosphate is added to a solution of a zirconium compound, complexes containing first 3 and then 6 metaphosphate groups per zirconium atom are formed (117). A precipitate obtained with a metaphosphate is reported to be useful in combination with silica gel or fullers' earth in a process for the catalytic cracking of hydrocarbons at 400-540° (118).

When hypophosphorous acid $H(H_2PO_2)$ is added to an aqueous solution

114. H. H. Willard and H. Freund, *Ind. Eng. Chem., Anal. Ed.* **18**, 195-7 (1946).
115. A. E. Levitt and H. Freund, *J. Am. Chem. Soc.* **78**, 694 (1956).
116. D. W. Brite, *U.S. Atomic Energy Comm. HW-30643*, Revised. 18 pp. 1954.
117. R. C. Mehrotra and N. R. Dhar, *Proc. Nat. Inst. Sci., India* **16**, 59-65 (1950)
118. J. R. Bates, U.S. Patent **2,349,243**, May 23, 1944.

of zirconyl nitrate, an amorphous precipitate forms, then redissolves when more hypophosphorous acid is added. If alcohol is added to the solution, colorless, strongly birefringent crystals of composition $Zr(H_2PO_2)_4 \cdot H_2O$ separate. The crystals rapidly acquire a violet color when exposed to sunlight, but the color develops only slowly if the sunlight is diffuse. No other perceptible change accompanies the development of the color. The crystals readily lose water (119). The suggested structure is

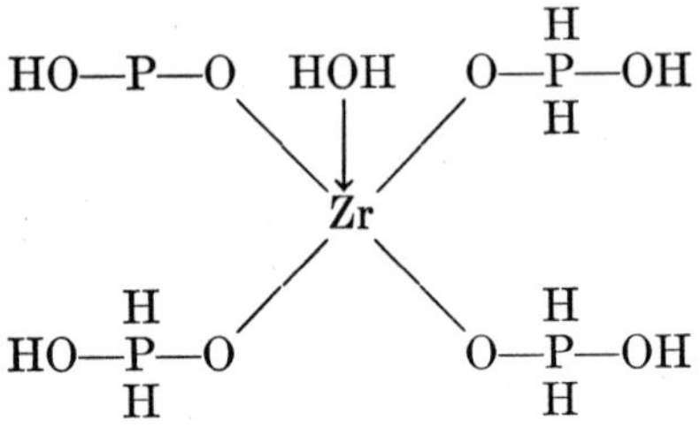

$$
\begin{array}{ccccc}
& & & & H \\
HO-P-O & HOH & O-P-OH \\
& & & & H \\
& & Zr \\
H & & & & H \\
HO-P-O & & & O-P-OH \\
H & & & & H
\end{array}
$$

The precipitate first obtained on adding hypophosphorous acid to a solution of a zirconium compound doubtless contains fewer hypophosphite groups.

On the addition of sodium hypophosphate to a zirconyl nitrate solution containing some hydrochloric acid, a hypophosphate of composition $Zr(PO_3)_2 \cdot H_2O$ is precipitated (119). Superficially it would appear to be the zirconium replacement product of the parent acid

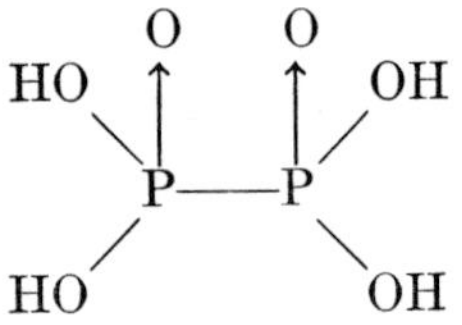

$$
\begin{array}{ccc}
& O \quad O \\
HO \quad \uparrow \quad \uparrow \quad OH \\
P-P \\
HO \quad \quad \quad OH
\end{array}
$$

but the steric difficulties involved in obtaining a simple zirconium derivative of this acid would be great, and a complex multimolecular structure appears more likely.

When diphosphatozirconic acid is calcined at 1000-1380°, the pyrophosphate ZrP_2O_7 is formed, and this compound seems to be the most stable phase in this temperature range, forming even from precipitates with the ratio $ZrO_2:P_2O_5$ different from 1:1. A precipitate of the same composition is reported to form as small, very birefringent octahedra or cubo-octahedra when a mixture of zirconium dioxide and orthophosphoric acid is heated just below the temperature of dehydration of the acid (87, 110). A similar substance was obtained on heating zirconium dioxide with a phosphate salt (110).

Chemical evidence that zirconium pyrophosphate is a true pyrophosphate

---

119. O. Hauser and H. Herzfeld, *Z. anorg. allgem. Chem.* **150**, 210-6 (1926).

(and not, for example, zirconyl metaphosphate $ZrO(PO_3)_2$) has been adduced by dissolving the compound in hydrofluoric acid, neutralizing rapidly with sodium hydroxide, and treating with luteocobaltic chloride (101). This reagent gives a typical reddish-yellow precipitate with the pyrophosphate ion. The available information appears to support the following proposed arrangement of atoms:

$$
\begin{array}{c}
\diagdown \quad \diagup \\
\text{Zr} \\
\diagup \quad \diagdown \\
\text{O} \quad \text{O} \qquad \text{O} \quad \text{O} \\
\text{P} \qquad \text{P} \\
\text{O} \qquad \text{O} \qquad \text{O}
\end{array}
$$

with linking of pyrophosphate oxygen atoms of 1 molecule with zirconium atoms of adjacent molecules.

Zirconium pyrophosphate, $Zr_2P_2O_7$, formula weight 265.18, occurs as cubic crystals at the ordinary temperature, with 4 molecules per unit cell and $a_0 = 8.258$ A. Interatomic distances are: Zr-O, 2.018; O-O, 2.495 and 2.619; O-P, 1.562; Zr-P, 3.443; and P-P, 3.033 A. The index of refraction is 1.657 ± 0.003 (120, 121). Its coefficient of thermal expansion is of the order of 5×10^{-7} (121, 122). It is insoluble in dilute and concentrated acids other than hydrofluoric acid (92, 101), and it is attacked with difficulty by potassium bisulfate. It can be decomposed by sintering with sodium carbonate, or better still, a mixture of sodium and potassium carbonates (87, 96, 106). At about 1550° it loses phosphorus pentoxide (121). When heated with the ClBrI halides of calcium or magnesium, the pyrophosphates of these metals are formed and zirconium tetrahalogenide vapor is evolved (122b).

Although zirconium pyrophosphate is a refractory substance of low coefficient of thermal expansion, its poor cohesion has prevented its use in making refractory articles. It has been shown, however, to have value as a support for platinum, palladium, or copper used as catalysts for the reaction of phosphorus vapor with steam to form orthophosphoric acid and hydrogen (106, 123, 124). In conjunction with silica it catalyzes the poly-

120. G. R. Levi and G. Peyronel, *Z. Krist.* **92**, 190-209 (1935).
121. D. E. Harrison, H. A. McKinstry, and F. A. Hummel, *J. Am. Ceram. Soc.* **37**, 277-80 (1954).
122. N. R. Thielke, *Bull. Am. Ceram. Soc.* **27**, 277-9 (1948).
122b. L. Aagard and G. E. Bronson, U.S. Patent **2,608,464**, Aug. 26, 1952.
123. J. F. Schultz, G. Tarbutton, T. M. Jones, M. E. Deming, C. M. Smith, and B. Cantelou, *Ind. Eng. Chem.* **42**, 1608-15 (1950).
124. L. B. Hein, G. H. Megar, and M. M. Stripling, Jr., *Ind. Eng. Chem.* **42**, 1616-22 (1950).

merization of olefins (125). A zirconium pyrophosphate phosphor has been shown to be useful in ultraviolet spot microscopy (126).

On heating zirconium pyrophosphate to 1550° or higher, it is decomposed with the formation of a composition corresponding to $(ZrO)_2P_2O_7$, zirconyl pyrophosphate. A product produced in this fashion was highly birefringent, had an index of refraction of 1.80, and an exceedingly low coefficient of thermal expansion at temperatures below 600° (121). A substance of the same composition has been reported to form on cooling a solution of zirconium dioxide in hot phosphoric acid in which the solubility is about 2 g ZrO_2 per 100 g of the acid. Two crystalline varieties of this precipitated zirconyl pyrophosphate were observed (87).

A composition of empirical formula $K_4Ca_5ZrO_6(PO_4)_2$ has been prepared, and may be a compound similar to a previously prepared silicon analog (127).

When an equivalence of arsenic acid or an arsenate salt is added to a hot, acidic solution of a zirconium compound, a precipitate is formed with the composition of a normal zirconium arsenate with various amounts of water of hydration. Weibull obtained a pentahydrate of composition $Zr_3(AsO_4)_4 \cdot 5H_2O$ on adding sodium hydrogen arsenate to a solution of difluozirconic acid in hydrochloric acid (128). It is doubtless not a salt, but a polyarsenatopolyzirconic acid with a chain structure such as

$$\begin{array}{ccccccc}
HO & O & HO & O & HO & O & HO \\
| & \| & | & \| & | & \| & | \\
HO-As-O-Zr-O-As-O-Zr-O-As-O-Zr-O-As-OH \\
\downarrow & \uparrow & \downarrow & \uparrow & \downarrow & \uparrow & \downarrow \\
O & HOH & O & HOH & O & HOH & O
\end{array}$$

Schumb and Nolan prepared the compound with this proportion of zirconium and arsenic oxides without noting the extent of its hydration, using the following procedure: 25 ml of zirconyl chloride containing the equivalent of 0.1200 g of ZrO_2, was diluted to 360 ml and made 2.75 N with respect to hydrochloric acid or 3.75 N with respect to nitric acid. Then, 50 ml of a 1% solution of ammonium arsenate was added, the mixture was heated to the boil, and an additional 15 ml of 10% ammonium arsenate solution was added. A flocculant, heavily hydrated precipitate formed. The acid strengths specified were the maximum concentrations which gave complete precipitation. When sulfuric acid was used in place of hydrochloric or nitric, precipitation was not complete even at acid strengths less than 0.5 N (129;

125. M. S. Bielawski and J. M. Mavity, U.S. Patent **2,656,323**, Oct. 20, 1953.

126. A. Bril, A. Klasens, and P. Zalm, *Philips Research Reports* **8**, 393-6 (1953).

127. G. Saring, *Versuche über den Aufschluss von Phosphaten durch Kieselsäure bein höhen Temperaturen*, Dresden, 1906.

128. M. Weibull, *Acta, Univ. Lund.* (2) **18**, 21 (1882).

129. W. C. Schumb and E. J. Nolan, *Ind. Eng. Chem., Anal. Ed.*, **9**, 371-73 (1937).

cf. 130). This reflects the competition of sulfate and arsenate ions for complexing the zirconium atoms.

Orthoarsenic acid, H_3AsO_4, is dehydrated to pyroarsenic acid, $H_4As_2O_7$, below $100°$ and to metaarsenic acid, $HAsO_3$, at about $200°$ (71, p. 787), and these changes are reflected in the products of aqueous preparations of arsenatozirconic acids at elevated temperatures. When a zirconyl nitrate solution was heated with a 30-40% solution of arsenic acid in an autoclave for 10 hours at 180-190° (under 10 atm pressure), a compound of composition $ZrO(H_2As_2O_7)$, zirconyl pyroarsenate, was formed. At $280°$ it was found to have become dehydrated to the composition $ZrO(AsO_3)_2$, zirconyl metaarsenate. X-ray diffraction substantiated the conclusion that the product was a metaarsenate (131).

The compositions of arsenatozirconic acids have been shown to vary considerably with the conditions of preparation. Hydrous zirconia was found to adsorb 2 moles of arsenic acid in 5 minutes at the ordinary temperature, and was presumed to give the compound, $Zr(HAsO_4)_2$, but the representation $ZrO(H_2AsO_4)_2 \cdot nH_2O$, diarsenatozirconic acid, appears to be more satisfactory. It was insoluble in acids and alkalies (132). The addition of disodium hydrogen arsenate, $Na_2HAsO_4 \cdot 7H_2O$, to a strong nitric acid solution of a zirconium compound has been reported to give a precipitate of composition $ZrOHAsO_4 \cdot nH_2O$, zirconyl monohydrogen arsenate (130, 133), and the precipitate of this composition has been stated to contain 25 or 30 molecules of water (55, 108). On heating, it first went over to zirconyl pyroarsenate, $(ZrO)_2As_2O_7$, and finally to zirconium dioxide (133). A study by Jean (134) showed that on mixing solutions of arsenic acid with solutions of zirconium compounds at the ordinary temperature, precipitates were obtained of compositions which varied with the proportions of reagents used. He noted that $2ZrO_2 \cdot As_2O_5$ was never obtained, $ZrO_2 \cdot As_2O_5$ rarely, and compositions approximating $3ZrO_2 \cdot As_2O_5$ most commonly under the range of experimental conditions which he investigated.

In general the precipitates obtained by the action of arsenic acid on zirconium solutions are almost insoluble in hydrochloric acid, but are dissolved by concentrated nitric or sulfuric acid (particularly when hot), hydrofluoric acid, and potassium and ammonium fluoride solutions (135). Some evidence of the formation of fluoarsenatozirconates has been reported (96).

Organic derivatives of arsenic acids retain the precipitating power of the parent acids for zirconium and have been found useful in analytical chemis-

130. L. Moser and R. Lessnig, *Monatsh.* **45**, 323-37 (1925).
131. G. Peyronel, *Gazz. chim. ital.* **72**, 89-93 (1942).
132. E. Wedekind and H. Wilke, *Kolloid Z.* **34**, 283-9 (1924).
133. (Mrs.) I. Sarudi, *Z. Anal. Chem.* **131**, 416-23 (1950).
134. M. Jean, *Anal. Chim. Acta* **3**, 96-9 (1949).
135. J. H. de Boer, *Z. anorg. allgem. Chem.* **165**, 1, 14 (1927).

try. The following organic acids have been reported to be useful analytical agents for the determination of zirconium: methylarsonic (136, 137); methylarsinic (138); propylarsonic (139, 140); phenylarsonic (140, 141, 142, 143); phenylarsinic (144); p-hydroxyphenylarsonic (145); p-dimethylaminoazophenylarsonic (144, 146); and o-o'-diarsonic acid of hydroxyglutaconaldehyde dianil (147).

Berzelius was of the opinion that the orange-yellow precipitate which he obtained on adding a solution of arsenic trisulfide in aqueous sodium hydrogen sulfide to a solution of a zirconium compound was a zirconium sulfarsenite, and that the lemon-yellow precipitate which he obtained on adding sodium sulfarsenate to a solution of a zirconium compound was zirconium sulfarsenate (148). No subsequent studies were made on these precipitates.

Arsenous acid is adsorbed by hydrous zirconia, but there has been no evidence of the formation of arsenitozirconic acids (132).

Little is known of the zirconium derivatives of oxyacids of antimony or bismuth. The casual references to compounds of the oxyacids of antimony as acid-insoluble substances, except for their solubility in hydrofluoric acid, have been incidental to studies of phosphoric acid compounds of zirconium (96). When bismuth trioxide is heated, it forms a γ variety which has a body-centered cubic structure and a unit cell of the composition $Bi_{26}O_{39}$. If zirconia is present during the heating, 1 Bi_2O_3 unit is replaced by 2 ZrO_2 to give a composition $Zr_2Bi_{24}O_{46}$. The unit cell of this compound has a cube edge of 10.21 A instead of the 10.243 A of $Bi_{26}O_{39}$ (149).

Ammonium metavanadate formed a gelatinous precipitate when added to a moderately dilute solution of zirconyl nitrate. It was soluble in mineral acids. When heated, it decomposed into zirconia and vanadia (150). When a nearly saturated solution of ammonium metavanadate was mixed with zirconyl nitrate solution so as to have a Zr:V ratio of 4:3, then heated for several hours in a closed vessel at 70°, a golden-yellow, viscous liquid

136. R. Chandelle, *Bull. soc. chim. Belg.* **46**, 423-7 (1937).
137. *Ibid.,* **47**, 172-93 (1938).
138. *Ibid.,* **46**, 283-300 (1937).
139. F. W. Arnold, Jr., and G. C. Chandlee, *J. Am. Chem. Soc.* **57**, 8 (1935).
140. H. H. Geist and G. C. Chandlee, *Ind Eng. Chem., Anal. Ed.* **9**, 169-70 (1937).
141. A. C. Rice, H. C. Fogg, and C. James, *J. Am. Chem. Soc.* **48**, 895-901 (1926).
142. P. Klinger and O. Schiesman, *Arch. Eisenhuttenw.* **7**, 113-15 (1933).
143. J. S. Knapper, K. A. Craig, and G. C. Chandlee, *J. Am. Chem. Soc.* **55**, 3945 (1933).
144. A. Okac, *Chem. Listy* **39**, 61-3 (1945).
145. C. T. Simpson and G. C. Chandlee, *Ind. Eng. Chem., Anal. Ed.* **10**, 642-3 (1938).
146. V. A. Nazarenko, *J. Applied Chem. U.S.S.R.* **10**, 1696-9 (1937).
147. V. I. Kuznetsov and N. A. Vasyunina, *J. Gen. Chem. U.S.S.R.* **10**, 1203-9 (1940).
148. J. J. Berzelius, *Ann. chim. phys.* (2) **11**, 225 (1819) and *ibid.* **32**, 166 (1826).
149. B. Aurvillius and L. G. Sillén, *Nature* **155**, 305-6 (1945).
150. M. B. Rane and K. Kondiah, *J. Indian Chem. Soc.* **8**, 289-92 (1931).

formed. When such a liquid of pH 1.25-1.51 was concentrated and allowed to stand, a transparent, gelatinous mass formed. On further dehydration it changed to a transparent, gelatinous, fragile solid which was very deliquescent and very soluble in water. From a liquid of Zr:V ratio 3:1 in the pH range 2.1-6.9, a solid of composition $3ZrO_2 \cdot 2V_2O_5 \cdot 9H_2O$ separated on evaporation. It was a yellow, amorphous, insoluble solid (151). Little can be concluded regarding the nature of a solid containing zirconia, vanadia, and chlorine, reported by Tanatar and Kurovskiĭ (59).

Blue and green pigments, useful as ceramic stains, have been made by calcining mixtures containing 60-70% zirconia, 26-36% silica, and 3-5% vanadia, by weight, at 700-900° (152). A variety of shades was obtained by calcining mixtures containing 80-99% zirconia and 1-20% ammonium metavanadate at 1400° (153).

A compound of composition $ZrO_2 \cdot 5Nb_2O_5$ was recovered from the following process: zirconyl chloride solution was added to a solution of potassium niobate and the precipitate which formed was fused with boric oxide. The mass so obtained was extracted with dilute hydrochloric acid, leaving acicular crystals of specific gravity 5.14 at 17° (154). A similar product was obtained on fusing together niobia, zirconia, and sodium fluoride (155).

COMPOUNDS AND COMPLEXES WITH TETRABASIC ACIDS

The only tetrabasic acid of present significance is ferrocyanic acid. The zirconium derivatives of the closely related tribasic ferricyanic acid will be considered along with those of ferrocyanic acid.

The common ferrocyanide salts give solutions of alkaline reaction, and it would be expected to precipitate solutions of zirconium compounds, whether or not true zirconium ferrocyanides were formed. Weibull has reported that the precipitate obtained on adding a solution of a potassium ferrocyanide to a solution of zirconyl chloride or a disulfatozirconic acid has the composition $(ZrO)_2Fe(CN)_6$, zirconyl ferrocyanide, with 10 molecules of water of hydration when the precipitate is formed from the chloride solution and 26 molecules of water when it is formed from the sulfato complex solution (32). Later Venable and Moehlmann were able to obtain only precipitates of higher zirconia content, and these precipitates varied in composition with the zirconium concentration in the mother liquor. One of their compositions

151. G. Peyronel, *Gazz. chim. ital.* **72**, 77-83 (1942).
152. C. A. Seabright, U.S. Patent **2,441,447**, May 11, 1948.
153. J. A. Earl, U.S. Patent **2,438,335**, March 23, 1948.
154. A. Larrson, *Z. anorg. allgem. Chem.* **12**, 188 (1896).
155. P. J. Holmquist, *J. Chem. Soc.* (London) **78**, a (II) 1388 (1898).

obtained at the ordinary temperature corresponded to $(ZrO)_2Fe(CN)_6 \cdot ZrO_2 \cdot H_2O$ (156).

When potassium ferricyanide is added to a concentrated solution of zirconyl chloride or disulfatozirconic acid, no precipitate forms. A precipitate was obtained from dilute zirconyl chloride solution and particularly readily when the solution had been heated to the boil and cooled several times (156). It may have been an adsorption complex of ferricyanide ion on hydrous zirconia.

156. F. P. Venable and E. O. Moehlmann, *J. Am. Chem. Soc.* **44**, 1705-7 (1922).

8

Carboxylates of Zirconium

INTRODUCTION

Compounds of zirconium in which the zirconium atom is linked to the
group R—$\overset{\overset{O}{\cdot\cdot}}{C}$—O—, in which R represents hydrogen or simple or ramified
organic radicals, are conveniently grouped together under the name *zirconium
carboxylates*. This group is necessarily subdivided into a number of subgroups
based on the presence and nature of substituents on the radical R. Certain
properties of the zirconium carboxylates are general and others vary considerably from subgroup to subgroup.

The simplest subgroup is that consisting of the zirconium compounds with
the formate and acetate radicals, the radicals of the carboxylic acids of
lowest molecular weights. Compounds of this group are characteristically
soluble in water (with or without decomposition, depending on the number
of carboxylate radicals bound to the zirconium atom and conditions in
the aqueous milieu) and insoluble in organic solvents. As against this,
the higher members of the same series of alkanoic acid radicals form
compounds with zirconium which are insoluble in water but soluble in
organic solvents, such as hydrocarbons and chlorinated hydrocarbons. Other
subgroups of the zirconium carboxylates with characteristic properties
are the zirconium polycarboxylates, the aromatic carboxylates, the compounds with esters of carboxylic acids, and the hydroxycarboxylates. It
is advantageous to examine the methods of preparation and the properties
of each of these subgroups separately.

Some significant aspects of the general behavior of the zirconium atom
as it bears on the formation and properties of zirconium carboxylates require attention. In aqueous systems, the zirconium atom has a strong
tendency to be complexed by the fluoride anion and by all or nearly all
oxygen-containing anions. The possibility of forming zirconium carboxylates
in aqueous systems, therefore, depends on the presence or absence of other
anions in the system and the relative strength of the bonds formed with
the zirconium atoms by these anions and by the carboxylate anion or
radical. The carboxylate anion or radical will meet with minimum competition for the zirconium atoms in solutions of the ClBrI halogenides of

311

zirconium, for in such solutions the only competing complexing species are water and hydroxyl ions. The study of the formation of zirconium carboxylates in aqueous systems is best begun by consideration of what is likely to occur when a water-soluble carboxylate is added to a solution of a zirconium ClBrI halogenide, such as zirconyl chloride.

The prevailing zirconium ion species in solutions of zirconyl chloride of moderate concentration is the basic zirconyl cation, $ZrOOH^+$. When it comes into contact with a carboxylate ion, it combines rapidly to form a monocarboxylatozirconium compound:

$$\begin{bmatrix} H_2O \quad\quad OH_2 \\ O{=}Zr{-}OH \\ H_2O \quad\quad OH_2 \end{bmatrix}^+ + \begin{bmatrix} O \\ {-}O{-}C{-}R \end{bmatrix}^- \rightarrow \begin{matrix} OH_2 \\ H_2O \quad | \quad OH \\ O{=}Zr \\ H_2O \quad | \quad O{-}C{-}R \\ OH_2 \quad\quad O \end{matrix} \tag{1}$$

Water may be lost from the complex during or after this reaction so as to attain the most stable hydration state in the product. The monocarboxylato-zirconium compound may subsequently react with a second carboxylate anion or carboxylic acid molecule, but more slowly:

$$HOOZrOOCR \cdot nH_2O + HOOCR \rightarrow$$
$$OZr(OOCR)_2 \cdot n'H_2O + (n - n' + 1)H_2O \tag{2}$$

Zirconium carboxylates of the latter type sometimes exhibit acid ionizations, indicating dissociation of an aquo group. For the case of diacetatozirconic acid, this behavior can be represented by the equation

$$OZr(OOCCH_3)_2 \cdot 3H_2O = H^+{}_n[HOOZr(OOCCH_3)_2 \cdot 2H_2O]^- \rightleftharpoons$$
$$H^+ + HOOZr(OOCCH_3)_2 \cdot 2H_2O^- \tag{3}$$

Less commonly, additional molecules of carboxylic acid will combine with the lower carboxyzirconates:

$$OZr(OOCR)_2 \cdot nH_2O + HOOCR \rightleftharpoons$$
$$HOZr(OOCR)_3 \cdot n'H_2O + (n - n')H_2O \tag{4-5}$$

$$HOZr(OOCR)_3 \cdot n'H_2O + HOOCR \rightleftharpoons$$
$$Zr(OOCR)_4 \cdot n''H_2O + (n'' - n' + 1)H_2O$$

In reactions 2, 4, and 5, either the carboxylate ion or the undissociated acid might be, hypothetically, the reacting species. Under some conditions the organic ligands may simply add to the zirconium atom by direct formation of a new coordinate covalent bond, and under others by an exchange of one or more aquo groups for the carboxylate groups.

It is apparent that for a zirconium carboxylate to form in an aqueous system, at least one bond between a carboxylate radical and a zirconium atom must be substantially more stable than a bond between an aquo group and a zirconium atom at a specific bonding position. The number of carboxylate radicals which will combine with the zirconium atom depends on the stabilities of the successively formed carboxylato ligands. Not more than 2 alkyl carboxylate radicals have ever been observed to combine with 1 zirconium atom in an aqueous solution, unless the alkyl carboxylate contains other reactive groups than the single carboxylate group. When 2 carboxylato ligands are bound to zirconium in cold aqueous systems, this tends to be reduced to 1 on heating. If the organic radical contains a second functional group, such as a hydroxyl group or a second carboxyl group in a vicinal position, chelate structures with the zirconium atom tend to be formed and these are more stable than the simple coordination structures. Three or four chelate ligands are often observed to be bound to the zirconium atom. Similar chelates are formed by polyfunctional organic radicals other than carboxylate radicals, as for example diketones and polyols.

The significance of pH in aqueous systems in which zirconium carboxylates are formed is quite considerable, and the reported investigations of a number of research workers are of much less than their potential importance because this factor was ignored. When a salt of a weak acid, such as most of the carboxylic acids are, is added to a zirconyl chloride solution, the alkaline reaction of the salt may be sufficient to form hydrous zirconia in accordance with the general equations:

$$2NaA + H_2O \rightleftharpoons 2Na^+ + 2OH^- + 2HX$$

$$ZrOCl_2 + 2OH^- + (x - 1)H_2O \rightarrow ZrO_2 \cdot xH_2O + 2Cl^- \qquad (6\text{-}8)$$

$$ZrO_2 \cdot xH_2O + yHO_2CR \rightleftharpoons ZrO_2 \cdot (x - y)H_2O \cdot yHO_2CR + yH_2O$$

The last equation represents the chemisorption of the carboxylic acid. Hydrous zirconia ordinarily begins to form at a pH of about 2.0 from solutions of moderate zirconium concentration. The stability of the hydrous zirconia may actually be increased by the formation of the adsorption complex, so that its formation at even lower pH's will be favored. An adsorption complex of an organic acid on hydrous zirconia could easily be mistaken for a true chemical compound. Only when a reaction product of a zirconium compound and a carboxylic acid occurs in a fairly strongly acid environment, e.g., at a pH of 1.5 or lower, can one be reasonably allowed to presume that the product is not an adsorption complex on hydrous zirconia.

Reactions of the zirconium ClBrI halogenides in nonaqueous systems involve little competition of the halogen atoms with organic radicals for bonding with the zirconium atom. Four carboxylato ligands are usually readily attached to zirconium in the absence of water. It is generally difficult, however, to disengage the liberated hydrogen halide completely.

It is of some interest to note the thermal decomposition temperatures of zirconium carboxylates. The following values have been reported (1) as the minimum temperatures for the complete conversion of zirconium carboxylates to zirconium dioxide when they are heated in air at a rate of 4.5° temperature rise per minute:

benzoate	500°	phthalate	550°	m-cresoxyacetate	585°
benzilate	500°	p-bromomandelate	550°	cinammate	600°
diphenate	505°	phenoxyacetate	565°	salicylate	790°

SHORT-CHAIN ALIPHATIC MONOCARBOXYLATES

Hydrous zirconia, $ZrO_2 \cdot xH_2O$, is attacked with difficulty by either hot or cold acetic acid of any strength (2, 3). The small amount of dissolved reaction product from this attack has been recovered after evaporation of the solution as an amorphous solid, which was soluble in water or alcohol (4, 5). Hydrous zirconia is also attacked slightly by monochloracetic acid (6).

Carbonated hydrous zirconia, $2ZrO_2 \cdot CO_2 \cdot nH_2O$,* reacts readily with acetic acid to form solutions if 2 or more moles of acetic acid are provided per atom of zirconium. Formic acid reacts similarly only if the carbonated hydrous zirconia is prepared with exceptional care to avoid alkaline impurities. While the acetate solutions are well known in industry, scant attention has been given to the formate solutions because they are relatively difficult to prepare and apt to be unstable after they are prepared.

The solutes formed by the reactions of 2 moles of formic or acetic acid with carbonated hydrous zirconia have the empirical compositions $ZrO(O_2CH)_2 \cdot nH_2O$ and $ZrO(O_2CCH_3)_2 \cdot nH_2O$, respectively, and they were long regarded simply as zirconyl salts composed of zirconyl cations and formate or acetate anions. Later studies of the properties of these solutions, however, led to the belief that they do not contain appreciable concentrations of zirconyl or other zirconium cations, but rather that they

---

*n has been reported to have the value 8 (7), and probably has other values, too. Carbonated hydrous zirconia is usually employed as a water pulp for chemical reactions, since when it is dried it is altered and loses much of its chemical activity.

1. W. W. Wendlandt, *Anal. Chim. Acta* **16**, 129-34 (1957).
2. A. Mandl, *Z. anorg. allgem. Chem.* **37**, 252 (1903).
3. F. P. Venable and A. W. Belden, *J. Am. Chem. Soc.* **20**, 231 (1898).
4. M. H. Klaproth, *Gehlen J.* **4**, 383 (1807).
5. P. Truchot, *Chem. News* **77**, 134, 145 (1902).
6. E. Wedekind and H. Wilke, *Kolloid Z.* **34**, 283-9 (1924).
7. E. Chauvenet, *Bull. soc. chim.* **13**, 454-7 (1913).

contain complex zirconium anions. The following observations are particularly significant in interpreting the chemical nature of the zirconium species in these solutions:

1. Hydrous zirconia is precipitated quantitatively from solutions of chloride compounds at moderate concentrations at pH's of about 2.1-4.0, but it is not precipitated from acetate solutions up to pH's of at least about 5.0. The zirconyl ion concentration must therefore be vanishingly small in the acetate solutions.

2. Acid dye anions are precipitated by the zirconium cations of zirconyl chloride solutions, but not by the zirconium species present in acetate solutions.

3. The pH of an approximately molar solution of the soluble diacetato zirconium compound approaches the value 3.2 as the impurities (particularly alkali and alkaline earth acetates) are eliminated. Since the solution does not contain zirconyl ions or other zirconium cations, and since the known hydrolysis products of the diacetatozirconium compound are insoluble, it appears likely that the acidity is a reflection of the compound's being a weak acid in which there is a diacetatozirconate anion.

4. Carbonated hydrous zirconia cannot be put into solution by less than 2 moles of acetic acid per mole of zirconia contained, indicating that the soluble compound must contain 2 acetate radicals per zirconium atom.*

5. Evaporation of the solutions obtained on dissolving carbonated hydrous zirconia with acetic acid leaves a water-soluble solid residue of composition approximating $HZrOOH(OOCCH_3)_2 \cdot 2H_2O$. A solution of this residue in water is similar in properties to the mother solution. The noncrystalline properties of the solid suggest that it is a polymer.

6. When the zirconium acetate solutions are heated, an insoluble hydrolysate containing 1 acetate radical per zirconium atom is formed (8), but not hydrous zirconia. The hydrolysate redissolves in the mother liquor after cooling and standing. Substances which are similar to this hydrolysate and very probably identical with it chemically are formed by adding base to the acetate solution or by adding sodium acetate to zirconyl chloride solution. These observations can be interpreted on the basis of the diacetatozirconic acid being a monobasic acid and its hydrolysis product an entirely covalent compound.

From the above observations and from other supporting evidence, we may

---

* Carbonated hydrous zirconia reacts with hydrochloric acid to give water-soluble chlorides containing either 1 or 2 chlorine atoms per 2 zirconium atoms. This is due to the formation of salts of the cation $Zr_2O_3^{+2}$. It is noteworthy that corresponding acetates such as $Zr_2O_3(OOCCH_3)_2$ do not form. It appears that an effect of the reaction with acetic acid is to cause loss of the identity of the $Zr_2O_3^{+2}$ cation. The structural unit in the acetate compound consists of a single zirconium atom and 2 acetate radicals.

8. H. L. van Mater, U.S. Patent **2,482,816**, Sept. 2, 1949.

presume the solute in the diacetatozirconic acid solution to have a unit structure corresponding to the graphical representation

$$H^+ \left[\begin{array}{c} O \qquad O \qquad OH_2 \quad O \\ \ddot{} \qquad \diagdown \qquad \diagup \qquad \ddot{} \\ H_3C-C-O-\!\!\!-Zr-\!\!\!-O-C-CH_3 \\ \diagup \qquad \diagdown \\ H_2O \qquad OH \end{array} \right]^-$$

which is appropriately represented by the name *diacetatozirconic acid.*

It has already been noted that diacetatozirconic acid does not crystallize from its aqueous solution. When the solution is evaporated, its viscosity progressively increases until it sets to an amorphous solid. When the solid is pulverized and added to water, while stirring vigorously, it dissolves completely in a few minutes. But if the agitation is inadequate and the mass of powder is allowed to form a clump, it agglutinates and then dissolves only very slowly (9).

Because of the large number of oxygen atoms in a molecule of diacetatozirconic acid, it is to be expected that it would have a strong tendency to polymerize (cf. polymerization of zirconium alkoxides, Chap. 9). The formation of long chains is doubtless responsible for failure of crystals to form, the molecules becoming entangled and unable to be oriented in a lattice. A manifestation of the same phenomenon is the setting of a solution of diacetatozirconic acid in methanol to a jelly on standing. The polymer structure is presumably of the form

$$
\begin{array}{c}
\qquad O \qquad\qquad\qquad O \qquad\qquad\qquad O \qquad\qquad\qquad O \\
H_2O \quad OCCH_3 \; H_2O \quad OCCH_3 \; H_2O \quad OCCH_3 \; H_2O \quad OCCH_3 \\
\cdots O\!\!-\!\!-\!\!\to\!\!Zr\!\!-\!\!-\!\!O\!\!-\!\!\to\!\!Zr\!\!-\!\!-\!\!O\!\!-\!\!\to\!\!Zr\!\!-\!\!-\!\!O\!\!-\!\!\to\!\!Zr\!\!-\!\!-\!\!O\!\!-\!\!\to \\
H_2O \; O \quad OCCH_3 \; H_2O \; O \quad OCCH_3 \; H_2O \; O \quad OCCH_3 \; H_2O \; O \quad OCCH_3 \\
H \quad O \qquad\quad H \quad O \qquad\quad H \quad O \qquad\quad H \quad O
\end{array}
$$

On heating solutions of diacetatozirconic acid to near the boil (if pure; if contaminated with alkalies, lower temperatures suffice), a gummy, solid hydrolysate separates, which is basic zirconyl monoacetate, $HOOZrOOCCH_3 \cdot nH_2O$. Little attention has been given to determining its exact composition or its properties, although its existence has long been known (10, 11). The same substance can be obtained by adding sodium acetate to zirconyl chloride solution (9, 10). An interesting and instructive preparation is the following:

> Dissolve 0.2 moles of sodium acetate in 50 ml of water and add to this an aged solution containing 0.1 moles of zirconyl chloride in 50 ml, while stirring. The two solutions should be at room temperature before mixing. Note

9. Titanium Alloy Mfg. Division of the National Lead Co., unpublished researches.
10. L. Haber, *Monatsh.* **18**, 687 (1898).
11. H. T. S. Britton, *J. Chem. Soc.* **1926**, 269-99.

that a few seconds after mixing the entire mixture sets to a clear jelly. The reaction may be represented by the equation

$$(ZrOOH^+ + H^+ + 2Cl^+) + (2Na^+ + 2OOCCH_3^-) + nH_2O \rightarrow \tag{9}$$
$$HOOZrOOCCH_3 \cdot nH_2O + 2Na^+ + 2Cl^- + HOOCCH_3$$

As the jelly stands, it rapidly changes from transparent to opaque, due to chemical changes which continue over a period of weeks. At first only the homogeneity of the jelly is lost, but on prolonged standing the entire product forms a limpid solution. The acetic acid has slowly transformed the insoluble basic zirconyl monacetate to soluble diacetatozirconic acid (9).

An insoluble compound is also formed by the action of sodium monochloracetate on zirconyl chloride solution (6).

Diformatozirconic acid is similar to diacetatozirconic acid, but more susceptible to hydrolysis. Even after the clear solution is formed by the action of formic acid on carbonated hydrous zirconia, it is likely to hydrolyze and gel unless very pure. The gel does not redissolve in the presence of its equivalence of formic acid.

Compounds of other short-chain alkyl carboxylic acids have been studied only superficially. While carbonated hydrous zirconia is dissolved by formic acid (ionization constant 1.76×10^{-4}) and acetic acid (ionization constant 1.75×10^{-5}), it is not dissolved by propionic acid (ionization constant 1.4×10^{-5}). Evidently factors other than the strengths of the acids are involved, and the relationship of the propionate radical to the zirconium atom is different from that of the formate or acetate radicals in some significant respect. It is reported that the sticky, amorphous solid that remains after the action of propionic acid on carbonated hydrous zirconia is soluble in benzene or acetone (12). In this respect it approaches the solubility behavior of the longer-chain carboxylate compounds of zirconium, which will be described below. Some monocarboxylates of zirconium with up to 6 carbon atoms, having α-β unsaturation, are reported to be water-soluble (13).

Zirconium tetrachloride reacts with boiling formic, acetic, chloracetic, propionic, and butyric acids to yield the respective zirconium tetracarboxylates (14). It is sometimes difficult or impossible to remove all of the by-product hydrogen halide from the reaction product (9). On cooling the product prepared from the reaction of zirconium tetrachloride with glacial acetic acid, microscopic crystals were observed to form. They dissolved in water and acetone but not in ether. They were unstable in air and even over sulfuric acid in a desiccator.

A polymerized zirconium ethoxyacetate of molecular weight 1100-1200 has

12. S. Tanatar and E. Kurovsky, *J. Russ. Phys. Chem. Soc.* **39**, 936-47 (1907).
13. M. T. Goebel and R. K. Iler, U.S. Patent **2,597,721**, May 10, 1952.
14. A. Rosenheim and J. Herzman, *Ber.* **40**, 810-14 (1907).

been described. It was prepared by heating zirconium tetraethoxide with anhydrous acetic acid in heptane (15).

Molten ammonium formate has been used as a solvent for zirconium salts for polarographic study (16).

Diacetatozirconic acid has been sold in considerable tonnages for industrial use, for the most part as an aqueous solution containing the equivalent of 13-14% ZrO_2. Its chief application has been to the water-repellent treatment of textiles, particularly cellulosic textiles. When the textiles are dipped into a dilute solution of diacetatozirconic acid (about 1 g ZrO_2 per 100 ml), then removed, rinsed, and dried, they are found to have retained a small amount of a zirconium compound and to resist the passage of water through their pores. Additional advantages can be obtained by admixing a suitable resin or wax emulsion with the diacetatozirconic acid solution. When textiles are treated in similar fashion with such a mixture, they not only resist passage of water through their pores, but the surfaces of the textile are not wetted by water. Compositions of the treating baths and characteristics of the treated textiles have been described in patents and other literature (17, 18, 19, 20, 21).* Diacetatozirconic acid catalyzes the cure of silicone resins (22) and improves the properties of tack-free acrylic resins (23). It catalyzes the formation of high-viscosity polyethylene terephthalate by polymerization of bis(2-hydroxymethyl) terephthalate (24). While diacetatozirconic acid has mordanting properties (9, 25), no use has been made of this in industry.

Zirconium forms a stable, water-soluble chelate with ethylenediamine tetraacetic acid, $(HO_2CCH_2)_2NCH_2CH_2N(CH_2CO_2H)_2$, at pH 6.0, which contains one organic ligand per zirconium atom (25b). It can be used in analysis to prevent the precipitation of zirconium at somewhat higher pH's than those which usually cause formation of hydrous zirconia. It has been used to prevent the precipitation of zirconium along with titanium by

---

* In contradistinction to the water-repellent processes, diacetatozirconic acid and diformatozirconic acid have been applied to paper photographic plates to reduce excessive water-repellence of the plates (26). In this case, surface repellence and not pore penetration is involved.

15. J. Balthis, British patent **755,558,** April 22, 1956.
16. E. L. Colichman, *Anal. Chem.* **27,** 1559-62 (1955).
17. W. B. Blumenthal, *Ind. Eng. Chem.* **42,** 640-2 (1950).
18. Blumenthal, *Rayon and Synthetic Textiles* **32,** No. 1, 85-6, 88 (1951).
19. A. Doser, U.S. Patent **2,708,642,** May 17, 1955.
20. L. A. Fluck and A. L. Logan, U.S. Patent **2,759,851,** April 21, 1956.
21. W. Schulenberg, U.S. Patent **2,713,008,** July 12, 1955.
22. H. W. McNulty and D. J. Killian, U.S. Patent **2,687,388,** Aug. 24, 1954.
23. G. L. Brown and B. B. Kine, U.S. Patent **2,754,280,** July 10, 1956.
24. E. Siggel, British Patent **727,790,** Aug. 6, 1955.
25. P. Wengraf, *Farben-Ztg.* **25,** 277-9 (1914).
25b. L. O. Morgan and N. L. Justus, *J. Am. Chem. Soc.* **78,** 38-41 (1956).

quinaldic acid (25c). Zirconium interferes with determinations of some other metals with ethylenediamine tetraacetic acid, e.g., thorium (25d, 25e).

LONGER-CHAIN ALIPHATIC MONOCARBOXYLATES

As the length of the carbon chain attached to a carboxylate radical increases, a zirconium atom attached to the radical becomes more remote from the organic end of the chain. The effect is to give decreased polar character and less hydrophilic tendency to the compound, while its organophilic tendency increases. Even when the chain is only 3 carbon atoms long, the zirconium compound is insoluble in water and soluble in benzene. The 4 carbon atom zirconium carboxylates, formed from isobutyric acid $(CH_3)_2$ CHCOOH, and crotonic acid, $CH_3CH:CHCOOH$, are also reported to be soluble in benzene (12).

Hydrous zirconia reacts directly with the longer-chain carboxylic acids and with their alkali soaps to form compounds which are soluble in organic solvents such as carbon tetrachloride. The compounds of zirconium with these organic acid radicals are usually called *zirconium soaps*. The best methods for their preparation make use of soluble salts of zirconium which are allowed to react with aqueous solutions of the alkali soaps.

Zirconium soaps of composition ZrOOHA have been prepared, mixed with free fatty acid HA, by the reaction of alkali soaps with zirconyl chloride solution. The free fatty acid can be extracted with alcohol, leaving the substantially pure zirconium soap (8; cf. 27). The reaction is comparable to that of zirconyl chloride and sodium acetate, illustrated by equation 9. Similar soaps have been prepared by heating solutions containing alkali soaps and ammonium carbonatozirconate (28):

$$NH_4OOCR + (NH_4)_3ZrOH(CO_3)_3 \rightarrow \tag{10}$$
$$ZrOOHOOCR + 4NH_3 + 2H_2O + 3CO_2$$

A different series of soaps have been prepared from trioxodizirconium dichloride solutions (Chap. 3). Solutions of this salt are added to solutions of the alkali soaps, maintained at 95°, and the soap forms by combination of the ions:

$$Zr_2O_3^{+2} + 2A^- \rightarrow Zr_2O_3A_2 \tag{11}$$

Soaps such as trioxodizirconium stearate, oleate, and 2-ethylcaproate have been prepared in this way (29). These soaps are not hydrated and their

---

25c. A. K. Majumdar and S. Banerjee, *Anal. Chim. Acta* **14**, 427-9 (1956).

25d. J. S. Fritz and J. J. Ford, *Anal. Chem.* **25**, 1640-2 (1953).

25e. H. V. Malmstadt and E. C. Gohrbandt, *Anal. Chem.* **26**, 442-5, 818 (1954).

26. S. V. Worthen, U.S. Patent **2,635,537**, April 21, 1953.

27. C. J. Kinzie and E. Wainer, U.S. Patent **2,221,975**, Nov. 19, 1940.

28. H. L. van Mater, U.S. Patent **2,457,853**, Dec. 14, 1948.

29. W. B. Blumenthal, U.S. Patent **2,802,847**, April 13, 1957.

properties suggest that they are polymerized. They generally dissolve in hydrocarbon and chlorinated hydrocarbon solvents, but not in alcohols. They are insoluble in water, and vary considerably in their solubilities in ether. The solubility data for these soaps are difficult to reproduce because, it appears, the dissolved soap can peptize the undissolved excess, obscuring the true saturation value for the solution. Some empirical values for the solubilities of zirconium soaps are given in Table 8.1.

The trioxodizirconium soaps begin to decompose at about 300°, and do not melt up to this temperature. While their empirical formulas are close to those of the basic zirconyl soaps of formula ZrOOHA (differing only by one molecule of water per two zirconium atoms), the structural differences between the two types are reflected in different thermal decomposition curves, as determined by differential thermal analysis, and different infrared absorption spectra (9).

Trioxodizirconium 2-ethylcaproate has been shown to promote strongly the catalysis of cobalt compounds on the drying of drying oils (30, 31).

Zirconium soaps derived from pelargonic acid, $CH_3(CH_2)_7COOH$, and valeric acid, $CH_3(CH_2)_3COOH$, have also been reported (32, 33).

Alkoxide groups can be replaced from zirconium alkoxides by heating them with fatty acids in solvents such as heptane. In particular, alkoxyzirconium carboxylates have been prepared from zirconium isopropoxide (34) and zirconium ethoxide (15) in this manner. Soaps prepared by this procedure include a propionate, butyrate, valerate, caprylate, heptylate, caprate, laurate, myristate, linoleate, stearate, β-eleostearate, and archidate. These derivatives occur as polymerized molecules. The molecular weight of ethoxyzirconium stearate was observed to be about 2700-2800 (15).

Naphthenic acids* do not lend themselves readily to the preparation of their trioxodizirconium soaps by the process discussed above, but they do react with hydrous zirconia to form soaps, presumably of the ZrOOHA type (9). A zirconium naphthenate is reported to act as a catalyst in curing silicone resins (22).

Solutions of zirconium soaps in petroleum are of the nature of greases,

---

* *Naphthenic acids* are loosely defined as carboxylic acids derived from cyclopentane, homologs of cyclopentane, or bicyclic cyclopentane derivatives. Other acids may be present, including those derived from cyclohexane. In many respects, the naphthenic acids behave like other carboxylic acids. Their chief use has been in the manufacture of metal soaps (35).

30. G. P. Mack and E. Parker, U.S. Patent **2,739,905**, Mar. 27, 1956.
31. Mack and Parker, U.S. Patent **2,739,902**, Mar. 27, 1956.
32. M. L. Stumpf, *Am. Paint. J.* **39**, No. 30, 22 (1955).
33. J. B. Trommsdorff, *Ann. Phys.* (2) **54**, 208 (1833).
34. R. C. Mehrotra, *Nature* **172**, 74 (1953).
35. R. E. Kirk and D. F. Othmer, *Encyclopedia of Chemical Technology*, The Interscience Encyclopedia, Inc., New York, Vol. 9, 241-47 (1957).

TABLE 8.1. SOLUBILITIES OBSERVED FOR THE TRIOXODIZIRCONIUM CARBOXYLATES IN ORGANIC SOLVENTS (9)*

Compound	Solubilities, g per 100 ml of solution			
	Benzene	Carbon Tetrachloride	Petroleum Ether	Others
2-Ethylcaproate $Zr_2O_3(CH_3(CH_2)_3C_2H_5HCCO_2)_2$	17.6 (34°)	18.8 (34°)	17.0 (34°)	18.5 ether (34°); insol. et., meth., and isoprop. alcs.
Laurate $Zr_2O_3(CH_3(CH_2)_{10}CO_2)_2$	13.5 (20°) 14.1 (34°) 18.1 (45°)	Miscible in all proportions	0.2 (20°)	Sl. sol. carbon disulfide; insol. eth., et., meth., and isoprop. alcs.
Palmitate $Zr_2O_3(CH_3(CH_2)_{14}CO_2)_2$	Miscible in all proportions	Miscible in all proportions	2 (20°)	Sl. sol. ether; miscible carbon disulfide; insol. et., meth., and isopropyl alcs.
Stearate $Zr_2O_3(CH_3(CH_2)_{16}CO_2)_2$	Miscible in all proportions	Miscible in all proportions	13 (34°)	22.9 carbon disulfide (34°); 11.6 ether (34°); insol. et., meth., and isoprop. alcs.

* These data are published with the kind permission of the U.S. Army Chemical Center, which sponsored studies from which these solubility data are taken.

but to date no application of these greases has been made. It is reported that on calcination of deposits of zirconium soaps on glass fiber, an oxide surface is formed which is receptive to dyeing (36). The components of zirconium soaps are to be found as constituents of certain water-repellent treatments for textiles, and the soaps are presumed to form during the process (17, 18).

ALIPHATIC POLYCARBOXYLATES

The aliphatic polycarboxylate radicals form zirconium compounds which are markedly different from those of the monocarboxylates. Only a few of the many possible polycarboxylates of zirconium that might be formed have been prepared, and of these only the oxalate compounds have been studied to any considerable extent. There are serious gaps in our knowledge even of these.

In some polycarboxylates of zirconium, the possibility of chelate formation exists when 2 carboxylate radicals are separated by not more than 2 carbon atoms of the aliphatic chain. Chelation has a marked effect on the character of the zirconium compound. When chelation does not occur, the free carboxyl group tends to make the molecule more hydrophilic than a molecule of a zirconium soap.

The simplest polycarboxylate radical is oxalate, $-O-\overset{\overset{O}{\cdot\cdot}}{C}-\overset{\overset{O}{\cdot\cdot}}{C}-O-$. Its compounds with zirconium bear some resemblance to the sulfatozirconic acids, and some aspects of this resemblance will receive consideration below. The oxalato zirconium compounds are most suitably prepared from zirconyl chloride or nitrate solutions, and it is particularly desirable to avoid the presence of sulfates, since sulfate ions compete with oxalate ions for bonding the zirconium atom, a behavior noted as early as 1904 (37).

During the first century of study of zirconium compounds, a number of investigators noted that precipitates formed on adding oxalic acid or oxalate salts to solutions of zirconyl salts, and that the precipitates dissolved when excesses of the reagents were added (38, 39). In fact, many water-insoluble and acid-insoluble zirconium compounds dissolve in oxalic acid. Evidently oxalato compounds with a relatively small number of oxalato ligands tend to be insoluble while those with a larger number of oxalato ligands tend to be soluble and only exceedingly slightly dissociated.*

---

*Limitations of the solubilization of zirconium compounds with oxalic acid have sometimes not been adequately recognized. The use of oxalic acid in leaching zirconium from soil (43) is a dubious procedure, since oxalic acid will not dissolve some zirconium compounds, notably zircon.

36. J. H. Waggoner, U.S. Patent **2,671,033**, Mar. 2, 1954.

37. R. Ruer, *Z. anorg. allgem. Chem.* **42**, 87 (1904).

38. F. DuBois and A. A. de Silveira, *Ann. chim. phys.* (2) **14**, 110 (1820).

39. F. P. Venable and C. Baskerville, *J. Am. Chem. Soc.* **20**, 231 (1898).

Like the sulfatozirconic acids, the oxalatozirconic acids tend to hydrolyze in the absence of a substantial concentration of the acid from which they are derived, and the hydrolysates are only sparingly soluble. The oxalato hydrolysates are not nearly as well known and understood as the sulfato hydrolysates, and a discussion of the oxalato hydrolysates must necessarily be very sketchy at the present time.

When a mole of oxalic acid or of an oxalate salt is added to a zirconyl chloride solution, a precipitate of empirical composition $ZrOC_2O_4 \cdot xH_2O$ is formed. Products in which $x = 0, 3$, and 4 have been reported (11, 40, 41), and it is probable that x varies continuously and that there are no true chemical hydrates (42). The precipitate has a characteristic gelatinous nature and does not settle well. It can be coagulated by adding sodium acetate to the slurry, after which it can be filtered and washed without difficulty. A dried product prepared in this fashion had the composition $ZrOC_2O_4 \cdot 4H_2O$ (40).

The monooxalatozirconium compounds are amorphous and doubtless polymeric. It is to be expected that terminal $ZrOC_2O_4$ units can be hydrolyzed, giving compounds of the general type

$$
\begin{array}{c}
\text{H--O--Zr--} \\
\uparrow \\
(\text{HOH})_x
\end{array}
\left[
\begin{array}{c}
\text{O--C--C--O--Zr--} \\
\uparrow \\
(\text{HOH})_x
\end{array}
\right]_n
\begin{array}{c}
\text{O--C--C--O--Zr--O--H} \\
\uparrow \\
(\text{HOH})_x
\end{array}
$$

A compound of such composition with $n = 1$ and $x = 1$ was first reported in 1909 (44). It was made by adding oxalic acid to a weakly acidic solution of zirconyl nitrate, and was recovered as birefringent crystals. Application of the same terminology to the oxalato compounds as has been employed for the sulfato compounds (Chap. 6) gives the name *polyoxalatopolyzirconic acids* to compounds of this class.

Gable reported preparing anhydrous dioxalatozirconium, $Zr(C_2O_4)_2$, by the reaction of zirconium tetrachloride with its equivalence of anhydrous oxalic acid in methanol. He described the product as soluble in water, slightly soluble in acetic acid, aniline, and methyl carbonate, and insoluble in carbon tetrachloride, carbon disulfide, methanol, and ethanol (45). The tetrahydrate, $Zr(C_2O_4)_2 \cdot 4H_2O$, was subsequently prepared by the reaction of oxalic acid dihydrate with zirconium tetrachloride in glacial acetic acid

40. A. Rosenheim and P. Frank, *Ber.* **40**, 803-10 (1907) .
41. S. R. Paykull, *Bull. soc. chim.* (2) **20**, 65 (1873).
42. E. Lowenstein, *Z. anorg. allgem. Chem.* **63**, 92-4 (1909).
43. B. Kahn, *Anal. Chem.* **28**, 216-18 (1956).
44. E. Lowenstein, *Z. anorg. allgem. Chem.* **63**, 105-16 (1909).
45. H. S. Gable, *J. Am. Chem. Soc.* **53**, 1276-8 (1931).

(46). It is a colorless solid which dissolves in water or methanol, but forms a gel or deposits a precipitate on standing (9).

Since zirconium does not form a tetravalent cation, the compounds containing 2 oxalate radicals are best regarded as an acid anhydride and an acid, respectively, of the structures

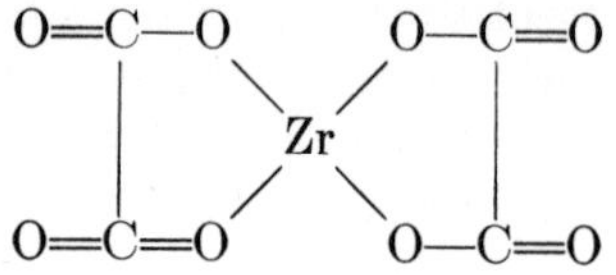

Dioxalatozirconium

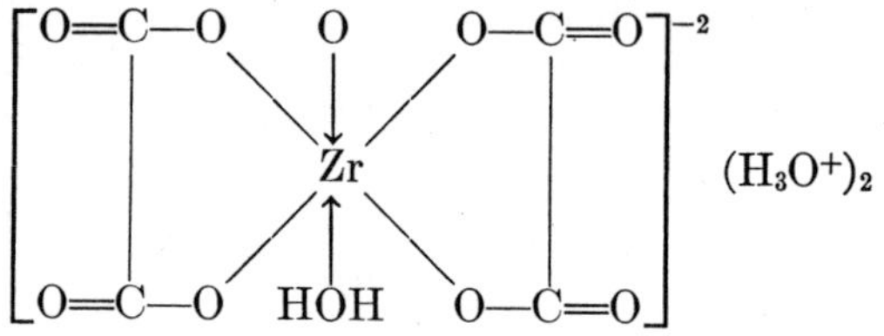

Dioxalatozirconic acid

The anhydrous oxalate compound is not similar to the anhydrous sulfato compound containing the equivalent of 2 sulfate radicals and 1 zirconium atom, the latter being a pyrosulfate, $ZrOS_2O_7$. The preparational methods for dioxalatozirconium and zirconyl pyrosulfate are entirely dissimilar.

Proof of the occurrence of the zirconium atom in a complex anion in oxalato compounds has been adduced from electrochromatography, which has shown the zirconium to migrate toward the anode in solutions containing oxalate ion (47).

It is not unlikely that tautomerism exists between monodentate and bidentate oxalate structures:

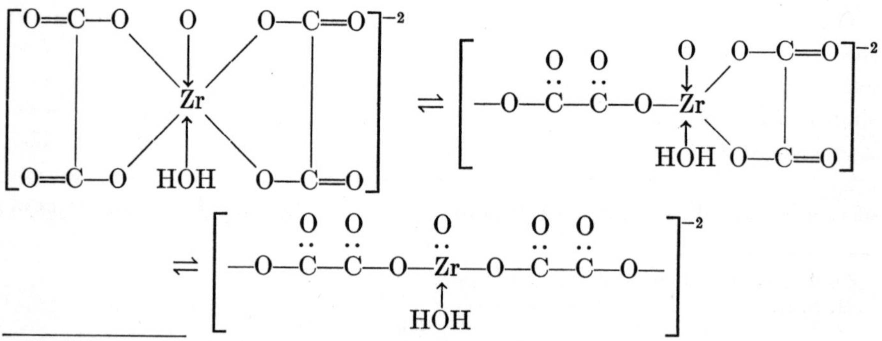

46. C. Rammelsberg, *Ann. Phys.* (3) **150**, 211 (1873).

47. T. R. Sato, H. Diamond, W. P. Norris, and H. H. Strain, *J. Amer. Chem. Soc.* **74**, 6154-5 (1952).

What evidence there is for the formation of monodentate oxalato ligands can be adduced from potentiometric measurements during the addition of sodium oxalate to a zirconyl salt solution. Potential peaks corresponded to the formation of di-, tetra-, hexa-, and octaoxalatozirconate complexes (48). It would be impossible for **6** or **8** bidentate groups to become attached to a single zirconium atom, but quite possible for this number of monodentate groups. It might be expected that the tautomeric coexistence of monodentate and bidentate oxalato groups would lead to solubilities between those of the completely bidentate alphahydroxycarboxylatozirconic acid compounds and the completely monodentate alkoxyglycolato compounds. This is borne out by known examples, e.g.,

Dimandelatozirconic acid, insoluble

Dioxalatozirconic acid, somewhat
soluble

Dimethoxyglycolatozirconic
acid, very soluble

The existence of the anhydrous dioxalatozirconium is itself an indication of chelation of the oxalato radical with the zirconium atom, for it would be difficult to explain the formation of a substance of composition $Zr(C_2O_4)_2$ by any other mechanism.

Dioxalatozirconic acid solutions are not stable and tend to deposit a hydrolysate on standing, possibly due to disproportionation of the complex to trioxalatozirconic acid and a lower oxalatozirconic acid. Adding hydrochloric acid to the solution causes trioxalatozirconic acid, $H_2Zr(C_2O_4)_3 \cdot nH_2O$ to crystallize, where n is 7 or 8 (49). The same acid deposits from a solution which has been made by saturating a warm oxalic acid solution with hydrous zirconia and allowing it to stand and cool (40).

Systematic study has been made of the phases separating from systems

48. S. R. Mohanty, D. Singh, J. Gopala, and K. Murty, *Current Sci.* (India) **24,** 229 (1955).

49. F. P. Venable and C. Baskerville, *J. Am. Chem. Soc.* **19,** 12 (1897).

containing $ZrOC_2O_4$, $M_2C_2O_4$, and H_2O at various temperatures, where M is any one of the alkalies lithium, sodium, ammonium, potassium, cesium, or rubidium (50, 51, 52). The compounds formed and their states of hydration at various temperatures of observation are given in Table 8.2. Some of the same compounds as well as similar compounds of organic bases have been prepared by a number of other investigators: tetrapotassium tetraoxalato- zirconate tetrahydrate (53) and pentahydrate (11), anhydrous ammonium tetraoxalatozirconate (54), the tetrahydrate (41) and hexahydrate (2), and tetraquininium and tetrastrychninium tetraoxalatozirconates (55). The organic salts were recovered as hygroscopic powders which were sparingly soluble in water and appeared not to hydrolyze. The general method of preparation is to dissolve hydrous zirconia in an excess of oxalic acid and to add the appropriate base (2, 49).

TABLE 8.2. COMPOUNDS FORMED IN THE SYSTEM $ZrOC_2O_4$—$M_2C_2O_4$—H_2O

Empirical formulas	Temperatures at which observed
$Li_4Zr(C_2O_4)_4 \cdot 8H_2O$	19°, 42°
$Li_4Zr(C_2O_4)_4 \cdot 4H_2O$	45° (decomp. 65°)
$Na_3ZrOH(C_2O_4)_3$	19°
$Na_4Zr(C_2O_4)_4 \cdot 4H_2O$	20°
$Na_4Zr(C_2O_4)_4 \cdot 3H_2O$	66° (decomp. 103°)
$(NH_4)_4Zr(C_2O_4)_4 \cdot 3H_2O$	19°, 20°, 39°
$(NH_4)_4Zr(C_2O_4)_4 \cdot H_2O$	42°
$(NH_4)_4Zr(C_2O_4)_4$	58°
$K_4ZrO(C_2O_4)_3 \cdot H_2O$	19°, 52°
$K_4Zr(C_2O_4)_4 \cdot 5H_2O$	20°
$K_4Zr(C_2O_4)_4 \cdot 3H_2O$	42°
$K_4Zr(C_2O_4)_4 \cdot H_2O$	65°
$K_4Zr(C_2O_4)_4$	85°
$Rb_4ZrO(C_2O_4)_3 \cdot 2H_2O$ (and $3H_2O$)	19°, 40°
$Rb_4Zr(C_2O_4)_4 \cdot 3H_2O$	20°
$Rb_4Zr(C_2O_4)_4$	32°
$Cs_4ZrO(C_2O_4)_3 \cdot 4H_2O$	19°
$Cs_4Zr(C_2O_4)_4 \cdot 5H_2O$	20°
$Cs_4Zr(C_2O_4)_4 \cdot 4H_2O$	75°

Carbonated hydrous zirconia is reported to react with succinic acid, $HOOCCH_2CH_2COOH$, to form a solid reaction product which is insoluble

50. Jeanne Boulanger, *Compt. rend.* **202**, 2156-9 (1936).
51. *Ibid.* **203**, 87-9 (1936).
52. *Ibid.* **204**, 356-8 (1937).
53. T. N. Burakova, *Echenye Zapiski Leningrad Gosudarst. Univ. im. A. A. Zhdanova* No. **178**, Ser. Geol. Nauk No. 4, 157-95 (1954).
54. G. Tammann, *Z. anorg. allgem. Chem.* **43**, 372 (1905).
55. A. Tchakirian, *Compt. rend.* **204**, 356-8 (1937).

in water and ethanol and very soluble in acetone (1; cf. 56).* Fumaric acid, HOOCCH:CHCOOH, precipitates zirconium quantitatively from a zirconyl chloride solution. The precipitate can be dissolved in 6 N hydrochloric acid (57), which would not be expected if complete chelation had occurred. Chelation of zirconium by this acid would give an improbable 7-membered ring.

AROMATIC CARBOXYLATES

The literature on zirconium compounds containing aromatic carboxylate radicals, such as benzoate and substituted benzoate, have been reported in only a superficial fashion. For example, the pH and other chemical and physical conditions in the environment in which these compounds were formed were not well controlled, and it is not clear from many of the reports whether a true zirconium aromatic carboxylate was obtained or an adsorption complex of the aromatic carboxylic acid on hydrous zirconia.

If sodium benzoate is added to a solution of zirconyl chloride, there might be only a simple combination of ions to form basic zirconyl benzoate:

$$ZrOOH^+ + C_6H_5CO_2^- \rightarrow ZrOOHO_2CC_6H_5 \tag{12}$$

or alternatively, hydrous zirconia can form and adsorb the benzoic acid:

$$NaO_2CC_6H_5 + H_2O \rightleftharpoons Na^+ + OH^- + HO_2CC_6H_5 \tag{13a}$$

$$ZrOOH^+ + OH^- + (x - 1)H_2O \rightarrow ZrO_2 \cdot xH_2O \tag{13b}$$

$$ZrO_2 \cdot xH_2O + yHOOCC_6H_5 \rightleftharpoons ZrO_2 \cdot yHOOCC_6H_5 \cdot (x - y)H_2O + yH_2O \tag{13c}$$

Reaction 13c is meant to represent chemisorption, and the adsorption complex might alter to a true compound. It is possible, too, that the processes of equations 12 and 13 will occur simultaneously. Moreover, additional molecules of sodium benzoate or benzoic acid might react with the first reaction product in several different ways. If the sodium benzoate solution is added slowly to the zirconyl chloride solution, the reaction environment will be more strongly acid at the beginning of the addition than toward the end, and the conditions during the earlier part of the process might favor reaction 12 while those during the later part might favor reactions 13.

---

* The product of reaction of carbonated hydrous zirconia with succinic acid was reported to contain 2 zirconium atoms per succinate radical. This suggests that the ion species originally present in the carbonated hydrous zirconia is preserved in the succinate, and that it contains a structure

$$-Zr-O-Zr-C_4H_4O_4-Zr-O-Zr-C_4H_4O_4-.$$
$$\ddot{O} \qquad \ddot{O} \qquad \quad \ddot{O} \qquad \ddot{O}$$

56. P. K. Katti, *Proc. Indian Acad. Sci.* **38A**, 148-60 (1953).
57. M. Venkataramaniah and Bh. S. V. Raghava Rao, *Analyst* **76**, 684-6 (1950).

Early studies in this field were made by Venable and Blaylock, who experimented with the addition of benzoic acid solutions to zirconyl chloride solutions. They stated that when the solutions were mixed cold, finely granular precipitates were formed on prolonged standing, and they settled slowly. The yield of precipitate was low. When the reaction was conducted at the boil, gelatinous precipitates formed which settled rapidly and could be filtered and washed without difficulty. Among the compositions which they noted, after drying at room temperature, were $ZrO(OH)_2 \cdot 2ZrO$-$(C_6H_5CO_2)_2 \cdot 6H_2O$, $ZrO(OH)_2 \cdot 3ZrO(C_6H_5CO_2)_2 \cdot 16H_2O$, and $ZrO(OH)_2$-$\cdot 6ZrO(C_6H_5CO_2)_2 \cdot 6H_2O$ (58). It is interesting that each of these contained one more of zirconium atoms than of benzoate radicals, and it might be surmised that the products belonged to a series of generic formula (ignoring water of hydration)

Venable and Blaylock were of the opinion that the compositions varied continuously. Other investigators of zirconium benzoates were interested in their significance in analysis rather than their structure and properties (59, 60).*

The author has added 1 mole of concentrated zirconyl chloride solution (75 g $ZrOCl_2 \cdot 8H_2O$ per 100 ml) to a boiling solution of benzoic acid containing 1 mole at nearly saturation, while stirring vigorously. The zirconium was precipitated quantitatively, a mere trace passing into the filtrate. The weight of the dried precipitate indicated that it contained between 1 and 2 benzoate radicals per zirconium atom. Unlike Venable and Blaylock, the author found the precipitate to be insoluble in ammonium hydroxide and not to darken when dried at 110°. Sodium benzoate precipitates zirconium quantitatively from sulfate solutions at lower pH's than does sodium hydroxide. Increasing the ratio of benzoate radicals per zirconium atom from 1:1 to 4:1 progressively decreases the pH at which precipitation is quantita-

---

* A composition $Zr_4O_5(C_6H_5CO_2)_6$ has been reported but not substantiated or explained (61, 62).

58. F. P. Venable and F. R. Blaylock, *J. Am. Chem. Soc.* **40**, 1746 (1918).

59. A. Jewsbury and G. H. Osborn, *Anal. Chim. Acta* **3**, 642-55 (1949).

60. Susumu Suzuki and Chozo Yoshimura, *J. Chem. Soc. Japan, Pure. Chem. Sect.* **72**, 428-31 (1951).

61. S. Tanatar and E. Kurovsky, *J. Russ. Phys. Chem. Soc.* **39**, 1630 (1908).

62. N. V. Sidgwick, *Nature* **111**, 808 (1923).

tive at room temperature. It appears likely that the hydrous zirconia is rendered more insoluble by formation of benzoatozirconeate micelles (9).

Zirconium has been precipitated from aqueous solutions by diphenic acid, o,o'-$HOOCC_6H_4C_6H_4COOH$ at pH's lower than 2.0 (63, 64). Dichlorozirconium benzoate $Cl_2Zr(O_2CC_6H_5)_2$ is formed by heating together benzoic acid and zirconium tetrachloride in ether solution until hydrogen chloride ceases to be evolved. While the benzoate radical thus replaces only 2 chlorine atoms from zirconium, formic or acetic acids replace 4 chlorine atoms under similar circumstances (14). Four chlorine atoms have been replaced by benzoate radicals by reaction of benzoic acid with zirconium tetrachloride in boiling benzene. The tetrabenzoatozirconium is recovered from this procedure as fine needles which are insoluble in benzene (65).

Phthalic acid, $C_6H_4(CO_2)_2$, precipitates zirconium quantitatively from a solution which is 0.35 N in hydrochloric acid. The precipitate can be dissolved in 6 N hydrochloric acid (66). In a series of preparations, 1.2 to 4.0 times the stoichiometric amount of hot 6% aqueous phthalic acid solutions was added to hot zirconyl chloride solutions which were 0.1 to 2.15 N in hydrochloric acid. The precipitate was always of the composition $ZrOC_6H_5$ $(CO_2)_2 \cdot 2H_2O$. When digested in hot mother liquor containing ammonium nitrate, the precipitate became suitable for filtering and washing. When larger excesses than the above of phthalic acid were used during the precipitation, excess phthalic acid tended to adhere during washing of the precipitate with water, but the ratio of phthalic acid to zirconia in the precipitate could be brought down to 1.1 by washing with ether. When less than the theoretical equivalent of phthalic acid was used for the precipitation, much of the excess zirconium was brought down in the precipitate, which accordingly had a variable composition (67). It appears probable from the solubility behavior that the phthalate compound of zirconium is largely non-chelate, and is of the structure

$$\left[\begin{array}{c} \overset{O}{\overset{\|}{}} \quad \overset{O}{\overset{\|}{}} \\ HO-\underset{\underset{HOH}{\uparrow}}{Zr}-O-C-C_6H_4-COOH \end{array} \right]_n$$

The free acid radical makes it possible for the precipitate to carry down excess zirconium.

Zirconium is also precipitated quantitatively by terephthalic acid (68).

63. G. Banerjee, *Naturwiss.* **42**, 417 (1955).
64. Banerjee, *Z. anal. Chem.* **147**, 404-9 (1955).
65. G. Jantsch, *J. prakt. Chem.* (2) **115**, 7-23 (1927).
66. A. Purnshottam and Bh. S. V. Raghava Rao, *Analyst* **76**, 684-6 (1950).
67. I. A. Sheka and V. Pevzner, *Zhur. Neorg. Khim.* **1**, 2767-71 (1956).
68. L. Gordon, C. H. Vanselow, and H. H. Willard, *Anal. Chem.* **21**, 1323-5 (1949).

The relative positions of the 2 carboxyl groups in terephthalic acid (para) would make chelation geometrically impossible.

COMPOUNDS WITH ESTERS

The reactions of zirconyl salts or the zirconium ClBrI tetrahalogenides with carboxylic acids involves initially the replacement of the hydrogen of the acids by zirconium. Subsequently additional carboxylate radicals may become bonded to zirconium by coordination. When zirconium compounds are brought into contact with esters of the carboxylic acids, they encounter no replaceable hydrogen atoms, and the alkyl groups which have taken the places of the replaceable hydrogen atoms are themselves not replaceable. Only the possibility of reaction through formation of a coordinate bond remains. This generally does not occur in aqueous systems because the zirconium atoms preferentially form coordination compounds with water. It is feasible, however, for addition products of the ClBrI tetrahalogenides of zirconium and esters to form under anhydrous conditions. This commonly proceeds in accordance with the general equation

$$ZrCl_4 + 2RO_2CR' \rightarrow ZrCl_4 \cdot 2RO_2CR' \tag{14}$$

For example, when a solution of 2 moles of ethyl benzoate in anhydrous ether was mixed with a solution of zirconium tetrachloride in the same solvent and the mixture boiled, a white crystalline precipitate formed of composition $ZrCl_4 \cdot 2C_6H_5CO_2C_2H_5$ (14). Methyl and phenyl benzoates form similar addition products, and hafnium analogs are known (69, 70). They are soluble in nitrobenzene. When heated they decompose and alkyl chloride, benzoyl chloride, and alkyl benzoate have been detected among the decomposition products. The hafnium compounds decompose at slower rates than the zirconium compounds. The decomposition products tend to form new addition compounds with the metal, and substances with compositions corresponding to $Zr_3O_2(C_6H_5CO_2)_8$, $Zr_2O(C_6H_5CO_2)_6$, and $Zr_2O(C_6H_5CO_2)_5Br$ have been noted. Such compositions suggest the formation of chains of zirconium atoms linked through oxygen atoms, with the organic radicals as substituents of the chains, e.g.,

$$
\begin{array}{ccccccc}
O{=}C{-}C_6H_5 & & O{=}C{-}C_6H_5 & & O{=}C{-}C_6H_5 & & \\
| & & | & & | & & \\
O & & O & & O & & \\
| & & | & & | & & \\
C_6H_5CO_2{-}\!\!-\!\!-Zr\!\!-\!\!-\!\!-O\!\!-\!\!-\!\!-Zr\!\!-\!\!-\!\!-O\!\!-\!\!-\!\!-Zr\!\!-\!\!-\!\!-O_2CC_6H_5 \\
| & & | & & | & & \\
O & & O & & O & & \\
| & & | & & | & & \\
O{=}C{-}C_6H_5 & & O{=}C{-}C_6H_5 & & O{=}C{-}C_6H_5 & & \\
\end{array}
$$

69. W. S. Hummers, S. Y. Tyree, Jr., and S. Yolles, *J. Am. Chem. Soc.* **74**, 139-41 (1952).

70. F. W. Chapman, W. S. Hummers, S. Y. Tyree, Jr., and S. Yolles, *J. Am. Chem. Soc.* **74**, 5277-9 (1952).

Although, as we have noted, the esters of the carboxylic acids have not been observed to form complexes with the zirconium ions or molecules in aqueous solutions, the so-called esters of phosphoric acid are able to form quite stable complexes in the presence of water. Tributyl phosphate, for example, forms one or more complexes with zirconium in a nitrate solution.* A similar complex is formed with hafnium, but that formed with zirconium is more stable, and if a solution of tributyl phosphate in dibutyl ether is shaken with an aqueous nitrate solution containing the two elements (in solutions of preferred composition, calcium chloride is present and the acidity is 2.5-5 N in HNO_3), the zirconium complex is concentrated in the organic liquid, while very little hafnium goes along with it. The reduced proportion of hafnium in the organic liquid can be virtually eliminated by shaking it with another aqueous solution containing calcium chloride and nitric acid in about the same proportions as the original aqueous solution (71, 72). Various alkyl and aryl phosphates can be used similarly, and organic solvents other than dibutyl ether can be employed (71, 72, 73).

HYDROXYCARBOXYLATES

Alphahydroxycarboxylic acids readily form chelate rings with the zirconium atom, and a result of the chelation is the ionization of the hydrozyl hydrogen atom. The chelate structure takes the form

In structure A, the hydroxyl oxygen atom has become an oxonium oxygen atom with a coordination number of 3 and an electric charge of +1. The stability of the ring is increased by the passage of this positive charge to the hydroxyl hydrogen atom, which thus becomes a hydrogen ion.

When an aqueous solution of a zirconyl salt is treated with an excess of an alphahydroxycarboxylic acid, a monohydroxycarboxylato complex forms

---

* Evidence, not regarded as final, has been adduced for the existence of the complexes $Zr(NO_3)_4 \cdot 2(C_4H_9)_3PO_4$ (73b) and $Zr(NO_3)_4 \cdot 3(C_4H_9)_3PO_4$ (73c). Perchlorate may replace nitrate.

71. D. F. Peppard, C. W. Mason, and J. L. Maier, *J. Inorg. Nuclear Chem.* 3, 215-28 (1956).

72. H. A. Wilhelm, K. A. Walsh, and J. V. Kerrigan, U.S. Patent **2,753,250**, July 3, 1956.

73. K. Alcock, F. C. Bedford, W. H. Hardwick, and H. A. C. McKay, *J. Inorg. Nuclear Chem.* 4, 100-5 (1957).

rapidly by combination of the ions, and thereafter additional hydroxy-carboxylato groups become attached to the zirconium atom more slowly, generally until 3 or 4 organic ligands have become bound to each zirconium atom. The processes appear to proceed as follows:

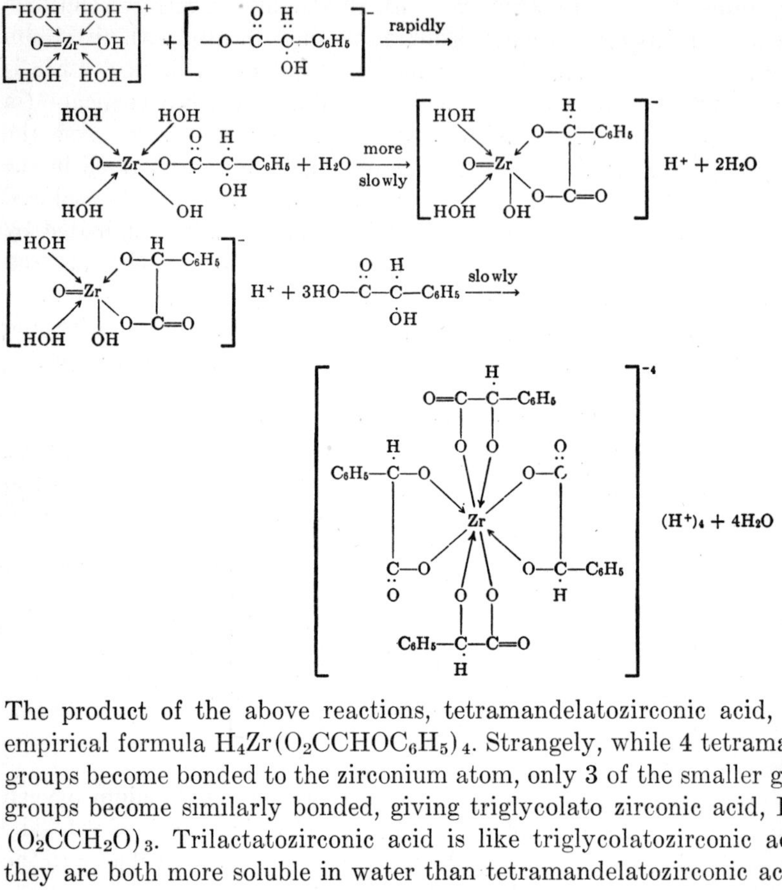

$$
\begin{bmatrix} \text{HOH} & \text{HOH} \\ \text{O}=\text{Zr}-\text{OH} \\ \text{HOH} & \text{HOH} \end{bmatrix}^{+} + \begin{bmatrix} \text{O} & \text{H} \\ -\text{O}-\text{C}-\text{C}-\text{C}_6\text{H}_5 \\ \text{OH} \end{bmatrix}^{-} \xrightarrow{\text{rapidly}}
$$

$$
\begin{array}{c} \text{HOH} \quad \text{HOH} \\ \text{O} \;\; \text{H} \\ \text{O}=\text{Zr}-\text{O}-\text{C}-\text{C}-\text{C}_6\text{H}_5 + \text{H}_2\text{O} \\ \text{OH} \\ \text{HOH} \quad \text{OH} \end{array} \xrightarrow[\text{slowly}]{\text{more}} \begin{bmatrix} \text{HOH} \qquad \text{H} \\ \text{O}-\text{C}-\text{C}_6\text{H}_5 \\ \text{O}=\text{Zr} \\ \text{O}-\text{C}=\text{O} \\ \text{HOH} \quad \text{OH} \end{bmatrix}^{-} \text{H}^{+} + 2\text{H}_2\text{O}
$$

$$
\begin{bmatrix} \text{HOH} \qquad \text{H} \\ \text{O}-\text{C}-\text{C}_6\text{H}_5 \\ \text{O}=\text{Zr} \\ \text{O}-\text{C}=\text{O} \\ \text{HOH} \quad \text{OH} \end{bmatrix}^{-} \text{H}^{+} + 3\text{HO}-\text{C}-\text{C}-\text{C}_6\text{H}_5 \xrightarrow{\text{slowly}}
$$

(with middle group O H / OH)

(15-16)

$$
\begin{bmatrix} & & \text{H} \\ & \text{O}=\text{C}-\text{C}-\text{C}_6\text{H}_5 \\ \text{H} & \text{O} \quad \text{O} \quad \quad \text{O} \\ \text{C}_6\text{H}_5-\text{C}-\text{O} \quad\quad\quad \text{O}-\text{C} \\ & \text{Zr} \\ \text{C}-\text{O} \quad\quad\quad \text{O}-\text{C}-\text{C}_6\text{H}_5 \\ \text{O} \quad \text{O} \quad \text{O} \quad \text{H} \\ \text{C}_6\text{H}_5-\text{C}-\text{C}=\text{O} \\ \text{H} \end{bmatrix}^{-4} \quad (\text{H}^{+})_4 + 4\text{H}_2\text{O}
$$

The product of the above reactions, tetramandelatozirconic acid, has the empirical formula $\text{H}_4\text{Zr}(\text{O}_2\text{CCHOC}_6\text{H}_5)_4$. Strangely, while 4 tetramandelato groups become bonded to the zirconium atom, only 3 of the smaller glycolato groups become similarly bonded, giving triglycolato zirconic acid, H_3ZrOH $(\text{O}_2\text{CCH}_2\text{O})_3$. Trilactatozirconic acid is like triglycolatozirconic acid, and they are both more soluble in water than tetramandelatozirconic acid.

The formation of hydroxycarboxylato chelates of zirconium is impeded by the presence of acids such as sulfuric which complex the zirconium atom and with which the hydroxycarboxylato radical must compete for positions on the zirconium atom. Since sulfato groups readily replace aquo groups on the zirconium atom, it would be expected that the former would be displaced by hydroxycarboxylato groups with greater difficulty than the latter.

All of the tri- and tetrahydroxycarboxylatozirconic acids form water-soluble salts when treated with bases such as sodium or ammonium hydroxide, or even hydroxylamine. But if the hydrogen atom of the hydroxyl group of the hydroxycarboxylic acid is replaced by an alkyl group, the ether so formed will not chelate the zirconium atom. Methoxyacetic acid, for example, will not precipitate zirconium from a zirconyl salt solution, and if a mixture of the zirconyl salt and methoxyacetic acid solution is rendered alkaline by addition of a base, hydrous zirconia forms rather than a soluble complex (74).*

Triglycolatozirconic acid, $H_3ZrOH(OCH_2COO)_3$, formula weight 333.36, is a white, soft solid. It dissolves in alkalies with formation of salts in which 1, 2, or 3 hydrogen atoms are replaced by alkali. The water-soluble alkali salts can be recovered as solids by evaporating their aqueous solutions. Triglycolatozirconic acid and its salts are very similar to the lactato analogs (74).

Trilactatozirconic acid, $H_3ZrOH(OCHCH_3COO)_3$, formula weight 375.44, is prepared by adding lactic acid to a solution of a zirconyl salt. It is a very sparingly soluble white solid. When dry it is extraordinarily soft and readily breaks down to a fluffy powder (75). It is insoluble in benzene, carbon disulfide, carbon tetrachloride, ether, ethanol, or petroleum ether (9). It is dissolved readily by aqueous alkalies with formation of salts by replacement of the hydrogen atoms of the complex acid. Lithium, sodium, ammonium, triethanolamine, potassium, and calcium salts are known. If a mole of the complex acid is treated with more than three equivalents of a strong base, the complex ion is decomposed and a colloidal solid forms which is extremely difficult to separate from its mother liquor. An excess of a weak base, such as ammonium hydroxide, does not cause this decomposition (9).

The alkali lactatozirconates do not form by reaction of alkali lactates on hydrous zirconia or carbonated hydrous zirconia.

When solid sodium or potassium lactatozirconate are calcined, an enormous increase of volume occurs as these compounds are converted to an ash containing alkali zirconate (9).

Sodium lactatozirconate has been found useful as the active principle in body deodorants (78, 79, 80, 81).

Some particularly illuminating experiments on the precipitation of zir-

---

* Zirconium is precipitated by 2,4 dichlorophenoxyacetic acid, $Cl_2C_6H_3OCH_2COOH$ (76) and by cresoxyacetic acid, $CH_3C_6H_4OCH_2COOH$. The cresoxyacetate of zirconium is soluble in 6 N hydrochloric acid (77). These acids precipitate zirconium similarly to benzoic acid rather than similarly to glycolic acid and its derivatives.

74. W. B. Blumenthal, *J. Chem. Ed.* **26**, 472-75 (1949).

75. R. E. Kirk and E. F. Othmer, *Encyclopedia of Chemical Technology,* Interscience Publishers, Inc., New York, 1956, vol. 15, p. 302.

76. S. K. Datta and G. Banerjee, *J. Indian Chem. Soc.* **31**, 773-8 (1954).

77. M. Venkataramaniah and Bh. S. V. Raghavo Rao, *Anal. Chem.* **23**, 1539-40 (1951).

78. H. L. van Mater, U.S. Patent **2,498,514**, Feb. 21, 1950.

79. F. M. Berger and S. L. Plechner, U.S. Patent **2,736,651**, Feb. 28, 1956.

80. W. B. Blumenthal, *J. Soc. Cosmetic Chemists* **4**, No. 2, 69-75 (1953).

81. W. K. Teller, U.S. Patent **2,732,327**, Jan. 24, 1956.

conium with mandelic acid, $C_6H_5CH_2COOH$, have been published by Hahn and Baginski (82). They prepared a series of solutions containing the identical amount of zirconyl chloride (equivalent to 25.30 mg of ZrO_2), added varying amounts of hydrochloric acid, and finally brought each to 50 ml by addition of distilled water. To each solution 25 ml of 1 M mandelic acid was added, the mixtures were brought to 85-90° and held at this temperature for about 45 minutes, then allowed to cool. The slurries were filtered and washed successively with a saturated solution of tetramandelatozirconic acid, ethanol, and ether. They were then dried to constant weight and the final weight recorded. Their experimental results are summarized in Table 8.3. The data indicate that at the acidity prevailing

TABLE 8.3. EFFECT OF HYDROCHLORIC ACID CONCENTRATION ON THE NUMBER OF LIGANDS IN PRECIPITATED MANDELATOZIRCONIC ACIDS*

Concentration of excess hydrochloric acid in the final solution, molarity	Weight of dried mandelatozirconic acid, g
0	0.0732, 0.0671, 0.0698, 0.0699
0.3	0.1041, 0.0995, 0.1035, 0.1040
0.8	0.1243, 0.1239, 0.1239, 0.1241
1.5	0.1305, 0.1308
3.0	0.1384, 0.1383
4.5	0.1398, 0.1411, 0.1426**, 0.1429**
7.5	0.1423, 0.1426, 0.1422**, 0.1425**

* The zirconium was precipitated quantitatively at all acidities, but was combined with different amounts of mandelate radical. Theoretical yields of dried precipitates are as follows: $HZrOOH(C_8H_6O_3)$ 0.05653, its trihydrate 0.06393; $HZrOH(C_8H_6O_3)_2$ 0.08406; $H_3ZrOH(C_8H_6O_3)_3$ 0.1153; $H_4Zr(C_8H_6O_3)_4$ 0.1428 g.

** For these only the mandelic acid was added dropwise over a 30 minute period.

in the unadjusted zirconyl chloride solution, the monomandelatozirconic acid formed first and it was only partially converted to the dimandelatozirconic acid by the time the samples were filtered. The relatively wide diversity of yields under these conditions indicate that the further reaction of the monomandelatozirconic acid had proceeded to different extents. The state of hydration of the monomandelatozirconic acid is not known, but presumably it does contain water of hydration. As the acidity of the solutions is increased, the number of mandelato ligands bound to the zirconium became more numerous for the same reaction time. This was doubtless due to the effect of higher acidity in converting aquo and hydoxo groups to hydronium ions, which are relatively weakly bound to the zirconium atom.

82. R. B. Hahn and E. S. Baginski, *Anal. Chim. Acta* **14,** 45-7 (1956).

Tetramandelatozirconic acid is converted to water-soluble alkali salts when it is treated with bases. The salt $(NH_4)_3HZr(C_8H_6O_3)_4$ has been observed to form, but an excess of ammonia appears to convert only half of the triammonium salt to a tetraammonium salt. Excess of strong bases causes hydrolysis of the compound to what appears to be hydrous zirconia (83).

The apparent formation of a salt containing 3.5 NH^+_4 ions per zirconium atom suggests the dimerization of the complexes in moderately alkaline solution, a process which would be somewhat similar to the polymerization of the zirconium alkoxides (Chap. 9). This dimerization would entail the opening of one of the rings per 2 monomer units, giving

The precipitation of zirconium by mandelic acid is almost a unique reaction (yttrium is precipitated under more restricted conditions than zirconium), and hence it has been very useful in the quantitative determination of zirconium (84, 85, 86, 87). As would be expected, tetramandelatohafnic acid is precipitated in the same way as the zirconium analog (88).

The broad applicability of compounds containing the group —CHOHCOOH

83. R. B. Hahn and L. Weber, *J. Am. Chem. Soc.* **77**, 4777-9 (1955).
84. R. B. Hahn, *Anal. Chem.* **21**, 1211-15 (1949).
85. R. E. Oesper and J. J. Klingenberg, *Anal. Chem.* **21**, 1509-11 (1949).
86. C. A. Kumins, U.S. Patent **2,630,370**, Mar. 3, 1953.
87. R. Belcher, A. Sykes, and J. C. Tatlow, *Anal. Chim. Acta* **10**, 34-47 (1954).
88. R. B. Hahn and P. T. Joseph, *J. Amer. Chem. Soc.* **79**, 1298-9 (1957).

to zirconium analysis has been studied (89), as well as the specific behaviors of individuals of the group such as the o-, m-, and p-fluoromandelic acids (90), and chloro- and bromomandelic acids (87, 91). All these acids show similar behavior toward the zirconium atom. Zirconium can be weighed as the complex acid or, after calcination, as the oxide. By weighing under both conditions, the hafnium content of the zirconium can be estimated.

The light absorbance of solutions of the ammonium salts of tetramandelatozirconic acid at 258 mμ is a measure of the zirconium present. The absorbance is due to the phenyl groups of the complex, ammonium mandelate exhibiting the same spectrum (92).

Naphthylglycolic acid, $C_{10}H_7CHOHCOOH$ (93) and benzilic acid, $(C_6H_5)_2COHCOOH$ (63, 64, 94) precipitate zirconium in similar fashion to mandelic acid. The naphthylglycolatozirconate is very voluminous. Zirconium compounds of pyroracemic acid (pyruvic acid, $CH_3COCOOH$) (95) and β-hydroxyamino-β-phenylpropionic acid (96), have also been reported.

Hydrocarbon and halogen substituents on the organic chain of alpha-hydroxycarboxylic acids have relatively small affects on the precipitation of zirconium by these acids. However, the presence of hydroxyl groups or carboxyl groups as substituents tends to render the zirconium compounds more soluble, doubtless due to the hydrophylic character of these substituents. It is relatively difficult, therefore, to isolate compounds of zirconium with alphahydroxycarboxylate radicals which contain hydroxyl or carboxyl substituents. A few zirconium compounds of this category have been of interest in physiological studies, and special techniques have been reported for their preparation.

A precipitate was obtained by adding a dilute zirconyl chloride solution to a boiling solution of sodium gluconate, $NaOOCC_5(OH)_5H_6$, in the proportion of 1 mole of zirconyl chloride to 2 moles of sodium gluconate. The precipitate was dissolved in hot 0.2 M sodium gluconate solution to obtain a solution of sodium gluconatozirconate (97).

Citric and tartaric acids have little visible effect on carbonated hydrous zirconia; they do not precipitate zirconium from solutions of its salts except

89. M. D. E. Jonckers, *Chim. anal.* 32, 207-12 (1950).
90. P. Srirama Murty and Bh. S. V. Raghava Rao, *Z. anal. Chem.* 141, 93-6 (1953).
91. R. A. Papucci, D. M. Fleishman, and J. J. Klingenberg, *Anal. Chem.* 25, 1758-60 (1953).
92. R. B. Hahn and L. Weber, *Anal. Chem.* 28, 414-5 (1956).
93. R. B. Hahn and P. T. Joseph, *Anal. Chem.* 28, 2019-21 (1956).
94. M. Venkataramaniah and Bh. S. V. Raghava Rao, *J. Indian Chem. Soc.* 28, 257-60 (1957).
95. J. J. Berzelius, *Ann. Phys.* (2) 6, 16 (1835).
96. G. Banerjee, *Z. anal. Chem.* 147, 348-54 (1955).
97. L. T. McClinton and J. Schubert, *J. Pharmacol. Ex. Therap.* 94, 1-6 (1948).

under certain conditions which have not been clearly delineated (9, 98). It is rather difficult, therefore, to prepare pure citrato- or tartratozirconic acids or their salts. A precipitate has been obtained by adding a solution of zirconyl chloride to an excess of boiling citric acid solution. The washed precipitate was dissolved in trisodium citrate solution to obtain a solution of sodium tricitratozirconate (97). On the other hand, after addition of citric or tartaric acid to a zirconyl chloride solution, the solution can be made alkaline without precipitation of hydrous zirconia, proving that complex citrato- and tartratozirconate ions have formed. This is verified by the strong rotatory action of the mixtures on polarized light (99, 100). Crystals of composition $K_2ZrO(C_4H_4O_6) \cdot 3H_2O$ have been noted to separate from solutions which had been prepared from 2 moles of tartaric acid, 1 mole of zirconyl nitrate, and 4 moles of potassium hydroxide (40, 58). The sodium analog could not be prepared similarly, and an ammonium salt is said to decompose with loss of ammonia (40).*

Injection of alkali citratozirconate solutions into experimental animals has been shown to promote excretion of Sr^{89} (106) and other radioactive elements (see Chap. 1, p. 44).

An ortho hydroxyl group on an aromatic carboxylic acid causes it to react with zirconium compounds in a manner similar to that of the aliphatic alphahydroxycarboxylic acids, but a 6-membered ring is formed instead of a 5-membered ring.

A precipitate is formed when salicylic acid is added to a boiling solution of zirconyl chloride, or vice versa (107). Unlike the precipitate obtained with benzoic acid, the salicylate precipitate dissolves when treated with an aqueous alkali, indicating a chelated salicylatozirconic acid has formed. The unneutralized salicylatozirconic acid can be extracted from the aqueous mixture by shaking with an immiscible alcohol, such as benzyl alcohol, or with nitrobenzene (108). A salicylato complex is also formed by the reaction of zirconium tetrachloride with salicylic acid in ethanol solution (14).

---

* Other preparations of citrato and tartrato complex are reported in the literature, but they do not establish the nature of the compounds formed (101, 102, 103, 104, 105, 114).

98. M. Weibull, *Acta Univ. Lund.* II, **18**, 34 (1881).
99. E. Rimbach and P. Schneider, *Z. phys. Chem.* **44**, 477 (1903).
100. G. Wernimont and T. de Vries, *J. Am. Chem. Soc.* **57**, 2386-7 (1935).
101. S. H. Harris, *Am. Chem. J.* **20**, 871 (1898).
102. F. P. Venable, *Zirconium and Its Compounds,* Chemical Catalog Co., Inc., New York, 1922.
103. C. J. Kinzie, U.S. Patent **2,013,856**, Sept. 10, 1935.
104. R. Hornberger, *Ann.* **181**, 232 (1876).
105. F. P. Venable and R. A. Lineberry, *J. Am. Chem. Soc.* **44**, 1708 (1922).
106. S. H. Cohn and J. K. Gong. *Proc. Soc. Exp. Biol. Med.* **83**, 550-4 (1953).
107. F. P. Venable and L. N. Giles, *J. Am. Chem. Soc.* **40**, 1653 (1918).
108. W. K. Plucknett, U.S. Patent **2,741,628**, April 10, 1956.

Precipitations of zirconium with the following derivatives of salicylic acid have been reported: sulfosalicylic acid (109), hydroxytoluic acid (110), bromo-, nitro-, and aminosalicylic acid (111), β-resorcylic acid and 5-bromoresorcylic acid (112), 1-hydroxynaphthoic acid, 1-hydroxy-4-bromo-naphthoic acid, and 1-hydroxy-4-nitronaphthoic acid (113). The author has also observed the precipitation of zirconium by p-aminosalicylic acid.

109. S. Prakash, *J. Indian Chem. Soc.* **10**, 281-5 (1933); *Z. anorg. allgem. Chem.* **215**, 249-54 (1933).

110. G. S. Deshmukh, *Naturwiss.* **42**, 69-70 (1955).

111. S. K. Datta, *J. Indian Chem. Soc.* **32**, 785-90 (1955).

112. *Ibid.* 687-93 (1955).

113. *Ibid.*, **33**, 394-8 (1956).

114. D. H. Drophy and W. P. Davey, *Phys. Rev.* (2) **25**, 882 (1925).

9

Organic Compounds Other than the Carboxylates

DERIVATIVES OF HYDROCARBONS

To date no compound has been isolated in which there is an identifiable covalent bond between zirconium and carbon. Even in zirconium carbide and in biscyclopentadienyl dichlorozirconium there appears to be no definite bond between the zirconium atom and the carbon atom, whence it might be said that such bonds fail to form under what might be regarded as the most favorable conditions. Considerable research effort, largely unpublished, has been expended in the effort to form compounds in which zirconium is covalently bonded with carbon, but with only negative results up to the present time. At most there is evidence for fleeting bond formation in some of the catalytic effects of zirconium compounds on organic reactions, as discussed elsewhere in this book, particularly in connection with zirconium dioxide and its effects on hydrocarbons at elevated temperatures.

In considering the chemical relationship of the zirconium atom to the carbon atom, much can be gained from viewing the relationship in the framework of the perspectives afforded by the periodic chart of the elements. Scanning the typical and A subgroup elements of Group IV from top to bottom, one notes the sequence: carbon to carbon bonds are extremely common and long known; carbon to silicon bonds are quite stable but much less common and known only as a relatively recent laboratory and industrial development; carbon to titanium bonds are extremely rare, tend to be unstable, and have been produced only very recently after long investigation (1); zirconium (or hafnium) to carbon bonds are unknown up to the present time.

More broadly, bonds between carbon and transition elements are generally uncommon, and have been unknown for some of the transition elements. Efforts to prepare alkyl and aryl iron compounds have not met with success. In considering that area of the chemistry of zirconium that involves its reactions with organic substances, a need is felt for an explanation, or at least a rationale, of its failure to form bonds with carbon. A completely

---

1. D. T. Herman and W. K. Nelson, *J. Am. Chem. Soc.* **74**, 2693 (1952).

satisfying answer to this question is not currently available, yet the phenomenon can be understood at least in part by making use of observations and concepts discussed in the preceding chapters. It has been noted that zirconium does not behave as an ion in any of its reactions at ordinary or moderately elevated temperatures.* Zirconium rarely is found at any oxidation number other than 0 and 4, and even in those few instances of compounds in which the oxidation number is 3 or 2 (the tri- and di- ClBrI halogenides of zirconium), their properties imply that they are polymerized and the structural units are tightly bound to one another. In this condition the coordination number of the zirconium atom is higher than its valence, and the valence electrons which did not form primary valence bonds are probably largely paired. The zirconium atom, therefore, is practically never available for reactions which occur by the pairing of oppositely charged ions or by the pairing of odd electrons. These two important categories of reaction, which account for so many reactions of other elements, are not applicable to reactions of zirconium. In illustration of the categories of reaction which apply to many of the reactions with carbon with other metals, but not to its reactions with zirconium, we may note the following:

Formation of carbon-containing compounds by ionic reactions

$$HCN \rightleftharpoons H^+ + CN^-$$
$$Ag^+ + CN^- \rightarrow AgCN$$

$$(1a\text{-}b)$$

Carbon reactions involving unpaired electrons (2)

$$D_2 \rightleftharpoons D^{\cdot} + D^{\cdot}$$
$$C_2H_6 \rightleftharpoons H_3CH_2C^{\cdot} + H^{\cdot}$$
$$H_3CH_2C^{\cdot} + D^{\cdot} \rightleftharpoons H_3CH_2DC$$

$$(2a\text{-}c)$$

In equations 2 a, b, and c, the dot $\cdot$ indicates an unpaired electron of hydrogen, deuterium, or carbon.

Averting our attention from the conditions for reactions for which zirconium never qualifies to those conditions for which it does qualify, we note that after its reactions, zirconium must always contain at least 8 electrons in its valence orbitals (4d and 5sp), and all reactions of zirconium may be regarded as initiated by the donation of lone pairs of electrons from other atoms to the zirconium atoms. As examples:**

Halogenation of zirconium

$$Zr + 2Cl\text{—}Cl \longrightarrow Cl\text{—}Cl \rightarrow Zr \leftarrow Cl\text{—}Cl \xrightarrow{\text{rearrangement}} ZrCl_4 \quad (3)$$

* The formation of zirconium ions at electric arc temperatures and in the atmospheres of stars is irrelevant to the present considerations.

** The examples given in equations 3 and 4 are simplified versions of more ramified reactions.

2. K. Miyahara, *J. Chem. Phys.* **26**, 1774-5 (1957).

Reaction of zirconium tetrachloride with water

$$Cl_2ZrCl_2 + 2H_2O \longrightarrow \overset{\overset{\displaystyle HOH}{\downarrow}}{\underset{\underset{\displaystyle HOH}{\uparrow}}{Cl_2ZrCl_2}} \xrightarrow{\text{rearrangement}} (O:ZrOH)^+ + 3H^+ + 4Cl^- \tag{4}$$

Our attention should now be directed to the first row elements. As we scan from right to left, we note that in their simpler compounds the number of lone pairs of electrons remaining on these atoms diminishes, becoming zero when we arrive at carbon. Examples:

$$H:\overset{..}{\underset{..}{F}}: \qquad H:\overset{..}{\underset{..}{O}}:H \qquad H:\overset{\displaystyle H}{\underset{..}{N}}:H \qquad H:\overset{\displaystyle H}{\underset{\displaystyle H}{C}}:H$$

Thus only carbon compounds are unable to participate in a process which begins with the donation of a pair of electrons. This disqualifies carbon compounds from reacting with zirconium with formation of a chemical bond.

It can be surmised, therefore, that a major reason for the nonexistence of compounds containing a zirconium-carbon bond is that the necessary prior circumstances for the formation of such bonds have never existed.*

It has been noted in Chapter 3 that some nitrogen compounds form addition compounds with zirconium tetrachloride, but not all nitrogen compounds form such addition compounds, even when the nitrogen atoms have lone pairs of electrons. This was explained as due to competition between lone pairs of electrons of the nitrogen atoms with lone pairs on the chlorine atoms within the zirconium tetrachloride molecule or crystal, this latter tendency causing double bonding of chlorine:

$$-\overset{|}{\underset{|}{Zr}}-Cl \;\rightleftharpoons\; -\overset{|}{\underset{|}{Zr}}=Cl \tag{5}$$

Were a carbon atom to donate a lone pair of electrons to a zirconium atom, it would have to overcome the same competition from lone pairs of electrons of the chlorine atoms. Since there is negligible availability of lone pairs of electrons from carbon, carbon does not succeed in the competition. A potential reaction is to be noted:

---

* Other circumstances also mitigate against the formation of zirconium-carbon bonds, where they do not similarly prevent the formation of other metal-carbon bonds. Aluminum trimethyl is formed by the reaction of aluminum metal with mercury dimethyl. For this reaction to occur, the relatively weakly bonded aluminum metal lattice (Mohs hardness 2.0, m. p. 660°) must be broken down, whereas a similar reaction with formation of zirconium tetramethyl would require a sufficiently energetic reaction to break down the refractory zirconium metal lattice (Mohs hardness ~3, m. p. 1830°).

$$ZrCl_4 + H-\underset{H\ H}{C}{=}\underset{}{C}-H \rightleftharpoons Cl_4Zr^- -\overset{H}{\underset{H}{C}}-\overset{+}{\underset{H}{C}}-H \qquad (6)$$

In such a reaction, a pair of pi electrons from the ethylenic double bond would have to attain an orbital position in the zirconium atom against the competition of lone pairs of electrons of the chlorine atoms. Actually, such a compound has never been isolated, but bonding with olefins as a fleeting stage appears to be involved in the catalysis of hydrocarbon reforming by zirconium compounds, and it may play a similar role in the hardening of vinyl polymers with zirconium salts (3, 4).

Some reports in the literature of compounds of zirconium with organic radicals or ligands, such as $ZrCl_4 \cdot 4C_4H_9Cl$ (5) and zirconium (and hafnium) carbonyls (6, 7) have not been supported with sufficient experimental data to permit their discussion at this time.

When cyclopentadiene is treated with sodium metal, hydrogen is liberated and a monosodium derivative is formed. The cyclic carbanion which is produced by the reaction contains three pairs of electrons which are conjugated in a pi-electron system analogous to that found in benzene:

$$\underset{\substack{H\quad\quad H\\ \diagdown\,\diagup\\ C\\ \diagup\,\diagdown\\ HC\quad\quad CH\\ \|\quad\quad\|\\ C\text{------}C\\ H\quad\quad\quad H}}{} + Na \rightarrow Na^+ \left[\underset{\substack{C\text{------}C\\ |\ :\quad :\ |\\ HC\quad\quad CH\\ \diagdown\,\diagup\\ \overset{..}{C}\\ |\\ H}}{\overset{H\quad\quad\quad H}{}}\right]^- + H \qquad (7)$$

The dots show the places of origin of the extra pairs of electrons. Since the carbon atoms are now all identical, none of the pairs of electrons is particularly associated with any one carbon atom. The cyclopentadienyl sodium reacts with chlorides of many transition metals to form biscyclopentadienyl compounds, in which the positively charged metal or metal-containing radical is sandwiched between two negatively charged cyclopentadienyl rings. It has not been possible to associate the bonding of the metal uniquely with any particular carbon atoms (8). The odd pair of electrons can be donated, however, to the metal:

---

3. G. T. Eaton and J. I. Crabtree, British Patent **559,689**, Mar. 1, 1944.
4. J. Q. Umberger and A. W. Grumbine, U.S. Patent **2,154,682**, April 18, 1939.
5. R. G. Jones, *Iowa State College J. Sci.* **17**, 88-99 (1952).
6. S. T. Jazwinski and J. A. Sisto, U.S. Patent **2,793,106**, May 21, 1957.
7. *Ibid.* **2,793,107**, May 21, 1957.
8. W. Moffitt, *J. Am. Chem. Soc.* **76**, 3386-92 (1954).

Biscyclopentadienyl
iron (ferrocene)

Biscyclopentadienyl
chlorozirconium (9)

Biscyclopentadienyl dibromozirconium can also be prepared by the reaction of cyclopentadienyl magnesium bromide with zirconium tetrachloride in ether solution (10).

Biscyclopentadienyl dichlorozirconium is soluble in water and insoluble in many common organic solvents such as benzene, while ferrocene is soluble in most organic solvents and insoluble in water. Biscyclopentadienyl dibromozirconium has been examined polarographically in its aqueous solution and found to exhibit no reduction curve (10). The sandwich structure is stable in aqueous acids and bases of moderate concentrations, but is decomposed by concentrated sulfuric acid and by molten alkali. They appear to be promising starting compounds for the synthesis of a wide variety of new organic compounds containing zirconium.

Zirconium tetrachloride does not react with nor dissolve in aryl or alkyl hydrocarbons. It catalyzes their thermal decomposition at elevated temperatures. Methane is normally stable up to at least 700°, but it darkens when passed through a tube with zirconium tetrachloride vapor at 400°. An exothermic reaction has been noted when acetylene was heated gently with zirconium tetrachloride (11), but no reactions occur between zirconium compounds in aqueous solution and freshly generated acetylene (12) or methane, or with phenyl diazonium chloride (13).

The author has observed dissolution of zirconium tetrachloride to occur in toluene at approximately −85°, under an atmosphere of hydrogen chloride. This might be due to the formation of a carbonium salt:

$$ZrCl_4 + HCl \rightleftharpoons HZrCl_5$$
$$HZrCl_5 + C_7H_8 \rightleftharpoons C_7H_9ZrCl_5$$

(8a-b)

9. G. Wilkinson and F. A. Cotton, *Chem. & Ind.* **1954**, 307-8.

10. G. Wilkinson, P. L. Pauson, J. M. Birmingham, and F. A. Cotton, *J. Am. Chem. Soc.* **75**, 1011-12 (1953).

11. F. P. Venable and R. O. Deitz, *J. Elisha Mitchell Sci. Soc.* **38**, Nos. 1 and 2, 74-5 (1922).

12. Titanium Alloy Mfg. Division of the National Lead Co., unpublished researches.

13. H. Gilman and R. G. Jones, *J. Org. Chem.* **10**, 505-15 (1945).

COMPOUNDS IN WHICH ZIRCONIUM IS BOUND TO ORGANIC RADICALS THROUGH NITROGEN

ZIRCONIUM DERIVATIVES OF AMINES

Ammonia and the organic amines do not combine with zirconium in aqueous solutions of its compounds because of the greater affinity of zirconium for the oxygen atoms of the water than for the nitrogen atoms.* The organic nitrogen bases behave like other bases in precipitating hydrous zirconia, when they are used to raise the pH of the aqueous solution containing zirconium. They also can furnish cations for the formation of salts of complex acids containing zirconium, e.g., the fluozirconates and lactatozirconates. In anhydrous environments, zirconium ClBrI tetrahalogenides react with ammonia and the amines to form addition products of the general empirical formula $ZrX_4 \cdot nA$, in which X represents a halogen atom and A an amine. The value of n for the amine additives is usually 2 or 4. In the presence of an excess of a liquid amine, such as propylamine or pyridine, the complex compound is dissolved.

By dissolving zirconium (or hafnium) ClBrI tetrahalogenides in methanol and saturating the solution with hydrogen chloride, then adding pyridine (and similarly, other organic nitrogen bases) pyridinium hexachlorozirconate (or hafnate) is precipitated as an anhydrous salt in which the protonated amine serves as a cation (14). It is seen from these behaviors that in an anhydrous amine environment, the lone pair of electrons of the nitrogen atom is donated to zirconium, but under acidic conditions; whether the environment is anhydrous or not, the lone pair is donated to a proton. The cation so formed may pair up with a complex zirconium anion to form a salt.

For further discussion of the ammino complexes and the salts formed by protonated amines with halogenozirconate ions, refer to Chapter 3, under the subhead *halogenozirconates*.

There has been no evidence of a reaction of the diazonium group in an aqueous solution with zirconium compounds or ions in the solution. Phenyl diazonium chloride, for example, has been observed not to react with zirconium compounds (13). The cyanide and thiocyanate ions behave toward zirconium as halogenoids, as discussed in Chapter 7. Zirconium tetrachloride reacts with acetonitrile to form an addition compound of empirical formula $ZrCl_4 \cdot 2CH_3CN$ (15).

---

* Little is known of the reactions of zirconium halogenides with organic compounds in which several amine groups are present on a chain or ring in vicinal positions.

14. A. Rosenheim and P. Frank, *Ber.* 38, 812 (1905).

15. E. M. Larsen and L. E. Trevorrow, *J. Inorg. Nuclear Chem.* 2, 254-9 (1956); E. M. Larsen, *U.S. Gov't. Research Report PB 123124*, August 1955.

DERIVATIVES IN WHICH THE ZIRCONIUM IS CHELATED
BY NITROGEN AND OXYGEN

In contrast with the urea complex with zirconium tetrachloride which decomposes and dissolves in water, 8-hydroxyquinoline precipitates zirconium quantitatively or almost so from aqueous solutions of its compounds. The precipitate is voluminous, and the mole ratio of quinoline to zirconium has been observed to vary from 1.5 to 4.0 (16, 17). At the latter composition, the zirconium atom is at coordination number 8. The crystalline solid recovered after precipitation from an excess of the 8-hydroxyquinoline has been observed to be stable and slightly volatile at 150°. Unlike the

8-Hydroxyquinoline

carboxylatozirconic acids, it is insoluble in ammonium hydroxide, and this is doubtless due to the absence of a replaceable hydrogen atom. The properties indicate a chelate structure containing 5-membered rings, in which the zirconium atom is bonded covalently with the phenol oxygen atom and the nitrogen atom. The compound is soluble in mineral acid solutions. It has a green fluorescence, as do the 8-hydroxyquinolinates of a number of metals (18, 19). Both zirconium and hafnium 8-hydroxyquinolates can be extracted from aqueous media with chloroform or hexone (20).

Dibromo 8-hydroxyquinoline precipitates a zirconium compound which is insoluble in water and in ammonium hydroxide (21). Iodoxime, 5,7-diiodo 8-hydroxyquinoline likewise precipitates zirconium and is reported to detect 0.2 mg of zirconium in 200 ml (22). The somewhat related 4-hydroxybenzothiazole precipitates a zirconium compound with a greenish-yellow fluorescence (23). Quinaldic acid precipitates zirconium from hot aqueous solutions of the chloride, but not in the cold. The precipitate is soluble in acetic acid (24).

16. G. Balenescu, *Z. Anal. Chem.* **101**, 101-8 (1935).
17. R. Bock and F. Umland, *Angew. Chem.* **67**, 420-3 (1955).
18. R. E. Thiers, E. M. S. Arthur, J. R. Mills, D. H. Hamly, and F. E. Beamish, *J. Ind. Hyg. Toxicol.* **29**, 129-33 (1947).
19. F. Feigl, C. Farok, and H. Zocher, *Anais assoc. quím. Brasil* **9**, 21-7 (1950).
20. D. Dryssen and Viktoria Dahlberg, *Acta Chem. Scand.* **7**, 1186-96 (1953).
21. P. Süe and G. Wetroff, *Bull. soc. chim.* (5) **2**, 1002-7 (1935).
22. A. J. Mukherjee and B. Banerjee, *Naturwiss.* **42**, 416-7 (1955).
23. Q. Fernando, *Anal. Chim. Acta* **12**, 432-5 (1955).
24. O. Erämetsä, *Suomen Kemistilehti* **17B**, 30 (1944).

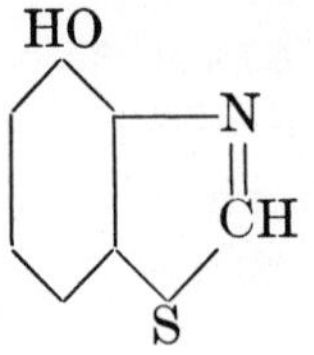

HO

—N
‖
CH
S

4-Hydroxybenzothiazole

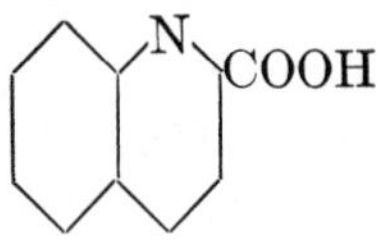

N
COOH

Quinaldic acid

Cupferron (nitrosophenylhydroxylamine) bears a certain structural resemblance to mandelic acid. It does not precipitate zirconium quite as quantitatively from mildly acid solutions (the solubility of the precipitate in mildly acid solutions is about 10^{-7} moles per liter), but the precipitate is remarkably insoluble in strong sulfuric acid solutions. It can be precipitated for analytical purposes in 40% sulfuric acid. The 1-naphthyl and p-xenyl analogs of cupferron have been found to form similar precipitates (25, 26). Zirconium cupferronate can be extracted from an aqueous medium with chloroform or hexone (20).

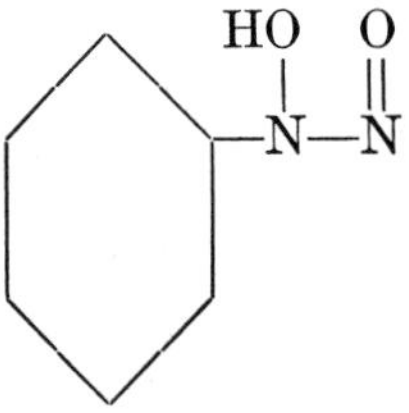

HO   O
| ‖
—N—N

Cupferron

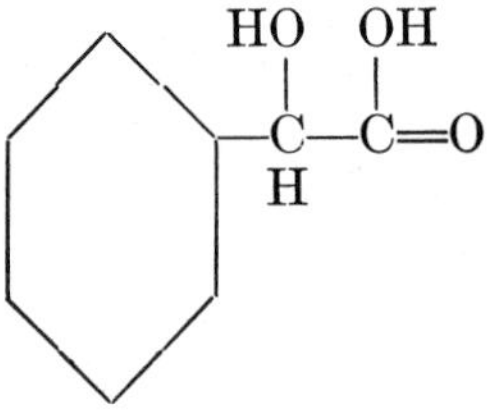

HO   OH
| |
—C—C=O
H

Mandelic acid

Very little is known about the reactions of amino acids and proteins with zirconyl ions in aqueous solution. Their carboxyl groups doubtless tend to become bonded to the zirconium atom in the solution, but there is little tendency for compounds so formed to precipitate from solution. Glycine (aminoacetic acid) does not dissolve carbonated hydrous zirconia, probably because it is not a strong enough acid. Zirconyl chloride has little or no tanning effect on leather when applied in an aqueous medium, and it does not precipitate such acids as glutamic ($HOOCCHNH_2CH_2CH_2COOH$) or aspartic ($HOOCCHNH_2CH_2COOH$). (See Fig. 9.1). The behavior of disulfatozirconic acid, 2123, is significantly different. Disulfatozirconic acid hardens gelatine (27), is an excellent tanning agent for leather (28, 29), and

25. S. Fujiwara, *J. Chem. Soc. Japan, Pure Chem. Sect.* **72**, 77-80 (1951).
26. P. J. Elving and E. C. Olson, *J. Am. Chem. Soc.* **78**, 4206-10 (1956).
27. J. Q. Umberger and A. W. Grumbine, U.S. Patent **2,154,682**, April 18, 1957.
28. I. C. Sommerville, *J. Am. Leather Chemists Assoc.* **37**, 381-90 (1942).
29. H. G. Turley and I. C. Sommerville, *J. Am. Leather Chemists Assoc.* **37**, 391-7 (1942).

it precipitates glutamic and aspartic acids quantitatively (12). The nature of the compounds formed under these circumstances is unknown. It is imaginable that a pseudochelate structure forms by the establishment of a covalent bond between the zirconium atom and the carboxyl oxygen atom, and a polar bond between the zirconyl oxygen atom and the protonated amine nitrogen atom.

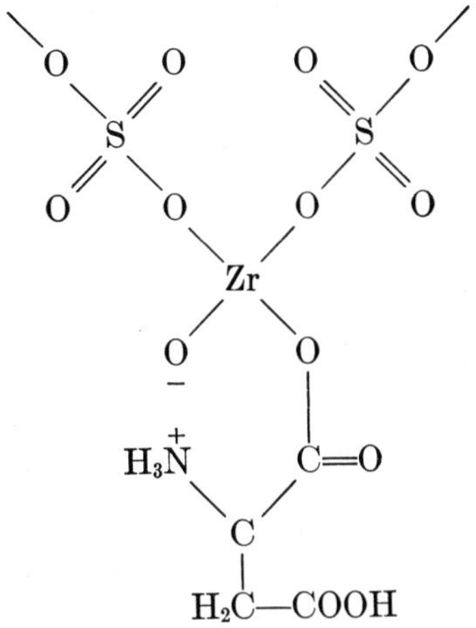

FIG. 9.1. Suggested structure of a fragment of the precipitate obtained with disulfatozirconic acid and aspartic acid.

ZIRCONIUM DERIVATIVES OF ORGANIC COMPOUNDS IN WHICH THE METAL IS LINKED TO THE ORGANIC RADICAL THROUGH —O—N—

Simple compounds of zirconium with oximes or nitroso compounds have not been reported. Zirconium (and hafnium) tetrachloride and many of its addition products and other derivatives are soluble in nitrobenzene (30, 31, 32), and the solutes are doubtlessly chemically combined with nitrobenzene. Many metallic compounds have been observed to react with solutions of o-nitrophenol in petroleum ether to form organic derivatives of the metals, but zirconium compounds showed no evidence of reacting similarly (33).

Chelates are readily formed with zirconium by organic compounds which have nitroso or nitro groups and oxygen atoms in vicinal positions. In very

30. T. R. Sato, H. Diamond, W. P. Norris, and H. H. Strain, *J. Am. Chem. Soc.* **74,** 6154-5 (1952).

31. S. K. Dhar and A. K. Das Gupta, *J. Sci. Ind. Research India* **11B,** 500-1 (1952).

32. I. A. Sheka and B. A. Voïtovich, *Zhur. Neorg. Khim.* **2,** 26-33 (1957).

33. G. Cronheim, *J. Org. Chem.* **12,** 1-6 (1947).

dilute solutions, colored soluble complexes are formed by 1-nitroso-2-naph-
thol (34) and 2-nitroso-1-naphthol (35), and have been identified spectro-
photometrically. The complex with 2-nitroso-1-naphthol in 3 M perchloric
acid solution contains four of the organic groups per zirconium atom, but
fewer organic groups in less strongly acid medium. The red color of the
2-nitroso-1-naphthol is of value in detecting the presence of zirconium in

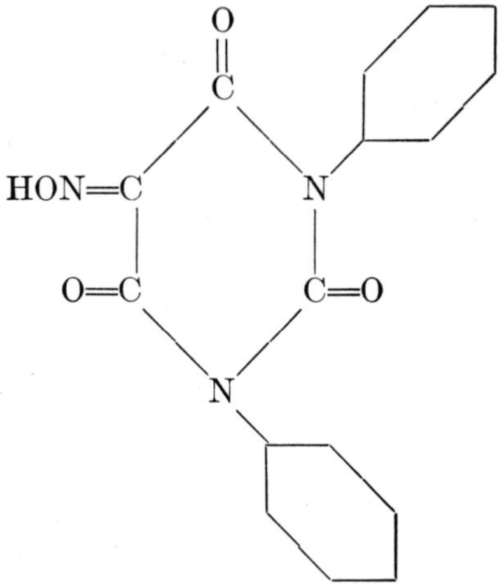

Diphenylvioluric acid

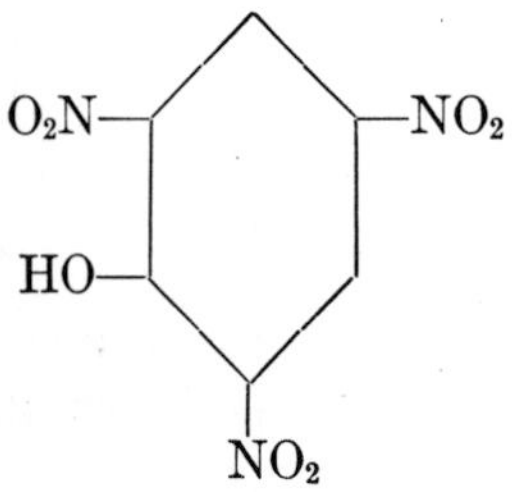

Picric acid

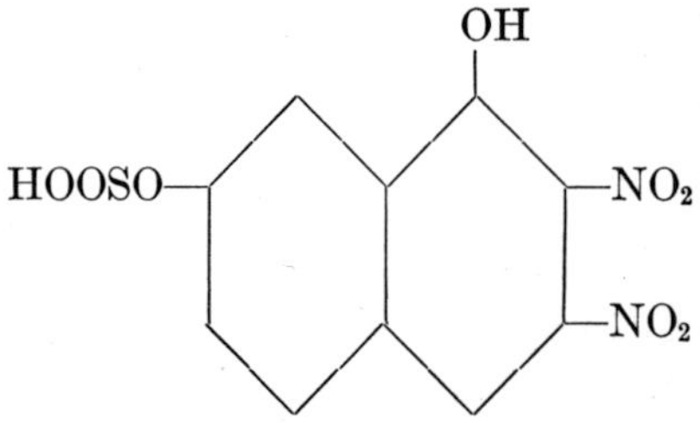

Flavianic acid

34. H. B. Jonassen and W. R. DeMonsabert, *J. Am. Chem. Soc.* **76**, 6025-7 (1954).
35. J. Gillis, A. Claeys, and J. Hoste, *Mededel. Konickl. Vlaam. Akad. Wetenschappen Belg.*, Klasse Wetenschap I, No. 11, 13 pp. (1947).

chloride solutions, except when sulfates or other strongly complexing ions are present (36). When sizable quantities of zirconyl chloride and 1-nitroso-2-naphthol or 2-nitroso-1-naphthol are mixed, the solid zirconium derivatives of these agents are precipitated, and they can be dried at 100° without decomposition (37).

Related insoluble chelates are formed by adding oxalohydroxamic acid (31) or ammonium diphenylviolurate (38) to solutions of zirconyl salts.

Picric acid precipitates zirconium quantitatively from solutions of its salts. The dried precipitate is zirconium tetrapicrate, $Zr(C_6H_2(NO_2)_3O)_4$. It can also be prepared by the action of picric acid on carbonated hydrous zirconia. The yellow crystals are stable up to 317-322°, at which temperature explosion occurs. The precipitate is stable in the presence of mineral acids, and it is said not to explode if when heated it is moist with sulfuric acid. It does not form soluble complexes with alkalies (39, 40, 41, 42). A related precipitate is formed by the reaction of sodium flavianate with zirconium in aqueous solutions of its salts (43).

COMPOUNDS IN WHICH ZIRCONIUM IS BOUND TO ORGANIC RADICALS THROUGH SULFUR OR PHOSPHORUS

It has already been discussed in Chapter 2 that sulfur and phosphorus have relatively weak tendencies to form chemical bonds with zirconium, that they undergo certain peculiar reactions with zirconium metal, and that other chemical reactions are known only at high temperatures under reducing conditions where it may be supposed that elementary zirconium is formed, and the zirconium reacts with the sulfur and phosphorus while in the elementary condition. No organic radicals are stable under the conditions required for forming zirconium-sulfur or zirconium-phosphorus bonds, and therefore, it is in accordance with expectation that we find no organic compounds containing zirconium bound to the molecule through sulfur or phosphorus.

A thioglycolatozirconate comparable to triglycolatozirconic acid or its salts (Chap. 8) fails to form when thioglycolic acid is added to solutions of zirconium salts. Other metals can be sequestered in aqueous solution by thioglycolic acid, leaving zirconium alone available for precipitation by the

36. V. O. Oshman and T. K. Zerchaninova, *Redkie Metal* 3, No. 6, 36-7 (1934).

37. I. Bellucci and G. Savola, *Atti. Congresso. naz. chim. pura applicata* **1923**, 483-8.

38. R. P. Singh, *J. Sci. Ind. Research* **15B**, 245-7 (1956).

39. M. Speter, *Continental Met. Chem. Eng.* **1**, 83 (1926).

40. T. N. Burakova, *Uchenye Zapiski Leningrad. Gosudarst. Univ. im. A. A. Zhdanova No. 178, Ser. Geol. Nauk* No. 4, 157-95 (1954).

41. O. Silberrad and H. A. Phillips, *J. Chem. Soc.* **93**, 474 (1908).

42. J. H. de Boer and A. E. van Arkel, *Z. anorg. allgem. Chem.* **148**, 84-6 (1925).

43. O. Erämetsä, *Suomen Kemistilehti* **16B**, 12 (1943).

reagents of analytical chemistry, such as ammonium benzoate (44). Zirconyl nitrate has been observed not to react with thiocarbohydrazide, CS-$(NHNH_2)_2$, in aqueous media (45).

Oxyacids of sulfur and phosphorus react with zirconium salts in aqueous solution, and are bonded to the zirconium atom through oxygen, as discussed in Chapters 6 and 7. Both water-soluble and water-insoluble organic compounds, in which zirconium is bonded through the oxygen atoms of the oxyacids of sulfur and phosphorus, are known. Among the compounds of this category are those derived from phytic acid (inositolhexaphosphonic acid) and cocarboxylase (aneurine pyrophosphate), both of which form water-insoluble zirconium derivatives, the former being insoluble in aqueous ammonia and the latter soluble (46). Phosphinic acids have been observed to form both water-soluble and water-insoluble compounds with zirconium, depending on the composition of the organic radical (12).*

COMPOUNDS IN WHICH ZIRCONIUM IS BOUND TO ORGANIC RADICALS AND LIGANDS THROUGH OXYGEN ONLY

SOME GENERAL ASPECTS

The bonding of an oxygen atom of an organic molecule to zirconium has much of the nature of the bonding of an oxygen atom of an inorganic ion or molecule, but it has especial interest because of consequences of this bonding on the organic radical. Also, resonance properties of the organic radical have effects on the zirconium-oxygen bond. Some conspicuous chemical behaviors of oxygen-containing organic compounds of zirconium are the following:

1. If an organic compound contains 1 and only 1 oxygen atom, it does not react with zirconium ions in aqueous solutions, but in anhydrous systems it forms addition compounds with zirconium ClBrI tetrahalogenides. For example, methanol does not react with zirconyl ions in aqueous solutions, but zirconium tetrachloride dissolves in cold methanol to form addition compounds.

2. When addition compounds are formed by zirconium halogenides with alcohols containing only 1 oxygen atom, they are stable at low temperatures only, e.g., $0°$ to $-15°$ or lower. On warming they tend to lose hydrogen halogenide and thus to form alkoxides. One to three chlorine atoms can be

---

* The author is indebted to Dr. Clarence Stiegman of the Oldbury Electrochemical Co. for making available laboratory preparations of phosphinic acids used in experiments on which these statements are based.

44. A. Jewsbury and G. H. Osborn, *Anal. Chim. Acta* **3**, 642-55 (1949).
45. Ng. Ph. Buu-Hoï, T. B. Loc, and Ng. D. Xuong, *Bull. soc. chim. France* **1955**, 694-7.
46. G. Beck, *Anal. Chim. Acta* **4**, 21-2 (1950).

replaced from zirconium tetrachloride by alkoxide groups in this way, and the fourth is commonly replaced after making the environment alkaline. Trichlorozirconium acetonate and monochlorozirconium trimethoxide are examples of compounds formed by the decompositions of addition compounds of alcohols (including the enol forms of ketones) with zirconium tetrachloride.

3. Many organic compounds containing more than 1 oxygen atom, pairs of which are separated by 2 or 3 carbon atoms (or in some cases nitrogen or other atoms may take the place of carbon) form very stable chelates with zirconium in anhydrous systems, and under more restricted conditions in aqueous solution. For example, acetylacetone forms chelates with the zirconium atom when allowed to react with zirconium tetrachloride suspended in benzene or with zirconyl chloride in aqueous solution. The zirconium atoms in zirconyl salt solutions are also chelated by glycol, glycerine, or mannitol under suitable conditions.

4. Oxygen atoms bearing an electronegative charge and singly bonded to carbon react most readily with zirconium; twice singly bonded oxygen atoms, which are bonded to 2 carbon atoms or a carbon atom and another atom such as hydrogen, react less readily with zirconium; and doubly bonded oxygen reacts least readily and often not at all. Thus the unionized alcohols and polyols do not inhibit the formation of hydrous zirconia when base is added to a solution of a zirconium salt to bring the pH to 2-4. These organic molecules cannot compete with the hydroxyl ion for the zirconium atom. The partially ionized carboxylic acids, such as acetic, inhibit the formation of hydrous zirconia until relatively high pH's are reached, i.e., about 7-9. The glycols, which do not inhibit the formation of hydrous zirconia at pH 2-4, prevent it completely in the pH range 10-12, at which the anion —OCH$_2$ CH$_2$O— chelates the zirconium atom with formation of highly stable complexes. While an insoluble chelate is formed following the addition of lactic acid, $CH_3CHOHCOOH$ to a zirconyl salt solution, a similar product is not formed by pyruvic acid, $CH_3COCOOH$.

ZIRCONIUM DERIVATIVES OF ETHERS

When zirconium tetrachloride is added to anhydrous diethyl ether, heat is evolved as the zirconium compound is dissolved. A compound of composition $ZrCl_4 \cdot 2C_2H_5OC_2H_5$ is formed (47), which presumably has the structure

---

47. A. Rosenheim and J. Herzmann, *Ber.* **40**, 810-14 (1907).

A similar reaction product has been obtained from zirconium tetrachloride and isoamyl ether, but its isoamyl ether content approaches without quite attaining to 2 ether ligands per zirconium atom (15).

The etherates do not form in aqueous systems, even when the possibility of forming the etherate is apparently increased by the opportunity for formation of a chelate, as in the case of methoxyacetic acid (48). Zirconyl salts are entirely insoluble in ether, and if the surfaces of particles of zirconium tetrachloride are hydrolyzed, its dissolution in ether is impeded.

The formation of etherates with zirconium tetrachloride appears to be irreversible, and no method has been reported for recovering zirconium tetrachloride from its solution in ether or from its compound with ether. Zirconium etherates dissolve in water with formation of zirconyl chloride solution.

ZIRCONIUM DERIVATIVES OF ALCOHOLS

When zirconium tetrachloride is treated with alcohols under suitable conditions, 1, 2, 3 or all of its chlorine atoms are replaced by the alkoxide group, —O—R. A comparison of the reactivities of zirconium tetrachloride and other tetrachlorides with alcohols has indicated the order to be $SiCl_4 >$ $TiCl_4 > ZrCl_4 > ThCl_4$, and this same order holds for their reactivities with water (49). The compounds resulting from the replacement of chlorine atoms by alkoxide groups will be designated *chlorozirconium alkoxides* and *alkoxides* in the following discussion. These products are frequently recovered in the solvated condition, and when the solvating substance is the alcohol from which they are derived, they will be referred to as *zirconium alkoxide alcoholates*.

At temperatures near to 0°, zirconium tetrachloride dissolves exothermically in alcohols and ketones (which may also be regarded as alcohols, when they are in their enol form), and if the temperature is not permitted to rise, there is little or no evolution of hydrogen chloride. An addition product is believed to form (49):

$$ZrCl_4 + nROH \rightarrow ZrCl_4 \cdot nROH \qquad (9)$$

As the temperature is raised, one or more molecules of hydrogen chloride are liberated with formation of chlorozirconium alkoxides or zirconium alkoxides:

$$ZrCl_4 \cdot nROH \rightleftharpoons Cl_{4-m}Zr(OR)_m \cdot rROH + (n - m - r)ROH + mHCl \quad (10)$$

For some of the reactions of this type, equilibrium constants have been determined. Values for pK_1, pK_2, pK_3, and pK_4 as determined by potentio-

---

48. W. B. Blumenthal, *J. Chem. Ed.* **26**, 472-5 (1949).

49. D. C. Bradley and W. Wardlaw, *J. Chem. Soc.* **1951**, 280-5.

metric and conductivity measurements for the reaction

$$ZrCl_4 + nROH \rightleftharpoons ZrCl_{4-n}(OR)_n + nHCl \qquad (11)$$

at 25° are given in Table 9.1 (50). The table includes values for the corresponding reactions with hafnium tetrachloride.

TABLE 9.1. VALUES FOR EQUILIBRIUM CONSTANTS IN THE REACTIONS OF ZIRCONIUM AND HAFNIUM TETRACHLORIDES WITH ALCOHOLS TO FORM ALKOXIDES

Alcohol, ROH	Values for equilibrium constants							
	pK_1		pK_2		pK_3		pK_4	
	$ZrCl_4$	$HfCl_4$	$ZrCl_4$	$HfCl_4$	$ZrCl_4$	$HfCl_4$	$ZrCl_4$	$HfCl_4$
CH_3OH	1.69	1.29	5.18	4.64	10.41	9.74	18.25	17.57
C_2H_5OH	2.40	2.30	6.68	6.35	12.20	11.81	20.80	19.68

The zirconium alkoxides and chlorozirconium alkoxides can be treated in various ways to increase or decrease the ratio of alkoxide groups to chlorine atoms bound to zirconium. Removal of hydrogen chloride by boiling the reactants or by addition of suitable alkalies* tends to increase the ratio. Treatment with acetyl chloride increases the ratio and at the same time esterifies some of the alcohol. Thus, treatment of $Cl_3ZrOC_2H_5 \cdot C_2H_5OH$, $Cl_2Zr(OC_2H_5)_2$, or $Zr(OC_2H_5)_4$ with acetyl chloride gave mixtures of reaction products containing more chlorine than the original (chloro)zirconium alkoxides. The products included $Cl_4Zr \cdot CH_3COOC_2H_5$, $Cl_3ZrOC_2H_5 \cdot CH_3COOC_2H_5$, $Cl_2Zr(OC_2H_5)_2 \cdot C_2H_5OH$, $Cl_2Zr(OC_2H_5)_2 \cdot CH_3COOC_2H_5$, and $ClZr(OC_2H_5)_3$.

A monomeric zirconium alkoxide contains zirconium at coordination number 4, except for any increase by double-bond formation between the

---

* The reported formation of sodium hydrogen hexamethoxyzirconate, $NaHZr(OC_2H_5)_6$ (53) was later shown not to be correct (54). Sodium ethoxide reacts with zirconium tetrachloride giving $Na_4Zr_6(OC_2H_5)_{21}(OH)_7$, which undergoes change in composition when subjected to recrystallization from toluene (54). The reaction of pyridinium chlorozirconate with sodium ethoxide yields pyridinium ethoxypentachlorozirconate (55):

$$(C_5H_6N)_2ZrCl_6 + NaOC_2H_5 \rightarrow (C_5H_6N)_2Zr(OC_2H_5)Cl + NaCl.$$

50. C. R. Simmons and R. S. Hansen, *J. Phys. Chem.* 59, 1072-3 (1955).
51. D. C. Bradley, R. C. Mehrotra, J. D. Swanwick, and W. Wardlaw, *J. Chem. Soc.* 1953, 2025-30.
52. W. Wardlaw, *J. Chem. Soc.* 1956, 4004-14.
53. H. Meerwein and T. Bersin, *Ann.* 476, 113-50 (1929).
54. D. C. Bradley and W. Wardlaw, *J. Chem. Soc.* 1951, 280-5.
55. D. C. Bradley, F. M. Abd-el-Halim, E. A. Sadek, and W. Wardlaw, *J. Chem. Soc.* 1952, 2032-5.

zirconium and alkoxy oxygen atoms. This leaves the zirconium atom in a reactive state which is made manifest in tendencies for the compounds to form solvates with the alcohol in the reacting mixture, or to form polymers or solvated polymers. (In this connection, see reference 51). The extent of polymerization is determined by the steric properties of the molecule. Alco-

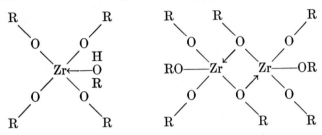

Alcoholated zirconium alkoxide   Polymerized zirconium alkoxide

hols of straight-chain alkyl radicals, such as methyl, ethyl, and n-propyl alcohols, and the simpler and lower molecular weight branched-chain alcohols, such as isopropyl alcohol, give rise to zirconium alkoxides which are

Zirconium tetra(tertiary butyl methyl methoxide)

commonly trimers or tetramers. That is, the molecule contains three to four times the number of atoms represented by the simplest empirical formula. This has been determined by measurements of vapor density and colligative properties in solution in solvents such as benzene (51, 52). Alcohols of higher molecular weight, having branched chains, form alkoxides whose molecules are monomeric. The actual physical shielding of the zirconium atom by the branched hydrocarbon chains prevents the approach of one molecule to another to form coordinated bonds. Thus, the alkoxide $Zr(OCH(CH_3)C_4H_9\text{-}tert.)_4$ was found to be monomeric by ebullioscopic measurements in benzene (56). An instructive picture of the shielding of the zirconium atom by the branches of a hydrocarbon chain can be had even from a two-dimensional representation of the arrangement of atoms in the molecule, as shown. The shielding effect goes so far as to obscure almost completely the nature of the metal atom in the center of the molecule. Thus, the compounds $Ti(OC(C_2H_5)_3)_4$, $Zr(OC(C_2H_5)_3)_4$, and $Th(OC(C_2H_5)_3)_4$ have the respective boiling points 166°, 166°, and 154° at 0.1 mm pressure, indicating that the metal is exerting little or no influence on the vapor pressure (52). The size of the metal atom is important, however, in determining how large an organic shield is required to prevent the polymerization of the alkoxide, as the data of Table 9.2 clearly show.

TABLE 9.2. BOILING POINTS* AND MOLECULAR COMPLEXITIES** OF THE ALKOXIDES
$M(OC(CH_3)_n(C_2H_5)_{3-n})_4$ (52)

Value of n	Metal whose alkoxide is measured							
	Titanium		Zirconium		Cerium		Thorium	
	b.p.	com-plexity	b.p.	com-plexity	b.p.	com-plexity	b.p.	com-plexity
3	52	1	50	1	150	2.4	160	3.4
2	98	1	95	1	245	2.3	198	2.8
1	128	1	128	1	132	1	148	1.8
0	166	1	166	1	154	1	154	1

* The boiling points are at 0.1 mm pressure.
** Complexity is used here to indicate the number of monomer units per molecule.

Although alkoxides are readily prepared by the reactions of primary alcohols with zirconium tetrachloride, it has been observed that when secondary alcohols are used, the products are apt to be appreciably hydro-

56. D. C. Bradley, R. C. Mehrotra, and W. Wardlaw, *J. Chem. Soc.* **1952**, 5020-3.

lyzed, and attempts to prepare alkoxides from tertiary alcohols by this reaction have failed completely. This appears due to the reaction of the hydrogen chloride formed by the initial process with the alcohol to form water and alkyl halogenide. It is well known that tertiary, secondary, and primary alcohols react with hydrogen chloride at decreasing rates, in that order (54). As against this, when pyridinium chlorozirconate reacts with alcohols and ammonia to form zirconium alkoxides, no hydrogen chloride is generated and no hydrolysis products are formed, even when tertiary butyl alcohol is used (55).

The striking increase of volatility of zirconium tetraalkoxides, as the alkoxy group is derived respectively from primary, secondary, and tertiary alcohols, is noteworthy (54).

The following is a summary of some of the methods for preparing the individual chlorozirconium alkoxides and zirconium alkoxides and of some of their properties.

Chlorozirconium methoxides

When 120 cc of methanol was added to 24.2 g of zirconium tetrachloride, a vigorous reaction occurred, with evolution of hydrogen chloride. After evaporating the filtered solution to dryness, 25 g of a pale-yellow solid was recovered. Its analysis indicated it to contain an equal number of moles each of $Cl_3ZrOCH_3 \cdot CH_3OH$ and $Cl_2Zr(OCH_3)_2$. It was insoluble in ether, benzene, or light petroleum, but dissolved in methanol. It could not be crystallized from the methanol solution (57).

Another process for the preparation of chlorozirconium methoxides involves the reaction of methanol with chlorozirconium triisopropoxide (57):

$$ClZr(OC_3H_7\text{-}i) \cdot i\text{-}C_3H_7OH + 3CH_3OH \rightarrow$$
$$ClZr(OCH_3)_3 + 4i\text{-}C_3H_7OH \tag{12}$$

Also

$$Cl_2Zr(OC_3H_7\text{-}i) \cdot i\text{-}C_3H_7OH + 2CH_3OH \rightarrow$$
$$Cl_2Zr(OCH_3)_2 + 3i\text{-}C_3H_7OH \tag{13}$$

Chlorozirconium ethoxides

The reaction of zirconium tetrachloride with an excess of ethyl alcohol gives a solid reaction product which consists of a mixture of equal numbers of moles of $Cl_3ZrOC_2H_5 \cdot C_2H_5OH$ and $Cl_2Zr(OC_2H_5)_2$. The second of these products appears to form from the first. When the alcohol is removed from the reaction mixture by azeotropic distillation with benzene or light petroleum, the residual solution contains only $Cl_2Zr(OC_2H_5)_2$ (49).

57. D. C. Bradley, F. M. Abd-el-Halim, R. C. Mehrotra, and W. Wardlaw, J. Chem. Soc. 1952, 4960-3.

In the presence of ammonia, dichlorozirconium ethoxide ethylate forms according to the equation

$$ZrCl_4 + 3C_2H_5OH + 2NH_3 \rightarrow Cl_2Zr(OC_2H_5)_2 \cdot C_2H_5OH + 2NH_4Cl \quad (14)$$

The coordinated alcohol can be removed by prolonged heating at $80°$ under 0.5 mm pressure. In contrast, the coordinated alcohol cannot be removed from trichlorozirconium ethoxide by heating in vacuum up to the point of catastrophic decomposition of the molecule.

Zirconium tetraethoxide reacts with hydrogen chloride to give trichlorozirconium ethoxide diethylate (58).

Chlorozirconium triethoxide can be prepared by the reaction of zirconium tetraethoxide with acetyl chloride:

$$Zr(OC_2H_5)_4 + CH_3COCl \rightarrow ClZr(OC_2H_5)_3 + CH_3COOC_2H_5 \quad (15)$$

In general, the tendency of chlorozirconium ethoxides to form addition products with ethyl alcohol decreases with increased replacement of chlorine by ethoxide groups. The chlorozirconium ethoxides also react with acetyl chloride to form ester addition compounds of zirconium tetrachloride:

$$Cl_3ZrOC_2H_5 \cdot C_2H_5OH + 2CH_3COCl \rightarrow$$
$$ZrCl_4 \cdot CH_3COOC_2H_5 + CH_3COOC_2H_5 + HCl \quad (16\text{-}17)$$

$$Cl_2Zr(OC_2H_5)_2 + 2CH_3COCl \rightarrow Cl_4Zr \cdot CH_3COOC_2H_5 + CH_3COOC_2H_5$$

Chlorozirconium ethoxides undergo metatheses with alcohols to form other chlorozirconium alkoxides, for example (57):

$$Cl_2Zr(OC_2H_5)_2 \cdot C_2H_5OH + 3i\text{-}C_3H_7OH \rightarrow$$
$$Cl_2Zr(OC_3H_7\text{-}i)_2 \cdot i\text{-}C_3H_7OH + 3C_2H_5OH \quad (18)$$

Other chlorozirconium alkoxides

Zirconium tetraisopropoxide reacts with hydrogen chloride to give a mixture of dichloro- and trichlorozirconium isopropoxides (58). Zirconium tetra-n-propoxide reacts with acetyl chloride to give an addition compound of zirconium tetrachloride and n-propyl acetate, $ZrCl_4 \cdot C_3H_7OOCCH_3$ (59). Zirconium tetraisopropoxide gives $ZrCl_4 \cdot 2i\text{-}C_3H_7OOCCH_3$, $Cl_3Zr(OC_3H_7\text{-}i)$, $Cl_2Zr(OC_3H_7\text{-}i)_2 \cdot i\text{-}C_3H_7OH$, and $ClZr(OC_3H_7\text{-}i)_3 \cdot i\text{-}C_3H_7OH$, depending on the proportion of acetyl chloride used. The last three products form rapidly and quantitatively from the reactants. No hydrogen chloride is evolved during any of these preparations (59). The products of these reactions react with one another, e.g.,

58. R. C. Mehrotra, *J. Indian Chem. Soc.* **30**, 731-4 (1953).

59. D. C. Bradley, F. M. Abd-el-Halim, R. C. Mehrotra, and W. Wardlaw, *J. Chem. Soc.* **1952**, 4609-12.

$$Zr(OC_3H_7\text{-}i)_4 \cdot i\text{-}C_3H_7OH + ZrCl_4 \cdot 2i\text{-}C_3H_7OOCCH_3 \rightarrow \tag{19}$$

$$Cl_2Zr(OC_3H_7\text{-}i)_2 \cdot i\text{-}C_3H_7OH \text{ plus other products (59)}.$$

After the reaction of isopropyl alcohol or n-amyl alcohol with zirconium tetrachloride, it has not been found possible to remove the excess of alcohol, even under reduced pressure, without decomposing the product (57). Tertiary butyl and tertiary amyl alcohols react in more than one manner with chlorozirconium triisopropoxide. When a minimum of tertiary amyl alcohol is used and the reaction occurs in a benzene medium, a simple metathesis occurs:

$$ClZr(OC_3H_7\text{-}i)_3 \cdot i\text{-}C_3H_7OH + 3C_5H_{11}OH \rightarrow \tag{20}$$

$$ClZr(OC_5H_{11})_3 + 4i\text{-}C_3H_7OH$$

In the presence of excess tertiary amyl alcohol and in the absence of benzene, a second reaction occurs in which a hydrolyzed zirconium compound is formed, as well as an alkyl chloride, olefin, and water. Chlorozirconium tri-tertiary amyl oxide itself decomposes very slowly in boiling benzene with formation of an olefin, but no volatile chloride. If tertiary amyl alcohol is added, there is an immediate decomposition with formation of a hydrolyzed zirconium compound, an olefin, water, and hydrogen chloride. A similar process occurs with tertiary butyl alcohol and chlorozirconium tri-tertiary-butoxide. A proposed mechanism for such reactions is expressed by the following equations (57):

$$ClZr(OC(CH_3)_3)_3 + C(CH_3)_3OH \rightarrow \tag{21}$$

$$\rightarrow HOZr(OC(CH_3)_3)_3 + (CH_3)_2CCH_2 + HCl$$

The hydrogen chloride so formed reacts with more of the tertiary alcohol to form alkyl chloride and water.

Tertiary amyl alcohol reacts with dichlorozirconium diisopropoxide to form the mixed dichlorozirconium alkoxide, $Cl_2Zr(OC_3H_7\text{—}i)(O(C_2H_5)C(CH_3)_2)$. This will react with more of the tertiary amyl alcohol to give an olefin, hydrogen chloride, etc. (57).

Zirconium tetra-tertiary-amyloxide is much less reactive toward acetyl chloride than the previously discussed alkoxides, and the reaction products do not go beyond one chlorine atom per alkoxide molecule, i.e., monochloro-zirconium tri-tertiary-amyloxide (59).

Zirconium methoxide*

Zirconium methoxide can be prepared by the metathesis of methanol with zirconium isopropoxide. It is a white, microcrystalline solid which is sparingly soluble in organic solvents. It is insoluble in methanol or benzene, even at their boiling points (54).

Zirconium ethoxide

Zirconium ethoxide forms readily when zirconium tetrachloride reacts with ethyl alcohol in the presence of ammonia. The following preparation has been described (54):

> Ammonia was passed into a solution of 52.5 g of zirconium tetrachloride in 200 ml of ethyl alcohol, whereupon an exothermic reaction occurred with the formation of a voluminous precipitate. The passage of ammonia was continued until the temperature of the solution reverted to the room temperature. Excess ammonia was removed by evacuation and the slurry was finally filtered. The filter cake was washed with 50 ml of ethyl alcohol, and 54 g of residue was recovered, which assayed 2.6% ZrO_2. The desired product was in the filtrate, which was evaporated to dryness under 1 mm pressure, and 47.3 g of a dry solid was recovered. Analysis showed it to contain 35.2% Zr, 63.4% C_2H_5O, and 0.25% Cl. The theoretical values for zirconium ethoxide are 33.6% Zr, 66.4% C_2H_5O. After 13.0 g of the impure product had been dissolved in 130 cc of boiling benzene and allowed to crystallize, 8.4 g of a pure product was finally recovered, which analyzed 33.5% Zr and 65.9% C_2H_5O.

Zirconium ethoxide has also been prepared by passing ammonia into a suspension of pyridinium chlorozirconate, $(C_5H_6N)_2ZrCl_6$, in a mixture of benzene and ethyl alcohol. It is a white, microcrystalline solid which is sparingly soluble in organic solvents including hot ethyl alcohol. It is moderately soluble in benzene, however. It sublimes at 120° under 10^{-4} mm pressure, and melts at 171-173°. A phase change has been noted to occur somewhat above 120°. The average complexity is 3.6 in benzene, but 2.5 in ethyl alcohol (54).

Zirconium propoxide**

Zirconium propoxide is readily formed by the reaction of zirconium tetrachloride with propyl alcohol in the presence of ammonia. Attempts to

---

* When referring to the zirconium alkoxides containing no radicals other than the one species of alkoxide radical, simplified names such as *zirconium methoxide* unambiguously convey the identity of the compound. In this case it is $Zr(OCH_3)_4$.

** In the absence of such prefixes as *iso-, sec-*(ondary) etc., the normal alkoxides and alcohols are to be understood.

resublime it or to crystallize it from benzene or carbon tetrachloride have not been successful (54).

Zirconium isopropoxide

Zirconium isopropoxide can readily be prepared by the reaction of zirconium tetrachloride with isopropyl alcohol in the presence of ammonia, or by the metathesis of zirconium ethoxide with isopropyl alcohol. When the crude product is recrystallized from isopropyl alcohol, the pure compound $Zr(OC_3H_7\text{-}i)_4 \cdot i\text{-}C_3H_7OH$ is obtained (54). The reaction of pyridinium chlorozirconate with isopropyl alcohol in the presence of ammonia gives $Zr(OC_3H_7\text{-}i) \cdot C_5H_5N$. This, too, on recrystallization from isopropyl alcohol gives $Zr(OC_3H_7\text{-}i)_4 \cdot i\text{-}C_3H_7OH$ (55).

Zirconium isopropoxide is a glassy solid which dissolves readily in organic solvents. It softens in the temperature range 105-120° to a liquid which can be distilled at 160° under 0.1 mm pressure. Zirconium isopropoxide reacts with various alcohols, such as methyl, ethyl, butyl, *sec*-butyl, and *tert*-butyl to form other alkoxides (54).

Zirconium isopropoxide monoisopropylate melts at 138-141°. It is only sparingly soluble in isopropyl alcohol at room temperature (59b).

Zirconium butoxide

Zirconium butoxide is readily formed by the reaction of zirconium tetrachloride with butyl alcohol in the presence of ammonia (54). It is also formed by the reaction of pyridinium chlorozirconate with butyl alcohol in the presence of ammonia (55), and by the reaction of zirconium acetylacetonate with butyl alcohol. A 92% yield has been reported for the last of these procedures (60).

Zirconium sec-butoxide

Zirconium *sec*-butoxide can be prepared by the metathesis of zirconium isopropoxide with *sec*-butyl alcohol (54) or by the reaction of pyridinium chlorozirconate with *sec*-butyl alcohol in the presence of ammonia (55). It is a gummy solid at the ordinary temperature, and when heated to 160° under 10^{-4} mm pressure, it sublimes with formation of a gummy, translucent sublimate. It is soluble in benzene but cannot be crystallized from the solution. A solvated solid can be recovered from its solution in *sec*-butyl alcohol, tentatively identified as $Zr(OC_4H_9\text{-}sec)_4 \cdot sec\text{-}C_4H_9OH$. This solvated compound is very soluble in a number of organic solvents, and it loses its alcoholation when it is dried (54).

59b. W. Wardlaw and D. C. Bradley, *Nature* **165**, 75-6 (1950).

60. R. Kh. Freĭdlina, E. M. Braĭnina, and A. N. Nesmeyanov, *Izvest. Akad. Nauk S.S.S.R. Otdel, Khim. Nauk* **1957**, 43-7.

Zirconium tert-butoxide

Zirconium *tert*-butoxide can be prepared by the metathesis of zirconium isopropoxide with *tert*-butyl alcohol. The reaction of zirconium tetrachloride with *tert*-butyl alcohol does not go well, and zirconium *tert*-butoxide is recovered at low purity (54). When ammonia is passed into a solution of zirconium tetrachloride in a mixture of *tert*-butyl alcohol and pyridine, and the solution is filtered and evaporated to dryness, a solid reaction product of composition $ClZr(OC_4H_9\text{-}tert)_3 \cdot 2C_5H_5N$ is recovered. This can be dissolved in benzene, and if ethyl alcohol is added to the solution, ethoxyzirconium tributoxide is formed. It is a solid whose melting point is between 110° and 130°, and which disproportionates at 180° with the formation of zirconium *tert*-butoxide (55).

Zirconium tertiary butoxide can also be prepared by refluxing together $Zr(OCH(CH_3)_2)_4 \cdot (CH_3)_2CHOH$ and $(CH_3)_3COOCH_3$ (61).

Zirconium amyloxide

Zirconium amyloxide is readily prepared by the reaction of zirconium tetrachloride with amyl alcohol in the presence of ammonia (54). It is a viscous liquid which volatilizes at 160° under 10^{-4} mm pressure.

Zirconium benzyloxide

Zirconium benzyloxide can be prepared by refluxing together benzyl alcohol, $C_6H_5CH_2OH$, with zirconium acetylacetonate. A yield of 89% has been reported (60).

The hafnium alkoxides are very similar to their zirconium counterparts in method of preparation and in physical and chemical properties. They are generally slightly more volatile than the zirconium compounds (62).

Except for their hafnium content, the zirconium alkoxides are usually recovered free of metallic impurities (63). Their boiling points and heats of vaporization increase with the molecular weight of the alcohol from which they are derived, and the entropy of vaporization increases only slightly (64). The heats and entropies of vaporization are much greater for the polymerized alkoxides, such as the ethoxide and the propoxide, than for the monomeric alkoxides such as the *tert*-butoxide (51).

Zirconium (and hafnium) alkoxides generally react with esters to form metathesis products:

$$4Zr(OR)_4 + 4R'OOCR'' \rightleftharpoons M(OR')_4 + 4ROOCR'' \qquad (22)$$

61. R. C. Mehrotra, *J. Am. Chem. Soc.* **76**, 2266-7 (1954).
62. D. C. Bradley, R. C. Mehrotra, and W. Wardlaw, *J Chem. Soc.* **1953**, 1634-6.
63. W. Wardlaw and D. C. Bradley, *Endeavor* **14**, 140-5 (1955).
64. D. C. Bradley, R. C. Mehrotra, and W. Wardlaw, *J. Chem. Soc.* **1952**, 4204-9.

The reaction tends to go to completion when the ester at the right is volatile (61). A process has been patented for the preparation of alkoxyzirconium soaps of generic formula $(Zr(OR)_{4-n}(OOCR')_n)_m$ by the reaction of zirconium alkoxides with aliphatic monocarboxylic acids of 8-20 carbon atoms (65). Polymeric products have also been prepared by the reactions of the alkoxides of zirconium with alkyl phosphonic acids (66).

There are no well-established uses for the zirconium alkoxides, largely because of the paucity of experimental investigation of these compounds until recently. However, a number of uses have been demonstrated, and these are summarized in Table 9.3.

TABLE 9.3. USES OF ZIRCONIUM ALKOXIDES

Use	Comments	Literature
Additive for paint	Rust inhibitor	65
Catalyst	For polycarbonate formation by condensation reactions	67
Coating material	The zirconium alkoxide in an organic solvent is sprayed on stainless steel plate in humid air to form an adherent, flexible film	68
Ink stabilizer	Promotes drying and prevents smearing of nitrocellulose inks; the alkoxide is applied in a solvent on top of the print	69
Insulation	As a component of insulating material, it reacts to overheating by forming an oxide which provides emergency insulation	70
Water-repellent treatment of leather	Zirconium alkoxides are used in conjunction with methylpolysiloxane and alkyl silicates, and are applied as solutions in Stoddard solvent	71
Water-repellent treatment of textiles	Zirconium ethoxide or isopropoxide used along with other substances in an organic solvent	72

65. J. H. Balthis, U.S. Patent **2,681,922**, June 22, 1954.
66. I. Kreidl and W. Kreidl, U.S. Patent **2,512,063**, June 20, 1950.
67. D. D. Reynolds and J. Van den Berghe, U.S. Patent **2,789,964**, April 23, 1957.
68. J. H. Haslam, U.S. Patent **2,768,909**, Oct. 30, 1956.
69. *Ibid.,* **2,732,799**, Jan. 31, 1956.
70. R. E. Berringer, U.S. Patent **2,572,906**, Oct. 30, 1951.
71. M. J. Hunter and C. F. Dudley, U.S. Patent **2,728,736**, Dec. 27, 1955.
72. L. Orthner and M. Reuter, U.S. Patent **2,774,689**, Dec. 18, 1956.

ZIRCONIUM DERIVATIVES OF POLYOĒS

When glycol or glycerine is added to aqueous solutions of zirconyl chloride, there is no evidence of a chemical reaction. If the pH of the solution is slowly raised by addition of a base, hydrous zirconia is precipitated in the same manner as in the absence of the organic compounds, and the rate of change of pH with the addition of the base is unaffected by the organic compounds. If an excess of strong alkali is added rapidly, however, so as to bring the pH to 10-12, hydrous zirconia is not precipitated, and it is apparent that one or more stable, water-soluble complexes with zirconium have formed. The reaction may be presumed to be of the type

$$ZrOCl_2 + 3HOCH_2CH_2OH + 6NaOH \rightarrow 2NaCl + 6H_2O +$$

$$(23)$$

For simplicity, hydration of zirconium species is ignored in equation 23. The reaction product remains stable in the solution only in the presence of strong alkali. If the alkalinity is reduced, a jelly of undetermined constitution is formed. Similar behavior is exhibited by glycerine, mannitol, sucrose, and other polyols (42). A solution containing zirconyl chloride and mannitol is mutarotatory, and polarimetric observation shows progressive changes to occur over periods of time ranging from days to months, depending on conditions. When solutions are prepared from zirconyl chloride, sodium hydroxide, and mannitol, increases in rotation of polarized light can be observed until the addition of 2 moles of mannitol per mole of zirconyl chloride. Electrodialysis of the solution causes movement of zirconium toward the anode, proving it to be present in an anionic complex (73, 74). Colloids are formed at lower alkalinities, and they can be precipitated with alcohol or with salts. When dried they swell on contact with water (75). Polyoses have less tendency to combine with zirconium than the simpler hexoses, but as they hydrolyze their decomposition products chelate available zirconium

73. A. Tchakirian, *Compt. rend.* **199**, 1620-2 (1934).
74. Marie Falinski, *Compt. rend.* **201**, 69-71 (1935).
75. Falinski, *Ann. chim.* **16**, 237-325 (1941).

atoms. Chelates formed by the hexoses with the zirconium in a zirconyl chloride solution exhibit brilliant green fluorescence; those formed from zirconyl nitrate solution do not. The hafnium analogs behave similarly (76). Cryoscopic measurements indicate 4 moles of sugar to be associated with 1 mole of zirconium in the chelate. A molten mixture of glucose and zirconyl chloride cooled to a solid which exhibited fluorescence for several weeks (*loc. cit.*).

Zirconium compounds with polyols are said to be useful in applications to polyvinyl films, such as are used in photography, since they render them harder and less soluble (77).

ZIRCONIUM DERIVATIVES OF PHENOL AND OTHER HYDROXY CYCLIC COMPOUNDS

Phenol, C_6H_5OH, is similar to the alcohols in containing the OH group, and its reactions with zirconium compounds are rather similar to those of the alcohols. When a mixture of zirconium tetrachloride and an excess of phenol is heated in dry benzene, chlorozirconium triphenoxide monophenolate, $ClZr(OC_6H_5)_3 \cdot C_6H_5OH$, is formed. On prolonged heating, it is converted to the phenoxide, $Zr(OC_6H_5)_4 \cdot C_6H_5OH$, a white, crystalline, hygroscopic solid (78).

Relatively little attention has been given to the zirconium phenoxides and their substitution products. Zirconium derivatives of picric acid have already been discussed in this chapter, and derivatives of salicyclic acid in Chapter 8.

Aromatic rings containing 2 or more phenolic OH groups in vicinal positions form stable chelates with the zirconium atom. Water-soluble complexes form in alkaline solution with pyrocatechol (1,2-dihydroxybenzene) and pyrogallol (1,2,3-trihydroxybenzene) (42); but chelates do not form with hydroquinone (1,4-dihydroxybenzene) or phloroglucinol (1,3,5-trihydroxybenzene) (*loc. cit.*) and reportedly not with chromotropic acid (4,5-dihydroxynaphthalenedisulfonic acid) (79). Addition of zirconyl chloride to a boiling ammoniacal solution of pyrocatechol gives ammonium tripyrocatecholatozirconate. A pyridinium analog is also reported (80, 81). As in the instances of the polyols, the alkali pyrocatecholatozirconates revert to hydrous zirconia when the alkali is neutralized (42, 81b). The hydrous zirconia adsorbs pyrocatechol and its derivatives very strongly.

76. G. A. Abbott, *Proc. N. Dakota Acad. Sci.* **7**, 41-4 (1953).
77. W. G. Lowe, U.S. Patent **2,455,937**, Dec. 14, 1948.
78. H. Funk and E. Rogler, *Z. anorg. allgem. Chem.* **252**, 323-8 (1944).
79. S. Ya. Snaĭderman and N. P. Mouchan, *Ukrain. Khim. Zhur.* **19**, 429-33 (1953).
80. A. Rosenheim and O. Sorge, *Ber.* **53B**, 932-9 (1920).
81. R. Weinland and H. Sperl, *Z. anorg. allgem. Chem.* **150**, 69-83 (1925).
81b. A. Rosenheim, B. Raibman, and G. Schendel, *Z. anorg. allgem. Chem.* **196**, 160-76 (1931).

Practical applications have been made of the adsorption of catechol by hydrous zirconia in chemotherapy. Urushiol, a pyrocatechol derivative with a hydrocarbon side chain, is exuded by the poison-ivy plant, *Rhus toxicodendron*. It is responsible for the familiar dermatitis. The dermatitis can often be prevented by the application of an ointment containing carbonated hydrous zirconia (82, 83) or hydrous zirconia (84) to the area of the skin which has been exposed to the plant or its exudate. These ointments also tend to alleviate the inflammation when they are applied to the afflicted skin after the dermatitis has developed (12).

A resinous substance is said to form on heating zirconium 2,4,6-trichlorophenoxide with trimethyl phosphate (66). Zirconium compounds with the dyes dihydroxyazobenzene (34, 85) and Pyrocatechol Violet (86, 87, 88, 89) have been noted.

ZIRCONIUM DERIVATIVES OF ALDEHYDES AND KETONES

It has already been noted that oxygen atoms which are doubly bonded to other atoms appear to coordinate relatively feebly with the zirconium atom in its compounds, and the coordination process is often reversible, whereas in general the formation of a coordinate bond between the zirconium atom of a ClBrI tetrahalogenide and an oxygen atom bound to one or more other atoms by single bonds is not reversible. Zirconium tetrachloride can be dissolved, for example, in liquid sulfur dioxide and can be recovered from the solution chemically unchanged by evaporation of the solvent. Solutions of zirconium tetrachloride in phosphorus oxychloride, $POCl_3$, react with a number of reagents in such a way as to indicate that the solvent is playing only a passive role in the reaction. The doubly bonded oxygen atom of pyruvic acid, $CH_3COCOOH$, does not act to form a sparingly soluble zirconium chelate similar to that formed by lactic acid, $CH_3CHOHCOOH$.

It might be expected from this behavior that zirconium would exhibit only a weak tendency to form coordinate bonds with aldehydes and ketones through the oxygen atom in the keto arrangement, but that it would have a considerably stronger tendency to form such bonds with the oxygen atom in the enol arrangement. The enolization reaction of ketones is of the nature indicated by the equation

82. G. A. Cronk and Dorothy E. Naumann, *J. Lab. Clin. Med.* **37**, 909-13 (1951).
83. J. W. E. Harrisson, B. Trabin, and E. W. Martin, *J. Pharmacol.* **102**, 179-84 (1951).
84. W. B. Blumenthal, Canadian patent **503,469**, June 1, 1954.
85. P. Bevillard, *Compt. rend.* **236**, 711-13 (1953).
86. H. Flaschka and F. Sadek, *Z. anorg. allgem. Chem.* **150**, 339-45 (1956).
87. V. Suk and M. Malat, *Chemist-Analyst* **45**, 30-7 (1956).
88. H. Flaschka and M. Y. Farah, *Z. anorg. allgem. Chem.* **152**, 401-11 (1956).
89. L. Kahulec, *Ceskoslov. hyg. epidemio., mikrobiol., immunol.* **4**, 376-7 (1955).

$$R-\overset{\overset{\displaystyle O}{\|}}{C}-\overset{\overset{\displaystyle H}{|}}{\underset{\underset{\displaystyle H}{|}}{C}}-R' \rightleftharpoons R-\overset{\overset{\displaystyle OH}{|}}{C}=\overset{}{\underset{\underset{\displaystyle H}{|}}{C}}-R' \tag{24}$$

In some β-diketonates of zirconium, the presence of an enolized oxygen atom has been detected by ultraviolet absorption spectroscopy (90).

A study of some of the reactions which occur when zirconium tetrachloride is added to simple ketones has been made by Dr. P. T. Joseph and the author (12). Zirconium tetrachloride was observed to dissolve in acetone or ethyl methyl ketone at 0-15° or lower temperatures without evolution of hydrogen chloride, but on warming to above this temperature range, hydrogen chloride was evolved and a trichlorozirconium ketonate was formed:

$$H_3C-\overset{\overset{\displaystyle OH}{|}}{C}=CH_2 + ZrCl_4 \xrightarrow{0 \text{ to } -15°} H_3C-\overset{\overset{\displaystyle HO \rightarrow ZrCl_4}{|}}{C}=CH_2 \tag{25}$$

$$\xrightarrow{\text{warm}} Cl_3Zr-O-C\underset{\diagdown CH_3}{\overset{\diagup CH_2}{}} + HCl$$

When the solution of zirconium tetrachloride in acetone was freshly prepared, it was colorless, but as it stood it developed an intense coloration and a pungent odor. Numerous by-products appeared to form, and mesityl oxide and phorone were detected.

$$\underset{H_3C}{\overset{H_3C}{\diagdown}}C=\overset{\overset{\displaystyle H}{|}}{C}-\overset{\overset{\displaystyle O}{\|}}{C}-CH_3 \qquad\qquad \underset{H_3C}{\overset{H_3C}{\diagdown}}C=\overset{\overset{\displaystyle H}{|}}{C}-\overset{\overset{\displaystyle O}{\|}}{C}-\overset{\overset{\displaystyle H}{|}}{C}=\overset{\overset{\displaystyle CH_3}{|}}{C}_{CH_3}$$

Mesityl oxide   Phorone

These products are formed by splitting out water between 2 or 3 molecules of acetone. The water causes formation of hydrolysis products of other components of the system, thus rendering its composition very complex.

The reaction of zirconium tetrachloride with diketones in which the oxygen atoms are separated by 3 carbon atoms leads to replacement of all 4 chlorine atoms from the zirconium and the formation of a stable, chelate structure in which zirconium attains to coordination number 8:

$$CH_3COCH:COHCH_3 + ZrCl_4 \rightarrow Zr(CH_3COCH:COCH_3)_4 + 4HCl \tag{26}$$

---

90. E. M. Larsen, G. Terry, and J. Leddy, *J. Am. Chem. Soc.* **75**, 5107-11 (1953).

Zirconium tetrachloride dissolves in acetaldehyde with formation of reaction products which have not been identified, and it also forms unidentified compounds by reaction with salicylaldehyde in aqueous solutions (47, 91). When a mixture of zirconium tetrachloride and salicylaldehyde is heated, a reaction product is obtained which can be recrystallized from chloroform. The crystalline product is tetrasalicylaldehydozirconium. It melts at 210-212°. Further heating is required to dispel all the chloroform, and this also causes decomposition of the product (60).

It has been noted that there is some reaction between acetylacetone and hydrous zirconia or carbonated hydrous zirconia, but only amorphous, poorly defined reaction products were obtained (92). Zirconium tetra-acetylacetonate decahydrate is obtained, however, as a well-formed crystalline product by the reaction of acetylacetone with aqueous zirconyl nitrate (93, 94, 95) or zirconyl chloride (90, 96). A convenient preparation is the following (96):

Dissolve 5.8 g of zirconyl chloride octahydrate in 50 ml of water, and cool the solution to 15°. In a separate vessel, add 10 g of acetylacetone to 50 ml of a 10% solution of sodium carbonate, adding the organic compound slowly and stirring until it dissolves. Surround the vessel containing the acetylacetone solution with an ice-water bath and continue the stirring until the temperature comes to equilibrium. Filter off any precipitate. Add the solution to the zirconyl chloride solution, which should also be at equilibrium with an ice-water bath. Allow to stand. After about an hour, the zirconium acetylacetonate will have precipitated and can be filtered off, washed with cold water, and dried. The mother liquor will deposit more zirconium acetylacetonate if allowed to stand 24 hours. The product is apt to contain a small amount of hydrous zirconia as a contaminant. To obtain a pure product, dissolve the crude in benzene in the proportion 5 g per 25 ml, filter the solution, and add petroleum ether to the filtrate. Pure, anhydrous zirconium acetylacetonate will separate.*

Zirconium acetylacetonate dodecahydrate effloresces in air, and it can be dehydrated completely by holding under a vacuum of 0.1 mm. The anhydrous compound can be obtained by recrystallizing from absolute alcohol, but the temperature should be held below 40° to avoid chemical reaction with the alcohol (95). The dodecahydrate is also obtained by the

---

* The hafnium analog has been prepared similarly (loc. cit.).

91. M. Bobtelsky and C. Heitner, Bull. soc. chim. France 1952, 938-42.

92. A. Mandl, Z. anorg. allgem. Chem. 37, 252 (1903).

93. W. Biltz and J. A. Clinch, Z. anorg. allgem. Chem. 40, 221 (1904).

94. G. T. Morgan and A. R. Bowen, J. Chem. Soc. 125, 1252-61 (1924).

95. G. von Hevesy and Marie Lögstrup, Ber. 59, 1890 (1926).

96. R. C. Young and A. Arch, in Inorganic Syntheses, Ed. W. C. Fernelius, McGraw-Hill Book Company, New York, Vol. 2, pp. 121-2.

reaction of chlorozirconium triacetylacetonate with acetylacetone in an aqueous medium.

Zirconium acetylacetonate, $Zr(CH_3COCHCOCH_3)_4$, formula weight 487.63, is a colorless, crystalline solid, characteristically occurring as birefringent monoclinic needles (93). Its density at 25° is 1.415 (90, 95). It melts at 194-195° (90, 93, 94, 95) and sublimes at 82° under 0.001 mm pressure. It begins to turn yellow and decompose at about 125°. Its Raman spectrum shows absorption at 1520 cm^{-1} (97). It dissolves in water to the extent of approximately 10 g per 100 ml of solution at 20°. It is insoluble in acetone, and various values have been obtained for its solubility in alcohol, probably in part due to its tendency to react chemically with this solvent, as indeed it does with a number of organic solvents. Some reported solubilities in g per 100 ml of solution are: benzene 10 (15°), carbon disulfide 3.3 (15°), carbon tetrachloride 9 (15°), ether 1.13 (room temperature), isopropanol 2 (20°), petroleum ether 0.1 (20°), and 4 (50°), and ethylene dibromide 4.8 (25°) (95).*

The Raman and infrared spectra of zirconium acetylacetonate have been interpreted as showing evidence for hydrogen bonding in the molecule (98). Polarization measurements of its solutions in nonpolar solvents have given higher values than those anticipated for its electron polarization, and this has been regarded as indicating intermolecular movements called *atom polarization* (99). The molar magnetic susceptibility is -212.00×10^{-8} cgs units (100).

Zirconium acetylacetonate does not form additional products with ammonia. Its reactions with alcohols have already been noted above.

The zirconium compounds of a considerable number of β-diketones other than acetylacetone have been prepared by substantially the same methods as used for the acetylacetonate. They may also be prepared by distilling mixtures of zirconium acetylacetonate with the desired β-diketone. Zirconium compounds containing four organic radicals per zirconium atom are generally recovered from these processes (60). A list of zirconium and hafnium β-diketonates is given in Table 9.4, with melting-point data, when available.

Acetyl chloride reacts with zirconium β-diketonates to form chlorozirconium tri-β-diketonates (60). Equilibration studies of aqueous solutions of zirconium β-diketonates with organic solvents have provided useful data

---

* Hafnium acetylacetonate melts at 188-190° and its density is 1.691. The molecular volumes of tetra-β-diketonates of hafnium are generally greater than those of the zirconium compounds (90).

97. D. N. Shigorin, *Zhur. Fiz. Khim.* **27**, 554-64 (1953).
98. Shigorin, *Izvest. Akad. Nauk S.S.S.R., Ser. Fiz.* **17**, 596-603 (1953).
99. A. E. Finn, G. C. Hampson, and C. E. Sutton, *J. Chem. Soc.* **1938**, 1254-63.
100. S. Mehta and D. M. Desai, *J. Indian Chem. Soc.* **34**, 189-92 (1957).

TABLE 9.4. ZIRCONIUM TETRA-β-DIKETONATES AND THEIR MELTING POINTS

Name of diketone	Melting points, °C		Literature
	Zr compound	Hf compound	
Acetylacetone	190-93	188-90	90, 101
Trifluoroacetylacetone	128-30	125-28	90, 101
Benzoyltrifluoroacetone			102
2-Furoyltrifluoroacetone	199-201	195-97	90
2-Pyrroyltrifluoroacetone	184-85	185-86	90
2-Thenoyltrifluoroacetone	225-26	220-23	90, 102, 103, 104, 105
Isovaleroyltrifluoroacetone			102
2-Furoylacetone	198-201	200-02	90
2-Thenoylacetone	244-45	239-42	90
Benzoylacetone			60
Dipavaloylmethane			106

from which the zirconium species in aqueous solutions can be deduced, and they have been of interest in the development of methods for separating hafnium from zirconium (101, 102, 103, 105, 107).

The reaction of the sodium salt of benzoylacetone with zirconyl chloride in aqueous solution gives zirconyl dibenzoylacetonate, $OZr(C_{10}H_9O_2)_2$, and not the tetra- compound. It is a white solid which is slightly soluble in alcohol, benzene, and glacial acetic acid (94). Benzoylacetone reacts with zirconium tetrachloride in ether solution with the formation of dichloro-zirconium dibenzoylacetonate, $Cl_2Zr(C_{10}H_9O_2)_2$, but in boiling benzene it forms chlorozirconium tribenzoylacetonate (108). In general, the β-diketones tend to form chlorozirconium tri-β-diketonates under anhydrous conditions, and acetylacetone, dibenzoylmethane, and benzoylacetone compounds of this type have been prepared. Chlorozirconium triacetylacetonate is monomeric, and it melts at 126-127°. When it dissolves in water the

101. B. G. Schultz and E. M. Larsen, *J. Am. Chem. Soc.* **72**, 3615-19 (1950).

102. E. H. Huffman, G. M. Iddings, R. N. Osborne, and G. V. Schalimoff, *J. Am. Chem. Soc.* **77**, 881-3 (1955).

103. E. H. Huffman and G. M. Iddings, *U.S. Atomic Energy Comm. UCRL-377*, 6 pp. (1949).

104. F. L. Moore, U.S. Patent **2,708,243**, May 10, 1955.

105. E. M. Larsen and G. Terry, *J. Am. Chem. Soc.* **75**, 1560-2 (1953).

106. G. A. Guter and G. S. Hammond, *J. Am. Chem. Soc.* **78**, 5166-7 (1956).

107. Dorothy C. McCarty, B. E. Dearing, and F. F. Flagg, *U.S. Atomic Energy Comm. KAPL-180*, 45 pp. (1949).

108. W. Dilthey, *J. prakt. Chem.* **111**, 147-52 (1925).

chlorine is separated from the molecule, and the solution reacts with acetylacetone to form zirconium (tetra)acetylacetonate. All three of the chlorozirconium tri-β-diketonates mentioned are soluble in chloroform and in benzene. The solid compounds can be preserved indefinitely in the solid, dry state. The chlorine can be replaced by chloroferrate, $FeCl_4$, or chlorau-rate, $AuCl_4$. The chloroplatinate $PtCl_6Zr(C_6H_5COCH_2COC_6H_5)_2$ has also been prepared (94). The chloroferrate, chloraurate, and chloroplatinate are oily compounds which appear not to crystallize.

ZIRCONIUM DERIVATIVES OF QUINONE AND RELATED COMPOUNDS

Compounds containing the quinone structure are related to the ketones, and are distinguished by having the carbonyl carbon atom form part of an aromatic ring. Some compounds of this class which are particularly signifi-cant for the present discussion are represented graphically below.

Quinone   Anthraquinone   Alizarin
(1,2-dihydroxyquinone)

Rufigallic acid   Chloranilic acid
(1,2,3,5,6,7-hexahydroxy-
anthraquinone)

No compounds with quinone have been reported but numerous compounds are known in which zirconium is chelated with hydroxyquinones or their analogs. It appears that the zirconium is bound through two vicinal hydroxyl groups, when these are present, rather than through a hydroxyl oxygen atom and the doubly bonded quinone oxygen atom (109). Colored compounds are formed by zirconium with alizarin, quinalizarin (1,2,5,8-tetrahydroxyanthraquinone), and purpurin (1,2,4-trihydroxyanthraquinone) in which there is one organic group per zirconium atom (110). By measurement of the light absorbency of dilute solutions of these compounds, and particularly of the alizarin compound, convenient quantitative determinations of zirconium can be achieved, and the method is especially applicable to the determination of zirconium when it is present in small quantities (110, 111, 112, 113). Rufigallic acid has been used similarly (114). The complexes are stable in strong perchloric acid solution, but are destroyed by sulfuric acid (113) and by hydrofluoric acid. The complex formed by 1,4,5,8-tetrahydroxyanthraquinone is decomposed by tartaric acid, but it reforms when the acid is neutralized with calcium carbonate (115). Some data on the dissociation of the complexes of zirconium and hafnium are available (116, 117).

The destruction of the color of the zirconium-alizarin complex by hydrofluoric acid provides a means for the colorimetric determination of fluorine. This is accomplished by treating the substance of unknown fluorine content so as to convert its fluorine to hydrofluoric acid, and measuring the decrease in light absorbency when the hydrofluoric acid solution is added to a solution containing a known concentration of zirconium-alizarin complex (81, 118, 119).

Chloranilic acid forms red solutions from which the colored solute is precipitated by zirconyl salts. By measuring the diminution in color of a solution of known strength by precipitation with zirconium, a value can be obtained for the amount of zirconium that was introduced (120, 121, 122).

109. W. B. Mors and Perola Zaltzman, *Bol. Inst. quim. agr.* (Rio de Janeiro) No. **34,** 7-15 (1954).
110. J. F. Flagg, H. A. Liebhafsky, and E. H. Winslow, *J. Am. Chem. Soc.* **71,** 3630-2 (1949).
111. R. Charonnat, *Compt. rend.* **199,** 1620-2 (1934).
112. H. A. Liebhafsky and E. H. Winslow, *J. Am. Chem. Soc.* **60,** 1776-84 (1938).
113. A. S. Komarovskiĭ and I. M. Korenman, *Z. Anal. Chem.* **94,** 257-9 (1933).
114. A. Okac, *Chem. Listy* **39,** 61-3 (1945).
115. I. S. Mustafin and L. M. Kul'berg, *Ukrain. Khim. Zhur.* **19,** 421-8 (1953).
116. V. Dorta-Schaeppi, H. Hürzeler, and W. D. Treadwell, *Helv. Chim. Acta* **34,** 797-805 (1951).
117. O. Gübeli and A. Jacob, *Helv. Chim. Acta* **38,** 1026-32 (1955).
118. R. L. Franci, *Off. Bul. N. Dakota Water Works Conf.* **19,** No. 6/7, 4-6 (1951-2).
119. A. Ya. Savchenko, *Zhur. Anal. Khim.* **10,** 355-7 (1955).
120. B. J. Thamer and A. F. Voigt, *J. Am. Chem. Soc.* **73,** 3192-3202 (1951).
121. R. B. Hahn and J. L. Johnson, *Anal. Chem.* **29,** 902-3 (1957).
122. R. E. U. Frost-Jones and J. T. Yardley, *Analyst* **77,** 468-72 (1952).

ZIRCONIUM DERIVATIVES OF THE FLAVONES

Flavone is the basic substance of which a number of plant coloring matters are derivatives. Most flavones are yellow, crystalline solids of high melting points for organic compounds. They are soluble in alcohol and in water or dilute aqueous solutions of acids and alkalies. The structural formulas of flavone and flavonol are shown below with the conventional numbering of the carbon atoms. (When the carbon atom No. 3 is completely reduced, with elimination of the double bond, the structure is identified by the name *flavanone*). Flavones can occur in nature as parts of more complex structures, for example the flavone glucoside rutin, $C_{27}H_{30}O_{16} \cdot 3H_2O$. The quercitron bark yields a well-known flavone dye.

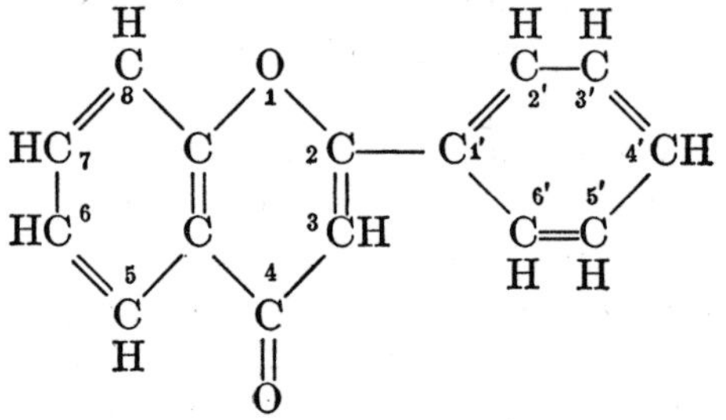

Flavone (2-phenylbenzopyrone)

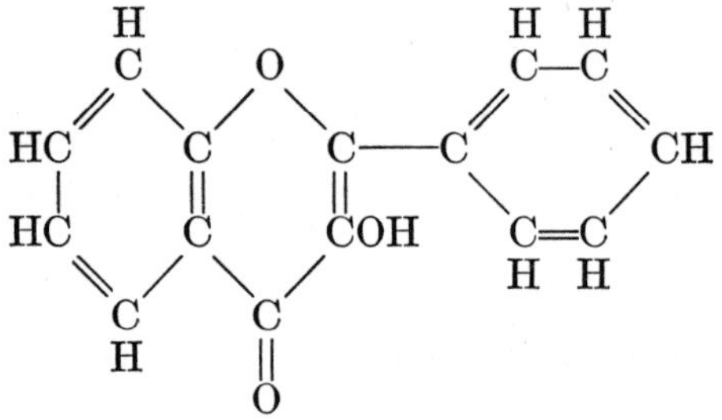

Flavonol (3-hydroxyflavone)

Zirconium forms colored complexes with hydroxyflavones. The polyhydroxyflavones have 3 chelate-forming groups in the molecule: (1) the hydroxyl group on the No. 3 carbon atom, in conjunction with the quinone oxygen atom, (2) the hydroxyl group on the number 5 carbon atom plus the quinone oxygen atom, and (3) the hydroxyl groups on the 1'-6' ring. Attempts have been made to establish the nature of compounds formed with zirconium through each of these chelating groups. Evidence has been adduced for the formation of complexes containing one or two flavone radicals per zirconium atom when compounds of class 1 are formed, only one flavone radical per zirconium atom for class 2; and no complexes from class 3. The tendency is to form mainly compounds of class 1, and the ratio of the dissociation constants for complexes of this class (in which the chelate ring is 5-membered) to that for complexes of class 2 (in which the chelate ring is 6-membered) is about 1:100 (123, 124). Some zirconium derivatives of flavones are listed in Table 9.5.

TABLE 9.5. ZIRCONIUM COMPOUNDS WITH FLAVONES

Common name of the flavone	Chemical name	Moles of flavone combining with 1 gram-atom of Zr	Literature
Flavonol	3-hydroxyflavone	2 or 1	124
Morin	3,5,7,2',4'-pentahydroxyflavone		125
Myricetin	3,5,7,3',4',5'-hexahydroxyflavone	2 or 1	124
Quercetin	3,5,7,3',4'-pentahydroxyflavone	2 or 1	126, 127, 128
Rutin	flavonol glucoside		127

The color formed by zirconium with quercetin has been used in chromatography (128). Titanium is perhaps more suitable for the determination of flavones than zirconium (128b).

ZIRCONIUM DERIVATIVES OF TANNINS

Tannins comprise a large group of water-soluble, complex organic substances which are widely distributed throughout the vegetable kingdom. Virtually all trees and shrubs contain some tannin in their leaves, wood, bark, or fruit. The hydrolysis of tannins usually yields either gallic or ellagic acid, which are seen from their structural formulas to be substances of the types which form stable complex compounds with zirconium.

U.S.P. Tannic Acid is gallotannic acid, a tannin usually obtained from nutgalls and widely used as a laboratory reagent. It has not been fully characterized and is defined only loosely by certain of its properties and reactions. It precipitates zirconium completely from solutions of zirconyl salts, such as that obtained by the dissolution of chlorides of zirconium.

123. L. Hörhammer, R. Hänsel, and W. Hieber, *Naturwiss.* **41**, 529 (1954).
124. Hörhammer, Hänsel, and Hieber, *Z. Anal. Chem.* **148**, 251-9 (1955).
125. G. Charlot, *Anal. Chim. Acta* **1**, 218-48 (1947).
126. F. S. Grimaldi and C. E. White, *Anal. Chem.* **25**, 1886-90 (1953).
127. L. Hörhammer and R. Hänsel, *Arch. Pharm.* **285**, 438-44 (1952).
128. J. Michal, *Chem. Listy* **50**, 77-80 (1956).
128b. P. Hagedorn and R. Neu, *Arch. Pharm.* **286**, 486-90 (1953).

Gallic acid   Ellagic acid

The precipitate can be ignited and weighed as zirconium dioxide in analytical procedures. Titanium and tin are coprecipitated with zirconium, but good separations are obtained from vanadium, uranium, and thorium (129). Zirconium has also been precipitated by tannic acid plus Methyl Violet from 0.2 N hydrochloric acid solution (130). Tannic acid is not a suitable reagent for precipitating zirconium from solutions containing sulfate or oxalate ions (131), but satisfactory precipitations have been reported in the presence of acetate or nitrate ions (132).

129. W. R. Schoeller, *Analyst* **69,** 259-62 (1944).
130. V. I. Kuznetsov, Sessiya *Akad. Nauk. S.S.S.R. po Mirnomu Izpol'zovaniyu Atomoĭ Energĭi 1955, zasedaniya Otdel. Khim. Nauk* 301-18.
131. W. R. Schoeller and H. Holness, *Analyst* **70,** 319-23 (1945).
132. L. Moser and J. Singer, *Monatsh.* **48,** 673-87 (1927).

Author Index

375

Becker, G., 57
Becker, K., 55
Becker, R. S., 34, 138, 170
Becket, F. M., 90, 91, 170
Bedford, F. C., 331
Bedr-Chan, S., 208
Behrens, H., 150
Belcher, R., 335
Belden, A. W., 183, 314
Belen'kaya, A. P., 34
Belle, J., 80
Bellucci, I., 349
Belozerskiĭ, N. A., 117
von Bemmeln, J. M., 182, 183
Benešovsky, F., 62, 73, 87, 89
Benford, J. R., 180
Ben-Saude, A., 208
Bensey, F. N., Jr., 139
Bensing, L. P., 157
Berg, Yu. N., 34
Berger, F. M., 333
Berglund, V. E., 18, 150
Berington, C. F. P., 31, 55
Berkowitz, J., 154
Berlin, N. J., 208
Bernard, W. J., 34, 138, 170
Berringer, R. E., 362
Bersin, T., 353
Bertaut, F., 75, 170, 203
Berthier, P., 192, 291
Berzelius, J. J., 2, 50, 93, 150, 243, 292, 293, 302, 308, 336
Bettendorf, A., 161
Betterton, J. O., Jr., 101
Betz, H., 32, 161
Beutel, E., 192
Bevillard, P., 365
Beyer, G. H., 140, 275
Bezborodov, M. A., 216
Bielawski, M. S., 306
Biltz, M., 188
Biltz, W., 79, 91, 93, 367
Binks, W., 202
Birnbräuer, E., 56
Blakely, J. P., 283
Blaylock, F. R., 328
Bloch, H., 42
Bloomfield, G., 193
Bloomstrand, C. W., 208
Blue, R. H., 175
Blum, A., 75
Blum, P., 75
Blumenfeld, J., 157, 158
Blumenthal, H., 72, 73
Blumenthal, W. B., 34, 35, 41, 43, 112, 116, 132, 135, 140, 157, 172, 180, 191,

194, 195, 248, 255, 276, 295, 297, 318, 319, 333, 352, 365, 367
Bobtelsky, M. 367
Bock, E., 286
Bock, R., 286, 345
Bode, H., 142
Bodin, V., 160
Bodkin, E. A., 193
Boedeker, E. R., 174
de Boer, J. H., 3,18, 19, 20, 32, 54, 78, 107, 117, 298, 299, 301, 307, 349
Boggild, O. B., 232
Böhm, J., 161, 186
Bond, D. C., 117
Bond, P. A., 292
Booth, G. W., 137
Borders, E., 101
Borelius, G., 76
Born, F., 164
Borovik, S. A., 13
Borovik-Romanova, T. F., 13
Bosch, C., 67
Boswell, P. G. H., 204
Boudreaux, E. A., 107
Bouissieres, G., 195
Boulanger, J., 130, 326
Bourgeois, L., 235
Bourian, F., 160
Bowen, A. R., 367
Bowerman, E. W., 111
Bowman, R. E., 142
Boyd, G. E., 215
Bradley, D. C., 118, 352, 353, 355, 356, 357, 360, 361
Bradt, W. E., 17
Braĭnina, E. M., 360
Brandenberger, E., 204
Brandes, E. A., 161
Brauer, G., 100
Braun, W. W., 129
Brauns, R., 206
Breithaupt, A., 3, 208
Brewer, L., 71, 96, 172
Bridge, J. P., 78
Bridgman, P. W., 28
Briggs, H. C., 296
Bril, A., 306
Brinton, P. H. M. P., 288
Brintzinger, H., 22
Brite, D. W., 303
Britton, H. T. S., 194, 262, 293, 297, 316
Brögger, W. C., 207, 231, 232, 233
Bromley, L. A., 96, 172
Bronder, O., 215
Bronson, G. E., 305
Brotzen, O., 213

Subject Index

393

Systems (*cont.*)
  H_2O-SO_3-ZrO_2, 264, 265
  Na_2O-SiO_2-ZrO_2, 234-235
  O-Zr, 151-152
  Si-Zr, 86-87
  SiO_2-ZiO_2, 216

Tachyaphaltite, 208, 209
Tannic acid, 373-374
Tartrate, 336-337
Tellurides, 98
Tellurites, 293
Terephthalate, 329
Tetraacetatozirconic acid, 317
Tetrabromide, 106, 115
Tetrachloride, 102, 103-106, 110
Tetrafluoride, 138-140
Tetraformatozirconic acid, 317
Tetraiodide, 20, 106, 115
Tetrasulfatozirconic acid, salts, 256
Thiocarbohydrazide, 350
Thiocyanates, 283
Thioglycolate, 349
Thiosulfate, 277-278, 281
Thorianite, 12
Thortveitite, 6, 12
Toluene, 343
Tribromide, 121
Trichloride, 119, 120, 121
Trioxodizirconium compounds, carboxylates, 319-321
  bromide, 133
  chloride, 133
  hydroxide, 194-195
  hydroxyhalogenides, 133
Trihalogenide, 119, 120
Triiodide, 122
Trisulfatozirconic acid, 247, 254-256
  salts, 252
Tritonite, 12
Tungstated hydrous zirconia, 293-295
Tungstatozirconates, 295-297

Uhligite, 12, 198
Uraninite, 12
Urushiol, 365

Valerate, 320
Vanadates, 308, 309
Violurate, diphenyl-, 348-349

Wadeite, 12
Wöhlerite, 12, 233

Xenotime, 12

Zircon, color, 204-206
  crystallography, 201-203, 217
  dissociation, 217, 218
  gem, 201
  geochemistry, 210
  identification, 201-204
  impurities in, 204, 205, 213
  luminescence, 296
  metamict, 207, 217, 218
  occurrences, 7-11, 210
  ore treatment, 225-227
  properties, chemical, 215, 216, 221-225
    physical, 201, 214, 215
    surface, 226
  radiation effects on, 205, 206, 220, 221
  radioactivity in, 220
  structure, 202-203, 219
  synthesis, 217, 218, 219
  use, 219, 226, 228-229
  varieties, 206
  weathering, 210, 211
Zirfesite, 233
Zirkelite, 12, 198
Zirkite, 11
Zirconates, 165
Zircocene, *see* Cyclopentadienyl compounds
Zirconeates, 190-191, 197
Zirconia, *see* Dioxide
  stabilized, 180
Zirconite, 201
Zirconium (element), atomic weight, 5
  corrosion, 30
  coordination number, 36
  crystallography, 2, 13
  discovery, 1
  colloidal, 27
  history, 1, 2
  identification, 2, 13
  occurrences, 1, 5, 7-11, 12, 13
  oxide surface on, 31
  pickling, 32
  preparation, 2-3
    electrochemical, 2, 17, 23, 24
  pure, 18, 22
  pyrolysis, of chlorides and bromides, 19
    of iodides, 3, 19, 20
  reduction, of halogenides, 2, 3, 18, 19
    of oxides, 21, 22
  removal of dissolved carbon, 60
  properties, atomic, 35
    biological, 39
  chemical, 13, 16, 25-35, 46
  physical, 13, 25
  thermodynamic, 28
  valence, 36